Enigma Books

Also published by Enigma Books

A. J. Barker

The First Iraq War
1914–1918

Britain's Mesopotamian Campaign

Introduction by Joseph Morrison Skelly

Illustrated with maps and photographs

Enigma Books

Printed in the United States of America

ISBN 978-1-929631-86-5

Original titles:
The Bastard War (U.S.)
The Neglected War (UK)

Library of Congress Cataloguing-in-Publication Data

Barker, A. J.
  The first Iraq war 1914–1918 : Britain's Mesopotamian campaign / A.J. Barker.

  p. : ill., maps ; cm.

  Originally published in 1967 under the titles: "The bastard war" (US) and "The neglected war" (UK).
  Includes bibliographical references and index.
  ISBN: 978-1-929631-86-5

1. World War, 1914-1918--Campaigns--Iraq. 2 Great Britain--History, Military--20th century. I. Title.

D568.5 .B33 2009
940.4/15

It was believed to be a sideshow and "no man's child."

Major General Sir George Gorringe

Contents

Maps and Sketches

Introduction

"In Mesopotamia a Safe Game Must Be Played"

by Joseph Morrison Skelly

In late April, 1915 a combined Anglo-Indian expeditionary force had just consolidated its hold on the city of Basra and was preparing to move up the Tigris River into the heart of Mesopotamia, which had been a province of the Ottoman Empire for more than four centuries. The recently appointed commanding officer, Lieutenant General John Nixon, was eager to press ahead, with Baghdad coming into focus as his ultimate objective, even though it was over three hundred miles upstream. He therefore requested higher headquarters to send another cavalry brigade and an infantry battalion to his area of operations.

In New Delhi and London, however, caution was the watchword of the day, with numerous military and economic interests hanging in the balance, including the security of an oil pipeline running down the Eastern flank of the British lines just across the border in Persia, from the oilfields North of Ahwaz to the port of Abadan, located on the Shatt-al-Arab Waterway, fifty miles inland from the head of the Persian Gulf. Lord Charles Hardinge, the British Viceroy in India, whose government was in overall command of the military operation, counseled restraint by declining Lieutenant General Nixon's request, although this was only a tactical decision since he was an avid supporter of Nixon's strategic plan. Lord Robert Crewe, the Secretary of State for India who was based in London and also Hardinge's superior, concurred, but from a different perspective. In a cable to Hardinge he insisted on a more detailed assessment of the situation and concluded that, for the time being, "No advance beyond the present theater of operations will be sanctioned, although an advance to Amara with the object of controlling the tribes between there and the Karun River might be supported because it adds to the safety of the pipeline. Our present position is strategically a sound one, and we cannot afford to take risks by extending it unduly. In Mesopotamia a safe game must be played."[1]

Lord Crewe's telegram offered sage operational advice. His last line, as events would demonstrate, represented the font of wisdom for waging war in Mesopotamia. It is important, however, that readers understand what Lord Crewe meant by the word "safe." He did not mean fighting in a cautious or timid manner; no, far from it. The word must be understood in its military context. "Safe" signifies a methodical, well planned, fully resourced, prudent course of action—combined, naturally, with ferocity, audacity, and élan on the battlefield. It implies correlating strategic ends with the logistical means to achieve them, ensuring that military objectives do not outrun their communication and supply lines. This is one of the fundamental principles of warfare. Matching ends to means is the proper path leading to the objective of all military operations, namely, victory.

Did the Anglo-Indian force hew to Lord Crewe's guidance in Mesopotamia? The answer, alas, is not consistently, especially during the first half of its campaign.[2] In fact, the Army's tactical success correlates to the degree to which it embraced a "safe" approach to planning, logistics, communications, and supply. When it did so—at Qurna, al-Amara, the Second Battle of Kut, and Baghdad, for instance—victory ensued. When it did not—at Ctesiphon in November, 1915 and the Fall of Kut in April, 1916—defeat followed. These triumphs, tragedies, and Britain's eventual, hard-won success are all recounted in gripping detail in this book, A. J. Barker's *The First Iraq War, 1914–1918: Britain's Mesopotamian Campaign*. It narrates the story of one of the most important battlefronts outside of Europe during World War I. Often overshadowed by T. E. Lawrence's adventures in the Arabian desert, by Field Marshal Edmund Allenby's conquest of Palestine, and by the tragic carnage in the Dardanelles, the battle for Mesopotamia is one of the key episodes in the

---

1. See below, p. 58.
2. For an extended discussion of the application of ends to means in Mesopotamia, see the excellent study by Paul K. Davis, *Ends and Means: The British Mesopotamian Campaign and Commission* (Rutherford, NJ: Fairleigh Dickinson University Press, 1994); for a compelling analysis of this relationship in the context of general warfare, see Angelo Codevilla and Paul Seabury, *War: Ends and Means,* 2nd edition (Washington: Potomac Books, 2006).

Great War and the world that it remade. Its history is expertly retold in A. J. Barker's volume, whose republication by Enigma Books at this time is most welcome, for it chronicles crucial chapters in the story of World War I, the history of the British Empire, the birth of modern Iraq, and the foundation of the modern Middle East. In it mirages of memory are stripped away to reveal the stark truth of a grueling campaign that lasted the entire length of the First World War, one in which enormous, at times unbearable, sacrifices were demanded from all of the combatants, only to be matched by the heroism they so consistently displayed on the battlefield.

The Geopolitical Context

Why was an Anglo-Indian army in the Land of the Two Rivers in the midst of World War I? The geopolitical context accounts for its presence. While heavy fighting was taking place on the Western Front, the Middle East emerged as a major theater of operations. Several British objectives were at stake. The government sought to alleviate pressure in Europe by opening a new front against the Central Powers; to weaken the Ottoman Empire as a rival in the Middle East; to check German designs in the region (epitomized by the building of the Berlin-to-Baghdad railway); and to defend myriad imperial interests, including Britain's protectorate in Egypt and the safety of the Suez Canal, the main artery of the Empire.[3] To secure these strategic aims, the British War Office poured soldiers into Egypt, where they repulsed an Ottoman attack on the Suez Canal in February, 1915, and in April sent an amphibious force consisting of British, Australian, and New Zealand troops into the Dardanelles, south of Istanbul, in order to capture the Ottoman capital and to open a sea lane to Russia.

The Northern Persian Gulf and lower Mesopotamia were also strategic arenas. Control of these regions was considered essential to defending British oil interests in nearby Persia, notably, as mentioned above, the Anglo-Persian Oil Company's oil fields near Ahwaz and its refineries at the port city of Abadan. A. J. Barker deems protecting Britain's oil supply "the original object of the expedition" into Mesopotamia.[4] As the campaign progressed other interests came into play, according to students of the conflict, including the need "to show support for the Gulf sheikhs; to impress the Mesopotamian Arabs, who respected only tangible victory; and to insure that the Arabs did not join the Turks in *jihad*."[5]

---

3. See John Keegan, *The First World War* (New York: Vintage Books, 1998), pp. 217-21, 234-5.
4. See below, p. 58.
5. Col. James D. Scudieri, "Iraq 2003-04 and Mesopotamia 1914-18: A Comparative Analysis in Ends and Means," Student Issue Paper, Center for Strategic Leadership, U.S. Army War College, Vol. 04 (August,

With the flow of oil an imperative, several British warships moved into the Northern end of the Persian Gulf in November, 1914. They were ferrying a combined force from India, called Indian Expeditionary Force "D" (I.E.F. "D"), which made progress in the early stages of the campaign. Following a landing on the Fao Peninsula, a foothold was established in the city of Basra. The first commander of Indian Expeditionary Force "D," Lieutenant General Arthur Barrett, soon realized that holding the city required control over its hinterlands, territory the Ottomans called the Basra *vilayet*, or province. Thus over the next several months I.E.F. "D" moved up the Tigris River in a systematic fashion, methodically crossing a latticework of irrigation canals and meticulously clearing palm groves before lush lower Mesopotamia gives way to the scorching sands of the desert. It captured the town of Qurna, the reputed site of the Garden of Eden located at the juncture of the Tigris and Euphrates rivers forty miles North of Basra, and repulsed an Ottoman counterattack at Shaiba, nine miles to the southwest of Basra. In all of these tactical engagements, it must be noted, the British and Indian soldiers displayed impressive skills and the highest degree of military ingenuity; their performance was exemplary, especially in the light of the challenging conditions they faced and the difficult terrain over which they had to traverse.

At this point, in April, 1915, Lieutenant General John Nixon arrived from India to assume command of I.E.F. "D." In June his subordinate, Major General Charles Townshend, commander of the 6th Indian (Poona) Division, captured Amara, situated north of Qurna on the Tigris River, while the next month Major General George Gorringe captured Nasiriyah, ninety miles northwest of Basra on the Euphrates River. As A. J. Barker notes, the original goal, the Basra *vilayet*, was now secure.

Still, success led not to consolidation, which would have been the proper military posture, but to temptation. Over the horizon, the prize of Baghdad beckoned, looming 340 miles north of Basra. The capture in September, 1915 of the town of Kut, located 100 miles southeast of Baghdad on the Tigris River, made this a possibility. Standing in the way was a Turkish encampment at the ruins of the ancient Persian city of Ctesiphon, whose great arch, the Taq-i-Kisra, is situated today in the Iraqi town of Salman Pak. Lieutenant General Nixon believed that the capture of Ctesiphon would pave the way to Baghdad, only twenty miles further north. Thus, in November, 1915 the moment of truth of this first stage of the campaign had arrived, and General Nixon made his fateful decision: he ordered Major General Townshend to assault the Turkish objective.

2004), p. 4. For a broader discussion of these interests, and related issues, see Davis, *Ends and Means: The British Mesopotamian Campaign and Commission*, pp. 31-2, 49-51.

Indian Expeditionary Force D, alas, ran into the sands at Ctesiphon. It fought the Ottomans more-or-less to a draw, but, having exhausted its supply lines, could not hold its position, and retreated to the supposed safety of Kut. In early December swarming Turks invested the town, and it was in that dusty desert redoubt that General Townshend, the hero of the siege of Chitral on the Northwest Frontier in 1895, decided to make his stand, hoping that history would repeat itself on the Tigris River. Despite the gallant efforts of a relief force to break through the Turkish lines on numerous occasions over the next several months, all expertly detailed in Barker's book, the siege could not be lifted. In January 1916 Lieutenant General Percival Lake replaced Lieutenant General Nixon as commander-in-chief, but he fared no better, and Kut fell on April 29, 1916. More than 13,000 soldiers became prisoners of war, with many of the rank and file later succumbing to the harsh conditions of their Turkish captivity. This was a bitter loss. Headlines in London screamed the news. It came at a bad time, with the Dardanelles campaign ending in defeat at Gallipoli three months earlier and the Western Front reduced to a meat grinder. The British campaign in Mesopotamia stalled.

Not Playing it "Safe"

Why did fortune turn against the British at Ctesiphon and Kut, which Barker describes as "one of the greatest mistakes in British military history?"[6] There were several key factors, all recounted with expertise in this volume. The first reason for failure was I.E.F. "D"'s complex chain of command: while it was officially under the control of the Indian government in New Delhi, it also communicated regularly with authorities in London, a procedure that generated strategic and operational confusion since the two capitals had different visions of the campaign. In 1912 New Delhi and London had reached an agreement in the event of war. The former promised to send "two divisions and a cavalry brigade" to the European theater. In the Middle East, according to Barker, they agreed to divide authority, with India being "responsible for the Persian Gulf and the portion of Arabia which included Basra; Britain was to look after the rest of Arabia."[7] Mesopotamia, while not a priority, "was regarded as being within India's radius of action although not within her designated sphere."

Ominously, however, the conception of operations in this region differed. To London, due to its strategic priorities in Europe, Egypt, and the Dardanelles, Mesopotamia was a secondary theater where a defensive campaign to protect the oil in Persia was envisioned. India conceptualized an offensive

---

6. See below, p. 232.
7. See below, p. 17.

operation in Mesopotamia to safeguard its interests within the context of the British Empire, especially following the appointment of Lieutenant General Nixon as commander-in-chief in 1915. It did not coordinate its plans with London at all times, nor did London demand that it do so. For example, as we have seen above, in April 1915 Lord Crewe urged caution in his cable to Lord Hardinge, the Viceroy in India, but only weeks beforehand General Harry Beauchamp-Duff, the commander-in-chief of the Indian Army who reported directly to Hardinge, had instructed Lieutenant General Nixon, before he departed to assume command in Mesopotamia, "to consider a plan for an advance on Baghdad." Barker asserts that Nixon's "arrival can be regarded as the turning point, not only in the methods and scope of the military operations which were to follow, but also in the changing aspirations of the Indian government."[8]

While there was obviously a temporary lack of communication between Hardinge and Beauchamp-Duff, London did not adequately manage the situation. It also sent mixed signals by eventually acquiescing in Lieutenant General Nixon's request to attack Ctesiphon and tolerating his eagerness to march on Baghdad, despite earlier having articulated its own serious logistical reservations. Barker delineates this strategic ambiguity in his book. General Nixon, he reports, "was given the green light [to Ctesiphon] on October 24 and Whitehall said that they would send him the two Indian divisions then serving in France, although when exactly they would be sent was not disclosed."[9] At the same time, the War Office in London did not correlate the Mesopotamian campaign to its overall war strategy. The failure to reconcile strategic objectives and to resolve fundamental differences generated a cloud of confusion that provided cover for the government in India, and the leadership of its expeditionary force in Mesopotamia, to pursue their own path. Because it never dispelled this uncertainty, London bears responsibility for the consequences.

New Delhi, on the other hand, bears primary responsibility for the second major failure: it did not insist that Lieutenant General Nixon follow Lord Crewe's principle of playing it "safe" in Mesopotamia. That is, the India government failed to correlate ends to means. The primary logistical train ran directly from India to Mesopotamia, but the campaign there was underfunded, undermanned, and undersupplied from the start, which proved deadly when Indian Expeditionary Force "D" outran its support system at Ctesiphon. Lieutenant General George MacMunn, who served as an inspector-general in the theater, drew an important conclusion from this error after the war: "It should be written in letters of fire before every War Cabinet and before every

8. See below, p. 57.
9. See below, p. 90.

General Staff. He who wills the ends must will the means."[10]

Yes, the Indian government sent some reinforcements to Mesopotamia at key junctures, such as the spring of 1915, which proved decisive at that time, but it did not sustain the lines of communication. A lack of river transport and insufficient medical supplies proved to be especially troubling. As Barker notes, "It is also important to stress that the fresh troops had been rushed out without a proper scale of equipment. Fighting men were welcome, but they came without the supply train which normally accompanies such troops and the new corps had the medical facilities sufficient only for one division. Nor had any provision been made for the additional river steamers and transport which would be so necessary for the support of the augmented force in the days to come or for a port organization for Basra. As will be seen, this was to become a problem of crucial importance, while the lack of medical facilities was to result in a near-Crimean scandal."[11]

The medical issue became especially acute at Ctesiphon and Kut, with thousands of injured soldiers denied the most basic field medical care. Barker is harshly critical on this point: "For all the utterly inadequate arrangements made for the transport and treatment of the wounded and for their hideous sufferings, the Indian government must be regarded as primarily responsible."[12] His conclusion is even more scathing: "No one in this day and age … can realize what was endured by those who were wounded in Mesopotamia in 1915; nothing, absolutely nothing, can excuse those who were responsible for the state of affairs which has been described."[13]

Supplies were not an issue in the first months of the campaign, when initial Ottoman resistance was overcome, but the first string of victories in 1914 and early 1915 set a trap for Indian Expeditionary Force "D." "Unfortunately," Barker laments, "those who were running the campaign in this third priority theater were to be encouraged by success after success steadily to extend the operations, at the same time without increasing the means of doing so."[14] Yes, London bears some of the blame, but the high command in India, and Lieutenant General Nixon in Mesopotamia, bear the fundamental responsibility. Having set the tempo with General Beauchamp-Duff's aggressive orders to Nixon in the spring of 1915, and being aware of the supply problems plaguing their troops, they still decided to move ahead at Ctesiphon. Their lines of communication, alas, were like a rope, flimsy and frayed, when they needed to be a horizontal pile driver, relentlessly propelling provisions forward.

---

10. Quoted in Davis, *Ends and Means: The British Mesopotamian Campaign and Commission*, p. 187.
11. See below, p. 58.
12. See below, p. 106.
13. See below, pp. 106-7.
14. See below, pp. 58-59.

At bottom, the logistical issues are symptoms of the fact, as one scholar of the campaign has written, that "the Indian Army was not designed for distant expeditionary operations, especially against a modernized, regular army."[15] Unsuited to confront the Ottoman Empire head on in Mesopotamia, it was more intended to police the colonial frontier in India. A. J. Barker stresses this shortcoming of the Indian Army, too, by highlighting its administrative defects: "No proper scheme for general mobilization existed; arrangements for training reservists were indifferent, and the proposed scheme for supplying the reinforcements which would be necessary was thoroughly unsound."[16]

At the tactical level, all of these deficiencies came to a head at the moment of decision before Ctesiphon. Not having received the extra troops he had been promised, along with other basic materials, General Nixon should have halted at Kut instead of assaulting the Turks. He had enough information to make this call. The officer responsible for the mission, Major General Townshend, being acutely aware of the gap between aims and available resources, counseled caution just days before the attack in an urgent cable to Nixon. "I consider that on all military grounds, we should consolidate our position at Kut," he argued. Failing that, "the advance from Kut by road should be carried out methodically by two divisions of one army corps, or by one division, closely supported by another complete division…"[17] According to A. J. Barker, "From this it is clear that Townshend was against any further advance unless he had at least two divisions under his command." He had correlated ends to means, in other words; he was playing a "safe" game in Mesopotamia.

In response, Barker writes, "Townshend received a sharp reply to the effect that it was the Army commander's intention to open the way to Baghdad, and that a division was expected from France." Nixon had overruled Townshend; he ignored the "safe" advice of his subordinate and ordered him to proceed to Ctesiphon. Barker calls this decision "absurd; there was no possible chance of any division arriving from France in time, especially as it had not even started." Intelligence reports from Whitehall, moreover, had suggested that 30,000 Turkish soldiers "under Khalil Pasha were en route for Baghdad, and that the German General von der Goltz was on his way out to Mesopotamia to take command."[18] Nixon refused to believe these dispatches, perhaps because, like many other Western officers, he had a tendency to underestimate the fighting skills of the Turks. In any event, his judgment became an

---

15. Scudieri, "Iraq 2003-04 and Mesopotamia 1914-18," p. 3.
16. See below, p. 16.
17. See below, p. 91.
18. See below, p. 91.

issue at the Parliamentary Commission on Mesopotamia, which met in London from August 1916 to April 1917. It found that although he had to cope with "wholly insufficient means ... The weightiest share of responsibility lies with Sir John Nixon, whose confident optimism was the main cause of the decision to advance" to Ctesiphon.[19]

These failures—unclear command and control, lack of coordination between London and India, resistance to playing it "safe," a refusal to match ends to means—account for the original titles of this volume, *The Neglected War* in the United Kingdom and *The Bastard War* in the United States. These titles are appropriate, since the campaign was not the priority of the War Office in London, yet the government in India, which was responsible for the war, did not provide the men and matériel necessary to wage it. To the British and Indian soldiers engaged in combat, who knew they were being shortchanged, the conflict in Mesopotamia truly appeared to be a "Bastard War." Some of the officers felt the same way: Major General Gorringe told the Mesopotamia Commission, in words that also serve as this book's epigraph, "It was believed to be a sideshow and 'no man's child.'"[20]

Heroism in the Desert

All of that said, and as this book documents on nearly every page, the heroism of the British and Indian soldiers was stirring. The conditions in which they fought were bleak, austere, and daunting. The desert heat hangs over this narrative like a death sentence. Time-after-time the troops endured forced marches of many miles followed immediately by pitched battles and hand-to-hand combat, often in temperatures higher than 120 degrees Fahrenheit. The rank and file was blasted by sand, whipped by the wind, plagued by flies, and haunted by mirages. The sun and thirst were constant enemies, with some soldiers literally dying on their feet from heat stroke and the wounded often being forced to crawl desperately to the banks of the Tigris River to gulp down some putrid water. Both the British and the Turks had to defend against marauding Arab tribes who were friends one day, foes the next, depending on their ever-changing assessment of who was winning. The British learned this fact of life the hard way during their retreat from Ctesiphon, with Arabs who only days before had been their allies now sniping at them from their flanks. As A. J. Barker points out, "according to custom, the local Arabs had turned

---

19. Quoted in Spencer Tucker (editor), *The European Powers in the First World War: An Encyclopedia* (New York: Routledge, 1999), p. 516.
20. See below, p. 17.

against the beaten side."[21] On their worst days the Arabs circled the battlefield like vultures, moving in to kill the injured, to strip the dying soldiers of their possessions, and to desecrate the bodies of the fallen.

Still, the valor of the British and Indian soldiers provided an operational advantage: it served as platform on which to stage a comeback. Events first had to unfold in London, where the widespread public outcry over the fall of Kut and the subsequent deliberations of the Parliamentary Commission concentrated the minds of the mandarins in the War Office, who proceeded to make the right course corrections in Mesopotamia. London assumed overall control of the campaign and in July, 1916 appointed a new commanding officer, Lieutenant General Stanley Maude. Once on the scene he carried out an impressive reorganization of the Army and spearheaded a five-month build-up of resources and infrastructure in the theater, including the construction of ports, roads, irrigation canals, bridges, and even a railway from Basra to Nasiriyah. These facilities were designed to match ends to means, to ensure that this time the Anglo-Indian force played it "safe" in Mesopotamia. London had finally taken Lord Crewe's advice to heart. A. J. Barker details these administrative and logistical achievements in the second half of his book, which depicts for the reader the imposing might of the British war machine once unleashed by bureaucrats in the War Office.

These military modifications, in combination with aspects of Britain's civilian response to the debacle at Kut such as the widespread media coverage and the convening of the Parliamentary Commission on Mesopotamia, all represent a positive feature of democracies at war. They are part of the process by which a self-governing society is able to audit the progress of a conflict and, if necessary, adjust fire in order to secure success. This resiliency is invaluable. Neither Czarist Russia, the Kaiser's Germany, nor the Ottoman Empire possessed it to the degree necessary to avoid revolution and defeat in World War I. Mistakes are made in every war, but one of the keys to democratic success is the ability to learn quickly from these errors, to apply new tactical knowledge on the battlefield, and to strike out for victory, which is just what the British proceeded to do in Mesopotamia.

The rebuilding effort paid dividends. General Maude started his drive up the Tigris River in December, 1916, and, by fighting methodically and relentlessly against enemy fortifications, retook Kut only two months later. His troops then passed by Ctesiphon on the way to their triumphal entry into Baghdad on March 11, 1917, where the inhabitants of the city welcomed them after centuries of oppressive Ottoman rule. General Maude's proclamation to

---

21. See below, p. 109.

the people of Baghdad declared, "Our armies do not come into your cities and lands as conquerors or enemies, but as liberators." The liberation of Baghdad was followed by further operations in Tikrit, Ramadi, Diyala Province, and the Hamrin Mountains near the Iranian border. The campaign officially concluded on October 30, 1918, when Britain and the Ottoman Empire signed the Armistice of Mudros, but in the following days Major General H. D. Fanshawe led a dash to the city of Mosul, which British troops occupied on November 14. Meanwhile, on the Western Front the war had ended three days earlier.

Mesopotamia in Retrospect

The aftermath in Mesopotamia is well known—and complicated. With the Treaty of Sèvres in 1920 the victorious Allies dismembered the Ottoman Empire and laid the foundation for the modern Middle East by creating a patchwork of new states and colonial territories.[22] The British Arabist and friend of T. E. Lawrence, Gertrude Bell, stitched together Ottoman lands to form the country of Iraq, which was designated a League of Nations mandate territory under British authority.[23] In 1921 the British granted nominal control to a Hashemite monarchy, and placed Faisal bin Al Hussein, the son of Sharif Hussein bin Ali and one of the leaders of the Arab revolt against the Turks, on the throne. Colonial rule proved to be problematic, however, with the Iraqis launching a series of uprisings that forced the British to employ draconian measures. The situation eventually stabilized, and in 1932 Iraq gained its independence. The Hashemite dynasty ruled the country until it was overthrown by a coup d'état in 1958.

In retrospect, the cost of the Mesopotamian campaign was high, and to many observers the gains were short-lived. British military cemeteries dot the landscape today across Iraq, in places like Basra, Kut, Habbaniya, and al-Amara. Lieutenant General Maude, who died of cholera in February, 1918, is buried in the North Gate War Cemetery in Baghdad. The entire operation is thus a matter of intense debate among historians, who ask a series of questions. What did it achieve? Were the costs justified? Was it central to the Allied war effort in the First World War? Did it secure British interests in the Middle East? What impact did Britain's post-war administration of the country have on the formation of modern Iraq?

An extensive scholarly literature on Mesopotamia offers an array of

---

22. For a comprehensive review of this period, see David Fromkin, *A Peace to End All Peace: The Fall of the Ottoman Empire and the Creation of the Modern Middle East*, 20th anniversary ed. (New York: Holt Paperbacks, 2009).

23. See Liora Lukitz, *A Quest in the Middle East: Gertrude Bell and the Making of Modern Iraq* (London: I. B. Tauris, 2006).

answers to these questions.[24] In numerous ways, A. J. Barker's book is a central starting point in this discussion. In it he addresses many of the issues surrounding the planning, execution, and consequences of the campaign that scholars continue to grapple with today. He is even-handed throughout his study. He apportions blame where necessary and credit where it is due. He situates the conflict within its local, regional, and international contexts. The epitome of a British Army officer, who saw action across the Middle East during World War II, he never loses sight of the trials, travails, and triumphs of the individual soldiers at the forward edge of battle, men who were fighting for King, Country, and their comrades-in-arms. It is their achievements that remind us of exactly what could be attained on the battlefield in Mesopotamia when a "safe game" was played. In a word: victory.

Joseph Morrison Skelly is treasurer of the Association for the Study of the Middle East and Africa, based in Washington, DC. He is an Associate Professor of History at the College of Mount Saint Vincent in New York City. He writes frequently on international terrorism, diplomatic history, and military affairs, and is the editor of the forthcoming volume, *Political Islam from Muhammad to Ahmadinejad: Defenders, Detractors, and Definitions* (Praeger Security International). An officer in the United States Army Reserve, he has completed a tour of duty in Operation Iraqi Freedom, where he was based in the city of Baquba in Diyala Province.

---

24. See, for example, Davis, *Ends and Means: The British Mesopotamian Campaign and Commission;* Michael Eisenstadt and Eric Mathewson (eds.), *U.S. Policy in Post-Saddam Iraq: Lessons from the British Experience* (Washington: Washington Institute for Near Eastern Policy, 2003); Toby Dodge, *Inventing Iraq: The Failure of Nation Building and a History Denied* (New York: Columbia University Press, 2005); Peter Sluglett, *Britain in Iraq: Contriving King and Country* (New York, Columbia University Press, 2007).

Preface

This story is offered as a humble tribute to the valor of the British and Indian troops who took part in the Mesopotamian Campaign between 1914 and 1918.

It describes one campaign of that terrible cataclysm which is now generally known by the prosaic title of World War I—that period which was a turning point in history, after which nothing was ever the same again. Until 1939 those four years, of blood and toil and tears, were usually described as the years of the "Great" War. This is a peculiarly apt title—not only because of the unprecedented scale of destruction and mechanized savagery that ensued—but also because of its far-reaching aftereffects, the end of which has not been seen even yet. World War II, the so-called "Cold War," and most of our present troubles are all rumblings of a troubled world as it tries to readjust to a stable pattern of conditions after the great upheaval which took place between 1914 and 1918. Since some of the more persistent of these rumbles emanate from the region of the Persian Gulf—an area vital to Britain's economy, but where British influence has been steadily declining in recent years—I regard this campaign as being of special significance.

Modern historians appear to agree that most of World War I was waged in a muddled fashion and—if only because it was so remote—the "picnic" in Mesopotamia was probably the biggest muddle of all. On other fronts the Allies sometimes profited by their mistakes, but in that part of the world the Army staggered on from blunder to blunder. The facts present a picture of political ineptitude and mismanagement; militarily, many of the lessons which derive from the campaign may now be considered to be technically outmoded. But politically and morally they are as applicable today as they were fifty years ago.

In such a complex and relatively compressed account, some faults, omissions, and errors are bound to have crept in unwittingly but I believe that I have been able to give an accurate and clear indication of the major issues involved. For those who would criticize on the grounds of inclusion of detail which appears scarcely relevant, I can only say that every cause has an effect, and to make history intelligible it is as necessary to trace the causes as to describe the effects; the student of history soon realizes how fine are the threads on which hang great destinies and so details are relevant. In war a Government primarily exercises control over operations by defining the policy to be pursued and the Services carry out its dictates. In this campaign the policy was by no means constant and there were other extraneous influences which affected the operations; the need to include these soon became apparent when the manuscript was sent around for criticism to those who served in Mesopotamia.

I must crave the reader's indulgence in regard to the correct spelling of place names; in general I have used the spelling adopted in the Official History. I have also found it necessary to describe locations close to the all-important rivers by the old-fashioned but less customary method of reference to "right" and "left" bank. The sinuous writhings of the course of the Tigris and Euphrates through the flat plain of Mesopotamia generally precludes any consistent defining of position by compass point and, for the reader who is not accustomed to the descriptive method I have used, it is perhaps necessary to say that the banks are considered to be right or left from the standpoint of looking *downstream*. Finally it is perhaps desirable to say that the expression "British" troops has often been used to describe soldiers from all parts of the British Empire, as it was then. On occasions where it has been necessary to distinguish between Indian and European troops, the expression "native" troops has been used; the expression is by no means intended as disparagement. The Gurkhas are described as such; they are not natives of India and are now members of both the British and the Indian Armies of today.

Acknowledgments

If I had not been able to borrow so generously from the library of the Royal United Service Institution, or able to call upon the services of the Reading Public Library and the British Museum, this book could not have been written. In regard to source material, I must express a special obligation to the volumes of the Official History, *The Campaign in Mesopotamia, 1914–1918,* by Brigadier General F. J. Moberly, G.B., C.S.I., D.S.O., from which I have quoted by courtesy of H.M. Stationery Office. Permission to include other copyright material has also been kindly granted by the following: Sir Reader Bullard, K.C.B., K.C.M.G., C.I.E., Ernest Benn Ltd., William Blackwood and Sons Ltd., Cassell & Co., Longmans Green and Co., Oxford University Press, Williams and Norgate Ltd.

Of all the very many people who have helped me, I must make special mention of the following: Brigadier John Stephenson, O.B.E., for his suggestions in regard to a number of books to consult, and for his encouragement; Lieutenant Colonel I. H. Stockwood for his patient and meticulous corrections of my drafts; Field Marshal Sir Claude Auchinleck, G.C.B., G.C.I.E., C.S.I., D.S.O., O.B.E., for his criticisms and suggestions; Countess Audrey de Borchgrave-Townshend for the loan of some of her father's papers and photographs; Sir Ernest Goodale, C.B.E., M.C., for the loan of his diaries, photographs and wartime maps.

Others who have proffered advice or contributed in some other way and so eased my task include: Sir Noel Arkell, T.D., Colonel G. W. R. Bishop, Major J. R. H. Bolingbroke, M.B.E., D.C.M., Major J. Castaldini, Major General G. O. de R. Channer, C.B.E., M.C., Reverend S. C. R. L. Clarke, Brigadier K. B. Crawford, Major W. G. Cripps (*The Royal Norfolk Regimental*

Association), Colonel H. J. Darlington, O.B.E. (Regimental Secretary, *King's Own Royal Border Regimental Association*), J. Dean Esq., D.C.M., Major G. J. B. Egerton (Regimental Secretary, *The South Wales Borderers*), Lieutenant Colonel P. J. Gething, Captain Sir Basil Liddell Hart, Colonel C. E. Knight, M.B.E., Lieutenant Colonel R. A. N. Lowther, M.C., E. J. Marjoram Esq., Major H. P. Patterson (*RHQ, 1st Green Jackets* [43rd and 52nd]), Captain R. E. Phillips, V.C., Lieutenant Colonel G. C. B. Sass (Regimental Secretary, *The Lancashire Regiment*), Lieutenant Colonel R. I. Scorer, M.C., Field Marshal Viscount Slim, K.G., Colonel W. C. Spackman, Lieutenant Colonel F. T. Stear (Secretary, *R.E. Historical Society),* Lieutenant Colonel P. G. Upcher, D.S.O., D.L., (Regimental Secretary, *Royal Leicestershire Regiment*), Major M. A. Urban-Smith, M.C., (Regimental Secretary, *14th/'20th King's Hussars)* and Lieutenant Colonel J. A. T. Miller, O.B.E., Lieutenant Colonel J. G. Vyvyan (Regimental Secretary, *RHQ The Royal Welch Fusiliers*), Lieutenant Colonel D. V. W. Wakely, M.C., (Curator, *The Dorset Military Museum),* Brigadier L. J. Woodhouse, M.C.

For the interpretation of character and the assessment of events I alone am responsible, and, if any of my assessments appear to be out of keeping with the facts, the faults are mine and not of those whose valuable assistance has been recorded here.

To Miss M. E. Heather and Miss S. M. White, who did so much of the typing and checking of facts, and Mr. C. G. Lovegrove and Mrs. V. Blackmer, who drew the maps, I am particularly grateful also. And finally, I must record my acknowledgment of the efforts of the men who served in Mesopotamia. My admiration for them was high when I began my researches and it was intensified as I read more and more about the campaign. At a time of revived interest in the First World War and the quickening pace of events in the Middle East it seems extraordinary that so little attention has been given to their exploits or acknowledgment of their sacrifice

The First Iraq War

1914–1918

Britain's Mesopotamian Campaign

Prologue

The thing that hath been, it is that which shall be; and that which is done is that which shall be done, and there is no new thing under the sun.

Ecclesiastes 1:8

The scene was Mesopotamia—the land not only of Adam and Eve, but also of Noah and Father Abraham; the land of Babylonia, where Daniel lived in captivity and was delivered from the den of lions; where Shadrach, Meshach and Abednego were cast into the furnace; a land which bristles with references to me Bible and which is now more usually known as Iraq. The time was 1916 when a disconsolate British Army faced a grimly determined Turkish Army entrenched astride the great Euphrates and men cursed the land of the Creation. They cursed because of the apparent futility of existence in that place at that time. In France, where soldiers knew that it was only a question of time before they stopped something in one of the great offensives that was always going to end the war, the troops were cheerful; in Gallipoli where they had clung precariously to a few miles of fire-swept beaches, they had been cheerful. But here in the "land of the two rivers" there was precious little to be cheerful about. It was not the climate—although the summer heat, which was too much even for the flies, played its part. Nor was it the lack of comforts and amusements, or even the deadly monotonous tins of bully beef, whose contents shot out in a liquid jet when they were pierced, together with the hardtack biscuits rescued from South African War surplus.

The Army in Mesopotamia was the Forgotten Army of the First World War, or so it seemed to those who were there. All it got was anything that was too old, too worn or too inadequate for use elsewhere; even the ammunition was labeled "Made in the USA. For practice only." All this perhaps, the men could have endured and still smiled, but the tide of war had turned against them. Kut had fallen—fallen in spite of all the desperate and costly efforts made to break through to its gallant defenders. The men in Mesopotamia were exhausted physically and mentally; failure and frustration lay heavy upon them.

When Allah made Hell, runs the Arab proverb, he did not find it bad enough, so he made Mesopotamia—and added flies. What was a British Army doing in this Godforsaken place and how had it all come about? For the answer, we must turn back the pages of history.

Britain's interest in this part of the world was centuries old. Starting with a trade agreement between the British East India Company and the Shah of Persia, her influence in the Persian Gulf had steadily increased over the years. The energy and enterprise of the English traders contributed much to this spread of influence, but basically it had grown with Britain's sea power. England had shown that she was willing to police the Gulf—in the same way as she policed nearly all the otherwise unpoliced waters of the earth in the heyday of her Empire—and her power grew.

The inhabitants of the desolate coastal regions are Arabs—Muslims of many tribes and tribal groups, divided among themselves but, at the head of the Gulf, into two great confederations. Those on the Mesopotamian side resented their Turkish overlords, those on the Persian side resisted Persian interference with their ancient rights and liberties; neither accepted any authority except that of their own chieftains. Of these, the Sheikhs of Kuwait and Muhammerah were the most important and, like their fathers before them, both were old friends of Britain. With good cause too, for such control as they were able to exercise over their turbulent followers was almost entirely due to the help they got from her. For generations the favorite pursuits in the upper Gulf were slave-trading, gun-running and piracy and to a coast Arab the only honorable and peaceful alternative to these traditional occupations was pearling, an industry which centered on the islands of Bahrain and Mubarak near Kuwait. As might be expected, the activities of the pearl fishers attracted their less industrious and get-rich-quick relations like bees to a honey pot so that in the pearling season the waters of the upper Gulf regularly became a pirates' paradise. In the interests of everybody economically concerned—not least the Sheikh of Kuwait, to whom pearling represented a major source of income—it was desirable to suppress the pirates. But, although Turkey claimed sovereignty over the waters of the Gulf, she did not patrol them; Persia could not, and the Sheikhs had no gunboats; only Britain was prepared to try.

In the meantime, while Britain's Royal Navy was laying the foundations of British supremacy in the Persian Gulf, another great European nation was casting an avaricious eye in that direction. Germany wanted "lebensraum." An expression, "Drang nach Osten," was coined and, if the causes of the First World War could be summed up and compressed into a single phrase, then this would be as appropriate as any: "The thrust towards the East." It expressed all the essentials for the realization of German ambitions; to Germany's militarists it was a clear, concise aim for the expansion of Greater Germany by force of arms and to the hardheaded businessmen it meant much more. Bismarck had striven to make the fatherland the most formidable nation in Europe. Germany had steadily become more and more industrialized, but German commercial interests needed new outlets. Germany's industries, railways, banks and her fiscal system had all been welded together into a machine for cheap production, but to work the machine efficiently she required markets which would enable her to dispose of her products at a profit. Yet most of the places where dividends were to be earned were barred to her; by coming late into the field of colonial expansion all the places in the sun which offered the most profitable returns were occupied by other nations, and it was humiliating to see a paltry power like Portugal holding possessions which would have been of incalculable value to Germany. What colonies she had managed to grab were not what she wanted; African swamps did not breed the sort of people who buy dyestuffs, the cannibals of New Guinea could hardly be expected to need steel rails; what such places really needed was heavy capital investment. There was enough of this to spare, but the development of primitive colonies is a long, slow process which promises only small profits and slow returns and at the turn of the century Germany was in a hurry. Despite the splendor of the Industrial fabric, the majority of the industrial and working classes of her population were poor. The excuse of "encirclement," which her rulers protested was menacing Germany's rightful place in the sun, was as re-alistic to them as it was attractive to those Germans who thought only in military terms. Out of the so-called encirclement there was one clear way—East to the Ottoman Empire and beyond. The Turks controlled a vast area, politically and economically centuries behind Europe, which was far better than any colony. Opening it up would provide many varied opportunities for German exploitation—railways and bridges to be built, mines to be dug, "concessions" to be obtained. At the same time, markets which could take the products of German manufacturers would become available, as would the wherewithal in the way of fresh sources of raw material on which the German industrial machine could feed.

These ideas seem to have been formulated about 1875, and from then on for nearly forty years German diplomats plotted and schemed to develop Germany's influence in Constantinople. Initially, their endeavors were directed toward developing Germany's commercial interests and persuading the Turks to take an unfavorable attitude toward corresponding British interests, British power and British prosperity in the East. The next step was to try to foment distrust between Britain and Russia, over Turkey, Persia and India, and then to create discord between Britain and Turkey over Egypt, Arabia, Mesopotamia and the Persian Gulf. Every aspect of their policy was aggressive, every point of it was co-ordinated and controlled from Berlin, where the men behind the scene made certain that German financial interests supported German diplomatic action.

Any opportunity which presented a means of weakening Turkey in order to secure her greater dependence on Germany was exploited to the limit; nothing was missed. Attempts were made to persuade the Sheikh of Kuwait to become a Turkish national—although this was in direct contravention of a Turco-British agreement to maintain the status quo in Kuwait; intrigues designed to upset the regime in Muhammerah were organized against the pro-British Sheikh; Turkish claims to the Qatar peninsula, next door to the British dominated island of Bahrain were voiced; objections were raised to the long-standing privileges enjoyed by Britons living and trading in Baghdad or along the Tigris.

By skillful diplomacy Britain's carefully nurtured influence with tradition-ally friendly Turkey was gradually undermined while her commercial interests steadily eroded. Because the British Government failed to provide the sort of help and backing by which the Germans were developing their commercial prosperity the trade of British firms wilted; that of German firms flourished. While Britain was occupied in other fields and dissipating her energies on other matters, the Germans were relentlessly pursuing their aim of "Drang nach Osten" and when the British Government woke up, it was too late.

In the world outside Britain, British diplomacy often enjoys a reputation for the skillful manipulation of foreign relations. If this reputation is justifiable—and, judging by the diplomatic blunders of recent years, this is questionable—then it can only derive from the fact that Governmental policy has not usually been tied to narrow commercial interests, which gives flexibility. Furthermore, improvisation, an art in which the British are truly the masters, has always been allowed full rein. To the outside, a policy of prevarication combined with one of day to day improvisation, unhampered by any partisan interest and stiffened by those "fair-play" public school ideals of the *old* British diplomat, probably encouraged respect—particularly when the might of the Royal Navy and the power of a great Empire were in the background. But, at the turn of the century, Britain had started to slide down the path of her decline and in the pre-war diplomatic skirmishes with Germany over Turkey, there is no doubt she lost almost every action. In 1912, at the advent of the Balkan war, she did succeed in recovering some lost ground when the Turkish attitude mysteriously underwent a change for the better. But the sands were fast running out and it was too late to re-establish the former relationship with Turkey before Germany had brought her into the war against Britain.

The concessions which Germany obtained to build a railway in Asia Minor and Mesopotamia were particularly important in Germany's scheme to insinuate herself into Turkey's economy, and the negotiations for them illustrate how Germany was able to extend her power over Turkey. Once again it is a sad tale of Britain losing an opportunity, for the first proposals for a railway which would link the Mediterranean with the Persian Gulf, open up the fertile valley of the Euphrates, and establish an even shorter route to India than the Suez Canal, were made by a British company. The company obtained a concession for its construction from the Ottoman Government in 1857 but nothing was done, the concession lapsed, and by 1914 German interests were predominant in the Anatolian and Baghdad railways. Financial reasons were the prime cause of this situation, combined with the fact that it was strategic and political motives which decided the alignment of the railways rather man considerations of commercial profit. Direct railway communication between Berlin and Constantinople was established in 1888 and over the next five years a number of concessions were awarded to German railway construction groups. However, it was in 1899, when a convention was signed conceding to the German controlled and financed Anatolian Railway Company the right to extend the existing railway to the Persian Gulf, that the British and Indian Governments' suspicions were finally aroused. And these suspicions were clinched three years later when a definitive scheme for a Berlin-Baghdad railway was agreed to with the Germans. There is no question that it was a magnificent concept, but it was not one over which Britain could be expected to show much enthusiasm, for it had the appearance of a highly dangerous precedent. The only possible excuse for not seeing its approach was that the concession to extend the railway to the Persian Gulf was obtained when Britain's attentions were concentrated on South Africa. Yet this can only be regarded as a lame excuse; a parsimonious outlook was probably the real reason for allowing the Germans to get in when the British should have done so. At the time when the concession was being considered, the Turks were in no position financially to provide the guaranteed revenue in return for the building of the line and the British Government declined to participate until it was too late—until the issue had been decided in favor of the Germans.

Apart from the threat to the Indian Empire which this railroad might represent if ever there was a clash of interests, there was another item of special and growing importance. In 1901 an Englishman had obtained a concession from the Shah for working petroleum in all its forms in Southern Persia. After seven years of disappointments he finally tapped an immense and seemingly inexhaustible oil field in Arabistan, within the territories of Britain's friend, the Sheikh of Muhammerah. From the oil fields a pipeline was laid to bring the crude petroleum down to the island of Abadan in the mouth of the Shatt-al-Arab at the head of the Gulf. There, the Anglo-Persian Oil Company set up its tanks and refineries, a new town was created and, by 1912, Abadan was on the way to becoming a great oil-shipping port. From the outset it was an all British concern, but in 1914 the British Admiralty stepped in to buy a controlling interest in what, till then, had been a purely private commercial enterprise. In Whitehall the move was criticized as unjustifiable extravagance but the Lords of the Admiralty had considered the importance of fuel for His Majesty's new oil-driven warships and the trend of events in the immediate vicinity of its source. Theirs was one of the few preparations England made for war and coming events were to provide ample justification for it.

By 1914, the Turks had been hypnotized into complete acceptance of the brotherly compact between their Sultan and the Kaiser. Most of the country's administrative services were running under the auspices of German "advisers," the Turkish Army was commanded by a Prussian and German officers held all the major command and staff appointments. German officers were also infiltrating into the senior ranks of the Turkish Navy, which for many years had been developed and served by a British Naval Mission. Supervising and encouraging the German take-over was Turkey's War Minister, the unscrupulous firebrand Enver Pasha[1] who had a miscellaneous following of extremists. Most of this collection of "Young Turks"—insincere individuals who had lived in Europe and whose respect for their own religious persuasion was not of a very high order—were generally well placed in senior commands in the Turkish forces.

---

1. A colorful character, but a queer mixture of quisling and patriot. Enver had helped to found the "Young Turk" movement and the Committee of "Union and Progress" at the time of the Balkan Wars. In 1913, at the end of a phase of these wars, he burst in on a cabinet meeting in Constantinople and shot the Minister of War, whom he considered was about to conclude a peace treaty unfavorable to Turkey. Subsequently he consolidated his position with the old regime by marrying one of the Sultan's daughters.

At the end of the First World War he fled the country and, after a fascinating series of adventures and intrigues with and against the Bolsheviks in Central Asia, he eventually disappeared in the summer of 1922. Very little is known about his ultimate fate but he is paid to have been beheaded by Cossacks in a wild and lonely valley in Turkestan.

As August gave way to September and then to October, the position of the British in Turkey steadily deteriorated. The members of the British Naval Mission in their executive command were suddenly replaced by Turkish officers, and a situation engineered which made their position untenable. Matters finally came to a head on October 29, when the Turkish Navy sailed out to bombard the Russian Black Sea ports, so creating, according to the British Foreign Office Statement, "an unprovoked violation of the most ordinary rules of international law, country and usage." Quite obviously the bombardment had been intended to provoke a crisis and the Allies responded accordingly; the British, Russian and French ambassadors demanded their passports from the Grand Vizier and departed.

So far, Britain was not at war with Turkey. Nevertheless, within a week, she had severed the last tenuous bonds of friendship and a formal declaration of hostilities had been made; the reason for this was given as the invasion of Egypt by Turkish troops massing in Palestine, a threat which had existed for some months. German agents were known to have been active in Cairo since August and through intelligence channels it had been learned that Enver was being urged to declare a Jihad—a Holy War—against the British, with the ultimate aim of restoring Egypt to its old condition as a Turkish province. Rumors of agents slipping into Egypt in disguise were rife, and the British ambassador in Turkey reported that he was concerned about such individuals impersonating Indian soldiers. "In substantiation of this," he wrote, "I have to state that His Majesty's Consul at Aleppo has learned that a tailor in that town has been commissioned to make a variety of Indian costumes and headdresses on designs and measurements supplied by German officers there." In fact, this rumor was never substantiated. (Unlike that just over twenty-five years later, when Germans were reported to be using similar subterfuges in the Low Countries. There, they were suspected of traveling among the streams of refugees disguised as nuns, having a stubble of beard on their chins and concealing submachine guns beneath their habits.)

The idea of a Holy War was extremely potent propaganda and the Germans were prepared to go to extraordinary lengths of mendacity in order to rouse the Mohammedan world; in true Teutonic fashion there were no half-measures and everything was done very skillfully. First, a report was circulated to the effect that the Kaiser had embraced the Muslim faith. Hadji Mohammed Guilliano, as he was now supposed to be calling himself—Hadji being the term applied only to those who have been to Mecca—was intent on restoring Islam to its proud position of a thousand years before, or so it was said.

According to the whispers around the bazaars, the Kaiser had seen the light when he had visited Mecca as a guest of his "brother" the Sultan some years previously. There, while he lay three days and nights seeking God's will before the great shrine, a voice from heaven had come to him, as the "Savior of Islam and Sword of the Lord," telling him to "Arise and Fight." For those who were not sufficiently convinced by these stories of the Kaiser's new role as Defender of Islam, other supporting rumors were assiduously circulated. Britain's main object in waging war against the Turks and their subject peoples, the Faithful were told, was that she was determined to rifle the tomb of the Prophet and add his bones to the collection of those of the Pharaohs and other ancients in the British Museum. At the same time an astonishing new family tree was found for the Hohenzollerns. The whole family was descended from Mohammed's sister, the word went out, and therefore it was the sacred duty of all Mohammedans to rally around the Turks and, of course, their allies. Perhaps the most incredible story of the lot was that Germany had a giant aircraft with an all-powerful magnet. This was supposed to have visited Petrograd, Paris, and London in turn, and sucked up the Tsar of all the Russias, the French President, and his most gracious and unwilling Majesty, King George V, taking all three off to Berlin as prisoners. In this day and age such blatant falsehoods might seem to be so puerile as to be utterly ridiculous. But, like the Voice of Cairo today, they had a far reaching and dangerous effect on many of the ignorant people of the Muslim Middle East.

Among the Arabs, the propaganda calling for a Jihad undoubtedly did have a measure of success. However, there was one major flaw in the argument and because of it the Turks and Germans preached to a lot of deaf ears among those of the Faith under British rule. The Mohammedans of the world` are divided into two main sects; the Sunnis and the Shi'ahs, the Shi'ah world including a part of Muslim India. The Sunnis acknowledge the Sultan of Turkey as the spiritual and temporal successor to the Prophet. But the Shi'ahs, who are regarded by the Sunnis as heretics, acknowledge only the Imam Ali who married Mohammed's daughter Fatima. Ali had two sons, both of whom—according to Shi'ah belief, that is—were treacherously slain by the Sultan's forefather. Consequently the Shi'ahs, whose temporal prince is the Shah of Persia, regarded the Sultan as usurping a holy office and they were less disposed to answer the call to rally round Hadji Guilliano. Clearly this was a schism that could be exploited and the pro-British Aga Khan speaking for the vast number of Muslims who looked to him as their spiritual head in India, quickly declared his loyalty to the British crown. "Turkey," he said, "has lost the position of trustee of Islam, and evil will overtake her. Nothing that the Turks or their German masters can do will ever weaken the loyalty of the Muslim Indians. . . ." To the Government of India, worried that a Jihad might sweep down from the North-West Frontier into the plains and the heart of the country, the Aga Khan's declaration of loyalty was more than welcome and His Highness, Sultan Mohammed Shah, Aga Khan, G.C.S.I., G.C.I.E., was suitably rewarded. But concern for the religious issue persisted and its effect will be apparent later.

So much for the stage; before the play starts it is also desirable to take a brief look in the wings and a glance at the actors. This means India, the Empire's "brightest jewel" whose quiescent millions were kept under the "galling yoke" of England by a there hundred and twenty-five thousand men from Britain, of whom more than three-fifths were soldiers. Approximately eighty thousand English troops and one hundred and fifty thousand Indians constituted the Army in India; native reserve forces amounted to another thirty-six thousand men; there were eighteen thousand Imperial Service Troops furnished by the Princes of the native states and, finally, an Indian Defence Force trained by regular officers, of thirty-six thousand European and Anglo-Indian volunteers. That was the total Indian military establishment in 1914—little enough to guard the frontiers, garrison the vast country and still provide substantial expeditionary forces for service in France and the Middle East. And all was not well in India's military world.

For close to 300 years there had been a British Army in India; at first this consisted only of European troops employed by "John Company"—the Honorable East India Company, whose commercial control of the great subcontinent preceded a British Governmental takeover. Gradually, as the numbers of troops increased with the inclusion of more territory, the troops were divided into three separate and individual bodies called Presidency Armies, and each Army was further subdivided into "Royal" troops—regular regiments of the British Army serving in India, "Company's" European troops, and "Company's" native troops. In i860, when the term "Royal Army" ceased to be used, the first two of these subdivisions became "The British Army in India." The third subdivision became part of Queen Victoria's military establishment and was thenceforth known as "The Indian Army," whose soldiers were men of India and whose officers and certain N.C.O.s in technical units, came from Britain.

This leaves one other category to be explained and, because it comprised troops of the Indian Princes, there is a special romance attached to the States Forces and Imperial Service Troops. The origin of both stems from the break up of the great Mogul Empire, when the various heads of the Principalities formed by its disintegration created their own armies; these were used primarily to war among themselves and to hold off the rising power of the British and French. Sooner or later all the Princes and Rajahs concerned attempted to organize their forces on the European model and to do so called in numbers of

Europeans, some of whom were capable and trustworthy, others who proved to be scallywags. As time passed, almost all the Princes attempted a trial of arms with the British which ended in their undoing; only when defeated did they settle down to a place in the British Empire, and when this happened their private armies were limited by treaty. Even so, the existence of most of the States Forces, composed largely of ragamuffins and used primarily for ornamental purposes, perplexed the Indian Government for a long time.

A war scare immediately prior to the turn of the century led to Governmental subsidies to keep them in being as a form of second-line defence. Then the Indian Foreign Office came up with the idea that a portion of the States Forces should be trained and equipped "so that they shall always be available for the service of the Empire" and from this germ sprang the idea of Imperial Service troops, trained by British officers, equipped from British arsenals, but still forming part of the States Forces. Needless to say the Imperial Service Troops remained subjects of the Princes they served and, in general, they constituted a military commitment which the Indian Government had to face at a time they would have preferred to be without it.

It is said that a young subaltern, joining the Indian Army only a few years before the outbreak of the war, asked an old general who had served in India since the Mutiny, "What was soldiering like in your day?" The reply was, "Very much as it is now, except that you fellows wear such beastly clothes." It was true; life in the cantonments had changed little in thirty years. Those who were subalterns then say that it had changed little twenty years after that. All of which suggests that there was perhaps some persistent factor peculiar to India herself which resisted change—even military progress. If so, then it was never more apparent than in 1914. With the coming of the new century, a more friendly understanding with Russia and the gradual extinction of the opium revenue, the Government of India had endeavored to cut expenditure; a cold wind of economy blew through India's military establishments and the army stagnated.

Late in 1902, with all due pomp and ceremony, Lord Kitchener of Khartoum took over as Commander-in-Chief of Britain's Army in India. "K. of K.," one of Britain's most famous soldiers, a somewhat awe-inspiring figure and a lonely man in consequence, was a man of stupendous energy. Capable, ambitious, dogmatic, he had built his reputation as a great public servant after winning fame as a soldier. It was for this reason he had been selected for the role of a new broom to sweep clean the Army in India, just as Lord Curzon, the Viceroy, had brushed up the civil administration. There were plenty of cobwebs to clear away. In Britain, matters had moved fast since the South African war, but in India the Army had stood still. In training, organization and equipment it was far behind European standards and Curzon, apprehensive of Russian designs on Persia, Afghanistan and Tibet was afraid that it might be called upon to cope with a Russian invasion. Except on the frontier, the Army was scattered throughout India in a number of independent commands and districts rather like the old Presidency armies.

Kitchener's aim was to concentrate, reorganize and redistribute the various units and formations, and modernize the staff in such a way as to provide protection from invasion, preserve peace on the Frontier, and maintain internal security. To rationalize these three aims he decided that most of the units should be massed on the Frontier and the remainder concentrated at various strategic points. Among the changes introduced was the reduction of the five existing commands to two, and the concentration of executive power in the hands of the Commander-in-Chief. The regiments were rearmed, equipment modernized, and new arsenals set up. But all this—particularly the movement of large numbers of troops from their existing stations to new ones and building new ones—was necessarily very costly and consequently it was not long before Kitchener came into conflict with the Viceroy's Council. Through the Council the Commander-in-Chief had to channel his proposals to the Government, and the Military Member who acted as War Minister invariably dabbled in military matters that Kitchener rightly considered to be only the concern of the Commander-in-Chief.

Kitchener, very conscious and jealous of his own responsibilities, thought that this system of dual control was iniquitous. "The system of putting the Army under a separate administrator," he wrote, "is simply *monstrous,* and full of the utmost danger in wartime. I have an Army without means of feeding, mounting and supplying it. For this I have to trust to a totally distinct and separate Department of Government, which is, I believe, very inefficient, and certainly knows nothing of war. When war comes, disaster must follow, and then I suppose the soldier will be blamed." His solution was simple—the abolition of the Military Member; the Commander-in-Chief would be War Member of the Viceroy's Council and if he had to be absent in the field then he should be able to appoint his own deputy. Curzon jibbed; like his Commander-in-Chief he too was exasperated with the system but, if he could help it, Kitchener was not going to meddle with the machinery. To Balfour in London he complained "If the Commander-in-Chief has anything to do with the machinery, he will become too powerful. . . ." As a compromise, it was suggested that all military functions should be passed to the Commander-in-Chief and that the Military Member should control matters concerned only with supply. This reduced the position of the Military Member to a there sine-cure but, what was far more serious, it reflected in the powers exercised by the

Viceroy as Governor-General. Curzon was up in arms at once but his protests were of no avail and when he offered his resignation on this score, to his pained surprise it was accepted.

Subsequent events in Mesopotamia were to prove that Curzon had been correct in regard to this aspect of Kitchener's proposals. Apart from the constitutional aspects, Kitchener's scheme for control by the Commander-in-Chief had grave defects. Under his system the Commander-in-Chief had to act in a dual capacity, and in consequence, when he was a "soldier's soldier" like his successor, administration suffered; when he was an administrator, like Beauchamp-Duff—his deputy who eventually succeeded to the post—field training was neglected. Under the test of war it broke down altogether. However, this was not apparent at the time and in 1909 the post of Military Member as such was abolished. By a strange irony of fate, Beauchamp-Duff found himself fulfilling the dual roles of Commander-in-Chief and Military Member now both rolled into one and to the Mesopotamia Commission he admitted that he was so overwhelmed by administrative detail that he was practically cut off from contact with the combatant services. "The layman in Bombay," he said, "knew more about what was going on in Mesopotamia, than Army Headquarters in Simla."

When the time came, "K. of K." was succeeded by the sixty-one-year-old General Sir O'Moore Creagh. "No more K." was a tough old soldier who had gained the Victoria Cross in the only action in which he had ever taken part and had shown character commanding troops in China during the Boxer rebellions. But that was his total experience; Grande Guerre and its preparation were strange subjects to him. Only in appointing Sir Douglas Haig to be his Chief of the General Staff did he give some proof of a desire to follow Kitchener's progressive attitude. But he had not the drive of his predecessor and under his hand Kitchener's reforms proceeded at a much slower pace. During his period of office, the Indian Government's financial overlords held the reins and with the approval of the new Viceroy, Lord Hardinge, the Army in India was subjected to constant, vigorous, economic pressure and on the assumption that it was unlikely to have to fight other than on the North-West Frontier, the military budget was slashed and slashed again. Training and the provision of equipment ignored the possibility of fighting a European army; the number of divisions available on mobilization was reduced from nine to seven; artillery units were cut; ancillary units were either undeveloped or nonexistent, and by 1914 it was worse off than it had been at the time of the South African War. There was no air force—a token establishment was set up a few months before the war but its limited scope was such as to make it virtually useless—and there was no mechanical transport service. Hospitals and medical services for the Indian Army had always been below the standard of those of the British Army but even these were chopped in those bleak years. For officers and most of the munitions of war, India was almost wholly dependent on Britain, so that when the war came the demands of the new armies raised in England meant the almost total cessation of these two essentials.

Since the Army in India was expected to fight only on the North-West Frontier, its equipment and organization was designed solely for the type of warfare that could be expected in that region. In the British Army a new design of webbing equipment, which allowed men to carry their rifle ammunition in easily accessible pouches and their "field-service" equipment—socks, spare shirt and the like—in a pack on the back, had been introduced in 1908. None had reached the Army in India; it expected long marches and so the men's impedimenta was carried by pack mules, ponies, camels or in Animal Transport carts. For the purpose and the theater for which they were intended, the "A.T." carts were excellent robust vehicles; in Mesopotamia, in the absence of anything else, they often had to be put to use as makeshift ambulances, a role for which they were highly unsuitable. The artillery's guns were small handy weapons, firing light shells—sufficient, if not ideal, to deter tribesmen fighting a running war in the rock-bound, hilly terrain of the Khyber, but of little use against a resolute, organized and entrenched enemy. There were no light machine guns, very few even of the medium guns, although this is hardly surprising considering the British Expeditionary Force went to France with only two per battalion. Centralization of facilities was almost nonexistent. Divisions were based on the geographical areas in which the units were stationed in peace, each individual Indian regiment relying on its Depot for its needs. Even the sick were cared for in regimental hospitals; general hospitals largely existed on paper only.

War was expected to be a business of movement in which the cavalry would assume the major role—it could only be the cavalry because the way the infantry was organized their movement must necessarily be confined to a slow tramp. Consequently the Order of Battle included a high proportion of Indian cavalry regiments. Some were organized and supplied on orthodox regular lines but others were equipped on what was known as the "Silladar" system, a method which was a relic of the post-Mutiny reorganization. Under the Silladar system a benevolent Indian Government supplied the firearms and certain items of mobilization equipment—the rest, in theory, being provided by the troopers, in reality by the regiment concerned out of sums deducted from the troopers' pay. In theory also, since the Silladar troopers had to provide their own horses and equipment their pay was suitably augmented. As might be expected, pay had lagged behind the cost of living and as prices rose over the years, the quality and numbers of horses in the Silladar regiments had declined. In order to keep their regiments efficient, Commanding Officers needed to be astute businessmen, horse-dealers in the real sense, and this was a role for which very few of them were qualified. Consequently, when the time came for the regiments to mobilize large numbers of horses and vast quantities of equipment which should have been in good condition either had to be replaced or else the regiments would take the field with horses and equipment that had seen better days.

Nor was this the end of it. Kitchener's reorganization had not removed many of the other weak spots in the Indian organization. Apart from a lack of any real reserve of officers[2] the number and quality of the reserves of men were totally inadequate. An Indian infantry regiment's reservists rarely amounted to half its establishment in serving soldiers and under the existing system many were too old or physically unfit for active service anyway. No proper scheme for general mobilization existed; arrangements for training reservists were indifferent, and the proposed system for supplying the reinforcements which would certainly be necessary was thoroughly unsound. No organization to cope with the recruiting and training of the men that would be needed to meet the heavy wastage or any large scale expansion, existed; recruiting was no problem but civilians do not become soldiers fit for active service overnight and at least nine weeks was needed to train the recruits properly.

Glum though it may seem, these were the untoward circumstances which formed the background to the many comprehensive commitments India found she had to meet in August 1914. As an introduction, it is a sorry tale, one which it is necessary to conclude quickly before the catalogue of error and omission grows too long. Nevertheless, it is essential to put in context the reasons why India apparently neglected to allow its policy of cutting the service to the bone to march with its acceptance of Imperial commitments. In Britain nowadays, one hears much talk of "tailoring" overseas military commitments to the reduced resources available and one wonders whether or not there is a parallel. If a military commitment is considered necessary men the men and material necessary must be available; if not, then men's lives will be wasted even if military disaster does not result. When the War Office in London realized that war with Germany was not unlikely, India's cooperation in a major war in Europe had been mooted in 1912 and she had promised two divisions and a cavalry brigade. At the same time, in the event of war, an

---

2. The Indian Army List shows only forty officers in the Indian Army Reserve of Officers at the outbreak of the war.

arrangement was made for India to be responsible for the Persian Gulf and the portion of Arabia which included Basra; Britain was to look after the rest of Arabia. Mesopotamia, at the head of the Persian Gulf, did not seem to warrant any particular attention, so it was regarded as being within India's radius of action although not actually in her designated "sphere." As a war with Turkey in alliance with Germany did not seem much of a possibility at that time, who was to look after Mesopotamia seemed of little consequence anyhow. If war came, Imperial policy was to protect the Suez Canal from the Arabs, the Anglo-Persian oilfields from the Turks, maintain authority in the Persian Gulf and to watch out for troubles on the North-West Frontier and possibly in India itself. That was all. Then, when the holocaust broke, the authorities in Britain were far too involved with plans for concentrating all the available forces for a decisive operation in Western Europe to be really concerned with Mesopotamia, and India was bounced into a campaign against her better judgment. Of these circumstances, there is no better summary than that contained in General Gorringe's bitter comment: "It was believed to be a sideshow and 'no man's child.'"[3]

---

3. Evidence at the Mesopotamia Commission.

Chapter 1

The Capture of Basra

On September 29, 1914, His Britannic Majesty's sloop *Espiègle* steamed slowly up the Persian Gulf to enter the estuary of the Shatt-al-Arab—the gateway to the oldest country in the world. Her mission—in what were regarded technically as Turkish waters—had been defined by the British Government as a purely precautionary measure. Since August and the cataclysmic turn of events in Europe, anti-British feeling in the Middle East had been steadily growing, fostered by official German and Turkish agencies; with it also came significant rumors which could be associated with military activity, all of which suggested that a break with Turkey could not be far distant. Baghdad was said to be under martial law. Foreign vessels using the Tigris had been turned back; Turkish preparations to block the Shatt-al-Arab and rumors of Turkish troops assembling in Basra for an expedition against Kuwait were all rife; a circumstantial suggestion that there were plans for an attack on Abadan was perhaps the most menacing information of all. But the prime reason for the *Espiègle's* mission was the Royal Navy's concern for two German raiders at large in the Indian Ocean. Since August the two cruisers, *Emden* and *Konigsberg,* whose courses could only be plotted by the trail of havoc in their wake, had successfully evaded the Navy's attempts to catch them and sooner or later it was felt that at least one of them would make for Basra, to lie up and refit in Sinbad the Sailor's old home port. Color was even lent to the possibility by a voluble stream of Turkish protests about ships of the British Gulf Division remaining in Turkish waters. They had never protested before; it had always been accepted that ships which kept to the Persian bank of the Shatt needed no Turkish permission to sail even as far as Muhammerah.

This entrance to the biblical lands of Mesopotamia is formed by the confluence of the Euphrates and the Tigris: hence the lyrical and romantic allusions to "The Land of the Two Rivers." Where they join, silt brought down by the two great waterways over the centuries has built up a vast alluvial plain which continues to creep into the sea year by year; it has also created an underwater barrier which precludes anything other than shallow draft vessels crossing into the Shatt, except at high tide. The *Espiègle* had to wait until high tide and even then, as she crossed this bar, the blue waters turned to a tawny yellow as her screws churned up the mud. Following her into the estuary came the rest of the Royal Navy's Gulf Division; first, the armed merchantman HMS *Dalhousie,* and then the sloop *Odin,* which stood off to watch and patrol outside the bar. Once across the barrier, the *Espiègle* and the *Dalhousie* steamed on—past the low palm-fringed flats on either bow, past the cable station near the old Turkish fort at Fao; on and up, through countryside where the cabbage-like tops of thick belts of crowded date palms obscured all but the near banks of the river.

Monotony of the scenery was broken only by glimpses of picturesque creeks and Arabs in their canoe shaped *bellums* or gondola-like *mashoofs* whirling past in the fast tidal stream, until, forty-five miles further on, the buildings, clustering chimneys, tanks and wharves of the oil refinery on the island of Abadan came into sight. Here the *Dalhousie* anchored on the Persian side of the river, while the *Espiègle* sailed on to drop anchor opposite the Sheikh's gaudy palace at Muhammerah, where the river Karun empties its clear waters into the yellow flow of the Shatt. Metaphorically, the Karun was then, and is now, something of a backwater. But it is closely connected with the greatest periods of Persian history, and was once the highway to cities, where now only great mounds of ruins in the desert show they ever existed. Muhammerah, itself the site of a number of ancient cities, was a pleasant enough spot for the *Espiègle* to lie up. Sheikh Khazal, whose grandfather had saved a British ship from pirates, was thoroughly sympathetic toward Britain, there were shops and bars and what is more, a cheerful European colony, happy to see a British warship in such proximity.

It was not long before the Turks objected to the presence of all three ships. On October 7 a formal letter, which ended with the curiously stilted instruction, "Please you leave the Shatt before 24 hours" was delivered to the *Espiègle* by a Turkish naval officer. The British commander replied that he could not leave without orders from the Admiralty. Nevertheless, if only because the question of whether or not the *Espiègle* was anchored in Turkish waters might be disputed, he moved his ship half a mile up the Karun where there could be no doubt about being in Persian territory; at the same time the *Dalhousie* moved back to the bar of the Shatt. A week elapsed before the Turks made any further move. The British Consul at Basra was then curtly told that if the *Espiègle* was not out of the Shatt-al-Arab by October 21 she would have to stay for good and any attempt to leave after that date would be prevented by force of arms. This ultimatum was followed by warlike preparations which could be seen quite plainly by the crew of the sloop; field guns were brought up and mounted on the river bank opposite Muhammerah and boat loads of troops sailed past going downstream.

On the day before the ultimatum was due to expire, Colonel Subhi Bey, the Wali[1] of Basra and commander of all Turkish Forces in lower Mesopotamia, sent a note to Sheikh Khazal. In it he proposed that Turkish troops in disguise should be allowed to move into the town and occupy the rooftops of houses on both sides of the Karun, opposite where the *Espiègle* lay at anchor. Then, when the time came it was planned that the guns on the opposite bank would open fire on the sloop and, when she fired back, these troops on the rooftops would rake her decks with small arms fire. "The slaughter" said the Wali "would be unexpected and eventually the gunboat could be seized without difficulty." "This" he concluded "would be an excellent opportunity for the Sheikh of Muhammerah to render a valuable service to the Turkish Government."

Fortunately—so far as the *Espiègle* was concerned anyway—the Sheikh was not inclined to be so accommodating; the information was passed to her captain, the ultimatum expired without incident and nothing further happened for another ten days. Action was then prompted by a signal from the Admiralty telling the *Espiègle's* commander that the Turks had opened hostilities in the Black Sea and ordering him to take such action as he considered desirable for safeguarding British interests in the area.

Two nights later, on an ebb tide and stern first, the sloop slipped her cables and dropped quietly downstream; apparently she got away without attracting the attention of the Turkish battery on the far bank or else they were prepared to let her go. Stopping only to allow a landing party to cut the telegraph lines between Fao and Basra, the sloop continued downstream to Abadan. There she anchored and, even as the cable rattled down, a ragged fusillade of rifle fire broke out from the Turkish side of the river and bullets sang over the *Espiègle's* deck. A few rounds from her guns soon put an end to it, however.

---

1. Governor

Meantime, both British and Turks had been busy elsewhere. Just above the Karun the Turks were getting everything ready to block the Shatt. A string of ships, consisting of the German 5,000 ton Hamburg-Amerika liner *Ecbatana,* the British lighter *John O'Scott* and two other small tramps had been assembled. These were to be towed across the Shatt and moored before the ships' seacocks were opened; when they went down it was expected that the channel would be blocked and the only practicable highway into the heart of Mesopotamia impassable to anything more than light native craft. This was one plan which was to go awry. Meantime the British were preparing for action.

In Whitehall, an expedition to Mesopotamia had already been discussed at the end of September, when a memorandum entitled "The role of India in a Turkish War" was submitted to the British Government by Sir Edmund Barrow, the Military Secretary of the India Office. "This seems a psychological moment to take action" he said, and went on to detail the advantages of an unexpected occupation of Basra. Turkish intrigues "would be checkmated" he postulated, the Arab world would be encouraged to rally behind Britain and the allegiance of the Sheikhs of Muhammerah and Kuwait would have a justifiable boost. Most important of all, such action would serve to protect the refinery at Abadan.

Undoubtedly this last reason was most important since oil interests were becoming the prime concern of Britain's economy. In the steam era Britain's possession of a first-class supply of steam coal had been the prime factor which enabled her to attain naval control of the world; with the advent of oil this inestimable strategic advantage had been lost. When oil superseded coal, the supremacy Britain had enjoyed by virtue of her coalfields went for good and during the transition period at the beginning of the century, three-quarters of the Royal Navy's oil supply came from the Middle East. Basically the problem is still the same, but at that time the safety of the supply depended on a subsidy paid to the Arabs living near the wells and to the influence of the Sheikh of Muhammerah; the fact that neither the wells nor the refinery at Abadan was in Turkish territory could hardly be regarded as likely to deter the Turks from endeavoring to cut off the supply. But it was known that they were being urged to do so by the Germans, and they, in the firm of Robert Wonckhaus, already had a tailor-made organization on the spot well suited to direct anti-British intrigues. Starting in 1896 with a simple business which bought shells on the beach, this firm had enjoyed a meteoric success and by August 1914, Wonckhaus and his partners had become the Middle East agents of the Hamburg-Amerika line with business agencies in all the main towns. The firm was known to have contributed large sums of money to the Baghdad railway and although the source of the money remained a mystery it was certainly not all from business profits. Time was to show that its representatives were trained intelligence agents.

Whitehall's decision to send an expedition to Mesopotamia now led to a considerable correspondence between the United Kingdom and Indian Governments. Initially, the idea of occupying Basra had not been entertained—the prime purpose was to safeguard the oil and Turkey was not yet a belligerent anyway; what was proposed was merely a demonstration at the head of the Persian Gulf. Both Governments knew that Turkey was favoring the proponents of a Holy War and that German arms and ammunition were pouring into Turkish territory but what worried the Indian Government was a fear that the so-called demonstration might look like an unprovoked attack on Turkey and it was apprehensive of the effect on Muslim opinion in India. Consequently, reactions to the idea were at best lukewarm; neither a recrudescence of disaffection in India nor a major war with Turkey were problems which that Government wished to face. Particularly now. There was the constant menace of the tribes on the North-West Frontier and the expeditionary forces which India had already agreed to provide for service in France, Egypt, and East Africa would seriously deplete the country's military establishment. Only time would show that these extra demands would drain India's resources to an impossibly low level and that the fears associated with religious feeling were exaggerated. Toward the end of 1914, the concern was real enough and India protested vigorously. Eventually however, her protests were overruled and once the decision had been taken the steps to mount the demonstration were left to the India Government. It was from here on that all the generally recognized rules for planning such a military operation appear to have been broken—though not for the first, or last, time of course. The War Office in Britain was not in charge of the operation; there was no cooperation between the War Office and the two governments and the plan which was evolved was not coordinated with either. That which was evolved was based on purely political considerations and gave little real consideration to military factors.

On October 2 the Indian Government was ordered to embark a brigade of the 6th Poona Division; its destination was to remain a secret until the troops were at sea but it would sail with the convoy which was going to France. Meanwhile the rest of the division was to be ready to follow up and a suggestion circulated to the effect that its destination was to be either Egypt or France. To do this, various subterfuges were adopted but the only people they effectively bewildered were the troops and they learned the truth in Bombay, for there the bazaars were buzzing with rumors that they were bound for Mesopotamia. From the types of ship in which the force were to embark and the quantities of rations which were taken aboard, the Indian tradesmen, in their own inimitable way, had quickly deduced what was afoot.

To most of the Indian Expeditionary Force "D," as it was now called, the orders to move came as a welcome climax to the waiting the troops had endured since August. The battalions and regiments of Lieutenant General Sir Arthur Barrett's division were all regulars and after the first spasm of excitement when war was declared the troops had found that hostilities were still tantalizingly distant. India had absorbed the news of a flare-up in Europe with almost complete indifference and life went on much as before; there was no sudden paralysis of business, no rush on the banks, no public demonstrations of patriotic fervor, no roar of troop trains; *war* was still a word. Among the troops there was a bit of excitement at first, while the units mobilized. After only a few days, life in barracks had resumed its monotonous routine and the men had settled down to wait and wonder when and where they would be invited to join in. When, at last, the orders came to Brigadier General W. S. Delamain's 16th Brigade: "The Brigade will proceed on active service" the tempo changed. It was required to entrain for an unknown destination in an almost impossible time. The final assembly on the parade ground was followed by the march to the railway station, through almost deserted streets to the martial strains of, first in the case of the Dorsets, the regimental march and then with a South African flavor, "Goodbye, Dolly Gray"; a hurly-burly of loading men and animals and they were off—all trains converging on Bombay. Generally, the departure was not impressive; there were no flagged streets nor enthusiastic crowds to wave goodbye to the troops and the attitude of the local population reflected a dispassionate interest in anything to do with the war. Despite what the politicians might say about India's "heart and soul" being in it, the war meant little to the ordinary man in the street.

Apart from countless stops and the backings and shuntings of the trains, the move to the port of embarkation was generally uneventful although, by the light of later events, the failure of such arrangements as the provision of meals en route—resulting in many of the men spending at least twenty-four hours on remarkably short rations—was a preliminary indication of the too often pathetic lack of administrative foresight which was to epitomize the earlier part of the campaign. At Bombay, where the destination was revealed as Mesopotamia, jumbles and muddles were overcome by the sort of improvisations at which the British Army is so adept, and eventually the 16th Infantry Brigade Group[2]—for the brigade's strength had been swelled by the addition of some supporting units—was loaded into the waiting transports. Because of the authorities belated realization that ships with more than eighteen feet draft

2. The brigade later referred to as I.E.F. "D."

would not be able to cross the bar at the mouth of the Shatt-al-Arab, it was six days behind schedule; collecting the right sort of transports and rearranging the loading tables all took time. Getting all the impedimenta accompanying regiments going to war, including squeaking, kicking country-bred ponies and equally obstreperous mules, between the decks of small ships also took time and yielded the sort of problems which can best be imagined. But eventually everything was aboard. Before the convoy sailed there was a brief spell of shore leave and the shops were besieged by those making last minute purchases—tins of "Keatings" anti-insect powder, carbolic soap and mosquito nets being in great demand. For the officers, a bath and a last civilized lunch or dinner at the "Taj" hotel was the finale.

The convoy sailed on October 16. Force "D" had assembled in Bombay with part of the main convoy bound for France and East Africa, the remainder of the ships for France coming from Karachi. On the third day out from Bombay the two sections of the convoy met and the battleship *Ocean* joined company as escort to the Gulf transports. The journey was as uneventful as could be expected. The troops, crowded and cramped, did physical exercise only by half companies as it was thought that the energetic and concerted efforts of more than a hundred men at a time might well rattle some of the old ships to pieces. En route, there were no ports of call and no opportunities to explore the mysteries of the pirate coast of the Gulf as some had hoped, and seven days after leaving Bombay the convoy anchored off the pearl fishers' island of Bahrain—there the Gulf expedition waited until the news of the attack in the Black Sea came through on the thirtieth. There also, Delamain ordered the arrest of the Wonckhaus Bahrain agent, a German, called Harling, who was picked up in his office in the act of signing a letter to the German Consul at Bushire. This letter, which turned out to be a report on the strength and composition of Force "D" ending with the remark that, so far, only about five thousand troops had come up the Gulf but that ten thousand more were on their way, showed that the German intelligence system was working well. None of the troops were allowed to disembark but while they waited some of them were given practice in rowing the ships' boats; if and when an assault landing had to be undertaken this practice might lessen the confusion—or so it was hoped.

Delamain's orders were vaguely simple. He had been told to occupy Abadan in order to protect "the oil refineries, tanks, and *pipe line*"—though how he could possibly accomplish the latter from the island of Abadan is difficult to understand. He was also required "to cover the landing of reinforcements, if these should be required" and finally, of course, to assure the local Arabs of British support against Turkey. Only if hostilities with Turkey were to become fact was he to occupy Basra and in this event the rest of the 6th Division would be ready to come to his assistance.

With the news of the Turkish hostilities against Russia, came instructions for Delamain to go ahead and fulfill the provisions of the first part of his directive; and next day, as the *Espiègle* was moving to Abadan, the convoy sailed for the Shatt-al-Arab. It arrived at the sandbar in the estuary on the evening of November 3, and there waited for two days until the minesweepers had made sure of a clear channel. To the troops, heartily sick at being cooped up, the operation seemed to be one long succession of waits and when the news that war had been declared on the fifth reached them, a sigh of relief went up. At long last it seemed as if they would see some action.

The first operations of the campaign started next morning. The *Ocean* was too big to cross the bar and so, leaving her outside, the rest of the convoy entered the Shatt; while the sloop *Odin* stood in to bombard the four-gun Turkish battery near the ruins of the old fort at Fao. In an hour the battery had been silenced and a composite force of 600 British troops, which included a party of the *Ocean's* marines and a couple of mountain guns, was landed. There was no opposition; most of the Turks had decamped soon after a shrapnel struck and killed their luckless commander—"The Bimbashi of Fao fort,"[3] and Fao's defenses turned out to be merely a walled enclosure badly battered by the *Odin's* guns. Reinforcements followed quickly on the heels of the assault party and the Krupp guns were torn from their mountings and thrown into the sea.

If only because Fao was the land terminal where the Turkish telegraph lines from upper Mesopotamia connected with the British cable to India and Persia, this minor victory had considerable significance. As was to be expected, the cable had been cut and the telegraph instruments destroyed but within a few days the system was working again under the Royal Navy's auspices. In the meantime the *Espiègle* had been in action again off Abadan, a few rounds of shrapnel from her guns rapidly dispersing a party of Turks which had established itself on the right bank of the Shatt. Next day Delamain sailed up the Shatt with the rest of his brigade, until he came to the refinery; behind him the landing force at Fao was re-embarked to follow. From a brief reconnaissance in the *Odin,* a bend in the river three miles further on was chosen as a suitable landing place. There was nothing particular to distinguish it from countless other bends in the river except perhaps by the fact that the tiny village of Sannayeh nestled in it, and that it was only about nine miles below Muhammerah. But, tactically, it seemed as likely a place as anywhere and the troops started to disembark from the long line of transports next morning.

---

3. It had not been the Bimbashi's day. He lived in Basra and this was his first visit to his operation station.

They and their kit were disgorged under every imaginable difficulty. A swift flowing current, no barges, no tugs and no landing stages on shore all made the few yards between ship and river bank extremely difficult to negotiate and it took two days to get the whole force ashore with its guns and animals. And in these two days the weather was anything but kind. During the day it was very hot but the mornings broke with an icy wind blowing down the river, so that as the troops waited to get off their ships they cursed the authority that had sent them to war in this place clad in thin tropical cotton.

Once ashore the expedition settled into a perimeter camp. Delamain had intended to start advancing toward Basra but he had the safety of the oil refinery to think about, and when he learned that a Turkish force was moving down toward the camp he deemed it wise to stop where he was. And there was every good reason for doing so; outnumbered and outgunned by the Turks round Basra, according to an Intelligence assessment, there was no sense in taking unnecessary risks when his divisional commander, with another infantry brigade and a brigade of artillery, was at sea only two days behind. Nevertheless he was not to remain undisturbed and at dawn on the eleventh about 400 Turks charged down on the camp. Fortunately for Delamain, as he had had prior information of the attack, the defence was ready and waiting. Eighty Turkish bodies remained on the battlefield when the Turks decided that they had had enough and withdrew to a defended area at Saihan, nearly four miles away.

In 1914 radio was not what it is today and ship to shore wireless communications broke down over this period. General Barrett knew nothing about Delamain's most recent battle when the convoy bringing the rest of the division steamed up the river to anchor at Sannayeh three days later. Until Turkey declared war there had been no question of invading Basra. Barrett's original orders were to *try* to occupy Basra only if she became a belligerent; otherwise the expedition was merely intended as a "demonstration" at the head of the Persian Gulf. Barrett had received the news that a state of war now existed between the two countries but, until the convoy arrived in the Shatt, he had no idea of how far Delamain had progressed. Disembarkation started at once and the infantry, using the ship's boats, were soon ashore. But, as their predecessors had found out already, getting the guns, wagons and horses off was a long, tedious business. Nevertheless, even as his force struggled ashore Barrett, now appraised of the situation, concluded that if Basra was to be taken, the sooner he started to advance, the better. Not only was it rumored that strong Turkish reinforcements—albeit "Catch 'em alive-o's," hastily scraped together in Basra with a few obsolete guns—were on their way down the river, but the attitude of the local Arabs might well depend on his having a quick success or otherwise. Delamain was ordered to reconnoiter ahead and, if possible, to eject the Turks from Saihan.

Early next morning (November 15), three battalions of Delamain's old stagers (Dorsets, Punjabis and Mahrattas) and the two mountain batteries marched out from Sannayeh with this end in view. By the same evening they were back, having dispersed the Turkish force and inflicted two hundred and fifty casualties in a very successful little action. The British troops had had more than a battle inoculation; they had experienced some of the difficulties of footslogging across a muddy plain and for the very first time they had met up with that strange phenomenon known as a mirage. The ground, sodden by recent heavy rain had turned into a tenacious, sticky quagmire; in dry weather the same ground breaks up into dust to provide a perverse, inverse alternative to the mud. The mirage is another of the country's perversities. Nothing is immune from it; every object a mile or so away becomes confusedly different and it even conveys a false impression of movement. The result is that animals seem to be men, trees become hills, bushes and birds, cavalry. Most of Mesopotamia is as flat as a billiard table and there are no trees, and practically no landmarks away from the rivers. Consequently, by obscuring the very few landmarks which can be recognized, a mirage often induces a strange sense of isolation. The combination of dust, mud, mirage and climate of which Delamain's men had a brief foretaste, was "to cause our troops endless trouble ... in the months to come."[4]

Encouraged by the success at Saihan, Barrett was now determined to attack what was believed to be the main Turkish position just above Muhammerah and the order was given to advance on "Sahil." (The name Sahil has stuck, although its vagueness—for it is the local word for "shore"—suggests that the same mistake had been made as on another occasion when a surveying party, coming to a village not marked on the map, hailed a local Arab and asked him its name. "M'adri" replied the Arab and Madri was marked on the map although what the Arab had said was "I don't know.") The Turks, about 4,500 of them, proved to be dug in near some palm groves close to the mud fort at Kut-az-Zain, about nine miles from where the British troops had disembarked. Barrett's plan was to attack their right flank driving them toward the river, where the *Odin* would be able to hammer them with her guns.

So far, only one battery of 18 pounder guns of the 10th Brigade, Royal Field Artillery had been landed but, the whole of Major General C. I. Fry's 18th Infantry Brigade and two squadrons of the divisional cavalry regiment, the 33rd Light Cavalry, had joined Delamain's brigade ashore. And so, at 6 a.m. on

---

4. F. J. Moberly, *The Campaign in Mesopotamia 1914–1918*, Vol. I, p. 117.

the morning of November 19, the two brigades, the cavalry and all the guns that could be mustered, set out for the village of Zain. There was no sign of the Turks until the vanguard of Barrett's force came within sight of the old fort and then the air was rent with the familiar crack of bursting shrapnel. Quickly, the column shook out into battle formations and, as they did, the heavens opened and it seemed as if the elements had turned against the British. Almost in an instant the ground was turned into a slippery, slithering, sloppy mess by the rainstorm which deluged the desert. Even the infantry could move only slowly and then with the utmost difficulty, while the gun teams were stuck and there was no option but to manhandle the guns into position. As a result, the advance across the two thousand yards of flat bare desert in front of the fort was painfully slow; luckily for those concerned the Turkish shells were bursting too high to inflict many casualties and the Turks' rifle fire was very inaccurate.

Persistence had its reward; as the attackers pressed on toward their objectives, the British guns came into action and shells smashed down accurately on the Turkish positions. The key position was the fort itself and when this fell the whole Turkish line got up and ran for it. It was no orderly retirement; the Turks just scrambled out of their trenches and streamed away; everything seemed set for the coup de grace. Then, suddenly at this crucial moment, a mirage appeared and as the British gunners were totally unable to distinguish any target at which to fire, the Turks were able to make off without much difficulty. A couple of guns and 150 prisoners were taken. Losses would have been a great deal more if the 33rd Cavalry had been able to get after them. With the ground a quagmire, the going far too heavy for the horses, a pursuit at walking pace is rarely effective. Yet, in spite of the elements, Barrett had every reason to be satisfied with the results of the day's fighting. The Turks had lost heavily; in Basra it was rumored that their casualties were over a thousand. This was probably an exaggeration. Nevertheless they had certainly suffered considerably more than the three hundred fifty-three British casualties. Of these three hundred fifty-three, the casualties who could least be afforded were four British officers of the sappers. Specialist officers were at a premium in Barrett's force and their loss meant that technical work was considerably hampered so that he was soon wiring urgently to India for sapper reinforcements.

As they withdrew, the Turks hurriedly tried to effect their plan for blocking the Shatt channel. The string of ships was towed across the river and all went well until they were settling down. Then the cables parted and the *Ecbatana,* swung by the tide, sank. Because of this, a clear channel—to be known later as Satan's Gap—was left and although navigating through it was a difficult performance, the gap was just sufficient to allow ships to get up to Basra. At first it seemed that the Turks were retiring to a position just opposite

Muhammerah and the mouth of the Karun. When this information and the news of the river block reached Barrett the *Espiègle* pushed on up the river to see what could be made of the obstacle. As the sloop approached the sunken block the *Marmariss,* a Turkish gunboat, and an armed launch which were lurking on the far side, together with a battery of guns covering the block, all opened fire. The *Espiègle* replied vigorously with such effect that the guns were silenced and both the *Marmariss* and the launch made off at all speed up river. Once this happened the *Espiègle's* crew were able to examine the block more or less at leisure and its weaknesses were soon probed.

Next morning, while Barrett was getting ready to resume his advance and attack the position opposite Muhammerah, Sheikh Khazal sent news that the Turkish Arab troops who had been occupying it had deserted; no longer were there any Turkish troops between Barrett and Basra. Nor was this all. As the *Espiègle's* crew worked to clear Satan's Gap, a launch appeared with a deputation from Basra begging the British to come up and save the town before it had been torn apart by looting Arabs. The 104th Wellesley's Rifles and the 117th Mahrattas were embarked without delay and, escorted by the *Espiègle* and *Odin,* they set off upstream. Satan's Gap was negotiated without mishap and by 9 p.m. on November 21, Indian soldiers were taking possession of the town. Delamain's directives had been fulfilled and the first objectives of the campaign had been achieved.

There had not been enough time for the local toughs to do much damage in Basra. As the *Odin* and *Espiègle* came in sight of the port, clouds of smoke could be seen arising from the town. A few rounds of blank shells from the ships' four-inch guns had a salutary effect and apparently frightened the looters into good behavior. But the ships were only just in time; the Custom House had been broken into and set on fire, the Consulates were expecting their turn to arrive very shortly. Most of the townsfolk were relieved to see British troops—though not the rowdy elements, a number of whom were caught and summarily punished "pour encourager les autres." By noon the next day the remainder of the force arrived after a grueling thirty mile forced march across the desert which, without maps or guides, made in searing heat and partly in the dark, showed a high standard of training. However, men and horses were both about all in when the column finally bivouacked outside the town's wall and an official entry was left until the morning of the twenty-third. The troops then marched to the center of Basra and in the presence of the town dignitaries the British Political Officer, Sir Percy Cox, standing alongside Barrett, read a Proclamation declaring the reasons for the presence of British troops. The ceremony concluded with the Union Jack being run up, a salute fired by the ships in the river, three cheers for His Majesty, and with that Sinbad's old port was officially under British protection.

To understand the disasters and misery which were to fall on the army in Mesopotamia it is now necessary, momentarily, to digress and consider the problems which Basra presented the invaders. Basra itself, formerly the fortified town of Ashar on the right bank of the Shatt, is a cosmopolitan port which, in 1914, had a mixed Christian and Muslim population of about sixty thousand souls. Near Basra the narrow belt of palms, already described as fringing the waterway, runs inland for two or three miles. For some distance on either bank numerous tidal creeks run up from the river for three or four miles and these are often a hundred feet wide; side canals radiate from these creeks to fill the gridiron ditches in which the palm trees are planted. When the tide is up—and it rises as much as twelve feet—everything is afloat, the gardens are flooded and the palms irrigated twice a day. The tide merely backs up the fresh water of the river and no salt water comes up. Beyond the creeks there are ten miles of alluvial desert of mud flats until one reaches higher ground; nothing grows here and behind Basra the flats are impassable in the rain. When the "gates of heaven are opened" and "the fountains of the deep are loosed,"[5] in the season of river flood and strong sea winds, the high waters of the Euphrates are forced back by a bar of sea water blown up from the head of the Persian Gulf and Sinbad's modern Bussorah is cut off from the mainland.

In those days, ships coming up the Shatt-al-Arab anchored off Ashar where there was a narrow strip of dry land on which stood the few mercantile houses. Above this strip, known as the "River Front," the Ashar Creek led up to the city of Basra, then the town of Ashar and another strip of dry land. Above this there was three miles of flooded palm gardens intersected by several creeks and finally a piece of higher ground known as the Makina; between Ashar and Makina the only dry spots were those that have been referred to. The deep channel in which ocean going vessels could lie was in the middle of the river, too far out to be reached by any jetty. Ships were unloaded by a few Arab port lighters. Since the normal pre-war traffic was limited to about two ships every three weeks, more ambitious facilities had not been necessary anyway.

It was into these primitive surroundings that Barrett's expeditionary force had come. Supply, ordnance and engineer depots were quickly located on such dry spots as were available and some of the larger houses were requisitioned for hospitals. Thus the demands of a small base were satisfied, but communication between them mostly had to be by water, and the supply of small craft and motor boats was almost nonexistent.

---

5. Genesis 7:2 and 8: 3.

One of the country's peculiarities is the fact that there is little drinking water in Mesopotamia except that which comes from the rivers. Water from wells dug in the drier parts, behind the palm trees, is too salty to drink and the well-to-do inhabitants of Ashar and Basra were accustomed to drawing the water from midstream; inshore the banks of the Shatt were too foul for those who respected their health. Consequently, when they disembarked, the troops were encamped on the dry patches within reach of the river.

Officers of the Royal Indian Marines, who came with the force, handled the few river craft then in use, but no one in authority at that time seems to have grasped the needs of what would be required if the force increased, or advanced up the river. Improvisation and sweat were the only essentials for dealing with the inconveniences of the moment and the few thousand troops then involved.

If, in the absence of motor boats, communication was difficult by water, it was worse on land. Moving in the dry zones behind the palm gardens meant crossing deep, wide creeks and, as there is not even a stone to throw at a dog in the region between the Tigris and the Euphrates and as there was no other material on hand, roads had to be built of alluvial mud. In the spring, when the floods came, even dry patches were saturated so that it was not even possible to bury the dead until a raised cemetery—several feet above sea level—had been built.

How impracticable a place to base a large force Basra was, and how necessary to have a clear program of work, and some idea of what one was working for will be obvious. Labor was badly needed for construction work, but military labor units were unknown in India. Nor was there any form of work organization to handle a locally hired labor force, and clearing the deep-sea ships which now crowded the river was far beyond the stevedoring resources of Basra. As more and more troops arrived the result can be imagined. Yet for close to two years there was no proper planning to improve conditions; conditions deteriorated but nobody seemed able to think big enough, and engineer officers with inadequate resources sweated far into the night to erect contrivances more suited to a small scale expedition in Upper Burma than a war against a first-class enemy which would necessitate the deployment of a huge army. Nobody grappled with the problems of Basra; nobody grappled with the problem of river craft even when the troops started to press forward. But this is going beyond the sequence of the story and the sad result of this lack of planning will unfold in the disasters which were to eventuate.

Returning to Basra and November 1914: Apart from the restoration and continuance of good order which the occupation brought to the locals, the British and Indians represented new business opportunities. And certainly the sight of civilization was welcome to the troops although they soon found themselves busily engaged in clearing up the age-old ordure of the town, for under Turkish rule even the most elementary rules of sanitation had been disregarded. The whole place was filthy and, like the well-to-do of Basra, they soon found that the only water fit to drink had to be fetched from the middle of the river. Yet, in spite of the precautions which were taken, there was soon an outbreak of dysentery and, to cope with this and the casualties which had been incurred since the landing, a hospital was opened in the Sheikh of Muhammerah's Basra palace. For those not employed on clearing-up duties there was plenty of other work. Stores had to be unloaded from the ships lying in midstream; sappers were put to making roads, improving bridges and devising elementary jetties. But there were shops, some beer, opportunities to wash and bathe, and an open market was soon doing a thriving trade with local produce.

Basra quickly settled down to life under its new rulers. The customary administrative proclamations were made and among them was one that illustrates the fear that the Indian authorities still held of religious differences having a detrimental effect. A letter was issued to the tribal chiefs warning them not to be misled by Turkish calls for a holy war. It declared:

> You, the Sheikhs of the Arabs, are wise men and will not be misled, but some of your ignorant tribesmen may be. It is therefore considered expedient to remind you of the following facts, which are patent to all and cannot be denied.
>
> Great Britain never came into this war willingly. The war was forced on her simply by the intrigues of Germany, who for her own purposes incited Turkey to commit repeated acts of hostility against England, so that she might be involved in war with her.
>
> Immediately on the arrival of the British forces in Shatt-al-Arab we proclaimed that the British Government had no quarrel with the tribes of Iraq and no design against their religion . . . and that the British forces would not attack or molest the Arabs, so long as they maintained a neutral attitude.

So far as the majority of Arabs, including quite a number of the Sheikhs, were concerned, it was soon to be seen that religious scruples were of lesser concern than material gain.

Contact with the Turkish Army had been broken when the sorry remnants of their force had fled across the desert from Sahil and the task of finding out where the new front line had been established fell to the Navy. Two days after Basra had been taken over, the *Odin* and *Espiègle* with the armed launches *Miner* and *Mashona* steamed up the river toward Qurna.

Forty miles upstream the "old" Euphrates joins the Tigris; the terms "old" and "new" Euphrates may seem confusing but the explanation is simple enough. In the course of time the river had silted up its "old" channel which, by the turn of the century, had become almost a backwater. When this happened the Euphrates changed course and cut a new channel running further to the southwest. Nowadays most of its waters are discharged into the Tigris at Gurmat Ali, five miles above Basra, and it is this channel which is regarded as the "new" Euphrates. Even now the channel is still ill-defined because it is constantly shifting and, for half the year it floods its shallow bed, turning the surrounding desert into one immense lake—all of which makes navigation up the lower reaches extremely difficult. In the triangle of firm land, where the "old" Euphrates joins the Tigris, lies the reputed Sumerian Paradise of Qurna or Kurnah—pronounced "Gurna"—which is the legendary site of the Garden of Eden. It was a place which had changed considerably since our first parents were driven out by the Angel with the Flaming Sword, the latter in all probability being the burning sun. But it was here that His Majesty's ships were making for.

From Basra, the Turks had fallen back to places where they could stand against a further British advance and at the same time get food, supplies and reinforcements quickly. Qurna was such a place which offered yet another important advantage besides—being so situated as to not be easily attacked from the flank. If an attack from the rear was unlikely, the back door remained a secure way of retreat if and when the need arose. And so, after his defeat on the seventeenth, Colonel Subhi Bey had collected the disorganized remnants of his force and made for Qurna as fast as his boats would carry him. His men were badly shaken and he had hoped for a breathing space but, as events were to show, he was not going to get it; the pursuit was too quick for that.

Steaming up toward Subhi Bey's new stronghold, Captain Hayes-Sadler, commanding the British ships, suddenly sighted the *Marmariss* six miles below Qurna, retiring up the Tigris after her unprofitable venture of five days before. Shots were exchanged but the Turkish gunboat had no intention of getting involved and Hayes-Sadler's ships were unable to get after her fast enough. Three miles further on the *Odin's* rudder was put out of action in a collision with an underwater obstruction. The whole flotilla came under the fire of field guns deployed in front of Qurna while a furious fusillade of rifle fire broke out from both banks. A few rounds of shrapnel soon silenced the rifles but as it was getting dark and Hayes-Sadler had found what he set out for—a landing place on the left bank out of sight of Qurna, and only two and a half miles away—the flotilla turned about and returned to Basra. In less than a week the Navy was back and, this time they were escorting four steamers full of troops.

General Barrett's original objective had been Basra but, to consolidate his position there, his orders allowed him to move as far up the river as was necessary to protect the port. Qurna, at the junction of the two rivers, certainly seemed to be the logical place to establish an outpost and on December 3, a composite force of two Indian battalions (104th Wellesley's Rifles and 110th Mahratta Light Infantry) and a double company of the Norfolks, with some sappers and a couple of field guns, two of which had been mounted in the steamers, embarked and set off upstream. The sloops *Espiègle* and *Odin* led the way, behind them came the *Lawrence*[6] and three armed launches—the *Miner, Shaitan* and *Lewis Pelly*. By nightfall the convoy was anchored about ten miles below Qurna ready to resume the journey next morning. However, at daybreak, as the ships steamed on up the Shatt, toward the landing place selected by Hayes-Sadler on his earlier sortie, there was now the familiar crash of bursting shells fired from a couple of Turkish guns emplaced two miles further on at the village of Muzereh. Here, part of the Turkish force had dug in to prevent access to the bank opposite their main position in Qurna. Since Qurna lies inside the fork of the two rivers, the assaulting troops had to cross one of the rivers—either the Euphrates or the Tigris—and as they had landed on the left bank of the Shatt it was the Tigris which barred the way. The landing went more or less according to plan. Under a barrage of fire put down by the gun-boats, everybody was safely ashore and the advance toward Muzereh had started by nine o'clock in the morning. The *Odin,* with her damaged rudder, stayed back to guard the landing place but the *Espiègle* and the rest of the ships moved steadily upstream in order to lend their fire support to the attack. It was not long before they were in the thick of it. Turkish guns had been concealed among the thick belt of date palms fringing the river and they were extremely difficult to locate. Time and time again the boats were hit and, before long, the *Miner,* holed below the water line, had to struggle back out of the battle. Not that the opposition were getting it all their way; shells from the *Espiègle* set fire to Muzereh village and a hail of shrapnel soon forced the Turks out of the date palms which surrounded it. If they had had time to finish their defenses it might have been a different story but, as it was, their uncompleted trenches were too shallow to afford much protection.

Until they reached the forward edge of the date gardens, the attackers had to move across a flat open plain utterly devoid of cover, and it was only the ships occupying the Turk's attention and drawing off most of the fire that enabled the position to be taken. But once into the date gardens the British and Indians steadily worked their way forward and around, until they reached the river bank opposite Qurna. There they were stuck; just as soon as a man showed himself on the bank a hail of bullets from the other side of the river

---

6. The *Lawrence* was one of six Indian Marine ships, transferred to the Royal Navy at the outbreak of war.

drove him back to cover. Loopholes had been made in every wall in the town and every house on the river front was strongly held. A stretch of yellow, racing water, as wide as the Thames at London Bridge, separated the two sides and with no boats and no bridge, there was little hope of getting any further. The order to retire was given and by late evening the troops were bivouacked where they had disembarked that morning. Except for desultory shelling, that night and the following day passed without incident. No further attempt to assault was made until the reinforcements which had been sent for arrived on the river steamers that were taking the wounded back to Basra.

At dawn on the 6th, Major General Fry arrived with the rest of the Norfolks, two more Indian battalions (7th Rajputs and 120th Infantry) and one of the mountain batteries; another battery of mountain guns was coming up behind him. Facing Qurna there were now about 2,316 guns—a force which was slightly superior to the Turks, although they too had been reinforced from upstream. Having been left undisturbed for twenty-four hours, Subhi Bey's men had also crossed the river and reoccupied their old positions in the charred remains of Muzereh. Consequently when Fry launched his attack, the battle which had taken place two days before, had to be fought all over again; the result was much the same as before. With great courage the launches chugged up the river until they came within sight of Qurna, and a tremendous barrage compelled them to retire. The *Shaitan,* caught in a devastating cross fire from both banks, narrowly escaped running aground when she received a direct hit on the bridge; her steering gear being put out of action and her commander killed.[7] But on land the soldiers were making steady progress. Muzereh was cleared and the Turks driven back across the river, but again as no crossing to Qurna was possible a retirement was ordered once more. This time a detachment was left to hold the bank, however, so that the Turks could not recross and bring about a repeat performance at Muzereh.

The problem was to get the troops across the Tigris; the solution was provided by the Royal Navy. On the morning of the 8th, Hayes-Sadler ordered his tiny fleet to move up toward Qurna's "back door" and after three hours of groping forward, the ships managed to get past the river junction to a position from where shells could be lobbed into the town. And, while he was maneuvering on the river, two of the Indian battalions (104th and 110th) with a few sappers, a section of mountain guns had marched up the left bank, well away from the river and then turned toward it. The Tigris was reached without mishap and an Indian sepoy swam across carrying a light line; an officer followed and eventually their efforts resulted in a wire hawser being pulled across to the

---

7. Lieutenant Commander Elkes, R.N.R.

far bank. There a conveniently abandoned *mahela* was found and within the
hour the first troops were being ferried across. Thus, by the time the first
rounds from Hayes-Sadler's ships were beginning to fall in the town, a land
threat was developing a mile and a half above it. Before the Turks had realized
what was happening the Indians were astride the northern approaches to
Qurna, communications were cut and their back door had been slammed shut.
All day long the ships' guns thundered and shells burst among the buildings in
Qurna but the Indians made no attempt to press on into the town. It was late
afternoon and, as street fighting is a slow grim process at any time, Fry had
decided that it would be better to hold off until the next day. When the time
came, it turned out that no more fighting was necessary anyhow; the Turks had
had enough. At midnight a steamer put out from the town and headed downstream with siren blowing and lights burning; she was carrying Turkish officers
to discuss terms of capitulation. If his men could march out under arms, Subhi
Bey said, he was prepared to surrender the town. Unconditional surrender—
nothing less—was what Fry demanded and after some discussion this was what
was agreed upon.

There the story of the battle for Qurna ends; during the afternoon of
December 19, with due ceremony, the British flag was hoisted in the town and
the assembled Turks marched out into captivity. It was a sizeable bag: forty-
two officers and nearly a thousand men laid down their arms, and these had
been heavy losses in the two engagements at Muzereh. British casualties
amounted to only twenty-seven killed and two hundred ninety-two soldiers
wounded plus two sailors killed and ten others wounded. To clinch the British
hold on Basra the cost had been comparatively cheap.

There was nothing attractive about Qurna even though it was supposed to
be the home of our first ancestors. None of the troops relished a prolonged
stay there but, as many of them thought that the campaign was over anyway, it
seemed sensible enough to organize things in such a way that they would be as
comfortable as the circumstances would permit. Consequently the jobs of
clearing the place and converting it to a defensive position were tackled enthusiastically.

It was not unreasonable to think that this was what the future promised
and it is true to say that this was the end of a phase—the end of a period of
cheap successes. Barrett's force had done well; they knew it, and morale was
high. Most of the Turkish 38th Division had been eliminated, over 1,200
prisoners and 21 guns captured, Basra had been secured and the oil refinery at
Abadan was safe. With a formidable list of achievements like this it might have
been better to have let matters rest. But it was not to be; apart from the fact
that the Turks were not prepared to acquiesce, the domes and minarets of

Baghdad were already beginning to glisten in the minds of those in Simla.

Every day the expeditionary force was getting stronger and reinforcements were pouring into Basra and by the end of the first week in December the Poona Division was almost complete. *Almost,* because the one exception was transport, and confusion over this essential element was to have a lasting effect. By the middle of the month over 3,000 mules had arrived and about 1,600 camels but, to function properly in the field, it had always been reckoned that an "Indian" Division needed just over 3,000 mules and a similar number of camels. Since there was no grazing for camels in and about Basra however, it was obviously no place for them and Barrett wired to India to ask if he could send back all but 300 of those which had already arrived. He would not be likely to ever need them, he said, because the division would never move very far by land; what he did not say was anything about the requirement for more boats which he would need—to move on the river. Even in retrospect, this seems a little odd for an experienced general. On the one hand he was prepared to restrict his means of moving by land; on the other, he had apparently not appreciated the vital need for the boats which would permit him to move by the only other medium open to him.

There were some wise heads among those who were with him—in November an Indian Marine officer recommended that the three available steamers should be augmented by twelve more, as quickly as possible. The basic trouble was that Barrett did not have enough wise heads among his staff—or even enough heads. For the expedition he had little more than the normal divisional headquarters complement of staff officers whose training, experience and numbers made them totally unsuited to any other task but that of coping with the current situation. Organizing a base was a job for specialist officers and Army HQ in India had not thought fit to provide any. Before Gallipoli Lord Hankey prepared an appreciation for the War Office listing all the requirements of specialist nature: assault craft, endless supplies of small boats, engineer services and the like. Most of his appreciation was ignored in any event, but at least there had been some thought given to the problem. For I.E.F. "D," India did nothing; Simla was still thinking in terms of the Frontier, Afghanistan, and the Russian Bear—in terms of pack transport and screw guns.

In their view, water was for drinking, not for transport, and the idea of rivers functioning as roads never entered the lists. According to the Mesopotamian Commission, Barrett had realized by this time that he might have to go on to Amara and Nasiriyeh; if he did, then presumably his staff and the staff in Simla also knew of the possibility. Yet nothing was done, no provision made. This may seem to be a strange lack of foresight, but the answer would seem to lie in the system which prevailed at the time. The prime requirement of a good staff officer was to be a colorless self-effacing character prepared to serve—not to suggest—and to work according to regulations. As India had submerged the workings of its army in a sea of regulations there was little opportunity to show much initiative and even if one tried only frustration could result. Whether it was the system, the shortcomings of individual staff officers, or the lack of direction by the commander that is considered to be at fault with regard to the errors of omission made at this time, the shortcomings were going to have to be paid for. As invariably happens in war those who were to pay were the soldiers, and the debt was to be settled in blood and suffering.

Chapter 2

The Turks Try to Recapture Basra

A *friend* cannot be known in prosperity; and an enemy cannot be hidden in adversity.

Apocrypha, Ecclesiastes 12:8

After the fight for the Garden of Eden, an uneasy quiet prevailed in Lower Mesopotamia and there was no really important action until April 1915. Qurna was regarded as the front line and to see how the war in Mesopotamia was getting on this was the place to which the visiting generals and other dignitaries came.

Among them at the beginning of February was India's Viceroy, Lord Hardinge of Penshurst, whose arrival finally confirmed a rumor that he was coming to visit Mesopotamia before taking a decision on its future in the British Empire. His arrival at Basra was attended with the customary ceremonial becoming the senior representative of the British Raj, and before he went up to the front, there was the usual round of guards of honor and inspections—culminating with a presentation of "robes of honor" to loyal Arab Sheikhs "for services rendered." At Qurna he walked around the defenses and, as it was a Sunday, a special parade service was held in his honor. The lesson was taken from the second chapter of Genesis and the sermon which followed was based on events at the traditional site where it was being given; as the descendants of the "Tree of Knowledge" were only a stone's throw away, it all seemed appropriate enough.

By the middle of the month the sultry stillness of the nights and the steaming heat of the days were a clear indication of the approach of the hot weather. The camps in and around Qurna were infested with fleas and tiny sand-flies, while the irrigation ditches brimful of malodorous water were the breeding grounds of the relentless mosquito hordes which attacked the troops by night. The countryside had that dreary unprepossessing appearance of a huge marshland with nothing Paradisiacal about it. In the early days of January the ground had been comparatively firm underfoot, although roots of dry rushes springing from the fissured soil, jungles of dried reeds and occasional patches of swamp intersected by sluggish streams were pointers to the fact that quite different conditions existed at other times of the year. By March the whole area was to become one vast inland sea, whose high-water mark could be measured by the protective banks surrounding Qurna's outlying villages. Even the date palms outside these walls, which provided the only soft touch of color in an otherwise harsh and forbidding landscape, would be covered when the floods were at their heights and it would be October before the water receded. By mid-May there is hardly any dry land at all between the Euphrates and the Tigris; something like ten thousand square miles of land are underwater and the story of the great flood told in Genesis is probably a true account of but one seasonal episode. In all probability, Noah was a weather prophet of considerable experience and when he foresaw that there were possibilities of an abnormally bad season he prepared accordingly. The country is exceptionally flat and, without any natural barriers, a rise of a few extra feet of flood water would be sufficient to spread with alarming rapidity and turn the whole of Mesopotamia into an immense sea, with a devastating effect on the crowded and unprepared population of Biblical times.

When the floods finally subside, marshes and inland lakes of brackish water are left. The ground between, which dries out to rock hardness, is intersected by deep watercourses which are sometimes as wide as great rivers. Odd though it may seem, most of these *nullahs* are distributaries of the two great rivers and not tributaries draining water from the country as might be expected. From the Persian hills however, there is a single tributary, which enters the Tigris just above Sheikh Sa'ad, and this—the Wadi—was to have much importance in some eighteen months time. Lesser streams draining toward this nightmarish plain lose themselves in the Suwaikiyeh Marsh near Sannaiyat. For campaigning, winds were an added curse. In June, the northerly prevailing winds which sometimes produce forty-mile-an-hour gusts were welcome because they dried the atmosphere and afforded some relief from the summer heat. But at other times east winds brought heat, and the oppressive south wind brought dust which covered everything and left a thick sandy sediment in the mugs of the tea-drinking Tommies. All winds brought problems for the river boats; the airmen suffered by their engines being choked with dust, and the effect on the inland lakes was to raise great tidal waves which would advance at about fifteen yards a minute. Camps pitched at midnight near a lake could be under water by six the next morning with their occupants frantically striving to rescue kit and stores.

Steady rain is almost unknown in Mesopotamia, and the rain has little to do with the floods, which are caused by the melting of the snows in the mountains of their upper waters. Earlier civilizations coped with floods by controlling the rise in the river and, by the evidence of former prosperity, it is apparent that they succeeded. Before the dawn of any Western civilization a huge system of canals intersected the country in all directions. Who built them is still a mystery, but in the first millennium B.C. their origin was considered both mysterious and divine, and for thousands of years, through this enormous network, the rivers were harnessed and controlled for irrigation. During the whole of this period, man was master of the great waters and throughout all Mesopotamia's vicissitudes a succession of conquerors were content to leave the canals alone. Persians, Seleucids, Parthians, Sassanides, Saracen Caliphs—all were wise enough to appreciate that once out of control the waters could well become their master. Then came those who neither understood nor cared. In the middle of the thirteenth century, in an orgy of destruction and wanton cruelty, Mongol hordes swept through Persia with savage and unscrupulous thoroughness. Their target was Mesopotamia's prosperity and wealth. When they left, only the ruins of the irrigation system remained. Canals had been cut, their banks leveled, the channels blocked and the waters diverted. With the waters unharnessed, Nature did the rest and the granary of the world was reduced to a howling wilderness of scrub and marsh.

> Thorns shall come up in her palaces, nettles and brambles in the fortresses thereof; and it shall be a habitation of dragons and a court for owls.

Nothing could be more true.

The years of Turkish occupation had done little to restore any of the former prosperity; only their Teutonic allies had spotted the possible value of these thousands of acres of desolation, and had plans for it. The inhabitants of the wide expanses of silent and apparently lifeless marshland are no less strange than the country itself—and the men of the Expeditionary Force found them to be no less unpleasant. These people, the Marsh Arabs, are a different race from the Bedouin from whom they claim descent although the latter have always looked upon them as the scum of the earth, considering them to have no religion and, because of their amphibious existence, even of having webbed feet. Except for webbed feet, the Bedouin assessment of their riparian cousins was not far from the truth. In theory, they made their living as herdsmen of water buffaloes, or fishermen, or as odd-job men, but their environment and natural traits produced a highly developed predilection for any form of thieving and dirty work—so much so, that even to people who regarded robbery with violence as a gentlemanly pastime, the Marsh Arabs had the reputation of being degraded villains.

An article in a British newspaper about this time fancifully described "the warm welcome accorded by the Arabs to British troops." A sniper's bullet—one of "the slugs that is hammered from telegraph wire"—which greeted the British troops on their way up to Qurna was usually the first evidence of the warmth of their welcome. Any doubts which may have existed about the friendliness of the "Buddhoos," as they came to be called, were finally dispelled by their adept performances in sneaking past sentries, under barbed wire and into the British camps, in order to steal whatever they could lay their hands on. Sniping was an almost continuous performance but, as they could be more easily spotted and dealt with during the day, the Arabs soon learned to confine their activities to convenient moments when they thought they would be safe from retaliation. At night the casual popping off of a few rifles in the direction of the British lines gradually increased in volume and accuracy as the days passed, until it soon assumed a regular routine. Half an hour before sunset, straggling bands of Arabs collected at a safe distance from the British lines, where they would start to work themselves into a frenzy by shouting, stamping and gesticulating. At this stage of the proceedings there would be no shooting—or none that counted anyway—and the "Salvation Army" meetings, as the British soldiers called them, invariably broke up after a banner-hoisting ceremony. Perhaps this was the Arabs' way of "trooping the color," because shortly after they had dispersed into the rising mists, the sniping would start. By eight o'clock there would be an almost continuous plip-plop, plip and bang of bullets from a variety of weapons, whanging their way in the general direction of the British lines. Heavy Martini bullets droned, Mausers fizzed, and individuals were sometimes recognized by the characteristic noise made by their particular weapons, the deep boom of one ancient piece earning its owner the nickname of Blunderbuss Bill. Eventually, with the nightly shoots becoming increasingly hazardous, the British and Indians set about breaking up the congregations which heralded the proceedings; as soon as a crowd had assembled, field guns would open up on them. On more than one occasion the shrapnel must have done great damage, but next morning there was never any sign of it as the Arabs always seemed to manage to remove their casualties.

A few nights of this treatment were enough to teach the Buddhoos that crowds assembling in daylight had little future and by mid-January they had changed their tactics. The weather had broken, nights now were pitch dark and more often than not there was pelting rain and icy winds. To the British and Indian troops shivering in their trenches, the new tactics were even more bloodcurdling than before, but they soon learned a drill, the success of which helped to nullify the dread of the eerie threat of the Buddhoos massing in the darkness before them. First indication of their presence was the rising and falling chant of hundreds of voices, borne on the wind; then, as the sound grew nearer it swelled from the black silence into a roar, "Allah illulah!" "Allah illulah!" This was the moment for action and, with a boom, a star shell would burst high over the desert. The light was sufficient for three rounds of rapid fire and as the Arabs dispersed there was a lull until they were able to stage another demonstration of the warm welcome they were supposed to be affording the invaders.

Apart from dealing with the attentions of the Arabs, the troops' life was mostly spent in improving the defenses. Digging only two feet down met water and this meant that the parapets of trenches had to be built up gradually; a complete system of redoubts and trenches was developed right around Qurna sufficient for the brigade it was considered would be necessary to hold the Qurna front. Muzereh was included in the fortified line and here, for the first time, many of the troops faced the sort of grim and grizzly sight to which they were to become accustomed. Apart from the fact that the Turkish troops had not bothered about such refinements as latrines, they had had little time to bury their dead during the battle, and Arabs seeking loot, pi-dogs and jackals had all done their work; it was only the British soldiers' customary irrepressible humor which helped him to overcome these morbid sights and putrid smells.

The presence of pi-dogs and flies in Mesopotamia were not new phenomena; the troops had come from India and that country had plenty of both. But not in the quantity nor of the quality that Mesopotamia is able to provide. Around Qurna—at Muzereh particularly—the flies had an especially fat and sleek appearance and the packs of miserable, red-eyed, mangy dogs snuffing around the shallow graves were enough to upset the stomachs of even those who were not new to such conditions. Consolations and amenities were few; of creature comfort there was little, no canteens, a dreary, monotonous ration. But the officers were able to shoot pig and snipe, all of which went to the pot and helped to ameliorate the troops' eternal round of bully beef and biscuits or equivalent Indian hard tack.

Reinforcements trickled into Basra, many of them Territorials at whom some of the regular old sweats looked askance. Otherwise Qurna, with its streets and alleys renamed with appropriate titles like Eden Gardens, Eve's Walk, Temptation Square and Serpents Lane and its mud, was as unattractive as it had been on the day it was captured. The troops wondered why they had been sent to this cold, cheerless land and their general attitude may be summed up by a piece of doggerel current at the time:

> Is this the land of dear old Adam,
> And beautiful Mother Eve?
> If so, dear reader, small blame to them
> For sinning and having to leave!
>
> I've tried to solve a riddle,
> You wish to know it? Well,
> If Qurna's the Garden of Eden,
> Then where the dickens is Hell?

There was little news from the outside world, and in its absence Indian Expeditionary Force "D" lived principally on rumor. The whisper which preceded the Viceroy's visit was augmented by a rumor that thirty thousand men were coming with him as reinforcements and there was something in this because Major General Gorringe's 12th Division was on its way. So far as the Turks were concerned, rumor had it that the Intelligence Staff had lost track of a complete Turkish Army Corps. They had thought that it was marching on Port Said, but it seemed that it was not; nor had it been captured by the Russians, which had also been a possibility. However, according to the very best latrinograms, Arabs had seen it marching toward Basra where it was expected at any moment; accompanying it was a whole host of guns, some of which had barrels as big as full-grown palm trees. Finally, the strongest rumor of all was that the Turks were about to make simultaneous attacks on Basra and Qurna. This, in fact, was not altogether an unlikely event, although just how they were going to get across the river to do so was difficult to see, both sides being separated, as they were, by eight miles of water, marsh and muddy desert. However, if they could get across, then the British and Indian troops, in their newly prepared positions, looked forward to receiving them with a certain amount of pleasurable anticipation.

The British capture of Basra meant more in terms of loss of face than of strategic advantage to the Turks, and they were indeed preparing for an attack, although events were to show that the main thrust would not be directed toward Qurna. A division of the Mosul Army Corps had been hastily concentrated at Baghdad and during December reinforcements were sent down to the river. A barrier to further British advances had been established at the Ruta creek, about eight miles from the British front line. So far as rumors about vast Turkish reinforcements marching down from Baghdad toward Basra were concerned, these were quite untrue. British intelligence was fed with information from a variety of sources; agents in Mesopotamia, the Egyptian front and a military liaison officer with the Russian Army in the Caucasus, and it was the two latter sources which had suggested at various times that no less than four divisions were on their way to Mesopotamia. The only reinforcements that were sent were a couple of battalions of the elite Constantinople Fire Brigade—the Sapeurs Pompiers—who left Constantinople in November.

On New Year's Day, 1915, a combined river and land reconnaissance "in force" which set out from Qurna came to a sudden halt when it arrived at Ruta. The Turks had dug trenches on both banks of the Tigris, at a position where two deep creeks prevented a direct approach and, when the British advance guard came within small arms range of the Turkish positions, it was found impossible to get any further. The creeks were found to be too deep to ford and pronounced impossible to bridge without pontoons. Nor was it possible for the amphibious party to make any progress. Four lighters sunk in the fairway effectively barred the channel and the reconnoitering parties returned to Qurna little wiser than they had been before they set out on their day's outing. In a few days the *Espiègle* returned to have another look at the river block and on this occasion a Turkish steamer was sunk on the far side of the barrier.

It seemed clear that the Turks at Ruta were up to something, and a fortnight later Barrett decided to attack them. The *Espiègle ,* supported by the armed launches *Miner* and *Lewis Pelly* and the old stern-wheeler *Mejidieh,* on which a couple of field guns had been mounted, moved up the river to support a strong column[1] from Qurna which marched out through the slush and mud in the early hours of January 21. In the darkness, the British and Indian infantry were almost to the Turkish positions without being detected but when the sun came up, and their presence became known, the Turks started to shell the advancing lines. The ships replied and the mutual bombardment which

---

1. Composed of Brigadier General W. H. Dobbie's 17th Brigade, the Norfolks and two companies of the 7th Rajputs from the 18th Brigade, two squadrons of the 33rd Cavalry, Artillery and Engineers.

developed went on for nearly an hour and a half. But for the fact that the Turkish shrapnel burst too high and many of their shells failed to explode the British casualties would have been heavy. As it was, although the forward Turkish defenses were driven in, their main positions were much too strongly held for any hope to be entertained of their capture with the force deployed and, under cover of the ships' guns, back it came to Qurna.

So far as Barrett was concerned, the situation was full of anxiety. Apart from the constant threat to Qurna which the force massing at Ruta presented, it was known that a large number of Arabs in Turkish employ were concentrating at Nasiriyeh on the Euphrates, thirty miles above the Hammer Lake and the site of the famous "Ur of the Chaldees." Rumor had it that this gathering had been joined by a party of Turks and the combined force was said to be preparing to move south across the marshes toward Basra. At the same time another Turkish force, coming from Amara on the Tigris, was said to have crossed the Persian border and making for Ahwaz on the Karun river where the pipeline linked the oil fields with the refinery at Abadan. There seemed to be little doubt that the Turks intended to take the offensive and, if so there was a strong possibility that Basra, Qurna and Ahwaz might well be attacked simultaneously. Yet there was little that Barrett would do about it with the troops he had at his disposal, and the whole purpose of "I.E.F. D's" now seemed to be in jeopardy. Thanks to the scheming of the Germans, the Arab world was in ferment and whether Britain or Germany would profit by it seemed to depend on what could be done in Mesopotamia. Already the Pan-Islamic movement had produced a deep impression in Central Arabia and the threat to the oil fields and the pipeline was extremely serious. Before long, saboteurs had cut the pipeline, necessitating stopping the pumps at the wells, and the oil ceased to flow.

Across Mesopotamia's frontier with Persia, the Arabs were no different from the rest of the Muslim world. The idea that Islam was being attacked and that it was their duty to rally behind those who were to protect the Faith had been dinned into their ears. They were always ripe for bellicose activity anyway, and with the incentive of a few Turkish bribes, trouble could be expected. Persian neutrality was certainly not going to stop the Turks sabotaging the pipeline if they had the chance. This was Barrett's problem. He grudged having to deplete his force and so weaken his positions at Basra and Qurna but protection of the pipeline had been laid down as one of his original objectives. When he heard that it had been cut it seemed something had to be done. Unless troops were sent to Ahwaz quickly, it was more than likely that tribesmen who were wavering would throw in their lot with the Turks, and those who had already decided which side they supported; by hesitating he might well have to face an even worse situation. And so, in the middle of February a platoon of Dorsets and a couple of mountain guns were shipped up the Karun river to "stabilize" the position around Ahwaz. The fact that the force was a hodgepodge from different formations did not make the task of its commander, Brigadier General Robinson, any easier in the action which was to follow.

On arrival at Ahwaz, word came in from the locals that the rumored Turkish-Arab concentration was indeed massing in the hills northwest of the town. Robinson, briefed to act quickly and decisively, decided that a prompt reconnaissance was called for, since this would demonstrate his strength of purpose. Leaving only a small reserve to garrison the town he sallied forth with the rest of his column. In a defile, about eight miles from the town, the column walked straight into an ambush. Suddenly, at the same time as they came under heavy fire from both sides and their front, Arab cavalry were seen to be deploying with the obvious intention of cutting them off. When, from the hills on both sides of the pass, a howling mob of Arabs descended on them and Turkish artillery opened up, Robinson decided the time had come to pull out. It was not a moment too soon. But for the gallant action of the single platoon of Dorsets, and the fact that the Turks in their enthusiasm had shelled their Arab allies by mistake, the force would never have survived. By the time it did get back to the trenched camp at Ahwaz, Robinson's men had been severely mauled and lost both mountain guns in the process. As might have been expected, too little too late had resulted in a sharp reverse and Barrett was compelled to send up another brigade to extricate what was left.

In the meantime the Turks and their Arab friends had been concentrating what they called their "Right Wing Command" at Nasiriyeh for an attempt to recapture Basra. In command, was a certain Lieutenant Colonel Sulaiman Askari, a stouthearted man and dedicated soldier who had had an adventurous career chasing Bulgarian bandits before the Balkan war. Unfortunately for him, during the course of his career he had fallen out of favor with the "Committee of Union and Progress" and this had led to his being posted as far away from Constantinople as the Turkish War Office could send him. Hence the command at Nasiriyeh, to which he had succeeded after Subhi Bey's surrender at Qurna. Wounded in the knee during the fighting for Qurna he had been evacuated to Baghdad. When the Turkish War Office sent an officer to replace him in his command Sulaiman refused to hand over and insisted on being carried down to Nasiriyeh in a litter; Confined to this litter he directed the forthcoming battle.

By the end of March, Sulaiman Askari had assembled the best part of two divisions and twenty-one guns. His force included "Fire Brigade" together with various odd batteries and sections of artillery—over six thousand men in all—of whom nearly half were tough Anatolian Turks. A motley and fluctuating collection of between ten and twenty thousand Arab tribesmen had also rallied to his banner. Sulaiman was confident that they would be of the utmost value when it came to a battle—in the event they were to fail him at a critical juncture.

Facing this formidable assembly Barrett had concentrated about 7,000 men in an entrenched camp at Shaiba, about nine miles southwest of Basra's Zubair Gate. To meet a possible attack by up to twenty thousand of the enemy this could hardly be considered a large force and, to make matters worse, communication with Basra was extremely difficult owing to the road being underwater for nearly the whole distance. Reinforcements had to wade the whole way and nearly all stores and ammunition had to be punted across the floods in bellums. However, more troops had been pouring into Basra from India and by the beginning of April the original Expeditionary Force had virtually doubled itself, to become an Army Corps of two divisions. At this stage the problem was not really men, but how to move, concentrate, and feed them. And it was lack of transport which made this difficult. All the shortages derived from the Indian Government's pre-war policy of economizing and cheese-paring began now to make themselves really felt. The newly arrived 12th Division had hardly any artillery, and was short of men and equipment8: two of its brigades (the 30th and 33rd) were each only three battalions strong, as two battalions had stopped off at Bushire to deal with disturbances engineered by the German Consul. And, of the two British regiments in the division, one was a Territorial unit which had only arrived in India a few months previously and had had little time to become acclimatized, let alone train, before being sent to one of the worst climates in the world just as the hot weather was coming on. Another battalion—the 67th Punjabis—among whom cholera had broken out during the voyage to Mesopotamia, was also hors de combat.

Returning to the front. Shaiba was a small place; the town comprised a few large houses and an old fort which had been the summer residence of Basra notables, surrounded by a small area of cultivated land and screened by a few tamarisk trees. The British had started to turn it into a defensive camp in February and the trenches had gradually been extended as the garrison grew; by the end of March the whole of the camp perimeter had been encircled with a long single trench and barbed wire fence. The Turks had established a forward camp in the Barjisiyeh Wood to the southwest of the town and about six miles of bare undulating desert separated the two lines. From their base at Nasiriyeh the Turks had dumped food supplies at points forward of Barjisiyeh and the most advanced of these was at Nukhailat, which was only about fourteen miles from Shaiba. But water rather than food was the problem. Only at Barjisiyeh and Zubair was it available and consequently it was this latter place that Sulaiman Askari intended to make the jumping-off point for his eventual advance. To harass the Turks during this preparatory phase a river column, with the grandiose title of the Euphrates Blockade Flotilla, was formed. Under command of a gunner colonel it consisted of small steamers, armed launches and gun barges on which a variety of armament was mounted; its duty was to patrol and blockade the "New" Euphrates and "interfere with" the Turkish base at Nukhailat. It did nothing spectacular at this time—unless shelling camps and sinking a few *mahelas* may be called spectacular—but no doubt its work did delay the Turkish advance. Its activities were to become important later.

The expected offensive opened at the beginning of April and, because of the failure of the naval attack on the Dardanelles, it came at a critical period in the war with Turkey. If the British were dislodged from the Shatt-al-Arab, the effects would undoubtedly have reverberated throughout the whole of the Eastern world. After the events of Ahwaz, the Admiralty in London, acutely conscious of the threat to their oil supply, ordered the sloop *Clio* up from Egypt and four armored "horse-boats" (so called because they were usually towed along the river bank like barges) armed with 4.7-inch guns to be shipped to Mesopotamia from the same place. The Government of India, preoccupied with what they considered to be the long term view of the Turks' actions in Mesopotamia and anxious about the internal unrest it would cause, were unwilling to take more troops from the Army in India. However, the urgings of those in Whitehall in March had had their effect and this was the background of the expansion of the original Expeditionary Force. Barrett, meantime, had fallen sick and to command the corps that was formed when the reinforcements eventually arrived came a new commander, General Sir John Nixon. Nixon was a different type of man from Barrett and he came to Basra on April 9 with a new brief. He was to retain control of the whole of Lower Mesopotamia, which included the Basra region "and all such portions of the neighboring territories as affected his operation." So far as possible, he was also to try to secure the safety of the oil fields, pipelines and the Abadan refinery and—more significantly—to formulate a plan for an advance on Baghdad.

Two days after Nixon stepped ashore in Basra, Sulaiman Askari's offensive opened. It was heralded with a bombardment of Qurna which continued all day. Next morning the British bridge across the Tigris was blown sky-high by a floating mine, and parties of Arabs were found to have infiltrated into the palm groves of Barjisiyeh Wood on the north bank of the Euphrates, just outside the town. To counter this the *Odin* steamed up, and put down such a barrage of shells that the Arabs decided it was time to go. Later when they tried to reoccupy the woods, a repeat performance was staged and on this occasion their Turkish masters, seeing them retiring *not* "according to plan" turned their own guns on to the fleeing Arabs. On the 13th and again on the 14th, Qurna was bombarded nearly all day but with little effect. And, by the second day the distant thud of guns coming from the south indicated that something was afoot in that direction. It was three days before what had happened was known to the British in Qurna, although the Turks must have heard the result sooner, for on the 15th all was quiet—no gun fire, no sign of any Arabs. And, after this Qurna was left in peace.

Sulaiman Askari's main thrust had been toward Basra. After advancing on Nukhailat he had moved his force up to Barjisiyeh Wood and on the 10th, when their cavalry patrols reported the advance, the British garrison stood ready. British intelligence had assessed the Turks' strength as twelve thousand regulars and ten thousand tribesmen supported by twelve guns, so a tough battle was anticipated. About 5 a.m. next morning the attack started in earnest, with a bombardment which went on intermittently throughout the day; as on previous occasions its effect was diminished by many of the shells failing to explode. There was no determined attempt to put in an infantry attack—a fact which caused some concern since its absence suggested the Turks might be making some move or other which could bring fresh hazards. The only real threat came from a large party of Arabs trying to get close up to the British lines. This was soon dispersed by a squadron of the 7th Hariana Lancers, who sallied forth to charge down the slope in front of the town. Not until dusk when the guns opened up again did anything untoward really happen. Then, under cover of heavy rifle fire, sections of Turks and Arabs tried to crawl up to cut lanes through the wire, shouting "Don't fire" in Hindustani as they did so. Those that got through the wire were soon disposed of however, and by dawn on the 13th the firing had died down and the Turks had withdrawn to a safe distance.

Meanwhile Major General Charles Melliss had brought up reinforcements. Fifty-four-year-old Melliss came of an old army family—his father had been a Lieutenant General—and he had won a Victoria Cross fighting in West Africa sixteen years before. A stern disciplinarian, he was one of the few generals who regarded the welfare of his men as his first concern and they thought the world of him. Getting his 30th Brigade and the battery of mountain guns he brought with him across the flooded area which separated Shaiba from Basra was quite a feat in itself. After trying to wade across toward Zubair and finding the gunners were unable to make it, and that Zubair was occupied by the Turks, he had retraced his steps to collect bellums in order to cross to Shaiba by the more direct route. At this juncture only sufficient boats could be found to carry Melliss' headquarters and one battalion while the *bellumchis*—the native rowers—refused to have anything to do with the operation, so that Melliss had to provide his own men to pole the boats. However, by midnight on the 12th the brigade were all in Shaiba and Melliss, as the senior officer, took over from Fry.

At first light next morning, when the Turks could be seen moving southeast across the front toward Old Basra, it appeared as if an advance on Basra across the floods was being contemplated. At the same time, while bellums carrying this force were maneuvering on the water, a large party of Arabs seemed to be getting ready to attack Shaiba itself from a northwesterly direction. This was all very worrying. For the Turks to advance across the front, ignoring Shaiba, was a risky business but if they succeeded in getting to Basra, both Basra and Shaiba would be in dire straits. The possibility of the Arab attack on Shaiba was less of a problem, and as they were not in range of the British guns the Cavalry Brigade was ordered to deal with the threat. The cavalry commander must have been supremely confident as it appears that he thought that only one squadron was necessary for the task. In due course the squadron of 7th Hariana Lancers, which had charged the Arabs on the previous day, formed up and trotted out. Events were to show that this was not the occasion for a mounted attack. As soon as the Lancers left the shelter of the trees, a hail of concentrated small arms fire brought horses and men crashing down, and the squadron had to withdraw. The Squadron Commander, Major Wheeler, and his senior Indian officer, were well ahead in the charge and unaware of the swathes being cut in the ranks behind them. The two of them galloped on and toward a group of Arabs gathered around a green standard. Both got through to the standard, sabering several Arabs in the process, but as Wheeler grasped the standard he was shot and the Indian officer was pulled from his horse. Once they had got him to the ground the Arabs seized the Indian officer, poured oil over him and set him on fire; later in the day his still smouldering body was recovered. Wheeler was awarded a posthumous Victoria Cross and the Indian officer the Indian Order of Merit.

Following the cavalry's failure, an infantry attack was ordered, but, again only half measures were deemed sufficient, and the 104th Wellesley's Rifles which went in first suffered a similar fate to that which had been the lot of the Lancers. Having suffered two costly setbacks, Melliss at last recognized that stronger measures were necessary and an artillery bombardment was ordered to "soften up" the Arabs before a two battalion attack. Then the 2nd Dorsets and the 24th Punjabis successfully routed the Arabs, taking 400 prisoners and inflicting heavy casualties as a result. After this action the Arabs took no further part in the battle—not until their allies were retreating—and then they changed sides to hinder and harry the fleeing Turks for nearly a hundred miles.

After the Arabs had been dispersed, Melliss ordered his troops back into the perimeter. None of them had had any rest for over forty-eight hours and so far as he could see the immediate threat had been overcome; things were quiet and Turkish attempts to cross to Old Basra had apparently failed. Next morning it was still quiet, and the battlefield with its dead, wounded and maimed, was an unromantic sight, for there is nothing picturesque or glorious about the aftermath of any battle. With no enemy in sight, it seemed that both Turks and Arabs had given up. Yet it was not over; Sulaiman Askari had indeed had enough of attacks but in Barjisiyeh Wood he intended to reverse the position.

At 9 a.m. on the 14th, Melliss' garrison marched out from Shaiba in three columns, to reconnoiter toward Old Basra. The columns marched eight abreast, carrying two hundred rounds of ammunition; the Cavalry Brigade covered the right flank, the 16th Brigade were on the right and the 18th Brigade took the left, with the troops deployed in artillery formations. Behind the marching men came the mules carrying water and more ammunition. Two miles out from Shaiba, as they approached a feature known as the South Mound, the leading troops of Delamain's 16th Brigade on the right came up against their first opposition. Rifle fire from a low ridge was directed at the leading platoons but as they doubled out into extended order it slackened, and a group of Arabs on horses was seen to make off. The columns marched on and by noon the South Mound had been occupied. No Turks were in evidence and as it seemed that they had concentrated in Barjisiyeh Wood, Melliss rode off toward the cavalry to make a personal reconnaissance in that direction. As he approached, the bullets coming in his direction indicated that they were all right, although neither he nor those who accompanied him could see exactly where their trenches were. Delamain's brigade[2] was directed toward the Wood and two battalions of Fry's brigade were countermarched across from the left to take up positions on Delamain's right—Melliss' idea being for Delamain to hold the front while Fry attacked the Turks' flank. Because of the floods, the cavalry who were out on this flank were unable to work around and presumably it was thought that men on foot could do better in mud than horses. The infantry struggled on and Fry's brigade suffered severely from the exemplary fire discipline of the Turks as the two battalions changed front. Heavy, accurate rifle and machine gun fire compelled them to move in a series

---

2. For this operation the 24th Punjabis took the place of the 104th Wellesley's Rifles.

of short rushes and as each rush went forward the Turks opened fire, shutting it off like a tap as soon as there was no target. The Turkish trenches were well sited and the mirage which had descended over the battlefield effectively hid them from view until the British troops were almost on them and, of course, the gunners were not able to discern any targets.

As Melliss' men advanced, the Turks' fire grew more intense and by 4 p.m. when the gap between the two sides had narrowed to five hundred yards, the firing line could get no further. And by this time things looked black. Ammunition was running short; nearly every mule that had been brought forward carrying it had been killed, as had their muleteers, and few had got close enough to the forward troops to enable the men to replenish what they had used of their original two hundred rounds. Casualties had been heavy; nearly every available man was in the fight, and most of them were feeling the effect of four hours of grueling heat and thirst. Melliss, disheartened by the way events had developed, was on the point of ordering a retirement and it is possible that an order to do so was actually given; if so it never reached the Dorsets. But for their behavior, success would have been conceded to the Turks and Melliss would have faced a six mile rearguard action back to Shaiba, with the Arabs taking the hindmost. However, at this juncture, with things at their worst, the Dorsets leapt up and dashed forward. It was a catalytic action to the rest of the brigade and, with a shout that swelled to a roar, the whole British line rose and swept forward in a wild bayonet charge which took them on and into the Turkish lines. Once across the fire-swept "No-man's Land" and hacking their way forward, the battle was as good as decided, for the Turks broke and fled. Some returned to surrender but the remainder streamed off into the desert in a terrified rabble. They might have launched a counterattack, for there were still some organized Turkish reserves, but it is said that the commander of these reserves mistook the British transport carts coming forward to pick up the wounded as fresh batteries of artillery, and he decided that flight was preferable to another round of fighting. For Sulaiman Askari— still in his litter—it was too much of a disgrace to go on living. After collecting some of his officers together and telling them that the failure was due entirely to Arab treachery, he announced that he could never fight again, then shot himself. It was a dramatic end to a brave man.

There was no pursuit. The British cavalry were still tied down on the right flank where they had achieved nothing all day; yet if they had been on the other flank they might have contributed much more to the infantry's success and have given chase. Someone must have blundered, for they knew the ground well—or should have, since they had spent a good deal of time reconnoitering it during March and April. And there was no other way to follow up the disorganized Turks and exploit the victory, since Melliss had no transport. Shortage of this vital sinew was only one of the evils bequeathed by the pre-war system imposed by the Government of India, but it was one which was to continue to bedevil the campaign right until the men in Whitehall insisted on taking over from those in Simla.

In many ways this battle, the "Miracle of Shaiba" as it became known, belonged to a by-gone era, out of the context of even the First World War. Not a single airplane was available to either side and the troops moved and operated from a fixed camp almost as their predecessors had done in the Crimea, the one campaign which it so closely resembled in its administrative failings. The presence of the host of predatory Arabs, sullenly hanging back at the edge of the battlefield waiting on events, was another unrealistic factor out of keeping with the times. The Turks had brought them into the field but they had done precious little to help Sulaiman Askari when it came to the crunch; all they were concerned about was looting whichever side was vanquished. And the Turks paid a high price to be disillusioned about their reliability.

For the newly appointed British Commander-in-Chief, Shaiba was a wonderful beginning; too wonderful perhaps, since this first flush of victory may well have contributed to the underestimation of Turkish fighting capacity that he undoubtedly formed. The cost had been high; British casualties in the three days fighting amounted to over twelve hundred although the Turks had suffered twice this number dead and wounded, while eighteen officers and over seven hundred men and two mountain guns had been captured.[3] Nevertheless it was a resounding success; doubly so when the consequences of a defeat are considered. Shaiba, cut off in the floods, would have been difficult to maintain against an enemy with their tails up and it would have been almost impossible to fall back on Basra where there were only three battalions, whose work would have been cut out keeping order in the town let alone defending it. Then, if Basra with all its stores and shipping had fallen, there would have been no base, the troops at Qurna and Ahwaz would have been cut off and the re-sult would have been a disaster, whose repercussions would have been felt throughout the whole of the East. The consequences of the critical four hours in front of Barjisiyeh Wood, finally resolved by the gallant Dorsets, have probably never been truly appreciated, except by the very few who breathed a sigh of relief when they saw the Turks in headlong flight.

Shaiba, like Inkerman, has been described as a "Soldiers" battle, by which is meant a hard fought infantry battle. The number of guns on either side was

---

3. Actual figures were: British casualties 1,57; Turkish casualties among the regular troops 54 officers, 2,381 other ranks—a figure which does not include slightly wounded.
  The strength of the British force on the morning of April 14 was 6,156 all ranks.

insignificant and it was the infantry who decided the day. Three British Indian brigades of infantry defeated a weak Turkish Army Corps and a horde of Arabs at a time when great issues were at stake. In Basra the population was quaking in its shoes; though the British had been welcomed, it was with a certain amount of apprehension, for the locals knew what would happen if they were ever driven out. If Melliss had been defeated at Shaiba, the returning Turks would have exacted a terrible toll on those who had shown any form of cooperation with the invaders. Whether the rest of the Muslim world was watching to see if the British would be hurled back into the mud at Shaiba is a matter for conjecture. It is true that the Caliph's words, summoning those of the true Faith to arms on the side of Turkey and her Teutonic ally, had gone form from mosques and minarets throughout the East. But it is unreasonable to suppose that a Turkish victory at Shaiba would necessarily have set the Muslims' ecclesiastic drum rolling against the white lords of the East, or at this moment persuaded the Emir of Afghanistan that duty demanded an invasion of India—as his son was persuaded four years later. Some loss of prestige would have been inevitable, but in retrospect it seems that little is engendered by minor defeats during the war. The evidence of the rebellions in Egypt and India after this Great War and the breaking up of the British, French and Dutch Empires after the Second World War, all suggest that matters of prestige are decided after a holocaust.

Chapter 3

Consolidation

Guard against a decisive blow, and acquiesce in smaller misfortunes to avoid greater.
Frederick the Great
"Instructions to his Generals"

Toward the end of November, Sir Percy Cox, to whom the Arabs had given the almost Babylonian name of "Supposi Kokus," had suggested to the Indian Government that an announcement should be made declaring that British occupation of Basra would be a permanent feature of the postwar world. Whitehall peremptorily vetoed the suggestion on the grounds that such a statement would be wholly contrary to the understanding between the Allies that settlements as to the future of occupied territory should await the end of hostilities. Suggestions by the Indian Government that political as well as military advantages would be gained by extending the area of occupation beyond Basra were also frowned upon by the Home Government in London. Lord Crewe, the Secretary of State for India, deprecated any idea of an advance up the river and it was only with difficulty that he had been persuaded of the tac-

tical advantages afforded by Qurna. With the establishment c
at the top end of the Persian Gulf, the men in Whitehall rega.
the expedition to Mesopotamia as having been achieved; safety o1
their paramount consideration and there had been no thoughts of terr.
aggrandizement.

Nevertheless, with the assumption of the command in Mesopotamia by Sir
John Nixon, the campaign was to take on a new aspect and his arrival can be
regarded as the turning point, not only in the methods and scope of the
military operations which were to follow, but also in the changing aspirations
of the Indian Government. Before Nixon left India, Sir Beauchamp-Duff,
India's Commander-in-Chief, had given him a fresh set of instructions super-
ceding those of Barrett and which, as has been mentioned already, included
orders to consider a plan for an advance on Baghdad. The terms of his new
directive were unknown to the British Government in London and, according
to his evidence at the Mesopotamia Commission nearly two years later, also
unknown to Lord Hardinge, the Viceroy. A copy of it was mailed to London
but as it did not arrive until the middle of May and those in Whitehall presumed Nixon was working on the original instructions issued to Barrett, its
existence was the basic reason for the authorities in London seeming to have
been at cross purposes with both Simla and Nixon for close to two months.

So far, most of the initiative in running the campaign had been taken by
Whitehall. When it was known that the Turks were believed to be preparing for
an attack on Basra and that the oil pipeline was threatened, it had been those in
London who had ordered the reluctant Indian Government to send reinforcements to the theater; after the debacle near Ahwaz, it had again been instructions from London that had prompted the dispatch of another brigade from
India—instructions which had required an undertaking relieving the Viceroy
and Beauchamp-Duff of responsibility for what might happen in India because
of the depletion of India's military reserves to provide troops for Mesopotamia. But with Nixon's appointment the initiative seems to have passed from
Whitehall. The decision to provide still more troops, in order to reorganize the
Mesopotamia Force as an Army Corps of two divisions, was taken solely by the
Indian Government and apparently without any consent or even any consulta-
tion with London. That these extra troops materially contributed to the success
at Shaiba and had enabled the precarious grip on Basra to be consolidated has
already been seen.

It is also important to stress that the fresh troops had been rushed out
without a proper scale of equipment. Fighting men were welcome but they
came without the supply train which normally accompanies such troops and
the new corps had the medical facilities sufficient only for one division. Nor

ﾉ any provision been made for the additional river steamers and transport ﾉhich would be so necessary for the support of the augmented force in the days to come or for a port organization for Basra. As will be seen, this was to become a problem of crucial importance, while the lack of medical facilities was to result in a near-Crimean scandal.

Because of what had happened at Ahwaz in April, Lord Crewe had telegraphed the Viceroy about the Admiralty's concern for the Persian oil supply; when he did so he was not aware of Nixon's fresh instructions. If he had known, he can hardly have failed to realize that the safety of the oil wells had become subsidiary to the control of the whole Basra region—the Basra vilayet, as it was known—and he might have been expected to have issued sharp instructions to the Indian Government for an adjustment of Nixon's priorities. As it was, the Secretary of State's telegram was merely forwarded to Nixon with the advice that he should use his own discretion as to coping with the threat to the oil.

Meantime, working from his new directive, Nixon had asked Simla for another Cavalry Brigade and a Pioneer battalion, both of which he considered would be needed for the operations he now had in mind. Both requests were turned down—although a Coolie Corps of Indus boatmen was offered in place of the Pioneers—and when Lord Crewe heard of it his reaction was to send a telegram to the Viceroy concurring with the Indian Government's refusal and saying that the demand indicated "an important offensive movement." Asking for an appraisal of the situation to be sent to him, he added "No advance beyond the present theater of operations will be sanctioned, although an advance to Amara with the object of controlling the tribes between there and the Karun river might be supported because it adds to the safety of the pipeline. Our present position is strategically a sound one and we cannot afford to take risks by extending it unduly. *In Mesopotamia a safe game must be played.*" From this telegram, it is evident that the safety of the oil—the original object of the expedition—was still uppermost in the minds of the Home Government.

There can be little doubt that the Secretary of State's attitude was right. The day after his telegram was dispatched, the first landing in Gallipoli was scheduled and Gallipoli was to be the main theater against the Turks. The Suez Canal also had to be considered and its protection was certainly more important than Mesopotamia, for the canal was a vital artery of imperial communications. Mesopotamia was third in order of importance, and, in any case, the object of the original expedition there had already been achieved. Unfortunately those who were running the campaign in this third priority theater were to be encouraged by success after success steadily to extend the operations, at the same time without increasing the means of doing so.

In response to Lord Crewe's telegram, Nixon started to concentrate troops under Gorringe for an operation up the Karun, and toward the end of April the required appreciation of the situation was wired to India. Nixon's conclusion was that the Turks in Mesopotamia were incapable of undertaking any effective offensive and he thought that both those in Nasiriyeh and those up the Tigris would remain where they were. Nothing definite could be said about the Turks on the Karun side until Gorringe got to Ahwaz. This, he maintained, was due to the lack of cavalry—a snide reference to the request which both India and Lord Crewe had rejected. His own preference was to push on to Nasiriyeh in order to take advantage of the Turks' disorganization which had followed the battle of Shaiba, although he accepted that this was not practicable at the moment because of the lack of land transport and the failure, so far, to find a clear channel up the river. At the same time however, if the western part of the Basra vilayet was to be controlled, he was firmly of the opinion that Nasiriyeh must be occupied eventually. And, if there was much of a delay, the Turks might again become a formidable threat in that direction. For the time being there was no urgency for any operations against the Turks up the Tigris beyond Qurna and in any case, before they could be tackled, there would have to be a good deal of preparation. Finally, before he could decide on what was the best course of action, he must await the outcome of Gorringe's operations.

What Nixon's conclusions really amounted to was that the Turks on the Karun were the only force that he could strike at, at that moment, and that the operation for which Gorringe was scheduled deserved priority. It was most important that Persian Arabistan should be cleared of Turks and pacified, so that pumping could be restarted at the oil wells. The Turks around Ahwaz were not supposed to be very strong—six battalions and two cavalry regiments with about 5,000 Arabs supporting them, at the most—but their very presence encouraged the tribesmen in the area to disobey the orders of their rightful liege, the Sheikh of Muhammerah. Shaiba had caused many of them to have second thoughts as to who would be the eventual victors; nevertheless no real cooperation could be expected until the Turks had been completely ousted and the recalcitrants treated to a sharp lesson.

Gorringe's column of about 9,000 men, comprising two brigades of his own division (one, already in Ahwaz, had been sent to pull the chestnuts of the first expedition out of the fire), the Cavalry Brigade, and the 6th Division's artillery, left Basra on April 22. Some marched, some went by river. The rain had cleared and, up to the end of the month, the weather was comparatively cool. The prediction was that the following month would be "hot-warm" and that, after that, June and July would be really hot. So it turned out, with the temperature rising from 100° to 120° F in the shade—where shade existed— and the only relief coming from the north-west wind which the Arabs call "The Blessing." Ahwaz was hotter than Basra and sudden sandstorms, eternal thirst, the infinite torment of flies, and mosquitoes were all to combine to make the lot of the troops, British and Indian alike, an unenviable one.

As Gorringe closed up on Ahwaz, the Turks steadily withdrew northwest toward the Kerkha River, and by the beginning of May, it was fairly obvious that he would not be able to bring them to battle. The difficulties of getting supplies, occasioned by the lack of transport, meant that the troops could not operate for long away from the Karun. However, Gorringe had been given a double object and, even if he could not strike at the Turks, it was still possible to deal with the locals. One tribe, the Beni Taruf, which had added to their sins by a treacherous attack on some of his cavalry reconnoitering in their stretch of desert, needed a salutary lesson and, in the middle of May, a punitive column set out to administer it. For two days the troops marched across the hot un- charted desert, chasing the tribesmen, who were dotted about in small camps over a wide area. Except for the country and the climate it would have been a simple little operation, but there was the ever pervading horror of the desert: thirst. When the column arrived at the spot where the men had anticipated refilling their water bottles one morning soon after the operation had started, it was only to find the nullah virtually dry. Practically all their supplies were ex- hausted and "by this time," runs a contemporary account, "the sun was terribly fierce, and we were absolutely done." There was nothing for it but to march back to the Karun about ten miles away and, on the way, many of the men— some of whom were Territorials totally unaccustomed to conditions of this sort—fell from sheer exhaustion. After four miles it was impossible to con- tinue and the order was given to halt while the cavalry rode on to fetch the water to the stricken infantry. One of the officers writes graphically:

> At last I volunteered to take all the water bottles on mules and fetch water inde- pendently of the other lot. I felt desperate. This is how I nearly lost my life. We were six miles from the river, but they appeared like fifty. How I got to the river I don't know. I just clung on to my saddle, and balanced myself the best way I could, with bottles dangling all round the saddle and my neck, with six mules following me. When I got to the river the horse plunged in, and I rolled off into the water. The cold water revived me a little. The charger and I stood side by side (I was up to my waist in water) and sucked away until I thought I was going to burst. But it was glorious; the water was very muddy, but what cared I! I then filled up all the bottles I had brought, had another long drink, and was off again back to our camp. I got back before the other water arrived, and I think just saved a lot of

fellows. One British officer was in a very bad state and if I had been half an hour later I think he would have gone. The misery in the camp was terrible.

As things turned out, Gorringe's operations against the Turks had been a blow in the air. Nevertheless they had had one important result; the oil pumping was resumed, although it was some time before the oil actually reached Abadan because the damaged pipeline had to be repaired.

With London's concern over the oil supplies satisfied, Nixon was now anxious to turn from Arabistan to strike the Turks nearer home. Lack of steamers precluded the advance on Nasiriyeh, which he favored, so he decided that the Turks above Qurna would be his next objective. To this, the Viceroy lent his support. Besides being a suitable location for a military outpost from which to control the tribesmen between the Tigris and Karun, on whose submission the security of the oil fields largely depended, Amara was an important administrative and commercial center covering the main route to Persian Arabistan. In a telegram dispatched on May 23 to Lord Crewe, Lord Hardinge outlined the commander-in-chief's intentions. Nixon, he said, proposed to mount an offensive up the Tigris. *But* he would not advance beyond Amara without the sanction of the Secretary of State. Lord Crewe's reply, sanctioning the operation, sounded peevish:

> On the clear understanding that the General Officer Commanding Force "D" is satisfied that he can concentrate a sufficient force at Amara to defy any attack from Baghdad during the summer. . . . We can send him no more troops and he must clearly understand that his action must be guided by this fact. Arrangements for this move must have been made some time back and I am of the opinion that General Nixon should have submitted his proposals before the last moment. . . .

As Nixon had been discussing an attack on Amara with India for some weeks, this statement seemed rather hard; it supported his suspicions that his instructions and Lord Crewe's ideas did not tally. And so, on the 25th, he sent a long wire to India asking for definite orders as to whether Nasiriyeh and Amara were to be occupied or not—because the orders given him when he assumed command and the policy laid down by the Secretary of State did not seem to agree. He ended up by saying that it was *not* his intention to advance any further than these two places. The reply came from India—to the effect that his orders and the British Government's policy were not really conflicting; it was merely that the Secretary of State wanted to emphasize that no reinforcements would be forthcoming. Mollified, Nixon continued with his preparations for attacking the Turks above Qurna.

In London there was still some uneasiness about what really was intended.

Four days after his petulant authorization of the advance on Amara, Lord Crewe was succeeded at the India Office by Joseph Austen Chamberlain, whose first action was to endorse his predecessor's policy of caution. On May 28, Chamberlain telegraphed the Viceroy:

> Till I know the immediate objects contemplated and the force with which General Nixon is advancing, I am unable to give further instructions. Our policy must depend partly on local factors, forces locally available, and partly on the situation elsewhere. I should like to be informed what force General Nixon considers necessary for garrisoning Amara, and how generally he proposes to distribute his troops during the summer if the occupation of that town is contemplated.

The Viceroy's reply was that it would be undesirable—possibly even dangerous—to tie Nixon down with precise orders, in case they might not fit in with the local situation. "Under the original instructions he will, as soon as he is in a position to do so, submit a plan for the occupation of the Basra vilayet, which includes Amara. . . . We should not propose to authorise any advance beyond Amara for which his force is not adequate." By the time this reached London, Nixon's troops were in Amara but even before it was penned it would seem as if the authorities in India were already contemplating more ambitious objectives.

It was about this time that a new general entered the lists to take command of Barrett's old 6th Division—one whose name was to become even better known in the months to follow than even that of the Commander-in-Chief. Fifty-four-year-old Major General Charles Vere Ferrers Townshend, C.B., D.S.O., grandson of the Lord George Townshend, who succeeded Wolfe after the latter's death at Quebec, had served through at least half a dozen campaigns before he came to Mesopotamia. For his defence of Chitral Fort he had been awarded the C.B. and for his services in the Nile expedition of 1898, the D.S.O. Coming to Mesopotamia with the reputation of a brilliant tactician who had made a deep study of Napoleon's campaigns, he was ambitious and a great showman. The British troops in his division soon developed a great confidence in his leadership, but the Indians never took to him in the same way—nor he to them. (They never saw him, they said; some who did see him during the siege of Kut are said to have referred to him as "the new General Sahib.") This was the man who was to make his debut in the fantastic adventure known as the second battle of Qurna—one of the most amphibious actions ever fought, for not only the navy but the army was afloat.

For some distance north of Qurna the country was completely flooded; only here and there did a yellow sand hill stand out over the water. The main

Turkish position lay just beyond the range of the British artillery, with outposts on the island of "Norfolk Hill," "One Tower Hill," and "Gun Hill" on the right bank of the Tigris, and "One Tree Hill" on the left bank. Between these undulations lay a sea of swamp up to three feet deep intersected by occasional ditches with a depth of eight feet or more. The only possible way to get at them was by boat—the local bellums; ten men to a boat, sixteen boats to a company. Five hundred or so bellums were commandeered, a flotilla was gradually assembled and men were trained to punt them through the reeds. Some boats were fitted with armored shields which, as it turned out, was a mistake, because the extra weight of the armor made for difficulties in pushing them through the reeds.

To coincide with a move by Gorringe, suggesting that he was advancing on Amara from the direction of the Karun,[1] the attack was planned for May 31. Townshend's idea was to attack the Turkish positions methodically, stage by stage. The first day he would take the outposts, on the second the main position, and then finally he would pursue the Turks up the river, making the maximum use of his ships. To support the operation there were mountain guns and machine guns on rafts, field guns in tugs, barges and steamers as well as the warships, and artillery dug in at Qurna; never before in Mesopotamia had there been such an assembly of fire power.

The operation against the Turkish position above Qurna got off to a good start. As the *Clio* and *Espiègle* steamed slowly upstream, preceded by the launches *Shaitan* and *Sumana* which were sweeping mines ahead of the sloops, the troops poled their way forward through the reeds. Meanwhile, each island was plastered with artillery fire from every available gun on ship and shore. Under cover of the bombardment the 22nd Punjabis carried One Tree Hill, and the Oxford and Bucks Light Infantry waded in waist-deep water to capture the trenches on Norfolk Hill at bayonet point. There was little real resistance: the Turks had been completely overwhelmed by the colossal amount of fire that was put down and, as the bombardment switched to One Tower Hill and Gun Hill, they could be seen scrambling into boats and paddling away as fast as they could. Then, half an hour before the British and Indians could reach them, white flags were seen flying over Gun Hill. By noon the first phase of the battle was over.

Townshend had no airplanes with him; there was nowhere for one to land near Qurna. Consequently air reconnaissance had to be made by uninterrupted flights from Basra, forty miles further back. On the morning of June 1, as the troops began to make their way slowly forward through the jungle of reeds, like

---

1. On May 29, his cavalry were reconnoitering less than fifty miles away.

rats, toward the main Turkish position, one of the aircraft dropped a message to say that the Turks were in full retreat up the Tigris. It was a little late; the Navy had already found this out for themselves and were getting ready for the pursuit. The brigade which had done the fighting the previous day hurriedly embarked in three of the paddle steamers and the flotilla steamed on up the river as fast as it could go. Townshend with his staff and no more than a dozen escort hastily embarked on the *Espiègle* and with the *Clio* and *Odin* the flotilla set out in a manner more usually associated with cavalry than warships. There were mines and obstructions to delay their passage, but as the Turkish officer responsible for laying them had been captured and put into one of the leading launches his cooperation helped to ensure that no time was lost in clearing a channel. The sunken lighters below Ruta were the main holdup and as the flotilla approached this obstruction the now familiar silhouette of the gunboat *Marmariss* could be seen hastily making off upstream in company with other vessels. Even here the delay was short-lived. A channel, through which the three sloops could just scrape by the inshore wreck, was found near one back and the remarkable operation which came to be known as "Townshend's Regatta" now began in earnest.

It was a unique situation. The general with his staff was going hell-for-leather after a fleeing enemy; his army was far behind, he had little idea of what lay ahead and no preconceived plan for dealing with whatever situation arose. Everything had to be improvised. Townshend himself had never intended to pursue the Turks in person but he had little option as the *Espiègle* carried him on, mile after mile, around bend after bend, against the surging current of the snaking river which narrowed and became more tortuous the further the ships traveled. Even for the Royal Navy it was a strange adventure; built for an ocean environment, their ships were irresponsibly charging up an uncharted waterway, in chase of an army in flight, into the very heart of an ancient empire a hundred and fifty miles from the open sea.

In the fierce shimmering heat the pursuit was a long, arduous business. Gradually the tail end of the fleeing Turkish convoy came into sight—first, the white sails of the mahelas struggling against the current; then the steamer *Mosul* crowded with troops and towing a couple of barges equally crowded; finally, the *Marmariss* similarly employed. As the sun started to go down, the leading ships of the "Regatta" opened fire and when the first shots whistled over them, both the *Mosul* and the *Marmariss* promptly cast off their tows and scurried on alone. In the fading light, as the graceful blue, balloon-shaped dome of Ezra's tomb in its clump of palm trees loomed up, the mahelas and barges were seen to be making for the banks of the river. The last ship in line, the *Odin,* stopped to take possession of this party while the rest continued on into the dusk, firing continuously at the two ships ahead until darkness shrouded them from the gunners' eyes. When darkness finally descended, the British flotilla had to stop for a couple of hours until the moon came up—it was just not possible to navigate at night. Then they were on the move again and in the early hours of the morning, as they rounded a bend about six miles further on, there was the *Marmariss* once more and, beyond her, the *Mosul*. The *Marmariss* was done for; she had been run aground and set on fire before she was abandoned. As for the *Mosul:* the immediate response to a round of gunfire from the *Clio* was a white flag, and one of the launches went to take possession of her.

The sloops could go no further now; in these waters the limit had been reached and there was nothing but mud under their keels. Amara was still fifty miles further on and the army was fifty miles behind. Yet, with the evidence of the Turks' complete demoralization and organizational breakup all around, it was a sore temptation to press on to Amara. Much may be dared on the heels of a routed enemy, so Townshend and Captain Nunn, the Naval Commander, together decided to take the risk. Both transferred to the *Comet* and with the launches *Shaitan, Sumana* and *Lewis Pelly*—each of which was towing a horse boat with a 4.7-inch naval gun—the chase got under way again. There were no signs of opposition or troops; at almost every bend white flags and signs of obeisance from the villagers gave a clear indication of their acceptance of a Turkish defeat.

By the following afternoon the launches were steaming into Amara. Turkish troops were there all right—far too many of them for the comfort of the combined force of 100 British sailors and soldiers and only British impudence and a colossal bluff saw them through. Though the tiny British force was practically surrounded and grossly outnumbered, the Turks were induced to throw in the towel, a boat which put ashore with a corporal and 12 men being greeted with an offer of surrender which was accepted. It was an amazing affair. In the barracks there was a whole battalion of the Constantinople "Fire Brigade." More and more Turks, in constant fear of the Arabs, flocked in to surrender; a town, twenty thousand inhabitants, its garrison and stores had capitulated to a general, a naval captain, a political officer and about 100 bluejackets and soldiers. On the face of it the surrender was complete and absolute. It was not without its lighter and more comical touches since one Turkish officer is reputed to have been permitted to send a telegram to his wife back in Anatolia, saying "Safely captured." The difficulty was keeping up the bluff. The Turks had been led to believe that the British Army was only just around the next bend in the river when it was in fact still twenty-four hours steaming distance away. Before long they were bound to realize they had been bamboozled and when once the troops of the "Fire Brigade" recovered their spirit and saw what slender opposition they had to deal with there was no telling what their reaction would be. Consequently the little band of conquerors breathed a sigh of relief when the Norfolks steamed in next morning.

Their arrival was not a moment too soon. In the town, the Arabs had already assessed the real state of affairs and when the first of Townshend's infantry disembarked they had started on an orgy of looting. Then all was quiet; Townshend's Regatta had proved to be an unqualified success. In four days' operations, a gunboat and two steamers had been sunk, a number of other vessels, Amara, nearly two thousand Turkish prisoners and a considerable stock of booty had all fallen into British hands. It seemed as if the impossible had been achieved comparatively easy, but the root cause had really been the careful preparations for the first attack above Qurna. After the punishment meted out at Norfolk Hill, the Turks had been in no mood to fight, and Townshend had exploited this state of affairs to the hilt. Consequently his stock rose; the troops felt that he meant business and that his audacity went with a lucky streak. Things had gone better than everyone expected and, in retrospect, it would seem that it was this success that stimulated the feeling of overconfidence leading to the stream of events which would culminate in the disasters at Ctesiphon and Kut. However, it is true to say that the capture of Amara came as the result of a well-planned and well-timed operation. In the words of the Mesopotamia Commission "it deserves high praise, as it achieved great objects with comparatively small loss of life."

General Nixon now had to consider his next objective which in a signal to Simla on the nth, he concluded was Nasiriyeh. That he *would* select Nasiriyeh might be expected from what has been recounted already, but his reasons for doing so are worth mentioning. It is situated at the southern end of the Shatt-al-Hai and it was the best place from which the Turks could threaten Basra; once it was secured Nixon reckoned that the vilayet of Basra would be safe. It was also the headquarters of the Turkish civil administration, from which the powerful Arab tribes who dwelt along the Euphrates were controlled and, now that Amara was in British hands, its occupation would close the communications between the Tigris and the Euphrates. After Nasiriyeh, Nixon was undoubtedly considering an advance on Kut—again on the premise that this would make the Basra region even more secure. Perhaps his ideas went beyond Kut, but even if he was not exactly eager to press on to Baghdad, those in Simla were. "So far as we can see, all advantages, political and strategical, point to as early a move on Baghdad as possible," was the general staff's opinion early in June. This, however, was a decision for those in Whitehall and on June 14, they expressed the view that the occupation of Nasiriyeh was not necessary, as it would necessitate leaving a considerable garrison there if an advance on

Baghdad were sanctioned. In spite of this, the Viceroy cabled Mr. Chamberlain recommending the advance to Nasiriyeh, and as no reply had been received by the 22nd, Nixon was told that he could start as soon as he was ready.

Nasiriyeh is about seventy miles west of Qurna and in June most of the district was underwater. More so than usual, for 1915 turned out to be a phenomenal flood year and if Noah had been alive no doubt he would have been very restless. Once the floods subside, this region turns into a lush green oasis; its soil is among the richest in Mesopotamia and, because its gardens and cultivations have a peculiarly English look, Nasiriyeh had a special appeal for the British troops of Nixon's army. The town itself was built about 1870 by the chief of the Muntafik tribe; with its broad straight avenues and modern buildings, as Middle East towns go it was quite modern. But, when the events to be described were current, Nasiriyeh was an island—an island in an abstract as well as physical sense. Outside the confines of its walls an Arab anarchy which had simmered for generations was rife. Thousands of fierce and degenerate "Buddhoos," who preferred disorder to a settled life of cultivation and commerce, inhabited the marshes for miles around; every island in the vast inundation of the Nasiriyeh district was a scene of perennial strife. This had nothing to do with the coming of the British, it was just that there was precious little communal spirit among the marsh Arabs and no respect for authority. Loyalty was something which had to be bought and 'the trappings of Turkish or British authority merely represented potential plunder; only by a show of strength and the knowledge that interference would bring swift and relentless punishment could they be induced to confine their quarrels to themselves. Between twenty and thirty thousand of the fiercest of them lived in this area and it will be remembered that it was to bottle up these characters that Nixon had reckoned that the occupation of Amara and Nasiriyeh was necessary.

Gorringe, back from his punitive sally in Arabistan, was entrusted with the command of the operation to seize the town. He started out with what would now be called a strong brigade group[2] but later on this had to be considerably reinforced. The operation he was to undertake was something akin to Lord Wolseley's Nile expedition to Khartoum—on an even more difficult scale. His men would have to travel sometimes by land and sometimes by water, dragging their improvised gunboats overland at one stage, traversing mined reaches of the Euphrates or its offshoots at another; all in a shade temperature of something like 113° F. By water the route to Nasiriyeh from Qurna, which was the only feasible approach, followed the low-lying valley of the Old Euphrates

---

2. 30th Brigade (24th Punjabis, 76th Punjabis, 2nd, 7th Gurkha Rifles) two companies of the 48th Pioneers, 63rd Battery R.F.A., 30th Mountain Battery, four 4.7-inch guns in horse boats and the 12th and 17th Companies, Sappers and Miners.

Channel for thirty miles to Chahbaish; across the Hammer Lake for fifteen miles to its western side; thence by the tortuous channel of the Hakika—some fifty yards wide and fifteen miles long—until the main channel of the Euphrates was reached some twenty-five miles below the objective. From Qurna to Chahbaish, deep draft vessels could go up the old Euphrates, and when the operations began on June 27 steamers could negotiate the Hammer Lake as far as the entrance to the Hakika Channel, provided they had a draft of less than five feet. However, by mid July, there was little more than three feet of water in the lake and only the smallest steamers could cross. With conditions getting progressively worse, even these were often aground for days at a time and the small tugs fitted as gunboats could only be taken across by removing the guns, ammunition, armor plating, fuel and water, and towing them by the few light-draft stern-wheelers available. Later, troops and stores had to be moved in bellums and, more often than not, they had to be manhandled over the mud and water.

The first phase of the operation was to force a passage from the lake into the Hakika, the approach to which had been blocked by a solid dam of sunken mahelas covered in mud. In front of this dam lay a minefield, behind it lurked a couple of Turkish launches armed with quick firing pom-poms. Captain Nunn, fresh from his triumphs at Amara, brought his gunboats up as far as he could to drive off the launches, and by sunset on "D Day" (the 27th) the whole of Gorringe's force was anchored in the creek just below the obstruction. To get through the dam a passage had to be blasted and all next day the Sappers slaved away to make a channel. In almost unbearable heat their work was aggravated by swarms of mosquitoes and the pom-poms of the Turkish launches. Thirty-six hours of unrelenting toil at last brought dividends, but then the rush of water through the new cut was so strong that none of the ships could get through under their own steam. Every one had to be hauled up the rapids and it was another twenty-four hours before they were all assembled on the far side.

The Turks' forward defenses were on the right bank of the river near the Euphrates junction, opposite the Hakika. Two field guns with a two thousand yard clear field of fire down the creek commanded it; against them the frail gunboats would not have stood an earthly chance and only by getting troops across the river to seize the trenches defending the guns would it be possible to advance. This took four more days, so that it was July 5 before the attack could be launched. At dawn that day, two Indian battalions[3] set off independently up the left bank—one of them, the 24m Punjabis, carrying the bellums in which

---

3. 24th and 76th Punjabis.

they were to cross the river above the Turks' positions in order to cut the avenue of supply and retreat to Nasiriyeh. On the right bank, the Hampshires and 2nd and 7th Gurkhas steadily worked their way forward through high reeds while the flotilla, slowly drawing up behind, kept up a hot fire over their heads. By nine o'clock the Turks' guns were silent and the Turks themselves were streaming away to the rear toward Nasiriyeh; finding the Punjabis in their path, most of them surrendered. Then, under the direction of a Turkish officer brought in by the fickle Arabs, the mines at the entrance to the Hakika creek were lifted by nightfall and the way out to the open river was clear.

The next step was to turn the Turks out of Suk-es-Sheyukh, a trading port and Sabean[4] settlement about three miles down the river. No fighting was necessary; when the flotilla arrived white flags were already flying and once again "Supposi Kokus" stepped ashore for another ceremonial flag raising.

The next opposition was about six miles below Nasiriyeh. The Turks had dug in on both sides of the Euphrates near the Majinina creek and about a mile and a half in front of this position a couple of ships had been hastily sunk to form an obstruction blocking the channel. Since Nunn's flotilla was able to get around without much difficulty this did not prove to be much of an obstacle. However, once the ships were past it, it became apparent that the gunboats were not going to be able to make much impression on the Turks' entrenchments—they could not get past until the Turks' artillery had been dealt with. One of the difficulties was that the river banks were much higher here, making firing directly at the Turkish positions impossible for the guns in the horse boats. It was also dangerous to fire those mounted in the old stern-wheel steamers, whose decks were beginning to give way under the stress of recoil.

The Turks had chosen a good position for their defenses, both difficult to turn and impossible to assault directly. The only approach open to Gorringe's troops lay along the river banks, and as these were no more than spits of dug land between the river and the marshes—which were cut by dikes at frequent intervals—clearly the troops were in for a lively time. Gorringe paused and his men dug in two miles below the objective while Brigadier K. E. Lean's 12th Brigade[5] and two 5-inch howitzers came up to join him. With the water falling

---

4. A curious tribe with an obscure history, whose mother tongue was said to be ancient Syrian, in whom Queen Victoria had had a special interest. They called themselves "Christians of St. John"—St. John being John the Baptist. Their religion was a strange mixture of Pagan, Muslim and Christian faiths. (The Sabeans have since fallen mostly under the prevailing Muslim influence.) The men never cut their hair and one of their more interesting customs was a form of annual exchange of women. After a stupendous feast attended by both men and women, the men would leave the gathering while the women removed their underpants and hung them on a line. On their return, the men would select a garment whose owner would then declare herself and become the wife of the individual concerned until the next ceremony.

5. 2nd Battalion Queen's Own Royal West Kents, 67th and 90th Punjabis and 44th Merwana Infantry.

fast, the reinforcements had a difficult time getting through the Hammer Lake so that it was July 13 before the operation could progress.

On its left bank, the river was fringed by a narrow belt of palms. What was attempted next depended on an outflanking movement on the right bank which, although devoid of cover, did offer a steppingstone to the main position by way of a group of sand hills. These sand hills, in which a strong Turkish outpost was located, could be reached by water and at first light the 24th Punjabis paddled off toward them in their bellums. They got there all right but almost before they could organize themselves to rush the Turks, swarms of Arabs were seen to be coming down on them out of the marshes on their left. To avoid being cut off and hacked to pieces there was nothing for it but to beat a hasty retreat, and a lot of men were lost in doing so. Nothing had been gained and to Gorringe it now seemed that the other side of the river offered the best hopes for success, after all.

By this time the situation was becoming critical. Apart from the fact that the water level was making communications very difficult, the intense heat had had its effect; sickness was rife and Gorringe's force was diminishing daily. To make sure of the outcome of the next phase of the battle, reinforcements had to be sent for. More infantry and more guns were wanted and with conditions as they were it was doubtful whether they could get through. But it was done; by a superhuman effort in furnace-like conditions the reinforcements were forced through the slime of the lake bottom and at dawn on July 24 a new attack was launched.

Both sides now had about 5,000 men each, but Gorringe had the advantage of a preponderance of artillery and also the services of an aircraft with which he was able to gather a picture of what lay behind the palm fringed river bank. This time the grand assault was to be on the left where there was better cover, the main snag about this route being the presence of a creek which was too deep for men to wade. The only means of bridging it was with a barge and for the ticklish job entailed, Nunn made his preparations. Fortunately it was to be the sort of operation at which the Royal Navy excels and fortunately, too, it worked brilliantly.

At 4:30 a.m. on Saturday morning, July 24, the first shells of a softening-up bombardment crashed down on the Turkish trenches. An hour later, spearheaded by the Royal West Kents who were reported to have advanced "as if on parade," the infantry went in to complete the work of the guns. And, as the men advanced on the left bank, the old *Sumana* steamed upstream towing the bridging barge. Despite the storm of fire which was directed at the two ships, the barge was laid across the mouth of the creek which was to be crossed. A third of the Sappers taking part were lost in fruitless attempts to convert it into some sort of bridge but, fortunately, though no actual bridge was possible, the barge so effectively barred the flow of water from the river that when the troops came up to the creek they were able to wade across. From there on it was just a matter of a dog fight. Most of the Turks' defenses had been roofed with matting to protect their occupants from the scorching sun. Once the British and Indians reached them they dashed along these covered trenches— much as the Australians did just a fortnight later among the roofed-in earthworks of Lone Pine plateau in Gallipoli—thrusting their bayonets down and receiving, in turn, a fierce fusillade from below. However, unlike those captured by the Anzacs, the Nasiriyeh trenches were not bayonet-proof and in spite of stubborn resistance the fight for the first line was soon over.

Pursuit of the second position, a mile and a half further on, came next and this was difficult with the heat, a succession of ditches, and the galling fire kept up by the Turks all making it an arduous performance for Gorringe's men. But now the flotilla came into its own and its presence was soon felt. As the troops slogged slowly on, the flotilla came up and Nunn, in the little *Shushan,* was soon in the fray, pumping lead into the Turkish trenches alongside the river bank from close range. By the late afternoon it was almost all over. Demoralized Turks were in full flight across the marshes; the British were bivouacking in the trenches they had just evacuated, and white flags could be seen flying over Nasiriyeh. Next morning a deputation of Arab townsfolk came out to report that the Turks had left and to invite the British to take over. After what had been a long period of suspense and anxiety for Gorringe, Nixon's plan had at last been brought to a successful conclusion.

The cost to the British was about 500 killed and wounded—about the same number of Turkish dead. The Turks had lost much more and, apart from those killed, nearly 1,000 men and fifteen guns had been captured. They had fought well—not perhaps as well as on other occasions, but their morale had been sapped by the reverse at Amara. Those that got away withdrew up the Hai toward Kut and there prepared to make another stand against the invaders. But the cost could not be assessed in terms of battlefield casualties alone. For Gorringe's men the operation had been more of a test of endurance than anything else. In the intense heat and atmosphere of high humidity they had been moving and fighting for just about three weeks and, because no animals could be employed, they had had to do much of the work normally performed by horses or mules.

Apart from battle casualties at Amara and Nasiriyeh, sickness among the entire expeditionary force had increased to almost frightening proportions. With few comforts and little transport, life was a soul-destroying business. Sickness took no account of rank, color or creed, and even General

Townshend was one of those who went down with fever. At first it was thought he would not recover from it, and he was invalided back to India; Major General Fry (18th Brigade) temporarily took over command of the 6th Division from him. Sickness increased and as the weeks passed the weather grew hotter. Along with the sicknesses of the body came that more insidious disease, sickness of the mind—both occasioned by the conditions of the campaign. Men were affected in different ways. The symptoms were the usual ones of restlessness, anxiety, shortness of temper and a feeling of utter depression, all very similar to the "jungle happiness" known to British and American troops who fought in the forgotten areas of Burma and the Southwest Pacific in the Second World War. The sicknesses of the body and their causes were many. According to the reports in the *Times,* no efforts were being spared to make the troops in Mesopotamia comfortable; spine protectors and goggles, mosquito nets, ice, mineral waters and fresh vegetables from Bombay were all being regularly supplied, it said. Those who were supposed to be enjoying the luxuries enumerated could only smile wryly and wish that the writer of such fantasy could be among them, and by the end of the year the *Times* had a different tale to confess. The truth was that vegetables were almost unobtainable, there were no electric fans, no soda water, no ice—not even in the hospitals.

By five o'clock on a Mesopotamia morning the sun was too hot for sleep and those living in the single-fly tents just grilled in the heat. It was too hot even for the flies which at other times swarmed around. Sunstroke and heatstroke were common, fever, dysentery and paratyphoid were rife, yet medical facilities were totally inadequate to deal with the heavy casualty list. Men lay on mats of rushes in tents which were scarcely sunproof; and to house the overflow, grass barracks had to be built. Those who did not go sick were permanently on the border line so that any extra exertion bowled them over. One officer wrote:

> I remember very vividly a burial party. We started out for the cemetery, about a mile away about 6 p.m. Before we had gone half the distance a man went down with heat-stroke, and was carried back, limp and twitching, to hospital. As the corpse was lowered into the grave, one of the men on the ropes stumbled forward and fell limply into the grave on top of the dead body, and, as we fell in to march back, another man went down. Luckily we had brought a spare stretcher, and with one man on this and the other on the stretcher on which the dead man had been carried to the grave, we returned. We had buried one man, and lost three others over the job.[6]

---

6. Oxford and Buckinghamshire Light Infantry Chronicles, Vol. XXIV, 1914–1915 (published privately).

Under such conditions regiments were soon getting short of both officers and men, and of the drafts of reinforcements which arrived many were half trained and ill equipped to face such conditions. For all of them it was a hardship to be dumped into this, one of the hottest, unhealthiest regions on earth, but especially for those who came from France.

Yet, after the fashion which is so curiously British and in spite of the doctors being overworked, civil hospitals were opened for the local Arabs. This, after all, was one way of demonstrating British concern for His Majesty's new subjects.

Chapter 4

The First Advance on Baghdad

The dust raised by the boots of the troops marching in to occupy Nasiriyeh had barely had time to settle before plans were afoot for another step toward Baghdad. According to his own earlier appreciation, Nixon's first objectives had now been attained; the Basra region was securely held, the oilfields and refineries were as safe as could be reasonably expected. If "a safe game" was to be played then undoubtedly this was the time to call a halt to the operations and consolidate. But Sir John was a man whose temperament would not allow him to remain still; he wanted Baghdad and, if this was his intention, then Kut was the next logical step toward it. But he did not declare that it was a steppingstone to Baghdad and the reasons which he gave for pressing on to capture it were not nearly so convincing as those he had put forward for taking Nasiriyeh. The Turks were concentrating at Kut, he said. Yet Kut was a hundred and twenty miles upstream of the most advanced British positions at Amara and the defenders of any invaded country will always be concentrating somewhere in advance of the invaders; the difficult decision is to know where and when to stop, for invariably the temptation is always to press on to occupy the ground just ahead. Kut, he urged, was a better strategic center than Amara. It lies at the junction of the Shatt-al-Hai with the Tigris and, once it was occupied, only a small garrison would be needed in Nasiriyeh; with both ends of the waterway connecting the Tigris and the Euphrates in British hands, the main force could be concentrated at Kut. Yet, whether or not he exaggerated the strategic value of the Hai, it is quite certain that occupying Kut at its upper limit could hardly compensate for adding another hundred and fifty miles to his already weak and tenuous line of communications. Nothing was said then about Baghdad being the objective; if it was, on the basis of the arguments Nixon had given, preparations on a vastly different scale to those being made should have been put in hand there and then. On the other hand, if the security of the Basra delta was the sole object—as was implied—then Amara was quite far enough. With Ahwaz and Nasiriyeh to think of as well, the line of communications was long enough and it was not as if the resources of the expeditionary force were growing with the extra commitments.

Nixon was not the only one with an eye on the minarets of Baghdad; the Viceroy had been attracted to the idea of capturing it ever since Barrett had first occupied Basra. And if one is trying to trace the source of the idea, then "Supposi Kokus" seemed to have been the prime instigator, for it was he who, in November, had first put forward a reasoned argument enumerating the political advantages to be gained by taking it. Whitehall had shown no enthusiasm for Cox's arguments and they had received short shrift from the Secretary of State when they reached London. Possibly this reaction was a disappointment to Lord Hardinge; nevertheless he appeared to accept that the idea was just not feasible and indeed, in a letter dated December 2, 1914, it was Hardinge himself who set out the most cogent reasons for rejecting it.

> You did not give me time to send you our views on Cox's proposal to advance to Baghdad, for you sent me a telegram crushing it. As a matter of fact, after consultation with Beauchamp Duff, I have arrived at the conclusion that it would be impossible to execute at present. Unlike Basra, which is easy to capture from the south and very strong against any attack from the north, Baghdad has no advantages as a position against an attacking enemy, and, being an extensive town situated on both banks of the Tigris, would be particularly difficult to defend. All communications with Baghdad would have to be by water, and Baghdad is about five hundred miles up the river from Basra and five hundred and seventy from the Gulf. It would not be possible to entrust this long line of communications to the Arabs, since, if they failed, a disaster must result. To avoid undue risk, it would, in the opinion of the Commander-in-Chief, have been necessary to have a whole division in Baghdad and another on the line of communications, to keep them open in the first instance and also ready to reinforce Baghdad if attacked. In view of the large number of troops that we have sent overseas and the very reduced military forces remaining in India, it would be impossible for India to carry out this scheme even with reasonable safety. In the absence, therefore, of extraneous assistance, those political advantages which are really considerable, that might

accrue from the capture and occupation of Baghdad must be subordinated to the military objections that would be involved in such a course.

Situations change quickly in war but with his almost enthusiastic acceptance of Nixon's recommendations less than six months later, this rejection has a false ring about it.

When the news that Nasiriyeh had fallen reached him, the Viceroy promptly wired to the Secretary of State: "As Nasiriyeh has now been occupied, we consider it a matter of strategic necessity that Kut should be occupied." He then went on to say that as sickness in the Mesopotamia force made reinforcements necessary, he proposed to "borrow" the Indian brigade[1] garrisoning Aden. Whitehall's reaction was lukewarm. The strategic importance of Kut was recognized, said Chamberlain in his reply on July 30. "But a cautious strategy was imposed because the brigade in Aden was *not* available, nor were any other reinforcements." Nasiriyeh might be evacuated, he suggested—seemingly a ludicrous idea considering it had only just been captured—and he would be grateful for the Commander-in-Chief's up-to-date views. Nixon answered tartly that his views were the same as they had been in June; Nasiriyeh could not be abandoned as the Secretary of State had suggested, although he did think that the troops at Ahwaz might be withdrawn if the Anglo-Persian Oil Company was prepared to pay the local tribesmen not to interfere with the oil wells. However, if he were allowed to go on to capture Kut, the situation ought to become easier because it was his opinion that the best remedy for disorders in Persia was an advance on Baghdad. Because the telegram was couched in fairly direct terms, the significance of the reference to Baghdad seems to have been lost. Chamberlain's reply, bringing a guarded assent to an advance to Kut, only expressed his continued concern for the oil wells and Nixon's riposte to this was that he could not undertake to look after the oil wells and capture Kut at the same time. Finally the decision that Nixon might go on to take Kut was clinched on August 20, when Chamberlain— assuming that the wells would be safe from local disorders and feeling reassured about the oil—authorized the advance.

This exchange of correspondence has been given in fair detail, if only to demonstrate the fundamental differences which still existed between Whitehall, India, and General Nixon, with regard to the role of the Expeditionary Force in Mesopotamia. Nixon and the Indian authorities both saw the campaign as an offensive one with Baghdad as the goal, Whitehall was trying to restrain and curb the operations; to Chamberlain the safety of the oil wells was really all that

---

1. This was the 28th Indian Infantry Brigade and the Viceroy's expressed intention was to return it to Aden in November (1916).

mattered. The trouble was that the Indian Government now had the bit between its teeth and if it had been reluctant to send troops to Mesopotamia at the outset of the campaign it was certainly not so now. Once the expedition was afoot, Simla was urging every new advance and it was left to Whitehall to apply the brake. Up to Qurna and Nixon's appointment, the purpose of the Expeditionary Force had been specific and definite; after that Whitehall relaxed its grip, the Indian Government became overenthusiastic, and in Mesopotamia the men on the spot were given almost free rein. Successive advances to Amara, Nasiriyeh and Kut—and finally the adventurous thrust at Baghdad— were all prompted by Nixon, supported by India and conceded by Whitehall. It is fair to add that the Secretary of State did have reservations on each and every occasion when an advance was raised. He was "opposed" to an advance to Qurna, he was "not in favor" of advances which necessitated reinforcements or appeared to detract from the task of safeguarding the oil supplies; but, ultimately, he gave his consent. The occupation of Nasiriyeh stemmed from the capture of Amara, the advance to Kut followed on the heels of Nasiriyeh, eventually the decision to advance on Baghdad was to succeed the occupation of Kut. One objective followed another and, in the final analysis, Nixon must be regarded as the inspiration of it all. The Viceroy, a complacent accessory, should have been restrained by Beauchamp-Duff, his Commander-in-Chief; but, at the same time, the responsibility of those in Whitehall, who accepted the dangers into which the extra commitments were leading them, is no less grave because they allowed their hands to be forced.

To appreciate the disastrous effect of enthusiasm, complacency and laissez-faire, it is necessary to return to the theater of operations. In the summer months of 1915, life for the British and Indian troops garrisoning Amara—the "Garden of Tears," from which Adam and Eve are supposed to have made their exit from Eden[2]—was probably more comfortable than anywhere else in Mesopotamia. Amara's trees and gardens were refreshingly green and the town itself quite modern. On the left bank, the row of fine brick houses fronting the river gave the town an impressive air as one steamed up the river, even though the usual Arab town tangle of narrow streets lay behind them, while on the opposite bank there was a pleasant expanse of date groves and lime orchards. The troops were under canvas or quartered in the larger buildings on both sides of the river and, during Townshend's sickness, command had devolved on the irascible Fry, whose deafness was a recurrent source of embarrassment to his staff. (His response to shouts of "Look out General, there's a shell coming this way" is reported to have been a quizzical

---

2. There is a story that Eve, when she left, wept copiously, and that her tears grew into the bush, which was still growing prolifically on the Mesopotamia front, and whose berries are known as "Eve's Tears."

look and from this behavior stemmed his reputation for imperturbability in battle.)

Sickness, shortages and, above all, boredom, were the real enemies of the British in Mesopotamia during this period. Nowhere were they greater than in Amara. In a temperature of 120⁰ little work was possible, so that everything had to be done in the early morning or late evening. Between seven in the morning and six at night men just lay and sweated; sleep, with myriads of flies hovering over them, was out of the question. Mail to and from England took over two months and there was the inevitable censorship. One letter written by a British soldier who said he was "encamped among the date palms" had "date" cut out by an Indian censor, because—according to regulations—no mention of dates was permitted. For the regimental officers, faced with the high-stacked pile of correspondence which had to be read through every evening, censoring was a tedious business. The continual adjuration "hoping this finds you in the pink as it leaves me at present" tries the patience of the average mind but in the course of time the rare unearthing of indiscretions from a mass of pencilled, spidery scrawl became second nature. Always a distasteful business, reading soldiers' missives offered a curious insight into the characters of those concerned and messages like those conveyed by the lines:

> From Mesopotamia,
> I write a line of love to you
> I wish I could do tonight to you
> What I should like to do

reputedly blandly penned on a postcard, showed that some of the men, at least, retained hale and hearty basic feelings, despite the conditions in which they served.

There was one consolation: no Turks were within thirty miles or so of Amara and Arab raids were the only threat. And, to counter these, a chain of defence posts was thrown up around the block houses built to protect the original Turkish rulers against their Arab subjects. To deal with more serious threats, a mobile column was organized, and at the upper end of the town a rickety Turkish pontoon bridge, originally constructed to exact tolls from passing river craft rather than as a convenience for the populace, was improved so that the column could move out quickly. The next place of any importance above Amara was the village of Ali Gharbi; in the heart of Beni Lam country. The members of this tribe were some of the most turbulent and inhospitable of all the riverain Arabs and were as treacherous as they were savage and cruel; the sacred laws of Arab hospitality meant nothing to them and they would cut the throat of a guest without a qualm. It was against a collection of these cutthroats that the mobile column first tried out its paces. Shortly after Amara had been captured, a British patrol had reconnoitered Ali Gharbi and found that the Turks had evacuated it. However, within a fortnight, the locals reported that Turkish officials were back there. As the telegraph line from Ali Gharbi to Kut was still intact, the village's value as an outpost was obvious and so it was decided to remove the so-called officials and let the mobile column see some action. The column had another aim also. At Kuwait on the way to Ali Gharbi, twenty thousand Arabs, under the leadership of a notoriously villainous Sheikh called Gazban—the "Angry One"—were said to be terrorizing the rightful Sheikh of Kuwait who "wanted" to be friendly. Gazban was known to have been implicated in the disturbances around Ahwaz and although he had shown some inclination to come to terms with the British it was known that he had been well paid by the Turks. If his allegiance was wavering, then it was thought that he might be persuaded to cast his lot with the British—on a basis of so much down and so much a month for good behavior. At Kuwait, Gazban was persuaded to return to Amara to talk matters over and it seems that he was very nearly won over to the British side. Almost, but not quite. When he heard that the payment of his bribe was to be conditional on his son living in Amara, his answer was an emphatic "NO" and, after asking for a dozen bottles of soda water for his "bad stomach," he returned to Kuwait. There his collection of cutthroats stayed, to constitute a potential menace throughout the subsequent operations.

As predicted, *the* Turkish "officials" were indeed in occupation of the sun-scorched wind-swept little village of mud huts which called itself Ali Gharbi. They had returned there, they said, because they were anxious to be made prisoners. Their wish was granted and with both of its missions accomplished the British column returned with them to Amara. There conditions remained much the same until July. Then, once it started to get cooler in the mornings, the troops' health began to improve. Mention has already been made of the fact that food and dietary deficiencies were the fundamental causes of their sickness. About the only vegetables available were onions and "Lathes Fingers," the latter being popular enough with the Indians but never particularly so with the British, whose ideas on food are consistently rigid. Of potatoes there were none, and news of a barge load being sent up from Basra was eagerly anticipated. However, after five days in the well of a barge with horses packed on the deck above, the arrival of the potatoes in Amara was heralded by a stench which outdid even that associated with the town's Arab quarter and every one was found to be rotten.

As the July days slipped past, the preparations for the coming advance got underway. A start on the building of an airfield had been made in June and when this was finished the two ancient Caudrons which had flown up to it practiced artillery fire control by means of smoke signals every morning. In Mesopotamia the Royal Flying Corps had started life with two obsolete Maurice Farmans sent down from Egypt only a few weeks before. Both had been assembled in time to reconnoiter over Qurna during Gorringe's advance at the end of May but one of them, which was constantly having engine trouble, was lost subsequently during the Nasiriyeh operations. To replace them came the two Caudrons. Like the Maurice Farmans they also needed constant attention and repairs were not easy in the circumstances in which they were compelled to operate. Men to fly them, mechanics to service them and spare parts were all scarce; little was known about flying in tropical climates—still less of the effect of sun and dust on engines and fabrics—so that it was a near miracle they were able to function as well as they did. Not until the end of August did the first modern aircraft—two 80 horsepower Martinsyde Scouts, which were considered pretty powerful machines in those days—arrive; this was the genesis of 30 Squadron—a unit which was to prove its worm in this and another great war.

In Amara the chief topic of conversation was Kut. Kut-al-Amara, to give it its full name, which was to dominate conversations in Mesopotamia for many a long month, lies at the southern end of a loop in the Tigris, by river about two hundred and fifty miles from Baghdad although it is only about ninety miles from Amara by road. It is from the loop—nearly two miles deep and about a mile wide at this northern, open end—which Kut occupies, that the Hai[3] takes off from the Tigris to run due south for about a hundred and forty miles before joining the Euphrates near Nasiriyeh. According to whichever alternative one was prepared to favor, rumor had it that the Turks were either evacuating Kut and retiring to Ctesiphon only twenty-three miles from Baghdad, or that they had been reinforced and joined by two batteries of German artillery, with German gunners. There was plenty of gossip but it was difficult to get exact information as to what the Turks were doing and some of the Arab "agents" sent forward to spy out the land returned with the news that their colleagues who failed to show up had been caught and hanged by a certain Yusef Nur-Ud-Din, ex-chief of police of the Basra vilayet, who, as the new Turkish Commandant, was making his presence felt in Kut. The Turks were, in fact, building a strong position about eight miles downstream from Kut.

On August 27, Townshend returned to pick up the reins of command at Amara. On that day, for the first time in five months, clouds were seen in the sky and to those who had come to hate the vast cloudless blue dome above

---

3. The Shatt-al-Hai, which is really an ancient canal, is probably the cause of the loop.

them, Townshend's return seemed to be an omen. It was. Two days later came the news that an advance on Kut had at last been authorized; the troops were to start upriver at once. Before he had fallen sick Townshend had asked for a six-months reserve of supplies to be dumped at Amara, together with a similar supply of gun and rifle ammunition. Nixon, however, had opposed the demand and said that six months reserve of rations was based on a misapprehension of the arrangements authorized for the force under his command. Six weeks—not six months—was the total reserve authorized by G.H.Q. in India for the whole of the Mesopotamia Army and everything had to be done strictly according to regulations. Demands for more transport were treated in a similar vein and Townshend was calmly told by Nixon "to cut his coat according to his cloth!" With this background, orders for what was to prove a fatal advance were approved.

Some of those concerned must have had qualms for even Townshend himself noted that "All the elements demanded by the strategic offensive were lacking . . . and the essential principle of rapidity was, owing to the lack of transport, out of the question. . . ." He also added his own opinion as to what should have been done under the circumstances. ". . . Having taken Amara and Nasiriyeh we should have consolidated our position in the Basra vilayet . . . only in the event of success of the Allies in France or Gallipoli should the strategic offensive have been taken in Mesopotamia." This extract from his diary shows that Townshend's thoughts were occupied with the provisions for an effective pursuit, for which he needed a sufficiency of transport—both on land and on the river. After the battles of Shaiba and Nasiriyeh no pursuit had been possible because the means were lacking and in consequence of which two thousand fugitives were added to Nur-Ud-Din's force; Townshend was determined that this should not happen again if he could help it.

At the beginning of August, Delamain's brigade had been sent forward to Ali Gharbi to cover the assembly of the main striking force and this was a move which Townshend, with a Napoleonic tendency to gather all his force together before making any advance at all, had considered at the time to be most imprudent. Behind Delamain, the rest of the 6th Division was to assemble. Townshend's plan was to pass Hoghton's 17th Brigade through Ali Gharbi and to concentrate the whole force, including Delamain, forward at Sheikh Sa'ad. Once the force was assembled, he proposed to move, lock, stock and barrel, up the left bank of the river; the Turks before Kut on that side were to be rolled up, and those on the right bank ignored. It would be a slow business, he predicted, but, he noted, "how could it be otherwise" considering he had to play "battledore and shuttlecock" with his transport and "fetch up troops in homeopathic doses." By September 11, the three infantry brigades

(16th, 17A and 18th) had assembled at Ali Gharbi and, with the divisional troops, he had a total of about eleven thousand combatants. The advance started next day; part of the force being carried in ships but the majority having to march. It was very hot—110° to 120°—but in spite of the heat the troops were reported to be in good spirit at the prospect of action. In three days they had reached Abu Rummanah, just before Sheikh Sa'ad, and about eight miles from where the Turks were digging in hard. Here the division bivouacked for ten days—on the *right* bank, because the ships were compelled to moor on that side—to await some of the artillery which had not yet arrived from the south.

Air reconnaissance established that the bulk of Nur-Ud-Din's troops were strongly entrenched on the left bank of the river in a sort of "Torres-Vedras like" line of earthworks which extended northwest from the river bank for about six miles inland to the Suwada Marsh. At Es Sinn, on the right bank, more Turks occupied about two and a half miles of trenches dug along the site of an ancient canal and they were linked to the forces on the other side of the river by means of a bridge of boats. The chief feature of the left bank and the reason for the strength of the Turkish defence was the marshes, three of which broke up the Turkish positions. Between them, the dry land had all been entrenched with deep narrow positions and most of the front was covered by extensive wire entanglements, some of which were hidden from view in deep depressions; lines of deep pits containing sharpened stakes and contact mines had also been used to strengthen the position, although this fact was not dis-covered till later.

The novel feature of Townshend's plan was that it depended on the maxi-mum use of deception and surprise, features which had hardly entered into the British plans of attack hitherto. At Shaiba there had been no plans for an attack at all, the battle had just "happened"; at Qurna the ground had precluded anything but a straight frontal attack; at Nasiriyeh similarly, the attacks had been made in a slow methodical fashion up both banks of the river. But Townshend was intent on using some professional science in his operations and his ideas of attacking on the left bank depended on inducing the Turks on the right bank to stay there until it was too late to do anything to save the roll-up on the left. However, the difficulty of implementing his stratagem was the very one he feared—lack of land transport. When operations started Townshend was three hundred mules short of what was required, consequently virtually all the transport had to be allotted to the main force on the left. (It is also relevant to add that there were no water carts and that no arrangements could be made for the carriage of extra drinking water.) The holding force on the right was depleted of its transport and was almost immobile.

On the morning of September 26, while the eyes of the world were focused on a titanic struggle on the Western Front, the battle for Kut-al-Amara began. On the right bank the feint attack was to be made against the Es Sinn position and the decisive attack would be directed against the flank positions nearest to the Suwada Marsh, six miles from the river. To attain surprise, the approach to them necessitated a night march and, because they were so far from the river, Townshend's plan was in direct contradiction to the established procedure for the British fighting a battle in Mesopotamia. As a result, it appears that Nur-Ud-Din was completely taken in. The Turkish commander had counted on a disembarkation from the ships, an advance in two columns on both sides of the river and two separate frontal attacks.

On the right bank a two-hour unopposed march brought the 16th, 17th and Cavalry Brigades to the Chahela Mounds, about two and a half miles from the Es Sinn. A camp was pitched and every available tent put up to give the appearance that the force had come to stay. Before long, shells began to burst among the tents and Nur-Ud-Din, believing that the main thrust was to come from this direction, marched his general reserve away from the left bank by way of the boat bridge in order to reinforce his positions against the force seemingly massing against him on the right. Meantime, on the left bank, Fry's 18th Brigade had marched to Nukhailat village, meeting with very little opposition, and there dug in. All was set, although from the point of view of the Royal Flying Corps it did not seem to be a particularly auspicious day to start. One of the Maurice Farmans had been smashed up during the advance from Ali Gharbi, two of the new Martinsydes were out of commission, one had been shot down and its pilot and observer made prisoners, and on this day one of the three remaining airplanes was put out of action when it capsized on landing. There was only one left but it did a magnificent job.[4]

That night, under cover of darkness, an Indian battalion and a squadron of cavalry moved across the Turks' front on the left bank and a pontoon bridge was thrown across the river; over this the majority of the force—ostensibly deployed on the far bank—was to cross and swell the column on the left bank. Everything went more or less according to plan and Sir John Nixon, who had earlier announced his intention of being present at the battle, came up to stay with Townshend, in the latter's observation post. Normally this would have been a very unsatisfactory arrangement, but Nixon had said that he did not wish to interfere in Townshend's conduct of the battle—that he only wished to be on the spot to settle questions of policy there and then—and Townshend had had to accept him. It would have been difficult to do otherwise and the situation might have been difficult if it had not been that Townshend's per-

---

4. Its observer was F. Yeats Brown, author of *Bengal Lancer.*

sonality was such that the presence of his commander made no difference. (In a similar situation a few weeks later, when Nixon and Townshend together marched with Hoghton's brigade, Nixon frequently expressed the opinion that the Brigadier was marching in the wrong direction and the wretched Hoghton was very upset at the interference.)

The two columns which were to attack on the left bank started to form up soon after midnight of the 27th; there was just time for a quick meal and then they were off on what was intended to be the decisive phase. Delamain was in overall command, and his column "B"—the Dorsets, 117th Mahrattas and a company of sappers—was to make a demonstration while Hoghton with column "A," comprising his own and the rest of Delamain's brigade, was to march across the Turks' front to capture the redoubt near the Ataba Marsh on the extreme left of their position. Once the flank attack was underway, Delamain's force was to follow. Meanwhile, close to the river bank Fry's brigade was to press on with a frontal attack which would be covered by the heavy guns, dismounted from the gun barges during the night.

The difficult part of the operation came when Hoghton had to strike off on his own. No reconnaissance of the route to be followed had been made, and yet greatest accuracy as to when to deploy and what direction to take was essential. So it was not really surprising that things went wrong. Shortly after 5 a.m. Delamain wheeled off left, to face the Turks and start the attack which was to occupy their attention while the turning force marched on. Hoghton marched on but, before long, Delamain and behind him Townshend, in his observation post, saw his column suddenly veer off to the right. Instead of marching parallel to the Turkish front line, Hoghton was apparently heading obliquely away from it. What had happened was that the head of the column had gone too far north before wheeling left and, when dawn came, Hoghton's men were marching along the only strip of dry land between two marshes. This gradually led them further over and further away from the Turks but unless the whole column was to be turned around there was no option but to continue and march completely around the Ataba Marsh. Realizing that it would be some time before the encircling attack in which Townshend had pinned his faith would go in, Delamain now had to decide whether to continue with his own attack or wait on Hoghton. The trenches in front of him were very strongly held, but any delay might result in their being reinforced so there was a good case for an immediate attack. Making the decision to do so was complicated by the fact that both brigades were out of touch with divisional headquarters as well as each other. An attempt had been made to lay a telephone line behind the marching columns but the cable was constantly breaking and the heavy mirage made helio communication almost impossible. There were, in fact, two pack radio sets with the force but both of these new-fangled creations were on the ships and all the news that Townshend got came from his airplanes—and that was to the effect that matters were going well!

As Hoghton appeared to be making such slow progress, Delamain decided to carry on with his attack and when Hoghton saw what was happening he sent back a couple of battalions[5] to help. Once they had arrived, the Turkish trenches in front of Delamain were quickly captured and, when Hoghton did eventually get into position the whole of the front line was soon rolled up. But by now the troops were pretty well exhausted and very, very thirsty. Except for the contents of their water bottles, they had had no water since the night before, and all day there had been a blazing sun and a hot dust laden wind. Like the men, the animals were nearly mad with thirst and a number of the mules made a dash for the nearest marsh, where they got bogged down in the mud and were sniped at as they lay. Some of the men sent after them tried to drink the water the mules had been after, but it was found to taste and have the effect of pure Epsom salts. Dead-beat and tired out, many of the men dropped and lay where they fell; thirst and exhaustion had produced such a stupefying effect that they could not even understand an order.

On the river bank, Fry, whose brigade had also got into difficulties was looking for assistance from the right where, according to the plan, the Turks were supposed to collapse. In a message to Delamain he said that he would not be able to get any further unless Delamain could put in a flank attack toward the positions opposing him. Somehow Delamain's men were coaxed into a last supreme effort and, just before sunset, a bayonet charge over a thousand yards of desert successfully brought them to the Turks' positions at the limit of Fry's front. Night then descended over the battlefield like a great black curtain and the troops, nearly all in, lay down to snatch some rest. There was still no water for them; the river was over a mile away and the Turks still lay across the direct route to it. Along the way they had come, lay the wounded, many of them lying in long grass and spread over a wide area and despite exhaustion it was essential that they should be collected and brought in or they would perish. Already the Arabs were on the prowl and many of the wounded were robbed and murdered—in some cases horribly mutilated as well. Furthermore, the medical arrangements had largely broken down; collecting stations and field ambulances had been lost and wounded men wandered around for hours before they got any attention. Others, whose lives could have been saved if they had been found sooner, died from exhaustion and the bitter cold of the night.

---

5. Not, for some strange reason, the two other battalions of Delamain's own 16th Brigade, but the Oxford and Buckinghamshire Light Infantry, and the 119th Infantry.

But the battle was as good as over. As soon as Townshend knew that Delamain's attack had been successful he had ordered the river flotilla to try to force a passage upstream to get at the Turks' bridge just below Kut. The difficulty was an obstruction just below the front line. Two iron barges had been run aground, one on either bank, and linked by iron cables to a sunken mahela in midstream. Turkish artillery commanded the whole reach and from trenches on the bank the obstruction itself was under point-blank fire from machine guns and rifles. The ships steamed up undercover of darkness but as soon as they came within range the Turks opened fire with everything they had. Steaming on at full tilt, the *Comet,* leading the convoy, tried to break the chains by ramming. But they held fast and the *Comet's* commander, Lieutenant Commander Cookson, then ran his ship alongside the mahela to see what could be done. With his guns out of action and most of the crew wounded, Cookson himself grabbed an axe and leapt aboard the mahela to try to cut the cables; no sooner had he done so than he fell dead, hit in a score of places.[6] When it was clear that nothing further could be done, a withdrawal was ordered, and the flotilla pulled back downstream.

The Turks were also pulling out. During the afternoon they had started to pull out of their positions on the right bank but, owing to the mirage, they had not been spotted. And on that side of the river it seems that they made a remarkable withdrawal, since they successfully got all their guns away. On the left bank too, they had had enough. During the night most of them slipped off and, under the very noses of Fry's and Delamain's tired men, got clean away.

Next morning, when Townshend's troops had established that Nur-Ud-Din was indeed retreating, a pursuit was organized and the cavalry was sent to follow up the Turks. (So far they had contributed virtually nothing to the battle—although they had suffered quite a few casualties when they cantered in dense formation toward Delamain's brigade in the dusk of the previous evening and were mistaken for Turks or Arabs.) Kut was reached without mishap and found to be empty of Turks but, outside the town, just along the Baghdad road, the cavalry ran into the rear guard and its commander decided to hold off and await reinforcements. Meanwhile Townshend, who had probably anticipated a pursuit on similar lines to that in which he had found himself after Qurna, had reserved the river chase for himself; maybe he had hopes of entering Baghdad on the heels of the fugitives as he had at Amara. If so, then he was doomed to disappointment for on this occasion he had not taken into account the difficulties of navigating up the exasperating Tigris. With little water in the river and many shoals to get past, his ships were stuck

---

6. For this action Commander Cookson was awarded a posthumous Victoria Cross.

for two days near Kut and when they finally got off it was too late for any effective chase. Not that such a chase could have been anything like that between Qurna and Amara anyway; Nur-Ud-Din's troops were retiring in good order along both banks and there was no rabble and no panic.

Yet, even if it had not brought the perfect victory for which he had hoped, Townshend's stratagem had been highly successful. Although the outcome had hung in the balance while Hoghton was maneuvering, the actions of Delamain and Fry had finally brought victory. Only the behavior of some of the Indian troops had caused any misgivings and Delamain told Townshend afterwards that he did not think they would storm trenches again if they were put to it. Two or three men of one of the Punjabi regiments were also reported to have deserted to the Turks and told them of the feint and intended march on the left bank but Nur-Ud-Din had regarded their story a ruse to mislead him, so that the plan was not jeopardized. Yet the behavior of a few can hardly condemn that of the majority. Most of the Indians fought gallantly and although Townshend was apt to eulogize later on the "Prodigies of valor" performed by his British regiments, he would not have got far without the Indians. Having said this, it is probably also true to say that the day would not have been carried if the Dorsets had not made such a splendid showing at a crucial point in the turning attack.

The final word must be in relation to the mobile part of Townshend's force; the cavalry, whose contribution to the battle was disappointing to say the least, and whose behavior may be used to instance how apparently insignificant events may ruin a general's plans. The reason given for the failure sounds most curious. The cavalry were Indian regiments; because of the want of transport, Delamain had not been able to carry their cooking pots and they refused to use the Arab equivalent found in the village en route. This, it is said, was the main reason for their not taking a more offensive attitude during *the* pursuit; if it is really true then it only shows how caste prejudices can affect a crucial situation. Whether or not the cavalry was really intended to be used for pursuit is another matter. If Townshend had intended to make full use of their mobility, then they would presumably have had first call on such transport as was available and they did not. His hankering after a repeat of the Qurna to Amara follow-up possibly blinded him to the cavalry's role, which seems a pity because any of the river steamer captains could have told him of the difficulties he would have to face when the Tigris water was low.

Back on the battlefield, the first move Delamain's men made on the morning of the 29th was to the river. After a bitterly cold night, during which the temperatures had dropped fifty degrees, dawn brought them the vista of an empty battlefield strewn with the impedimenta of a beaten army. Cold and hungry, their real agony was still thirst. Soon after the order to push on to the river was dropped on Delamain's headquarters from the only airplane which was operating, men were scrambling down its bank and gulping mouthfuls of the muddy Tigris. Fry's brigade was detailed as the pursuit force to accompany Townshend and they embarked on the ships and set off upstream that afternoon. Delamain was given the task of occupying Kut with the 16th Brigade while Hoghton was left to clear up the battlefield, bury the dead and salvage as much material as could be salvaged.

"Clearing up" any battlefield is invariably an unpleasant business, likewise it is also a very necessary one. Never more so than on this occasion! The Arabs started clearing before the British and they were believed to have gotten away with many hundreds of rifles and considerable quantities of ammunition—all of which would be used in due course against British, Indians or Turks, according to the way the wind blew. Even so, a great deal of material was recovered and the Turks' defenses were found to be even more elaborate man had ever been imagined. Trenches were deep and narrow and the redoubts provided with the sort of overhead cover that was prescribed for the systems which were to exist in Korea thirty-five years later. Mines, wire, and concealed pits housing sharply pointed stakes had all been incorporated in the defenses and at appropriate intervals along the trenches huge jars of water had been stored for the creature comforts of the defenders. On the right bank the field works were not so formidable as those on the other side of the river, although their capture would undoubtedly have been a murderous business. The best artillery pieces had been removed; all that remained were obsolescent or ante-diluvian, and out of a total of fourteen guns left on the field, eight were brass muzzle-loaders and two small brass cannon bearing a Persian date of 1181—equivalent to A.D. 1802.

As a newly captured town, Kut naturally held a good deal of interest and when Hoghton's men got there, a day behind the first victors, it was a hive of activity. The town itself was smaller and dirtier than Amara, but its bazaars were crowded and the shops were doing a roaring trade. After the Turks, who had been in the habit of encouraging loyalty by executing those who showed too mild an interest in their cause, the inhabitants greeted their new masters almost effusively. Indeed, it seemed that news of British justice had preceded their arrival as one Arab is said to have been waiting to greet the cavalry officers in order to present a claim for compensation because they had ridden across one of his fields.

It took some time for the ships carrying Fry's brigade to get off the mud and it was October 5 before the flotilla reached Aziziyeh, sixty miles from Kut overland. By this time the retreating Turks had halted at Ctesiphon and were installed astride the river on both banks in formidable defenses which had been prepared for this very emergency. If Nixon had entertained hopes that after the battle for Kut Townshend would be able to get on to Baghdad without another major action, he had been very optimistic. From Es Sinn, where the battle had been fought, it was just over 100 miles to Baghdad. It was true that if the Turks followed previous precedent they would go back quite a long way; after Shaiba they had retired 90 miles; after Qurna another 90 miles. But not on this occasion, and in assuming that it would be something like 90 miles before they offered battle again Nixon was wrong. And, up to October 4, he was confident that Baghdad would fall. In a cable to India on the 3rd, he said he considered himself "strong enough to open the road to Baghdad" and that he proposed to concentrate at Aziziyeh. Next day he followed up with another telegram asking whether he would be reinforced by a division from France, so that once in Baghdad he could stay there. Both telegrams were obviously sent in the belief that the retreating Turks were demoralized, and even on October 5, when he knew that the Turks had stopped and were digging in at Ctesiphon, Nixon still considered that it was advisable to "smash him and that nothing could justify letting slip such an opportunity."

Townshend thought differently, and in his diary he noted on October 3:

> The Army Commander does not seem to realize the weakness and danger of his line of communications. We are now some 380 miles from the sea and have only two weak divisions, including my own, in the country. There is my division to do the fighting and Gorringe's to hold the line of communication from Kut to the sea. There is no possible support to give me if I receive a check, and the consequences of a retreat are not to be imagined. Thus, I feel it my duty to give my opinion plainly to the Army Commander, whether he likes it or not! . . . The line of communication should be secured before everything, and a line of five or six days good marching must be considered a long one. An advance along a long line of communications is always productive of trouble. A navigable river like the Tigris may form a very good line, but it must be amply patrolled by war vessels to keep the Arabs in check.

People in Whitehall were also beginning to get worried. On October 4, Chamberlain wired "If on account of navigation difficulties there is no probability of the enemy being caught up and smashed, there is no object in the pursuit being continued" and next day, this telegram was followed by another ordering Nixon to stop. But Nixon, unwilling to see his prize whipped away from him, had answered the "navigation difficulties" argument by saying that if he marched his troops with land transport and lightened the vessels, there would be no "navigation difficulties." And it was this telegram that led to considerable misunderstanding in Whitehall. With Nixon answerable to Delhi or Simla and not Whitehall, the British Government was unaware of Nixon's previous requests for river transport, and from his latest cable it appeared that sufficient transport was in fact available for an advance on Baghdad. Consequently, in the subsequent discussions leading to its sanction, the question of more ships was not considered. On political grounds the situation in the Middle East and the precarious situation in Gallipoli both made the capture of Baghdad a very attractive proposition and so, on October 8, a telegram was sent to the Viceroy stating that every effort would be made to supply the reinforcements[7] Nixon wanted. But he was not to make the attempt with insufficient troops. The decision had been taken entirely on the basis of whether or not there were enough fighting troops to ensure the success of the operation; logistics were not even considered—presumably because of the misunderstanding over the navigation difficulties telegram. In the War Office in London, the experts—including even those who had earlier said the operation was not feasible—had now concluded that Nixon had enough men at his disposal to capture Baghdad; all that he did need was two more divisions to hold it afterward. The result was that Nixon was given the green light on October 24, and Whitehall said that they would send him the two Indian divisions then serving in France, although when exactly they would be sent was not disclosed.

If one now stops to consider the transportation difficulties which faced him, it is difficult to understand what induced Nixon ever to recommend the advance on Baghdad in the first place. Certainly it was not a case of cutting his coat according to his cloth, as he had recommended Townshend to do for the advance on Kut. And, if the situation in May had been unsatisfactory, it was relatively much worse in November when there was a longer line of communications and the low water season to contend with. Two more divisions and a line of communications extending to Baghdad would have exacerbated the situation even further. Not only this; the question of the strength of the Turks opposing him and the likelihood of their being reinforced also suggest that Nixon made a most unwise appreciation of the facts. Whitehall, Simla and the Intelligence Authorities in Mesopotamia all agreed that the Turkish troops in Mesopotamia at that time numbered only about nine thousand men. But, according to Whitehall's calculations, as many as sixty thousand could be deployed there by the end of January 1916 and this information was wired out to India in a "private" telegram to the Viceroy on October 21. If it had been passed on to Nixon it is possible that he might have changed his view. On the

---

7. About this time both Mr. Chamberlain and the Viceroy were considering asking for two divisions of Japanese troops for employment in Mesopotamia.

other hand when Whitehall again wired to India on November 22—and this time repeated the information to Nixon—that thirty thousand troops under Khalil Pasha were en route for Baghdad, and that the German General von der Goltz was on his way out to Mesopotamia to take command, he refused to believe it.

The hazards of going on were not lost on Townshend, and he decided to halt; land Fry's 18th Brigade at Aziziyeh, and report to Nixon that it would be best to return to Kut and consolidate. Only because Nixon was on the spot in Kut was it necessary to ascertain his views; if he had been at Basra or even Amara, no doubt Townshend would have taken the responsibility on himself and turned back, without reference to Nixon. This was the situation when he sent the telegram that was to become a prime topic for discussion in the Press and Parliament.

Addressed to Nixon's Chief of Staff from Townshend at Aziziyeh, it read as follows:

> By the aviator's report attached, you will see that the chance of breaking up the retreating Turkish forces which by now have taken up a position at Sulaiman Pak (i.e., Ctesiphon), no longer exist. That position is astride the Baghdad road and the Tigris and is estimated to be six miles of entrenchments. They have also been probably reinforced from Baghdad. If I may be allowed to express an opinion, I think that up to the battle of Kut our object had been to occupy the strategical position of Kut and consolidate ourselves in the province of Basra. Ctesiphon is now held by the defeated Turkish forces. Should it not be considered politically advisable by the Government to occupy Baghdad at present on account of the doubtful position at the Dardanelles and the possibility of our small force being driven out of Baghdad by strong forces from Anatolia, which would compel us to retire down a long line of communications, teeming with Arabs more or less hostile, whose hostility would become active on hearing of our retreat, then I consider that on all military grounds, we should consolidate our position at Kut. The sudden fall of the water which made the advance of our ships most difficult, slow and toilsome, upset our plans of entering Baghdad on the heels of the Turks while they were retreating in disorder. If, on the other hand, it is the desire of the Government to occupy Baghdad, then unless great risk is to be run, it is in my opinion absolutely necessary that the advance from Kut by road should be carried out methodically by two divisions of one army corps, or by one division, closely supported by another complete division, exclusive of the garrisons of the important places of Nasiriyeh, Ahwaz and Amara. It is absolutely impossible to send laden ships up river now. . . .

From this it is clear that Townshend was against any further advance unless he had at least two divisions under his command.

Before sending the telegram, Townshend, according to his own account, deliberated for a long time; to him it was a breach of discipline to protest. He felt that it was his duty to warn Nixon that carrying out the orders to advance on Baghdad might entail disaster, but having done so he was then ready to carry out the order. Like all responsible soldiers he recognized the difference between military and civil life which such a situation posed. In political office a subordinate who differs from his chief can, and often does, resign; in the army a subordinate must bow to his superior officer, even though the orders he receives may be totally against his own better judgment. During his convalescence in India, Townshend had explained the Mesopotamian situation to Beauchamp-Duff who is reputed to have said to him, on the question of advancing to Baghdad: "Not one inch shall you go beyond Kut unless I make you up to thirty or forty thousand men." To Townshend it was quite clear that such reinforcements were out of the question at this stage, and even if he managed to battle his way through to Baghdad, it would not be long before he had to pull out, for undoubtedly Turkish reinforcements would pour in from Anatolia and the Caucasus. If Gallipoli had been successful, then the situation could have been very different and Baghdad might have fallen an easy prey.

In answer to his long telegram of protest, Townshend received a sharp reply to the effect that it was the Army Commander's intention to open the way to Baghdad, and that a division was expected from France. This, of course, was absurd; there was no possible chance of any division arriving from France in time, especially as it had probably not even started. This clinched Townshend's protests; he claimed later that his doubts persisted, but, as the Mesopotamia Commission states, he did not press his objections very hard. According to him, "it was useless to argue any further and a risky advance was decided upon, much against the wish of the general who was going to be in charge of the actual operations." A statement in the House of Commons made it appear that the British Cabinet endorsed the idea that the advance should be made and Townshend quaintly noted in his diary "What the House of Commons had to do with my tactical pursuit after a victory I could not quite make out!"

Meanwhile, Nixon's staff were issuing orders to units in Townshend's command without reference to him, and this apparently irritated Townshend to the extent that he determined to make absolutely certain as to who was going to be responsible for the operation. If there was going to be any kudos to be gained, then he wanted it; if things went wrong, then he wished to be sure that it was because of his fault. In reply to a wire "Will you kindly inform me if the Army Commander is commanding this operation in person, or if he intends me to command it as I did in the Kut operations . . ." he got a somewhat ambiguous reply, "You will of course command the 6th Division as before." So far as the troops were concerned, they were all for going on. They had wiped the floor with the Turks so far, and few of them saw any reason why they should not do so again. They were tired and none too fit after a year in Mesopotamia, but they felt that the same must apply to the Turks in front of them; they knew their enemies almost as old friends and the chances of the Turks being reinforced seemed scarcely worm considering. Besides, there was Baghdad with the promise of fabulous houris and a spot of soft living—theories incidentally which never materialized even when Baghdad was finally taken.

A day or two before the advance was authorized, Nixon ordered Townshend to concentrate his troops at Aziziyeh and on October 7, the 16th Brigade left Kut to march up, to join the 18th Brigade already there. Next day the 17th Brigade was ordered to follow them, only the weak 30th Brigade remaining to garrison Kut. Delamain's troops made a bad start. The day they set off the hot weather suddenly reasserted itself and as it was the end of the season, the change from the cool the troops had been enjoying, was something of a shock........ Then, on the first day's march, orders were received telling the brigade to press on. There was only one way to do so and that was to cut across the bends in the river, rather than follow its serpentine writhings. In effect this meant making a march of 20 miles without water and while this may not sound to be much, it must be remembered that from ten in the morning till four o'clock in the afternoon the sun was beating down, there was a hot dust-laden wind and the men, debilitated by the climate and campaigning of the last six months were in no fit state for an ordeal of this nature.

The order was accepted cheerfully enough: the Dorsets stepped out with a chorus of "Here we are, here we are, here we are again. All good pals and jolly good company . . ." followed after a while by the older, less jaunty but much loved "Dolly Gray." "Goodbye Dolly I must leave you. . . . Though it breaks my heart to go. . . ." The mood was changing and after a few hours even the cheeriest gave up trying to sing. It was now just a grim shuffle and no one could think of anything except reaching the river and the blessed water. Somehow the column had lost direction and the river should have been reached more than an hour before. When dusk fell the men were still marching. Time and again hopes, rising with a glimmer in the distance, were dashed when it turned out to be not the river but a white salt deposit shining in the moonlight. An hour more and men were beginning to collapse. Despite the danger from Arabs who were bound to be prowling around somewhere, those who fell out had to be left, to follow up as best they could. Next day the column again lost its bearings and there was a similar story. Then, when the tired men at last stumbled into the mud hut village on the left bank which was Aziziyeh, it was to find that there had been no real urgency after all; Townshend had no intention of attacking just yet. It was just that his staff thought it a good idea to "encourage" the brigade to step out.

Townshend himself was already concerned about the morale of his men and in a letter to the Viceroy he wrote: "their tails were slightly down." In this he was quite wrong. Certainly the men of his three British battalions were all absolutely confident that their "Charlie" would take them on into Baghdad without much difficulty. Thoughts of defeat in the forthcoming battle never entered their heads. Only on two counts, perhaps, was there any real cause for concern. The drafts of reinforcements which arrived to fill the gaps in the Indian battalions caused by the casualties of the earlier operations were often of poor quality. The best drafts—those of trained soldiers—were sent to units serving in France, and Mesopotamia had to be content with recruits who had no more than eight months service. The other concerned the site of the coming battle. Many of the Indian troops were Muslims to whom Sulaiman Pak—close by Ctesiphon—was a holy place and to Townshend whether they would fight around the ancient barber's tomb was a matter of conjecture. His real faith lay in the three British battalions—Dorsets, Norfolks, and the Oxford and Buckinghamshire Light Infantry—which to him constituted the backbone of the division. Yet even these three British units had been milked to provide men for various base duties in hospitals, as batmen, as clerks, marines on gunboats and various other odd duties so that all three battalions were down to half strength.

On the Turkish side, Nur-Ud-Din had Approximately the same number of troops with which to defend Ctesiphon, as Townshend had to attack it—something like twelve thousand men. More than half of them had been in the battle for Kut and their morale was supposedly low but others, including some of the Arab hangers-on, were decidedly aggressive. At Zeur, about fifteen miles upstream from Aziziyeh, Nur-Ud-Din had pushed out a detachment of cavalry to keep an eye on what Townshend was up to. Using Zeur as a base, the British camp was attacked by Arabs the very first night the division was concentrated in Aziziyeh and a few days later an Indian cavalry patrol found that El Kutuniya only six miles away had been occupied by Turkish cavalry and Arab horsemen. This was too close for Townshend's comfort and he determined to oust them by a surprise attack. But to effect surprise again meant a night march. If it came off, he felt a successful little operation like this would do much to improve the morale of the troops, although so far night marches had had rather disappointing outcomes. On this occasion the march on Kutuniya was completely successful. Townshend's men pushed on and following a brisk action the Turks evacuated Zeur in good order and retired back toward Ctesiphon, taking their guns with them. No effective follow-up was possible because the ground was too broken for the cavalry to get round.

All was now more or less ready for the main advance to begin. The men's health had improved with the better weather and the Royal Navy had been reinforced with the first of the new "Fly" class monitors—HMS *Firefly*[8] Following a long struggle—for only six ships of any size could work above Kut with any degree of reliability—considerable quantities of stores had been amassed in the forward area. Not everything that was needed in the circumstances; that would have been expecting too much. Many items, which Townshend had demanded for the defence of Aziziyeh—the wire-cutters and Verey lights and a myriad of other items needed for the attack—Nixon had refused to send up. Such items as were available in Basra his staff had said were not necessary. Why send them up now; the whole situation would be changed when the troops marched into Baghdad. Furthermore, everything that did not come within the field service scale of equipment for an Indian division— including tents—was ordered to be sent back. On the Western front, millions were being poured out like water. But Mesopotamia was the Cinderella of all the British campaigns and it was being constrained in an atmosphere of false economy.

---

8. Mounting one 4-inch gun, one 6-pounder and a machine gun. Of the other gunboats: *Comet, Shaitan, Sumana* and *Shushan* only the latter could navigate above Kut with any certainty.

Chapter 5

The Battle of Ctesiphon

A bold heart is half the battle
Latin Proverb

The ruins of what was once the flourishing city of Ctesiphon stand opposite those of the historically more interesting town of Seleucia founded by the Greeks in Alexander's time. For seven hundred years Ctesiphon was a great city, fought for in turn by Parthians, Armenians, Romans and Sassanians but its end came in a Jihad, when the great flame of Islam swept through the Middle East. Then it was reduced to a heap of ruins—everything that is, except its greatest monument. The palace and great hall, built by the Chosroes and once famous throughout the East for its magnificence was looted but it could not be destroyed. To this day the immense, imposing Arch of Ctesiphon, eighty-five feet high, seventy-two feet wide, still stands in an empty desert, brooding over the ruins of a forgotten world. It was here, at the palace gate, that the men of the 6th Indian Division were to fight. No doubt the ghosts of those who had fallen in previous battles around Ctesiphon were watching for the newcomers soon to join them, as Townshend's columns tramped up the old caravan road.

With the greater part of their force on the left bank, the Turks almost exactly as at Kut, had taken up a position astride the river to cover Ctesiphon. Their front line lay about two miles east of the great Arch, and behind it—a mile or so west of the ruins—a second line of trenches had been dug. In both lines the trenches were more or less at right angles to the river's course, running northwards from the river for about six miles. They had been well sited, well dug and well camouflaged and to an observer approaching from the direction Townshend would have to follow, they were completely invisible; all that could be seen across the monotonous scrub-covered terrain was the Arch. On the other bank the Turks were also well dug in, but, on this side, where Nur-Ud-Din was relying on the nature of the terrain as the backbone of his defence, the ground was an expanse of dried-up marsh broken by ruined canals and so fissured and cracked as to be impassable by any troops.

Three miles below the Arch the river turns sharply south and the village of Bustan is located at the bend. Halfway between Bustan and the Arch there are the ruins of an old city wall, about twenty feet high; because of the observation it afforded over the flat countryside, High Wall, as it was to be known, was extremely important tactically. From there the trenches of the Turkish front line, the so-called "First Line," ran to a fortified redoubt on a small mound, which came to be called the "Water" Redoubt. From the "Water" Redoubt they then continued to the "Vital Point"9 (V.P.) redoubts—two mounds three hundred yards apart and nearly two miles from the High Wall—and this formed the extreme left of the front line. About two miles behind V.P. lay the "Second Line" already referred to. Further back, six miles or so behind the Second Line, the Diyala joins the Tigris and in this stretch of river the Turks had a couple of boat bridges—one just below the Diyala junction and the other immediately above the Second Line. Other than the features which have been described as being incorporated into the Turks' defenses, the whole battlefield was generally as flat as a pancake—a factor which Nur-Ud-Din had made full use of. To prevent any obstruction interfering with the murderous fire, which was to sweep every yard of the ground immediately in front of the elaborate entrenchments, even the soil thrown up from the deep, narrow trenches had been removed and this was the prime reason for the vast number of British casualties incurred during the battle.

From such information as could be gleaned from the locals and from air reconnaissance reports, Townshend estimated that Nur-Ud-Din had about eleven thousand men and 40 guns with which to defend Ctesiphon. As it could be expected that the Turkish commander, less than twenty-two miles from Baghdad, could be reinforced more quickly and more effectively than the

British who were at the end of the long river line from Basra, this figure could be regarded as conservative.[1] For the benefit of the troops, Townshend did his best to play down rumors that more men were arriving daily to swell Nur-Ud-Din's force but, despite his own apparent flippancy: "Nur-Ud-Din is within punching distance, I'll put him out for the count"—an utterance which strongly foreshadowed some of Field Marshal Montgomery's sayings during the Second World War—he himself was worried. Nor were his men deceived. The hush-hush attitude of Townshend's staff was enough to arouse suspicions in itself. They could guess that things were not so promising as Townshend's communiqués would have them believe. And, if only because it illustrates how little incidents can lend false weight to such a situation and cause rumor to run riot, it is worthwhile digressing on one which occurred about this time. For some reason or other, Townshend had decided that cutting the telegraph lines east and north of Baghdad would help to isolate the capital, possibly delay the arrival of Nur-Ud-Din's reinforcements and generally lower the morale of everybody in the Turkish rear areas. In retrospect it all seems rather futile, but the job was given to the Flying Corps. To a suitable area, where an aircraft could land with reasonable expectation of not being interfered with, the round trip was over two hundred miles, so that the old Maurice Farman detailed for the job had to be loaded with extra gas and oil as well as the explosives needed to blow up the telegraph posts. It was a slow old crate which could land almost anywhere in the open desert and the idea was feasible enough, even though the chances of its making the return journey were really pretty thin.[2] Consequently, when the troops got to hear of it they deduced that it was a "forlorn hope" operation, intended to blow up not the telegraph wire but the railway line.

Townshend's original intention was to attack the Turks on November 19, which was the earliest date feasible. However, a series of unforeseen delays, concerned almost entirely with shortage of transport, prevented him from leaving Aziziyeh until the 18th, and it was four more days before he could give battle. Leaving a small garrison, largely composed of convalescents able to handle a rifle but not to march and two guns which he had no means of moving, every other man and gun he could muster started out on what they hoped would be the last leg to Baghdad. The Turks had been expected to put

---

1. It was. The estimate was seven thousand men and 12 guns short of the real total.
2. The old airplane reached the place where the wire was to be cut without mishap, made a perfect touch-down and, with a tail wind, ran on evenly toward the telegraph posts. Then disaster overtook the two luckless individuals who were its crew. There was a rending crash as one of the wings struck a telegraph post and the ensuing damage precluded any idea of flying back. Cutting the telegraph lines was still possible, but no sooner had this been done than Arab horsemen appeared from the four quarters of the desert and the two airmen were borne back in triumph to Baghdad, to be paraded through the street and, as was the custom, be spat on by the populace.

up some sort of fight at Zeur but although a false air reconnaissance report of their presence there caused some alarm, nothing happened. The few who were there promptly decamped when Townshend's cavalry arrived, and eventually the division arrived within a few miles of Ctesiphon without having encountered any opposition worth mentioning. This was taken as a good sign and things were remarkably quiet—too quiet perhaps for there was not even any sniping by the Arabs. Even the circumstances of the march were passable, for the scorching heat had finally given place to cooler weather and there was no repetition of the freak conditions which had arisen on the march from Kut to Aziziyeh; the only real hardship was the cold at night, when the thermometer went down to the freezing point. And with no enemy interference and tolerable weather conditions, morale was good; the troops whose off-beat conversation centered on the "Bags" of Baghdad, were quietly confident that "Charlie" would see them through O.K. "Are we downhearted?" "No! No!" was the popular cry on the line of march. But "their Charlie" was not so sanguine. Referring to the troops' confidence, the Mesopotamia Commission reported "a spirit of intense optimism" animated by his [Townshend's] headquarters and staff when the advance from Aziziyeh started and in his diary Townshend commented:

> I knew nothing about this "intense optimism." All I do know is that I was determined to carry through the operation if it could possibly be done, and it was my plain and simple duty to carry out the orders of my superior to the best of my ability, although his orders were against my better judgment. Personally, I had no doubts in my mind as to the extreme gravity of the results of this advance, an offensive undertaken with insufficient forces, and not only that, but an offensive undertaken in a secondary theatre of the war, where our strategy should have been to have remained on the defensive with minimum forces sufficient for that purpose. All my study indicated disaster to me. However the die was cast. And so, when Sir John Nixon asked me on the eve of battle: "Are you confident of winning, Townshend?" I replied: "Yes, I shall win all right". And I did win . . .

With the size of the force at his disposal, an attack up both banks of the river was out of the question. Some sort of tactical ruse would have to be employed and the plan Townshend ultimately decided on was very much the same as that which had been used at Kut. Basically, there were two courses open to him; to attack on either the right or the left bank. At first he was in favor of taking the right, in order to compel Nur-Ud-Din to deplete the left bank defenses and give battle where he was less well prepared, and this method also had the advantage that it would have avoided the necessity of having to cross the Diyala when once the troops were through the Ctesiphon position.

Ultimately he settled for an attack up the opposite bank because of the bad reports of the state of the ground on the right. Despite the strong positions there, what he hoped to do was to paralyze the greater part of Nur-Ud-Din's force by holding the Turks' attention on his immediate front near the Arch, while a right hook was made toward their left flank. There was nothing wrong with the plan; if Townshend had had the numerical superiority afforded by the two divisions he had asked for, then probably he could have attained a decisive victory. As it was, the 6th Division alone was just not strong enough to take on anything like the formidable defenses which those at Ctesiphon undoubtedly were.

To implement the plan, Townshend divided the force into four columns: three of them—A, B and C—were to do the attacking and a cavalry "Flying" column was to sweep round to the right, create havoc behind the Second Line and finally go on to occupy Baghdad after the battle. It seems logical to expect that the Cavalry Brigadier, General Roberts, should have commanded this force but as Townshend did not trust him, Melliss was put in command and an infantry battalion added to the column in order to make it a mixed force. (Townshend distrusted Roberts after the action at Kut; Melliss was noted for his energy and drive. With the clash of personalities that must have arisen when Roberts was superseded by Melliss and the fact that the infantry can only have been a drag on the cavalry, altogether this must have been a most unhappy arrangement.) Closest to the river was column C, under Hoghton, who was ordered to attack the front line between High Wall and Water Redoubt. When Hoghton's attack was under way, column B, under Brigadier General W. G. Hamilton who had relieved Major General Fry in command of the 18th Brigade, was to assault the Second Line behind V.P. Then, when this attack had started and the Turks' attention was fully occupied with Hoghton on the left and Hamilton on the right, Delamain with column A was to make the decisive attack on V.P. itself. Meanwhile, the "Flying" column, operating further away on Hamilton's right was to get around the flank to cut off the Turks' reserves behind the Second Line. As a deceptive measure, Hoghton was to leave the jumping off place of Lajj during the afternoon on the day before the battle, and march up the Baghdad road in a blatantly ostentatious fashion—the idea being that the Turks should gain the impression that his column was the main assault force; finally, the approach march of both A and B columns was to be made at night. This then was Townshend's conception of how the plan would unfold; needless to say matters did not go the way that was expected.

As had been planned, Hoghton's men swung off down the road from Lajj in column of fours at 2 p.m. on the 21st, with the troops cheerfully singing. After marching five miles the column halted and the men went down to the river bank to fill up their water bottles. Their first set-back occurred here when they were shelled by the flotilla who had not been told of the move and this took the edge off their cheerfulness. When they had recovered, the advance was resumed and, by midnight, the column was about two miles east of Bustan. With no moon and clouds obscuring the stars, the night march which followed turned out to be extremely difficult; the only landmark was provided by the Arch of Ctesiphon and when dawn came Hoghton called a halt in order to sort out exactly where the column was. All the troops could see in front of them was a forbidding hedge of wire entanglements, behind which loomed the huge brown bulk of the ancient Arch.[3]

Hamilton, waiting to take his cue from Hoghton, was impatient to start his attack and not having heard any sounds of attack from the direction of column C, sent back to ask Townshend if he could advance. Permission was given and by 8 a.m. Hamilton's men had started to move toward their objective of the Second Line. Meantime, Hoghton's men were standing about on the skyline eating bully beef sandwiches and debating whether or not the Turks had again pulled out and left Baghdad to the British. It was not improbable and indeed if it had been so, then it would have been typical of Townshend's proverbial luck. But it was not to be. As soon as they started to move forward there was the chilling stutter of machine guns, the crack of rifle fire and the customary whoosh and crump as shells coming from behind the Arch started to land among them; the Turks had laid low until they could see the whites of British and Indian eyes. In no time at all, Hoghton's men were brought to a halt and driven to ground. Fortunately for them, the mounds of ruins and ditches which had impeded their progress this far now provided a certain amount of cover.

Delamain's Gurkhas and Punjabis, who had set off an hour later, very quickly moved forward through a curtain of fire to capture their objective and soon the Turks were seen to be streaming away from V.P. toward the Second Line where Hamilton's men were already heavily engaged. However, because of a mirage and the fact that there were no proper communication arrangements between the guns and the forward infantry, both Delamain and Hamilton had lost a lot of men in getting into a situation which was to have a telling effect later. And, at this point, came a hitch in the plan which was to cost Hoghton's men dearly. Delamain, interpreting the flight from V.P. as a collapse of the whole Turkish front line, carried straight on through it toward the Second Line instead of turning aside to roll up the First Line. The result was that Hoghton was left to face Turks who were well dug in and who had

---

3. The British gunners had been told that the Arch was to be immune even if it was suspected of being a Turkish observation post. This had not prevented bets being taken on whether the "heavies" would knock it endways before the day was out.

obviously no intention of budging. Without any help from the flank the idea of a frontal attack was soon seen to be out of the question, and the best hope seemed to be to move across V.P. to get in behind Delamain. To do this was not easy as it meant a sideways, crablike move but an order was given "Advance at right angles to your present line of advance." Across the fiat desert without a blade of grass for cover, marching across the Turks' front may well seem to be a suicidal tactic; certainly it was one which the Turks at High Wall made the most of. Townshend, horrified by the turn of events commented: ". . . If only the gunboats would appear by the Arch. . . ." Don Quixote had stood a better chance tilting against the windmills than the gunboats did of getting up to help. Beyond Bustan, Turkish guns on the right bank were able to fire straight down the stretch of water they would have to negotiate before reaching the Arch and this effectively checked any attempts to do so. But even if they could have withstood the gun fire, a mined obstruction would have prevented further progress.

Delamain and Hamilton were both in the thick of the fray by this time and, like Hoghton's, their thrusts had also been brought to a standstill. Melliss was in difficulties too. Not having gone far enough over to the right, the cavalry had run up against the Second Line defenses, and when some Turkish cavalry and Arabs started to form up away on his right flank he had deemed it expedient to pull back. He and his column, which had done very little "flying" so far, were now lying back some way behind Hamilton. After some hard fighting, the whole of the Turks' First Line was in Townshend's hands by the late afternoon but the impetus of the assault was spent. With no reserves it was utterly impossible to get any further. In his diary Townshend recorded:

> I had not a man left to throw into the principal mass. If I had had (I will not say the extra Division I needed and had asked for) even another brigade, we should have swept the Turks into the Tigris. This is a fact that no one who was present at the battle can deny. It was hard, very hard, to stand there and realize that victory was slipping from my grasp for the want of a few troops. . .

Events had certainly not turned out as Townshend had hoped, as yet the Turks were not showing even the slightest sign of retiring according to precedent—indeed, not only were they obstinately refusing to budge but were getting ready to counterattack. And when they did, what was left of Delamain's column was pushed back toward V.P. and he lost everything, including eight Turkish guns captured earlier in the day, in the process. For the British, this marked the beginning of the end. It was not just Delamain's troops; most of Townshend's division were in the same state; they could not take any more, and hundreds of men were already walking slowly back to V.P. Hoghton was ordered to form up and attack again, in order to relieve the pressure on Delamain and stop the rot, but it was no use. The men were exhausted; casualties had taken their toll and in some cases battalions were down to platoon strength. Nixon, who had attached himself to Townshend's headquarters at V.P. agreed with Townshend that the only thing to do would be to try and hold on to what had been taken.

At dusk, as the firing died away, orders were given to concentrate around V.P. for the night and bivouac on the battlefield. Dead Turks mutely testified to the fact that the enemy had also taken a hard knock and the ever optimistic Townshend felt that things might well seem better in the morning; indeed both he and Nixon still hoped that Nur-Ud-Din would decide to pull out and concede the victory to the British. It was a forlorn hope. The night passed quietly enough, but next morning the Turks were still occupying the trenches of their Second Line and, during the day, while Townshend tried to reorganize and rally his pathetically depleted division, they counterattacked again. Fortunately for the British it was a halfhearted attempt which got nowhere. But there was nothing halfhearted about the series of attacks they launched that night when repeated attempts were made to oust the British from V.P. and the main vantage point of "Gurkha Mound"[4] which lay in front of it. Once again Townshend's men held firm and at dawn the Turks withdrew. They too were in a spent and chaotic condition and many of them are said to have wandered in circles over the countryside during the night attacking objectives that had not been given to them.

Suddenly it seemed that Townshend might have been right after all and that by hanging on he might yet take Baghdad. Next day Nur-Ud-Din ordered a general withdrawal. The trouble was that Townshend was unable to take advantage of it.

Out of 8,500 men of the 6th Division who had gone into the battle, more than half had been killed or wounded—practically the whole of the casualties being borne by the infantry. Of the depressing state of the wounded Townshend wrote:

> If I live a hundred years, I shall not forget that night bivouac at V.P. amongst hundreds of wounded, who were being brought in loaded on the commissariat carts in which they were collected throughout the night. Their sufferings in these small springless carts can be easily imagined: but the way in which the medical officers worked was beyond all praise.. . .

---

4. The 2nd/7th Gurkha Rifles and two companies of the 24th Punjabis, whose overall strength had been reduced by half to about 400 men, had captured and held this feature. The whole Turkish division counterattacked but could make no headway.

After the battle for Kut the medical arrangements had been chaotic but this time the confusion was on an even bigger scale. Wounded who were able to walk wandered about looking for collecting stations which did not exist and the more severely wounded had to lie where they fell until search parties found them, often hours later. One group of unfortunates caught by a machine gun in a shallow ditch just south of V.P. lay throughout the night in icy water. The Turks having spotted that the ditch was full of men had opened the dikes to the river in an attempt to flood it. Consequently those who lay there either had to evacuate the ditch at the risk of being shot, or stay where they were and risk being drowned; some of the more seriously wounded, unable to move, were drowned before help could reach them anyway.

As the exhausted British and Indians collected to bivouac around V.P. after the first day of the battle, those who were able to walk were ordered to make their own way to the rear. And, as the cloak of night shrouded the field a crowd of limping, bandaged figures staggered back to Lajj ten miles distant. Most of the more seriously wounded, unable to move without assistance, lay where they had fallen until they were located next morning and lifted on to the dreaded "A.T." carts. These contraptions, which were merely iron frameworks suspended between two iron-tired wheels, drawn by mules and driven by an Indian driver, had no springs in their make-up. As they had never been intended to be used as ambulances, there was no reason why they should have been more than just the simple load-carrying vehicles which they were. Into these carts, the wounded were heaped, three or four in each; there was no other way, but for those with fractured limbs, head wounds or abdominal injuries the carts were like the tumbrils of the French Revolution. On the journey back to the river they bumped and clattered over the rough ground, the nervous mules often got out of hand and ditches had to be rushed in order to get them up over the far edge. With every bump sending an agonizing jolt through to the occupants, men soon were screaming in agony; here and there some of them threw them-selves off, unable to bear the torture any longer. The forecast had been that the battle would produce five hundred casualties but even before it had started there were more than that number of sick and wounded aboard the hospital ships. There was nothing else for it but to cram the fresh casualties on to other ships and barges from which stores and animals had scarcely been unloaded. Only the worst cases could be put aboard the two hospital ships and even there the arrangements were totally inadequate. There were only a few doctors; the numbers involved were beyond their capacity to provide adequate attention; food and drink was not to be had and there were not enough mattresses for any but the most severely wounded to lie on.

Laden with their cargoes of broken humanity the ships left Lajj on the morning of the 25th; Basra was 400 miles downstream. That night the first rains of the season teemed down and the awnings were of little protection to the wounded lying on the decks below. Their bedding was soon soaked and with no spare blankets nor any means of drying the wet ones, all they could do was to lie in their misery. In order that the lighter draft ships could return upstream, the casualties had to be transshipped at Kut and they started downstream again on the morning of the 27th, expecting to reach Basra in five days. Five days was the best estimate, and conditions dictated that a quick journey was necessary. Most of the ships had been carrying stores and animals and they were in a very unsanitary state; now they were packed with wounded for whom doctors, dressings, medicine, and food were all scarce. On the journey the very worst cases could only be dressed once every two days and even to attain this the doctors had to work without a break. Most of the men did not have their dressings looked at between the time they left the battlefield and their arrival in Basra, which was longer than expected, for the change in Townshend's luck appeared to dog the heels of his wretched wounded. That night, as the leading ship was approaching Sheikh Sa'ad, a couple of Arabs paddled out from the bank and frantically signaled for it to heave-to; when they got on board they said that between two and three thousand Arabs were waiting to ambush the convoy round the next bend. Following a hurried conference, the steamer captains decided that the uncertain state of the channel made getting round the bend in question in the dark, under the rifles of a couple of thousand treacherous Buddhoos, an extremely hazardous one. The only thing to do was to return to Kut. So back they went.

Two days elapsed before another start could be made but this time the monitor HMS *Butterfly* led the convoy. The ships' luck had not changed. Just before they reached the danger area, the *Butterfly* ran hard aground and in no time most of the ships had piled up on the steep bank behind her. This was just the sort of chance the Arabs had been waiting for and they took it. All day long as the ships lay helpless, Arab snipers on both banks of the river had a field day and there was little that could be done to stop them. The *Butterfly* was too close to the bank to be able to use her four-inch guns and so the Arabs were able to pour lead into the ships almost at will. The effect was bad enough though everybody knew only too well what would happen if they eventually got aboard. Rolls of blankets and every available store were piled up against the ships' rails to form a parapet, but, in spite of this many of those who had already been wounded were wounded again or else killed. Things only eased off when the *Butterfly* managed to get off the bank just before sunset; standing out in midstream, she opened fire and the shrapnel from her guns drove back the Arabs. The immediate danger was over, but with night approaching it was still not possible to get beyond Sheikh Sa'ad. So, once more, the convoy streamed back to Kut.

A long wait followed—so long that to many it seemed that they would never get further than Kut; many of the worst cases had already died and it was probably the less seriously wounded that suffered most as a result of this delay. Finally, a week after the battle, the ships attempted the run down to Basra once again and this time, with two companies of infantry and a couple of mountain guns to ensure their safety, they got safely past the danger spot near Sheikh Sa'ad. Even so, the casualties' troubles were not yet at an end. Time and time again the ships were stuck on mud banks for long weary hours; most of the food ran out, so did the filtered water; dysentery raged among the crowded men and the situation deteriorated to one which is almost past description.

The convoy eventually reached Amara on December 4. It had been intended to evacuate the worst cases here, but there were so many of them that most had to continue down the river. Two days later, just above Qurna, came the ultimate episode of this chapter of misfortunes. With Basra still a day's journey away, the engines of the leading ship broke down; there was a long wait before the rest could get past, and the ship which had broken down had to wait until repairs could be effected. Only when their destination was reached at long last was the awful pilgrimage over. The worst cases were then trans-shipped to a hospital ship sailing direct to India and the others were sent to the already crowded Basra hospital.

For all the utterly inadequate arrangements made for the transport and treatment of the wounded and for their hideous sufferings, the Indian Government must be regarded as primarily responsible. Efforts were made later to pin the entire blame on to Nixon, but there can be little doubt as to where the fault really lay. According to labored phraseology of the "Field Service Regulations" then in force, "a Commander-in-Chief is relieved of the direct responsibility of providing the requirements of the forces in the field. . . . Responsibility . . . rests with the Government who, in approving a plan, assume responsibility, in principle for the provision of the requisite forces." On this basis, Nixon claimed that "requisite forces" included all the auxiliary services—medical facilities, river craft and the thousand and one other things his troops lacked. And, since the management of the expedition was the responsibility of the Indian Government, it is quite clear that by the book of rules, it was the men in Delhi and Simla who were the miscreants. This is not to say that Nixon was entirely blameless; in an effort to escape censure, his staff went to extraordinary lengths to conceal the deplorable facts—not only from the public but from higher authority also. No one in this day and age—not least those who have served in a war where the medical arrangements have hardly ever been the subject of even the mildest criticism—can realize what was endured by those who were wounded in Mesopotamia in 1915; nothing, absolutely nothing, can excuse those who were responsible for the state of affairs which has been described. There can be little lasting disgrace attached to a genuine blunder; however gross, in time it can be forgiven. But not this. The plight of the wounded must have been known to the authorities in Basra. Even while the ships were still in midstream a sickening smell tainted the air and before the casualties were taken off, they could be seen lying in their own filth, crowded together on the iron decks. The wounds of many of the more serious cases were found to be in the advanced stages of septic poisoning and in some cases men with comparatively slight injuries were dying from huge bed sores. That was how things were and yet a report was cabled to India: "General condition of the wounded very satisfactory. Medical arrangements, under circumstances of considerable difficulty, worked splendidly."

Nixon's staff seem to have been determined to conceal their own inadequacies with regard to the medical arrangements and it is puzzling to try to understand how they hoped to get away with it. No subordinate officer dared to protest or even ask for a bare necessity beyond what had been provided according to scale or "laid down by regulations"; if he did, then he was at once threatened with arrest. A certain Major Carter of the Indian Medical Service, in charge of a hospital ship at Basra, complained of the facilities available to him. He was sent for by two of Nixon's senior staff officers—Major General Cowper, the "Q" staff chief, and Surgeon-General Hathaway, the chief medical officer—and told that if he did not shut up and keep quiet he would lose his command, because he was an "interfering faddist." This same officer is the one quoted by the Mesopotamia Commission as volunteering the appalling evidence of what he saw when the convoy of wounded from Ctesiphon arrived at Basra:

> When the *Mejidieh* was about three hundred yards off, it looked as if she was festooned with ropes. The stench when she was close was quite definite, and I found that what I mistook for ropes were dried stalactites of human faeces. The patients were so crowded and huddled together on the ship that they could not perform the offices of Nature clear of the ship's edge and the whole of the ship's side was covered, . . .

During the thirteen days which it took for the casualties to get from Lajj to Basra, the depleted regiments on the field of Ctesiphon had been having their own troubles. The morning after *the* night of counterattacks, when Townshend concentrated what was left at High Wall and evacuated his wounded, no Turks were in sight. Nur-Ud-Din had ordered a retreat and it almost seemed as if the

British had come out on top after all. But it was a Pyrrhic victory. Because the enormous casualty list had made a follow-up impossible the retreat was short-lived. Nur-Ud-Din had decided to fall back only because of false information supplied by Arabs to the effect that a British column was advancing toward the Diyala; as soon as he discovered the truth—that the column they had seen was one of his own divisions withdrawing after the previous night's battles—his troops were ordered to turn about. Instrumental in persuading him to give the order was his newly arrived second-in-command, Khalil Bey, a dynamic young man of thirty-five, who was to take a leading role in the events to come. First news of the Turks volte-face came to Townshend through the medium of an air reconnaissance report and having deduced—wrongly, in fact—that Nur-Ud-Din had been reinforced, he made up his mind to withdraw. His only reason for delaying to this point was the now remote hope that he might yet march into Baghdad, together with the knowledge that any retreat would be seen by those in Whitehall and Simla as a political catastrophe.

Nixon had already returned to Kut but General Kemball, his Chief of Staff, had stayed behind to hear what was going to be done. "I told him what I intended to do—that I was not going to let political reasons endanger the force. If it were annihilated, the whole of Mesopotamia would fall like a ripe plum into the hands of the Turks. But I was not going to retire a moment before it was necessary or before I had sent out aerial and cavalry reconnaissances to see what the enemy was doing. . . ."

The hours of daylight on November 25, were a period of confusion and mixed feeling for everyone, British and Turks alike. The guns which had prevented the gunboats getting up the river past Bustan were still in position and they desultorily shelled High Wall throughout the day, and as soon as the battlefield had been cleared of its human litter Townshend gave the order to withdraw back to Lajj. His original intention had been to wait until the next day before moving; by then the situation might have changed. Throughout the day Townshend had been bewildered by inaccurate information or the lack of any information at all. His cavalry ought to have been able to have given him a reasonably accurate picture, but they were out of contact, and in any case Townshend preferred to put his confidence in the news brought by his aircraft—a reliance which was less than wise since the sorties they made were necessarily few and far between. Nevertheless, when air reconnaissance reported a Turkish column had been seen near the Diyala moving down toward Ctesiphon, Zero hour was brought forward and the withdrawal started that night. Townshend, always fond of *Orders of the Day,* and long rambling instructions studded with references to Field Service Regulations, took the opportunity to issue one of his typical communiqués:

I cannot express my admiration and gratitude for the heroism displayed by all ranks. To show with what stern valor you fought, you drove four divisions out of a very strong position and forced them to retire beyond the Diyala river But our numbers were too few to put them to rout; we have had 4,000 killed and wounded, the Turks losing many more than this figure.[5] You have added a brilliant page to the glorious battle roll of the Army in India and you will be proud to tell that you fought at the Battle of Ctesiphon... I have ordered a move back to Lajj. . . where the ships are in security. Three more monitors are promised to me in a few days.

It is said that Townshend meant to hold Lajj while reinforcements which would enable him to go back to the offensive were concentrated at Aziziyeh; if this were so, then Nur-Ud-Din's cooperation would have been necessary because it is quite certain that no reinforcements could possibly have reached him in under a couple of months. More probably Townshend had intended to fall back and stand at Kut from the moment he realized that the Turks were on the march. And it was lucky for him that Nur-Ud-Din's supply ships were delayed by their own obstruction near Sulaiman Pak, for if supplies had been forthcoming sooner then the Turkish commander would have been on Townshend's heels even more quickly than was the case.

From the very beginning the retreat was fraught with the most extraordinary difficulties. The British flotilla had to be covered by troops ashore and as the exhausted army slowly retired along the road it was only by the greatest exertions that the ships were able to keep up with it. Getting up the river had been bad enough, but going down was far worse. Vessels were constantly running aground and, when one did, all the others above it were held up. Over 90 dreary miles and from morning till night the gunboats were constantly employed hauling them off the banks. Meanwhile, the Buddhoos sniped and waited their opportunity; according to custom, the local Arabs had turned against the beaten side.

On the morning of November 26, the advance guard of the long column of weary troops arrived back at Aziziyeh and Townshend stood silently at the entrance to their old camp to watch the regiments march in. He could see that they were pretty well done in and very much in need of rest, but this was not the only reason for the halt which was now called. Just above Aziziyeh the *Comet* and the *Shaitan* had run aground and although the *Comet* was soon afloat again, the *Shaitan* was stuck fast. Under the constant sniping of Arabs lying up on the banks above them, the *Comet, Firefly,* and the *Shushan* all tried to get her off. It was no good, she was immovable and as soon as it became apparent that

---

5. Townshend's force incurred 4,600 casualties against the Turks 9,500.

the Turkish advance guard had started to arrive on the scene the *Shaitan* was abandoned. Valuable time had been lost in trying to save her and when Townshend's men got on the march again the Turks were hard behind.

The next leg of the retreat was only 8 miles. That it was not further was due to Townshend being under the mistaken apprehension that 10 miles as the crow flies was the limit of the ship's journey—a misunderstanding which had arisen because the senior naval officer was under the impression that he could not go further because the troops were exhausted. Fortunately for the British columns the Arab cavalry heading the pursuit had been diverted by the prospect of loot in Aziziyeh, and so at a crucial period the pressure on Townshend's rearguard momentarily eased. Not only that, while the Arabs were seeing to their booty they could not be reconnoitering ahead and Nur-Ud-Din was not aware of how close Townshend really was. During the night his infantry, believing their cavalry to be still in front of them, ran slap up against the British positions. Thinking that they had stumbled on Townshend's rearguard which would upsticks and flee at once, the Turks contented themselves with shelling the British outposts, and then settled down for the night; they did not realize the peril they were in.

Nobody was prepared for the sight which greeted both sides in the gray light of early morning, but the British were the first to take full advantage of it. Less than a mile from their perimeter was a huge camp, in which large numbers of Turks could be seen forming up ready to continue the chase. Shrapnel from Townshend's artillery and high explosive from his gunboats was soon bursting among them and within minutes the camp was a veritable inferno surrounded by a pall of dust raised by the bursting shells. Under its cover some of Townshend's infantry charged toward the camp, but as soon as the Turks started to rally the action was broken off and once again they set off marching back toward Kut. The Turks, shaken by the sudden turn of events, had suffered a severe check and it was some hours before they were ready to resume the pursuit. The flotilla had not been so fortunate. As the gunboats showered death and destruction among their comrades, a party of Turks managed to manhandle some field guns to the river bank and get them into action. One of the first shots fired went clean through the *Firefly's* boiler, disabling her, and when the *Comet* tried to take her in tow both vessels went aground. The little tug *Sumana* chugged up to the rescue and succeeded in getting the men off her doomed consorts, but only minutes before Turks were swarming on their abandoned decks. With the *Shaitan* lost earlier, now the *Firefly* and the *Comet,* Townshend's flotilla was virtually no more.

In the last two days of the retreat, Townshend dared not halt. Qala Shadi, 20 miles from Kut, was the next staging point. It was a dull twenty-six mile plod across the arid, scrub-covered desert, but if his men were to get down to the river bank Townshend was sure that they would lie by the water, drink their fill and sleep like logs. There was no time to lose. The Turks had been rudely checked, but, even so they were still only just a few miles behind, and their Arab hyena allies, dogging the rearguard and flanks of the columns, were always present, waiting to strip and mutilate any luckless individual who dropped out. The order was given that there should be no stop before Kut. When it was finally reached on the morning of December 3, Townshend stood again to watch the exhausted men dragging themselves past him. In his diary he recorded "Courage and firmness in adversity were not wanting . . . not in the 6th Division." Since this seven and a half day retreat was one of the most arduous that has ever been experienced in the history of the British Army, the praise was well deserved. Like Dunkirk, a quarter century later, the Battle of Ctesiphon and the retreat from it were epics. But Ctesiphon was not a victory, and instead of the success which had been hoped would counter the moral effect of withdrawing from Gallipoli, the British had met with a resounding rebuff. Furthermore, unless Townshend in Kut could speedily be relieved, the attempt to do so was likely to end in an even more resounding disaster.

Chapter 6

Besieged in Kut

Strategy is the art of making use of time and space. I am less chary of the latter than the former. Space we can recover, lost time never.

Napoleon

The British public had been led to believe that the fall of Baghdad was imminent. Consequently the news of Ctesiphon came as a dreadful shock. Unlike his German counterpart, the man in the street in Britain had not been prepared for a defeat; when the news came he was stunned. First indications of the true state of affairs were published in a communiqué that Townshend had "withdrawn his force to a position lower down the river" and this was followed by a statement that the British forces were "in full retirement,"[1] towards their old position of Kut-al-Amara. As questions were asked and explanations formulated the authorities started to look for a scapegoat. It was not difficult to see who was being cast for the role.

---

1. A curious phrase resulting from the fact that the word "retreat" is never favored in British military parlance since it implies finality of defeat. "Retirement" is preferable because it suggests a temporary, unfortunate phase which will be followed, very soon, by a return to the offensive.

"The early capture of Baghdad would have been a great stroke, both from the military and political point of view" said Lord Crewe to the House of Lords, in a speech on December 8, designed to soft-pedal the news that the expected victory had been turned into a repulse. "It was a complete error" he went on "to suppose that this was a rash military adventure undertaken by General Townshend on his own initiative. The advance on Baghdad had been contemplated some months ago ... a sufficient force had been collected to carry out the whole operation, the whole proceedings having been thought out by the Commander-in-Chief, General Nixon." He said nothing about the Cabinet's own errors in falling for the lure of Baghdad, and although his words did not actually condemn Nixon they certainly suggested that it was entirely his appreciation and plan that had led to the set-back. If Nixon thought it out, then presumably it was Nixon's planning that had gone awry. There was no mention of the fact that Nixon's orders from the Indian Government in April had included the instruction "to prepare for an advance on Baghdad." For taking a chance and neglecting what in the popular jargon would now be called the logistical train, he was certainly due for a share of the blame but hardly for having thought out "the whole proceedings." Like all generals, Nixon wanted victory and he was prepared to push his luck, even at the point when he knew that the Turks were no longer retreating and had occupied the Ctesiphon position. If he had insisted on waiting until the two promised divisions arrived from France, there would have been plenty of voices to condemn him as over-cautious. November seemed to him to be an opportune moment for a drive to Baghdad. Having failed, he was the obvious target of the witch hunt—just as he would have been the obvious man to be feted and honored if the gamble had come off.

The one advantage deriving directly from the immediate aftermath of Ctesiphon was that both Whitehall and Simla at last came to realize that they were no longer going to be able to run the Mesopotamia campaign on the cheap. India hurriedly scraped together a couple of Indian infantry brigades and three batteries of artillery, and by the second week of December they were at sea, en route for Basra; Britain ordered that the moves of the two divisions promised from Egypt and France should be expedited. Meantime the Viceroy had also cabled to Whitehall asking for yet another division and for the all-important river transport on which the relief of Kut also depended. "The ruling factor in the rapidity of our concentration" he said "is the supply of additional river transport." The pity was that this realization had not dawned on his minions long before. Unfortunately this was a time when there were many calls on Britain's limited resources. Everywhere the tide of war was flowing against the Allies. In the Balkans the position was critical; the British force at Salonika was in a precarious position and Egypt also needed reinforcements; there was little to spare for Mesopotamia. Frantically seeking some way of stalling, the War Committee portentously proffered the advice that Townshend should retire from Kut to a position further downstream where he could cover a new build-up and prepare for another advance on Baghdad. But it was too late. Townshend was already besieged and the next report from Nixon brought even more ominous news. He reported no less than eight Turkish divisions, released from the Dardanelles—then on the point of being evacuated by British troops—were probably concentrating on the Baghdad front. This was cause for real concern and Whitehall at last responded. At the eleventh hour, twelve "garrison" battalions were promised to India to permit a fifth. Indian division to be formed in Mesopotamia; at the same time the War Committee sternly directed that as soon as the chestnuts had been pulled from the fire and Townshend had been relieved, Nixon should return to a defensive posture. If withdrawing from Kut should make it necessary, defensive positions should be prepared at Qurna and up the Karun valley so that the oil fields and pipeline would at least be protected. There was to be no further wildcat offensive directed on Baghdad. Not yet anyway.

Back in Kut, after his battered units had limped in, Townshend declared: "I mean to defend Kut as I did Chitral" and a signal couched in the same terms was sent to Nixon. From Basra the Army Commander replied that he was "glad to hear" of his decision and was "convinced that your troops will continue to show the same spirit in defence as they have shown throughout your operations. *Reinforcements will be pushed up to you with all possible speed.*" It was not clear yet when they would arrive but he said nothing about this.

In theory, the principal advantage to be gained from holding Kut—which in effect meant holding the junction of the Tigris and the Hai—was that the Turks were prevented from moving down the Hai to Nasiriyeh to attack Basra from a flank. While Townshend's guns dominated the Tigris, Field Marshal von der Goltz,[2] the newly appointed commander in Baghdad, could not over-run lower Mesopotamia. Furthermore, while Townshend held at Kut, Nixon could regroup his scattered forces, organize the expected reinforcements and prepare a counterthrust. Tactically however, there were many disadvantages to a protracted defence of the area. The town itself was scarcely more than a densely packed conglomeration of houses crowded with about 7,000 inhabitants, a flour mill and a bazaar. Opposite, on the right bank, there was the tiny "Woolpress" village of Yakasum which possessed, besides a woolpress, a

---

2. An old man of seventy-two but a master of strategy. Between 1883 and 1896 he had been responsible for the reorganization of the Turkish Army and later, in 1909, he had headed the German Military Mission to Turkey.

licorice factory. Filthy beyond description, Kut was the most vile and un-sanitary of all the places occupied by the British in Mesopotamia, and about the only alleviating features were the date plantations and a few gardens northwest and southeast of the actual town. From a logistical viewpoint, Kut's importance derived from the fact that it was the center of the local grain trade and so long as it remained merely a post on the line of communications to the front, grain supplies were available there. But this advantage obviously could not hold if it were in a state of siege and indeed such a situation had never been visualized. The few defenses that had been erected around the town had been planned for its role as a supply post, and it was in no sense a fortified enclave. A line of four blockhouses, connected by a barbed wire fence to a mud-walled enclosure, dignified by the name of a "fort," extended across the mile long neck of the loop in the Tigris which contained the town.

Except for a few mounds near the river, and some irrigation channels which would afford ready-made cover from fire, the surrounding countryside' was flat, open and almost featureless. This fact meant that any army standing to fight at Kut would have to hold both banks of the Tigris if boats were to pass up and down the river. Furthermore, the Tigris, although two or three hundred yards wide, was now so shallow near Kut that it was quite possible to wade across near the Woolpress village. As the Hai was also practically dry at this juncture, it too did not constitute a serious obstacle. The worst tactical drawback was the one which might seem, on the face of it, to make Kut an attractive location to withstand a siege. Because they would be enclosed in a loop of the river and with their backs to it, the defenders were liable to be driven down into the loop. Once this happened they would be shut up in an area about two miles long and a mile wide, where they would be exposed to fire from all sides and from which it would be very difficult to escape, even if bridges were available—which they were not. Across the neck of land at the mouth of the loop the short front line had its advantages while on the defensive but, as this was the only way the garrison could sally out, its defensive advantages reverted to those opposing the break-out if the defenders were to try.

Strategically, the most serious disadvantage lay in the potential advantages that the neighborhood of Kut afforded the Turks besieging it to hold off and delay any relief force coming up from Basra, and in his earlier battle at Es Sinn Townshend himself had already run up against them. On the left bank from Sannaiyat to Hanna 25 miles below Kut, there was only a mile wide strip of dry land between the river and extensive marshland; on the right bank the ground was also broken up by dried-up water courses and marshes. Getting a relief force across terrain of this nature would be difficult enough in the dry weather, but when the floods, produced by the melting snows in the highlands, swept down in March or late February, much of the Kut landscape would be submerged, with a proportionate increase in the difficulties which the advancing relief force would have to face.

One of the few things that could be said in favor of sitting tight in Kut was that any delay is usually to the advantage of those on the defensive. Those who are attacking generally face greater hardships than those who are on the defensive and doubtful friends and potential enemies waiting on the touchline are held in suspense, unable to make up their minds which side to support: time is gained for the development of the defender's resources. If the Turks were to advance from Baghdad to retake Basra men they would have to pass Kut and this was its greatest merit. In this instance the question of cultivating the uncertain sympathies of the Arab tribes in the immediate area can probably be discounted; their attitude was conditioned purely by practical considerations as to who was in the ascendant. But the same argument did not necessarily apply to the Persians. For some time they had shown a most equivocal attitude and to deter them from declaring in favor of the Turks and Germans was as good a reason as any other for checking von der Goltz's advance as far away from Basra as possible. Kut was as far forward as it was possible to do this. Perhaps the most important consideration was the one which seems almost hypothetical. Any army which is locked up in a besieged city is not pulling its weight; it might be compelled to retire hundreds of miles but while it is intact and mobile, it still retains the power to change the balance of a campaign by a single successful maneuver. Apart from that, once it is immobilized and besieged, the tendency is for everybody else to hurry to its assistance, a move which hands the initiative straight across to the opponents. On these counts Townshend's decision to stop withdrawing and stand at Kut seems to have been wrong. Occasionally, as at Ladysmith during the South African War, success has followed such a decision, but this was not to be such an occasion.

Having said all this, the one factor of paramount importance which influenced Townshend on December 1, 1915, must be mentioned. In the telegram announcing his intention to fight it out at Kut he pointed out that his men needed rest there and then. Strategical and tactical considerations were secondary to this, the decisive factor, and with "one month's full rations for British troops and two months for Indians, as well as plenty of ammunition" the prospect was not so glum . . . *so long as the reinforcements Nixon had promised reached him within two months.* Kut was not yet surrounded and it appears that Nixon did not finally make up his mind that it should be held until four days after Townshend's characteristic announcement about defending the place "like Chitral." Meantime Townshend had issued to the troops one of his typical communiqués:

> I intend to defend Kut-al-Amara and not to retire any further. Reinforcements are being sent at once to relieve us. The honor of our Mother Country and the Empire demands that we all work heart and soul in the defence of this place. We must dig in deep and dig in quickly, and then the enemy's shells will do little damage. We have ample food and ammunition, but Commanding Officers must husband the ammunition and not throw it away uselessly. The way you have managed to retire some eighty or ninety miles under the very noses of the Turks is nothing short of splendid, and speaks eloquently for the courage and discipline of this force.

Second thoughts came after receipt of Nixon's next signal. Every effort would be made to relieve the force, the Army Commander said, and it was hoped that this would be achieved *within two months*. And, because the Turks would probably[3] invest the town it would be a good thing if Townshend were to send the cavalry and any transport that could be spared back to Ali Gharbi and to return as many of the ships as possible. This would not only reduce the numbers he would have to feed but would also help the relief force.

The prospect of being locked up for two months in Kut did not suit Townshend at all. Apart from the fact that this period was the limit of his rations as he assessed them at that time, his principal fear was that the advent of the flood season might well delay the relief beyond then. He was a great student of military history and he knew full well that the story of besieged camps was almost invariably one of repeated capitulations: Bazaine at Metz, Cornwallis in Yorktown, Mack in Ulm, Massena at Genoa—in each case the garrison surrendered. "In two months," he telegraphed Nixon "I shall be surrounded by an army of six divisions," so it would be best if he now withdrew the whole division and retired on Ali Gharbi to await the relief force. Meanwhile he was sending back the Cavalry Brigade as Nixon had suggested.

When the Army Commander's reply came to this, it was clear that Townshend's new proposal was not to Nixon's liking. So long as Townshend remained at Kut, Nixon propounded, by containing superior numbers of Turks he would be doing what was expected of him. Townshend and his tired division were committed; Kut was where he was, Kut was where he would stay. The only crumb which Nixon offered in an otherwise unpalatable message was that the two months he forecast was the *outside limit* and that yet another division and more heavy guns had been asked for.

On December 7, the Turks finally closed the ring around Kut and the siege

---

3. Some of Nixon's staff were doubtful that they would do so, in fact.

began in earnest. The Cavalry Brigade and the ships had got away only three days before, the ships full of sick and wounded sailing down to Basra, the Cavalry Brigade to fight its way back to Ali Gharbi where, a week later, it was joined by the first contingent of the relief force. In the Kut enclave Townshend was left with about ten thousand fighting men (excluding two thousand odd sick and wounded), of whom about 7,400 were infantry; there were also about 3,500 Indian noncombatants—drivers, cooks, servants and the like—together with 6,000 Arab inhabitants. Of the latter, only the genuine householders and their families had been permitted to stay, the rest had been evicted. Political interests were given as the grounds for the retention of those remaining, and humanity dictated that they should stay. Even their presence was to prove a serious handicap in the days to come. It may have been humane to let them remain, to eat up their own grain and that of the besieged force, but when the consequences of that decision are assessed in terms of soldiers' lives, it may seem that it would have been preferable to expel many more. No doubt the Turks were happy to persuade them to stay and eat the garrison's rations; indeed many who tried to escape later were shot in the attempt.

The only gunboat to stay behind was the old tug *Sumana* which had been kept back as a ferry, but a dozen other smaller boats which Townshend thought would be useful had also been retained. Neither food nor ammunition appeared to present an immediate problem. With two months supplies, "excepting firewood, medical comforts and vegetables," Townshend decided that me vitality of his command would best be maintained on a full daily ration.[4] The estimate of a sufficiency for two months had been arrived at as the result of a quick assessment and, when stocks of grain in the town were commandeered, even the first detailed survey suggested that two months was a somewhat conservative estimate. Nor had every source of food been tapped and it was not until things began to get desperate that any systematic search was made of the Arab houses; this was a mistake which materially contributed to all the abortive efforts to raise the siege by the middle of January. In all sieges food and ammunition stocks are critical considerations and with Townshend's experience at Chitral it is surprising that he did not take steps in the early days of December to find out the exact position and then to husband such stocks of food as were revealed. It is also relevant to add that when his troops first arrived in Kut, tired as they were, they were not so far gone as to forego the time-honored custom of scrounging, and stocks of the more attractive commodities were conveniently "liberated" and wastefully dispersed.

---

4. Which for British troops was 1 lb. meat, 1 lb. bread, 3 oz. bacon, butter, cheese, 6 oz. potatoes, 4 oz. onions, 2½ oz. sugar, 3 oz. jam, 1 oz. tea, ½ oz. salt.

The defenses of Kut, organized only as a means of holding off the marauding Buddhoos, have already been mentioned. Except for the mud-walled Fort at the northeast of the perimeter, linked by a single barbed wire fence to four blockhouses, there were none. This meant that trenches and shelters had to be dug, barbed wire entanglements erected, and arrangements made to defend the river front. The troops were tired out and, according to Townshend, only the British regiments were fit to do any digging on December 4. The Indian troops could not move at all, he said—a statement with which others present at the time subsequently disagreed. The blockhouses were too far forward and their position added hundreds of yards of unnecessary line to the front. Yet abandoning them was not feasible; to do so would mean giving up the Fort which held large quantities of supplies and stores. These could not be moved elsewhere because there were no men to spare from the digging program generated by this situation. Beyond the blockhouses a line of sand hills, too far away to be occupied by the British troops, was a further disadvantage. Not only would these sand dunes offer cover to the Turks but they would also limit the garrison's ability to sally forth across the left bank of the river. On the other bank, me licorice factory in the Woolpress village, was an area which Townshend decided would have to be an outpost connected to the town by means of a boat bridge. Apart from the fact that there was a large quantity of grain stored in Yakasum, Townshend had concluded that it was essential to the defence of Kut. Coming from such a brilliant tactician this seems an odd conclusion. The factory was on the wrong side of the river and while it was obviously necessary to hold it until the grain had been removed, it is difficult to understand why it otherwise had any advantage over many other areas on the right bank. The main defenses were sited in the U loop of the river, protected by the so-called "First Line" entrenchments running from the Fort; this was the line incorporating the four blockhouses and behind this a "Middle" and a "Second Line" were dug—the latter covering the final redoubt. For ease of control, the whole of Kut was then subdivided into three sectors; the peninsula being divided more or less east and west by the Second Line, the area south of this line, together with the Woolpress village and its licorice factory, forming the Southern Sector. North of the Second Line, the top half of the U was divided by a line drawn south from "Redoubt B" the second blockhouse—the east side, including the Fort, becoming the North-East Sector and the western half the North-West Sector.

To each sector a brigade was allotted: Hoghton (17th Brigade) to the North-East; Delamain (16th Brigade) to the North-West and Hamilton's 18th Brigade to the Southern Sector, where most of the artillery was also located. Mclliss' 30th Brigade was put into reserve, to rest in the town during the day and alternate with the 16th Brigade at the north end of the peninsula by night. Work on organizing the defenses started as soon as the force had arrived in Kut and for the next few days the infantrymen's lives were just one long round of digging. Under the glare of the sun, they dug; in the bitterly cold dark nights, they dug; under the pale wan light of the moon they were still digging. There was every incentive, everyone knew that when the Turks finally closed in, life above ground was going to be very difficult. And they were right.

As the Cavalry Brigade trotted off across the bridge which had been built to span the river the previous day, the first shells started to fall in the town. Having closed the northern land exit, the Turks then moved down both banks north and south of the Kut peninsula until the investment was complete. Finding that the violent fire of the British guns prevented any further progress down the neck of the peninsula, the Turks set about constructing a vast network of trenches and covered ways to close the loop; guns to cover the British positions from all points of the compass were also deployed. Once this was done Nur-Ud-Din was ready to eliminate the garrison.

At this stage the morale of Townshend's troops was high; a month later he was to signal that "my troops are not what they were two or three months ago," but in early December their tails were still up. After all, in their opinion, every time they had fought the Turks they had come out on top; the retirement after Ctesiphon was no fault of theirs and given this opportunity now, they would soon show Johnny Turk who was the better man. Their "Charlie" was no Montgomery or Patton—indeed he was a remote figure to the troops during the siege—they saw him only on rare occasions. In a stream of *Orders of the Day* he did make some attempt to keep the troops in the picture and in those days that was quite something for a general to do. There was no question, he assured them, of their not being relieved, but in any case they were not going to just sit back and wait. Using the bridge, he proposed to hit hard at the enemy on both banks of the river; the Turks would soon know what they were up against.

The bridge referred to was the one which had been thrown across the Tigris and used by the cavalry to get out of Kut. Because there were insufficient pontoons to span the width of the river, constructing it in its initial location had given Townshend's sappers opposite the Fort plenty of headaches and more were to follow. By this time the Fort was under heavy fire and as might be expected as soon as it was in position the bridge immediately became a priority target. Townshend, realizing that it-had no future in its existing location, decided that it should be dismantled and re-erected in a new and less exposed position further upstream. At first, the new location seemed promising. A company of Indian troops were ferried across to the far bank to reconnoiter the bridgehead area and they reported no sign of any Turks—a happy state which was not to be of very long duration. Even as the pontoons were being towed into position, a Turkish detachment was inarching around the right bank, across the Hai, with orders to destroy the bridge and close the last alleyway of retreat to Ali Gharbi.

The bridge was completed by the evening of December 8, and a company of Punjabis doubled across and fanned out on the far bank to act as a bridge-head guard. When dawn broke, however, Turkish infantry could be seen advancing toward them in open order and Townshend ordered the Indians to get back across the bridge. Under the circumstances it was a difficult order to carry out and throughout the day there was a brisk duel as parties of Turks tried to rush the bridgehead and stop the Indians' withdrawing, while on the Kut side, troops lined the river bank and attempted to give covering fire for the hard-pressed Punjabis. It was nightfall before what was left of them got back. Now, with the bridge still in position and the Turks holding the far end, Townshend faced a situation which was far too dangerous to be allowed to continue. Breaking the link between the two river banks was no problem but recovering, or alternatively destroying, the bridge, was a very different matter. If the pontoons on the near side were demolished then the current would carry the rest of it over to the Turkish side, so making a gift of a valuable asset—one which certainly could be expected to be used subsequently against the besieged garrison. The only sure way of making certain that this did not happen was to blow up the pontoons at the far end and cut the anchor ropes in midstream. Frogmen were unheard of in 1915 and the plan evolved depended simply on a demolition party creeping across the bridge at night in order to plant explosive charges, set the fuses on them, and then rush back across the bridge—cutting the anchor ropes en route—before the bridge went up. Since an enterprise like this could hardly be expected to pass unnoticed by the Turks it was not exactly an enviable task. However, two officers—a Sapper subaltern by name of Matthews, and Sweet, a young officer of the Gurkhas, who was to act as Matthews' escort—volunteered for the job. Their little party stole across the bridge during the pitch black night, laid a charge of guncotton slabs across one of the pontoons about three-quarters of the way over, lit the fuse and doubled back. Everything went according to plan; only one man was wounded, and as they reached the shore, up went the bridge. With its destruction the immediate danger had been averted, but any hope of getting across the river to help the relief force went with it. Matthews and Sweet were both recommended for the Victoria Cross and the men who had taken part for the Indian Order of Merit. All of them had volunteered for what appeared to be a suicidal role and had waited all day in cold blood for nightfall and an operation which everyone thought would be certain death—a very different business from a spontaneous act of bravery in a hot fight. But the two officers were only awarded the D.S.O.

It was about this time that Nur-Ud-Din first suggested that the garrison should surrender. In a letter to Townshend he complained that the "peaceful inhabitants" of Kut were being exposed to the horrors of war, that it would be better for Townshend to avoid useless bloodshed and that the garrison should lay down its arms forthwith. In his reply Townshend thanked him for his courtesy in suggesting how he might avoid needless sacrifice, declined the offer and reminded his opponent that the Turks' Teutonic allies had scant respect for the occupants of the towns and villages they had occupied. He might have added that the so-called peaceful inhabitants of Kut were nothing but a constant source of anxiety and that he would have been very happy to be rid of them:

> I knew that they were in communication with the enemy, that went without saying; and my anxiety was based on the fact that many rifles must have been buried or concealed. It was certain that the consequences might be serious if the enemy should induce them to rise in the night when an attack was in progress on our northern front. For that reason I took some of the leading inhabitants into custody and announced that I would shoot them if there was the least sign of treachery. In order to put a stop to the looting by the Arabs at the commencement of the siege, I had caused twelve men who had been caught in the act to be tried by military commission and shot—*pour encourager les autres.*

After the souring effect of Nur-Ud-Din's letter, a telegram from his own side brought balm. His old friend General Fenton Aylmer had left Basra to organize the relief force and on December 10 he signaled Townshend:

> Have assumed command Tigris line. Have utmost confidence in the defender of Chitral and his gallant troops to keep the flag flying until we can relieve them. Heartiest congratulations on brilliant deeds of yourself and your command.

Meantime the battle for Kut had started to broaden. Shells were falling with increasing regularity in and around the Fort and during the afternoon of December 9 the North-West Sector was attacked. The assault was quickly repulsed. The Turks dug in just beyond the range of the defenders' rifles and by that evening they were ensconced all along the front in trenches which were never more than six hundred yards away from the British line. As dawn broke next morning shells crashed down on the British trenches and soon afterward, through the pale gray light, long lines of Turkish infantry in extended order could be seen advancing toward them. Rapid fire eventually halted the attack but by the time it did the Turks had halved the distance across "No Man's Land" and the garrison had suffered nearly two hundred casualties and, equally as serious, had shot off a very considerable quantity of ammunition. Two nights later, and again on the morning of December 13, the Turks returned to the attack; on each occasion they were again repulsed, but once more at the cost of a relatively large number of casualties and a very heavy expenditure of ammunition. Battles are not won without casualties, nor without expending ammunition. In any siege, where the garrison is living on dwindling stocks of manpower and material, these problems are doubly important. In these actions the only compensating factor that could be said to be satisfactory from Townshend's point of view was that the Turks had also lost a lot of men.

Attack and counterattack now succeeded one another intermittently until the end of the year, by which time the operation had settled down to a state of regular siege warfare, with the Fort at the northeast corner of the First Line as the priority objective of Turkish shell fire and sapping operations. Christmas Eve 1915, when a series of infuriated efforts were made to hack a way through the British lines brought this phase to a close however. Nur-Ud-Din, rein-forced and believing that Townshend's ammunition and supplies must be giving out, had decided to press on and capture Kut before Aylmer's Relief Force, concentrating less than fifty miles away to the south, could come to the rescue. And the morale of his men had gone up with the news that the British army at Suvla Bay had slipped away only a few days before. During the night of the 23rd, every available gun concentrated its fire on the Fort and the bom-bardment steadily increased in scale and intensity until it reached a crescendo late the following morning. In the Fort, the two 15-pounders mounted there were knocked out; most of the mud walls were flattened; the telephone lines back to Sector headquarters were all cut and under the rain of steel the garrison was forced to evacuate the northeast wall and retire to the nearby trenches. When the Turks attacked at noon, it was this corner of the Fort that they made for but, as the infantry of the crack 52nd Turkish Division advanced toward them, in close-packed formation with bayonets fixed, the tired and grim defenders climbed back on to what remained of the firesteps of their trenches and started in on a fearful execution. The murderous fire of four of the Maxim guns still in action on the flanks of the Fort, ploughed swathes into the Turkish ranks, yet still they came on. British and Indians alike repeatedly fired fifteen round "mad minutes" of rapid fire while others in what was styled "regular bludgeon work" hurled grenade after grenade into the compact formations at only ten yards range. Through the carnage only a few brave Turks survived to get to grips and then there was some bitter hand-to-hand fighting. The battle swayed to and fro but in half an hour it was all over. The waves of advancing infantry suddenly petered out and the Turks who were left on the battlefield wavered and finally ran back; the Fort had been held.

The attack on the Fort was said to have been ordered, organized and watched by von der Goltz himself; if he had had anything to do with it then he must have been disappointed for all there was to show for it was the pile of Turkish dead strewn between the original trenches and what was left of the Fort's mud walls. At the licorice factory where a feint, designed to keep British reserves away from the Fort, had been made, it had been a similar story. But it was not yet over, shelling of the Fort continued intermittently until about 8 o'clock that night and then another assault was made, this time the Turkish infantry being led by bombers, hurling grenades toward the battered trenches and bastions in front of them in an effort to open a way for the rest of the infantry. By sheer weight of numbers the British parapet was breached and a desperate hand-to-hand struggle went on until well past midnight. For a time it was touch and go as to whether the defenders could hold out or not and it was only the arrival of reinforcements at a crucial moment that stemmed the tide. Once again the defence had held, once again the cost had been high: 315 of the garrison perished in killing 907 Turks in that Christmas fight. For their gallant performance, both the 103rd Mahratta Light Infantry and the 43rd—the Oxford and Buckinghamshire Light Infantry—need a special mention. Of the latter, the Official History says "the Oxfords maintained fully their reputation as one of the Old Light Division and someone else who had been with them from the first landing in Mesopotamia, wrote proudly, "They need no mention—they were the Oxfords."

By Christmas morning only dead and captured Turks remained in the British perimeter but scores of others lay or hung on the wire, before it. Their pitiful groans induced Townshend's men to try to fetch in those who could be reached and to pass out food and water to the others, but Turkish snipers were active and during the day little could be done. When darkness fell those who could be moved without a stretcher were brought in; of the rest who had to be left out in the open, the more seriously wounded never had a hope and they were doomed to a lingering death in extremes of temperature. Two days later a Turkish officer asked for and got permission to bury the dead. Townshend gave him four hours, with a strict warning that if the Turks used the flag of truce as a means of getting troops into the forward trenches—as had happened at Gallipoli—they would be fired on at once.

After the din of battle, the oppressive silence of the afternoon of Christmas Day was both uncanny and ominous; something worse was bound to follow, the garrison thought. But it was not so; with the Turks' failure the campaign entered a new phase. Warned of the preparations for a relieving column,

Nur-Ud-Din had decided to blockade Kut and take immediate measures to stop Aylmer, and on Boxing Day (the first weekday after Christmas), Townshend's men could see columns of Turkish infantry trudging up the right bank. Townshend's immediate reaction was that his opponent had given up, that the Turks were retreating. To Nixon and Aylmer he signaled elatedly:

> . . . I have seen at least two divisions moving up river since 11:15 a.m., moving by the right bank. Mist prevented seeing if other troops moved previous to 11:15 a.m. in same direction. . . . Steady movement westward all day by transport and infantry, field ambulance flags northeast of fort disappeared . . . conclude Turks cross to right bank at Abu Dhakar bend in order to avoid my force pursuing . . . Turks retreated by right bank after our victory at Es Sinn (Kut) September last. Nur-Ud-Din must now know of large British forces arriving Ali Gharbi; he would be foolish to try and fight a battle with relieving force, he knows he must be beaten and could never shake off our pursuit on left bank and that of our gunboats. Then his best division has suffered heavy losses in its repulse from the Fort. Clouds have garnered for rain last two days; he could never get his guns away if rain comes down. . . . To sum up, all above indicates a retirement. ... I think his repulse on December 25, and our concentration at Ali Gharbi have caused his retirement; will wire tomorrow.

Next day the situation did not look so rosy however, and his signal read more soberly: "... Enemy's object in dividing his forces on both banks would appear to be to entrench a position for defence against relieving force on same lines as at Es Sinn and Ctesiphon."

Two days later it became apparent that this was exactly what the Turks did propose to do. But not above Kut as Townshend had first assumed. On December 28, the Turks began to move back along the right bank of the river and for several days their columns marched past Kut on the way to a position at which they could best block Aylmer's path. At a point three and a half miles east of Sheikh Sa'ad, which till now had been occupied only by Arab cavalry, they stopped and started to dig in. Kut, which had been completely by-passed was now left more or less to its own devices, although a daily pounding by a variety of guns outside the town reminded its defenders that the blockade was still on, and the Arab houses suffered a good deal of damage. Heavy Krupp guns, whose black powder shells exploded with an ear-splitting crash, field artillery firing shrapnel and even an enormous old brass mortar, last seen at Ctesiphon, all contributed to the daily hate. To this thundering of the guns the garrison settled down to spend their time getting the defenses back into shape and to await their relief. Trenches which had been almost obliterated by the earlier actions were re-dug and deepened; equipment and stores buried under piles of rubble were recovered; barbed wire fences in front of the trenches re-placed—the latter being an unenviable task, possible only at night, and even then the thud of muffled mallets was liable to be detected and result in a hail of bullets singing toward where the fatigue parties worked on the wire. Yet through all this, Townshend's men remained cheerful. Life was not so bad, the climate was tolerable, they were on full rations, seemingly secure, and Townshend had apparently convinced everybody that relief would not be long deferred. Optimism was the spirit of the day; defeat was impossible, thought his troops; relief was a certainty said their commander—Aylmer's men will hack their way through in the good old British way. Disillusion was to come with the New Year.

Chapter 7

Persian Interlude

Two swords cannot be kept in one sheath.

Persian Proverb

The troops on the Tigris were much too busy to think about what was happening anywhere except on their own immediate front and they would only have been further depressed if they had known how things were going elsewhere. The summer and autumn months of 1915 were a crucial period for the Allies in almost every theater of war, but nowhere was the situation potentially more critical than on Mesopotamia's flank—Persia, a country which had known civilization before Greece and Rome, but whose prime importance now lay in the fact that it possessed the oil which was to become one of the chief essentials of modern war. Because the source of this oil lay in the hills 70 miles northeast of Ahwaz, it was essential to British interests that Persia should at least remain neutral with no internal disturbances to upset the flow of oil to Abadan. No one knew this better than the Germans.

"The plain of the oil," which held the all-important oil fields, lies in the

heart of the Bakhtiari country and, as the Khans of the Bakhtiari received substantial subsidies from the Anglo-Persian Oil Company, their prosperity
depended on the British being able to extract the oil without interference. The
Sheikh of Muhammerah, through whose territory the pipeline ran, also
depended on the oil for the major portion of his income—although his loyalty
could almost be taken for granted because of the long and honorable traditions
of good faith which had bound his family to Britain, and both he and the
Khans maintained a firm grip of their followers throughout the anxious
months of 1915. Consequently neither the Bakhtiari tribesmen nor the Sheikh's
men took part in any of the troubles which had necessitated Nixon's sending
troops up the Karun. The Bakhtiari were in fact inclined to sympathize with
the Germans—not so much because they were pro-German but because the
Turks held the same faith as themselves and also because they were tradi-
tionally anti-Russian. However, the dividends their chiefs received were a very
strong argument for keeping out of any intrigues which might put a stop to
them; clearly it was preferable to subjugate pro-German zeal for the sake of an
assured income. Similarly it was hardly to be expected that they would show
much enthusiasm at seeing their livelihood go up in columns of smoke. But
other tribes in the same region, unaffected by the exploitation of Persia's
richest asset, were not limited by such considerations and it was these that the
Germans and Turks tried to subvert, efforts which were only part of a much
larger plot to force Persia into the war on their side.

To extend the area of hostilities and make the war a "world" war in the
fullest sense was an aim for which the Germans had made considerable
preparations as soon as they saw how things were shaping up in Europe. By so
doing they hoped that Britain would become so deeply involved and her forces
so dissipated throughout other theaters of war that pressure on the Western
Front would be relaxed. So far as the Middle East was concerned, operations
across the northern frontiers of the Ottoman Empire, guarded as they were by
a Russian army, seemed to offer little prospect of any dividends in this direction. Persia in the south, where the eighteen-year-old Shah sat upon the jewel-
studded peacock throne of Aurangzebe, but had little control over his turbulent population, was a much more attractive proposition. The Government was
weak and most of the power lay in the hands of provincial governors; as these
were notoriously corrupt, bribes made it comparatively simple for commercial
and diplomatic agents to undermine the regime, particularly when the bags of
German gold were combined with propaganda for a Holy War.

German Agent-in-Chief, Director General of Propaganda and Chief Archi-
tect of the plot, was Prince Henry of Reuss, German Minister in Teheran, a
man well-suited to the task not only by virtue of his personal qualities but also

for the background knowledge he had gained while serving as Consul-General at Calcutta. Berlin had seen to it that he was well provided with the wherewithal for lavish handouts and he was ably assisted by a formidable entourage of desperadoes, which included quite a number of German officers. Prince Henry's propaganda campaign, based on the Holy War religious theme, had been well thought out and it was well directed into every channel which appeared to offer any hope of stirring up trouble. Bales of inflammatory leaflets, in five languages, were even distributed to Indian troops with the object of seducing the Indian soldier. This particular line met with a poor response—except among the Afghans serving in Indian regiments—and they were not the King Emperor's subjects anyway. But to the more fanatical Persian Arabs, the biblical directness of the propaganda had a definite appeal: "O Persians! Are we to suppose that all your prayers and breast-beatings, all your religious ceremonies, are in vain? Now, when the whole of Islam is threatened by the infidel, such lip service is of little count. Now is the time to give yourselves to the Holy Cause. If you shrink from the Sacrifice, what answer will you render the Prophet on the Judgment Day." To tribesmen, who are in the habit of relieving what to them in normal times was a pathetically monotonous existence by piracy and gun-running, this was a heaven-sent opportunity. Not only were the German agents prepared to pay well and provide modern weapons from across the Turkish border, they would be following the devices and desires of their hearts, and even God—according to the Germans, anyway—was on their side. When profit and religion pointed to the same path, few were proof against such arguments.

By February the whole of western Persia had been affected. The Sheikh of Muhammerah's followers and the Bakhtiari continued to honor their contract with the oil company but the Bawi and Chaab tribesmen urged on by their mullahs, rose in response to the Jihad. It was their behavior which led to the first operations up the Karun river in which the platoon of Dorsets so distinguished themselves and to the subsequent expedition by Gorringe. Efforts had been made to subvert and commit the Bakhtiari Khans to the same disturbances but these had come to nothing. "Why be content with sharing the income from the oil?" the German agents asked; "Come in with us and the whole of the wealth is yours." The wily Khans pointed out that the oil fields would be of little use without the British engineers serving the oil company. "We will work for you" the Germans said. The Khans were too astute to be taken in by this sort of talk; the Germans had no ships, they countered, and unless it could be sold, the oil was valueless. They knew full well that the German fleet had been swept off the seas and this was a fact which none of Prince Henry's political missionaries could explain away.

Meantime, unrest was developing in the south; indeed it had been coming for some time. When Delamain's brigade reached Bahrain in October 1914, evidence of a well-established German intelligence system had been uncovered which pointed to the necessity for taking over Bushire where the cable station connecting Basra with India was located. The cable station was too important a link on the line of communications back to India to be left unprotected and early in March the port was taken over, put under British administration and the German residents deported to India.[1] Somewhat naturally this seemed to the Persians a very highhanded action and it was one of which the German Consul, Herr Wassmuss, made the most. In company with the rest of the Germans in Bushire, Wassmuss had been taken into custody but he managed to escape and make off in the direction of Shiraz. After walking fifty miles or so—a feat worthy of recognition in itself—he procured a horse and so kept ahead of the patrol which had been sent to recapture him. On reaching Shiraz, Wassmuss made for his own Consulate. Technically, of course, the British had no business even trying to apprehend him, nor even any authority to chase him; Persia was a neutral country, although this was a consideration that seemed to count for little since Germans, Turks, Russians and British alike showed no compunction about invading her neutrality when it suited them to do so. However, this was not the basis of Wassmuss's evading re-arrest. Quite a large number of Germans lived in Shiraz and, once in the Consulate, Wassmuss raised such a hue and cry that the British patrol had to beat a hasty retreat.

Wassmuss, now in the role of a fugitive, righteously concerned about Persia's being menaced by the British lion, immediately set to work to turn the situation to propaganda advantage. What had happened at Bushire presented a glorious opportunity for troublemaking; here was direct evidence of sinister British designs on the country of his adoption. Before long the Khans of Tangistan in the territory behind Bushire were vigorously protesting that they were shocked at Britain's violation of Persian neutrality and were demanding that their innocent German "guests"—the same guests who had brought them arms from over the Turkish border—should be returned to Persia. When no move to evacuate Bushire was made, prompted again by Wassmuss, they called for sterner measures. Tangistani tribesmen started to mass in the coastal region behind Bushire and a patrol of Indian troops which went to investigate reports of this concentration, were ambushed and severely handled.

Wassmuss's subversive efforts had been remarkably effective and indeed

---

1. It was handed back to the Persians in October 1915, Persia having accepted the British terms for its administration.

they continued to be so all along. Nobody appreciated the potency of his propaganda and the danger of the man himself more than his indefatigable opponent Sir Percy Cox, and Sir Percy, whose reputation carried great weight throughout Arabia—so much so that among the Arabs, "Kokus" became the generic term for all political officers—was all for eliminating him without further ado. A proclamation promising a reward for the capture of Wassmuss, dead or alive, was issued, but when news of this reached Whitehall the Foreign Office ordered its immediate withdrawal. His Majesty's Ministers viewed his action "with abhorrence and detestation." Six months later when the Foreign Office cabled to ask if he could suggest some means of curbing Wassmuss' activities, he replied, "Fear of exciting the abhorrence and detestation of His Majesty's Ministers precludes me from making any suggestion."

For those who may consider that a proclamation inviting the local population of a neutral country to murder a diplomatic representative may seem unethical, it must be remembered that over and above the intense antipathy felt by the British toward the Germans, Sir Percy's demand was in keeping with the attitude best understood by those to whom the appeal to eliminate him was made. Rough justice was accepted as a way of life by the Arabs, and those who were fighting the British were known to offer rewards of gold pieces for British or Indian heads, and wounded who fell into Arab hands were usually killed at once. (And in this context one story deserving immortality is worth repeating. As he lay wounded and unarmed after an action near Ahwaz in March 1915, a British officer was surrounded by Arabs. When they indicated that they proposed to cut his throat he mentioned to them to wait while he took off his boots. Thinking that perhaps it was a British custom to say one's prayers in bare feet, the Arabs waited. However, when he got them off the officer concerned threw his boots with unerring aim straight into their faces as they closed in on him.)

The Persian Government was apparently not prepared to do anything about the Tangistanis threatening Bushire; it is doubtful whether they had the ability to do so anyway. Consequently Nixon ordered a punitive raid on their base, the fortified village of Dilwar. The raid was a complete success in so far as the village was destroyed, but it did not have the effect of deterring the Tangistanis from their warlike activities around Bushire and, during September, there was a brisk little action across the low-lying sandy tract which joins Bushire island to the mainland. A large force of tribesmen who had assembled in the nullahs near this spot were attacked by an Indian battalion and after several hours of fighting which concluded with a dramatic bayonet charge, the Arabs were routed. To administer the coup de grace an Indian cavalry squadron charged the fleeing tribesmen, but although the charge was a dramatic interlude it can hardly have been said to have had the same success as the infantrymen's bayonets. When the tribesmen stopped in their tracks turned about and opened fire the charge came to an abrupt halt and most of the officers and quite a few troopers lost their lives. The action was typical of its day for at that time British and Indian cavalry regiments seem to have been imbued with the spirit of Balaclava and a predilection for charging at the wrong time and the wrong place.

The British detachment at Bushire was well able to take care of itself but outside a radius of a few miles from the port it was quite powerless to affect the general situation in Persia. During the summer months of 1915, as Prince Henry's machinations got under way, the situation gradually went from bad to worse. The first and ominous developments came with a series of violent anti-British and anti-Russian outbursts at Ispahan, where the Russian bank manager was killed and the British Consul attacked; at Shiraz, in southern Persia, the British Consul was wounded and his deputy assassinated. All this was the work of Prince Henry's men. The Persian Government apologized for the outrages but the situation was obviously getting out of hand, and with the revolt of the so-called "Swedish"[2] gendarmerie in October the crisis came to a head. It was all a matter of money. As the gendarmes were not getting any pay from their own government, German gold made them easy victims and their Swedish officers apparently had few qualms about transferring loyalties.

The first scene in the latest act of the Persian drama opened in Shiraz with the arrest of all British subjects, including the Consul, and their removal to the Tangistani country halfway to Bushire. It was all rather ironic because the gendarmes who came to arrest them had been trained and equipped on money loaned by Britain and Russia for the express purpose of looking after the safety and well-being of foreign residents. However, the gendarmes concerned half-apologetically explained their behavior by saying that they were acting under orders, that Persia was about to declare war against the Allies and that the prisoners were to be held as hostages until all Germans and Persians taken on Persian soil were repatriated and the British evacuated Bushire. This was a demand the British and Indian Governments obviously could not accept, and so for the next few months the wretched prisoners were held in a fortress

---

2. Swedish only in its name and its officers. It had been created to replace a similar force of Persians, armed and dressed as Cossacks and officered by a proportion of Russians, when it was found it was necessary that it should be officered by men from a country which was neutral in the sense of not being concerned in Persian affairs or suspected of any ambitions of becoming so. It was for this reason Swedish officers were chosen; when they betrayed their trust and rebelled against their Persian employers they were disowned by their own Government which endeavored to prevent them engaging in "unneutral" activities. (It is also fair to add that most of the officers originally nominated for the force by the Swedish Government had returned when the troubles began and their Swedish successors were discredited adventurers.)

barely twenty miles from Bushire. The detachment at Bushire could not reach them, and in any case the Indian Government was opposed to any rescue operations or punitive expedition. It was not that defeating the Tangistanis was in question, merely that at the first alarm they would probably cut their captives' throats and make off into the hills.[3]

Meanwhile, the Russians had decided to take a hand. In their opinion there was only one argument that the troublemakers would understand which was capable of making absolutely sure that Allied interests would be looked after and that was armed force. As a column of Russian troops was marching from Kazvin toward Teheran, the Tsar's Legation announced "Russia has decided to put a stop to the activities of the Turko-German agents who are trying to drag Persia into the war." Knowing that the Persians regarded the Russians as their hereditary enemies the communiqué went on to try to allay the feelings of suspicion that would be bound to arise with this news of Russian troops on the move. "Russian arms will not be used against the Persian people; the Russian soldiers are solely for the purpose of defending the peaceful population" it said; it was not "Russian Arms" that the peaceful population need have feared, Russian soldiers' stomachs were to prove a much more potent threat than the rifles they carried!

The Russian statement was also preceded by a reference to the troops' move being "in agreement with the Government of the Shah." How this could be justified is not quite clear, since the Shah had certainly not asked for them and it is most unlikely that any of his government wanted them. In Britain the House of Commons was told that the Russian column was advancing on Teheran "to protect Allied interests in the Persian capital." The Persian Government, it was said, had been told of the specific intentions of these troops and that both Britain and Russia were anxious to maintain friendly relations with Persia. The explanation followed the usual wartime diplomatic lines. Friendly relations would continue it was hoped; however they would not be possible if the Persian Government concluded any special agreement with the Turks or Germans. "It must be obvious" said Sir Edward Grey, on November 11, 1915, in the House of Commons "that the Persian Government cannot make agreements with our enemies, who have instigated murderous attacks on our Consuls and their staffs, with-out risking the position of Persia."

To Prince Henry of Reuss the Russian incursion was exactly the sort of ready-made excuse he needed to trigger the final stages of his plans. He had to act anyway; if he waited, then presumably his organization would soon be

---

3. The Consul and his party were released in August 1916, after nearly eleven months of captivity, when they were exchanged for a number of Persians who had been deported earlier in the year.

stripped and in time German influence could be expected to wane, while that of the Russians and British correspondingly grew stronger. This seemed to be the ideal moment to make an extra effort to get Persia into the war, particularly as the Persians, softened up by his diligent propaganda war, were already showing a distinct leaning toward the Germans and resentment against the Allies. The Shah might want his country to stay neutral but with the news that the Russians were making toward Teheran he was in an unenviable position. If he could be persuaded to leave the capital because of the Russians' threat to his authority and to seek refuge with the gendarmerie, Persia was as good as in the war. Persian troops would rally around the Shah's standard—most of them were under German influence already and the Shah would provide just that final reason for their taking up the German cudgels; knowing that the Shah was in the war should also put teeth into the Jihad.

Together with the rest of the German, Austrian and Turkish members of Teheran's diplomatic corps, Prince Henry left the capital to transfer his headquarters to a town about thirty miles away. At the same time, ostensibly on government orders, the gendarmerie also left Teheran, forming up and marching to the same location as Prince Henry. They had been told that they were to concentrate and eventually take part in operations against the Russians. Meanwhile, that night, back in Teheran, the Colonel of the Persian Cossack Brigade had arranged to give a reception. As he was known to be one on whom the Shah could rely in any emergency and whose troops were completely loyal, Prince Henry's gang had concluded that the German cause would be best served by the Colonel's elimination, and one of his guests had been bribed to assassinate him during the party. The effect of his death, it was hoped, would be to throw his troops into confusion and so make the rest of the plot easy. Fortunately for the Colonel, and indeed for the Shah, the would-be assassin and his bombs were discovered before he had time to do any damage. At the same- time the capital was seeming with excitement at a rumor initiated by the Germans to the effect that the Shah was about to leave Teheran.

In the palace, surrounded by his Cabinet, the young Shah was trying to make up his mind whether or not to leave. Those of his entourage who were party to the plot were doing their utmost to persuade him to go while others, led by the Prime Minister, were urging him to stay. The Chief of Police, to whom the Shah appealed for advice, refused to commit himself, insisting that he was there to obey orders, not to advise, and those who had maintained a discreet silence during the early arguments steadfastly still refused to offer any opinion. Most of them had been overawed by the pro-German set and were acutely conscious of their insecure position whatever course of action the Shah should choose. The arguments to go or to stay continued throughout the night and next morning the Shah was still undecided. Finally, after a private audience with the British and Russian Ambassadors at which his fears with regard to the Russian troops were allayed, the Shah declared for Britain and Russia. Calling the Chief of Police, he announced his decision to stay in Teheran and this put paid to Prince Henry's hopes. Within a few days the capital was back to normal.

It was some time before the news got through to the new German, Austrian and Turkish diplomatic headquarters, where the gendarmerie was drawn up in review order, while the Prince and the other diplomats with their staffs, all in full dress, confidently waited for the Shah to arrive. Once he had joined them the intention was to set up his standard in the old capital of Ispahan which, for a long time, had been the main center of German intrigue. When eventually it was known that the Shah did not propose to honor them with his presence, there was no point in waiting about any longer; it was still possible to harass the British and Russians even without the Shah. Obviously it was no longer feasible to return to Teheran but a great deal could still be done to embarrass the British and Russian war effort.

By the beginning of December, about 8,000 irregulars and 3,000 of the original gendarmerie[4] had collected at Hamadan where they were being supplied by the Turks. They were not allowed to stay there for long. When General Baratoff occupied Hamadan, the rebels were compelled to fall back on Kermanshah along the caravan route from Baghdad to Teheran. Baratoff continued to press on toward the Turkish frontier but by this time the terrain was becoming more difficult, and opposition was stiffening. Not only had the news of the British evacuation of Gallipoli and Kut being under siege given Prince Henry's propaganda campaign a boost, but Turkish troops had been sent up to reinforce the motley crew of Persian bandits, malcontents and fanatics. In Baghdad, Baratoff's progress was disturbing von der Goltz and this was part of his "active defence."

In January, Prince Henry was recalled to Germany and replaced by Dr. Vassell, the former Consul General in Baghdad, but the hey-day of German inspired disturbances was over.

Until the fate of Kut had been sealed and while Aylmer was trying to batter his way through to Townshend, von der Goltz was not strong enough to tackle Baratoff. Nor could he afford to ignore him. It was essential that the road to the Mesopotamia plains should be blocked and if von der Goltz had been alive

---

4. Some, rather shamefacedly, trickled back to Teheran when they found the Shah was not going to join them.

when Townshend surrendered he would probably have been satisfied that this had been accomplished very effectively. Both Nixon and Townshend were praying that the Russian advance would take some of the pressure off Kut but it was the end of February before Baratoff broke through at Kermanshah and the middle of March 1916 before they reached Karind, "on the way to Baghdad" and by that time the garrison of Kut had little more than six weeks to go.

As the crow flies Karind is about 130 miles from Baghdad and the British fervently hoped that the Turks would have no option now but to divert a considerable force from the Tigris front in order to stop the Russians from taking Baghdad. Indeed, if Baratoff had relentlessly pushed on straight down the road soon after he got to Karind it seems almost certain that he would have captured Baghdad. The fact was that he did not do so and it was June before his army was on the move again. Then when the Turkish positions at Khanaqin, just across the Turko-Persian border were attacked, his men suffered a sharp reverse. Whether or not he needed the best part of three months to prepare for this attack is a matter for conjecture, but Baratoff, like Nixon, had his difficulties. He too was harassed by the ubiquitous "Buddhoo" and he too was at the end of a long line of communications. Not that supplies worried the Russians in the same way as the British. Their policy was to live off the country and what they took was seldom paid for—a policy which could hardly be expected to endear them to the Persian peasants, particularly as the troops often got out of hand and incidents of violence and rape were frequent.

By the end of 1916 this part of the country was utterly desolate, all reserves of food had been seized and eaten, trees had been felled, standing crops burnt; there was not even any seed grain for the next harvest. Then came a drought and the inevitable followed: famine. Cossacks and Turks had left a dreadful legacy behind them and it is small wonder that the Persians grew to hate all Russians, Turks and Germans with such intensity.

> It is sufficient to say here that much, if not all of the xenophobia prevalent in Persia in the years succeeding the Great War was due to the appalling inhumanity with which Persians were treated alike by Turks, Germans and Russians.[5]

As the Russians had advanced on Karind, northern and western Persia was gradually cleared of troublemakers and, although the activities of the Russian troops were building up a great fund of resentment which politically offset much of the military advantages gained by a return of peace to the area, British influence gradually began to reassert itself. This was only in the north and west

---

5. *Loyalties. Mesopotamia 1914–1917,* Sir Arnold Wilson, Oxford University Press, 1930, p. 163.

however; the rest of Persia was still a kind of neutral battlefield and at the end of 1915 ten of the seventeen branches of the Imperial Bank of Persia were in German hands; Sultanabad, Ispahan, Shiraz and Yezd were all under German influence and even in Teheran, where there was also still a good deal of Turkish and German influence, the British Ambassador, Sir Charles Marling, had an unenviable task.

At Ispahan, the Germans erected a wireless station over which came news for Kaiser Hadji Guilliano's Faithful of how well the war was going in Europe, of the destruction of the British Navy and the failure of the Bank of England. Further south, the redoubtable Wassmuss still reigned among the Tangistani to whom, by means of a dummy radio, he too brought news from the All-Highest. Rewards in Paradise were promised to the credulous Khans by the Kaiser, provided they continued with the crusade against the British. Only at Ispahan did the propaganda machine make any real blunder. There, the local population, promised that a German zeppelin would bring a load of sugar, turned out to acclaim its arrival and, being disappointed, German prestige suffered accordingly.

Not until the end of 1916 was the Persian flank of the Mesopotamia Expeditionary Force made secure and making it so was a long tedious business. With the approval of the Shah's Government, Sir Percy Sykes, with a mixed British, Indian and Arab force gradually cleared one town after another, mopping up pockets of rebels and gendarmes and killing or capturing their German organizers. The roads to Bushire and Ahwaz were reopened, the various propaganda centers fell and slowly British influence came into its own.

For results which were so cheaply attained, a there handful of Germans had had the most astounding success and, if only because their methods served as a model to others who were to come after them, their achievements with the propaganda weapon are worthy of note. We have come a long way since those days but the Germans' work in Persia was a milestone in propaganda warfare. The Soviets, quick to spot its potentialities, were among the first to take up where the Germans left off. Since then almost every nation has tried its hand and in the hands of a demagogue its power is frighteningly apparent. The cries may have changed but it is always possible to raise a bogey and give it a name like "Imperialism" or "Racialism"; given the correct context, a religious theme is also a guaranteed rabble rouser and from then on it is not a far step to proclaim the need for an "Army of Deliverance."

In one short chapter it is not possible to describe adequately all that happened in Persia over this period; such an account needs a book to itself. The war in this part of the world was fought out in Mesopotamia and some may regard the events in Persia as a diversion. Yet, because Persia was the source of the oil and this was the principal *raison d'être* for General Barrett's original expedition, Persia warranted much more consideration than a normal diversion in war usually gets. If Prince Henry's German coup d'état in Teheran had come off in November there is little doubt that the immediate situation would have been a serious one for Britain. Every man and every gun was needed for the relief of Townshend in Kut and it is possible that the oil fields might have had to be abandoned; if so they would have fallen into German hands, although it is doubtful if they could have held them for long. Furthermore, Persia's entry into the war would have meant that the main struggle in the Middle East would have shifted further east—a fact which, in the long run, would have been to Britain's advantage, since the Turks would have been drawn further from their base and any loss of prestige consequent on temporarily giving up ground in Mesopotamia might have been compensated for by the consolidation of British authority right up to the northwest frontier of India.

But this is there speculation as events did not turn this way. Russian troops, a day's march from Teheran, decided the immediate issue and were the prime reason for the Shah being persuaded to stay in the capital—an outcome from which some Persians even derived considerable benefit. For a while they basked at a blaze which had been lit for them and then found profit in the embers; the religious aspect seems to have been almost forgotten. But, when the fire eventually went out, when there were no more profits to be made and famine was rife: "Even God" they said "is tired of the war."

Chapter 8

With the Relief Force

In Basra, during the first week of December, where the atmosphere might best be described as one of controlled panic, the first of Nixon's long and anxiously awaited reinforcements started to arrive. Major General Sir George Younghusband, commanding the 28th Brigade, was among the first to disembark; with him from Egypt came his headquarters and a single Indian battalion, the rest of the 7th (Meerut) Indian Division were following.

There was no time to stage the troops in Basra; as soon as they arrived they were transshipped and sent upstream to Ali Gharbi. Nixon was set on losing no time; if the 6th Division were to be extricated from Kut, then the relief force had to be assembled without delay, or it would be too late. The first step was to establish a firm new front line and Younghusband was ordered to deploy his brigade[1] at Ali Gharbi as fast as possible; behind the screen it would provide, the main force would assemble as quickly as the fresh troops could be ferried forward. Since Townshend's original signal that he had only fifty-nine days' rations in Kut implied that relief had to be effected inside two months, clearly it was going to be a race against time. And once again Nixon was up against the old problem that had bedeviled the campaign all along. It was all very well to plan an advance and to call for reinforcements; getting them to the

---

1. Comprising: 2nd Bn. Leicestershire Regiment, 51st Sikhs F.F., 53rd Sikhs F.F., 56th Punjabi Rifles F.F.

front and maintaining them there all depended on transport and supplies. Everything in fact depended on transport and, if it had been barely adequate up to Ctesiphon, it was lamentably insufficient now. The root cause lay in the fact that the numbers of ships capable of navigating the Tigris had never kept pace with the lengthening communications and the increasing loads.

Those who had urged the original advance on Baghdad had made no provision for the type of shallow draft vessels which were required; none existed in any quantity either in India or elsewhere at that time, they said. As before, it was the troops who were to suffer. On this count, as with the deplorable medical arrangements, Nixon's staff cannot escape blame. There is a simple arithmetical connection between numbers of men, distances from the base and the supplies they require, which is an exercise familiar to every staff college student. Yet it was eight months after the start of the campaign before the realization of this connection really dawned on those in Mesopotamia and a call for more shipping was made; then, since they had to be built, it was over a year before the new craft could be available. Like those in Simla, Nixon's staff had been blinded by the lodestar of Baghdad; once Baghdad had fallen all would be well. It had even been suggested that sufficient boats would be captured in Baghdad to augment the existing British flotilla and provide for the move up of the two promised divisions once they arrived—though what justification there was for this supposition is difficult to understand, as the Turks had only two steamers and a few launches there anyway.

In December 1915 the outlook was grim indeed. By river, the round trip from Basra to the front and back took about twenty days and the shortage of boats was such that not only was a really quick concentration out of the question, but its potential striking power would be weakened when once it had been assembled. Nor was the problem confined only to the river. Basra, with its lack of facilities for the handling of sea transports was also a serious bottleneck and the means of unloading ships were only slightly less primitive than those which had existed when it had been captured a year before. Only a few wooden piers were available and ships had to anchor in midstream to discharge their cargoes into the tiny native boats, necessarily a long, tedious business. Even as late as July the following year it was still quite normal for a ship to spend six weeks at Basra before it could be turned around—this, at a time when every ton of shipping was vital to the war effort. An expert in these matters, Sir George Buchanan, sent out from India to investigate reported:

> The military expedition to Basra is, I believe, unique, inasmuch as in no previous case has such an enormous force been landed and maintained *without an adequately prepared base.*

Not until the end of 1916, when a ship's turn-around had been cut to three weeks, did improvements at the port start to be effective, and even then the river—which had to supply an army of 120,000 men more than two hundred miles from Basra—was still a bottleneck. It was no better than the single track railway which one might logically have supposed would have been put to use much earlier. In actual fact, the construction of a railway line from Basra to Nasiriyeh had been suggested as early as February but the wherewithal for it had not been forthcoming from India. It is fair to add that Simla had inquired whether a light railway—for which a hundred and thirty-seven miles of material existed—would be suitable. Apart from this the idea had been shelved until August when Nixon again asked for one. Despite repeated reminders, no reply from India was forthcoming until November and then Nixon was curtly informed that the expense prohibited Government sanction of such a project. Three months the reply had taken; when it did come disaster was hanging over the Army in Mesopotamia. Admittedly, if construction had been sanctioned in February it would still not have been possible to start work until the floods subsided and consequently it is doubtful whether sufficient track would have been laid in time for the railway to have had any real influence on the disasters which followed the Battle of Ctesiphon. But this is about the only argument that can be found to excuse the behavior of the Government of India; even fifty years after the events their complacency is still bewildering. If those in charge appreciated that a great war was in progress then they would appear to have been sadly lacking in sense of responsibility. Undoubtedly the perceptions of those who ruled India had been dulled by the years of stringent economy that preceded the war, and Nixon had made the mistake of linking his demand with the commercial prospects of a railway in the post-war era instead of confining himself to the military requirement. To the men who regarded themselves as patriotic guardians of India's resources this was a matter of exercising their powers of curtailment, and the contemporary comments of the Finance Member made on October 5, 1915, would seem to support this view.

> I confess to being somewhat sceptical as to the line being so remunerative as is at present represented. Apart from this, it is perfectly clear that in present circumstances we cannot embark on large expenditure on such a project for other than the most urgent military reasons. We have already cut our own railway programme in India to the quick. Further, *we have at present no right to act as if we were certain of getting Mesopotamia after the war.* If, however, His Excellency the Commander-in-Chief can definitely assure me that this project is absolutely necessary for the safeguarding of our military position, I cannot of course resist a reference home. In the event it will be necessary to indicate to the Secretary of State that the cost must fall on the Home Government. . . .

His guarded reference to a post-war settlement was the key to the way the minds of the Indian Government worked; nowhere in the Finance Member's minutes was there any evidence of concern for the safety and well-being of the troops. If there is any excuse to be found for this attitude then it must lie in the fact that when the minute was written the advance on Baghdad was being contemplated. Once Baghdad had been taken—and success then seemed certain to those back in India—no further geographical objectives were envisaged. Presumably it was on this basis that it was hoped the railway would no longer be necessary. Having said this, it should be remembered that many of the difficulties which faced the troops in Mesopotamia also ought to have been known in India—extreme heat in summer and the disease and discomforts which were likely to attend fit men, let alone the wounded—and a railway would have helped to alleviate these hardships. Yet General Sir Beauchamp-Duff, the Commander-in-Chief, apparently was not prepared to endorse Nixon's request, since it was Duff who failed to press for a railway on the grounds of urgent military necessity. Nixon probably erred in putting forward an argument which was not directly related to his own sphere but on Duff must fall the onus of the idea's final rejection.

Not until the British War Office stepped in to control operations was approval for the construction of a railway sanctioned and it took the fall of Kut for that to happen. Eventually, by late 1916, it was possible to travel from Basra to Nasiriyeh quickly in comparative comfort; and when the first train from Basra rolled into Baghdad in August 1917, it had covered the hundred and eighty miles separating the two towns in twelve hours. By river the same journey would have covered twice the distance and taken two full days. How Nixon—a sick man and out of the battle then—must have pondered on the difference a railway from Basra to Amara would have made if it had been built a year earlier.

So far, consideration of the Army Commander's problems seem to have dwelt wholly on river and rail transport difficulties when it might be expected that first thoughts would be concerned with roads. In these days of mechanized movement the problem would have been very different and there was plenty of oil available: for at Kirkuk, at the place of "Eternal Fires," oil had been burning for over two thousand years. But in 1915 the motor vehicle was still in its infancy and as yet unsuited to the undeveloped regions of the East. Everything comes back to the river. From biblical times animals had provided the only means of land transport in Mesopotamia and animals, like men, need food, and fodder had to be brought from India. Like men also, they need water so that movement in this flat, arid, featureless terrain was tied to the river and if the significance of the nightmare conditions which prevailed have not yet been fully appreciated, a glance at a map will serve as a reminder of its importance. In the hot weather movement is handicapped because there is no drinking water to be found away from it; in the flood season the whole plain becomes a morass of sticky mud which is virtually impassable to land transport. Add to these circumstances considerations of the lack of roads, shortage of animals, carts, drivers, fodder and grazing—creating a situation whereby much of an animal's burden consisted of its own rations which had to be brought from India anyway—and the common denominator of Nixon's problems stands out: the means to travel on the rivers.

By this time the Commander-in-Chief was beginning to show signs of strain. He had been subjected to all the stresses which those in authority have to bear in times of crisis and he was not a young man. Never an easy person to get on with, because of his impatience and apparent arrogance toward those who questioned his wisdom, his temper now was even shorter, and his staff found him even less approachable than usual. But one aspect of his character had not changed. Though he was somewhat puzzled by the perverse turn that events had taken, he was doggedly determined to see the crisis through to its bitter end and he was not prepared to relinquish command until the British were once more on the way to Baghdad. The situation was a challenge to him—akin perhaps to the annoying reverse experienced sometimes when breaking in a horse; something had gone wrong—the Turks had managed to swing things in their favor for the moment but it was only a temporary phase. He was quite optimistic, but he was not up to the challenge. His health was deteriorating rapidly and his decision to hang on to the reins of command was injudicious—a judgment not of his personal motives, for he was a real soldier "grown gray in the service of his country,"[2] but of his ability to make the right decisions during those critical weeks.

Calculations as to how his ships and boats could best be organized occupied him and the minds of his staff constantly and persistently; to other problems solutions might be apparent, but not to this one. Up as far as Ctesiphon there had been just—and only just—the bare minimum of shipping sufficient to maintain Townshend's force in its advance. During the retreat some of the barges and steamers had been lost and those that were left were now working to the limit of their capacity. As has been said before, it was a problem which could be reduced to mathematical terms but until now the need to do so had never been quite so apparent. The parameters were simple: At any one time there were five ships going up the river, three coming down, four loading and twelve unloading. There was no time for any overhaul so that ships had to

---

2. *The Tragedy of Mesopotamia,* Sir George Buchanan, Blackwood, 1938.

work until they broke down and then be patched up; the round trip from Basra to Ali Gharbi and back took about ten days, not counting the time taken to load and unload, and this was a period which could double the estimated ten days. Without any reserves of craft available, no amount of shuffling or improvisation could change the basic fact that there were just not enough ships to concentrate a relief force quickly or to supply it properly when once it had assembled. "X" tons of supplies could be delivered, or "Y" numbers of men could be carried to the forward area; alternatively a varying combination of "X" and "Y" could be moved. The further the journey up river the longer it would take, so that unless the river fleet got more boats "X" and "Y" would diminish with an advance. Clearly there was an optimum size for the relief force; if it exceeded this size then it could not be fed properly and this is, in fact, what happened. More than six months were to elapse before the men at the front were on full rations and during the whole of this time the supply machinery was taxed almost to breaking point. If the front had been a hundred miles further upstream, either the men would have suffered dreadful privations, even worse than those that they did go through, or the force would have had to be reduced. More probably, of course, by a combination of British compromise and privations, economies would have resulted in a balance and a depleted and underfed army would have stood half as far up stream.

There was one faint ray of hope for the future. By now, both the British and Indian Governments were trying to find more ships. Half a dozen Thames steamers, forty flat-bottomed boats, six motor lighters and twenty small barges were promised from Britain; ten river steamers were to be provided from Egypt, and India, who had fortuitously "discovered" forty river steamers, was to send those. Yet it would be some time before any of them would be available. The steamers from Britain, which in happier summer days had taken gay, boozy, cockle and mussel eating crowds from London downstream to the seaside of Southend, or more sedate crowds upstream to Windsor, did not arrive until the end of May 1916. As they had not been designed for sea voyages and had come under their own steam it was a credit to their crews that they got to Basra at all. Their adventures on the way are redolent of Agatha Christie's *Ten Little Indians:* five arrived at Basra in January, three in February, fourteen in March and seven in April; seventeen foundered, and three were burnt en route. But this was the future. At the beginning of December the strength of the river flotilla exclusive of the impressed piratical-looking mahelas, was thirteen paddle steamers, three stern-wheelers, nine tugs, three screw-boats and fifty-seven barges. For the equivalent of more than four divisions—even for three if Kut were compelled to capitulate—the flotilla was still lamentably inadequate.

Nixon had returned to Basra on the same day as many of those who had been wounded at Ctesiphon finally reached the base. If he had had any doubts about the parlous state of his river transport the reports about their privations and journey were sufficiently convincing to make him think of alternatives. His mind now turned to the possibilities of marching men up to the front. So far the idea had been regarded as impractical because there was no proper road, but fortunately there had been some forward thinking by his staff and the building of a "raised" roadway[3] up the Shatt-al-Arab and along the right bank of the Tigris to Amara had already been started. By mid-December the newly arrived sappers of the 7th Division working at top speed had made a track fit for use—eleven bridges having been needed to carry it over otherwise impassable creeks. By sending only essential units up by steamer and marching the main body of the relief force to Amara along this road, Nixon reckoned that he might concentrate the Relief Force—the Tigris Corps as it was now known—much sooner than by attempting to lift it all forward by steamer. By doing so his boats could concentrate almost entirely on moving material and supplies. The troops faced ten days tough marching to Amara and four more to Ali Gharbi but this was the only way. The pressing need was for speed—speed in concentrating the Relief Force and speed in launching and effecting the breakthrough to Kut.

Meantime a distinguished Sapper officer, Lieutenant General Sir Fenton Aylmer, had been sent from India to command all British forces upstream of Ezra's Tomb, and in mid-December he disembarked at Basra. In 1891, as a captain he had won a well deserved Victoria Cross in a tough little, campaign on the North-West Frontier. Tribesmen holding a mountain stronghold stood across the route of a British punitive force and to get past them their fort had to be stormed. To do this meant blowing up the main gate and this was an extremely hazardous operation. Getting up to the gate of the Fort was fraught with danger but Aylmer succeeded in putting a guncotton charge against it; then, having lit the fuse he returned to safety, being wounded in the leg as he did so. However, the fuse went out and Aylmer went back to relight it; this time the charge went up, the fort was stormed and Aylmer took a very active part in the fight which ensued. Some years later as Major Aylmer, he had distinguished himself again at the relief of Chitral where Townshend had also made his name. Apart from the fact that he was a friend of Townshend and had cooperated with him before, on three counts—proven determination, bravery, and experience with a relief force—he seemed ideally suited to the

---

3. In Southern Mesopotamia no metalled roads existed; there were only tracks across the plain and ramps in the banks of canals.

task which lay ahead. In Amara, at the receiving end of Nixon's pipeline to the front, Aylmer set about marshalling and organizing his new command as best he could but, like everyone and everything else concerned with the campaign, he was beset with every conceivable confusion and difficulty.

Neither he, nor Younghusband, who by now had been promoted to command the veteran 7th Division, had a proper staff, and battalions and regiments were being sent forward piecemeal as and when they arrived in Basra. To the staff in Basra, getting fighting men up to the front was all that mattered and as battalions arrived and disembarked they were ordered straight up the line. Fighting men first, equipment second, "first line" transport next—if it was there, and if there was time; last of all ambulances and medical facilities. In December, Mesopotamian nights were bitterly cold and as a result of this policy most units' "second line" transport, carrying the kit and blankets had been left behind in Basra. Mesopotamia's initiation to unacclimatized troops promptly put a large number on the sick list. Many were inadequately equipped, some were badly trained and morale was not at its best. The country, the climate, and the conditions under which they were expected to fight were enough to grumble at anyway, and some troops even professed to be discontented at being relegated to a second-rate theater of war. They were not even sure what they were fighting for; nobody had told them, nobody thought it necessary to do so. One Punjabi soldier, fresh from France, is reputed to have said contemptuously, "It passeth my understanding why the British Government should desire this Satan-like land." Presumably in the absence of a cause he assumed he was being expected to fight to add another piece of Empire to the British Crown, and it hardly seemed worthwhile.

As might be expected with a composite force like this, thrown together, none of the brigades had worked or trained together as formations; some had trained to fight in France, others in Egypt, and the remainder on India's North-West Frontier. But it was clear that for whatever they were to do, there was the minimum of transport even in the field. There were plenty of animals and carts in Basra but the shortage of boats again decided what could accompany them to battle. As it was impossible to carry sufficient fodder up to the forward area it was useless taking animals up there in the first place; added to which, to get up country the carts would have needed considerable escorts to fend off the Buddhoos. Short of transport, ammunition, bridges, signaling equipment, doctors and medical stores—almost everything that a force needs to deal with a stiff-necked enemy, and lacking experience and cohesion—Aylmer's expedition like almost all other hastily improvised expeditions was foredoomed.

The plan to relieve Kut was a straightforward "filletting" advance up both banks of the Tigris when once the force, comprising Younghusband's 7th

Division, two independent infantry brigades, the 6th Cavalry Brigade and a miscellany of engineers and administrative units[4] had finally assembled. Gradually the heterogeneous, untried assembly of nineteen thousand men, 46 guns and two British airplanes collected together. Because of strong winds it was two days after Christmas before either of the aircraft could do any reconnaissance, and their first reports were that only about a hundred tents had been seen at Sheikh Sa'ad—thirty miles in front of Ali Gharbi, twenty from Kut as the crow flies. However, as each tent could only hold a maximum of twenty-five men this was encouraging information, since it would be presumed that there was no more than a Turkish brigade barring the way. But next day, when Townshend signaled from Kut to the effect that the bivouacs of a division of Turks could be seen on the left bank of the river three miles northeast of his Fort and that from prisoners he had learned that the Turkish 26th Division was moving up, the picture was less hopeful. "We have quite sufficient numbers here upon us as it is, without this extra division," he said. "I am sure you do not require my reasons for my serious anxiety on the score of any more reinforcements reaching the enemy. I hope, if you start on January 3, as I understand you do, that you will get here much sooner than January 10."

Townshend was forcing the pace; he was anxious that his garrison should not have to withstand another attack like that which had taken place on Christmas Day. As far as he was concerned the sooner Aylmer got started the better.

Aylmer, meantime, wanted to know how much cooperation he could expect from the Kut garrison. With the destruction of his boat bridge, the protective moat of the Tigris on three sides of Kut became a prison barrier which severely restricted Townshend's own freedom of action. Aylmer could see only too well that the garrison was handicapped by this fact, and that any attempt at a full scale break-out was foredoomed. Nevertheless, there were nearly nine thousand fighting men inside Kut and a force of this size ought to be able to make a sizeable contribution toward their own succor. It was not unreasonable to expect Townshend to help relief operations by making a sortie outward as Aylmer strove to batter a gap in the Turkish block which barred the way, though how much of an effort was to be put in really depended on Townshend. He took two days to reply to a query as to how much help Aylmer could expect. After reiterating the difficulties of getting troops across the river when he had only thirty mahelas, and no bridging material, Townshend said that he was prepared to make five thousand rifles and some of his guns available, *if necessary;* however, the rest of his signal showed that he was not

---

4. And two "provisional" battalions—one, made up of Dorset and Norfolk regimental details being known as the "Norsets"—formed from drafts waiting to join their units in Kut.

keen on the idea of participating at all. He was locked up and isolated in Kut because he had been ordered to stay there; it was up to others to get relief to him, as Nixon had promised. His job was to sit tight until that happened. What about the Russians who were supposed to be advancing toward Baghdad, he queried—hoping, no doubt, that their maneuvers in Persia would draw off some of the concentration of Turks surrounding him.

Aylmer, whose prime and correct concern was not to get involved in any premature advance which could only result in failure, sent a closely reasoned review of the situation to both Nixon and Townshend. In it he pointed out all the disadvantages of launching an ill-prepared and ill-timed operation. His conclusion was that it would be best if he undertook a methodical advance in force; risks would have to be accepted in coming to the assistance of the Kut garrison if it became imperative to do so, and he was quite ready to accept them. But there was a limit to advancing the date of the proposed advance without prejudicing the whole operation. Nixon concurred. Townshend, obviously disappointed at any suggestion of delay, made no direct reply. His indirect response was a signal to the effect that the incidence of self-inflicted wounds among the garrison and of sentries sleeping at their posts was increasing; that the Turks were calling on the Indian troops to overpower their officers and mutiny, and that seditious talk had been heard among his troops. Next day he followed up with another curiously perverse message that the Turks seemed to be turning the siege into a blockade: "Only in the case of dire necessity would an appeal be made for immediate assistance," he said. After his initial disappointment it seemed that he was now resigned to wait in Kut.

Meantime, at Ali Gharbi, the Buddhoos were hoping for pickings and Arab horsemen were hanging around the outskirts of the British camps. Two or three days before Christmas they had been joined by some Turkish cavalry, but they had not attempted to interfere with the concentration and except for a few shots fired into the camp at night, the relief force had been left unmolested. There was nothing to show their presence but it was then estimated that five Turkish divisions totaling about 22,500 men in all,[5] with about 72 guns—35 of which were modern quick-firing field guns—faced Aylmer. Most of this force was believed to be around Kut but there were some astride the Tigris in the Es Sinn position east of the town and it was expected that these would be the biggest obstacle to the break-in. If experience was anything to go by, so far as the locals were concerned, the Arabs in front of Ali Gharbi could be regarded

---

5. The 35th Division (2,500); 38th (2,500); 45th (3,500); 51st (6,500); 52nd (7,500). The 35th and 38th Divisions were mostly Arabs; the 45th had had 3,500 casualties at Ctesiphon; the 51st and 52nd were Turkish Divisions lately arrived in the country. This figure of 22,500 is at variance with the figure of 20,000 quoted in the Official History.

as hostile; those behind as neutral-hostile—if it is possible to be ostensibly friendly and hostile at the same time.

On January 3, Aylmer issued the orders to start the operation which it was hoped would take him on and in to Kut. Next day Younghusband's division, preceded by the Cavalry Brigade, were to start moving forward astride the river towards Sheikh Sa'ad, with the three gunboats *Dragonfly, Cranefly* and *Butterfly* keeping station with them on the river as they went forward. Aylmer with the rest of the troops would follow two days behind. At Sheikh Sa'ad itself the opposition was thought to be no more man an advance guard of the Turkish main force: 900 cavalry, 1,100 "camelry" and a battalion of infantry supported by only two light guns. The possibility of a division having moved up to the neighborhood from Kut had not been discounted, but the information available did not suggest that Younghusband would have any trouble in getting to Sheikh Sa'ad; it was really what was to happen afterward that was problematical. After Sheikh Sa'ad the objective would be Sannaiyat, fifteen miles further on. West of Sannaiyat lay the Sinn position where, just over three months previously, the Turks had held out before the first battle for Kut. Aylmer knew that getting to Sannaiyat was going to be no easy task. It meant advancing up either a narrow strip of land no more than a mile wide, separating the Tigris from the Suwaikiyeh Marsh on the left bank, or over extremely broken ground covered by the Sinn defenses on the other bank. It was apparent that after he got to Sheikh Sa'ad, Younghusband would have to feel his way forward cautiously. For the moment the important thing was to get started.

High winds and heavy rain prevented either of Aylmer's airplanes getting off the ground the day before the operation was to start, but from some of the local Arabs it was learned that there were about 4,000 Turkish infantry in and around Sheikh Sa'ad, and that Arab and Turkish cavalry were patrolling both banks of the river. It was also rumored that many more Turks were encamped behind Sheikh Sa'ad—near the stream, known as the Wadi, on the left bank of the Tigris. Next day, when a message came in from Townshend to say that two Turkish divisions had been seen marching past Kut during the night, some substance was lent to this intelligence; as they had made no attempt to attack Kut they were, in Townshend's view, making for the very position Aylmer was about to attack. A little later there was another signal to say that not only had another large mixed column of infantry, artillery and cavalry been seen to march east past Kut but that it was quite obvious that the Turkish camps around the town were getting smaller as tents were being struck and their occupants departing. The inference was clear; the Turks had decided to move to meet the threat which Aylmer was now presenting and the pressure on Kut was diminishing.

After a late start, occasioned by the same bad weather which had prevented the aircraft taking off, Younghusband's columns started to advance
toward Sheikh Sa'ad on the morning of the 4th. Apart from some sniping and
an occasional hit-and-run foray by the Arab cavalry and Buddhoos, who were
moving on a parallel course to the columns just out of small arms range, they
met no opposition and Younghusband made slow methodical progress toward
his first objective. By nightfall his men had reached a point only about five
miles from the village; they camped and prepared to set off again the following
morning. At the same time Aylmer was now receiving a mass of conflicting information, most of which was extremely gloomy. That morning his airmen had
at last been able to take off and when they got back from their reconnaissance
it was to report having seen great activity around Sheikh Sa'ad. Soon afterward
word came from Townshend to the effect that a five mile column of Turks
which would comprise about 8,000 men was moving down the left bank of the
river and that nearly all the camps opposite Kut had disappeared. Later that
morning, however, other and more welcome intelligence information came in
from GHQ. According to those in Basra, agents had reported that Nur-Ud-
Din had about 30,000 men and 40 guns around Kut, that most of these were
Arabs and that reports of Turkish troops moving down toward the battlefield
could be dismissed as there rumors. However this news had scarcely been
digested before it was shown to be completely false. An airman flew over the
Turkish lines at midday and when he got back, he reported having seen what
he estimated was more than ten thousand men in and around Sheikh Sa'ad and
trenches on both sides of the Tigris. Younghusband was inclined to scoff at the
idea of the trenches having any significance, but there could be only one real
conclusion: the Turks were going to stand and fight. Younghusband was confident that once his men made contact the Turks would retire; his optimism
probably reflected the prevailing optimism of his men. They were British; those
in front were Turks; it was just a matter of clearing them out of the way. However, Aylmer did not share his confidence and he had no wish to run the risk of
being held up at Sheikh Sa'ad, as might well happen if the place were assaulted
by a force insufficient to deliver a hammer blow in the first instance. He felt it
would pay to make haste slowly. Younghusband was ordered to "hold the
enemy in their positions," pending the arrival of the rest of the Corps next day
and to get a bridge across the Tigris as far forward and as close as possible to
the enemy positions. This would enable reserves to be switched from one bank
to the other according to where the enemy was weakest. A signal was also sent
to Nixon, suggesting that deceptive moves by Gorringe's troops around
Nasireyeh might help to divert the Turks and provide a further safeguard. If
Gorringe were to advance up the Shatt-al-Hai it was possible that they would

be deluded into thinking relief for Kut was coming from that direction, and troops be diverted to meet the new threat which would otherwise be deployed against the real relief force. Nixon agreed with this plan and Gorringe was ordered to advance. Messages referring to the move were signaled to Townshend in a cipher which would easily be broken by the Turks. In any event there is little reason to suppose that the Turks were deceived or, if they were, that it made any difference.

Once again it must be stressed that in the minds of both generals the overriding factor was the necessity for speed, since their information at this juncture was that the garrison had full rations to last only until the end of January. What is more, as Aylmer's moves had apparently drawn off a large proportion of the Turks surrounding Townshend, something had been achieved already; at least the possibility of a successful attack being made on the town was now remote. But this was not enough; to relieve Kut a gap had to be punched through the Turkish lines. And this was not going to be easy. The means to accomplish it were of dubious worth, and blind precipitancy was not going to get through to Townshend. The Tigris Corps was untrained, many of its units hardly knew each other; few of them even knew their leaders. The supporting services—signals in particular—had all been improvised and were learning as they went, so that Aylmer had good reason to heed the Arab proverb, "Hurry, hurry, hath no blessing."

As Younghusband's advance guard approached Sheikh Sa'ad, two alternatives seemed open. He could leave a holding force on the left bank of the Tigris and concentrate everything else into smashing the Turks on the right bank where they seemed to be weakest, pinning them into the bend of the river which contained the village. They could be annihilated so that the troops on the far bank, supported by fire from the village, could press their attack, or, alternatively, a simultaneous attack up both banks was possible. In any event, this was the method that was adopted. The ever present requirement for speed being the main factor in Younghusband's decision to decide on what may seem to be the more conventional method. But, by simultaneously dislodging the Turks on both banks he hoped that they would not be able to stand again in front of Kut and, once on the run, Townshend's relief would be only a matter of days. Whether Aylmer's orders to Younghusband on how to conduct the opening phases of the battle were as clear as they might have been is a matter for conjecture. Loose phrases like those used today of "leaning on the enemy" are often dramatically expressive in the context in which they are used; equally they often cover a vague purpose and this was a case where an ill-defined intention was to lead to difficulties.

For the attack Younghusband's troops were more or less evenly apportioned to the two banks of the river. Brigadier General Rice's 35th Brigade was to attack on the left, Major General Kemball's 28th Brigade along the right; the rest of the division would march behind Rice on the left bank and constitute the reserve. Younghusband himself would move in the gunboat *Gadfly* at the head of the flotilla bringing up the baggage, stores and reserves of ammunition. In the rear was the old steamer *Julnar* which had been earmarked for duty as a hospital ship.

The British camp was shot up during the night but the disturbance did not interfere with preparations for the forthcoming battle. However, during the night a thick mist descended and this upset the timetable. The Cavalry Brigade, which was to operate on Kemball's left, cantered out into the fog about 8:30 a.m. and half an hour later the 28th Brigade moved off in two parallel columns; before the mist lifted it had covered four miles without anything untoward happening. Then, in a half haze before the backdrop of a mirage which formed as the wisps of mist dispersed, the long line of trenches which formed the Turkish front line came into view about two miles ahead. Behind them a mass of cavalry could also be distinguished forming up. The brigade shook out into extended formation and began to advance once more with the right of the line following the river bank. The Turks were alive to the attack now and as the British line continued to move steadily forward there was the whistle and crash of exploding shells and a rattle of small arms fire, the volume and direction of which indicated that the trenches extended much further than the air reconnaissance reports had suggested. As they felt for the Turkish flank, and reached toward the cavalry the British were gradually compelled to edge further and further outward from the river. A sudden threat developed when it was seen that some Turkish camelmen, with parties of the ubiquitous Buddhoos, were trying to slip around their left and get in behind Kemball's men. By 3:30 p.m. there were enormous gaps in the thin, khaki-clad British line, and although the forward troops had reached positions about five hundred yards from the Turks' trenches, it was becoming obvious that little further progress was going to be achieved in the remaining couple of hours before the sun set.

In similar flat and featureless terrain, utterly devoid of cover, Rice had fared no better. His men's first intimation of the enemy positions came when the advance guard was shot up from trenches less than three hundred yards away. They had been led on to them by "friendly" Arabs, who escaped toward the Turks when the firing broke out. By the middle of the afternoon the attack which Rice promptly put in when this happened was held up. Not only had he lost a lot of men in the action but it had been found virtually impossible to pin-point exactly where the wily Turks actually were. Wherever they were, one thing was clear: they were fighting back hard all along the line. Even the flotilla had been engaged and the ships had had their moments dodging mines floated down from Sheikh Sa'ad; there had been plenty of scares but fortunately none of the ships was damaged. With both Kemball and Rice heavily engaged, it was a stalemate and Young-husband decided to call it a day. The brigades were ordered to break off the action and dig in where they were. And this was the point where the misinterpretation of Aylmer's original orders bedeviled the future of the operation; Younghusband's idea of "holding the enemy in their positions" had committed the Corps Commander to a course of action from which there was no turning back.

Aylmer did not learn what had happened until after dark. While he had been marching up with the two brigades which formed the remainder of his force, signal communications had broken down—the break-down occurring once again as a result of shortages. However, about 9 p.m. a message came in from Younghusband telling him of the failure, that it was proposed to renew the attack next morning and that a bridge was being thrown across the river in accordance with the original plan. Aylmer seems to have been more astounded than disappointed and the message brought a swift reaction. Younghusband was ordered to meet the Corps Commander at the bridge soon after first light next morning and not to get involved in any serious action until Aylmer had seen the situation for himself.

Mention must now be made of the bridge, since its existence was about the only advantage which the British enjoyed—giving, as it did, a degree of mobility not available to the Turks, for they did not have a bridge across the Shatt-al-Hai until early February and had to cross the rivers in rafts and small boats. By modern standards the British bridge was but a poor thing, built of country boats of poor wood and awkward design, which were apt to collapse and precipitate whatever was crossing at the time into the Tigris. Even after fourteen months of war in Mesopotamia nothing better was available but it served its purpose until wrecked by high winds and the swollen river. Had its true potential been realized—if Aylmer had appreciated the advantages of being able to switch his troops from one bank to the other at will—it might have played a more decisive role in the forthcoming battle.

The morning of January 7 was hot, foggy and humid, as it had been on the previous day. It was the rainy season and everyone expected a downpour which would at least have relieved the oppressive atmosphere. Younghusband's men had been soaked to the skin by a thunderstorm in the early hours, but by noon when the intense heat had dispersed the fog, no rain had fallen and conditions for a battle were about as bad as they could be. The mist could have been the one opportunity for the attack to have been renewed on the right bank but Aylmer's orders of the night before precluded this and it was not until the afternoon that the troops again deployed for action. Meantime, the generals had met as arranged. While they conferred, the cavalry supporting Rice's brigade on the left bank reported that a couple of Turkish battalions and a force of cavalry were apparently trying to work their way round the British flank. Rice's Territorial Sussex gunners, who had been battering away at the Turkish trenches to their front, swung their 15-pounders around to meet the threat and fired salvos at this party. This was too much for the Turks who smartly turned about and made off back to their lines. The threat had been averted and Aylmer decided that his only course was a concerted attack on both banks. The plan of action which proposed that the attack should start at noon was explained to the brigade commanders at 11 a.m. On the left bank, where the Turkish defenses lay at right angles to the river with an outflanking trench flung far out to the right, Rice would "hold." Meanwhile Dennys, with the weak 19th Brigade (the Seaforths and the 125th Napier's Rifles and a company of 28th Punjabis) would sweep around Rice's right and, with the help of the 16th Cavalry, roll up the Turkish left flank. Norie's 21st Brigade (Black Watch, 6th Jats, 9th Bhopals and 41st Dogras) would follow Dennys and act as the reserve. Simultaneously, once the attack was ready to go in on the left bank, Kemball, with his own brigade and the 92nd Punjabis, was to advance "vigorously" and the Cavalry Brigade would try to help him forward. Behind Kemball, Major General R. G. Egerton's 9m Brigade and the 62nd Punjabis would constitute the reserve on his side of the river and this reserve would be controlled by the Corps Commander himself.

The attack on the left bank was complicated by the fact that no one on the British side yet knew quite where the Turkish trenches were, or indeed how far they extended. The Turks were adept at digging and concealing their positions, and both the flat ground and the mirage were to their advantage. Afterward, it was seen that their front line on Rice's side of the river ran for more than three miles from it, being connected by elaborate communication trenches to other reserve and flanking positions aimed at stopping any attempts to get around behind their front. In such circumstances a concentrated artillery pounding would have helped to even the odds. But the amount of artillery support that the British infantry could expect was ludicrously small—and not merely by Second World War standards—for it was only about a tenth of the support expected in comparable conditions in France at that time. In Mesopotamia the number of guns was inadequate and their types, in terms of performance and weight of shells which could be delivered, were generally inferior. Furthermore, in shooting at a series of barely located and hidden positions the gunners invariably suffered another disadvantage, often exacerbated by the mirage. Consequently the British infantry usually had to assault trenches which had not been touched by shellfire and whose exact location was only spotted when they saw the glint of Turkish bayonets. This is how it was on the left bank of the Tigris on the morning of January 7, 1916.

The Seaforths and the 125th Napier's Rifles of Dennys' 19th Brigade set off about noon and there was no opposition as they swung out to develop their turning movement. However, two hours later they had swung so far north that the gap opening between them and the 35th Brigade was becoming perilously wide. Spotting the inherent dangers of this gap one of Younghusband's staff officers galloped over to Norie and told him to get his 21st Brigade forward. Norie's men had halted and had started to cook a meal, so it was anything but a popular order. Nevertheless the Black Watch and 6th Jats quickly shook out into extended formations and moved up. The same staff officer then galloped across to Dennys and instructed him to wheel to the left, march forward a thousand yards and then attack. The method of giving the orders as well as the tactics themselves might seem to be reminiscent of a bygone age, more suited to a battlefield of the Napoleonic wars, but they were ordered in the belief that the Turkish flank had already been passed. As events were to show, Dennys had been turned inward before the limit of the Turks' defenses had been reached.

The men of both brigades plodded stolidly on until, out of the haze and less than a mile away, Turks could be seen digging away feverishly. But not for long, and soon bullets from positions on both flanks were singing through the ranks of the leading British troops and shells were crashing down among them. Without any artillery support of their own and facing in two directions the British had no option but to close with the enemy as quickly as possible. In the center, the Black Watch who had come virtually straight through from Marseilles, and had marched up the twenty-two miles from Ali Gharbi only the previous day, doubled forward with the Jats but they were finally and irrevocably checked about three or four hundred yards from the enemy line. The Turks had held their fire until they and Dennys' men on their right had reached a killing ground where their concentrated fire would have most effect. Highlanders and Indians alike tried gallantly to break through to the Turkish line but there was nothing to cover their gallant rushes forward and nothing could stand up to the hail of lead. Casualties were appalling and men who had been at Loos said that the rifle fire was more deadly than anything they had ever experienced on the Western Front. The Seaforths alone lost 20 officers and 380 men in this action. Of the 485 Jats who had gone into the battle, only 150 came out. 6

While the fighting was going on the Turks made another attempt to en-circle the whole of the British right. Turkish infantry and Arab horsemen were seen to be maneuvering toward the 16th Cavalry who were on the far flank and Dennys, who could not ignore the danger, was compelled to swing the small reserve and five of his brigade machine guns towards them while Norie, to whom Dennys appealed for help, rushed the 41st Dogras and 9th Bhopals up to prolong the line. The threat was averted when the British artillery got into action on this front and concentrated salvos from guns of two howitzer batteries, together with the two guns of the 104th Heavy Battery on the bank of the Tigris, and the 4-inch gun of the *Cranefly* superimposed on that of two field batteries eventually took effect. The Turkish attempt fizzled out as it had done the day before, with the flight of the Arab horsemen. But the Turkish infantry settled down and holed up about four hundred yards from the line which the British had hastily established. The immediate crisis had been overcome but the danger was not past, since an air reconnaissance reported even more Turks and Arabs in large numbers out on this flank. This new enemy made no further attempt to attack. Nevertheless the situation on the left bank that night was insecure and unsatisfactory.

Kemball on the other bank had done better. His attack had opened about 2:30 p.m. when the 92nd Punjabis had got into a position level with his own brigade. Then the whole line had risen and pushed home a vigorous attack which, by 4 p.m. had carried the Turks' forward positions. In the center, the 51st Sikhs were the first to gain a foothold in the enemy trenches; on their right the 53rd Sikhs and 56th Rifles showed the same élan as they had done so many times previously on the North-West Frontier, as part of the old Punjab Frontier Force. On the left, the actions of the Leicester's proved that they had lost nothing of their reputation for dash and fearlessness gained in France, but they lost 16 officers and 298 men in the course of the day. Six hundred prisoners were taken during that day, and next morning more than 350 Turks were buried. But the cost had been heavy—more than a thousand casualties in the 28th Brigade alone. And the Turks were not beaten yet. Attempts to press further on toward Sheikh Sa'ad were met with such a murderous fire from their second line and support trenches that by nightfall Kemball decided it was suicidal to press on any further, and to hold on to what he had won so far.

The wet cold night which followed passed reasonably quietly. The men— British and Indian alike—were tired out. It was just as well that as they dug to improve the trenches, searched for their wounded, replenished their ammunition and snatched a hasty meal, the Turks did little except maintain a desultory rifle fire. Next day was again extremely hot and the mirage returned—acting as a magnifying glass to distort and enlarge objects and movements—so that it was one of conflicting reports. The cavalry on both banks brushed with Arab horsemen during the morning; otherwise, except for sniping, there was little activity, and by the middle of the morning Kemball had concluded that the Turks were pulling out. Aylmer, told of this, was inclined to be cautious—and with considerable justification. His information was that there were 7,500 Turks on the left bank and another 4,500 on the right. He believed that his original plan to capture the Sheikh Sa'ad loop, from where the positions on the left bank could be enfiladed, still offered most promise. However, since his troops were sorely in need of both food and rest, the best way of continuing the advance now seemed to be by a night attack, and both Younghusband and Kemball were told to make their preparations accordingly.

While the generals were busying themselves considering the next move, water and rations were sent up the line to the troops and efforts were made to collect those of the wounded who still lay on the battlefield. During the course of the action the walking wounded had limped down toward the Red Cross flag on the river bank, where, possibly with some thoughts of conditions in France in mind, they had visions of relief from pain, clean dressings, hot tea, sleep and other comforts, followed perhaps by a smooth cruise back to a base hospital where doctors and pretty nurses would be ready with all the latest surgical equipment. If so, they were to be sadly disappointed. At the ambulance unit where the Red Cross flag flew, there were but three doctors and one assistant, and, by 10 p.m. on the night of the 6m, more wounded had assembled man they could cope with. Over a thousand casualties—many of them serious—lay in serried ranks, cold, miserable and disillusioned, and gradually this crowd spread along the bank as others poured in. The situation was even worse man it had been at Ctesiphon. The three doctors did all that was humanly possible but within a few hours, they were reduced to dealing with only the more serious cases. It was just not possible for them to cope with the tide of broken humanity. The five field ambulances of Younghusband's division were still on the high seas; provision had been made for only about 250 casualties[6] and when the time came these arrangements had to cater for over 4,000.

The British soldiers soon came to realize that something had gone very wrong. Although this did not make their plight any easier it did help them to accept the situation more philosophically than the Indians, who just could not understand that the Sirkar's arrangements had broken down. Pathetic bundles of humanity lay on the river bank clutching at the feet of anyone who walked

---

6. At Sheikh Sa'ad No. 20 Combined Field Ambulance (110 beds), two sections of No. 3 Field Ambulance (50 beds), four improvised field ambulance sections on the left bank and a cavalry ambulance converted to a clearing hospital made up the total hospital accommodation; all the units were short of men—qualified doctors in particular. No. 20 Field Ambulance took in more than 1,900 casualties during the three days (January 6–9, 1916).

past imploring: "Water, sahib, water"; "Sahib, sahib, the blood will not stop ... a blanket, sahib, a blanket, sahib . . ." after the manner of the beggars who roamed Bombay and Calcutta. As they waited for treatment their wounds became septic, gangrene set in and many died even before they could be carried on to the boats that were to evacuate them downstream to the already congested hospital at Amara. Then, when those who survived were finally carried on to the few overcrowded boats, many died for lack of attention en route, for few doctors could be spared for the voyage.

Eleven days after the battle, a field ambulance hospital unit from Meerut on its way to the front found nearly 200 British and 800 Indians, still lying on the muddy ground behind Sheikh Sa'ad. Only a few had had the first field dressings applied on the battlefield changed; over 100 were suffering from dysentery; there were no proper sanitary arrangements and those unable to walk lay in their film, past caring and without hope. Sacks of food had been dumped in the open for their sustenance, but much which was perishable had been ruined by rain; what was edible was hardly enough to go around. As there were only one or two cooks, and few of the miserable casualties could help themselves, its availability was of little consequence. Happily, the medical officer in charge of the field ambulance decided to halt and set up his hospital then and there, but it was a month before hospital tents and operating equipment arrived from Basra.

The men on the spot cannot be blamed for misery and suffering which amounted to criminal neglect. The doctors and medical staff worked until they dropped; there just were not enough of them nor did they have the equipment and stores which were so vital. The number of fighting troops had been increased out of all proportion to the services which accompany them in normal circumstances; the resources of the country were totally insufficient and they had not been augmented by supplies from India. Yet when the public in Britain eventually became aware of what was happening the Indian Government plaintively expressed surprise. "We never refused Mesopotamia anything on financial grounds" a government spokesman said from the comfort of Simla, and it was implied that Nixon and his staff were at fault for not insisting on more: "They never asked." The reply might have been "It was no good asking when nothing was ever forthcoming." The real fault lay in the system. The Army in India had been starved for so long that its commanders had lost the habit of asking—an argument which applied to other items besides those associated with the medical service. Under such circumstances it is difficult to judge who should have been indicted: those who failed to ask or those who failed to provide.

Yet the system cannot be wholly blamed for the disasters associated with this attempt to relieve Kut. Much of it was due to the dilemma of those faced with the need to come quickly to the aid of Townshend's beleaguered force. Once Kut was surrounded time seemed to be of vital consequence; omelets are not made without breaking eggs; in war, risks have to be taken and the pressing need was to get a force on the ground, moving up to Kut before Townshend's supplies ran out. Throughout the operations of the next three months one question hangs in the background like a habitual ghost. Townshend had implied that his force was in dire peril; but was there justification for the blind haste that followed his first *crie du coeur?*

Back on the battlefield Younghusband had decided to shuffle his units around, in order to rest those who had been most pressed in the two days fighting, and to have ready the units he needed for the forthcoming night attack. The Seaforths and the 125th Napier's Rifles fell back to be relieved by men of the 21st Brigade who in turn were to take over from Rice's 35th Brigade. It was late in the afternoon before Dennys' brigade had been collected together, and as darkness fell a strong wind brought rain. In the bitterly cold night everyone was soon soaked and before long the guides lost their way. In the darkness the brigade marched and countermarched through clinging mud throughout the night and when eventually they arrived at the 35th Brigade's bivouacs they were utterly exhausted, too tired even to curse and blaspheme, in the way of soldiers, against their sorry lot. And, as it subsequently turned out, much of the preparation was unnecessary since the Turks were withdrawing. Cavalry, reconnoitering routes for the night attack on the right bank, saw that many of the Turkish trenches were empty, and wounded men were limping away from the village of Sheikh Sa'ad. On the left bank Turkish cavalry could also be seen moving west. The opposition had crumbled and during the afternoon of January 9, Kemball occupied the village and the trenches in front of Norie's brigade.

Nobody quite understood why the Turks had decided to retire. The primary reason was the same factor as that which limited the British: transport. With the river blocked at Kut, Nur-Ud-Din had the utmost difficulty supplying his troops; his men were hungry and prisoners taken by the British during the action complained that they had not eaten for three days. Hungry or not, they had fought stubbornly enough—more so than in any of the battles up to Ctesiphon—and they had held off the relief force. By doing so they had made Aylmer pay a costly price for every inch of ground he had won. And they had gained time. The relief force was ten miles closer to Kut but over 4,000 men had been lost; only if tins had been the decisive battle could the cost be considered worthwhile. Time was to show that it was not.

Chapter 9

The Black Month: January 1916

The way the Turks had fought at Sheikh Sa'ad came as an unexpected and unpleasant surprise to Nixon. His problem now was whether he should permit Aylmer to go on trying to force a way through to Kut, or to wait until the reinforcements he was rushing up to the front could be garnered into a force which would make a breakthrough inevitable. As is usual in war, time was the decisive factor and one which Nixon did not consider was on his side. If Aylmer waited until he had a better balanced and numerically superior force, not only would Townshend's supplies be running down but the Turks would be able to strengthen their positions in front of Aylmer and bring up troops who could be used either to overwhelm Townshend or block the Relief Force. The fact that the weather was deteriorating and that a delay would give the Russian thrust an opportunity to develop were sound and cogent reasons for taking things slowly and methodically, but the critical point at issue was whether or not the garrison in Kut could hold out. Morally, it was difficult to resist Townshend's initial appeal, and although since making it he had said that he would not ask for help unless he was in real trouble it was obvious that he would be in trouble once the limit of his two months' rations was reached. Viewed in this light, the approach of bad weather lent weight to the argument for moving before it could get worse. Furthermore, even if Nixon were prepared to stay his hand, pressure from Delhi and London to get the mess in Mesopotamia sorted out quickly and decisively forced the pace.

These were compelling reasons enough, but there was another factor which was relevant. None of the arguments took into account Nixon's own personality. He was not a man with the Nelson or the Drake touch, but he was supremely optimistic—it was his optimism which had urged Townshend on, almost to Baghdad. A year's experience in Mesopotamia had convinced him that as soon as any pressure was put on the Turks they would bolt—an idea which was an extension of the old theory that the British would always win once they put their minds to it. Unfortunately for the British at this stage of the campaign, circumstances had changed, and his estimate of Turkish fighting efficiency was very, very wrong. Had he but realized it, his experience was of Turkish-led Arab troops; Osmanlis—many of them veterans flushed with their success at Gallipoli—well organized and well led, now faced Aylmer. If, previously, Townshend's division had never failed to breakthrough, as the yesmen on Nixon's staff constantly reminded him, then it was largely because in the main they had only been up against raw troops—there Buddhoos in fact. It was all very different now, as the troops fresh from France quickly appreciated. Unless the British had numerical superiority backed by equivalent superiority in guns, or were prepared to accept a prohibitive sacrifice, it was physically impossible to attack across open ground against machine guns in the hands of well-disciplined troops. They had learned this lesson the hard way on the Western Front, but it was one of the new parameters of modern warfare which neither Nixon nor his staff had appreciated. Nixon's basic miscalculation was in regarding the Turk as a second-class enemy and in relying solely on the gallantry of the British and Indian troops. He was hopelessly out of date. Neither he, nor his staff, appreciated that his new troops, blooded in France, worked differently; there was still gallantry but they tended to react in the ways they had learned on the Western Front. When these men came up against a determined enemy who was sweeping open ground which had to be crossed with murderous fire, from trenches which more often than not were invisible beyond a few hundred yards, their reaction was to stop and dig in. To those who had served only on the Frontier and in Mesopotamia this behavior was extraordinary; there could only be one explanation: the new troops were "trench-minded," lacking in spirit and the old qualities which had proved so successful till now.

In Sheikh Sa'ad, Aylmer had a more realistic picture than Nixon. With rain turning the ground into a quagmire, hampered by the chaotic supply conditions caused by the shortage of boats on the river, his men tired, he was under no illusions about the fact that he would have to fight every inch of the way to

Kut. In a signal, he put the situation- succinctly and clearly to Nixon on January 13:

> After consulting Generals Younghusband (commanding 7th Division) and Kemball, I have determined to continue the advance on Kut; but it is my distinct duty to point out that it is a most precarious undertaking, for which I, of course, accept full responsibility, as I consider that the situation demands a supreme effort to relieve Townshend. The Army Commander has full figures of the enemy's strength, and possibly 4,000 may be allowed for his losses and desertions at Sheikh Sa'ad. My fighting strength amounts to about 10,000. The enemy is reported by local inhabitants as occupying a position in advance of Es Sinn at the narrowest part between the Suwada and Suwaikiyeh marshes. This will probably be continued with an advanced line from near Clery's post to the river. My medical establishments, as you may calculate, are deplorably low and the wounded cannot receive proper attention. Even if it is necessary to remove fighting men from the ships more must be sent up at once. I have only one aeroplane in action. On the other hand I have the greatest confidence that the troops will do what is humanly possible—and I know that the enemy's Arab troops are much demoralized.

Nixon's sanguine reply, telegraphed from the comparative comfort of Basra showed that he was not a prey to the anxieties oppressing Aylmer and was as optimistic as ever:

> I must leave the matter to your decision. Am confident that you and the fine troops under your command will achieve your object.

Adding that four more battalions would shortly reach the front and that four more could be quickly sent up river if Aylmer could spare the ships, he concluded rather naively:

> Meanwhile, however, the enemy will be strengthening his position. You are as well informed as I am as regards the enemy's possible reinforcements.

Nobody knew better than Aylmer that the Turks would be strengthening their positions and that they were getting reinforcements. So did his men. Rumors of four Turkish divisions coming down from Aleppo, one of which was supposed to be arriving at the front within the next fortnight, had been circulating for over a month. In and around Baghdad there were probably about thirty thousand Turks at that juncture but within a fortnight, if there was anything in the rumors, that number would be doubled. Nixon, who was in touch with Baratoff by wireless, had suggested that the Russian column advancing on Kermanshah would help to take the pressure off the Tigris. But Kermanshah was over 200 miles away from Baghdad so whatever contribution Baratoff and his Russians could make would best be regarded as pie in the sky.

On the immediate front around Kut, the British and Turks seemed to be about evenly matched. In round figures Aylmer had 10,000 infantry, 1,500 cavalry and 46 guns, including a newly arrived howitzer battery. Townshend inside Kut could still muster 8,500 fighting men, so that for the attack, relief and defence of Kut there was a force of about 20,000, Approximately the same strength as that of the Turks investing Kut. Four more battalions—those which Nixon had referred to—were steaming up the Tigris to join Aylmer however; another four were either in Basra or marching up toward him and further reinforcements with more guns were known to be at sea. Physically Aylmer's men were far from being in the peak of condition; apart from being tired, their confidence had taken a severe knock as a consequence of the battle they had just fought. The morale of the Turks, on the other hand, was presumably in a sorrier state if only because they had lost the battle but, if there was any truth in the rumors, the balance should soon incline in their favor. Certainly the weather was on their side.

Once the rainy season set in—and the first rains had already fallen—the whole countryside would be turned into a slough of sticky, clinging mud, making any British advance across the plain toward Kut very difficult. By March, when the rivers, swollen by the melting snows in the highlands of Armenia and Persia, flooded the plains, the road up the bank of the Tigris would be impassable; what is more, if the Turks cut the dykes controlling the canals above Baghdad, even larger areas of the country would be inundated. Not that these factors really counted for anything; if it had not been relieved by March everyone believed that the garrison in Kut would have eaten its last rations and fired its last shots.

The rumor that a fresh Turkish division was shortly expected to make its appearance on the Tigris front was well-founded, and after the battle of Sheikh Sa'ad Nur-Ud-Din had decided to fight a delaying action in order to gain time for it to reach him. But his order to withdraw was one that earned him the sack and on von der Goltz's orders he was superseded by Khalil Pasha.- The new commander, realizing that the British were not following up, promptly stopped the retirement of his troops, faced about and dug in along the line of the Wadi, a steep-banked stream on the left bank of the Tigris. The real significance of this position lay in the fact that it was three and a half miles east of the strip of land known as the Hanna defile, separating the Tigris from the Suwaikiyeh marsh, and it was one which might have afforded an ideal opportunity for a British success. If Aylmer's troops could get around behind the Wadi and seize this defile between marsh and river, the whole Turkish force would be ensnared. Aylmer saw his chance and to Nixon and Townshend he signaled his intention of moving around the left flank. That he had great faith in the outcome of this operation may be deduced from his words "... I hope to give him [Khalil and the Turks] a good beating." At Sheikh Sa'ad the Turks had shown plenty of dogged tenacity but little enterprise and consequently his plan for defeating them here at the Wadi had considerable merit. Its success however depended on two important factors: surprise, and a determination to push the battle through to a successful conclusion with the utmost vigor. Failure to meet either of these two conditions could only result in the Turks escaping to the Hanna defile which would present a far worse defensive nut to crack than the Wadi position. And so it was to prove.

Three main causes contributed to the miscarriage of Aylmer's plan: insufficient troops being available for the enveloping move around the flank; the artillery crossing the Wadi too late—so holding up the advance for several hours; and finally, the fact that the only maps the British possessed were inaccurate with the consequence that nobody knew anything about the ground which had to be crossed. Of these, the last was undoubtedly the direct cause of the failure. Events were to show that the troops could have closed the rings and that the lost time might have been made good; the real difficulty was that nobody knew quite where he was.

Kemball's 28th Brigade was detailed for the frontal attack. This was merely supposed to "hold" the Turks while the main force, under Younghusband, comprising the 21st, 19th and 35th Brigades, circled around behind them. The cavalry brigade, under Roberts, was to "operate" on Younghusband's outer flank but as they were not given any definite orders about what exactly they were supposed to do, their operation degenerated into a swan. January 12th was given over to preparing for the battle and there was plenty of time for reconnaissance, although little benefit seemed to come out of it. Apart from a few huts, some ruins and a walled enclosure known as Chitab's Fort, the ground which was to become the battlefield appeared to have little to differentiate it from the rest of the countryside. On all sides the empty dun-colored landscape which stretched monotonously to the horizon was broken only by small banks and shallow irrigation channels. For the British these cuts would afford cover from fire; for the Turks they served effectively to conceal trenches and weapon pits. Near the Tigris and the Wadi there were deeper dry canals which would provide the attackers with covered avenues of approach. Since the maps conveyed nothing, the British officers assumed that their troops would have little difficulty getting across the Wadi.

That night it was cold, but at least it did not rain; there was a heavy dew and the moon was in the second quarter as Younghusband's infantry and the cavalry formed up and moved off toward the Turkish flank. By 1 a.m. the cavalry had reached the position from which Roberts reckoned he would start out in the morning and they off-saddled and settled down to snatch a few hours sleep. Meantime the three brigades of infantry—a thousand yards apart in line of battalions, with each battalion in column—continued to march for another three hours before they were in position; the 35th Brigade was on the right, the 19th in the middle and the 21st on the left. When dawn broke a thick mist shrouded the area; one might have expected this to be regarded as a god-send but apparently it was not looked upon as such, and the start of the operation proper was delayed to give it time to clear. Nevertheless, by 9 a.m. Roberts' men had splashed across the Wadi and driven off the Turkish cavalry they encountered on the far side. The leading infantry were not far behind but the banks of the stream were much steeper than had been anticipated and, to get the guns and wheeled transport across, the pioneers had to dig ramps on both sides. All this took time—the one thing that could least be afforded. Consequently it was nearly 1 p.m. before the artillery was over, and some of the transport was not across until nightfall.

Norie's 21st Brigade, the first across the Wadi, started out as soon as they had collected on the far bank and, with the 1st/9th Gurkhas leading, headed northwest straight for the Hanna defile. But by 11 a.m. shells from a couple of Turkish guns, which could be seen quite clearly in the distance, and the concentrated fire of Turkish small arms brought them to a halt; while the leading companies of Gurkhas dug in about two hundred yards from the Turks the rest of the brigade edged off to the right. Seeing Norie was held up, the battalions of the 19th Brigade coming up behind also veered off to the right. So far, so good; this was in accordance with the plan to get around behind the Turks and strike down the Tigris. But, having got to the flank there was a pause—a pause which was to prove fatal. Once in position the infantry could have attacked much sooner than they did but both brigades were ordered to wait until the artillery was ready to support them, and it was 1 p.m. before the guns were across the Wadi. Why the guns had to cross the stream is anything but clear; they could have bombarded the Turks' trenches just as well from behind it. However, when eventually they did come into action, the infantry assault went in and within half an hour the battalions of the 21st Brigade on the left were struggling with Turks, lining a low bank which ran between the Wadi and the marsh, as well as the trenches which faced the Wadi. Only two battalions of the 19th Brigade had been committed to this first assault but within the hour they too were closely engaged. It was a hard fight but gradually the 19th Brigade gained ground and Turks were seen to be scurrying away from their positions. Seeing this, Younghusband promptly concluded that he had almost cut off the

Turks at the Wadi from the Hanna bottleneck. In his view, they were sand-wiched between his men and those of Kemball; all that had to be done now was for his other brigade to go in, close the gap between the 19th Brigade and the Tigris—so completing the circle—and deliver the coup de grace.

Rice's 35th Brigade moved out to the right to do just this, but as they advanced there was the clamor of Turkish guns and the rattle of small arms from the direction which Younghusband had assumed was clear for a walk-over. Shrapnel shells inflicted quite a few casualties and caused the first line transport mules to stampede. But despite this, Rice's men resolutely pushed on and about 5:15 p.m.—just a few minutes before sunset—the Buffs came into line with the 28th Punjabis of the 19th Brigade. Together the two battalions charged into the eye of the setting sun and drove back the Turks, until they were halted by the cross fire of machine-guns fired from Turkish trenches on both sides. They were still a long way from the river.

Further still over on the right, the cavalry brigade were the only ones who could have done anything toward completing the encirclement and they did nothing. They could have charged down to the river across perfect going but while they waited and watched, the golden moment slipped by and when they did advance across the open, into the gathering gloom of the early evening, shell-fire and the long range fire of a few machine guns effectively held them. By this time, though he believed otherwise, the battle was over and the prize had slipped from Younghusband's grasp.

What had happened was what might well have been forecast. As Young-husband's brigades wheeled around the Turkish flank, so the Turks moved out with them, prolonging their line by manning the water-cuts which ran parallel to the river. Khalil had no intention of being caught napping; from previous experience, the form of Aylmer's attack had been obvious and the Turks were prepared to fight hard to keep their line of retreat open. Yet it was a near thing; the ponderous moves of the British and their own dogged resistance had saved them. The main reasons for the failure have already been adduced and little more can be added. Only one course of action would have most likely brought a British success. If Younghusband's brigade had taken a wider swing it is probable that a large proportion of the Turks would have been encircled; this, followed by a really determined attack by the whole force ought to have smashed through to the river. As it was, when darkness set in, the Turks made good their retreat through the gap which still lay open between the British lines and the Tigris and next morning when the force moved on, the Turks were found to be strongly entrenched across the mouth of the Hanna defile.

The Wadi had been captured but for the British it was a barren success—a disappointing outcome to a situation that had held such promise. At a cost of over 1,600 casualties, of whom 218 were killed, Aylmer was no nearer fulfilling his task than he had been two days earlier. Kemball's brigade, which had pressed the frontal attack had suffered most. If they had only been committed to the holding attack originally intended, no doubt they would have gotten off more lightly, but at the last minute they had been told that the positions in front of them were only lightly held and been ordered to drive the Turks out. It was found that they were full of Turks and were cleverly sited to command every yard of the steep banks of the watercourse. Consequently Kemball's men, advancing across open ground with very little cover, found themselves walking into a devastating curtain of fire which cut swathes in their ranks. The Wadi itself was invisible until one was almost on top of it and an irrigation channel in front served to confuse the attackers as to where exactly their objectives lay; in the narrow strip of land, between this channel and the Wadi proper, most of Kemball's casualties were incurred. Having crossed this suicidal stretch, the deep shelving of the Wadi proved to be yet another deadly obstacle. Time and again as the assaulting troops tried to rush it, their ranks were thinned, mowed down by bullets fired low above the ground. If they had only waited in the channel and pinned the Turks to their trenches by fire until Younghusband's brigades had gone around the flank, many of Kemball's men who were killed that day would have lived to fight another day. But they had been ordered to take the position. In the days when generals led the troops and indicated where to attack by a wave of the hand, they would never have been committed to a suicidal assault of this nature. But those days were over; as on the Western Front, the general's job was done -with maps and telephones far behind the lines and to ensure that the battle was run properly the theory was that he should keep out of personal danger. His role was that of the brain, not the pulse of the machine. If the battle had turned out a success the cost might have been regarded as worthwhile, but it was not, and the casualties here— following those of Sheikh Sa'ad—were a heavy drain on the relief force and one which could be ill afforded, particularly when it was now clear that heavier losses were still to come.

The reasons why the actions at Sheikh Sa'ad and the Wadi had been so costly may be attributed to the impatient urge to get through to Kut at any price, faulty intelligence and, to some extent, an unjustifiable contempt for the Turks' fighting capacity. Aylmer had played into the Turks' hands by launching a series of frontal attacks. Yet now with the visionary hourglass at Kut running low, it seemed that he had no option but to repeat the maneuver. It was hardly possible to stop and think things out, for Townshend was again clamoring for quick relief. In a signal on January 15, he complained that he was deeply concerned that no news of the Relief Force had reached him since the day before and that the date had already been reached beyond which it was hazardous to expect the garrison to hold out. What was holding Aylmer? So far as he could see, the Turks were only fighting a delaying action to gain time for reinforcements to reach them. Indeed, there were indications of their pulling out, convoys had been seen moving north and west past Kut and the right bank of the Tigris opposite the town had been practically denuded of troops.

To Aylmer this called for a straight answer and that night he unburdened himself in a signal to both Nixon and Townshend:

> The position of affairs must be frankly faced. The enemy is blocking the entrance of the Wadi-Nukhailat defile with very strong works . . . behind the defile is a single line of entrenchments probably a mile and a half long. Behind again is the Es Sinn position. It is impossible in my opinion to take the first position from this side along without losing half the force. It is my intention to cross the 3rd Division (now formed under Major General H. D'U Keary who had reached the front with his staff on January 14) and Cavalry Brigade on the right bank . . . and thus enfilade the enemy's position. *Even by this means I do not think that progress can be anything but very slow.* Information indicates that reinforcements may have begun to arrive at Kut and these may soon amount to a considerable number. On the right bank below Kut at present there do not seem to be at the outside more than 2,000 men and rain is evidently rendering Hai crossing difficult for transport. *The best plan seems to me for Townshend to cross the river during the night with such able-bodied men as he has got in mahailas or other river transport and march well round the Es Sinn position on the right bank.* I would cross one division and cavalry brigade at the same time and march to meet and bring him back here. The opportunity is now favorable and may cease directly the enemy sends troops down the right bank which may be very soon. On December 20 Townshend informed me that he had fifty mahailas besides other river craft. If these still exist it should be about sufficient for his purpose, though he would have to leave sick unable to march and destroy his guns and material. If Townshend thinks this possible I shall issue orders for him to do so. The Commander 6th Division is requested to wire at once feasibility of passage and earliest date he can be ready, remembering opportunity may not recur.

Nixon needed little time to consider this proposal and early on the 17th he addressed himself to both Aylmer and Townshend:

> I do NOT in any way agree with your appreciation of the situation or that the same calls for Townshend to take the extreme step that you propose. The only circumstance that could, in my opinion, justify this course would be the demoralization of your force which I have no reason to suspect. . . . The course you originally proposed, namely, to employ part of your force on the right bank, should not only promise success but afford you opportunity of inflicting a severe blow on the en-

emy and effecting the speedy relief of Townshend. I cannot believe that the position in front of you can equal in strength those attacked and captured by us in the past which had been in preparation for four months. *The course you now propose for Townshend in your telegram under reply would be disastrous from every point of view to Townshend's force, to your force, to the whole force in Mesopotamia and to the Empire, and I can NOT sanction it. ... .*

Townshend's reply to Aylmer, which concerned itself only with the method of effecting the juncture of his garrison with the relief column, pointed out that while he could ferry 4,000 men across the Tigris in one night, twenty hours would be needed to get the guns over and seventy-five hours for the horses and other animals of the division. This led to a considerable three-cornered correspondence between Aylmer, Townshend and Nixon as to whether Kut should or should not be evacuated after the Relief Force had met up with the garrison of Kut—Townshend maintaining that the sortie Aylmer had suggested would result in the destruction of the men who crossed the river. In the end Nixon ruled that to abandon Kut was quite uncalled for, that after Kut had been relieved it would be held, and preparations made for an offensive designed to secure a position west of the town from which it could be better defended.

Decisions of this nature, made in Basra miles behind the line, were of little immediate value to Aylmer who still had to force the Turks' position at Hanna. Apart from the fact that there were too many factors which could not be properly assessed individually by any of the three generals concerned—conditions at the front; how long the garrison in Kut could last; how soon reinforcements could reach Aylmer, how soon they could reach Khalil and what quality they would be; the effect of the Russian column moving up through Persia; the real worm of the Hanna defenses; and the possibility of the countryside's being flooded before a breakthrough could be made—none of the three was particularly well qualified to make such decisions. Sir John Nixon was a sick man—the fact that he was invalided back to India on January 18 is evidence of his ill-health. The decision to halt Townshend at Kut, and consequently the situation which had developed from this decision, -*was* his responsibility. Unless he went up to the front to see for himself, it is unreasonable to expect him to have been fully appraised of what conditions were really like. Because of his ill-health he could not go, so his judgment was faulty. Aylmer, in the thick of it, probably tended to see a gloomier picture man that which actually prevailed. He had already had a difficult time organizing the Relief Force and, of course, two heart-breaking disappointments in the battles of Sheikh Sa'ad and the Wadi. Townshend, the strong man of the three, was anxious for the future of his garrison, and annoyed that the promise of his early relief had not been fulfilled so that his judgment too could be considered anything but unbiased. With Townshend expecting too much and not in a mood to compromise, Aylmer unduly depressed, and Nixon too sanguine about the situation, the latter's signal was hardly calculated to encourage Aylmer—the man who actually had to do the job.

And Aylmer had other problems. As the Relief Force girded their loins and prepared for the next onslaught, everything seemed to go wrong. The bridge, which had been built over the Tigris to enable him to switch his troops from one bank to the other as tactical opportunities dictated, was broken by one of the steamers and carried away by the wind and current in a strong gale. Bad weather and the exhaustion of the tiny band of bridge-building Sappers and Miners made its immediate repair impossible. The same bad weather, which had turned the surface of the plain into a sodden morass, making any movement of the infantry one of excessive exertion, was also having its effect on the troops' health. Exposure to cold winds and rain was telling on the men of the Relief Force, just as it was on the garrison in the trenches at Kut, up to their waists in water. Even in the rear areas it was causing chaos. Because of the weather, reinforcements marching up from Basra were compelled to halt at Amara and Qurna and even the steamers ferrying other troops forward were delayed.

Yet, in spite of the weather, the troops opposite Hanna had tried to advance. All they had been able to do was to push their trenches forward a few yards and so far as could be seen the Turks had not shown any signs of giving way. It was a gloomy prospect; everybody knew it and in Kut, Townshend, fearing for his supplies, had ordered his stores to be recounted. Perhaps his news was the one bright gleam in an otherwise black picture. On the 16th he signaled Aylmer the all-important news that he had twenty-one-days' rations for British troops; seventeen days for Indians; fodder for five days, tinned meat for three; meat on the hoof for seventeen and tea for eight. Thus, to Aylmer it appeared that so far as food was concerned the relief of the garrison was no longer a matter of great urgency; the possibility of Khalil's getting reinforcements and the time available to the Turks for improving their defenses were factors of much greater significance. Nevertheless, Nixon in the sick-bay was all for Aylmer pressing on and in a reply to a signal from Aylmer telling him of the bad weather, he endeavored to apply the spur.

> The Army Commander recognizes the difficulties caused by the prevalence of bad weather, but can you give no estimate as to when you will be able to continue the offensive and your plans for the same?

The goad was not necessary. Aylmer had already made up his mind that this time he would break through allright but since the attack had to be driven home frontally he determined that there should be no lack of artillery support and gun preparation. Batteries were to be ferried over to the right bank to enfilade the Hanna position, and on the night of the 19th he planned a concentrated bombardment of the Turks' positions by guns on both banks. Then, during the following morning, the 7th Division would stage a massive onslaught against the mouth of the Hanna defile. That was the plan; unfortunately, owing to the weather, it had to be put back twenty-four hours, during which time Khalil's men were digging away and strengthening their defenses.

At noon on the 20th, as planned, the Turkish front line trenches were subjected to a twenty-minute bombardment from all the British guns, and a similar bombardment was arranged for the morning of the 21st before the infantry assaulted. There was no attempt to mislead the Turks as to where and when the attack would take place. Few deceptive measures were feasible anyway since there was only one avenue of approach—the river on one side and the marsh on the other precluded any outflanking movement, so the way the attack would have to go was predetermined. Only by battering a way through the narrow neck of the defile could the Turks be dislodged. The one possible advantage open to the British lay in their ability to bombard the Turkish positions from two directions, but even this was modified by the terrain. Because the country was so flat, the existence of even a small mound in "No Man's Land" concealed hundreds of yards of enemy territory and made observation of the customary direct fire very difficult. To overcome this difficulty, indirect fire, directed by gunner observation officers using an observation ladder, scaffolding or a mast, had to be resorted to, and as a counter to this the Turks dug deeper trenches in the easy stoneless desert. "We don't mind your bombardments" one Turkish officer said later, "when you shell our front line, we lie low and fire from the second line, and when you shell our second line, we get up again and fire from the first."

To neutralize a front just under a mile long, Aylmer had 46 guns plus the support of the two gunboats *Cranefly* and *Dragonfly* (each carrying one four-inch, one 12-pounder, one 6-pounder gun and a 2-pounder pom-pom); with twelve thousand rounds fired from these guns it was hoped to demoralize the Turk and destroy his defenses. Compared with the support available on a similar frontage on the Western Front,[1] the amount of metal which this concentration could put down on the Hanna defenses may be judged hopelessly

---

1. At Loos, where between four and five hundred field guns and howitzers with sixty odd "heavies" were available, the bombardment lasted two hours.

inadequate; in a similar comparison with a Second World War battle it appears ludicrous. And if times were different, the calibre of the men concerned was not. The Turks were a hardy race, good soldiers and not easily dislodged.

Two days before the battle was scheduled to begin, the weather cleared and as the troops dried out their sodden clothing some of their old cheerfulness returned. They believed, like their commander, that January 21 would decide the fate of Kut; if they did not break through that day, then they never would. Most of them appreciated that it would be hard going, few realized how inadequately they were placed. The three brigades of the 7th Division, which was to carry out the assault, should have been able to muster nine thousand men if they had been at their full war establishment but less than four thousand manned the trenches on the morning of "D" Day. Sickness and the earlier privations had reduced the division to a strength of little more man what one of its brigades should have been. Because of this, one of them (21st) had been broken up, and its battalions[2] attached to the other two (19th and 35th)—an unfortunate arrangement in many respects, since none of these battalions were used to working with their new formations.

By dawn on the 20th the British troops had closed up to within six hundred yards of the Turks' forward positions and had dug in. Echeloned back in the order in which they were to assault, the composite 35th Brigade was on the left of the British position and the composite 19th Brigade on the right; just over a mile behind were the guns. Everything had been planned by Younghusband himself in the most meticulous detail. Ten minutes after the preliminary bombardment the infantry would climb out of their trenches and advance; a company of bombers—infantry who would rely on sacks of Mills grenades—would move along the Turks' trenches, clearing them as soon as the first wave established a foothold; prisoners would be marched back to be looked after by the cavalry; and so on. Every detail was dovetailed into a strict timetable, nothing was left to chance; the battle was to follow a set pattern. As so often happens on these occasions both timings and the arrangements which fitted them were soon to go awry.

When the British guns opened up on the day before the attack the Turks' artillery made little attempt to reply and this was taken to be a good sign. Since every movement around the British trenches drew a storm of bullets it was obvious that the effect of the shelling was less than had been expected. However, during the morning some encouraging news came in from Townshend. About three thousand Turks had been seen moving back, he said, with guns; and a camp at the Dujaila canal had disappeared. Unfortunately Townshend,

---

2. Of these battalions, the Black Watch could only muster 300 rifles, the 6th Jats a there 170

subject on this occasion to lapses into wishful dunking, was always apt to see Turks moving to the rear, and it is possible that he might have been deceived by the mirage, so Aylmer should have treated his information with reserve. His inference was that the bombardment might at least have induced Khalil to withdraw some of his troops from Hanna and this theory was strengthened that night as the guns fell silent, when observers on the right bank of the river reported seeing the Turks striking tents and packing up. To Aylmer, at least, the prospect for the morrow seemed better man had been hoped for, particularly as the greater part of the wire running in front of the Turks forward line appeared to have been cut by the gunfire.

One might have expected the attack next morning to have gone in at dawn and indeed it would have been better for the British if it had, as the last six hundred yards to the Turkish trenches would have been less deadly in the half light. But the bombardment from land and river only began at 7:45 a.m. and when the first streaks of gray light illuminated the battlefield it was found that a thick mist lay like a shroud over the Turkish lines. As me gunners needed half an hour of daylight to check the registration of their targets, the infantry had to forego the advantages of the mist and the day started as it was to end—with the steady tap-tap-tap of machine gun fire and the crack of rifles, like hail on a corrugated iron roof. Nevertheless, as soon as the British shells started to crash down on the Turks' front line, the Black Watch on the left began their advance and, in a couple of so-called rushes, they got across the first two hundred yards. But because of the sticky, clinging mud, their pace was that of a slow amble rather than a rush. When the guns lifted to the second line of Turkish trenches, some of the Black Watch were able to squelch their way forward and gain the front line. But only some; the barrage was not proving to be the protection anticipated and the rest fell en route. The Turk was not lying low and sheltering as presumably he ought to have been; he was shooting back and his bullets, barely audible in the din of the bombardment, were taking their toll. The only effect of the bombardment had been to indicate the point of attack; the trenches were little damaged and the wire, such as it was, was uncut. The Highlanders, joined by a few Jats, endeavored to broaden their narrow foothold. As they jumped into the redoubt, the Turks dropped their rifles and ran back to the second line. But they were soon back, moving up along the communication trench traverses on the right and left, hurling bombs in front of them as they advanced. The little party of Black Watch and Jats, jammed between, were squeezed out over the parapet and as they left the trench a deadly fire which inflicted more casualties than they had incurred in the attack was directed toward them. Only two officers and fifteen men got away, back to where they had started that morning. Temporarily this spelled the end of the

Black Watch, one of the finest battalions in Mesopotamia, one of the best regiments in the British Army. Counting the noneffectives who had been committed to the battle there were only about 120 men of the battalion left; in three actions within a fortnight the battalion had been reduced a fifth of its size.

On the right, the assault had met with even less success than that experienced by the Black Watch- Such a storm of bullets met the two Dogra battalions leading the attack that only twenty-five men reached the Turks' wire entanglements. One or two who forced their way through the wire were soon driven back, or killed. More and more troops, including even the follow-up parties, were pitched into the fight but with the exception of two companies of the Seaforth Highlanders, no progress was made. As groups of men went forward they were either shot down or driven back by violent incessant small arms fire. The attack had failed and as more and more desperate attempts were made to deny this fact the situation rapidly went from bad to worse. Bombers who were rushed forward could not even find any cover at their start line as all the trenches were filled with dead or wounded. As a consequence they too suffered terrible casualties from the ceaseless fire of the Turks.

At divisional headquarters, a mile behind the front, Younghusband was out of touch with the situation almost from the moment the first waves of his infantry went over the top; Aylmer, miles further back at Tigris Corps headquarters, was even more in the dark. Owing to the wet soil and casualties among the operators, the field telephone system broke down and the only messages to or from the front line had to be sent by runner——a slow, hazardous, and unreliable business in any battle. When Younghusband did eventually come to realize what had happened, he saw that the only course open to him was to collect the remnants of the shattered battalions and reorganize them before the attack could go on; but for this time was needed. Disorganization was rife, there were no quick means of getting orders out to the troops and to make matters worse, at noon the rain came down. All day and all that night it bucketed down, putting the crown on dejection.

When the news first percolated through to Aylmer he was all for going on with the battle next day and, during the afternoon, he sent out an appeal to the troops:

> For the honor of the Empire and for the sake of your brave comrades in Kut, I ask the gallant troops under my orders to hold on to the present position and to make one more supreme effort to capture the enemy's line.

It is doubtful whether the message reached many of the troops who in any case were too far gone to be much concerned about their comrades in Kut, still less the honor of the Empire at this stage. Nevertheless, an hour after it had been sent out Younghusband was ordered to prepare for a fresh attack. Happily it was never to develop.

Torrential rain and sleet, driven by an icy wind, put an end to the battle that night; in so far as the broken force of numbed, soaked, shivering British and Indian soldiers were able to extricate themselves and reorganize, such weather was heaven-sent. But it was a miserable experience just the same—particularly for the wounded. Lying in ankle-deep pools amid a sea of mud, they must have plumbed the depths of agony, and in any history of sufferings endured by the British Army the collective misery of that night of January 21, 1916, is probably without parallel since the Crimea. The medical arrangements had been bad enough at Ctesiphon but "the Battles of Sheikh Sa'ad, Wadi and Hanna, resulted in the most complete breakdown of all."[3] Stretcher bearers were few and far between, so that those who were brought back while it was still light were fortunate indeed. In the area designated as a casualty clearing center, tents had been put up for them, but me ground was so muddy that they sank up to their boots in mire. Into these tents the casualties, cold and exhausted with pain and loss of blood, were dumped; all through the night the carts brought more to join them. Only two sections of one of the five divisional field ambulances were up at the front and doctors were overwhelmed by this flood of casualties; they could not be everywhere and it was no fault of theirs that the stream which poured in was something with which they could not cope.

When the tents were full to overflowing, casualties were carried straight on to the hospital ship *Julnar,* until every inch of her decks were covered and others were left out in the rain on the A.T. carts all night. Still they came and still there were others to be collected. As the night passed the camp grew and in the glare of hurricane lanterns it looked like a subdued inferno, which would have shaken even Dante. In chaotic disarray, shrouded bodies twisted and turned to a constant chorus of groans and sobs. In the lamplight all had that some stark gray look and the ashen bloodless hue of the faces of the dead made it difficult to distinguish British from Indian. Some cried to God, some to Allah; some tried to joke in spite of it all, like a group of the damned trying to make merry in hell; most were grimly stoical. Looking at this oppressive scene one subaltern is reputed to have said in an aside to his sergeant: "I suppose this is as near hell as we are likely to see." Drawing himself up, to answer in the disciplined matter-of-fact fashion of the parade ground, the

---

3. Extract from the Mesopotamia Commission Report.

sergeant replied: "I should say it is, sir." In many ways the wounded from the Battles of the Wadi and Hanna had to undergo far worse privations than those of Ctesiphon, and their sufferings were so grievous that it would be difficult to exaggerate them. The whole of the medical shortcomings were a tragedy whose cost in spiritual and material terms could not be counted in the wastage—the dead who might have lived, the maimed who might have retained their limbs; the ultimate pay-off was in the blow dealt to the morale of the living—to the spirit of those who were left to carry on—and it was a blow the effects of which were to be felt for many a long day.

Since the very beginning of the campaign the military authorities had done their best to stifle any form of criticism or prevent any unpleasant news from leaking out of the country, by means of a strict censorship. Anything which the censors thought might discredit the doctrine of official infallibility was strangled with red tape. All telegrams and letters from the front were censored at least three times before they left Mesopotamia, and news agency dispatches had to be riddled through a net stretching from the front to Delhi and thence to London, which effectively removed any worthwhile report. There was no "free" communication with the outside world, even the most oblique criticism was ruled out. "The Higher Command" was sacrosanct and aspersions could be cast only on the Turks and Germans. Candor was a quality which was not recognized—the enemy must have no hint of troubles, deficiencies, losses, resources, reinforcements, methods or preoccupations—and the censor was quick to discover an ambush in every phrase. Stories of pain, profanity, bungling, incompetence or mischance were prohibited outside the theater, even though they are common in a greater or lesser degree to every campaign. In almost every imaginable topic there were hidden dangers. Even if the story of the "date palms" is dismissed as the application of ignorant bureaucracy it is true to say that the censorship system was all-embracing; the official line was that even the most commonplace subject needed careful treatment. Because the Indians were supposed to be kept in the dark about the Jihad, religious references were to be avoided; because it was not considered desirable to disparage the Arabs in case they should hear of it and feel hurt, no mention of the characters who mutilated the wounded and dug up the graves was desirable. Even the expression "friendly Arab" was forbidden because it implied that there were some Arabs who were not friendly (the Buddhoo came to be officially designated "marauder in Turkish pay" and later in Baghdad the Arabs who resorted to violence were referred to as "Kurds and others"). News agency reports had to observe every propriety or the censor was there with his blue pencil. Everything must be as it should be; on Sundays—Divine Services; the troops' health—good; their morale—first class; no one was to be hungry or thirsty and of course no battle lost which might have been won; no casualties sustained which might have been avoided. All this has a familiar ring; some of the comments and reports emanating from Vietnam seem to follow very similar lines today. The trouble is that somewhere along the line one has to take account of the credulity of those who are following the news, and accept the fact that calamitous news will always leak out no matter what steps are taken to suppress it.

Early on the morning of January 22, Younghusband made a personal report to Aylmer. Rain had fallen in torrents all night; so much of it that it seemed as if the great Flood was about to repeat itself. The Tigris was overflowing, the trenches were flooded, the camps were underwater and the only dry places were in the holds of the ships. Many men who had been out all night were found dead next morning without a mark on them ("dead from exposure"). Barely a shot had been fired during the night and on both sides the damp and cold had taxed men's resources to an extent whereby fighting became a very secondary consideration. In view of all this Aylmer decided to ask for a six hour truce in order to collect the wounded and bury the dead.[4] It was some time before the Turks agreed but as soon as a white flag had been hoisted at the British side of the defile a number of Arabs swarmed out of the Turkish lines and began to rob the disabled and dead, and to collect the rifles lying on the battlefield. Whether these were irresponsible nomads or Turkish Arab soldiers has never been clear. As the Arab in the Turkish army was basically the same as his unregenerate brother not under the leash, he could well have been the latter. Working like jackals, the Arabs rapidly stripped clothing from the clothes of the casualties lying in No Man's Land. Any sign of life was rewarded by a knock on the head, or a handful of sand thrust into the mouth and a tight grip to hold it shut until the individual concerned succumbed. This was too much for Aylmer's men. British and Indians dropped their weapons so that no false interpretation of the white flag could be made and rushed forward to protect their comrades. From the wounded, the Arabs turned on them and many of them were assaulted and robbed. Fortunately a party of Turkish officers came forward about this time, the hangers-on who had broken the truce were driven off, and the work of collecting the wounded was allowed to go on until dusk. Finally, before leaving tins sorry little interlude it is fair to conclude that the Turks were ashamed of what had happened. The Turks were in a different category from the Arabs; they were hard fighters but, on the battlefield at least, they were also courteous and chivalrous. Nominally the Arabs were fighting for the Turks, but there was no trust between them.

4.Total British casualties in this action amounted to 2,700 killed and wounded.

Turk and Arab shared a common religion but that was the only common ground between them. The Arab followed a cause and given the opportunity he would turn on his friends for murder and loot without the slightest compunction. No one knew this better than the Turks. "It would be better," said one Turkish officer, speaking of his so-called allies, "if we could join hands and make an end to these scavengers. We could settle our own differences later."

In deciding to ask for a truce Aylmer had accepted that he had suffered a severe reverse; he had already signaled to Basra and to Townshend that he had had to give up the attack and during the morning of the 22nd he was compelled to supplement it by saying ". . . the troops' condition may be regarded as prohibiting further advance for the present. . . . Weather is atrocious and floods increasing." For everybody concerned—Nixon, Townshend and the garrison of Kut, and, not least, Aylmer and the men of the Tigris Corps—acceptance of the failure at Hanna must have been a bitter pill to swallow. Fifty years after the event it is easy enough to sit in judgment, make weighty pronouncements and point the finger of shame. Nevertheless it is questionable whether the battle of Hanna should ever have been fought. According to Napoleon, no commander should accept battle unless the odds are 7 to 2 in his favor, and on January 21, the odds were by no means 7 to 2 in Aylmer's favor. The Turks were occupying a very strong position which they had worked hard to develop during the pause in the British advance. The improvements they had effected were such as to negate any advantage which the feeble British bombardment might have given to Aylmer's men. Numerically, both sides were about evenly matched, but even if the weather and the state of the ground had been better, the there fact that the British were up against a resolute enemy and formidable defenses put the chances of successful action beyond their power. If every military commander hesitated to offer or accept battle until the prospects were as favorable as Napoleon postulated, then he might never find himself in a position to do anything at all. Clearly there must be occasions when an offensive must be launched whatever the chances of success. But Hanna in January 1916 was not such an occasion and, if Nixon had only appreciated the quality of Khalil Pasha's troops, the strength of their position and the fact that the garrison of Kut could last for weeks more, then it may be conjectured that he would never have urged Aylmer to make the attack. But Nixon did not know these facts and, as is usual in war, he was compelled to base vital decisions on inaccurate premises and a prejudiced point of view.

Chapter 10

Downfall at Dujaila

W stands for the wonder and pain
With which we regard our infirm and insane
Old aged Generals who run this campaign
We are waging in Mesopotamia.

> (A stanza from the Cynical "Alphabet,"
> circulated in Mesopotamia during 1916.)

If Napoleon's criterion of inquiring whether an officer was lucky before he was employed in high command had been used in Mesopotamia in 1916, most of the senior commanders would have been sacked there and then. Townshend, who had come to Mesopotamia with a proverbial reputation for luck, had had a phenomenal run of it as far as Ctesiphon—so much so that even the Turks had come to regard him as one of Fortune's children. But by the time he arrived back in Kut his lucky streak was finished, never to return during his service career, and he died heartbroken at never getting another command. Nixon might also be said to have been lucky up to Ctesiphon.

Under his direction the Expeditionary Force had enjoyed a remarkable series of successes, successes so remarkable that the English newspapers in a spate of journalistic extravaganza had referred to the campaign as the "Mesopotamia picnic." But, after Ctesiphon, when the truth about the defective medical arrangements leaked out, he was damned in the eyes of the British public; his luck was out, his health was broken, his reputation finished. The commander who probably needed as much luck as anybody, Aylmer, never really had much of a chance to demonstrate whether he had any. Like Townshend, he was largely a victim of circumstance, and after his first two dismal failures to breakthrough to Kut his reputation was tottering.

Whether any of the three could have done differently is open to conjecture. If any one could have changed the tragic course of events it is logical to suppose that would have been Nixon. Yet Nixon, like Sir Arthur Barrett before him and indeed, to a large extent, Sir Percy Lake who followed, was constrained by his background, his training, and his loyalty to Simla and Whitehall. He left Mesopotamia under a cloud and he was never again employed, although with the troops he remained popular to the end; that he did so was also typical of the times. The fact that he spoke fluent Hindustani was a great advantage, he was known to have had a distinguished career and he certainly looked the part of a general. To the troops these were the qualities that counted. Regular soldiers—Indians, perhaps more than British—accepted that they were in the Army to "serve" and their attitude to senior officers had a touching faith about it, somewhat akin to their forebears of the Crimea. To inspecting officers they were usually uncomplaining. Asked if they were "all right" they would cheerfully say "yes," even if they were lacking the most elementary comforts in circumstances when they could reasonably have expected them. There was an undertone of grumbles, of course, as evinced by the alphabet quoted at the beginning of the chapter, but the British soldier has always grumbled—he would not be a British soldier if he did not do so—and in spite of this he usually accepted his sufferings as part of what he had to pay for being one. Cheerfulness under trying conditions was expected; it was the order of the day, and it has always been fortunate for Britain that it was so.[1]

---

1. Food is usually a sore point with Thomas Atkins. Mesopotamia was no exception:

> R are the rations "By Order" we get,
> Though no one I know has sampled them yet—
> And I don't think we will, so it's best to forget,
> That they're somewhere in Mesopotamia.

The ration party of one regiment, sent to collect bread, is said to have been told "only five loaves were available." This drew the reply: "If you could give us a few small fishes as well, perhaps we could perform a miracle."

Another instance of the attitude of mind, which highlights the solid worth of the seasoned British N.C.O.,

Sir Percy Lake's appointment as Nixon's successor was originally intended to be temporary, until a British War Office nominee should be forthcoming. Even so, in the circumstances it was unfortunate. As Beauchamp-Duff's Chief of Staff in Delhi and Simla, a large share in the responsibility for what the Mesopotamia Army lacked in the way of equipment, as well as for some of the disastrous strategical decisions that had been taken over the past year could be laid at his door. Either this, or a sense of loyalty, to his brother officers as well as to the Indian Government, compelled him to take on the job. To do so at sixty years of age certainly needed guts. Apart from the fact that it had been he who had sent Nixon to relieve Barrett and had appointed Townshend to the command of the 6th Division, Aylmer, as Adjutant General in India, had been his close colleague until only a few months previously—facts which others construed as being to his disadvantage rather than otherwise. But coming straight from India, imbued with all the ideas and limited outlook of one who had directed the war from Delhi and Simla, was his worst qualification for the job. During the campaign he had never visited the theater and so it is greatly to his credit that he was able quickly to set aside his preconceived ideas, to take a grip of Nixon's old staff who had been running the war while he was sick, to put right a lot of mistakes and make provision for the future.

When he arrived, reinforcements and supplies were pouring into Basra and by the end of January 1916 there were more troops there than at the front, for it was just not possible to move them forward. Conditions were already chaotic and Lake's immediate decision to stock up three months' reserve of supplies, ammunition and other stores in Basra only served to add to the confusion. The fault lay with the Army in India organization and its staff—defects of which Kitchener and later Sir Douglas Haig had both complained. Lake had not realized that the port facilities of Basra were hardly equal to receiving the daily requirements of the Mesopotamia army, let alone bringing in the additional tonnage to accumulate a reserve. No one had told him the implications of stocking a three-month reserve, nor did his staff know how to control it. The various heads of departments, supplies, ordnance stores, engineers and the rest all zealously cabled India for three months reserves to be sent as soon as possible and India, alarmed at her earlier failure, eagerly and promptly responded. The reserves poured in and Bombay was stripped of ocean-going ships for the purpose. The result was a melancholy row of ships lying in the Shatt-al-Arab waiting to be cleared sometimes for as long as a month.

---

may be assessed from the story of the British battalion moving up to an attack. Coming under long range rifle fire a young recruit asked "What's that noise, Sergeant?" "Wasps, son" was the reply "if they get you then its Blighty, India or qualifying for the resurrection." Regrettably, the sergeant qualified himself soon afterward.

Congestion in and around the town was unbelievable and, with the hospitals full of sick and wounded, it was obvious that sorting out the base was one of the new Army Commander's first and most pressing problems. It was not one that could be solved overnight. Army headquarters in India—Lake included— had completely underestimated the difficulties of waging war in Mesopotamia and Lake now took the only way of resolving them by sending for experts. Together with the material for the railway which had been refused Nixon earlier they were dispatched with the same alacrity as the reinforcements and stores. The ultimate responsibility must be regarded as that of Lake but one cannot help wondering about the caliber of the staff officers who served him as well of those in India who contributed to the chaos. Lake's own quartermaster general, the embarkation staffs at Basra, Bombay and Karachi and finally the quartermaster general himself in Delhi must all have been aware of the mounting confusion yet there is no record that they were anything but inarticulate about it.

The Viceroy and his Government now appreciated that anything which could be done to retrieve the position in Mesopotamia would have to be done quickly if a scandal was to be averted. It was no use taking a lofty attitude; public opinion had been profoundly moved by rumors of the appalling sufferings of the wounded and the India Office in Whitehall had already ordered the appointment of a Committee of Investigation.

It should be added, however, that there was still an old guard who took the view that the tragic issues involved were grossly exaggerated. Sir Arnold Wilson of the Political service, on a visit to India at this time, reports the viewpoint of the quartermaster general in Delhi which in different circumstances would have been laughable. On being told that a shortage of vegetables had been responsible for an outbreak of scurvy and beriberi, he is said to have replied, "That's what they all say," adding with venomous emphasis "What *I* always say is—if you want vegetables—GROW 'EM." To suggestions that his idea had seasonal limitations if no others, he turned a deaf ear. Despite this the authorities in Delhi and Simla were worried about me results of the commission's investigation; they had every reason to be, and Whitehall was already convinced that the campaign would have to be run differently in the future. At the beginning of February the astute former Chief of the Imperial General Staff, Sir "Wully" Robertson, recommended to the War Committee of the British Cabinet that control of the operations in Mesopotamia should be taken over by the War Office in London and run in exactly the same fashion as the war in other theaters. The recommendation was quickly seized on by the War Committee and accepted with relief by India; to those who understood its implications it brought a sense of gratitude and relief. The whole might of the

British Empire would be behind the prosecution of the campaign, British methods and equipment—not merely Indian—would be applied and even if European standards were never reached, they would be the aim. It was the beginning of a new epoch in the campaign.

Lake could have spent weeks reorganizing the Basra base if the situation up the Tigris had not demanded his urgent attention. On January 24, three days after the battle of Hanna, he sailed up the Tigris to meet Aylmer and to see for himself how things were at the front; en route he learned that Townshend had declared a second reassessment of the food stocks in Kut which now made him self-sufficient for eighty-four days and not the twenty-two he had originally forecast. Since the Hanna battle Townshend had been reappraising his position, in which the question of his breaking out had again become a major consideration. In a long telegram to Aylmer he posed three alternatives. Either he could try to fight his way out of the town, making for Sheikh Sa'ad twenty-five miles away, with all the men of the garrison that could march and fight. Such a move would mean leaving all the sick and wounded behind and destroying his guns before leaving, since the column would only be able to take what it could carry with it on the men's backs—two-hundred rounds of ammunition and two days' rations.[2] The next obvious alternative was to stay where he was, continuing to block the passage of the Turks' ships and so preventing any further advance on Kut. Finally, when "all hope was past," the third alternative was to negotiate for terms of surrender. The telegram concluded by saying that Townshend "supposed" that the idea of breaking out was the best.

Sir Percy Lake got a copy of this message before he left Basra and he replied immediately. Unlike his predecessor, Nixon, he did not rule out the possibility of Townshend's fighting his way out of Kut but he signaled "I still hope to effect your relief. . . ." "In any case your other alternatives [*sic*] are unnecessary and out of the question." Aylmer thought differently. After Hanna, he was not convinced of ever being able to reach Kut. "Flesh and blood," he said, "cannot do more than the troops have done against the enemy and the extraordinarily adverse conditions of cold and floods." Seizing on Townshend's apparent readiness to cooperate in a gigantic "break-out—break-in" he wired to Lake:

---

2. It is not generally known that "Strictly Secret" orders for a break-out, referred to as "Project E," were actually prepared and issued. A "Maximum Force" was to cross to the right bank of the Tigris leaving a "Minimum Force" to hold Kut and "Cooperate with the Relieving Force." The "Maximum Force" under Townshend's command was to comprise two columns A and B of two weak brigades, a total of about 2,500 men. Left to defend Kut according to these orders would be about 4,000 active defenders including "about 300 convalescents and men with scurvy able to use rifles." Since Townshend's declared effective strength at the beginning of March was Approximately 12,400, two thousand fighting men appear to be unaccounted for.

I know the Army Commander disagrees with me but I must again affirm that in my opinion... I am not in a position to reach Kut, so as to effect entire relief of Townshend. *I believe even after reinforcements now on their way arrive, we shall have very little chance of success, I have now only* 9,000 *infantry left and have just suffered reverse. I am very doubtful of morale of a good many of the Indian troops especially as I have the gravest suspicion of extent of self-mutilation amongst them;* it is my deliberate opinion, formed after the gravest consideration, that the best course would be to adopt Townshend's plan, as suggested by me originally and vetoed by Army Commander. ... .

Although Townshend had said that he "supposed" the idea of breaking-out was "best," and had convinced himself that it would succeed, by the morning after, when he had had the signals from Lake and Aylmer, he had changed his mind about doing so. "I thought the matter over carefully in the night," he wrote, *"and I was certain that to stay and fight it out in Kut was the best course to pursue, so I determined to adopt it, irrespective of what orders I might get, convinced of its being the correct role to play—in other words I would make Kut into a second Plevna."*[3] Having made up his mind he wired Aylmer to this effect and it was in this signal that he revealed the astounding news that "great supplies of barley" had been discovered and that by killing his 3,000 animals he found "we can last for eighty-four days." Following on Aylmer's comments, Townshend also had something to say about his Indian troops: "As regards the want of morale of a good part of your Indian troops, I have the same here in a more modified form; it is my handful of Norfolks, Dorsets, Oxfords who are my sheet anchor here. We do not want inferior drafts of Indian recruits such as my battalions were filled up with after the battle of Kut in September last. Melliss, Delamain, Hamilton and Hoghton will bear me out in this. One or two good all-British Divisions are what we want. There now is the time to demand good white troops from overseas, an Army Corps to save and hold Mesopotamia if Government considers it worm holding. . ."

The situation facing Lake when he reached Aylmer's headquarters at the Wadi on the evening of January 27, was pretty gloomy. In the whole of the Persian Gulf he now had about sixty-three thousand men, of whom fifteen thousand were British, but of the sixty-three thousand, eight thousand were in hospital and another fifteen thousand were not available for one reason or another. This left about forty thousand and as the Turks were estimated to have something like thirty-five thousand men between Baghdad and the firing line, Lake and his opponent, numerically, seemed to be about evenly matched. However, on the Tigris front only about fourteen thousand men and 46 guns

---

3. Osman Pasha's defence of the Bulgarian town of Plevna halted a Russian advance on Constantinople in 1877. After five months, however, Osman was compelled to capitulate and, like Kut, the Siege of Plevna illustrates the futility of a purely passive defence.

could be mustered, although another 11,028 guns were available as reinforcements when once they could be got up to the forward area. Facing the fourteen
thousand, the Turks were estimated to have about ten thousand on the right
bank of the Tigris, forward of the Hai, and this figure did not take into account
the reserves they could bring up from Shumran or ferry across the Tigris. Nor,
in considering the relative strengths, must it be forgotten that the Turks were
on the defensive, well dug in, and that they had already shown a remarkable
propensity for trench warfare. That they would be reinforced before very long
also seemed extremely probable as news had been received from agents in
Constantinople that a force of thirty-six thousand men had left the Dardanelles
for Mesopotamia on January 20.

In view of all this, presumably Lake's first consideration was whether
Aylmer should carry on trying to break through to Kut or whether he should
order Townshend to try to break out; apparently he never wavered in his
decision to adhere to the first alternative. Having decided that the Tigris Corps
should battle on, the next question ought to have been whether or not the task
should have been delegated to Aylmer. Undoubtedly a solution to the
administrative problems was vital but the relief of Kut should have taken
priority over everything else and it is difficult to believe that the administrative
difficulties demanded the constant personal supervision of the Commander in
Chief then, or indeed at any other time. If not, then he would have been better
employed directing the operations on the battlefield. Lake apparently thought
otherwise however, since he sailed back to Basra on the morning of the 29th,
leaving Aylmer to carry on.

At this point it becomes clear that Lake no longer trusted Aylmer completely. Probably some straight talking took place between the evening of
January 27 and the morning of January 29, and, from the signals already
referred to, it is apparent that Aylmer was not exactly brimming with confidence about his ability to get through to Townshend. Aylmer was left in
command of the Tigris Corps but Gorringe, who had recently been knighted
for his earlier actions, was appointed to be his Chief of Staff and, one suspects,
to act as Lake's stooge.[4] Because of the cynical suggestion of the generals being
aged, "infirm and insane," it is interesting to note that Gorringe, at forty-seven
was the youngest of the lot. Lake was sixty and Nixon fifty-eight—three years
older than Townshend; Aylmer could, in fact, be counted as one of the
younger set and he was fifty-one. Most of the brigade commanders were in
their mid-fifties, in striking contrast to the situation on the Western front

---

4. This suggestion is based on the fact that soon after his return to Basra, Lake took the unusual step of
asking Gorringe to submit a report giving his personal views on the situation at Hanna. What Gorringe
suggested in his report was virtually the same as the plan suggested by Aylmer two days later.

where, by this time at this level of command the younger element was beginning to establish itself.

Aylmer's plan for the next attempt to get through to Townshend has probably been the most criticized action of all the tragic attempts to relieve Kut. The idea was to attack up the right bank and take the strongly defended Es Sinn position from where the town of Kut was plainly visible. Except for the mounds of ancient canal banks the country was as flat as a table, with one notable exception, the Dujaila depression. This depression ran from the right bank of the Tigris for some distance upstream of Magasis past the tomb of Imam-al-Mansur and it contained the strongly entrenched position which became known as the Dujaila Redoubt. The depression itself was about a hundred and fifty yards wide and six feet below the level of the surrounding countryside and was covered with a stunted thorny acacia type of scrub which gave cover to hosts of partridges, jackals and wild cats. (Later in the campaign the cavalry collected a pack of hounds together to hunt the jackals and many of the officers were in the habit of getting in some shooting at the few survivors of the partridges that remained after the battle of March 8, 1916).

The Dujaila Redoubt was the key of the whole position and Aylmer's plan was to carry this first and then pivot around it toward the Turks' rear, in order to cut their communications and make the right bank untenable. By this maneuver he hoped that the Turks would be compelled to evacuate the left bank, leaving him the command of the river and an open door to Kut. Considering that his plan would mean a formidable frontal attack, which in view of the wastage incurred at Sheikh Sa'ad, the Wadi and Hanna during January— wastage from which the Tigris Corps had not yet recovered—it is surprising that a less ambitious scheme was not considered. Instead of attacking the Es Sinn position, a bolder plan would have been to have tried to hold the Turks at Dujaila and march a column straight on toward the Hai and Kut, in order to extricate Townshend and his garrison so that they could have joined hands with Aylmer at a point in front of El Orah. But this would have meant delivering Kut as a prize to Khalil Pasha and surrendering command of that stretch of the river for the time being, a contingency which, apparently, was not acceptable. Lake argued that if Kut fell to the Turks during the flood months, from March to June, they could get boats down the Hai, so enabling them to outflank the British positions at Qurna. If this happened it might then be necessary for the British forces to fall back below Amara, leaving the roads to the oilfields and southwest Persia open and the Bakhtiari and other tribes exposed to Turkish influence. Furthermore, if the Turks drove the British south of Amara they would be able to operate in Persia without any concern about the security of Baghdad.

Since Townshend had made it known that his supplies would last throughout March there was no immediate urgency to relieve him. Waiting for the 13th "New Army" Division which had fought at Gallipoli, and which was now under orders for service in Mesopotamia, should have allowed a sufficiently strong force to assemble enabling the Turks to be held at Dujaila and for a strong column to march on to Kut. On March 8 the first two battalions of this division had arrived at Orah and three weeks later the complete division was in camp at Sheikh Sa'ad. But at the beginning of March the river was rising and Lake feared that the forthcoming operation would be hampered by floods. Aylmer was all for waiting for his reinforcements before he started the attack but the Army Commander was not; he wanted Aylmer to get on. This being so, it is a moot point who should have decided when the offensive should be undertaken and one that underlines the earlier contention that Lake ought to have assumed command of the troops on the Tigris front himself. Clearly, he alone should have been the man with the best information in regard to all the vital factors concerned with the opportune moment when to attack; he alone could assess the related problems of transport and supplies and of the movements and concentrations of his troops and those of the Turks. On the other hand only the commander at the front could really decide as to the details of the plan and the exact moment when it could be launched most advantageously and this was an instance where divided responsibility was to result in a serious defeat with grievous losses. The underlying problem was of course the matter of time, as is so often the case in war: Would time best be gained by early action or by delay? In the event Lake set the time limit as March 15, the latest date on which it was reckoned Aylmer could count with any certainty on the ground's being free from inundation.

If Aylmer's attack had failed after waiting for reinforcements he would most certainly have been criticized for waiting and not advancing at once. As it was the criticisms—always easy after the event—have resolved into censuring his rashness in attacking before the 13th Division had arrived. Perhaps this sounds too simple for if time and reinforcements had been the only factors probably they were as sound and sufficient reasons as any for pushing on with the advance, and other subsidiary motives need not be taken into account. It is difficult to assess the effect of all these subsidiary factors although no doubt they made a major contribution to the decision. Political considerations did count for a great deal. Turkey had received a severe knock from the Russians at Erzerum and probably it was hoped that a reverse on her other flank would help to destroy her morale. But perhaps the one factor which carried most weight was the lurking hope still retained by the staff at Basra that when once a British bayonet was thrust over the parapet at Dujaila the Turks would take to their heels, clear out of Es Sinn and Hanna and leave the road open to Kut.

Returning to the battlefield: Between the beginning of February and the attack in March, Aylmer maintained a consistent pressure against the Hanna defile. A continual bombardment was kept up on the Turkish positions but this had no other effect than to make the Turks dig deeper and Townshend wrote in his diary: "It was like putting salt on a bird's tail, or trying to do so, for they never showed themselves." Guns by themselves were not sufficient to force the Turks from their trenches. On February 26, Aylmer signaled to him what he proposed to do. An attack was to be made on the south of the Dujaila Redoubt and Townshend was to send troops across the river to help as soon as he saw Aylmer's attack taking effect. Townshend replied to the effect that his "full cooperation" could be expected. Rain fell steadily in the last days of February and first few days of March, turning the ground into a morass which became almost impassable for the British troops. Meantime the Turks had a shrewd suspicion that another attempt was about to be made to relieve Kut and the town was subjected to a number of air raids during which forty bombs were dropped. By modern standards this novel method of attack may well seem to be hardly worthy of consideration, but in those days its effect on the morale of the garrison in the restricted perimeter of Kut may well have been proportionately greater than it would have been twenty-four years later. It is difficult to say but Townshend noted:

> If one of the German pilots had fallen into the hands of my troops he would have been torn to pieces. It was not fear of their bombs, for everyone treated the aeroplanes as a joke, running to cover at the last moment with shouts of laughter, but the victims were often the poor wounded in the hospital and it was not possible to mistake the building for anything else.

Slowly the reinforcements trickled up to the front. As an illustration of the rigidity of the system which still governed the troops, two anecdotes are worth recounting. One of the newly arrived British battalions was issued with an innovation from Japan known as the "fly-catching machine," on a scale of one to each company. This machine comprised a box with a triangular piece of wood revolving on a clockwork-operated spindle and its purpose as might be deduced was to reduce the vast numbers of the fly population with which the troops in the forward areas were infested. Through a cutaway opening in the box, unsuspecting flies settled on the revolving wood triangle which was made sticky with fly-catching material, and were slowly revolved into the box where they were scraped off. The boxes were issued in Basra with instructional leaflets which included photographs of piles of flies caught in various places at various times. Generally the troops found these little boxes quite fascinating and it is said that their chief attribute was to relieve the boredom of the journey up to the front from Basra and bets were placed on different machines. Once arrived at the front however more important and more urgent matters precluded this form of entertainment and what happened to the fly-catching machines was of little concern to the fighting men. Not to the staff in Basra, however, and it is said that during a period of bitter fighting the adjutant of one battalion received a signal asking him to "Please report how many files caught in April." Across the signal the adjutant wrote "Balls" and this was duly sent back. Back came an immediate operation telegram "For 'files' read 'flies'" and to this the same adjutant wrote "For 'balls' read 'cock.' " Later when asked during an artillery bombardment to report on the attitude of the enemy this officer replied "Hostile." To the signal asking him to amplify this, he is said to have replied "Very hostile."

The attack had been timed for March 6, but the state of the ground was such that Aylmer made up his mind on the fourth that it would have to be postponed for twenty-four hours, and next day he decided on a further postponement, which meant that zero hour was not until dawn on the eighth. Townshend suggested later that the delay was fatal. According to him, three Arabs, who sneaked out of Kut by swimming the river reported the preparations for his sortie in support of the attacking force and so Khalil knew that something was afoot. There is no reason to doubt Townshend's intelligence; he had long intensive discussions with Khalil after the fall of Kut and this was a phase of the battle which was particularly subject to his penetrating analysis. Yet, despite the fact that the Turks probably guessed that a major attack was being prepared, it is unlikely, in view of what happened, that they knew either when it was to be launched or the exact point at which it was to be aimed.

Aylmer's plan was nothing less than a full-scale frontal assault of the Turkish positions on the right bank, employing virtually the whole of the Tigris force. In that it meant an attack on a strongly entrenched position, over ten miles from the existing front line, it was a novel idea; because it initiated a chain of consequences leading to strategic decisions of worldwide importance, its outcome was equally unusual. Failure at Dujaila resulted in the fall of Kut and from this stemmed the eventual employment of a force in Mesopotamia whose ration strength was only just short of half a million. The main assault was to be made while Younghusband with two brigades (19th and 21st) and a cavalry regiment (16th Cavalry)—a force of about 6,500 men in all, supported by 24 guns—kept the Turks busy in the Hanna positions across the river. Three columns of infantry A, B, and C, together with the Cavalry Brigade were to march on the Dujaila depression by night and assault the Redoubt and the

Turkish line running back to the river from it at dawn next day. Twenty thousand men were quietly to assemble at the Pools of Siloam about three miles due south of the Hanna position after dark on March 7; from here, directed and led by a small party moving on a compass bearing, they were to advance roughly southwest across the desert, marshaled as columns "battalions in line of half battalions," in columns of fours. Although the columns would be enormous, unwieldy, hollow squares of men with transport and guns jammed between the marching ranks, Aylmer considered with some justification that they would be controlled more easily that way at night. At a point some seven miles from the assembly area the force would split into its four component columns and continue to advance toward their individual objectives, until, at dawn—at least that was according to the timings which had all been very carefully worked out—they would have arrived at locations from which they would be able to assault the Turkish lines. The main striking force was to be Columns A and B, under Major General Kemball and they were to make for a point south of the Dujaila Redoubt. Meanwhile, Column C under a fiery Irishman, Major General D'Urban Keary, was to veer a mile or so toward the north, while the Cavalry Brigade went in the other direction to "operate" on the left flank; because they were given no definite objectives the cavalry operations were to become little more than a swan round the open desert.

The organization of the force was the first mistake, one which was to have a profound effect on the operations. Columns A and B were made up of brigades from three different formations which had never worked together before, and neither Kemball, the commander, nor his staff were known to the troops.[5] The choice of Kemball as commander was made because of the qualities of dash and vigor he had shown in the attacks on Sheikh Sa'ad and the Wadi but the fact that he was a stranger to the troops was a serious shortcoming. There had been no time for any proper preparation for the attack and although extremely detailed orders were issued it turned out that these were only to have a paralyzing effect on the subordinate commanders. A final limitation lay in the fact that the brigades moved with all their transport, ambulances

---

5. Actual composition of the force was as follows:

> *Column A* (under Brigadier General G. Christian)
> 36 and 37 Brigades (newly arrived). 9 Brigade (from D'Urban Keary's 3rd Division). A total of 22,000 men with 6 guns.
> *Column B* (under Major General Kemball, who was in overall command of both A and B columns) 28th Brigade (Aylmer's Corps Troops Reserve). Another 8,000 men and 24 guns.
> *Column C* (under Major General 'Urban Keary)
> 7th and 8th Brigades (from his own 3rd Division); 6,500 men with 32 guns.
> *6th Cavalry Brigade* (under Brigadier General R. C. Stephen)
> Four cavalry regiments with S battery Royal Horse Artillery; 1,150 sabres and 4 guns.

and guns—not behind, as one might have expected in a night march which involved crossing difficult ground and which might have developed into a night
attack.

Because the units converging on the assembly area were only given a bare
two hours to cover the distance between their bivouacs and the rendezvous—
in some cases a seven mile march—it is not surprising that some of them were
over an hour and a half late. In spite of an allowance of an hour's margin for
accidents this delay, which may be regarded as almost inevitable in the nature
of things, was never made good. Nevertheless, the night march was remarkable
and probably unique in British military history. In view of the fact that the only
reconnaissance for it had been by air, and the extraordinary difficulties inherent
in such an operation, it was astonishingly successful. The troops set off about
9:30 p.m. The going was slow and there was a succession of halts as the compass parties, on whom everything depended, stopped to check their bearings
and the columns "concertina-ed" up on them. Distances were checked by
means of a bicycle wheeled by one man of each compass party; as the column
stepped out two men checked the revolutions of its wheels while another
counted steps as a means of comparison and yet another swung a pace stick as
a further countercheck; by these methods an aggregate distance was arrived at.

Eventually, shortly before dawn and after many vicissitudes which included
bumping into an Arab encampment where the Arabs threw themselves down
in an attitude of supplication crying "A-rab, A-rab," the force arrived at me
point where they were to split up. As planned, the two leading columns then
turned south along the Dujaila depression while column C veered north, to
face the Dujaila Redoubt from the east. Columns A and B continued along the
depression as far as a bend two miles southwest of the redoubt—subsequently
known as Kemball's Corner—where they formed up for the attack. It was
nearly sunrise by this time but the Turks had given no sign of having spotted
the British force. The few Turks who could be seen were merely standing on
the parapet of their trenches yawning and shaking out their blankets. It seemed
as if complete surprise had been attained and a reconnoitering patrol which
went forward and entered the Redoubt confirmed an earlier report received
from a daring young officer, one Major Leachman, who was working as a
political officer. Disguised as an Arab he had wandered through the Turkish
lines during the night and found the strongpoint to be completely deserted.
Unfortunately although these reports were accepted as being authentic, the pre-
arranged program which, as had been mentioned already, was of a very detailed
nature, included an artillery bombardment before the attack was to be
launched. Still more unfortunately the occasion produced no leader with the
vision to seize the opportunity, give the one command "advance" and let those

back at the headquarters take care of the artillery. Instead, word was telephoned back to Aylmer's headquarters with a request for orders and the fatal reply came back "Stick to program." In retrospect, it seems unquestionable that if the Dujaila Redoubt had been occupied at dawn on March 8, not only would Kut have been relieved, but the safety of the whole Turkish army on the left bank of the Tigris would have been imperiled. Three precious hours were wasted before any forward move took place and not only this, when the artillery moved up it was allowed to register in a leisurely manner and so the whole advantage of the surprise which had been attained was lost.

As soon as Kemball's force had advertised its presence with the bombardment, Turkish reinforcements poured into the trenches of the Redoubt and at ten o'clock when the advance started again Khalil's men were ready to meet the attack. Three thousand of them had come from the Magasis Fort to strengthen the line and more were being ferried across from the left bank in native coracle-like mashoofs and on skin rafts towed by motor-boats. An air reconnaissance estimated that at least another three thousand of them came across the river during the day. Some were caught by the British artillery as they marched across the open ground in close order, but most were unharmed by the gun fire and when once they got to the line of well-concealed trenches south of the Redoubt they disappeared from view and were safe. Then, as the line of British infantry advanced it was met with heavy rifle and machine-gun fire at a range of about seven hundred yards. By noon Kemball's men had only gained a couple of hundred yards and in doing so they suffered very heavy casualties. The advance slowed to a halt but while they were frantically digging in with the "Sirhind" portable entrenching tools which every man carried, orders were given for the advance to be continued and for an assault on the Redoubt.

Meanwhile, in accordance with the original orders, D'Urban Keary's column on the east of the Redoubt was waiting for Kemball's attack to start before joining battle. It was supposed to have deployed at 5:30 in the morning but it had been an another hour before the point in the Dujaila depression, a mile short of the bend where the deployment was to be made, was reached. Even then the infantry were still mixed up with mules, artillery wagons, ambulances, and the guns with the column had yet to get into action. Surprise now was out of the question and because D'Urban Keary's column had held back the last hope of carrying the position was gone. In his dispatch following the action, Lake blamed the failure on Kemball's delay although this was not the full story. As Aylmer and Gorringe were both with D'Urban Keary part of the responsibility must lie with them. A lightly help gap in the Turkish defenses yawned in front of Keary's men and, if they had been allowed to go in, the

Redoubt could still have been taken. But they were held back, the preconceived plan was adhered to and the chance was thrown away. When once it did get moving again Kemball's column in the south still made very little progress in the face of the deadly small arms fire from the concealed positions to the left and in front of the redoubt. A series of attacks preceded by artillery fire were made throughout the day but the troops never really got to grips with their enemies and they took heavy punishment, while hardly ever sighting a Turk. So far as they were concerned the assault on the Redoubt proper, which was still a mile away, was now out of the question, and by 2:30 p.m. it became clear that any advance in this direction would entail the annihilation of Kemball's whole force. Once again it had been shown that the paltry bombardment of prepared positions with but a few field guns—which were not firing high explosives anyway and for which there was no aerial observation—was an ineffectual screen for the infantry to advance under. As always it was the wretched infantryman who suffered. In sultry heat, across a waterless stretch of land with his water bottle empty, weighted down with two days' rations, a load of ammunition and all his other impedimenta in his pack and his entrenching tool on top, he had a hard time. Every advantage lay with the Turks, although the numbers involved were probably evenly matched. Those who were occupying the Dujaila Redoubt were the pick of the Ottoman army, fresh troops flushed with the success of the Dardanelles and strongly entrenched in a secure position which dominated the plain to be crossed by the attackers. Morale was high and Turkish infantry in such circumstances proved to be as stubborn as the Japanese in their foxholes in Burma, and the Southwest Pacific during the Second World War.

By half past four, when Kemball's attack was completely spent, Aylmer decided to rely on Keary's column to batter a way through on the east side of the Redoubt. The Manchesters and the 59th Rifles formed up with the 2nd Rajputs in support and the tired waves of infantry shook out into formation and started to tramp steadily forward into the sunset. But this last attack which the troops had been ordered to push home at all costs had little hope of success for as soon as they got a third of the way across the three thousand yards they had to cover, a heart-sickening rattle broke out from the Redoubt and the advancing troops were caught in small arms fire from both flanks. At the same time Turkish guns, untouched by the British artillery, put down a heavy barrage in front of the line on which they were advancing. Despite this the Manchesters and the 59th Rifles managed to gain a foothold in the Redoubt and two lines of trenches were occupied. No sooner had they broken in however, than a counterattack was launched and a whole mass of Turkish infantry, hurling grenades in front of them as they came, threw back what was left of the assaulting force. British and Indian discipline was good and the thin line of infantry withdrew in good order under this intensive fire to halt for the night three thousand yards from the Redoubt. It was all over and Aylmer had lost about half of his men. The 8th Brigade alone, which had gone into action with 2,300 men, came out with 1,127; thirty-three British and twenty-three Indian officers fell in the attack and the 2nd Rajputs lost all their British officers and twelve out of the sixteen Indian officers; a company and a half of the 1st/2nd Gurkhas who went in with them were practically annihilated. Casualties in the whole force during the action were close to 3,500 including 123 British officers; the Turks were reported to have had about 1,200 dead and wounded. The cavalry, who had been given the job of looking after the left flank can be said to have had absolutely no effect on the battle at all. They hovered about in an ineffective manner, usually somewhere behind the infantry and always moving either with great deliberation or not at all. Had they been capably led and either been given the task of sweeping right around the flank between Dujaila and the Hai, to operate against the Turkish reinforcements rushing up from Magasis, or alternatively put under Kemball's orders and pushed on by him before daylight in a wide sweep around to Imam-al-Mansur to threaten the Turks' rear, they might have attained something. As it was they achieved nothing. Like the cavalry, the garrison in Kut also contributed nothing to the battle. The force deputed to cross the river, when the relieving force was seen to be coming around south of the Dujaila Redoubt, assembled in the palm groves southeast of Kut early on the morning of March 8. Altogether it comprised about two weak brigades and each man carried about a hundred and fifty rounds of ammunition and one day's rations. Through the haze the attack on the Redoubt could be seen developing and the cavalry maneuvering south of it but as the relieving force came no nearer Townshend made no attempt to cross. In his opinion "cooperation was of little practical use" at this stage. Whether he was right or not is a matter for conjecture. The Turks had been taken by surprise and if he had threatened them in the rear they might have pulled back. But success would have depended on a determination on the part of those who commanded the sortie to link up with the relief force. Surprise would have been difficult as he has recorded, yet it still seems as if a sortie could have been possible and it might have turned the day.

During the night Aylmer's men withdrew to Kemball's Corner, their morning assembly area. The Turks followed them, but made no attempt to attack, although they shelled the British rear guard and there was a good deal of sporadic sniping in the dark. However at dawn the Buddhoos again appeared on the skyline to fall upon the wretched wounded, bayoneting and stripping them of their equipment and clothing. Next day the retirement was continued back to the positions from which Aylmer's men had set out; and that was the end of that. Nothing had been gained and the troops were weary and dejected while the Turks were equally elated. The official explanation of their retirement as relayed through Reuter's channels, was that Aylmer's men had retired "through want of water"; when the British troops heard of it they greeted the announcement with blasphemy and derision; they knew they had been beaten. They had not lost morale—good regiments never do—but they had lost confidence as a result of what they regarded as the ineptitude of their commanders. They had suffered heavy casualties without so much as even seeing their enemies and what they felt they needed was effective generalship. It was to be some months before any was forthcoming.

The failure broke Aylmer and three days later he handed over command to Gorringe. On the 12th of March Aylmer sent a letter to Townshend by airplane:

My dear Townshend,

The War Office say that my conduct of operations had been unfortunate, and have ordered my suspension. I need not tell you how deeply I grieve that I have not been able to relieve you; but I have every confidence that my successor will be able to do so very soon. I have had a harder task than most people realize. It all looks very easy when you sit in an armchair at the W.O.! The business a few days ago very nearly came off. I cannot tell you how much I admire the splendid way in which you are defending Kut. I heartily pray that you will gain your reward in speedy relief. Give my best wishes to Delamain, Melliss and Hamilton. Goodbye and God Bless you all, and may you be more fortunate than myself.

Yours ever,

Fenton Aylmer

Townshend replied with a sympathetic telegram, for as he said, "I know his heart must be broken." If his heart was not actually broken, Aylmer was indeed bitter and, in his evidence before the Mesopotamia Commission, he said that he had fought the action on the Wadi against his better judgment, under orders from his superiors, and that his plans for operations after that had never been accepted. In fact, the action at Dujaila, which had brought his downfall need never have been fought when it was—if indeed, at all; the trouble was that everything hung on the urgency of Townshend's relief. Because it had failed to relieve Kut, Townshend might have been expected to feel upset; because Aylmer was an old friend, with whom he had soldiered in happier times, he could be expected to have felt a twinge of regret when he heard that Aylmer had been sacked. But Townshend was feeling disgruntled as well. To replace

Aylmer in command of the Tigris Corps Gorringe was promoted to Lieutenant General and as Gorringe was junior to Townshend, this was a matter of considerable concern to the ambitious and self-seeking commander of the 6th Division.

Chapter 11

Impasse

After the battle of Dujaila, the Tigris Corps spent the rest of March licking its wounds and, in the words of the official communiqué, "consolidating and improving its position." Apart from an occasional thunderstorm the weather was fine and clear and it was not so cold now. But, as the melting snows in the Caucasus poured into the headwaters of the Tigris, the river steadily rose. The whole area round Kut is part of the old Babylonian Plain and as it lies below the high water level of the Tigris when the river fills, the swamps spread out to cover the land. As this happened the length of the front line contracted before them and the troops on both sides had to work hard repairing the dikes along the river bank in order to stop the trenches from becoming water pits. The artillery was immobile and what fighting there was came as the result of patrol actions or occasional flare-ups resulting from attempts to eliminate Turkish snipers. Everybody on the British side—everybody except the Army Commander and his staff, that is—felt that the relief of Kut was fast becoming a hopeless proposition and the atmosphere was one of despondency and despair. And with good cause. The troops, depressed by the costly failure at Dujaila had little faith in the high command. Cold, wet, rain and mud, a dull ration, irregular mail from home, no canteen arrangements and nowhere to go for a rest: all these things were having their effect. India was making some effort to improve conditions but such effort was often badly organized. Some canteen stores for instance, had been sent out but no distributing organization had been provided to see that they got into the hands of those who needed them most, up the Tigris. Yet an absurd audit of their disposal was demanded of them even though most never reached their destination. The whole system behind the lines was completely disorganized. Of the reinforcement drafts which left Basra something like sixty percent never got to the front as those that did not fall sick from natural causes en route malingered. Sickness, real and feigned, was rife. Indeed, with few exceptions the whole of the British Mesopotamia Expedition Force was sick at heart—sick and stale.

On the "other side of the hill" the Turks were quite certain that it was only a matter of time before Kut fell, and in a courteous and almost friendly letter Khalil Pasha addressed himself to Townshend pointing out the facts. After referring to Aylmer's abortive attempts to break through after six weeks' preparation—attempts which had only resulted in four thousand casualties and a return to the original position—he went on:

> For your part you have heroically fulfilled your military duty. From hence-forth I see no likelihood that you will be relieved. Your deserters say that you are without food and that diseases are prevalent among your troops. You are free to continue your resistance at Kut or to surrender to my forces, which are growing larger and larger. Receive, General, the assurance of our highest consideration.
>
> KHALIL
> *Governor of Baghdad*
> *Commanding Turkish Forces in Irak*

To this Townshend replied with equal courtesy, thanking Khalil for his letter and commenting that he was glad to find again, as he had found at Ctesiphon, that the Turk was always a good soldier and a "gentleman,"[1] he concluded there was "still every chance of relief." Nevertheless even Townshend was beginning to have his doubts. Yet he was the only general in whom the Meso-potamia Army had any real faith—even Gorringe's men also believed that he was the only British commander really worth his salt. It was the Commander-in-Chief who was forcing the pace for, despite the weather and the recent set-back, Lake still believed it was possible to extricate Townshend's force and snatch a victory. It hardly seems credible to believe that he can have been aware of all the facts but on the eleventh—almost before he knew the extent of the defeat of Dujaila—he was signaling to Townshend:

---

1. A word which could be construed differently after the experiences of the prisoners following the fall of Kut.

I can realize to the full, and sympathize most deeply with the disappointment which both you and your command must feel at our recent failure to relieve you. Rest assured, however, that we shall not abandon the effort and that *for the next attempt the Maximum Force will be employed.*

This was as good as suggesting that Aylmer had not employed the "Maximum Force" at Dujaila and Townshend quickly picked up the point. In his reply he said "... I realize fully Aylmer's difficulties and I sympathize with his heavy loss of brave officers and men. I know you will relieve me if it is possible to do so but I think it will require the whole 13th Division united. ... I hope it will be a united force on one bank—no dissemination whatsoever. ..." And in his diary he noted his original suspicions that Aylmer had not made as bold an effort as he might have done and "as I had begged him to do," were well-founded.

All this may be considered something of a slur on poor Aylmer who had done his best; the trouble was that Aylmer's best was just not good enough. Gorringe, too, was soon to be found wanting and like his predecessor he was also destined to make the melancholy journey down river into obscurity which Nixon and Aylmer had already taken. Not that this was any consolation to the men who had to fight. The situation is a very good example of the maxim that there are no bad regiments, only bad officers—in this case, senior officers. Despite their staleness and disillusionment they were willing enough—not so willing perhaps as their predecessors at Qurna—but after all their reverses they had forgotten the taste of victory, and it would be stupid to suggest that the men facing the Turkish lines in front of Kut relished the idea of frontal attacks. They had seen how fruitless they were and suffered their waste; because of them their numbers were sadly depleted, so much so that brigades had had to be completely reorganized. The Seaforths and Black Watch were in such a parlous state that they had had to be amalgamated into a "Highland" Battalion; the 9th Bhopals had to be reinforced with oddments from Rajput regiments; the Norfolks and Dorsets reinforcements telescoped into a composite "Norset" Battalion, the Hants and Buffs into the "Huffs"; and so on. In many ways it was a ridiculous situation because in Basra other reinforcements were cooling their heels, unable to get up to the front line and, of course, there were all the sick and malingerers along the route. (One officer recalls that about the time of the battle of the Wadi a notice in the officers' reinforcement camp read "Will officers who wish to go up to the front please write their names below." Of those who did so—and it would be an affectation to suggest that there were many volunteers—some were told that they could not go upstream until Kut was relieved and were offered jobs supervising Arabs unloading ships above Basra. Only one or two managed to hitch-hike up the river; when they finally reached the Tigris Corps area they were employed on base duties, collecting and dealing with Indian deserters, before being posted to one of the battalions where they were so badly needed).

For his next attempt to breakthrough, Gorringe had at his command about thirty thousand men and 130 guns; for the latter it must be added, there was a great shortage of ammunition. Opposing him was about the same number of Turks, who had 96 guns. Although by mid-March all of its units had not yet arrived, Gorringe was relying primarily on the all-British 13th Division, one of Kitchener's "New Army" divisions, commanded by Major General Stanley Maude, the one man who was destined eventually to retrieve the British military fortunes in Mesopotamia. The division had already covered itself in glory at Gallipoli, where it had lost 6,000 men out of a grand total of 10,500, but after Gallipoli its strength had been made up with raw and only semi-trained drafts so that it could no longer really be considered a battle-tried formation. The one apparent advantage was that it was fresh to the country; but it was also fresh to the type of warfare which it was about to face, and obviously it had to learn. How it was to be taught was rather akin to a non-swimmer being thrown in at the deep end of a pool; a desperate method of initiation. However, desperate needs require desperate remedies, or so Gorringe thought. Apart from the gallant 13th, two divisions were also available for the offensive. The 3rd was on the right bank of the river and the 7th deployed on the left. Both were well-tried, both were tired, having borne the brunt of all the Relief Force operations so far and, apart from all the privations and hardships they had suffered, they had received fourteen thousand casualties over the last few weeks. Despite their weaknesses (and weakness in resolve probably counted more than depleted manpower states) they were going to have to buckle-to again, as were the three infantry brigades, 35th, 36th and 37th in the so-called Corps Reserve.

Preparations for the next operation, which once again was to be *the* one that would open the door to Kut, went steadily ahead. During this period conditions in the firing line had stabilized into trench warfare, akin in many respects to that in Flanders—but with Mesopotamian modifications. There was the same old business of patrols, listening posts in "No Man's Land" as in France, but, as sixteen miles of communication trenches were necessary for a mile long front on the Tigris, the area covered by the British positions there was much deeper than anything on the same line of front in Flanders. Furthermore the human aspects of the Mesopotamia force were vastly different. As has been stressed already there were absolutely no amenities to fall back on in Mesopotamia. In France there was always the possibility of leave to England—infrequent maybe, but nevertheless a possibility. Out of the line there were rest areas near towns and villages which had cafes; these did at least provide some opportunity to forget the war for a few hours. In Mesopotamia, where no comparable resources existed, once they got to the front most of the troops preferred to stay there and put up with the privations of the forward area where there was always the mild excitement of a little sniping as against the so-called rest areas a few miles behind the line where life was but a drab monotony.

Turning to the more pleasant aspects of this dreary existence: on the left bank of the Tigris "No Man's Land" was a long narrow, soggy strip of land which, because of the season and its comparatively untrodden state had attained a lushness described as almost English, where Shepherd's purse, mallow and wild mustard all vied with each other among the coarse grass. In spite of the war, birds were there in plenty—mallard, teal and wild geese on the marshes, even larks—while snow-capped peaks and deep purple gorges of the Pusht-i-Kuh mountains on the horizon provided a singularly attractive backdrop. Momentarily it could all seem very peaceful. But for any whose minds were straying to the lighter side of life the wire entanglements in front of the now flooded Turkish front line and the occasional *"zing"* of a sniper's bullet soon brought back the grimmer aspects of the scene. And any who might have been tempted to ride off toward the mountains for a day's shooting would also soon have found that the deserted plain between the foothills and the British lines were swarming with concealed Buddhoos merely awaiting the opportunity to cut the traveler's throat.

On the right bank the landscape was not quite so lush, but the prickly bushes had put on their green seasonal coats and, as on the left bank, there was no dearth of birds. Nature had even thought about the cavalry and horse-gunners and provided wild boar for their traditional sport of pigsticking, and this they occasionally indulged in behind the lines. The British infantry, in their off-duty moments when they were not digging, patrolling or on sentry-go, were compelled to amuse themselves with less glamorous sport by catching tortoises and pitting their strange pets against each other in races. Especially for these men in the line, life was anything but a gay round of idle amusement and it would be foolish to dwell too long on these lighter aspects because, if ever a place could be cited as an example of war being ninety-nine percent sheer boredom and misery and one percent excitement and possible glory, then that place was Mesopotamia. Furthermore, those three weeks in March and early April, 1916, were but a, prelude to another bloody struggle.

Before the attack on March 8, Aylmer had said that if he failed to break-through to Kut at Dujaila .the only alternative was to go back to the left bank to smash a way through on that side of the river. This not only meant forcing the Hanna position, scene of the failure of January 21, but subsequently capturing first a strongly defended position at Fallahiyeh three miles behind Hanna and then another defensive layout at Sannaiyat another three miles behind that. Even then, before the way to Kut was open there was yet another line of trenches which the Turks had dug in continuation of the Sinn Banks position on the other side of the Tigris and this was probably the strongest of all four localities. However, Gorringe apparently came to the same conclusion as Aylmer because this was where he decided to strike the next blow. The idea of Townshend launching a breakout expedition to coincide with this fresh effort of the Relief Force had now been dropped and Gorringe said that he only expected the 6th Division in Kut to cooperate passively, adding frothily: "You are the rock on which I hope to split the Turkish forces and your co-operation by gun fire on the ferry at Magasis and by containing the enemy on the left bank on the last day of the operations will greatly assist."

Four fifty-five on the morning of April 5, was fixed as zero hour for the first phase of the operation—the capture of Hanna. Despite the fact that the fine weather had broken on March 30, every possible preparation had been made that could be made; so far as could be foreseen absolutely nothing had been left to chance. Guns had been massed on both banks of the river, the barbed wire entanglements in front of the Turkish positions had been shelled and shelled again in order to break them down and the guns were now all ready to pulverize the actual trenches. The 13th Division, whose arrival it was hoped had been kept a secret from the Turks, had rehearsed its operational roles on a scale model; every unit knew its task and its place. The first lines of the Hanna trenches were to be assaulted "silently," there was to be no artillery bombardment until the attack was well under way. The trenches, it was hoped, would be carried by surprise infantry bombers[2] and bayonets finishing the job when the assaulting waves had reached their objectives. Only when the first line had been taken would the guns open up, and then on the third line while the attackers were pushing on to take the second position. Behind the 13th Division the 7th was to mop up and be ready to move forward to help if this became necessary; on the right bank the task of the men of the 3rd was to pin down the Turks facing them and to shoot any Turks across the river who were trying to move forward from the Fallahiyeh position. For all this to go well, all that was wanted was the initial surprise.

Attaining it could only be possible as- to the moment of the attack for, needless to say, the Turks were well aware that something was about to happen

---

2. At this stage of the war, the use of grenades and attacks by bombers enjoyed an unprecedented popularity. Grenades are obviously an extremely useful weapon for clearing trenches but dependence on them resulted in a decline in the standard of shooting with the rifle. Men went into an assault across open ground, hurling grenades in front of them when they would have attained better results from the one weapon which pre-war soldiers had been taught was their "best friend."

and, like the British, they were prepared. Nevertheless Gorringe's whole scheme seemed to go like clockwork, but when the first waves of the 13th Division crept up to their first objective in the hard gray light of dawn, they found most of the Turks had skipped off during the night. Less than a hundred men were left behind as a weak rear guard and prominently displayed over the first line trenches was a large notice in French, "Cheerio, until the next battle." The men of the 13th raced on to the next and succeeding objectives, but they too were almost deserted and by 7 a.m. they were almost on to the next barrier of the Fallahiyeh positions. For the British infantry, keyed up and spoiling for a fight it was an unexpected and easy success and the emptiness of the position was as much a disappointment as a relief; naively, because they were fresh, they assumed that the Turks were on the run. The old hands knew better, the Turks were playing for time. They were right; two and a half months had been spent preparing for an assault on Hanna and when overwhelming odds had been assembled, Khalil wisely gave way. For him it was better to forego a few barren miles of difficult terrain and save his men for a more propitious battle.

Gorringe was one who had factual evidence that the Turks were not running. Air reconnaissance reports had told him that Fallahiyeh and Sannaiyat were being reinforced. When the men of the 40th Brigade tried to cross the mile and a half stretch of flat open ground which separated the Hanna defenses from those at Fallahiyeh and came under heavy machine gun fire, they soon learned the truth also. To press on undoubtedly presaged heavy losses and so the brigade was ordered to stop where they were, dig in and wait until it got dark. This seems to have been a pity because in the light of after events the delay probably proved fatal to a success at Sannaiyat. Nevertheless, as seen during that afternoon, a good deal had been attained. Not only had the initial block at Hanna been broken, even on the other bank of the river the 8th Brigade had seized an opportunity to advance against lesser opposition man had been expected and managed to capture the Turkish positions south of Umm-al-Bahram. The brigade had had to withstand a heavy counterattack but the ground which had been gained was held on to. All things considered it had been a successful day for Gorringe, and for Khalil too, for that matter, even though he had lost ground.

Soon after dark the British started to shell Fallahiyeh, and at 7:30 p.m. the 38th and 39th Brigades started their advance to capture the series of deep trenches forming the position. This time however the Turks doggedly hung on to await the British bayonets and next morning the measure of their resistance was reflected in the long swathes of dead Tommies, riddled with bullets, which lay along the line of advance. The positions were taken but Fallahiyeh and Hanna together had cost almost two thousand British lives. In the morning,

the ill-fated 7th Division came up to relieve the 13th, the intention being that
they should assault Sannaiyat at dawn next day—pushing on to give the Turks
no rest. Their task was reckoned to be easy; the real obstacle and the key to
Kut, or so it was thought at the time, lay six miles behind Sannaiyat in the prolongation of the Sinn position and the 13th Division, less war-worn than the
others, was to force this. According to Gorringe's appreciation, the 7th had
been given an easy job. Since the Turks had no intention of giving way at
Sannaiyat without a very stiff fight, his appreciation was to prove woefully
wrong.

So far as the men who were to make the attack were concerned the first
difficulty lay in the fact that nobody knew anything about the ground which
had to be crossed to get to their objective. As the operation was taking place at
night some confusion was inevitable, but even as they started to move up to
the front the situation was exacerbated and considerable disorder caused by the
13th Division retiring through them. This was a setback from which they never
recovered. Worse was to follow. No maps of the Fallahiyeh defence system
were available and the old Turkish trenches had to be crossed in pitch darkness. As some of them were seven feet deep this meant that innumerable diversions had to be made around them and with the marching and counter-
marching that ensued, it is amazing that the assaulting battalions managed to
stumble through in as good order as they did. To do so they had to leave all
their heavy equipment, including their machine guns behind, and the latter
were weapons which they would have been glad of later on. At 4:30 a.m. when
the attack was supposed to begin, the men of the 7th were still a long way from
Sannaiyat and even an hour later as dawn broke, they were still eight hundred
yards away from their objective when the first Turkish shots rang out. The
Turks could see the long thin lines of British troops as they stumbled on
toward them quite plainly, the British had simply no idea where the Turks were
and they never had a chance. Another hundred yards and Khalil's men let fly a
solid sheet of lead. The British and Indians tried gamely to struggle on but it
was hopeless; there was nothing for it but to fall back and dig in. In less than
two hours the 7th Division lost over 1,200 men in this action, most of them
falling in the first twenty minutes. "What is that line of khaki?" queried a staff
officer, looking through his binoculars from the Hanna position shortly
afterward, "Why haven't they dug themselves in?" "They are our dead," was
the sad rejoinder.

The plan now was for the 7th Division to attack again in the early hours of
the following morning, and the opportunities that had been missed by post-
poning the earlier advance by the men of the 13th were emphasized during the
day. A strong wind suddenly blew up, driving the waters of the Suwaikiyeh

Marsh south toward the river and drowning many of the British wounded and flooding the trenches they had feverishly scratched in the soft earth. Above ground the whole area was swept by bullets which caused many more casualties during the day. Then, when night finally came and an attempt was made to resume the advance only two hundred yards were gained. Once more it was stalemate. Gorringe was loath to admit it but it was so. The official communiqué laconically described the operation as a "demonstration"—a word whose connotations are never particularly palatable to any soldier who has taken part in one. "It means," somebody once explained with an odd mixture of clichés, "that you get it in the neck without getting your own back."

At 9 p.m. that night (April 7) the Turkish trenches were bombarded, not as a prelude to another attack but in order that Gorringe's staff should be able to plot just where the Turks' positions lay. Khalil's men cooperate well: presuming there was about to be another British assault they opened fire and sent up Verey lights all along the line. From this Gorringe's staff were able to make a rough plot of what they were up against, and armed with this knowledge it was decided that the next attack would be at dawn on April 9. This time it would be delivered by the 13th Division. What remained of the 7th were to cooperate by giving covering fire as and when the opportunity arose. Oddly enough no deliberate bombardment or barrage was arranged on the immediate objectives of Kitchener's men but only on the trenches to the flank and rear. During the night the three brigades of the 13m Division silently deployed and got into position in perfect order. It was a good start which augured well for the outcome. However, just before they crossed the start line at a slow pace to go into the assault, the first shots were heard and a mass of flares shot up into the air from the Turkish lines illuminating the battlefield. Within minutes the sickening rattle of rifle and machine gun fire had swelled to a great volume—always an ominous sign in modern war and one which often spells failure, since it is an indication that the element of surprise has gone.

Three lines of trenches formed the core of the Turks' defenses at Sannaiyat; the second line lying seventy-five yards behind the first, the third a hundred and twenty-five yards behind that. Some of the British infantry actually penetrated the first line but they were given no chance to consolidate their position and open the way for those behind them. They were ruthlessly bombed out by Turks who had been concealed in a labyrinth of cunningly contrived dugouts, aptly named "snake pits" by the British, into which the Turks had slipped back when their line was rushed. Under a shower of grenades, the Tommies were compelled to withdraw and eventually the front was again stabilized three hundred yards or so away from the still intact Turkish line. In tins battle casualties again amounted to about 1,600 men, so that in the two actions of Fallahiyeh and Sannaiyat the 13th Division had lost over 3,600 men or some forty-six percent of the actual troops engaged. These were appalling casualties even if one accepts an attritional battle—since they could not be replaced. (The tempo of the fighting may also be judged from the fact that five Victoria Crosses were won.)

Just as it had been in the January operation, so it was now in April. Once again the elements turned against the British and tins time with the most devastating violence: stormy weather and the creeping waters of the marsh all working against Gorringe's men. It was not that the conditions were abnormal; Mesopotamia is a country of excess where the weather is seldom moderate. What was abnormal was the necessity for trying to wage war while they lasted. Under such conditions relieving men in the trenches was a difficult business and the troops, who had to fight the waters of both the Tigris and the marsh as well as the Turks, were hard pressed building and keeping up embankments in order to ward off the floods. On the left bank the trenches were so full of water that the men sometimes had to swim. On the right bank the Turks broke down the dikes at Bait Aisa and Umm-al-Bahram to assist the work of Nature. This resulted in the forward firing line on the right bank being cut off from its base and the formation of a dangerous salient in the British line. To the tired British troops the only consolation—if it was a consolation—was that the Turks were in a similar plight; they too were flooded out and were having to work hard to keep their lines intact.

In spite of these filthy conditions which, it might be added, promised only to get worse, Gorringe had not given up. However, for his next thrust he decided to change his tactics, and try the right bank again. The 7th Division was to hold the line between the river and the marsh on the left bank while the main thrust was made at the Turks' position at Sinn. However before the actual attack could be made on Sinn, a complicated network of trenches and picquets had to be cleared in front of it. These centered on Bait Aisa and so a preliminary operation had to be mounted in order to get possession of this place. This was not made easier by the swamp or the fact that the Turks commanded the stretch of the river which enabled them to control much of the flooding on this side. (For the reader who may be puzzled why no further attempt was made to assault Dujaila again among this frenzy of attacks—first on the left, then on the right and so on—it should be explained that Gorringe was now pinned down to the firm ground on the river bank by the flooding. He could not strike either directly at Sinn or the Dujaila Redoubt.) The new plan was for the 3rd Division to capture Bait Aisa on April 13, and significantly because of the date the 13th Division, now thoroughly blooded, was to be brought across the river and concentrated behind them ready to push through, deliver the coup de grace and carry on to Sinn. Largely because of the enormous natural difficulties imposed by the weather, this plan, like its predecessors, was also doomed. More Turks had come down from Baghdad, although irrespective of this fact Khalil had been able to switch his troops about between the positions investing Kut and those facing the Relief Force; meantime Gorringe had had next to no reinforcements. Approximately five thousand men were on the way up from Basra but so far they were pie in the sky and reliance had to be placed on the same old regiments and the same men who had fought in all the actions from Hanna onward. These men were tired, ill-fed and poorly organized; many of them were sick as well, but they kept going. Some of me units which had lost heavily since the original amalgamations had had to be combined with others in a similar state, so that old regimental identities were now almost completely lost in a few composite battalions. None of this helped, physically worn, sick in spirit: these are the times when the mystique regimental esprit de corps is most valuable and it had been submerged. In the strange combined units officers often did not even know the names of their men, sometimes not even each other, before they were called upon to go into battle.

Two days beforehand an exceptionally heavy thunderstorm made it necessary to postpone this, the latest operation, for about twenty-four hours. During the delay periods another gale broke the causeway behind the 3rd Division, completely flooding the country between the river and the Umm-al-Bahram and making it impossible to get the artillery forward to positions from which they could support the forthcoming attack. That was the first setback for this operation but not the last; a whole sequence of equally unfortunate events were to follow. Just before dawn on April 15, the attack got under way in a heavy thunderstorm. The 7th and 9th Brigades, moving abreast of each other on a comparatively narrow frontage, set out bravely enough, but soon they were knee-deep in water as they ploughed stubbornly across toward their outpost objectives. Many of them marched and marched—waded and waded would be a better description—but never got there. The compasses on which they had to rely in order to maintain direction in the dark are said to have been affected by the heavy lightning and some of the units actually moved in a complete circle; at daylight these unfortunates found themselves actually behind their starting point. Nevertheless in spite of everything one battalion managed to capture the outposts at dawn and in the teeth of all the difficulties or movement and communication, Bait Aisa was assaulted on the 17th. This was again the task of the 7th and 9th Brigades. The men advanced through a slight mist, as close as they could get behind a heavy barrage and as a result of risking themselves to their own shrapnel they managed to get up to the Turks' trenches with comparatively few casualties. When they jumped over their parapets Khalil's men were found to be sitting under them, oblivious to the close proximity of the assaulting waves. The fight which followed was short and sharp and many Turks were either bayoneted or quickly taken prisoner. For once, the Gurkhas of the 7th Brigade really came into their own, cutting and slashing with their kukris, and the Turks were so completely shaken that those of them who were defending the second and third lines of trenches rose to a man and bolted. The Gurkhas with their blood up, went after them hell for leather, way beyond their objectives and even managed to capture a couple of Turkish field guns in the rear area, although they were not able to get them away. Meanwhile the 9th Brigade which had cleared a large length of the main communication trench leading up to the Chahela Mounds had also done well. The attack, so far as it had gone, had been a complete success and that day was counted as one of reckoning. Dead Turks who had been clubbed or bayoneted to death were everywhere and surprisingly enough, British and Indian casualties had been comparatively light. It had been a battle of contradictions.

But it was not yet over. Khalil realized that the loss of Bait Aisa gave Gorringe freedom to maneuver on the right bank and this he was unwilling to concede. The British had to be stopped before they got any further and he immediately organized a supreme effort to do so. Every available Turk—some ten thousand of them, including units of the famous 2nd Ottoman Division, veterans of the Balkan war and opponents of the 13th Division at Gallipoli— collected between Magasis and the north end of the Sinn banks, and in a very short time Khalil managed to throw in an all-out counterattack supported by all the guns he had at his disposal. His first object was to pinch off the salient formed when the Gurkhas had dashed ahead so enthusiastically and masses of Turks now descended on the little men from Nepal. Before long there was complete confusion, the situation being described as rather like a football match on a ground where there were two or three gates. In the light of a half- moon sheer weight of numbers steadily pushed the 9th Brigade further and further back, and only the 8th Brigade who had taken up a position in a water- cut just across from Bait Aisa was able to stop the rot. On the British left, the Turks even managed to capture the 7th Brigade headquarters; it was only the resolution of the brigade commander who led a counterattack that enabled the headquarters to be retaken. Fighting continued until both sides were nearly exhausted and the position was only finally stabilized when the 13th Division, preparing to move up to carry on to Sinn, came up to reinforce the new front line. Then, when the counterattack eventually petered, out, the Tommies took over what was left of the previous morning's success. Once again it was a case of being back to square one; the only difference being that this time the Turks had also taken a knock.

During the night most of the punishment was taken by the 8th Brigade. Assault after assault had been delivered with the greatest determination against their front, and next morning hundreds of Turkish corpses lay in a three hundred yard wide band in front of their trenches—a truly gruesome testimony of the resistance which the men of the 59th Rifles and 47th Sikhs had put up. The men of the 8th Brigade expended an average of four hundred rounds of ammunition that night, and the four guns of the pack battery, supporting them close by on the right, had fired over open sights every single shell it possessed. During the morning one of the Sikhs, surveying the dead from his trench, is reported to have said to a British officer, "Sahib, I hear that the enemy are very numerous. May God put it into their heads to attack in this manner again. They will soon become very few." It was wishful thinking, the Turks preferred to fight from their trenches and let the British and Indians do the attacking. Attacking in this fashion was exceptional and in this action it was estimated that they lost about 4,000 men against British and Indian casualties of about 1,650. More Turks were killed at Bait Aisa than at Sheikh Sa'ad, the Wadi and Fallahiyeh combined, and so in some ways it may be counted a British success. Nevertheless Khalil had held the line and although the 13th Division made a number of attempts to advance during the succeeding few days, none of them had much success. Yet again Gorringe had to admit that it was a stalemate, and like a yo-yo his thoughts again turned toward the left bank.

This time he decided that the 7th Division, supported by the 35th and 36th Brigades, should attack Sannaiyat on April 20. As before, the elements it seemed, had their own plans as well as Gorringe, because once again the weather interfered and the attack had to be postponed for two days. On April 20, there was six inches of water with six inches of mud underneath it, covering the ground across which the troops would have to advance; on the 22nd it was still flooded and heavy going. Nevertheless an attack was pronounced to be a feasible proposition. Listening posts had been sent out and it had been deduced that the first and second Turkish trenches had suffered severely from the weather, so much so that they were only thinly held and deep in water.

The plan was for the assault to be made by the 19th and 21st Brigades at 7 a.m., after a fifty minute bombardment—forty minutes "slow" and nine "intense" according to the gunner's arithmetic—had cleared the way. There was then to be a barrage whose rate of lift had been carefully calculated to cope with a slow advance through knee-deep water; under this umbrella the troops would advance safely. All they would have to do would be to occupy the trenches when they got to them. The scheme was very scientific and, by present-day standards, quite modern. The water had fallen and consequently the advance was much more rapid than had been expected so that the main effect of the barrage was to hold the troops back. The real hitch came just before the time for the infantry to start moving, when the 21st Brigade reported that the mud was such that they would not be able to cross the ground in front of them at all. The ground across which they were supposed to assault was lower and had not dried out to the same extent as that on their left flank. Consequently the whole brunt of the attack fell on the 19m Brigade alone, most of it on the Highland battalion which was the spearhead of the assault.

The Highlanders climbed out of their trenches and started to slosh forward; soon they were seen to be waving their red flags furiously in order to stop the artillery fire. When they got to the first line it was, as had been expected, flooded; there were no Turks in it and the Highlanders struggled across to carry the second line which was also neck deep in water. However, behind the second line of trenches there was a network of dugouts and "snake pits" and as they floundered blindly among them they came under terrific fire. In the mud and water the Scotsmen had great difficulty in keeping their feet and that was not the worst of it. Choked and clogged with mud, their rifles jammed, making it impossible to return the Turks' fire; nothing could have been more exasperating or, as far as the Highlanders were concerned, more tragic. And this was the moment that the Turks chose to counterattack. They came in from both sides; from the right and from the left along the river bank, over firm ground which was not flooded or only lightly so. As they came they fired down into the Highlanders struggling in the water-logged trenches below them and the Scotsmen could do nothing about it until the Turks came close enough for them to get in among them and use cold steel. The counterattack along the river bank was eventually stopped by the fire of the British artillery and machine guns south of the river but there was little that could be done about coming in on the right. Behind the Highlanders, the supporting battalions of the 19th Brigade were having trouble with their rifles and so they too were unable to do anything much to help. An order is said to have been given for the Highlanders to retire. (Its source is apparently lost to posterity since the officer who is said to have given it was killed shortly afterward.) Many of the Highlanders refused to obey or, not being aware of the order, stayed on to fight it out and were eventually mown down in a bloody shambles. Gallant though this may have been, they had little hope of attaining anything and were eventually driven back to the original start line. Still yet again the attempt to breakthrough had been a failure. The only outcome on the British side being a bill for thirteen hundred casualties. Fortunately this proved to be the final effort to relieve Kut and, after such a chapter of failures, no doubt the reader will have concluded already that it was high time a halt was called. Nevertheless the basic reason for this ghastly series of abortive operations must not be forgotten—Kut. There time was fast running out, the state of the garrison was critical and if they were to be relieved, no time could be lost. But the time and opportunity, if they ever existed, were gone now.

At 10 a.m. on the morning of April 22, when the fighting had died down, a party of Turks carrying a Red Crescent Flag was seen to be walking toward the British lines; carrying a Red Cross Flag, an Indian Medical Service officer went out to meet them and, by mutual agreement, an informal armistice was arranged. The wounded on both sides were brought in and apart from the fact that the Turks were seen to strip the British dead close to their trenches, the truce passed off without incident. To many of the British who were there, why the Turks had asked for a truce seemed inexplicable but the answer would seem to be in the long streams of Turkish wounded seen retiring from the battlefield while the truce lasted. Yet the battle on April 22 was definitely a Turkish victory. There have been contradictory views expressed; many of the Highlanders believed that they could have carried the Turkish 3rd line at the point of the bayonet;, particularly if the supporting battalions behind them had been poured in at the right moment. But the general impression is one of a tragic impasse and hopeless physical odds in which the floods imposed the final veto, making a British success impossible. Any reader with the minimum of a military background will appreciate that the odds were heavily against such a success when the original plan for an assault by two brigades was changed at the last minute because the 21st Brigade said that they were unable to move; on a one-brigade front it was not really worthwhile trying. Furthermore, one wonders even if this particular action had been a success whether it could have made any difference.

The fate of Kut was said to have hung on the outcome of Sannaiyat and failure there meant that Townshend's garrison would fall. But after Sannaiyat there was the prolongation of the Sinn position and "flesh and blood" could do no more. The Tigris Corps casualties, in the three weeks from April 5 to April 23 were just under ten thousand men; this was twenty-five percent of the force and in some formations the percentage was much higher. As an example, taking into account the reinforcements they received during the period the 28th Brigade lost over one hundred percent of its strength and one hundred and ninety percent of its British officers. In Kut there were about 12,500 men and in the efforts to relieve them the Tigris Corps lost 23,000 in battle casualties alone in the four months between January and April 1916. There were large numbers of sick also but these are not included in this figure. Corresponding Turkish losses during this period are estimated to have been about ten thousand.

The garrison in Kut was now on minimum rations and to complete the sorry story the details of the last desperate attempt which was made to re-provision it must be recounted. At 8 p.m. on April 24 the paddle steamer *Julnar,* which had been specially prepared arid loaded with two hundred and seventy tons of supplies, made a most gallant attempt to force the blockade. The mission was a forlorn hope, bitterly criticized, but a magnificent adventure in the best British naval tradition. As in any daredevil enterprise of this nature there was no lack of volunteers and Lieutenant H. O. B. Firman, R.N. was given command and Lieutenant Commander Cowley,[3] who had been commanding the *Mejidieh,* appointed pilot. Cowley, a most unusual piratical character, had been in the service of the Euphrates and Tigris Navigation Company for many years and because of this he was regarded by the Turks as one of their subjects. Knowing that they looked upon him as a renegade and that he would get short shrift if he was captured, the fact that he volunteered for the job in spite of it makes his actions even more outstanding. He did so because he knew the river and the *Julnar* well and probably he was the man best suited to this suicidal operation. Owing to the floods, the Tigris was then at its highest level, the darkness and the shifting shoals would have made the venture risky enough even with friends on both banks. With a gauntlet of guns to be run for some twenty-five miles of river, and unknown obstacles to be navigated in the shape of mines and booms, the chances of the *Julnar* getting through were pretty remote. In the hope of distracting the Turks, her departure was covered by all the artillery that could be brought to bear by Gorringe's force, but the Turks were too alert to be caught napping.

It was moonlight when the *Julnar* set off. Any hope of maintaining surprise for more than a few minutes was, of course, impossible and as soon as she came opposite the first Turkish lines there was a terrific fusillade of rifle and machine-gun fire from both banks. As she passed through the Sinn position the Turks let fly with everything they had but the *Julnar* had been fitted with armor plates and sandbagged and she steamed on. Disaster came as she was nearing Magasis, about four miles off Kut (eight and a half miles by river). Steel wire hawsers had been stretched diagonally across the stream and when the ship's rudder became tangled in one of these she was held. There the Turks were waiting for her; it would hardly be surprising if her arrival had been unex-pected, since she had been prepared for the voyage at Amara, a known hot-bed of spies. After a quick and intense bombardment in which most of the crew were either killed or wounded, a boarding party administered the coup de grace, and next morning the *Julnar* could be seen from Kut lying alongside the

---

3. Both officers were posthumously awarded the Victoria Cross.

river bank by the Magasis Fort. Those of the crew still alive were hauled off into captivity; all that is, except for the wretched Cowley, who was summarily executed.

The only consolation that could be said to have derived from the *Julnar's* failure was that it definitely put an end to any further hope of the garrison in Kut maintaining the siege, so saving the Tigris Corps from a further sacrifice of life and morale in more abortive attempts at getting through to it. By now the very name of Kut had become a nightmare to those concerned with its relief for the lesson had become so very clear. To break through to Kut meant that vast numbers of men would have to be sacrificed in massed attacks against the stout defenses of the Turks and that was a course of action that was just not possible; there were insufficient transport on the Tigris to bring such vast numbers up to Fallahiyeh for the sacrifice. For those who are tempted to suggest that other methods might have proved more suitable[4] it must be remembered that this was an age when many modern weapons, of which we now mink instinctively, were just not available. Air supply was virtually unknown. It is true that some supplies of food were actually dropped into Kut from the air but the quantities involved were but a flea-bite compared with what was necessary. The few airplanes that were available were all slow and had a very poor performance. Even aerial photography had not yet reached Meso-potamia, and the only maps which were available of the country that had to be fought over were produced by officers sketching from the air. Consequently these were quite inaccurate. There was no such thing as an airfield as we know it today and such landing strips as were improvised suffered because the ground was either flooded or became a sea of glutinous mud. Tanks had not yet appeared in Europe, gas was in its infancy and in Mesopotamia heavy artillery was almost non-existent. Finally, excluding any consideration of the generals, some tribute must be paid to the men who fought and fell. So far as they were concerned, even though Kut surrendered, nobody can say that the

---

4. Whenever British foreign policy has outrun its military means—and the history of the British Empire affords many examples—there have usually been plenty of suggestions as to how the situation could be handled! In the Zulu War, for instance, Secocoeni retired to his caves and there were insufficient troops or guns to drive him out. The Secretary of State wrote "Can Secocoeni be only driven out of his caves by starvation? Would not rockets do it or some such appliance? I suggest cayenne pepper. Such a process would be shorter in its operation and more humane."

British and Indian soldiers did not do all that could possibly be expected of them—and more. There are still plenty of men about in the world today with guts, but whether they could have done as well as those in the Tigris Corps between December 1915 and May 1916 is very, very doubtful. These men showed grit and determination of a quality as fine as any recorded in the annals of any army.

The Kaiser and Enver Pasha discuss plans to take the Suez
canal and expel the British from the Near East.

The wreck of the *Ecbatana,* sunk in the Shatt-al-Arab.

Armored bellums being towed up river, 1915.

Mahelas at Amara, 1915

Kitchener of Khartoum

General Sir O'Moore Creagh, VC

General—later Field Marshal–Sir Arthur Barrett, KCB, KCVO

Lord Hardinge,
Viceroy of India

Sir Percy Z. Cox

General Sir John E. Nixon,
KCB

Enver Pasha *(left)* with a German officer.

"Fort Wight,"
May 1915.

"Fort Wight"

HMS Espiegle in
action during the
advance up the
Tigris to Amara
from Qurna on
May 31, 1915.

"Fort Wight,"

"Fort Wight," May 1915.

Arab fort on the Tigris, August 1915.

Major General Sir Charles John Mellis, VC, CB.

Lieutenant General Sir
Fenton Aylmer, VC, KCB.

Major General Sir
Charles V. Townshend.

Major General Sir George Younghusband, KCMG.

Major General Sir
George Gorringe.

A water supply cart.

Trenches at Qurna.

A British gunboat on the Tigris, 1917.

The licorice factory at Kut.

An 18-pounder gun in action before Kut, December 1916.

The *Firefly* in action up the Tigris.

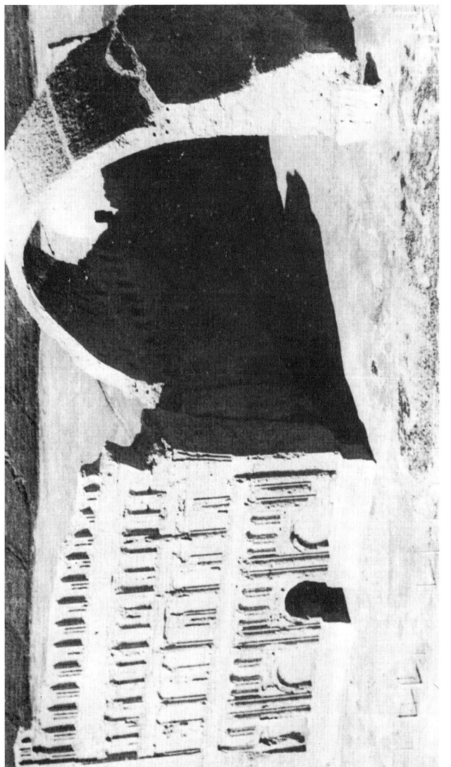

The Arch of Ctesiphon.

Ezra's Tomb.

Arab encampment on the banks of the Tigris, August 1915.

Lieutenant General Sir William Marshall, GCMG, KCB, KCSI.

Lieutenant General Sir Alexander Stanhope Cobbe.

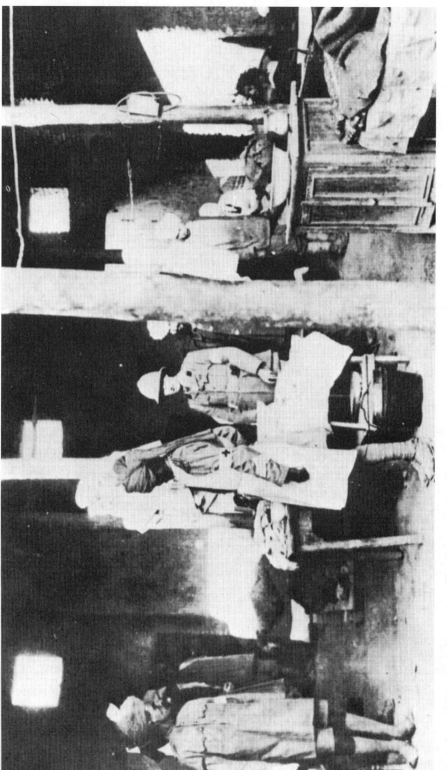

Scene in one of the Indian hospitals in Kut during the siege, 1916.

The entry of British troops into Baghdad, March 11, 1917.

"New Street," Baghdad.

Signaling by helio.

General Sir Stanley Maude (*second from right*) with British and Russian officers.

General Sir Stanley
Maude.

Lieutenant General
Sir Percy Lake.

Major General Sir George
Fletcher MacMunn.

Major General H.
D'Urban Keary.

General Maude's funeral.

British pack transport crossing the Dujaila.

An "A.T." cart.

Ottoman wounded and Indian army medics.

An armored car salving a Martinsyde airplane.

A South Lancashire soldier with some Persian Buddhoos.

Some of the men.

And their equipment

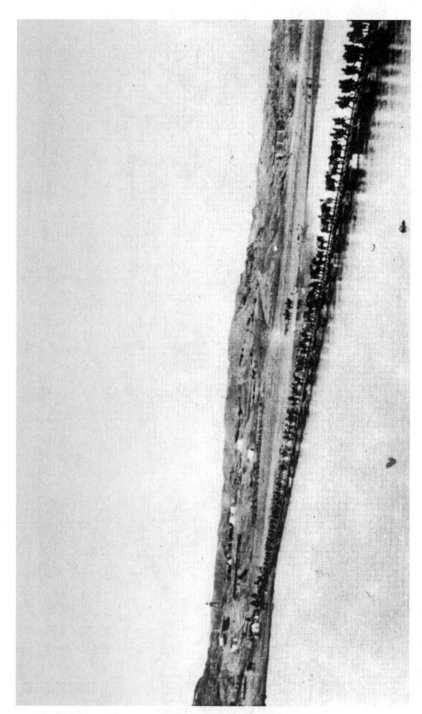

Crossing the Diyala by pontoon bridge.

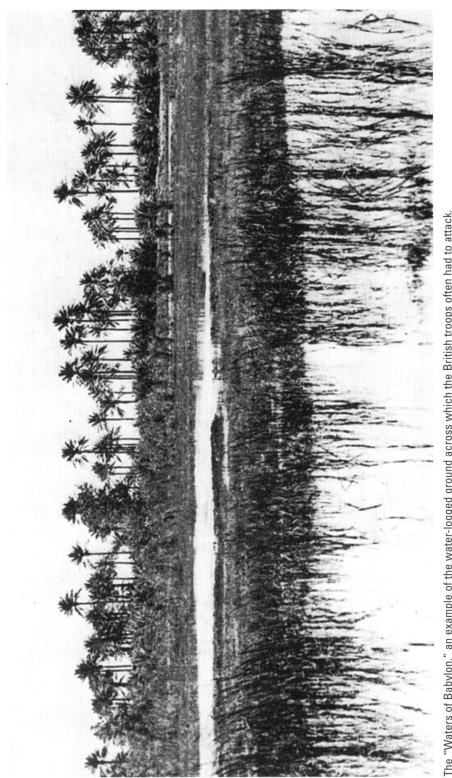

The "Waters of Babylon," an example of the water-logged ground across which the British troops often had to attack.

Persian transport, 1918.

Commodore Norris, RN, and Major General Dunsterville.

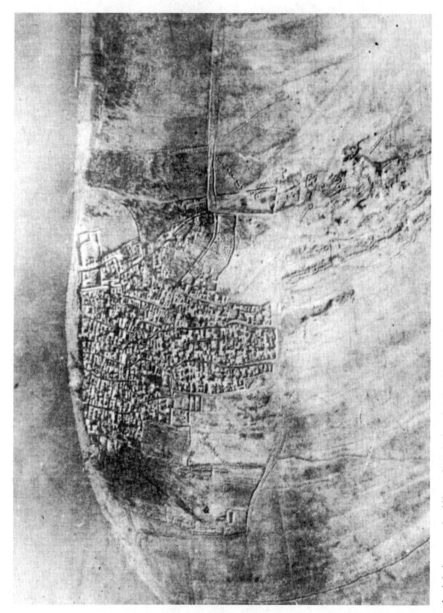

Aerial photograph of Kut, taken during the siege in 1916, by a German airman.

Kut prisoners, Kastamuni, Anatolia, 1918.

The Ottoman army evacuates Baghdad in 1917.

Chapter 12

The Fall of Kut

When the ox is down, many are the butchers.

Talmud

A fter the event it is easy to be wise and sit in judgment on those responsible for the operations which led to the surrender of nearly nine thousand fighting men—three thousand of them British, six thousand Indians. But the fall of Kut came as a terrible shock to the British public and it wanted to know how such a catastrophe could ever come about. In the whole history of the British Army there had never been a surrender like this; the nearest parallel was that of Cornwallis with seven thousand officers and men in the American War of Independence.[1] Nor had any of the peoples of the Middle

---

1. The siege of Kut has, in fact, been compared with the defence of the Residency at Lucknow: the "Baillie Guard." Sir Henry Lawrence had laid in huge stocks of grain in underground store houses, the extent of which his staff apparently were unaware and, at Lawrence's death, the military commander knew nothing of them. He, like Townshend, also reported his starvation point to be far nearer than it actually was, and when

and Far East ever associated the British flag with a reverse of this sort and the immediate effect was a sudden realization by the Arabs of the fact that Britain could be just as fallible as any other nation. In consequence the prestige of the Raj slumped and in the bazaars throughout the Middle East Turkish money regained its old value overnight.

The story of the first phase of the siege, when the garrison was fighting for their lives in the last days of 1915, has already been related. The note of optimism on which this period closed was only shattered in mid-January when doubts as to the ability of the Relief Force to effect a breakthrough first began to be apparent. With the coming of the rain and the flooding of the front line trenches, the garrison suddenly began to realize that the waterlogged country-side would prove a serious bar to the operations of the Relief Force. Seemingly the only stroke of good fortune at that time—and it was one which could hardly be said to have been derived from good management—was the discovery that there was enough food in Kut for the garrison to hold out until mid-April. As the Turks seemed to have settled down to a blockade of the town and there was no apparent intention to resume the attacks of December, holding out seemed feasible enough, even if it was not exactly a pleasant prospect. Perhaps it would not be for long anyway. If the Relief Force really made an all-out effort there was every chance that the siege would be lifted before April. Their "Charlie" was confident; it was really only a matter of time— or so the garrison wanted to believe.

Disillusionment slowly started to seep into their thoughts during the second phase of the siege. Between mid-January and mid-March, they settled down to a humdrum existence, with battalions alternating between a week in the line and a week bivouacking in reserve. All things considered, the actual living conditions were not so bad but individuals began to wonder whether the outlook was quite so sanguine as they had been led to believe, and morale began to flag. Duty in the line was preferred to being in reserve; the forward trenches were not shelled or the object of air raids to the same extent as the town. Out of the line, there was not very much to break the monotony; games and amusements were almost non-existent for it was only in a patch of dead ground on the right bank that any recognized team sport could be organized. By improvising a pitch where they could play cricket and hockey with pick handles and a rag ball, the two battalions holding the licorice factory made the most of it but for the rest, there was nothing—not even any serious fishing, as the licorice factory corner was the only place where this was possible. On the

---

the garrison and Havelock's reinforcements were relieved by Sir Colin Campbell these stocks of grain, which had only just been discovered, had to be destroyed.

other hand, in reserve it was possible to buy extra food to help supplement the diminishing scale of rations; everybody was hungry now and so extras bought from the Arabs in the town were very welcome. That it was possible to buy them at all may seem ludicrous; since the locals were being issued with rations on the same scale as the troops such trade suggests that there was still something wrong with the official methods of food distribution.

Food was one of Townshend's two main problems—the other being co-operation with the Relief Force. Fighting hunger was as important as fighting Turks and, by the end of January, his stocks of food were being supplemented by slaughtering the transport animals[2] locked up in Kut with the garrison. To provide beef the heavy battery bullocks were the first to go; after them came the horses and mules, and by mid-April every single animal had been butchered. Toward the end of the siege it is said that even dogs and cats were getting scarce and undoubtedly there were those among the British troops who were prepared to eat such meat. The last of the mules to come to its undig-nified destiny was one which had served in three Indian Frontier campaigns, the ribbons of which it wore around its neck; when its turn came the butcher refused to slaughter it and twice it was sent back. But in the end, like the rest, it had to go. Those who became connoisseurs in these matters opined that mule flesh had some special virtues over horse-meat; mule fat they said, also made good dripping and provided a substitute for lamp oil. Supplies of crude cooking oil, which gave out thick, rank fumes when it was burned—so giving the regimental cooks a chimney-sweep appearance—lasted throughout the whole of the siege but lamp oil was soon on the restricted list and so mule fat was doubly welcome.

With the killing of the animals, there was plenty of horsemeat for every-body in the beginning but, because of religious prejudices, many of the Indian troops were unwilling to eat it (their unwillingness to do so stemming more often from physical rather than spiritual loathing). As was to be expected, their reasons for not eating it were given as religious restraint and to overcome the restriction Townshend radioed the leaders of the chief religious communities in India, asking for a ruling that it was lawful for the men in Kut to be allowed to eat what meat was available, irrespective of the animal it came from or how the beast was slaughtered. This permission was given, but in spite of it most of the Indians were still reluctant to eat horsemeat, and at this stage Townshend hesi-tated to use coercion to get them to do so. The alternative was to find some-thing which was acceptable to the Indians, those who would not accept horse-

---

2. Once the gunners' animals were gone their drivers had no responsibility and they were formed into a new unit called the "Kut Foot."

meat were given a larger share of the flour ration, in lieu—the extra quantity needed being found by cutting the British soldiers' issue. Townshend himself was furious that such a measure was even necessary; he considered it was just the bloody-minded attitude of the Indian sepoys—"typical" he said, and noted that "the Indian troops throughout the siege have been dejected, spiritless and pessimistic"; that "there were considerable desertions to the enemy and many cases of self-mutilation and malingering." "There has been a difficulty of the Indian Mohammedans not wishing to fight against their coreligionists—the Turks" he continued, and warming up to this theme: "No Mohammedan troops should ever have been sent to Mesopotamia if it were possible to send Sikhs, Gurkhas or other Hindu troops..." Maybe the Indian troops were being difficult; they could be bloody-minded if they wished—so for that matter can British, American or soldiers of any other nation. But Townshend's prejudice and dislike was returned in full measure, by the Indian sepoys and by their British officers also.

After the setback at Hanna, when Aylmer had begun to doubt whether he would ever be able to reach Kut, the garrison had its grimmest foretaste of the desperate days ahead. The rations[3] had again been cut and the poor food was beginning to have its effect. As the troops' health rapidly deteriorated, 1,500 men, over 500 of whom had scurvy, were in the hospital at the beginning of March and among the British troops there had been an out? break of beriberi. Physically, as well as morally, the situation was galloping downhill and, realizing this, Townshend issued a final appeal to those Indians who had consistently refused to eat horseflesh. His message, which contained the threat to demote those who continued in their refusal and to promote others in their place produced the desired effect at long last and 9,000 Indians eventually came on the meat ration list as a result of it. But by this time the powers of resistance against disease of those who had refused it till now had been reduced by the semi-starvation diet which they had endured. Colic and dysentery complicated by jaundice were endemic, and if to this mélange one adds a plague of flies, swarms of sand flies and parasitical lice the journalists' earlier picture of a "Mesopotamian picnic" is almost complete.

Medical arrangements, difficult enough even at the start of the siege, became increasingly so as time went on. Owing to the confined space available the hospitals were often under fire and, as the town itself had no sanitation arrangements and the Arabs were in the habit of using the streets for their physical functions, it is surprising that there were not more infectious diseases

---

3. On March 18, the ration for British troops was 8 oz. bread, 20 oz. meat, 1½ oz. dates, and for Indian troops 8 oz. barley, 8 oz. meat (for those who would eat it), 1 oz. of ghee and 1½ oz. dates.

than there were. The numbers of sick swelled; with diminishing vitality their recuperative powers declined and the death rate increased accordingly. So far as many of the Indians were concerned it is probable that the horror of horseflesh cost them their lives; even in the end, when driven to eat it either by hunger or the terms of Townshend's order, their powers of digestion had been so reduced that they were unable to stomach it. Those who accepted it in the beginning fared better; the Gurkhas who had no scruples in the matter did best of all.

There is a theory that forced abstention will cure the craving to smoke, but this did not prove to be so in Kut. By the beginning of March there was, of course, very little tobacco and after the local supplies had been exhausted, ginger, tea, apricot and lime leaves were all tried out as substitutes; the meager supplies of the real weed which did remain were almost priceless. At the auction of a dead officer's kit, a single box of a hundred cigarettes fetched the equivalent of nearly seven pounds—a sum which, even in these inflationary days is something of a record—and Townshend recorded that a box of Indian cheroots fetched twice that price. Yet, apparently by some strange anomaly, local cigarettes could always be bought from the Arabs at about a shilling each. Black market supplies of these held out to the end and perhaps the fact that they did was not so strange after all, since it is thought that Buddhoos brought in fresh supplies by night. Black market transactions were not confined to tobacco, and even up to the last week of the siege the bazaar in Kut was doing a roaring business in almost every scarce commodity, with the merchants making a small fortune. The Buddhoos, with their extraordinary attributes of boldness, resource and endurance, were fully capable of exploiting the situation to their profit.

Hunger expressed itself in curious ways, sometimes in the fads and fancies more usually associated with pregnant women rather than fighting men. Of the cravings, that for sugar, almost non-existent during March and April, was very strong; and because there were none in the rations everyone had a yen for the green vegetables which also were virtually unobtainable. Efforts to make the local vegetation serve in their stead had varying degrees of success. The dishes concocted often looked anything but appetizing, smelt even less so and certainly contained little nutriment, but sometimes they satisfied or deferred the individual's yearning for what they were supposed to represent. Dandelion leaves were turned into a sort of spinach, other weeds into cabbage-like stews. However, when General Hoghton suddenly breathed his last after a meal, the cause of his death was attributed to poisonous vegetation in the green slops that were enjoying an ephemeral and brittle success among the garrison that week, and an abrupt halt was called to the improvisation of vegetables.

During the siege, the different units saw little of each other. In the first phase, when the whole area was under constant bombardment and swept by machine gun fire, men were permitted to leave their trenches and shelters only if they were undertaking a specific task such as repairing the wire. Later when movement was relatively safe, many had lost the urge to leave their trenches; weakened by hunger and dispirited, they were wholly apathetic. Too often their hopes, kindled by the sound of the gunfire heralding each and every attempt by the Tigris Corps to break through to them, were dashed when they learned that there had been another failure and morale was such that they were fully prepared to stay put until the Relief Force actually arrived. There was no attempt to shake them out of this state; their role was passive—little patrolling, no offensive moves—so that in time the suspense and strain were bound to tell. As the days flicked past they grew more and more weary; morally, even more than physically, many of them were done for.

By the beginning of April nobody inside Kut had any doubt as to the ultimate outcome of the siege; the only question was how long could it last and any optimism which still remained stemmed from Townshend. Obsessed by his memories of Chitral and the idea that he might repeat his former epic, some of the personality of the man may be deduced from his communiqués. On January 26, he took the garrison into his confidence in an address which explained how things stood and what part they were playing:

> Our relieving force suffered severe loss and had very bad weather to contend against; they are entrenched close to the Turkish position. More reinforcements are on their way up-river, and I confidently expect to be relieved some day during the first half of the month of February. I desire all ranks to know why I decided to make a stand at Kut during our retirement from Ctesiphon. It was because, as long as we hold Kut, the Turks cannot get their ships, barges, stores and munitions past this place, and so cannot move down to attack Amara, and thus we are holding up the whole of the Turkish advance. It also gives time for our reinforcements to come up-river from Basra, and so restore success to our arms.
>
> It gives time to our Allies the Russians to move towards Baghdad, which a large force is now doing. I had a personal message from General Baratoff, in command of the Russian Expeditionary Force in Persia, telling me of his admiration of what you men of the 6th Division and troops attached have done in the past few months, and telling of his own progress on the road from Kermanshah towards Baghdad. By standing at Kut I maintain the territory we have won in the past year at the expense of much blood, commencing with your glorious victory at Shaiba, and thus we maintain the campaign as a glorious one, instead of letting disaster pursue its course down to Amara, and perhaps, beyond.
>
> I have ample food for eighty-four days, and that is not counting the 3,000 animals which can be eaten. *When I defended Chitral some twenty years ago* we lived well

on atta (flour) and horse-flesh; but, as I repeat, I expect confidently to be relieved in the first half of the month of February. Our duty stands out clear and simple. It is our duty to our Empire, to our beloved King and Country, to stand here and hold up the Turkish advance as we are doing now, and with the help of all, heart and soul together, we will make this a defence to be remembered in history as a glorious one. All in India and England are watching us now, and are proud of the splendid courage you have shown; and I tell you, let all remember the glorious defence of Plevna[4], for that is what is in my mind.

I am absolutely calm and confident as to the result. The Turk, though good behind the trench, is of little value in the attack. They have tried it once, and their losses in one night in their attempt on the fort were 2,000 alone.

They have already had very heavy losses from General Aylmer's musketry and guns, and I have no doubt they have had enough.

On March 10, following the unsuccessful attack on the Dujaila Redoubt, he took the opportunity to issue another message designed to bolster the garrison's flagging morale:

As on a former occasion, I take the troops of all ranks into my confidence again. We have now stood a three months' siege in a manner which has called upon you the praise of our beloved King and our fellow-countrymen in England, Scotland, Ireland and India, and all this after your brilliant battles of Kut-al-Amara and Ctesiphon and your retirement to Kut, all of which feats of arms are now famous. Since 5th December, 1915, you have spent three months of cruel uncertainty, and to all men and all people uncertainty is intolerable. As I say, on the top of all this comes the second failure to relieve us. And I ask you also to give a little sympathy to me who have commanded you in these battles referred to, and who having come to you as a stranger, now love my command with a depth of feeling I have never known in my life before. When I mention myself, I would also mention the names of the generals under me, whose names are distinguished in the Army as leaders of men.

I am speaking to you as I did before, straight from the heart, and, as I say, I ask your sympathy for my feelings, having promised you relief on certain dates on the promise of those ordered to relieve us. Not their fault, no doubt. Do not think that I blame them; they are giving their lives freely, and deserve our gratitude and admiration. But I want you to help me again, as before. I have asked General Aylmer for the next attempt to bring such numbers as will break down all resistance and leave no doubt as to the issue. In order, then, to hold out, I am killing a large number of horses so as to reduce the quantity of grain eaten every day, and I have had to reduce your ration. It is necessary to do this in order to keep our flag flying. I am determined to hold out, and I know you are with me heart and soul.

---

4. This reference from his diaries suggests that Townshend had an eye to posterity. Few of his soldiers could be expected to know anything about a siege which had taken place nearly forty years previously during the Russo-Turk campaign.

On the last day of March rations were again reduced; a week later there was no fuel for the flour mill. Sufficient flour had been ground to last for one more week and, when this was gone on April 16, the flour ration was cut to four ounces for British and Indian alike. Opium pills were issued to the Indian troops to stay the pangs of hunger and by now everybody was eating, or trying to eat, horsemeat. Just under a week later the tiny flour ration gave out completely and for me next three days the garrison subsisted on their two days' emergency reserve. This was a situation which clearly could not continue very much longer and, as a last desperate effort to maintain the siege, Lake attempted to resupply the garrison by air. If, as his staff calculated, five thousand pounds a day were dropped from the few primitive aircraft which were then available, it was reckoned that there would be sufficient for a bare-existence diet of six ounces per man. When five thousand pounds proved to be an impossible target, Townshend bitterly commented that on April 15, "in ideal weather and perfect conditions," the target was a third short of even the minimum requirement. Furthermore, among the first stores that were dropped were seven bags of silver rupees—presumably with which to buy his own supplies. With food taking priority, Townshend justifiably saw little sense in wasting precious aircraft sorties on inessentials. This, one of the earliest of serious air supply operations ever attempted, probably prolonged the siege for another four days. But, it was a puny effort; the only hope of any real stay of the inexorable fate that awaited the garrison lay in the *Julnar*'s attempt to run the blockade. In Townshend's own words, "there was little left to say" once this had failed.

Two days before the *Julnar* was to make her fateful run Townshend had suggested to the Army Commander that negotiations for an honorable capitulation should be opened with the Turks forthwith. Following Gorringe's second repulse at Sannaiyat he had concluded that nothing short of a miracle could save Kut now and in these circumstances it was up to Sir Percy Lake to arrange the best possible terms with Khalil Pasha. The onus of initiating the negotiations, he felt, lay with Lake but he was determined to have his say in the formulation of the terms, and with his customary predilection for military parallels he suggested that the same sort of arrangements—the "honorable terms"—which Massena had obtained from the Austrians when he was compelled to capitulate after the defence of Genoa might well be repeated for the garrison of Kut. Presumably what Townshend hoped was to march out of Kut at the head of his troops with all the so-called honors of war—colors flying, drums beating, bayonets fixed—and he appears to have been obsessed with the idea that the Turks would be amenable. "Parole in India" was his aim, an aim which he assessed as quite feasible and practicable. However, if his hopes of parole were serious, then they were soon to be shattered.

To Townshend's suggestion, Lake replied that he had asked the Indian Government for permission to negotiate on the lines which Townshend had suggested but that he, Lake, was of the opinion it should be Townshend who did the negotiating. It was not a question of protocol, merely a case of Townshend's prestige carrying more weight than an independent negotiating body such as would have to be set up if the onus were on Lake. As a result of this, the first overtures for the surrender were made on the morning of April 26, when Townshend "much against my will, knowing that I had not a biscuit up my sleeve to argue with and that Khalil Pasha knew I was in extremis for food," asked for a six day armistice and permission for ten days' food for the garrison to be sent up from the Relief Force while surrender terms were arranged.

Khalil's prompt reply, couched in courteous terms, implied sweet reasonableness; Townshend should meet him to discuss matters he suggested; in the meantime an armistice would be in order. That night the guns were silent. After so many months of noise, "the stillness . . . was quite extraordinary. The day was calm, the weather fine and the river flood had fallen considerably; the atrocious weather and flood conditions had lasted just sufficiently long to prevent our relief."[5] Next day Townshend met Khalil on a Turkish launch a mile and a half upstream above Kut and talked with him alone. The Turkish commander demanded "unconditional surrender" as could have been expected, but when Townshend suggested a gold ransom might be paid by the British Government to secure exceptional terms, Khalil conceded that it might be possible to compromise on something better than "unconditional" surrender. Even so his minimum requirements would be the immediate evacuation of Kut and to facilitate the evacuation he was prepared to supply tents and food from the captured *Julnar*. Further, the garrison must get out of the town and concentrate in an area to be designated by him. Townshend had gone as far as he could go without consulting his superior, and at this point negotiations were broken off so as to enable him to get in touch with Lake. To Townshend's recommendations consequent on the meeting, the Army Commander suggested that Khalil should be offered Townshend's guns, money, and an exchange of prisoners as the price of the garrison's pass to freedom and parole in India. Unfortunately for Townshend a prolonged argument was jus; not possible; as he had forecast, he "had not a biscuit up his sleeve," his men were starving, time was on Khalil's side. The emergency rations were the only solid rations left in Kut; with these another two days was

---

5. *In Kut and Captivity,* Major E. W. C. Sandes, M.C., R.E., Murray, 1919.

the limit of the siege. After that the garrison would either have to surrender, irrespective of the outcome of any negotiations or, facing starvation, make some desperate do-or-the attempt to cut their way out to the Relief Force.

Early on the morning of April 28, Townshend wrote to Khalil and offered in exchange for the freedom of the garrison, a million pounds sterling, a promise to hand over undamaged the fifty guns in Kut and a gentleman's agreement that his men would not fight against the Turks for the rest of the war. Khalil, according to German accounts, was prepared on his own account to accept these terms and a recommendation to that effect was sent off to his government. But if Khalil was satisfied with an agreement of this nature, the wily Enver was not. Nothing less than the unconditional surrender of the garrison, together with all its guns and ammunition was what he insisted on. What he wanted—indeed what he needed—was a spectacular victory which would show the Arab world the superiority of Turkish arms. Furthermore, it seemed to him that the very suggestion that the British Government was pre-pared to pay in hard cash for a military concession had a propaganda value that outweighed its financial merit and he was not one to let an opportunity like this slip by. Khalil was curtly told to turn the offer down, and when an offer to double the ransom price was made, it was rejected—although Enver was pre-pared to concede that in exchange for the money and his guns and munitions Townshend himself could go free. Clearly the acceptance of a concession like this was unthinkable; even if Townshend had himself been prepared to con-sider it, Lake had already made it quite clear that whatever happened it was Townshend's duty to stay with his garrison.[6]

During the first two days of the armistice, a large proportion of the am-munition stocks remaining in Kut was dumped into the Tigris and as soon as it was clear that there was going to be no improvement on the unconditional surrender terms, the garrison systematically started to destroy everything that might be useful to the Turks. In a ruthless scorched earth policy, documents were burned, carts broken up, animal harnesses cut into ribbons, machine guns, rifles and bayonets all made useless. On the very last night what little remained of the ammunition was tipped into the river, only a few rounds being kept for the rifles in case they were needed for use against the Arabs when the final moments came, while the Turks were taking over. Finally on the morning of April 29, the guns were spiked, the launches blown up and sunk in deep water and all the engineer stores broken up, set ablaze or dumped in the river.

---

6. At the beginning of April Townshend had suggested that he should select about seven hundred "good" men, who would try to run the blockade on the *Sumana;* like the voyage of the *Julnar* this could have been a suicidal mission. From the correspondence it is not clear whether Townshend included himself in the composition of those who were to try to get away but the Army Commander stipulated that Townshend's duty was with his men.

Apart from the troops' rifles, on a scale of one rifle to three men, the only other weapons that were kept back were the officers' swords, and these had been retained merely because it was expected that they would be needed for a ceremonial hand-over to the Turks. A final communiqué thanking the troops for their devotion, discipline and bravery was issued from Townshend's head-quarters and a message received from Sir Beauchamp-Duff, the Commander-in-Chief in India, on similar lines was published with the addendum from Lake which had accompanied it: "We [himself, Gorringe and all troops of the Tigris Column] can only express extreme disappointment and regret that our efforts to relieve you should not have been crowned with success."

The final messages from Kut were transmitted during the last morning. First came the signal: "Have destroyed my guns and most of my munitions; officers have gone to Khalil to say I am ready to surrender. Cannot hold on any more. Khalil has been told I need food and a deputation of officers has gone on a launch to bring some food from *Julnar.*" And then: "I have hoisted the White Flag over Kut. ... I shall shortly destroy wireless ... we are pleased to know we have done our duty and recognize that our situation is one of the fortunes of war. We thank you and General Gorringe and all ranks of the Tigris Force for the great efforts you have made to save us." Finally came the coded message which the Kut operators had said would precede the destruction of their transmitters; then there was silence. The siege was over, Kut had fallen.

A few days later on May 4, 1916, the peroration of Townshend's final message was read over by Kitchener to a grimly silent audience in the House of Lords. Although the news had been expected it still came as something of a shock to the British public. Although the same British public had taken quite a number of knocks in the past few months—knocks which to some extent had inured them to bad news, the fall of Kut following the recent announcement of the withdrawal from Gallipoli, still came as a great blow to their pride. The wave of sympathy which flowed into Whitehall and Delhi did little to assuage feelings which swayed between bewilderment and savage resentment. General Joffre expressed "the admiration of the French Army" at the way the "gallant defenders" had stuck it out at Kut; the Russians pointed out that Townshend's force had done a useful job by keeping Turkish troops occupied which would otherwise have been employed either against Salonika or Egypt or against themselves on the Caucasian front. The Governor General of Australia tele-graphed that "this disaster would strengthen Australia's determination to do her part in hastening the overthrow of Britain's enemies." Yet everyone knew that something had gone very, very wrong.

But Kut was soon forgotten. In Britain there were too many other things to think about and the battles in Flanders were much nearer home than somewhere in the Middle East of whose location the man in the street was only dimly aware. Even to those who did appreciate what the fall of Kut meant, in the wider context of the whole war, Townshend's surrender was only a minor incident, an unhappy end to a situation that should never have been allowed to develop in the first place—but even though an isolated adventure it was a tragedy. The most serious effect of the news was not in England but in the Middle East where prestige really counted. The people in Britain, fighting for survival and fed with the idea that the war would be decided by victory or defeat on the Western Front, were not prepared to worry for long about a nebulous issue like Kut and what the Arabs thought of them.

Shortly after noon on April 29, as white flags fluttered over the British lines in Kut, a column of thick-set, dirty, tired-looking Turkish infantry in full battle order, trudged into the town to take over the defenses. After hammering the sights of their rifles in order to distort them, the British and Indian troops piled their few remaining arms and sat down to await orders. They were to move to a concentration area at Shumran, nine miles upstream, prior to a long trek into captivity in Anatolia. "Your troubles are over, my dears" Khalil had assured them through Townshend, and they were glad of it. Little did they know what lay ahead. Orders for the move came through in the early evening and next morning what was left of the 18th and 30th Brigades embarked in a river steamer for the journey up river. There were no other ships to lift the rest of the garrison and so they had to march. For the unfit, famished men who filed up the river bank this march—short as it may seem—was a severe test of endurance. It was late that night before the last files of the long marching column reached Shumran where the first of the Turkish rations on which the captives were expected to subsist in the days to come, were issued. Six brown biscuits of a barley flour, chaff and lard concoction were handed to each man and in the words of one British soldier who was there, "The British Army biscuit which is no doughnut at the best of times, was a sponge cake compared with that of the Turks." Food like this was no good for starving stomachs; the biscuits were soaked in water and eaten but very few of the prisoners were able to digest them and men died that night. Perhaps it was the result of the continual starvation, maybe it was the inedibility of the biscuits. The Turks said that it was the result of overeating although it is hard to believe that anyone had much opportunity to overeat that day or for many days to come.

As the British garrison marched out the victors moved in and before long both Turks and Arab hangers-on were busy in the town. The locals had already started in on an orgy of looting and they were quickly joined by the ill-disciplined elements of the new garrison. There was little enough to steal but nothing was sacred, and no doubt some of the best pickings were concentrated in the hospitals. General Melliss was among the patients in one hospital and even as he lay in bed a Turkish soldier tried to make off with his boots. This was too much for Melliss. Although sick, he was up and out of bed chasing after the thief, who surprisingly enough continued to run; perhaps he recognized ingrained authority in Melliss, or maybe he had some sort of conscience. Whatever the reason, it was his undoing. Meeting a Turkish officer in the street outside the hospital, the culprit was given summary punishment, Turkish variety, which in this case meant a sound thrashing. Turkish officers knew how to hand out punishments, a fact which the locals soon discovered. In his negotiations with Khalil, Townshend had tried to obtain a promise that no action would be taken against those who had helped the British maintain order in the town during the siege but if such a promise was ever given the Turks had short memories or else never had any intention of honoring it. The morning after the town had changed hands, most of the prominent citizens of Kut were either swinging from hastily improvised gibbets or had been strangled to death. No one who had any authority was forgotten or forgiven; these men were Turkish citizens and in Khalil's opinion they had to pay the price. They paid with their lives for having believed in the British.

Arrangements for the exchange of British sick and wounded for an equivalent number of unwounded and healthy Turkish prisoners of war of specified regiments had been included in the surrender terms. About eleven hundred of the worst hospital cases were eventually repatriated under the exchange agreement, and these men could count themselves fortunate indeed to escape becoming Turkey's "honored guests," as Khalil had put it. Many who returned were at their last gasp, and there were many others who should have been sent back who were marked fit for captivity by the Turkish doctors. Selection of those to be repatriated was made by rough and ready methods not generally associated with medical practice, and some preference seems to have been given to the Indian sick at the expense of the British; by being seen to exercise preference and favor to their brother Moslems the Turks hoped to gain some propaganda advantage. Of those who should have been evacuated back to the British lines many of the stretcher cases were put in ships for Baghdad and died in agony on the way; others, some of whom had legs in splints or were suffering from spinal injuries, were ordered to march. Needless to say these unfortunates were among the first to succumb. The hospital ship *Sikhim*, accompanied by a paddle steamer and lighters loaded with food and canteen stores, was allowed to steam up to Kut to collect the wounded who were to be evacuated. The food was intended for the benefit of those who were to go on into captivity, although few of the British troops saw anything of it. "Spot,"

Townshend's terrier and one of the few dogs that had survived the siege, was fortunate enough to be awarded a place in the *Sikhim* and he returned to Basra with the evacuees; from Basra "Spot" sailed for England where he was reunited with his master two years later.

Townshend himself was confined in Kut for a couple of days until arrangements could be made for him to be removed to Baghdad. With an eye to the niceties of a formal surrender, he had proffered his sword and pistol to Khalil soon after the Turkish commander arrived in the town but they were declined. "They are as much yours as ever they were" Khalil said with an airy gesture of magnanimity. "You will be sent to Constantinople and be the honored guest of the Turkish nation" he continued; the British troops would be sent to Asia Minor "to be interned in places in a good climate near the sea." So far as Townshend was concerned he was speaking the truth; it was a different story for the rank and file.

Together with his A.D.C., his principal staff officers, an Indian servant, two British orderlies and a Portuguese cook, Townshend traveled up to Baghdad in a launch provided by Khalil. To permit him to say his farewells, the launch was stopped at Shumran and Townshend recorded:

> Officers and men lined the bank as we passed the place where the remnants of the gallant Sixth Division were encamped, and cheered me long as I went by. I shall never forget that cheer. Tears filled my eyes as I stood to attention at the salute. Never shall I have such a command again. I loved the Sixth Division with all my heart.

These were fine sentiments; it is unfortunate that he did not have the opportunity to show some tangible evidence of his love by easing the lot of his erstwhile command during their captivity.

In Baghdad the intention had been for Townshend to be billeted in von der Goltz's old house which, it was said, was one of the best in the town. However, as the old Field Marshal had died only a few days previously, allegedly of typhus—though some said poisoned by the Turks—Townshend was lodged in the Italian Consulate. Following his arrival in the capital, Khalil gave a dinner party in Townshend's honor and the two generals sat long into the night, while Townshend propounded his theories on Napoleonic tactics. The journey was resumed a few days later; Townshend traveling by rail to Samarra and thence by road, in a horse-drawn victoria to Mosul. On this section of the journey the party met the survivors of the ill-fated *Julnar* who were trudging wearily along the road to their eventual internment camp; their trek had been made in a considerably less grandiose style than that of Townshend, and they were in a bad way. No doubt they were glad to see him but the meeting brought them little physical relief, since the general for whom they had risked their all was permitted to do little for them, and after a few words of sympathy his party was ordered on.

From Mosul, Townshend's progress to the Bosporus was almost triumphal. At Aleppo- a guard of honor, a car and convoy of lorries awaited his arrival and at Bozanti, where the entourage transferred to the railway again, Enver Pasha himself was waiting to pay his respects. "You must not grieve at being a prisoner" Turkey's Minister of War enjoined, after some flattering comments on his guest's ability as a soldier "it is the fortune of war." Since the journey to Constantinople was made in the company of the dead von der Goltz, whose coffin was on the same train, Townshend had good reason to cogitate on strange twists in the fortune to which Enver had referred.

The climax to the journey came when the entourage reached Constantinople. When he stepped off the train Townshend was greeted by the general commanding the First Turkish Army and a host of senior Turkish officials who were waiting on the platform for him. A Turkish Naval officer was assigned to him as a member of his staff and, after a brief session of holding court at a reception in the station waiting room, Townshend was driven through the streets of the city in an open landau escorted by a detachment of cavalry. It was an incredible performance; for the Turks this was clearly their moment of triumph, yet it was hardly a day of shame for Townshend since there must be few instances where a conquered general has been so well treated. Then followed a few months on the fashionable island of Halki, which lies opposite Constantinople in full view of its palaces and minarets, before the final move to the summer residence of the British Consul at Prinkipo. There, in a house which looked like an English country vicarage and in an atmosphere where the tempo of life also resembled that of an English country parson, Townshend remained until the end of the war. And at this point so far as this story is concerned, he fades out of the picture. In contrast with the sorry lot of his men, the "Hero of Chitral and Kut" had an enviable time. He may have suffered mental anguish but there was no physical hardship attached to his captivity and every feasible diversion was arranged for him by his Turkish Attaché. For Townshend it was me end of the Mesopotamia campaign and, had he but known it, the end of his army career; Kut was his last battle.

Momentarily, it is now worthwhile to turn back to the siege and consider its lessons, of which two stand out above all others. The first is that of the food supply. From what has been related it must be obvious that the planning of the Relief Force operations was hampered by not knowing how long the rations in Kut would last. Not until several abortive attempts to breakthrough to the garrison—attempts which frittered away men and material unnecessarily—had been made, was any real forecast of the "final" date at which the garrison would have to give up forthcoming. During the whole of me first phase of the siege, the men in Kut were on a full ration or more, and at no time was the food distributed on a sensible or reasonably scientific basis. Common sense dictates that supplies are the paramount consideration in a siege and one of the prime reasons why Kut fell was that neither Townshend, Nixon nor his successor Lake, seemed to realize that relief depended in the last resort on the full stomachs of the troops. There was fire in their bellies when they were full; with progressively less and less food, the men grew more and more despondent and the abortive efforts of the Relief Force only served to lower their morale still further. Yet if Townshend's staff had made a proper assessment of the food resources in the first place, the decisive time available for a major relief operation could have been better calculated, the troops properly fed and physically strong and fit for a complementary action to support the break-in.

The second major lesson is the garrison's passivity. Except for a few patrols, none of which had any real significance, there was hardly any offensive action outside the ring of trenches around the Kut perimeter and never a single raid across the river—even the Buddhoos were more enterprising than the garrison in this respect. Townshend was content to allow his men to sit tight in their trenches and wait for the Relief Force to come to him. It is well-known that such lethargy is bad for morale but his excuse was that he had no bridge by which he could get across the river to do anything of use to those trying to get through to him. Paraphrasing the French Marshal Bazaine: "If my finger were a bridge, I would" is the reply he is reputed to have given an officer who asked him why he did not try to cut his way out of the town. Yet there was a bridge when he fell back on Kut and he had it for just a week; it was he who had it blown up in such a way that most of the pontoons and boats from which it had been made up were lost to him. In his own account of the siege he has made the point that the only useful function performed by the garrison defending Kut was to detain as many Turks as possible—in numbers at least as great as his own. Yet because Khalil knew that he had no bridge by which he could cross the river and debouch on the southern bank of the Tigris behind the Turkish line facing the Relief Force he failed even in that. He might have provided an alternative to a bridge by using the tug *Sumana* with a couple of flying bridges which his engineers had actually prepared, and the thirty *mahelas* which were left behind in Kut. With these it should have been possible to have mounted a sizable offensive which, if it had been staged to coincide with the attack on the Dujaila Redoubt, might just have given that little extra weight which would have tipped the scales in favor of the Relief Force. This is surmise, for it was not to be.

How far Townshend's judgment was faulty when he decided to "sit out" the siege and "turn Kut into another Plevna" is the major factor governing any conjecture. By his own account he had no other real alternative to the course he pursued, and undoubtedly the difficulties confronting him were formidable. Yet, because of what befell the garrison after its surrender it might be considered that the men could hardly have fared worse even if Townshend had dared all in one glorious attempt to break out. He had toyed with the idea, after all, and on two occasions the chances of a successful sortie from Kut would seem to have stood a very good chance of success. After the battle of Hanna on January 21, it might have been possible to ferry a force of about four thousand men across the river and march down to link up with the Relief Force at Sheikh Sa'ad twenty-five miles away. At that time the Turks at Es Sinn and near Kut were thin on the ground, the floods covered almost a mile of the northern sector, and shortage of food and the weather being what it was, the morale of Khalil's men could not have been at its best. The question is whether the move would have been worth it. Only about three thousand fit men would have been left to defend Kut and if the Turks had put in a determined attack it is unlikely that they would have been able to hold out. I.E.F. "D" would have gained what was left of the "break-out" force, and Kut would have fallen during January. Since Gallipoli had just been evacuated and the Home Government was anxious for a victory in Mesopotamia to offset it, the idea of losing Kut was wholly unacceptable. Moreover, the staff in Basra was still optimistic and, to a lesser extent, so was the garrison in Kut itself. For these reasons Nixon's message to Aylmer and Townshend, rejecting the latter's offer to breakout, is understandable.

Six weeks later, came the more opportune moment which has been discussed. On March 8, when Aylmer surprised the Turks at Dujaila, an attack across the river by a force from the garrison might have caused them to retire. Admittedly, success would have depended on the determination of both the Relief Force and the troops from Kut who made the sortie. But the men were keen and on the whole the chances of success seemed high. This, despite the fact that the element of surprise would have been difficult to attain. The Turks were in constant communication with the Arabs in the town and a couple of *mahela* men had escaped at the end of February. Nevertheless, it was learned later that Khalil had not made any special provision for a breakout across the river south and east of the town. However, Townshend's appreciation was that "cooperation was of little practical use." After that the floods turned the right bank of the river near Kut into a marsh and any opportunity for a breakout had passed.

The defence and relief of Kut provide the basis of an ideal after-dinner game for amateur tacticians. Its surrender was a sad ending to the plan which had originally contemplated the capture of Baghdad and it came as a bitter blow to British pride. From beginning to end, the cost of these operations—including those who went into captivity—was over 40,000 British and Indian casualties and the question which deserves most consideration is whether Kut should ever have been besieged at all. As was pointed out at the beginning of this chapter, it is easy to be wise after the event; today with the modern weapons of war it is doubtful whether the idea of stopping Townshend's withdrawal at Kut would ever be entertained. Whether it should ever have been entertained fifty years ago is the real question; many will conclude that it was one of the greatest mistakes in British military history.

Chapter 13

Captivity

The Turks are savages with whom no civilized Christian nation ought to form any alliance.
Edmund Burke

Throughout the ages the treatment of prisoners of war has generally been inhuman. Even in modern times the edicts of the League of Nations did not deter the Japanese from perpetrating horrors which compare with those which are about to be described. Nor does the establishment of the United Nations Organization seem to have made much difference. Scenes which are scarcely less terrible than those recorded in the following pages were enacted in the Korean theater a few years ago; others of a similar nature have been repeated in the Congo and are taking place in Vietnam even today. But other later crimes can not excuse the Turks for the barbarous sufferings of the British and Indian prisoners who fell into their hands when Townshend capitulated. Two hundred and seventy-seven British officers, 204 Indian officers together with 12,888 rank and file surrendered on April 29, 1915; 2,592 of the "other ranks" were British and over 1,700 of them left their bones in Mesopotamia or Turkey. Khalil had said that their troubles were "over now, my dears; you will be treated as honored guests of the Sultan," but for all his flowery promises they perished miserably. They had every right to expect the same rations, clothing and treatment as Turkish soldiers (Article seven of the Hague Convention of 1909 prescribes that: "Les prisonniers de guerre seront traités... sur le même pied que les troupes du Gouvernement qui les aura capturés."). Although the standards of the Turkish troops were well below their own standards and those of the soldiers of other Western nations—yet the wretched captives did not even get this entitlement. They died in their hundreds from lack of food and from ill treatment; that any survived at all is almost a miracle.

All that can be said in defence of the Turkish authorities with regard to this sorry tale is that they often treated their own men with inhuman cruelty; otherwise the explanation must lie deep rooted in the Turkish character. In 1915 the British public looked on the Turk with a certain amount of admiration tinged with sympathy. Items suggesting that the Turk was really quite a nice fellow had been encouraged since the days of the Crimea: fighting on the opposite side in this war only because he had been misled, subverted by German propaganda and influence; he had no real quarrel with the British. This attitude, extended to the battlefield, where the fine military qualities of the Turk compelled the same admiration as they did thirty-five years later in Korea, quickly led British soldiers to develop a sneaking affection for his opponent. So far as he was concerned the Turk was a first-class soldier and a clean fighter; until he actually saw evidence to the contrary he was not prepared to believe otherwise. Hearsay was not nearly enough to overcome the British soldiers' esteem for the "old Turkey-cock." Yet, underneath a thin veneer, the Turk was a descendant of the Tartars.

In fifty years the changes wrought by Mustafa Kemal may have thickened the cultured veneer but the experience of the First World War was that, under the skin, the Turk is a savage, unscrupulous where his interests were concerned, and by western standards, scarcely civilized. He had little regard for human life or for the palliation of human ills and, being an innate respecter of persons and privilege, he was inclined to treat all prisoners according to their rank rather than by the generally accepted civilized standards of humanity. In Turkish the word for prisoner is synonymous with that for slave and so perhaps it is hardly surprising that the rank and file were treated like cattle. However, if there is any excuse in these characteristics for the way in which the miserable British prisoners were treated, where the Turks could not be excused was in their policy of delegating authority to Arabs whose behavior in charge of British and Indian prisoners was not merely semi-civilized but wholly, unpardonably, and brutally, barbarous.

Khalil had been warned by Townshend that many of his men were in no fit state to face a long march. In a written reply on this point Khalil promised that every care would be taken of them and that they would travel to Baghdad by steamer and thence by cart to their final destinations, although in actual fact orders for the desert march and the segregation of officers from the men must already have been issued when he penned this reply. Something of the initial concentration at Shumran has already been described; hundreds of men died during the few days they were there and few of them were buried, most of the bodies being thrown into a nearby ravine. From this ravine some of their skulls were recovered just over a year later.

Despite protests, most of the officers were separated from the rank and file at Shumran, only one officer per regiment being permitted to stay with his unit to see it through to Baghdad. The Turks must have realized, in consequence of the appalling death rate during the first couple of days, that their captives would never get as far as the capital unless they had some proper food and Gorringe was permitted to send up supplies; no doubt this food helped many a starving soldier to survive a little longer. Although before the rations arrived many of them had already sold their boots and some of their clothing to Arabs in exchange for a few handfuls of dates and black bread.

A long ragged column formed up on the morning of May 6, and after innumerable delays marched out under the full force of the noonday sun on the first lap of what was to be a death march. It is said they set off singing but the singing did not last for long. Outside the perimeter of the camp Arab guards took over from the Turkish sentries; and so started a journey which had had no parallel since the days of Genghis Khan and Tamerlane, when prisoners were treated like cattle and scourged from place to place, regardless of any human feeling. The first leg was quite short, nine miles in all, but at the end of it the men were glad to flop down and get some sleep; they were just not fit, which is hardly surprising. Next morning many of them found that the escort had stolen their boots during the night and thereafter those who still had them seldom took them off or else tied them around their necks during the night. From dawn until dusk the next day throughout a day of intense and suffocating heat, the column was kept moving. Fifteen miles had to be covered, fifteen miles without water or shade, fifteen miles of which every step was agony for the weak, sick and emaciated men. Parched with thirst, blinded by the sun, choked with dust as they stumbled and staggered forward, those who lagged were beaten with whips and sticks, or clubbed with the rifle butts of the Arab guards. Several who fell out were left to die in the desert and never seen again.

Even to the Turkish commandant it was obvious that his charges could not continue next day, and a thirty-six hour halt was called. Many more died during this halt and the only food that was issued was a portion of the bare Turkish ration although the Arab guards were prepared to sell the remainder of the ration at exorbitant prices.

By the time the column reached Aziziyeh on May 12, many of the captives had no boots and their bleeding feet were wrapped in the shreds of their putties. Complaints to the Turkish officers on these matters and of the behavior of the Arab guards were sternly rejected; the British prisoners were now subject to Turkish discipline, their spokesmen were told, and they were to go on. Nevertheless 350 men, who could not be judged as anything but totally unfit for any sort of march, had to be left behind at Aziziyeh to wait for boats to take them up the river; by the time the boats were forthcoming very few of the 350 were left to travel. Meanwhile, the main body staggered on to Ctesiphon and a vivid description of the state of the ragged, exhausted column of starved men at this stage of the journey has been supplied by one of the officers who witnessed it from the other bank:[1]

> We tingled with anger and shame at seeing on the other bank a sad little column of troops who had marched up from Kut, driven by a wild crowd of Kurdish horsemen who brandished sticks and what looked like whips. The eyes of our men stared from white faces, drawn long with the suffering of a too tardy death and they held out their hands towards our boat. As they dragged one foot after another, some fell and those with the rearguard came in for blows from cudgels and sticks. I saw one Kurd strike a British soldier who was limping along, he reeled under the blows. . . . Some had been thrashed to death, some killed, and some robbed of their kit and left to be tortured by the Arabs. Men were dying of cholera and dysentery and often fell out from sheer weakness. . . . Enteritis, a form of cholera, attacked the whole garrison after Kut fell, and the change of food no doubt helped this. ... A man turned green and foamed at the mouth. His eyes became sightless and the most terrible moans conceivable came from his inner being . . . they died, one and all, with terrible suddenness. One saw British soldiers dying with a green ooze issuing from their lips, their mouths fixed open, in and out of which flies walked.

Turkish and German flags were flying when the ragged column reached Baghdad on May 17—and was driven through the streets—a "dreadful spectacle to see British troops in rags, many barefooted, starved and sick, wending their way under brutal Arab guards through an Eastern bazaar."[2] As

1. *Secrets of a Kuttite,* by Captain E. O. Mousley, John Lane, 1922.
2. Official History Vol. 2.

the prisoners were herded toward a wired compound which had been prepared near the railway station, the lowest elements of the Baghdad populace crowded the route to jeer, and movie cameras whirred as official operators recorded the first tangible fruits of a Turkish victory. In this compound the sad and sorry remnants of the column were kept for three days; there was no protection from the sun, no sanitation arrangements and the stench and flies increased with the passage of time. However, for the first time since Kut a meager bread ration was issued and General Delamain with some of the British medical officers were permitted to visit them, as was the American Consul Mr. Brissell. It was as a result of the tatter's tireless efforts that a number of the worst cases were admitted to the Turkish hospital.

Five hundred sick were left in Baghdad and the rest were packed into trucks and sent off in batches to Samarra en route for Mosul and Anatolia. The treatment of those who were left behind in Baghdad was pitifully inadequate; nevertheless, their lot turned out to be immeasurably better than that of their supposedly fit companions who had continued on the journey to Samarra. The British doctors, by spending their own money on food and comforts, succeeded in raising the standards of the patients to a barely tolerable level and a large proportion of these five hundred—those who managed to survive— were eventually sent downstream in exchange for a corresponding number of Turks. Twenty-two officers and 323 other ranks eventually reached Basra in the middle of August, to be packed off to India just as soon as transport could be arranged. While in Basra they were forbidden to speak of their privations and what they had seen; the authorities had put it about that all prisoners were being well treated by the Turks and censorship enveloped the one source that could so easily have dispelled this falsehood. Indian military circles held that it was bad policy to speak ill of the Turks since the official attitude was that the Turkish Government was a misguided cat's-paw of the Germans. An imaginative commander-in-chief would have followed the precedent of Phillipon, who described the English prison hulks during the Peninsular War,[3] and capitalized on the point that death could be preferable to becoming the inmate of a Turkish prison camp. But neither Lake nor Beauchamp-Duff either took this view or had the imagination of a Phillipon.

The main body of the prisoners, who traveled to Samarra seventy miles north of Baghdad, went by rail in open cattle trucks and were allowed to rest for two days before starting on their five hundred mile march to Ras al'Ain via Mosul. Considering their physical condition and how ill equipped they were to withstand the climatic conditions of intense heat, it is amazing that any sur-

---

3. *Peninsular War,* Napier, Book XVI.

vived the journey. During it, some of the younger British soldiers were compelled to submit to the homosexual appetites of their captors; most were too weak to object, those who did resist were simply beaten into submission. As far as Mosul the journey averaged twenty miles a day and most of the route lay across rough and stony ground. Old putties and strips of blanket are poor protection against sharp stones, and so the feet of those who had no boots were cut to ribbons. For food they were given a daily issue of a handful of wheat, a handful of flour, and a spoonful of ghee; there was no firewood and few of the British troops had any idea how to prepare such rations. Later, through the merciful mediations of Generals Delamain and Melliss, Indian cooks were attached to the British units and they fared better, but in the meantime, to avoid starvation, men were forced to sell the clothes they wore to wayside Arabs for scraps of food. Fortunately, as it so happened, General Melliss and a party of officers who had been delayed by illness followed in the wake of this tragic march and Melliss' A.D.G., a Captain Shakeshaft, has recorded some of the sights seen by his party of officers. At Tikrit they met "a number of unfortunate Indian and British soldiers who were standing at the door of a miserable yard where they were herded together . . . they were in a miserable plight, many suffering from dysentery . . . others . . . had no boots for marching. . . . They received only a ration of wheat. The Arabs used to bring milk and eggs to sell and ask exorbitant prices; consequently they would soon have no money and would the of starvation and neglect. . . . Sometimes when a sick man would crawl out of the hovel they lived in Arabs would throw stones and chase him into the yard. I will spare . . . any description of the dark, filthy hovel where they slept."[4]

In an urgent letter to Khalil, Melliss protested strongly and, eventually, a British medical officer and hospital staff were sent to Samarra. Some of the men who had fallen out on the first stage of the march to Mosul were collected by this party but many others were out of reach; they had been buried by the roadside while still alive. That Melliss was able to organize any humane measures at all was a miracle in itself and not one of which the Turkish authorities approved, for they made quite certain that other batches of officer prisoners traveling from Baghdad to Mosul went by another route. Across the desert, the track taken by the columns of prisoners became a Via Dolorosa, along which the sights hardly bear telling. The dead lay unburied and stripped of their last clothing; parties of starving men in their last throes lay in mud hovels by the way to await their end, subsisting solely on the few scraps thrown

---

4. *The Campaign in Mesopotamia, 1914–1918*, Vol. II. In a letter, General Melliss said that the men "were afraid to go any little distance alone to relieve themselves for fear of being murdered for their clothes."

to them by passing Arabs. Thus it is that there is no record and nothing is known of the ultimate fate of three thousand of those who surrendered at Kut. As Melliss's party traveled on in the wake of the plodding columns, they continually overtook many of these human derelicts. "I shall never forget one soldier who could go no further" wrote one of the party, "he fell resignedly onto the ground . . . with a tiredness borne of long suffering, and buried his head in his arms to shut out the disappearing column. . . . One sick soldier was hanging on to the strap of my donkey, my orderly on another. His feet were all blood as his boots had been taken from him. Shortly after ... I saw another man crawling all over the desert in the dark . . . quite alone. ... At another place we came across another British soldier ... he had been left in a cave and had evidently eaten nothing for days but had crawled down to the river. He was delirious and jabbering, and thought he was a dog."

When the column arrived at Ras al'Ain, where they were to rejoin the railway, they were hurriedly herded, like cattle, into a train. Like the troop trains in France—known as "Hommes quarante-chevaux huit"—each truck contained an average of forty men and their doors were locked to be opened subsequently only at stations—sometimes, not even until the destination was reached. Inside the trucks there was no room to lie down, so that men had to sit on top of each other through twenty-four hours of summer heat; as many of them were in the advanced stages of dysentery, the conditions and stench may well be considered indescribable. In his book "Bengal Lancer," Captain Yeats-Brown, who was one of the two officers captured in the abortive attempt to cut the telephone lines from Baghdad prior to the battle of Ctesiphon, wrote:

> I saw a party of twenty English soldiers . . . they were literally skeletons alive, and they brought with them three skeletons dead. One of the living men kept making piteous signs to his mouth with a stump of an arm in which maggots crawled. Presently he died in a fit.
>
> Then there was the saddest tea-party at which I have ever assisted. We had bribed a sentry to allow us to give two of these men a meal of bread and buffalo-cream which we had prepared out of our slender resources. Our guests told us that they were kept in a cellar, with hardly enough room to lie down. Only drinking water and bread were supplied to them. They could not wash. Three times a day they were allowed to go to the latrines, and sometimes not then, for if a prisoner possessed anything that the sentry wanted, he was not allowed to go until he had parted with it.
>
> When our pay was given us, and an opportunity occurred to bribe the guards, it was a heart-breaking business to decide which of the sufferers we should attempt to save. Some were too far gone to help, others might manage to live without our smuggled food. But it was little enough we could do before we were transferred to Aleppo.

The soldier survivors followed. Many were clubbed to death by the sentries and stripped naked. Others, more fortunate, were found dead by their companions after the night's halt, when they turned out to face another day of misery.

Reports of this state of affairs were all sent to General Townshend and although it may be appreciated that he could do little to help it is surprising that his nature should have been so forgiving. In November 1921, to Mustafa Kemal, he wrote "I am devoted heart and soul to your cause and I am proud of the affection of the Turks for me"; small wonder that the Turkish troops cheered him "like blazes and shouted *Inshallah*" when he visited Adana province soon afterward.

The last leg of the march over the Amanus mountains was a there repetition of the earlier stages of the journey. Melliss compiled a detailed report which was sent to Enver Pasha, begging him to intervene with instructions that would insure proper treatment for his captives. Enver's reply, to the effect that having already given orders for their proper treatment it was inconceivable that there was any truth in what Melliss had written, was typical of an attitude of Turkish moral turpitude.

Across the mountains and within sight of the Mediterranean a new period of suffering began for the survivors. Despite their depleted ranks there were still enough of them to form an army of laborers and the task for which they were destined was to work on the Baghdad railway, supervision of which was in the hands of German engineers. It was to their charge that the captives, now reduced to between two and three thousand, were consigned and from these of their enemies they did at least receive some sympathy. Tents and proper food were issued, and for the first week the men were allowed to rest and recuperate. Work then began and went on from six in the morning till six at night "with an hour for breakfast and an hour for dinner, Sundays included." The men themselves were anxious enough to work, if only to earn a little money with which to buy extra food. But the hard fact was that few were fit for any sort of manual labor and, in the hot Anatolian summer, it was not long before fever and beriberi broke out among them. Those committed to the hospital found that they were again back under Turkish jurisdiction—in a system which admitted no treatment for them; soon they were dying like flies of cholera, dysentery, enteritis or the beriberi with which they were plagued. And the rest, those who struggled on and refused to break down, were useless as a labor force—a fact which was soon recognized by their German employers. By September they too had been handed back to the Turkish authorities. But the broken men were a liability to them also—a liability which they had no wish to keep in that particular district. Apart from the liberal attitude exercised by the

Germans, kindness and care was at hand from other sources and news of the captives' sorry state was getting out and the Turks were concerned with international opinion. Already, charitable Americans in the country had rallied around and collected a few of the sick and stragglers into American-controlled hospitals at Adana and Tarsus. As a result of the exertions of the United States Consul at Mersina supported by American doctors and nurses some of the prisoners were saved from inevitable death at these places. Consequently the main body of captives were dispersed and sent to camps in the interior of Asia Minor. The journey there, without doctors, medicines or food, packed as before into railway cars followed by a ghastly march across the Taurus mountains, was a there repetition of their earlier privations. According to one Austrian officer, who witnessed part of this journey, the scene was like something out of Dante's *Inferno*. A few of the men who fell out en route managed to take refuge in German and Austrian military camps in the Taurus. But most of the survivors were driven on across the mountain range by the butts of the Turkish gendarmes' rifles, and the most terrible feature of such records of the appalling march as exist, is the ghastly monotony with which prisoners are said to have been clubbed to death if they faltered, or how they were left, slowly dying by the roadside.

> Recrossing the yard I noticed a row of bodies lying in the sun near a mud wall. They were stark-naked and I noticed that one of them was heavily tattooed. I crossed over to them and saw that what I had suspected was true—they were dead Englishmen, at least three out of seven were; the others may have been. Thinking that I recognized the tattooed body, I bent over it to look more closely and saw a faint twitching of the lips. I ran back to the annexe and told the orderly that one of the men outside was alive. He swore and spat at me and told me to clear out, but I threatened to tell the Kaimakham if he did not have the man brought inside and looked after. At that he picked up a water bottle and asked me to show him the man. Suspecting nothing, I did so, and the Arab walked round to his head, and forcing open his mouth, inserted the neck of the bottle inside. A few bubbles, a convulsive twist, and the poor fellow was dead, deliberately choked to death.[5]

It would be possible to chronicle further chapters of the brutal treatment subsequently undergone by the British troops, but the mention of those who were quartered at Afium Qarahisar will suffice; all the others follow the same pattern. At this place the flogging and ill-treatment of the prisoners became so notorious that early in 1917 the Turkish Government was constrained, under pressure, to dismiss its Commandant, a Turkish naval officer who maintained

---

5. *Other Ranks of Kut*, P. W. Long, M.M., Williams and Norgate, 1938.

his authority by the rule of the whip. A homosexual sadist, this man was in the habit of selling the men's clothes and having them beaten with sticks if they as much as raised a whisper of complaint. And in the bitterly cold winter months the prisoners, who were allowed only a single blanket but no mattress and were crowded into tiny unheated cells, had just cause for plenty of complaint. It is recorded that one prisoner was flogged and imprisoned on a bread and water diet, for having the temerity to burn verminous clothing, while the camp hospital could have been better described as the camp shambles. Here the weak were beaten because they were helpless, medicines were non-existent, and men who were too ill to look after themselves were either left to the in their own ordure or else injected with some fluid from the effects of which they never recovered. All this, and more, could be attributed to the Commandant, who it was said was one of Enver's men, appointed to his command as a reward for services as an assassin. Those who sought to find excuses for him and explain his conduct said that he had served many years in the Yemen where sunstroke had affected his brain. Justice came late, too late for many, but after the war he stood trial and suffered the ultimate penalty for his crimes.

None of the neutral diplomats serving in Turkey were permitted by the Turkish authorities to visit the prison camps for some months after the fall of Kut. Complaints and appeals by the prisoners were treated with studied indifference and supine apathy, so that they could do little for themselves. That they would be ill treated had been the pessimistic forecast of the United States Consul at Baghdad even before Kut surrendered, when he had expressed the opinion that Townshend ought to have cut his way out *"at any cost."* According to the Turks the captives were being treated in accordance with the Hague Convention, although if this was true it seems curious that they should have objected to inspections by neutral observers. Only as the result of strenuous efforts on the part of the United States Ambassador, Mr. Morgenthau, his successor Mr. Elkus, and their staff did any relaxation come about. Then, when the camps were finally opened up to Red Cross delegates, conditions steadily improved; parcels and clothing began to arrive and some degree of comfort at last began to filter into the prisoners' pitiful conditions of misery. Even then the death rate continued to be high, the earlier privations were still taking their toll; only the lion-hearted survived the war to return to their homes. Seventy percent of the British rank and file in captivity died and of the Indian rank and file more than 2,500 of the original 9,300 also perished. Turkish negligence and brutality were the direct causes—a fact which is inescapable.

As the war dragged on, British doctors were allowed to take medical charge of the prison camps and the Turkish guards started to fraternize with their prisoners, so that by 1918 most of the survivors were properly clothed, adequately fed and reasonably cheerful. Nevertheless, few could forget their appalling march into captivity and its immediate consequences, although the Turks were anxious enough to do so when the war started going against Germany and themselves. Plenty of excuses were found afterward, some of which had little foundation. But it is totally unreasonable to accept the view that their higher command could have been ignorant of what was happening. The desert march and the treatment of their prisoners was not just a matter of Turkish apathy, it was a crime of the first order, a shame on Turkey. No one would wish to rake among the dying embers of history and rekindle flames of hatred; the Turks are now firm friends of the West and the present generation has lifted itself far above the subhuman level which many years of corruption and mal-administration by their ruling class had forced on its predecessors. But public memory is short and it is hoped that this account will remind readers that the oriental outlook and ideas of chivalry differ considerably from those of the West. To the historian, only time provides the true perspective, but facts like these are as true today as they were in 1916; reports of the current war in the Yemen serve as confirmatory evidence of the differences in outlook that continue to exist.

To complete the picture, some account of the vicissitudes of officer captives is necessary, although their lot was not nearly so tragic as that of the men. After they had been separated from their troops, the first party of officer prisoners, comprising 100 British and 60 Indians all under the command of General Delamain, were packed into the paddle steamer *Burhanieh* for the journey to Baghdad. As they chugged up the river, whose banks were lined with jeering Arabs, the women raised their shifts and pointed to their privy parts in gestures of derision. When the ship arrived at Baghdad five days later it moored alongside the old British Residency then in use as a Turkish hospital and there the party disembarked while the *Burhanieh* then turned round and went back to fetch the second echelon of officer prisoners, who had stayed at Shumran. The subsequent moves of the two parties were consecutive with those behind following in the tracks of the first party. At Baghdad the reception was less demonstrative than that which the troops, still on *the* line of march, were to receive. The junior officers were marched through the main bazaar roads to the Cavalry Barracks, and although the whole route was thronged with spectators, the crowd behaved well and there appeared to be no hostility. The barracks which were to be their temporary prison were clean and adequately equipped for their reception, although like nearly all Turkish public buildings they had no proper sanitation arrangements. However the first difficulty came with the arrangements for eating; either by intent or ignorance, but probably the former, the Turks insisted that all officers should use the same utensils. Both British and Indian officers would be treated alike by them they said. Religious and other considerations made this a difficult proposition to carry out in practice but fortunately courtesy and good manners shown by the Indian officers surmounted the problem. To many, this may seem a trivial problem; it was not, for it undermined the basis of respect which had been built up over many years. Meanwhile the senior officers in the party had been accommodated in the Grand Babylon Hotel, whose illustrious title belied the comforts it might be expected to offer. They had not been made a public spectacle as had the troops—a point which illustrates Turkish regard for rank and privilege.

Only two days were spent in Baghdad before the officers were packed into a train. At Samarra, where they spent the night on *the* platform or in the station outbuildings, they had the dubious privilege of seeing Townshend and his staff leaving from Mosul before setting off for the same place themselves. But they had to march, and for the journey the junior officers were allotted a donkey each on which to load their kits. Pairing off they shared two donkeys, one of which was used for baggage and one for riding. Starting in the late evening as *the* sun was sinking in the summer sky, the march continued hour after hour across an interminable desert of coarse brown grass. The British march routine of halting for ten minutes in every hour was adhered to but as the hours dragged by and the weary column trudged on through the night, parched with thirst and suffocated with dust, these short breaks seemed to become less and less adequate.

At 10 a.m. next morning the column was halted alongside the Tigris for a short break before the march continued. Then, as the sun climbed into the blazing sky, the column stumbled on. At the next halt in Tikrit, when the officers limped in on blistered feet after thirty-five miles of hard going, Arab women thronged the single street to jeer as the captives were hustled into *the* filthy courtyard where they were to remain for the next twenty-four hours. From Tikrit to Kharinina, twenty miles northwest; from Kharinina to Sunaidij and from Sunaidij to Sharquat; hour after hour in heat, dust, and darkness the dreary journey continued. The last lap was a blessed relief for, as they approached Mosul, the monotonous expanse of desert gave place to green fields and orchards and the climate became more bearable. When they marched in, on May 25, they had completed a hundred and seventy miles in seventy-seven and a quarter hours of marching time; most of them had had little sleep, the food had been poor, and almost everyone was overcome by a feeling of intolerable lassitude. Even if they had been fit, the journey under these con-ditions, accomplished at an average of a little over two miles an hour would have been an achievement. And after the siege they were not fit.

The barracks in which the officers were quartered in Mosul were exceptionally clean by Turkish standards, but Turkish standards took no account of the ubiquitous vermin which inhabited almost all of their buildings. With time, even the prisoners came to accept the presence of vermin with indifference and, despite a prolificacy of lice, known typhus carriers, there were surprisingly few cases among the officers during the whole of their incarceration. The column was warned that they would leave Mosul on the evening of May 27, and before they left, while the officers were packing their kits, Enver Pasha himself suddenly appeared on the veranda and addressed them in fluent French. He had, he said, "the highest admiration for the British officers"; that while they were in Turkish hands they would be treated as precious and honored guests of the Ottoman Government—an expression that by now had a somewhat empty and conventional ring about it. He also added that "with displeasure" he had heard that the officers had been deprived of their swords and that he would take steps to have them returned. Needless to say, none was ever received, nor was any further mention of them ever made. Doubtless one or two still hang on the walls of Turkish homes.

From Mosul, for the journey across the desert to Ras al'Ain, light horse-drawn wagons were allotted on a scale of one to three officers and an arabiya—a light victoria—for each general officer. When the officers' kit had been loaded onto the wagons there was only room for two to ride, the third had to march. Then followed another series of long, fatiguing night journeys, often without water, with daylight rests during which invariably there was no shelter from the sun. Sleep was an impossibility. Finally Ras al'Ain was reached and there the prisoners entrained in horse-boxes for Aleppo, where the senior officers were taken to hotels and the juniors quartered in barracks. As usual both hotels and barracks were infested with every known form of parasite but this was only a short halt—welcome nevertheless—at which they were permitted to spend what little money they had.

Aleppo to Islahiya at the foot of the Amanus mountains was the next step, once again by rail; from here, the journey continued on foot, across the mountains to Kulek, a few miles from the town of Tarsus, and at Kulek the prisoners had reason to be grateful for German influence and organization. Arrangements had been made for their accommodation in tents which had been pitched close to the station, and the sight of the tents seemed almost like a return to civilization. But the break was short-lived. In motor-lorries driven by Germans or Austrians the captives were now taken over the Taurus mountains to Pozanti on a hair-raising journey along rough narrow mountain roads which, for the greater part of the journey, were edged by sheer precipices. At Eskichehir, the generals—Delamain, Hamilton, Evans and Greer—

parted company, being sent to Brusa, near the Sea of Marmora, while the rest went on to Angora.

Meanwhile, the second officers' party had been following up the first and to some extent their journey was easier than that of those who had preceded them; alternatively, perhaps those who constituted the second party showed, or were allowed to show, more initiative in the arrangements for their march. For the journey to Mosul the prisoners supplemented the donkeys by hiring other animals, so that there were three donkeys for two officers. But otherwise the story was a repetition of that described. As with their predecessors the second party was allowed to buy food in Mosul at "horrid little places, more like a fried-fish shop than anything else." On the journey across the Amanus mountains, survivors of this party record that they found traces of recent massacres of Armenians and at one point in the journey met a column of Armenian women and children. These wretches had been driven from their homes and were suffering similar privations to those being experienced by the British troops who were at this time marching into captivity. Little has been recorded of the plight of these people; indeed little of the details is known. Over a million Armenians, men, women and children, were massacred but the world outside knew next to nothing of the event at this time. The Ambassador of the United States was one of those who did and he protested loudly, but as the only official Turkish concern was with regard to the benefits from the policies held by Armenians insured with United States life assurance companies his protestations had little effect. "They are practically all dead now" Tala at Pasha, a Turkish spokesman, is reputed to have said "and have no heirs to collect the money, which of course all escheats to the State. The Turkish Government is the beneficiary now."[6]

The two main parties of officer prisoners eventually joined up at Angora; at this place there was a short halt prior to their final dispersal into the camps in Anatolia where they were to spend the rest of the war. A party made up of a few stragglers admitted into the hospital in Baghdad which came up later and crossed and re-crossed the route taken by the other ranks also eventually linked up with the main body. Wherever they hit the track taken by the troops they found the usual sorry state of affairs which has already been labored and their testimony serves to corroborate the evidence of the barbarous treatment meted out to the men. Little parties of sick and dying, many of whom were covered with wounds from beatings, whippings or even the marks of bayonets littered the way. Most of them were just waiting to the and when death came to them, it was a happy release.

---

6. An account of the Turkish attitude toward the Armenian massacres is given in *Secrets of the Bosphorus, 1918,* Henry Morgenthau.

For the survivors the story concluded with two years languishing in prison. Probably only those who have been prisoners of war—more particularly perhaps those who were taken by the Japanese in the last war—can appreciate what life was like. Cut off from all intercourse with the outside world, unaware of the course of the war, deprived of everything that makes life worth living. There remained only hope—hope that the Turkish army would crumble—or hope that some exchange of prisoners would materialize which would enable them to return home, and to those who were unable to view their conditions philosophically, enforced inactivity became extremely irksome as the months slipped past. Many accounts have been published which give minute details of the daily life of captivity, books which bring out the ingenuity individuals exercised in attempts to improve their conditions or escape. Every means in their power was used in attempts to break the monotony of inaction and idleness and to preserve their interests in the world outside. As the war dragged on these attempts became more and more sophisticated, and even cryptograms were devised to send and receive news from England in the limited mail allowed to the prisoners. None of the officers gave their parole not to escape and a number of attempts were made to do so. One fantastic effort involving a complex plot to feign madness virtually succeeded after the two officers concerned had undergone the most diabolical treatment—treatment which almost succeeded in defeating the original object, by causing them to cross into the realms of insanity they had feigned.

Until pressure was put on the Turkish government, by neutral as well as belligerent powers, the treatment accorded to the British prisoners can only be summarized as being brutal, cowardly, tyrannical and wholly inexcusable by any standards; by those of a western civilization it was inconceivable. In November 1918, a British Parliamentary report on the treatment of prisoners of war in Turkey was published. In this report it was stated that "the history of British prisoners of war in Turkey has faithfully reflected the peculiarities of the Turkish character. Some of these . . . are due to the there dead weight of Asiatic indifference and inertia; others again are actively and resolutely barbarous. . . ." After the war, various excuses were found for the Turks but none of them really rings true. The captives were continually overcrowded, but overcrowding is as natural to the Turks as to all eastern races; because they require little space for themselves, they allotted to the prisoners only what they would have expected in similar circumstances. Vermin were rife and there was no sanitation in the quarters provided in the camps; but, of course, to the Turks, vermin was of no more consequence man smuts are to Londoners and they knew nothing of sanitation. They had neither beds nor tables in their own homes, therefore they provided none for their prisoners. The simple fact remains that they never took the slightest trouble to examine the needs or appreciate the culture of their captives. And, even if the excuses that were found for them with regard to the conditions under which the prisoners were compelled to exist were to be accepted, the Turks can never be acquitted of the indictment of murder as a result of their treatment of the defenseless rank and file prisoners. That any of the Europeans survived at all is surprising; it is a sad and sorry finale on which to ring down the curtain on the siege of Kut.

To the Garrison of Kut

Battle and toil survived, is this the end
Of all your high endeavor? Shall the stock
That death and desert braved be made a mock
Of gazing crowds, nor in the crowd a friend?
Shall they who ever to their will did bend—
From Zain to Ctesiphon—the battle shock
Fall prey to lean starvation's craven flock
And the dark terrors that her train attend?

You leave the field, but those who, passing by,
Take up the torch, where'er your name is named
Shall fight more stoutly, while your company,
Its task performed, shall carry unashamed
Into captivity a courage high;
The body prisoner, but the mind untamed.

R. W. Bullard[7]

---

7. Published in the Basra *Times,* May 25, 1916.

Chapter 14

New Blood, New Methods

At the end of April the men of the Tigris Corps were brooding under the bitterness of defeat. Through field glasses from their forward trenches, the Crescent flag could plainly be seen flying over Kut and their feelings of depression and resentment were exacerbated early in June by the news of Kitchener's death and the first reports of the battle of Jutland. There was no fire in their bellies: they felt they had been let down. In spite of all the privations they had endured, all the losses they had suffered, the outcome had been failure and that it should be so could only be due to mishandling by someone. Before they tackled the Turks again that someone would have to go.

After Townshend's surrender, the armistice, for the exchange of sick and wounded from Kut with Turkish prisoners, came as a welcome lull in the fighting. And when the cease fire had expired, the guns were still silent. An uneasy peace reigned over the battlefield, for neither side was yet ready for an offensive. On the left bank, the 7th Division, sitting in their trenches at Sannaiyat and the 3rd Division dug in before Bait Aisa on the other bank of the river waited for the Turks to make the next move. A few hundred yards away behind the low banks which denoted the parapets of their trenches in front of the British positions, Khalil's men also waited. Neither side wanted to initiate any more of the slaughter of the last few months—or so it seemed. Only in the south where flanks of the two armies diverged, leaving a vast "No Man's Land" was there any hostile activity. But this was Arab country where the Buddhoos, lurking like so many human vultures, were waiting to pounce wherever there was a chance of loot. The whole area was littered with the un-buried dead of the previous battles and when they thought they were safe these ghouls would sally forth to strip and rob the bodies. Patrols of Briton and Turk, equally revolted by the habits of the desert pariahs, made common cause against them and on more than one occasion the Buddhoos were caught in their diabolic activities by the steel-tipped lances of the Indian cavalry. Those who escaped death were set to burying in the pitiable clay which had been the object of their loot.

At this time, there were four British divisions in the forward area.[1] All four were under strength and most of the men were in a bad way. Sickness was rife; dysentery had followed on the scurvy which had been the direct consequence of inadequate and poor quality rations, and at the beginning of May there was an outbreak of cholera. Shade temperatures of over 115° Fahrenheit were now common, the scorching wind, blowing like a blast furnace, rasped and burned skin unaccustomed to a tropical clime. Reinforcements fresh from England suffered most and soon cases of severe sunburn, and worse still heatstroke were added to the list of diseases. In the daytime plagues of flies, originating and breeding among the vast number of corpses in "No Man's Land," added to all other miseries; apart from the diseases which these pests undoubtedly carried and spread, the discomfort of their presence was almost unbearable. Every dish, every cooking pot, every scrap of food was black with them; the air was filled with their buzzing and every man carried his own swarm for they settled on every portion of his anatomy where a hand could not reach to brush them off. The sick and wounded, for whom there were no mosquito nets and very few tents, suffered most of all and only those who have known and suffered the vicious attentions of the Middle East fly may appreciate the torment. Only at night when the flies retired with the setting sun was there any relief. But then their place was taken by sandflies and other nocturnal pests which sallied forth to take up the nauseating irritation when the flies left off.

A few hundred yards away, the Turks suffered similar anguish even though they were conditioned to flies and pests and more able to adapt themselves than the Tommies—such things, after all, being regarded as part of their way of life. They were certainly not downhearted, for the moral effect of Townshend's surrender had been tremendous. Not since 1842 had British arms

---

1. In the autumn the four divisions were formed into two Corps: 1st and 3rd. The 7th on the left bank; 13th, 3rd and 14th on the right. The 14th Division was formed from the 35th, 36th and 37th Brigades during May. This division with the 3rd was deployed behind the 13th on the left bank.

suffered such an unprecedented setback in Asia; the triumphs and successes which had taken Townshend to Ctesiphon were now forgotten and for the Turkish soldier, like the Arab subjects of the Empire for which he was fighting, British prestige was a thing of the past. But this was not to say that the war was over, that the British were defeated. On this front it was just not possible to exploit the victory at Kut without incurring heavy casualties. Turkish morale might be higher than that of the British, but Khalil knew full well that Nature favored both sides equally. British and Turk were about equally matched; numerically the British were superior but they were tired, the terrain favored those on the defence and the British artillery was superior to that of Khalil. The British might be dispirited and in worse physical shape than the Turks, but they were still strong enough to resist any attempt to rush their positions. Besides, Khalil thought that he knew better ways of winning battles than this. Better to hold on to what had been gained on this front, he reckoned, and to look elsewhere for opportunities to smash the infidels. A swollen head, an ex-aggerated idea of his own importance—too often the product of success—was having its effect on him. Reports from agents in Basra indicating the gathering strength of his opponents were contemptuously shrugged off; like the Indian Government earlier he was making the fatal mistake of underrating his adversaries and, as they had paid, so would he. Back in Baghdad ploughing through accounts of Napoleon's campaigns, he was too busy dreaming up a plan for a victorious sweep through Persia to be really concerned with his three divisions before Kut. They would be all right. While they held the front he would fall on the flank of the British line, of communications and finally drive the remnants of the British Expeditionary Force into the Persian Gulf. Marching irresistibly from conquest to conquest, in his mind's eye he saw himself as a modern Tamurlane fulfilling the long cherished Turkish dream of a Pan-Turanian Empire. But first he needed to regroup his army so Kiazim Karabekir, the commander of the 18th Turkish Corps in front of Kut, was ordered to redeploy and shorten his line. Thus it was that in the middle of May the Turks evacuated their positions at Bait Aisa and fell back to prepared po-sitions on the Hai.

The withdrawal was skillfully carried out and patrols of the 13th Division were the first to discover that it had taken place. As soon as it became clear that the move was not some sort of trap, the decision was taken to close up on the new Turkish front line and the 3rd Division was brought up and pushed forward to a line running from Magasis through Imam-al-Mansur to Dujaila. The new line was only ten miles further forward than their old position but in the move up, no less than ten percent of the troops fell out of the line of march suffering from heat stroke—a sure indication of their physical debility and the effect of the hot weather. But the problem was not only in getting the men forward and digging in. When it is unopposed, an advance of ten miles may appear to be a substantial gain, even though the ground has little tactical advantage. The trouble was that this move added another ten miles to an already overstrained supply line, and providing transport and escorts for the ration and water convoys which had to travel up from Sheikh Sa'ad to Es Sinn taxed the resources of the Tigris Corps to the limit. Because of the heat, the convoys were compelled to move by night and at this time of the year the long crocodile formation of animals and men invariably raised blinding clouds of dust. Even with escorts of battalion strength—and sometimes battalions could only produce about a hundred men for the job because of the high proportion of sick—it was almost impossible to protect the columns adequately in the darkness and screen of dust. As might be expected the predatory Buddhoos were not slow to take advantage of the opportunities presented by such conditions.

With the passage of time the number and severity of attacks increased with a corresponding increase of successful ones and as the Arabs steadily grew bolder the supply of the forward troops became more and more difficult. To make matters worse the Shamal—the strong northwest wind, which usually sets in about the second or third week in June and continues for six weeks or so bringing some relief during the day—did not begin until July 20 that year. Tents were scant protection against the scorching sun, shortages of tropical clothing and mosquito nets as well as food persisted and the casualty returns of sick men showed no signs of diminishing. Bigger escorts and extra convoys were out of the question, many of the men and all the animals in the forward area were on short rations and it was obvious that some drastic measures would have to be taken. By August, when over thirty thousand sick had been evacuated from the forward area, it was decided to face the problem squarely and a complete reorganization of the front was effected. The 13th Division and all the animals were withdrawn to rear areas in which they could be more easily supplied, so reducing the number of troops to be fed and clothed at the front and at the same time making it possible for those who had to stay to get better rations; it also gave the 13th Division a much needed opportunity to retrain. Most of the units decimated by the earlier fighting were now made up of half-trained drafts and the front line was hardly the place to give initiates the instruction they needed. But back at Amara, conditions could be—and were—made quite different. Supply was easy; decent living conditions and games were possible, even a canteen selling Japanese beer could be provided. Amara was no holiday camp, but compared with conditions in front of Kut, it was a welcome haven to the tired and debilitated British troops. The regimental sergeant major might come into his own once more but at least there was good food and some relaxation.

Reorganization was not confined to the Tigris Corps; the most important developments were taking shape back in the rear areas—at the Basra base and up along the lines of communication to the front. The problem of poor communications, inadequate transport and a hopelessly inefficient administrative machine had been the quicksands underlying the foundations of the Mesopotamia Expedition so far, and the reader will appreciate that most of the reorganization and build-up during these summer months of 1916 was long overdue. From the very conception of Townshend's advance on Baghdad it had been too little or too few, too late—a familiar pattern in British military history. Now, at long last, the situation was about to change. The advent of Sir Percy Lake had started the ball rolling but it was really the widespread indignation aroused by the first disclosures of the "Vincent Bingley"[2] Commission convened by the Indian Government to investigate the medical arrangements in Mesopotamia that facilitated the basic reorganization, but when Whitehall took over direction of the campaign the War Office supplied further impetus. For the British, the success which followed a period in the doldrums was entirely due to this build-up; consequently even at the cost of some repetition it is appropriate to turn from the front and briefly to consider those all-important matters which are now usually classified under that unglamorous word logistics.

In 1914, when Delamain seized Basra, neither road nor railway connected Sinbad's old port with Baghdad; any traffic between the two cities had to be by water. River steamers plied regularly up and down the Tigris, half a dozen of them belonging to Messrs. Lynch, the British firm which was gradually being shouldered out of the river trade by Turco-German restrictions. Lynch's vessels provided the backbone of support which led to the initial successes in the campaign and it is only fair to add that without the help provided by this firm no success would have been possible. This help was freely and willingly given to the firm's undying credit, for they had received little enough assistance or sympathy from the British Government when they were being forced out of the Tigris trade in distinct contrast with Messrs. Wonckhaus who were supported, backed and financed by the German Government. Without the paddle steamers *Blosse Lynch, Mejidieh,* and *Malamir* and the knowledge of the river, the country and the locals provided by the employees of Messrs. Lynch, Force 'D' would have suffered more than they did. The real difficulties started

---

2. This was appointed in March 1916; its members being Sir William Vincent, Kt, I.C.S., Major General Bingley, C.B., CI.E. and Mr. E. A. Ridsdale, F.G.S.

at Basra—or rather Ashar, the seaport—which is nearly seventy miles from the mouth of the Shatt-al-Arab. As now, the Shatt was a magnificent open stretch of waterway but at that time it could only be navigated by steamers not exceeding 26 feet draft; furthermore the bar at the entrance to the Shatt-al-Arab limited it to vessels of 19 feet draft. Steamers of four thousand tons or more could only enter the Shatt if they unloaded part of their cargo and to do so meant a tedious business of discharging into lighters and native craft at the bar before they could cross. The town itself had seen little development since the time of Sinbad and in no way could it be compared with the busy modern ocean terminal of today. In 1914, there were rarely more than a couple of steamers in the port at any one time and these moored in the middle of the river for their cargoes to be unloaded into native lighters. There was virtually nothing in the way of port facilities, indeed little to show that Basra was a port at all. On shore the land on both sides of the river was criss-crossed by innumerable irrigation channels serving the palm gardens; the dry land was cultivated, the rest was swamp. Further up into lower Mesopotamia shipping difficulties increased, particularly along the other great river, the Euphrates. From its junction with the Tigris at Qurna it was possible for native craft and launches to sail forty miles up the Euphrates but, beyond this point, the shallows of the Hammer Lake had to be contended with and the only craft which could get as far as Nasiriyeh were of the flat-bottomed variety.

Because Barrett's original invasion force was so small, it needed little in the way of base facilities and what were required could be provided by taking over existing buildings on the banks of the Shatt and dumping stores on existing dry spits of land. There was no planned organization and consequently the base expanded haphazardly; considering there was no one with any experience of port and base organization included in Barrett's staff at his headquarters, this is hardly surprising. Development continued in an unscientific fashion and except for minor improvements nothing was done to prepare for large scale operations; the Basra base just grew. Difficulties, which might have been foreseen, only began to appear as the size of the force increased and the scope of the operations spread. What had been sufficient for a small compact contingent operating close to Basra became wholly inadequate when more ambitious operations started. More and more transports and supply ships poured into Basra where there were insufficient smaller craft to serve them: no port facilities, no labor force, no wharves for lighters and none of the hundred and one things taken for granted in any busy port. On shore the swamps restricted a planned layout and the available dry land was already cluttered up.

Apart from shortages—no drinking water except from the river, lack of material with which to build roads, difficult climatic conditions, ranging from extremes of oppressively hot summers and cold, wet winters—it was the old Indian administrative system which imposed the greatest inertia. More river steamers gradually began to arrive in Basra from the Ganges, Brahmaputra and the Irrawaddy, but owing to the distance, the weather, and their incompetent fitting-out for the long sea voyage between their home waters and their destination, many of them arrived in no fit condition to be of any use. Before they could go into service in Mesopotamia they needed expert attention; so for that matter did the steamers which had been flogging up and down to Basra since the start of the campaign. All this meant base and up-river workshops, machinery, spare parts and skilled mechanics. To get these from India demanded some very determined organization and energy, but no one in Mesopotamia knew what to ask for, let alone how to go about submitting the demands.

With the retreat from Ctesiphon came the climax. Only then had the gravity of the situation really sunk into the minds of those who were responsible for the campaign and, as has been related, the Government of India feverishly started to rush men and material to the theater, and to look around for yet more steamers. Unfortunately, most of what they requisitioned in the way of river craft—stern-wheelers from Burma, and a few old paddlers from the Nile[3]—turned out to be virtually useless, while the sudden influx into Basra of a vast number of ocean-going ships resulted in congestion which sent the shipping and commercial world wild with rage. In April 1916, twenty loaded ships lay at anchor for six weeks waiting to be unloaded just below Basra. All of this time the staff at the headquarters in Basra was still wiring to India for more stores and these were being dispatched regardless of what had gone before or of the reception of the ships when they got to their destination. It was a case of panic supply.

Finally came the realization of the truth of the popular Staff College dictum: that nothing would be accomplished unless there were planned organization. Once this had sunk in, the base organization started to move on more rational and scientific lines. An expert on ports, Sir George Buchanan, was sent out to plan the Basra port facilities and the river supply routes. Arrangements were made for steamers to be built in Britain, and Indian rivers were combed for others to fill the gap meantime. (Generally, only the poorest were sent!) Some attempts were made to organize hospital steamers, and, what proved to be an ineffective arrangement was made with the Anglo-Persian Oil Company

---

3. Many more sank on the way. Of a batch of twenty-one stern-wheelers, mostly from the Irrawaddy and Brahmaputra, only four reached Basra and these four were found to be unsatisfactory for use on the Tigris without modification.

for barges to be built at Abadan. Concurrently with this reorganization changes in the higher echelons of command were putting younger, more able and more imaginative men into the seats of authority in Mesopotamia. Among the most important of these was the appointment of Major General G. F. MacMunn as "Inspector General of Communications" and much of the future success of the Mesopotamia Expedition was due to the vigorous action taken by this new administrative king.

Needless to say all did not go smoothly; the speed of the reorganization militated against such an eventuality. Mistakes were made. In the case of the ships being built in Britain, for instance, as was to be expected when the design was undertaken by people unaware of the vagaries of the Tigris, the resultant products were bound to have faults. At different seasons, different types of craft are suited to navigation up the Tigris. In the flood season, from the end of March until the beginning of July, a steamer faces a five knot current; in the late summer and early autumn, when the channel is only five feet deep, anything drawing over four feet six inches is useless. At the same time the serpentine windings of an ever changing channel made navigation a nightmare and attempts to design a boat which would cope with all these factors proved to be somewhat analogous to the tank designers' efforts to produce an all-purpose tank. It took time for the correct design to emerge but fortunately time was something that was not now the problem, for Whitehall had issued firm instructions to the new Army Commander that "no fresh advance on Baghdad could be contemplated—at least for the time being." Eventually a modified version of the paddle steamer which had proved its worth with Messrs. Lynch was decided upon. This vessel had a draft of only four feet and could carry four hundred tons of cargo; from it the P-50 class steamer was eventually evolved.[4] By the end of the year P-50s were starting to arrive at Basra in quantity; the shoestring days of the campaign were over.

Apart from the problems of draft, associated with the depth and course of its channels, one of the prime difficulties with the Tigris as a line of communication was the limitation on the number of vessels that could move up and downstream at any one time. Between Ezra's Tomb and Amara there was a stretch of eleven miles of narrows where vessels could pass only if the up-bound vessels ran into the bank to make way for those traveling downstream. The congestion in this stretch could only be removed by building a railway which would allow freight to be unloaded from the larger vessels at Qurna, carried through to Amara and reloaded into steamers and barges above the narrows. This railway was one of the first attempts to rationalize a planned

---

4. As an indication of the mounting expenses of the campaign, it is worth noting that the cost of a single P-50 was £75,000 in 1916

transport system, and when it came into being the site of Adam and Eve's old haunts became a port for seagoing steamers. A continuous line between Basra and Amara would have been more logical but with the resources then at hand this was not feasible. For such a project, the Euphrates would have had to be bridged either at Qurna or at the main junction just above Basra, and no material for a bridge of this size was readily forthcoming. As it was, the disconnected railway was adequate and offered certain advantages, for when the bar at the mouth of the Euphrates channel was dredged, Qurna could take ocean-going ships of up to fourteen feet draft while some of the smaller vessels from Bombay could discharge part of their stores at Basra, so lessening their draft, and then carry on to moor near the Tree of Knowledge close by the railway terminal. At the same time, by installing telephone control and electric lights to illuminate the channel, the capacity of the narrows was increased, permitting ships to navigate the tortuous channel by night when previously they had been compelled to tie up.

Turning now to the other arteries of supply: The withdrawal of the 13th Division was dictated primarily by the insufficiency of land transport at the front; to overcome this a light, narrow gauge railway was built to ease the movement of supplies up to the Sinn area. This was the same railway which had been used as the sight-seeing line at the Delhi Durbar and had been offered to Nixon when he had first asked for one for the theater as an alternative to the river.[5] From the advance supply base at Sheikh Sa'ad the railway ran to a point within the Sinn position between the Dujaila and Sinn Abtar Redoubts at first; subsequently it was extended to Imam al Mansur and later to Atab. For its protection from the marauding Buddhoos wire fence with blockhouses at intervals was erected while the lines were being laid. Once the trains were running the supply problem was easier although the capacity of this tiny makeshift route was not enough to take all the supplies which the troops needed. Thousands of horses, mules, carts and subsequently Ford vans, still had to be kept forward to supplement its deliveries, and in a country where there was no grazing, no fodder to be bought locally, and no fuel for the vehicles, their presence added to the administrative headaches.

All the major problems were still rooted in Basra, for it will be appreciated that the inland arteries were all linked with the development of the main base. Not until Basra had been made into a seaport proper could the supply system really develop, and turning an Oriental backwater into a modern port was not

---

5. Nixon had wanted it laid between Basra and Nasiriyeh, to maintain the force at the latter place, because of the breakdown of the Euphrates route in low water. Before many miles had actually been put down it became obvious to his successor that a much larger gauge than 2'6" was necessary if Nasiriyeh was to depend on this mode of supply and it was torn up to be relaid in the forward area, when it would be "on its own."

something that could be done overnight. Cosmos was not evolved out of chaos with the same ease as in the first chapter of the Book of Genesis, and it was a long time before the shipping congestion was reduced. Building port facilities was a slow process but as wharves, jetties and warehouses took shape, land was reclaimed and a labor force assembled, stores piled up and munition dumps grew. One of the most difficult problems initially was to find the men to do the work. The local Arabs were not keen on any sort of manual labor. Even if the pay for it was acceptable, their Mediterranean preference for lying in the sun made them unsatisfactory. The only alternative was to import a labor force, and from India Labor Corps companies under command of old Indian Army officer pensioners were brought in. At least they were willing, though some were very old and one anecdote is worth recounting. One white bearded Subahdar, asked by General MacMunn how long it was since he went on pension, excused his presence with the reply: "Eleven years Sahib. When the war got serious, father says to me 'Get out to the wars, I won't have you young fellows loafing around the farm.'" To supplement these companies, men serving sentences in Indian prisons were recruited into a Jail Labor Corps. For good service this recruitment scheme allowed prisoners to gain remissions of their sentences and many of the units formed came with their own jailers as officers. They are reputed to have worked so well that the scheme was extended to prisoners in Egypt, one labor unit even being provided by a women's colony of runaway wives. This unit, whose members ruled and controlled themselves, also proved to be a success, working as well as the men. Runaway wives they might be, but it is said that they would stand no nonsense, even from British officers, and the story is told of one officer who had made some ribald comments, being pulled off his horse and stripped to the pelt.

To start with, the development of Basra as a port was necessarily a slow business, not only because of the difficulties of unloading the material needed to build it up but of finding somewhere to put it when it was ashore. However, as ditches and swamps were filled in, the work went on at an ever increasing rate. Suction dredgers brought across from Burma by Buchanan deepened the river channels, navigation over the bar across the Shatt was improved and an automatic signal station to indicate the water depth was erected. Meantime a port staff with a competent pilot service was organized and a drill worked out for bringing the ocean-going merchantmen into the harbor, clearing their cargoes and turning them around within a few days. Improvements were also going ahead on shore alongside these developments. A metalled road with proper bridges –crossing all the creeks which lay between was built connecting Basra to Ashar, and a huge camp with piped water supply and electric light was set up as a base depot with several general hospitals. All these projects produced a whole host of engineering problems. Because India had sent rock hard road metal that could not be rolled, the six miles of metalled road between Basra and Ashar had to be given a cement foundation. However, once it was built this road proved to be most economical and from Ashar it was steadily pushed forward toward the front. Rest camps and supply dumps were set up at appropriate intervals along the two hundred and fifty miles which separated the base from the operational area up the Tigris, and, by autumn, columns of reinforcements were able to march up to the front with a consequent easing of the strain On the river transport system.

By this time also, the crash program for improving the river system was also bearing fruit. Barges and steamers were beginning to materialize at long last and more and more native craft had been taken into service to augment the river fleet.[6] As with the construction work the initial problem was me provision of labor—suitable individuals to man and run the boats. In the beginning the men sent out to take charge of the steamers were often the type of individual whose upper limit was the position of fourth-mate on an ocean tramp. Many of them were overfond of the bottle and apart from this weakness few had had any training in sailing small craft up narrow waters. Improvisation again provided the answer and a special marine corps was organized from among volunteers in the land service; to the troops they were to become known affectionately as "Kitchener's Bastards." Without them the coming British offensive could never have made any progress and the Turks might still be in Baghdad.[7]

In other respects, the tide of British fortune in Mesopotamia was steadily rising. As more resources became available the medical situation improved. Steamers could not be spared solely for use as hospital ships but in May and June a number of barges were fitted out to carry sick and wounded back from the front and, by the end of the year, these barges were supplemented by proper hospital steamers and specially equipped barges from Britain. Nurses

---

6. The amount of river transport available on May 1, 1916, and the increase in the next seven months is shown below:

	May 1	September 1	November 1
Paddle steamers	25	32	38
Stern-wheel steamers	3	3	5
Tugs	4	4	4
Total tonnage capacity	7,300	8,990	11,500

During the period May to November, 17 ships were lost on their way to Mesopotamia. Subsequently the tonnage carried up river rose to over 90,000 in March 1917.

7. During the advance they were often cursed up hill and down dale. The army, marching from Kut to Baghdad had only its bare rations and many attempts were made to flag steamers into the shore. But the canny MacMunn had anticipated this sort of upset to his carefully laid plans and every ship's captain had orders to take no notice of any summons, however peremptory, unless told to do so by his headquarters. No doubt such orders were hard to obey but by doing so the ultimate success was assured.

came out to staff the base hospitals, and special clinics were established to deal with the tropical diseases which abounded in Mesopotamia. With improvements in the medical field and better food, the troops' health began to improve and by July the flow of reinforcements was more than coping with the flow of sick in the reverse direction—a significant development indeed at this time.

Every kind of equipment was pouring into the country by now. Stocks of the latest type of grenades, Verey Lights, machine guns, mortars and guns were all welcome additions to the Expeditionary Force's armory—especially the medium guns and howitzers so essential to deal with the Turks' earthworks. Reserves of ammunition started to accumulate and bridging material to eradicate one of the most severe handicaps that the Tigris Corps had been suffering from—freedom to maneuver—was also either collected or manufactured. Gas masks were also sent out from England and issued but as the Turks never used gas, they were never necessary. In May 1916, there were only five antiquated aircraft available to Lake, and the Turks, with modern German machines, had air superiority. Within three months they had lost it and, by the end of the year, the British air force in Mesopotamia had twenty-four modern airplanes and all the latest bombing and aerial cameras to go with them. With the cameras it was now possible to make accurate maps, so this perhaps was the greatest blessing that the RFC could bestow.

By far the most important developments stemmed from changes in the higher command. Mention has already been made of MacMunn and Buchanan; the key appointment—that of Army Commander—was also revitalized about this time. Both before and immediately following Town-shend's surrender, Gorringe had been suffering from considerable strain and as the weather got hotter it was obvious to Lake that his subordinate was feeling the effect of all he had undergone. Because of the succession of failures to get through to Townshend the relationship between the two commanders was also strained, but not to the extent that Lake considered sacking Gorringe. It was just that the Army Commander felt that Gorringe needed a rest, and in July when he was politely ordered back to Britain, Maude was appointed to supersede him in command of the Tigris Corps. Within a month, at the instigation of the .War Office in Whitehall, Maude had been promoted yet again and had taken over as Army Commander. Lake was over sixty years of age and, like Gorringe, he had found the events of the previous months, coupled with the damp heat of Basra, to be a great strain and Whitehall considered that he should go. For Maude it was a case of being the right man in the right place at the right time—something which seemed to have become almost a habit with him, since the war had brought him meteoric promotion. Commanding a brigade in France in 1914 he was severely wounded; on his recovery, promotion to Major General and command of the 13th Division at Gallipoli awaited him. From Gallipoli he had come with the 13th to Mesopotamia and he regarded 13 as his lucky number. When Maude was promoted to become the "Army Commander"—he was always known by this title, for he was the sort of man to whom few people ever referred as "General" Maude—his place, as commander of the Tigris Corps was taken by Lieutenant General A. S. Cobbe. (Like Aylmer before him, Cobbe was one of the select company who had won the Victoria Cross.) Maude and Cobbe were the two most junior Major Generals in the Mesopotamia force and it is unquestionable that their appointments, together with that of MacMunn, set the board for the victorious phase which was about to start.

Maude was to become known as "The Man of Mesopotamia." Of a cold, highly-strung and meticulous nature, he had started his career in the Brigade of Guards, where his thoroughness, single-mindedness and eye for detail had marked him out for early promotion. He was one who worked every minute he was awake, and if any criticisms are to be made of his methods they must be centered on his inability to delegate authority. In war, he said, time was an element of first importance and the greatest offence anyone could commit was to waste a moment of his carefully planned day. Every detail of his operations was regarded as his personal business and unshared responsibility was delegated to nobody. To some of his staff such an attitude was infuriating but to Maude the job was the only thing and if he had known anything about the art of delegation, he would unquestionably have been a great man. He liked to say that he always preferred the quickest way—although the methods he adopted when he resumed the offensive would hardly bear out the truth of his claim. He hated motorcars and traveled to and from the front by airplane; when someone protested against the dangers of this method of transportation it is said that he invariably referred to a friend of his who "fell down a little stairway and died of a broken neck." Maude was not one with whom anyone could form an intimate association, and in his presence his staff were never able to be anything but militarily correct. Plans were formulated in a series of interminable conferences; he wanted, he said, to keep his staff gingered up, and there are not many people who like constant gingering. Exasperating he may have been, but this man was soon to prove that he could crush the Turks and when all is said and done a general's worth, like that of any one else, must be judged by his success.

Thus, changes among the generals, changes in the system, changes in morale, changes even in the weather, were the keynote of the Mesopotamian summer months of 1916. At the beginning of the hot weather the morale of British troops was at its lowest ebb. They had suffered casualties on an unprecedented scale, and knowing that they had failed to relieve their comrades in

Kut their morale was low. And they were suffering from the climate, inadequate rations and disease. Bad communications, an inefficient administrative organization and a hopelessly inadequate transport system were the foundations of their suffering. But in these months everything started to change. These were the days of preparation, analogous to the years in Egypt which followed the death of Gordon—except that what was accomplished in ten months of preparations in Mesopotamia was more than was accomplished by Kitchener in the thirteen years which elapsed between the fall of Khartoum and the decisive battle of Omdurman. Kitchener did not have the support and resources at his disposal to the same extent as Lake and his successor Maude, yet what was done in Mesopotamia bears a strong resemblance to Kitchener's work in the Sudan. Kitchener retrieved the errors of his predecessors by pushing up a railway toward his objective; once it was built it was possible to destroy the Mahdi. In Mesopotamia the Turks were stronger and more ably led than the Mahdi's followers and they were supplied with the most modern equipment. Only the disaster of Kut brought the realization of these facts to the British authorities, and then the transport system which eventually made the capture of Baghdad possible was developed.

Finally, there is one comment which must not be left unsaid, one credit which must not go unrecorded. Sir Percy Lake left the stage during this period and his retirement should not go unnoticed, for the foundation of all me reforms which guaranteed the success of the near future were all laid by him. While he was in India he may have made his mistakes, but in his brief spell as Army Commander in Mesopotamia he more man made up for them. The penalty for regarding Mesopotamia as a side-show for so long had now been paid.

Chapter 15

Maude's Offensive

The sword is for him who wears it, the bridge for him who
crosses it, the horse for him who mounts it.

Turkish Proverb

30th September, 1916:

From: The Chief of the Imperial General Staff,[1] War Office, London.
To: The Commander-in-Chief in India.

The instructions of His Majesty's Government.

The Mission of the Mesopotamia Expeditionary Force is to protect the Oil Fields and Pipe
Lines in the vicinity of the Karun river, to maintain our occupation and control of the Basra
Vilayet, and to deny hostile access to the Persian Gulf and Southern Persia. *At present no fresh
advance to Baghdad can be contemplated, but it is the desire of His Majesty's Government, if and when
possible, to establish British influence in the Baghdad Vilayet. This further advance should not be undertaken
unless and until* sanction for it is given. . . . No further reinforcements for the force must be
expected. On the contrary it may become necessary to withdraw the 13th Division which was
sent to Mesopotamia in order to assist in the attempted relief of Kut-al-Amara.

With a covering letter emphasizing that Mesopotamia was a "secondary"
theater of war and that any ideas regarding another advance on Baghdad
were to be put out of the Army Commander's mind forthwith, this telegram

---

1. General Sir W. R. Robertson—"Wully Robertson," the ex-ranker who had risen on merit to the highest
service appointment in Britain.

made it quite clear that so far as those in Whitehall were concerned it was once again a case of "a safe game being played in Mesopotamia." No more rash dashes up the Tigris were to be entertained; indirectly, Maude had been assigned a defensive role and there was no word about destroying the Turks opposing him.

For the time being the new Army Commander went along with this directive. He realized, he said, "that visions of Baghdad are beyond our sphere . . . and that severe losses must not be incurred." Nevertheless he stressed that an entirely passive attitude in Mesopotamia would not only be unprofitable but also bad for the troops, and this point was grudgingly accepted. By the end of September, when the effects of the reorganization and build-up described in the last chapter were beginning to have an effect, Maude was seeking to extend the terms of his directive for, despite these terms, he believed that his mission was to smash the Turks in Mesopotamia. Now was the time. His troops had recovered born physically and mentally, their tails were up. If he were to frustrate Khalil's designs, wipe out the slur of Kut, and restore British prestige in the Middle East, there would have to be an offensive; nothing could be gained by the continued stalemate of trench warfare. With a hundred and fifty thousand men under his command,[2] a seemingly adequate line of communications behind him, and these inducements, Maude was resolved to attack before the winter rains set in and made operations difficult.

In November the Army Commander moved his headquarters from Basra up the Tigris to the front. Like Allenby, who shifted his command post from Cairo to the Gaza front before his offensive in Palestine, Maude was determined to hold all the strings and control the forthcoming battle personally. Remote control from Basra was not for him, he was going to make quite certain that the battle went his way. With a superiority of three to one over the Turks, the railway, the transport columns—which now included a company of lorries—and two brigades of cavalry Maude was far more able to maneuver than his opposite number Kiazim Karabekir. His troops could operate away from the river, the Turks were tied to it. So far as tactics were concerned, and the ability to apply this maneuverability, the courses open to him were strictly limited however. On the left bank, because of Suwaikiyeh Marsh, now a huge lake, it was not possible to get around behind the Turkish flank, and a frontal attack on their Sannaiyat trenches was out of the question, if only because of the high cost in men's lives that was bound to be incurred. Furthermore, even if a high casualty rate was acceptable, bitter experience had shown that a

---

2. Of these, only 72,000 could be concentrated on the main front: a fact which exemplifies the growing tail of a modern army. Whether in view of the Turkish posture the Euphrates detachment (15th Division) was justified is arguable.

successful assault there was doubtful. In theory the defenses at Sannaiyat could be hammered by the British guns from the right bank but as the Turks had steadfastly sat through previous bombardments, any such theoretical weakness could hardly be assumed to be one which might be exploited. In view of these considerations an attack somewhere on the right bank seemed to be indicated and this is where Maude decided the blow should fall.

Though it may seem to be a simple statement of the obvious, Maude's object seems to have been the destruction of the whole Turkish Army on the Tigris front. Yet it does not appear to have been the one which was dominant in his mind when the offensive was launched. If it was, then he was flagrantly disregarding his directive. Obviously he was concerned with defeating the Turks, but the plan evolved suggests that his initial object was not to surround Kiazim Karabekir's force completely prior to annihilating it, but, rather less ambitiously, with maneuvering it out of the trenches before Kut and compelling a retreat. No doubt "Wully" Robertson's strict injunction about casualties and his warning that no more reinforcements were available weighed heavily on Maude's mind while he was working out the plan. And, furthermore, the possibility of the 13th Division being taken away from him must also have influenced his decision to try a cautious and deliberate approach rather man a bold advance which might offer spectacular results, but with a strong element of risk.

With a certain amount of trepidation, Kiazim Karabekir had watched the British build-up in front of him throughout the summer months, and he was fully alive to the dangers of his position. But there was little he could do about it. He had thirty battalions, and little hope of getting any more, no matter how many troops his opponents concentrated against him, for his master, Khalil Pasha, remained contemptuous of British arms. In the light of what was to follow, his self-complacency and fixed ideas must have been worth at least another division to Maude at this time. Kiazim Karabekir warned him what to expect, but his mind was centered on a Persian venture and he was not prepared to sanction any reinforcements. All Kiazim could do was to strengthen his defenses.

The British plan was transparently simple. Briefly, the 7th Division—the same, it will be remembered, which had twice attacked the Sannaiyat defenses in the attempts to get through to the beleaguered garrison at Kut, and which since April had been sitting facing the very same trenches—was to make a "strong demonstration" against them. Meanwhile the Cavalry Division[3] and the

3. Formed from the 6th and 7th Cavalry Brigades in December, under command of Major General S. F. Crocker.

13th Division[4] were to march across "No Man's Land" and seize the line of the Hai. Both the cavalry and the 13th were in good heart, but whether the 7th were best suited to their role is open to argument. After their earlier experiences they worked like Trojans to make their position practically impregnable during the summer months, and it is only human to imagine that if one's own position is unassailable that of the enemy is even more so. For this reason it might have been preferable for this division to have been changed over with one of the others. Preparations for the attack went on throughout October and to get some idea of the lie of the land, Marshall, the Corps Commander who was to control the flank move, decided to fly over the Turkish positions. This was probably one of the earliest recorded instances of a senior officer undertaking an aerial reconnaissance before a battle. (Such events are so commonplace now that it hardly seems worth mentioning—except to say that in his reminiscences, the general has commented on his sudden realization that the role of an aerial observer was not all cakes and ale: that to do the job efficiently, time and training were necessary.)

On the morning of December 6, the heavens opened and the first rain since the fall of Kut teemed down; it seemed as if the elements had again been reserving their malice for the new British offensive. Next day was fine, but two days later it poured again all day and the new-fangled lorries were soon as mudbound as the horses and camels. But next morning the skies were clear and blue once more, the wind quickly dried the mud and it was soon found that the rain had proved to be a blessing in disguise since it had settled the dust which for months had bedeviled every move of the transport columns. Five days later on the night of December 13, the offensive opened with a crashing bombardment all along the Turkish front line. Part of the deception plan had been to conceal from the Turks the disposition of Maude's troops as they moved to their forming-up places for the attack, and the Royal Flying Corps had been standing by to deal with Turkish reconnaissance aircraft. Looked at in the light of today's sophisticated techniques of radar cover and early warning systems, their efforts will appear puny. But they worked. Gunner forward observation officers in telephonic communication with the airfield near Sheikh Sa'ad called the pilots of the B.E. 2Cs sitting in their cockpits—ready to start as soon as any aircraft appeared on the skyline—and one or two of the B.E. 2Cs was ready to roar off to deal with it. Only one Turkish airplane appeared during the alert period and this quickly made off when the British airplane appeared, to the chagrin of the pilots. The RFC had been given another task in support of the coming operations however—one which brought considerably more satis-

---

4. Of Lieutenant General N. A. Marshall's 3rd Indian Army Corps.

faction. As part of an elementary interdiction plan, three of the B.E. 2Cs carrying "heavy" bombs (336 lbs. was a heavy bomb in 1916!) attacked the Turkish boat bridge during the night of December 13, from a height of six hundred feet. One pontoon received a direct hit but the bridge was still floating when the aircraft turned and flew off over the Turkish lines where the glow of charcoal fires was an indication of Turks brewing their breakfast coffee. As dawn broke the first smoke from British guns spurted over the battlefield and it is doubtful whether the coffee-brewers had much opportunity to enjoy their potion for many days afterward. The intense bombardment on the Sannaiyat front had led the Turks to believe that this was Maude's objective and Kiazim Karabekir promptly deployed part of his reserve to meet the threat on that side of the river. When the cavalry, closely followed by the leading infantry of the 13th Division, debouched on the banks of the Hai they had achieved almost complete surprise. The night march across the featureless desert went smoothly without a hitch and the infantry moving on one axis and the cavalry on another both reached their objective exactly according to plan. By daybreak (December 14) the cavalry was across the almost stagnant river at Basrugiya and the infantry columns had reached Atab, the point on which they had been directed. Within a couple of hours two pontoon bridges had been thrown across the river and Lewin's 40th Brigade had crossed over to follow up the cavalry, struggling forward along the north bank of the Hai, hampered by the deep-cut irrigation channels near the river. On the south bank the other two brigades, O'Dowda's 38th and Andrus's 39th trudged off upstream toward Kut, but halted as soon as they came under effective rifle fire from the main Turkish trench system, defending Kut from the south. There they dug in and waited. Meantime, the cavalry, now that their river flank had been secured by the advancing infantry of the 40th Brigade, turned east and swung out toward the Turks' bridge across the Tigris at Shumran where the captives of Kut had assembled for their death march. The vanguard actually got to within three hundred yards of the bridge, but in the late afternoon Crocker decided his horses needed to be watered and the force turned back to bivouac behind the infantry positions at Atab.

That night the Royal Flying Corps was active. On a moonlight reconnaissance one pilot spotted a Turkish steamer towing the Shumran pontoon bridge upstream. This was too good an opportunity to miss and the steamer was bombed, first from a hundred feet and then, after returning to Sheikh Sa'ad for more bombs, twice again. Between midnight and 6 a.m., twenty-four bombs in all were dropped as a result of which the steamer dropped her tow. As he flew off after his final sortie the pilot could see the pontoons scattered, and for the time being the Turks astride the Tigris were bereft of communication across the river. The only way they could transfer reinforcements from one bank to the other was by a ferry—a slow and tedious process.

At dawn on December 15, the two brigades of infantry on the east bank of the Hai resumed their slow advance toward the Turks' bridgehead while the 40th, now joined by Thomson's 35th Brigade from the 14th Division struck out to the west. Air reconnaissance reports had given Maude to understand that there were few Turks on the right bank of the Tigris and so the move of the 38th and 39th Brigades up the east bank of the Hai was supposed to be a normal advance. Every available gun had been turned onto the trenches opposite Kut, and the fact that the total British casualties for the day was less than two hundred suggests that there was little serious fighting. But the advance was anything but rapid; caution was the watchword and it seems as if "rapid" was not really the executive word because the orders for it were qualified by the instruction that "if enemy are found to be holding trenches even fairly strongly, objective may be modified." Maude wanted no more reverses, nor long casualty lists, and he was prepared to settle for an advance that was slow, so long as it was sure. Yet, in view of what was to follow, it might have been preferable to have taken a more positive approach, made a resolute attack at the right bank of the Tigris there and then, before the Turks could be reinforced or strengthen their positions. As it was, in the long run the result of this ponderous crawl forward was a series of slow and costly trench to trench assaults. But this anticipates the turn of events.

On the west bank of the Hai, both the cavalry and the 35th and 40th Brigades made a second penetration into the featureless country to the west. It was a day that the Arabs had selected for one of their demonstrations, and as the British troops advanced, a long procession of Buddhoos coming from the town of Hai was seen moving across the front, toward Shumran. The infantry enthusiastically turned their machine-guns on this column but, in the way of the Buddhoos, it melted away before the fire to reform again out of range. Nothing was attained but it was obvious that this flank offered possibilities and two days later Maude decided to exploit it. It is interesting to note that in his orders for the operation the word "strike" was used for the first time. By threatening the Turks communications his object so far had been confined to compelling the Turks to withdraw. Now however, his intention was expressed as being to maneuver westward so as to "*strike* the enemy's communications." After a late start on December 20, the cavalry and the 40th Brigade set off with a bridging train to attempt a crossing at the bend in the Tigris near some brick kilns four miles west of Shumran. The cavalry were to seize the brick kilns and the two sides of the neck of the peninsula while the infantry crossed the river at the apex. Despite the orders for a "strike" Maude was still inclined to be cautious and Crocker, who was in command of the whole operation, had been told that if he managed to surprise the Turks, all well and good. On the other hand, if anything more than the lightest opposition was encountered the whole operation was to be abandoned. Maude knew that of all operations of war an opposed river crossing is the one that invariably exacts a very high toll in blood as the price of success, and this was unacceptable. This halfhearted approach, combined with Crocker's concern for his horses and the way the operation was staged damned it from the very beginning. The earlier cavalry excursion in this area had already put the Turks on their guard, and as the approach march was carried out in broad daylight there could be no question of attaining the one element which might have made the operation a success—surprise. Spotted by the Turks, who quickly deduced what was afoot, the advance guard of the force was in action long before it got to the river. By the time the projected crossing place was reached snipers were out in force on the opposite bank. The South Wales Borderers made several attempts to get across during the day but fire from the Brick Kilns,which were finally held by a company of Turkish infantry, and the opposite bank soon made it clear that if a crossing was to be made heavy casualties would be incurred. And at this point, one wonders what would have been achieved even if a crossing had been effected. Since Maude's army was strung out across thirty miles of front and there was no general reserve, the job of cutting Kiazim Karabekir's supply line and blocking his retreat from Kut would have fallen on the single infantry brigade and one cavalry brigade detailed to make the crossing. All this lends credence to the idea that what Maude really wanted at this stage was to compel the Turks to withdraw rather than a battle for their destruction. Not everybody concerned in the operation thought that it should have been called off, and that evening when Crocker gave the order to withdraw Lewin, the infantry brigadier, was reportedly heard to say "I could have got over that bloody river, sliding on my arse." He was probably right, Crocker's force was immensely superior to that of the Turks; if the march to the crossing point had been done at night and a resolute attack put in, a bridgehead should have been possible. No doubt there would have been plenty of technical problems in the construction of an actual bridge, but at this period the river was at its lowest so that if it could not be bridged then there was a poor outlook for the future. The question remains what would have been the next move had the British established themselves on the left bank. Maude was quite enigmatic about it. Marshall, the Corps Commander, knowing the limitations imposed on the operation was so astonished by the sympathy on their failure expressed to Crocker and Lewin by the Army Commander next day that he blurted out "But you didn't really mean them to cross!" Fixing him with a cold stare, Maude replied blandly "Of course I did."

Whatever the intention it was just as well that no crossing had been effected. Rain poured down during the next few days, turning the ground into a morass and making operations well nigh impossible. At Shumran conditions would have benefited the Turks with their shorter line of communications back to Kut considerably more than the British, who would have been hard pressed to hold the bridgehead. Getting supplies up to the Hai proved difficult enough and to ease the strain on the supply line the cavalry division was ordered back to Sheikh Sa'ad. While the sodden infantry shivered in their trenches the Royal Flying Corps kept up the offensive. Date palm mats were spread over the muddy runways of the airfield at Sheikh Sa'ad and the pilots flew the 1916 equivalent of a round-the-clock bombing program. Three hundred pound bombs—the block busters of the age—were dropped on camps and shipping at Bughaila forty-five miles up river from Kut and on one of these days the record quantity of a ton of explosives was delivered. On Christmas Eve one pilot, the intrepid Hereward de Havilland, whose name these days is more usually associated with the aircraft firm of that name, flew up the Tigris to Baghdad. Not since Ctesiphon had a British airplane flown over the city, and the inhabitants were as much shaken as those to whom de Havilland recounted the urban delights of the place were delighted.

Two days prior to this notable reconnaissance Maude had decided to abandon the idea of crossing the Tigris and in a telegram to London he declared his intentions as being the consolidation of his present position, raids to harass the Turks' communications and watching for any opportunity to develop the offensive. In the meantime, however, "Woolly" Robertson in London had been reassessing the situation and a telegram to Maude removing the embarrassing embargo on casualties contained in his earlier directive put a new complexion on the planning. Twenty-five percent casualties was now acceptable and this meant that Maude was no longer tied to bloodless operations. A scheme for the systematic clearance of the Turks in the Hai bridgehead was the outcome.

But first came a long overdue strike against the Arabs. Throughout all the operations so far they had been a continual source of annoyance; large numbers of troops had had to be dispersed on protective duties and whenever any move was undertaken a wary eye had to be kept open for this second enemy. All this detracted from the main object, defeating the Turks, and Maude decided it was high time that they were given a sharp lesson. The main Arab stronghold lay about fifteen miles southwest of Dujaila at a place called Gassab's Fort and it was decided to destroy the Fort and annihilate as many of the Buddhoos as possible. A quick and resolute operation was clearly necessary if they were to be caught; at the first signs of an attack on them the Arabs would be off, and this is precisely what happened. The cavalry division, which was given the task of annihilating them, made a night march and arrived at Gassab's Fort soon after dawn on the morning of December 24. Surprise had been achieved but for some peculiar reason no attempt was made to surround the Fort, and when the artillery accompanying the cavalry opened up on it, the Arabs speedily decamped. Their smaller horses were not as fast as those of the British and Indian cavalrymen but they traveled light, whereas the British troopers' steeds were weighed down with the two hundred and fifty pounds of oddments considered vital for operations in this terrain. The Fort was destroyed, a few rifles, some sheep and a quantity of grain was captured but the Arabs got away. Had some of the cavalry been located to cut off their retreat a really salutary lesson would have been delivered. The Buddhoos were left to fight another day and Crocker's division trotted back to Sheikh Sa'ad to remain inactive for the next fortnight.

On the right bank of the Tigris the Turks were defending Kut from two main trench systems. The first of these opposite Khadairi Fort, where a loop of the Tigris takes a bend almost due north of the town was more usually referred to as the Mohammed Abdul Hassan loop. The second roughly formed a triangle south and southwest of the Kut peninsula with its base on the Tigris upstream and downstream of the town and its apex nearly two miles down the Hai; this system included Townshend's old licorice factory outpost. Since the Mohammed Abdul Hassan position could be considered an outwork of the second system described, it became the first objective in Maude's plan for clearing the right bank. Made up of two lines of trenches, this position covered the defenses in the Kut peninsula which in turn supported the Hai system; so long as the Turks held it, the British were denied positions from which their guns might enfilade the main defenses. It was a well sited defensive locality in an area of thick brushwood; the trenches and strong points were strongly built and protected by a mass of wire entanglements and the front line was over two miles long. Well placed machine guns flanked the front and the guns in Kut which commanded the whole of no man's land before the first line could be controlled from vantage points which—for Mesopotamia—provided extraordinarily good observation. Not only could the surrounding countryside be scanned from the so-called East Mounds which lay at the southern flank of the position, but also from the high buildings in the town itself. Among these was the single tall minaret, towering above the white houses against the dark background of palm trees and plainly visible to the men of the Tigris Corps. (Maude ordered that the minaret was to be spared, nevertheless the top was knocked off by one battery.)

On the night of December 22, the Manchesters of the 8th Brigade and the

Highland Light Infantry of the 9th delivered the first blow. Closing to within seven hundred yards of the Turkish front line on what was considered to be their weakest flank near the East Mounds, they dug in. Then, in the course of the next few days, the line they had established was gradually pushed forward by a tedious process of digging. Saps, radiating from the front line like the spokes of a wheel, were dug forward a few yards and then joined at their forward ends so that the result was a continuous new front line closer to the enemy.[5] This process went on until less than two hundred yards separated the opposing sides. On the morning of January 7, after much sweat but little blood, an advance of two thousand yards had been attained. Twenty-five thousand yards of trench had had to be dug in order to do so—much of it in heavy rain; but the cost had been only three hundred and fifty casualties. It was a commonplace method of advance on the Western Front: slow, tiring, some-times costly, but generally sure.

In an attempt to divert attention from the point of attack, British activity over the whole front rose to a crescendo on the nights of January 7 and 8. The Turks' defenses on the Hai were bombarded, a cavalry force was ordered to raid Bughaila (losing themselves in the mist their raid never materialized), another force was sent off to demonstrate near the Shumran bend and after the position had been shelled the 7th Division raided Sannaiyat. The latter turned out to be a singularly bloody and desperate affair and, of the four raiding parties which were detailed—one each from the Leicester's, 53rd Sikhs and 56th Punjabi Rifles of the 28th Brigade, the fourth being provided by the Sappers—all the officers and most of the rank and file were lost.

Following a heavy bombardment the main attack went in on a six hundred yard front at 9 a.m. on the morning of January 9. A heavy mist covered the ground and the Turks' trenches had been battered to pieces by the shelling. Most of their occupants were still in a daze from the tons of metal that had been showered down on them, and many surrendered but others rallied and there was some obstinate close quarter fighting with bomb and bayonet before the British objectives were taken. Having cleared the East Mounds and about six hundred yards of river front the two brigades which had assaulted were just about to exploit their success toward the second lines of Turkish trenches when a violent counterattack was put in against them. Out of the mist a mass of Turks suddenly appeared and bitter hand to hand fighting ensued. However the counterattack was held and by the evening the British were still holding on to what they had gained. Next day was comparatively quiet and, by pushing out to the flank, the whole of the old Turkish front line was occupied with little

---

5. The same system was used by Wellington in the Peninsular War.

opposition. The Turks still retained their hold on the inner line of trenches but it was assumed that the back of their resistance had been broken. By the evening of January 10, they had been pinned into a narrow triangle against the river bank and Maude's men believed that this part of the operation was all but over. However, as they were preparing to deliver the coup de grace during the following afternoon the Turks counterattacked on both flanks and broke through the British line. It was a gallant effort and an anxious time for the British troops involved, but after some sticky fighting the Turks were gradually forced back, step by step into the river. It took nearly three more weeks to mop up but on the morning of January 29, the whole of the Khadairi Bend was in British hands and Maude had completed the first phase of his clearance operations.

After the war a member of the Turkish General Staff said that this particular battle was not only a most critical and costly reverse but the turning point in the campaign. The Turks fought doggedly and well but, as has been seen so many times before and since, guts alone are rarely sufficient to counter the mass application of modern armament. These were the best Ottoman troops and with their backs to the swollen Tigris, they held their ground stubbornly until they were gradually forced back into a diminishing area where the British barrage became increasingly effective. Even then they rallied and counterattacked with the utmost gallantry. Found on one of the Turkish dead was a message from Kiazim Karabekir to the Commander of the Turkish troops at Mohammed Abdul Hassan stating that "the steadfastness of the troops ... in spite of bloody losses, is above all praise. The Corps Commander kisses the eyes of all ranks and thanks them." Despite its extravagant phraseology there is no doubt that the compliment was well deserved.

During January the rain fell with increasing regularity. Once again the Tigris battlefield turned into a sea of mud overlaid by floodwater which could not drain away through the nonabsorbent soil. High winds blew, the color of the tawny Tigris which rose eight feet in two weeks changed to the sickly yellow of the suspended sand it was carrying down from the upper reaches. Aircraft were grounded, and as in the previous year, to prevent their trenches being flooded out the troops had to turn their hands to building dikes. This region might have been a model for El Alamein twenty-five years later, but in Mesopotamia the terrain was more difficult and the tools of war more crude than in the Western Desert. Maude's men were poised on a narrow front where the ground was flat, devoid of cover and ideal for entrenched defenses; the serpentine winding of the Tigris imposed a series of natural obstacles and the Turks, strongly dug in, were stubborn fighters. They were still clinging to Sannaiyat and so with the Khadairi Bend clear, Maude turned his attention to the Hai Salient. Typically, the method by which he proposed to clear it was a repetition of the tactics which had been used for the Mohammed Abdul Hassan position. The advance was to be slow, each step taken was to be sure and deliberate. Because of the preponderance of British artillery, the outcome was almost inevitable. The intensity of the British barrages was such that flesh and blood had to yield eventually, and during this period of the fighting one of the factors which must have dismayed the Turks was the array of artillery observation ladders which steadily crept forward day by day as the batteries advanced their position during the hours of darkness.

The preliminary work of pushing the trenches forward to a distance from which the assault could be launched was completed by the third week in January. As with the attack on the Mohammed Abdul Hassan position a diversionary move, intended to distract the Turks' attention from the point of attack was made at this stage. The Cavalry Division was taken across the river and sent off around the Suwaikiyeh Marsh to threaten the Turks' communications on the left bank of the river. Yet again, the cavalry put up a poor performance. Owing to the waterlogged state of the ground and the featureless country they did not get very far and as a diversion the maneuver was ineffective. Men and horses covered a good deal of the countryside during these months but it is hard to say what good resulted from their peregrinations. The whole Cavalry Division carried out numerous reconnaissances and it is reported that they were a magnificent sight, riding in sections with pennants fluttering from their lances in extended order spread out as far as the eye could see. Yet what the division could do surely could have been performed more efficiently by a single squadron. Little use was made of their specialist capabilities, they could have been a strong and valuable asset to Maude, enjoying a tremendous superiority over the Turkish mounted troops but their performance was most disappointing. On the whole the going must have been good. Mesopotamia was cavalry country, where every advantage lay with the mounted man if full use was made of his mobility. Yet little value seems to have been attached to mobility—the capacity to move quickly to make wide movements round a flank and, if serious opposition were met, to go wider still. Not until young and energetic leaders were appointed later in the campaign were these characteristics developed.

After January 25, when the fighting for the elaborate trench system of the Hai bridgehead started, there was continual fighting until the whole of the right bank of the Tigris was clear of Turks. Two months passed while the British line was advanced to a position from which an assault could be made. Then came the bombardment, followed by clearance at the point of the bayonet. As at Mohammed Abdul Hassan, the Turks fought back with stubborn determination and for the British and Indian infantry it was far from being a walk-over. Only in the last few days before they were finally eliminated entirely on the right bank was the morale of the Turks broken. By now the British troops were beginning to feel the strain; nobody was "burning to be up and at the Turks" as those who read the newspapers in England were led to believe. If there had ever been any glamour in the war most of it had faded by now; for the fighting man the dead monotony of Mesopotamia and the consistent repetition of attacking a series of ditches in an infinity of caked clay was just a soul destroying experience. The method of attack was reduced to a drill. First there would be the bombardment and then the limited assault under a thunderous barrage of guns, the waves of infantry sweeping on forty or fifty yards behind the artillery screen to kill or capture such Turks as were left in the next line. Then would come the consolidation phase, bringing with it the expectancy of counter-attacks. The parados of the recently captured trenches had to be broken down and fire-steps cut in their walls while machine guns were set up and blocks built at points where communication trenches led off back to the positions the Turks were still holding. New communication trenches then had to be dug back to the old position and at night wire entanglements thrown across the front. So little seemed to be gained by so much effort that the ordinary soldier may be excused for feeling it was leading nowhere.

When the battle for the Hai Salient started the Turkish garrison was estimated at about 3,700. The first attack on January 25, was directed at both banks of the Hai and the two bridges involved—the 39th on the left and 40th on the right each having a nine hundred yard front.[6] All went well at first and eighteen hundred yards of the Turkish front line were captured. Then under cover of the heavy fire from a large Minenwerfer mortar the Turks made four successive counterattacks and Turkish infantry who carried no weapons or equipment other than their grenades dashed across the open to bomb the men consolidating their newly captured trench. On the 39th Brigade front the North Staffords and Worcesters who had led the attack reeled back and the whole position was in danger of being rolled up until support came in from the Warwicks as, led by their commanding officer Colonel Henderson,[7] they charged into the melee. In their first charge the Turks had captured the assaulting troops signaling flags and the artillery screens which marked the limits of the advance, and these were used to confuse the forward observation officers. There was no option but to hold off the British artillery support, but

---

6. The attack was supported by the fire of sixty-six 18-pounders, twenty-eight 4.5-inch howitzers, eight 60-pounders and two 6-inch howitzers.

7. Henderson, killed in this action was awarded a posthumous V.C. for his gallantry as was the adjutant, Lieutenant Phillips, who attempted to rescue him.

in the meantime the Turkish Minenwerfer continued to lob bombs on the front line. Believing that they were being shot up by their own gunners the British infantry withdrew and the line was not recaptured until that night. What had been gained was now lost. It had been a day of bitter fighting during which eleven hundred casualties had been incurred, among whom were three commanding officers of the British battalions taking part. Seven out of eight of the British mortars in action on this front had been knocked out and three of the four machine guns set up in the trench during the consolidation were also destroyed. (A fifth which was brought up at the last minute was saved by a sergeant of the Machine Gun Company after its crew was killed to a man; carrying it out of action he also fell dead.)

The attack was renewed next day, with the 14th Division taking over from the 13th on the west bank of the Hai. This time, after twelve hours of stubborn fighting, the 82nd and 26th Punjabis succeeded in retaking the line which had been captured and lost the day before and knocking out the fateful Minenwerfer in the process. But success was only achieved at the cost of heavy punishment. Of the 82nd Punjabis, 240 of the 500 men who had hopped the parapet that morning were either killed or wounded. On the east bank it was the same story. Nevertheless, by the end of the month the whole Turkish front line system to a depth of a thousand yards was in British hands.

On February 1, a fresh attack was launched with the object of completing the clearance; the 37m Brigade assaulting west of the Hai and the 40th along the east bank. Unhappily the events on the left bank were a repetition of January 25, and although the two battalions engaged—the 36th Sikhs on the left, and 45th Sikhs on the right—fought with the most desperate gallantry, the Turks had concentrated to defend what they considered to be the most vital point in their defence system and the assault was rolled back. Both Sikh regiments went over the top in full strength and were practically annihilated, losing more than a thousand men between them. After this setback Maude redistributed his troops and the 8th Brigade of the 3rd Division took over on the east bank of the Hai. The attack was renewed on the morning of February 3, and this time it was successful, possibly because the Devons and Gurkhas who spearheaded the assault were able to take advantage of the cover afforded by piles of corpses of the Sikhs, as they crossed the open ground. The Gurkhas, who behaved with their usual élan, swept on through the Turks like a pack of terriers and the story is told of one being so excited by his blind lust of hunting that he followed his grenade into a Turkish trench before it had burst and both he and the Turks in the trench were blown up together.

A detailed description of the operations in the Hai triangle would exhaust the reader's patience. After February 3, the story is mostly one of a hundred small affairs of outposts, pickets, patrols wiring and sapping up toward the enemy's position—all the operations which go under that ubiquitous term "consolidation." Always there was a constant drain of casualties; even in the quietest periods a dozen or more wounded would drift back to the advanced dressing stations and the padre would have his work reading the burial service over the dead. In the three weeks before the end of January, the 40th Brigade alone dug seven and a half miles of trenches as well as wiring and consolidating four miles of captured line. But, as the days passed, the rate of progress increased, the Turks' morale declined and the ground was covered more rapidly. Between February 9 and February 13 the bombers of the South Lancashire Regiment cleared over 5,500 yards of enemy trenches and three strongpoints; these are only the statistics of a single battalion but many of the others of the six brigades which took part are as equally impressive. In all these operations 3,700 casualties were incurred, but the final phase of this clearance operation was approaching.

By February 5, the Turks had evacuated the Hai triangle and had taken up a new line running from the licorice factory to the Shumran Bend at Yusifiya, and the fighting here is more usually referred to as the operations for the clearance of the Dahra Bend. On the morning of February 9, in fine weather, the 38th Brigade launched an attack against the center of the positions opposite the licorice factory and after some hot fighting and several counterattacks the Turkish front line was finally breached. Next day the licorice factory was captured, and during the ensuing four days the Turks were completely hemmed in and steadily pressed further and further back to their last line across the curve of the river. Six days later their resistance collapsed and although the bend was not captured without fighting, for the first time since before Ctesiphon they started to surrender en masse. After the first surrender the collapse was infectious; prisoners came forward all along the line waving white rags and for nearly an hour there was a continuous procession. The Turks on the other side of the river turned their guns on to these wretches but this only quickened the current. For the Turks in the Dahra Bend the war was over. "We do not wish to counterattack" one of the prisoners explained; like his comrades, he had had enough of the British artillery. And that was the end of that; Maude's nibbling operations had achieved their object at last. Whether he would have done as well by a full scale surprise attack pressed on with vigor when the offensive opened in December is arguable since the trench operations undoubtedly proved to be much more costly in men, as well as time, than he had ever anticipated. What the effect would have been if he had had a regiment of tanks under his command in the terrain of Mesopotamia is interesting to conjecture. When the weather is right, except for the river there is nothing to stop tanks and while they would have been conspicuous on the flat ground it would seem, on the whole, that they would have had an overwhelming effect.[8] The value of artillery has of course been obvious; trench systems could not be taken without very strong artillery support, as Aylmer had learned earlier, and the guns were Maude's greatest single battle winning asset.

How the Turks managed to maintain *the* high morale they did is one of the enigmas of this time; not until the very end did their spirit deteriorate. But soon after the final action, rain fell in torrents flooding the trenches, and a captured Turkish officer sadly recounted the Turkish point of view. "We have been praying for this rain," he said "for two months. Now it has come too late."

Rain or no rain, they would still have lost. Maude might have had a more dramatic victory at less cost in men's lives but he would have won in the end.

---

8. There would have been the problem of getting them to the front of course and it is realized that early in 1917 tanks were not fully accepted on the Western Front, let alone "sideshows."

Chapter 16

The Pursuit

The race is not to the swift, nor the battle to the strong . . . but time and chance
happeneth to them all.
Ecclesiastes 9:11

The Turkish position at Sannaiyat—or Fallahiyeh as it was called in
Baghdad—had all the natural attributes of a Thermopylae. Yet before the
Turks had dug the formidable trench system across the barren strip of land
between river and marsh, Sannaiyat was merely the place name of a featureless
stretch of desert where nomadic Arabs sometimes grazed their herds; otherwise it was unknown. Who had appreciated that it could become what was
virtually a fortress gate is also not known. During Townshend's advance, the
Turks had preferred to dig in a few miles further back and defend Kut from
the more extended position at Sinn. But someone—the wily old von der Goltz
possibly—had spotted the tremendous potentialities of Sannaiyat as the only
strong position between Basra and Baghdad and realized that so long as it was
held there could be no breakthrough to the capital. During the siege of Kut,
bitter experience had amply justified the assessment of its defensive capacity
and shown the British that frontal attacks on Sannaiyat were an extremely ex-

pensive way of breaking through. One might have expected therefore that any more frontal attacks would be out of the question. But, as this was not so, it is worthwhile recapitulating a description of the Sannaiyat position as it was in February 1917. The main Turkish defenses rested on two lines of trenches forty yards apart; a third lay two hundred yards behind the second line and something like three thousand men, supported by 19 guns, were distributed between the three lines. In the normal course of events, both forward trenches were lightly held, but from the third line machine guns could sweep the ground across which any British attack would have to be made, and from this rearward position, where the bulk of the Turkish garrison was located, a counterattack could quickly be mounted. As sited and organized, the position was almost impregnable. A series of attacks supported by an overwhelming barrage of artillery fire might possibly have forced a way through in the end, but it must necessarily have been at a tremendous cost in lives even if heavy artillery had been available—which it was not. Then behind Sannaiyat lay the Nukhailat and Suwada positions, both of which would have to be forced before the road to Kut lay open. Yet, to Maude there was little alternative but to attack again, or somehow or other get around behind Sannaiyat. Either the Sannaiyat door to the Kut fortress had to be hammered open or the wall behind scaled and the key turned from the inside. As will be seen, it was the second method that was to succeed eventually, but not before more lives had been sacrificed in further attempts to breakthrough.

Despite the rain bucketing down in mid-February, Maude had originally intended to continue the operations designed to clear the Dahra Bend, and at the same time to attack Sannaiyat. However, by the morning of February 17, the countryside had been turned into a veritable quagmire once again and he reluctantly decided to abandon the operations on the right bank of the river—at least for the time being. But the assault on Sannaiyat still held good; me ground there was reasonably firm, everything had been arranged and orders for the operation were already issued. Better, thought Maude, to let it go on. It was an unfortunate decision. The troops detailed for the attack came from the 7th Division and their possible unsuitability, in view of the fact that they had sat throughout the hot weather and wet winter facing Sannaiyat has already been noticed. The regiments taking part in this attack and that which was staged a few days later were the same as those which had made the original attack on April 6, 1916. For nearly a year they had bled and sweated over the ground around Sannaiyat and although me original division had been virtually reconstituted since the heavy losses of ten months before, it is reasonable to suppose that fresh troops might have done better—and indeed that they might have been better employed elsewhere. The fault was not that of the men concerned;

they needed a change of scenery.

"D" day was fixed for February 17, and zero hour for noon, when the 21st Brigade was to make a surprise attack. There was to be no preliminary bombardment which might forewarn the Turks and the attack was to be made with two battalions assaulting in line, despite the narrowness of the front—only three hundred and fifty yards. When the first two lines of trenches had been captured, the 19th Brigade was to pass through the 21st Brigade and go on to capture the third line. Meanwhile the third brigade of the division (28th) would make sure that none of the Turks on the right of this narrow front interfered with the main operation. After the initial break-in, the 19th Brigade would have the support of all the artillery which could be mustered—including the Corps' heavy guns which were sited to enfilade the Turks from across the river. With such powerful support it was hoped that the defenders would be pulverized even before the infantry got to the third line. In spite of the assumption that the mud and rain had not materially affected the Sannaiyat position, the 21st Brigade was not ready to start the attack at noon. Men had been sliding about the slippery communication trenches for much longer than had been anticipated and consequently zero hour had to be put back until 2 p.m. However, once the brigade did go over the top the two Turkish trenches were quickly overrun and held for over an hour and a half while the 19th Brigade was moving up. So far all had gone well. Then the Turks put in a counterattack along the river bank and their gunners directed a hail of accurately placed shells onto their old front. Suddenly there was panic and by 4:30 p.m. considerably shaken and very disorganized, the remnants of the assaulting battalions were back in their old trenches. This excursion had cost over 500 casualties and, so far as Maude was concerned, absolutely nothing had been attained—or so it appeared.

On this occasion appearances were deceptive; following so closely on the Dahra Bend operations the attack on Sannaiyat had had a far greater effect than Maude could possibly have realized. Up to now Khalil had been convinced that the Turkish front on the Tigris had been stabilized and he was still obsessed with the idea of a Napoleonic blow through Persia which would cut Maude's communications somewhere between Sheikh Sa'ad and Amara. Kiazim Karabekir had been sounding grim warnings, but so far Khalil had been deaf to them. As a result the Kut front had been starved of reinforcements and no plans had been made to cover Baghdad in the event of the front's cracking; not even the five positions prepared in 1916 between Aziziyeh and Baghdad by the more far-sighted Nur-Ud-Din had been maintained. So far as Khalil was concerned a British breakthrough was not even worth considering; his concern was for the future and that, to him, meant the attack through Persia. Suddenly it seemed, there was cause for alarm. Operations in the Dahra Bend had written off more than three thousand Turks as casualties and the effective strength of Kiazim's Corps was down to below ten thousand men. Now came Maude's blow against Sannaiyat. So far nothing had been lost, no ground given; the Sannaiyat position was still safe. But Khalil was sensitive to any attack on the left bank and he could no longer metaphorically bury his head in the sand. For the time being anyway, the pet Persian scheme would have to be shelved, and the 13m Corps, already diverted to Persia and facing Baratoff's Russians, was ordered back to Baghdad. Simultaneously other reinforcements were hastily ordered up to the Tigris front. But by now the snows in the mountains were impeding movement, and when the 13th Corps did manage to disentangle itself and get back to Baghdad, it was too late to influence events.

Khalil's troops were also beginning to feel the strain. It was not only the bombardments, the strain of waiting for an attack or the close quarter fighting which followed—although these were all having their effect—the Turkish supply line was proving unable to cope with the additional demands imposed on it by the increased tempo of the operations. Ammunition was running low, rations had been cut and, when one remembers that the ration of a Turkish soldier was little more than a bare subsistence diet anyway, the effect was bound to be serious. Behind the firing line, the increasing numbers of deserters were a portent of the doubts the Turks were beginning to have in their ability to beat the British in Mesopotamia. Drafts for the front arrived only at about half strength and an intercepted message stated that a certain unit was moving down to the front but that the battalion commander had deserted. The blame could be laid at Khalil's door; if he had but listened to Kiazim Karabekir's words of warning things might have been very, very different. Including the troops allotted to the Persian expedition, Khalil had thirty thousand fighting men under his command—quite sufficient to block Maude's advance, if not at Kut, then somewhere further along the road to Baghdad where his communications would have been shorter and those of the British correspondingly longer. As it was, he had barely 10,000 men facing Maude at the front, and perhaps another three thousand in and around Baghdad. What was about to happen was the price he was to pay for the folly of his strategic obsessions.

The Sannaiyat attack having proved a dismal failure, Maude returned to the idea of crossing the Tigris some way up the river. If a force could be established on the left bank, the threat to Kiazim's communications back to Baghdad ought to be sufficient to make him abandon Sannaiyat sooner or later. The idea was not novel; indeed it seems to have been the only logical alternative. Its hazardous aspect lay in the actual forcing of the passage across the river; apart from the physical difficulties of getting a sizable force with all its equipment over to the left bank, it was obvious that the Turks would do their utmost to crush the bridgehead as soon as its existence became known to them. Clearly, surprise was essential and every deceptive measure that would serve to mystify the Turks would have to be employed. In the meantime, the operations along the right bank were going to help; they increased the length of the front but the British were better able to stand the thinning out than the Turks and the more Kiazim's men were dispersed the easier would be the crossing. Turkish piquets and outposts could be expected to be keeping an eye on the river line all the way along the front line but it was quite clear to Maude that the Turks could not be at full strength everywhere along the front. If the concentration and preparations necessary for a crossing could be concealed until the very last minute, the Turks deceived by some sort of feint and the crossing made at night, a foothold on the left bank ought to be secured without much difficulty. After that it should be merely a question of rapid build-up, where British numerical strength ought to tell.

The Shumran Bend was selected as the most suitable area for the proposed crossing. The Dahra Bend was considered as an alternative site but rejected by Maude because it was a re-entrant and virtually a defile to the Turkish line. At Shumran the loop in the river which was the obverse of the Dahra Bend not only permitted, the artillery to give converging covering fire from the right bank during the actual crossing, but because the river itself secured the flanks of the bridgehead to extend it to the top of the loop; the sealed salient so provided should be ideal for the build-up. There were other advantages too; Shumran was a long way from Sannaiyat, to which the Turks were tied, and the conformation of the ground here was such that effective observation from the ridges which overlooked the Dahra Bend was denied to them. In any event, all the benefits forecast for Shumran held good on the day of the assault.

The site fixed, preparations started at once. The plan was for Marshall's 3rd Corps to force the crossing on February 23, while Cobbe's 1st Corps on the other side of the river renewed the attack on Sannaiyat in order to pin down Kiazim's reserves and prevent their being diverted to the crossing place. Egerton's 14th Division, already deployed on the right bank, was selected to force the crossing, and in order to allow it to concentrate and practice river crossing techniques, Caley's 13th Division took over from it. For three days parties of Egerton's men practiced maneuvering boats and pontoons across the Hai, by the end of which over 800 had been taught to row; 800 was more than ample but allowed for spares and casualties. Throughout the preparatory period the utmost secrecy was maintained with regard to the time and place of the crossing—so much so that the meticulous Maude dealt direct with the Sapper officer concerned and no one else, not even the Corps or Divisional Commanders knew the exact details of the plan until they were committed to it. In actual fact it had been arranged that there should be three pontoon ferries: no. 1 at the toe of the peninsula, no. 2 about seven hundred yards downstream of no. 1, and no. 3 a further five hundred yards downstream. Each ferry was to have thirteen pontoons and a complement of volunteer rowers drawn from the Hampshires, the Norfolks, the 128th Pioneers and the Indian Sappers and Miners. Sapper officers were detailed to prepare the necessary ramps and organize the ferries, while the pontoons for both the ferries and the projected bridge to be erected near the no. 1 crossing point were to be moved up from the Hai and hidden near the crossing places at night. To deceive Turkish airmen the pontoons were laid out on the ground in the design of trenches complete with traverses; whether this particular ruse was effective is not known—it seems too naïve to have been so. All that can be said is that the combination of all the deceptive measures which were taken did seem to work.

On the day of the crossing the assault was to be supported by fire from every piece of artillery in Marshall's Corps, and sites for the guns and howitzers were selected and prepared around both sides of the Shumran loop; once dug the gun pits were concealed with brushwood. The troops detailed for the assault were to come from the 37th Brigade and Marshall, impressed by the performance of the little men from Nepal, was keen for Egerton's three Gurkha battalions to lead the way. Egerton however wanted an English regiment in the bridgehead and it was decided eventually that the Norfolks should cross at no. 1 ferry while the Gurkhas took on nos. 2 and 3. As soon as the assault force had consolidated its position on the left bank and a bridgehead been finally established, the 36th Brigade, followed by the 35th, would cross over to exploit the success and extend the bridgehead to the top of the river loop. As a result of his Gallipoli experience Marshall was all for making the assault at night and in his original orders the ferries were timed to make the first crossings at 3 a.m. But neither Egerton, his brigadiers nor the battalion commanders concerned liked the idea of a night operation; daylight might bring grave risks but there was certainty that darkness would bring confusion. Whether it was to be a day or night assault was referred to Maude for a decision, as indeed all details were. In this instance he chose to sit on the fence, although his sympathy was with the men who had to do the fighting—at least this is what he told Marshall. Eventually Marshall gave way, with the compromise that the first ferries would start half an hour before daybreak.

On the other side of the river, Cobbe was making his arrangements for the 7th Division's attack on Sannaiyat, scheduled to take place six hours before the

Shumran crossing zero hour. The Sannaiyat defenses were given a series of "Chinese"[1] bombardments daily and as every bombardment thundered out the Turks would retire to their dug-outs, rushing back when it stopped to man their parapets in anticipation of the assault to follow. But instead of an attack the guns would open up again, catching the hapless Turks in the open trenches and wreaking devastating havoc. The Turks could not afford to neglect these bombardments in case one should turn out to be the preliminary to a real assault and for three days the feint bombardments went on in the hope that they would be off their guard when the real attack came. Uncertainty and mystification caused by the dummy bombardments, coupled with the effect of the genuine preparation for the assault which they knew was to come, all had their deleterious effect on the defenders; yet, when the time came, they still had plenty of fight left.

Some of the other deceptive efforts must also be mentioned. One of the less subtle, designed to make the Turks feel uneasy about their left flank resting on the marsh at Sannaiyat, was meant to give the impression that an attack was imminent in that area. For this purpose a couple of battalions marched up to the edge of the marsh and deployed themselves there in broad daylight; like so many things being done at the time, it is possible that this bluff made a contribution to the assault when the crunch came, although again it seems extremely naive. Probably more effective were the measures taken to persuade Kiazim Karabekir that the main attack was to be made directly against Kut. Everywhere on the stretch of the right bank just upstream and downstream of the town evidence of partially concealed activity was provided. Pontoons launched with much splashing and towed upstream undercover of the bank at night; carts with unoiled wheels creaking as they moved stealthily up and down the tracks behind the British front—all served to build up a picture of a concentration at the very point where it was reasonable to suppose Maude would attack for prestige reasons. So too did the growing forest of artillery observation ladders around the licorice factory. In all these activities no lights were shown and there was no talking—only the subdued noises associated with an army flexing its muscles preparatory to an attack was meant to rouse the Turks' suspicion that this was where the next blow would fall.

But before the final piece of evidence came the attack on Sannaiyat—the attack which the Turks had been led to believe was imminent and for which they were waiting. This drew off a large portion of Kiazim's reserve at a crucial moment, for the assault started thirty hours—not six—before the crossing was

---

1. So called because they were heavy concentrations of fire similar to the "softening up" barrages put down before an infantry assault. "Chinese" because Chinese soldiers were, on occasions, said to have simulated all the preliminaries for an attack but, when the moment came for the final attack, decided against it.

due to take place: Maude had ordered it to go in earlier for this very reason. At 10 a.m. on the morning of February 22, spearheaded by the Seaforths and the 92nd Punjabis, undercover of a barrage, the 19th Brigade swept across the open stretch of no man's land separating the two front lines. Having brought forward the original zero hour, the attack was supposed to have gone in at dawn but, because of the chopping and changing it had to be postponed at the last minute. Many of the men, already on the firestep waiting to go over the top, had to wait for nearly four hours—a wait which can have done little to improve their morale. When the order to assault came, however, the attack turned out easier than expected. There were no Turks in the first line—what was left of it, after the pounding it had received—and, when the bombardment lifted from the second line and the infantry were able to move up through the smoke and dust laden haze, where the second line had been was also found to be deserted. Among the shell craters, little evidence of the trench which had been the objective existed; this made it all very confusing for the assaulting infantry. Eventually a line was decided on and the Highlanders and their Indian comrades started to dig in, in the certain expectation of the Turks returning to the fight.

Shortly after noon the counterattack developed. Forming up behind their third line, the Turks advanced bravely through the thick shrapnel curtain which enfolded them as soon as the British forward observation officers could call their guns into action. Within an hour they had ejected the Punjabis and recovered their old front line on the left of the British position. But it was only a temporary success; once the Punjabis had disengaged, machine guns from across the river were able to cut the Turks to pieces before they could get to ground and, when the Punjabis rallied and returned to the attack, what was left of the Turks were forced back. Seeing the battle swaying in his favor Cobbe now gave the order for the second phase of the attack to start, and shortly before 3 p.m. the 28th Brigade moved up to clear and extend the new front line on the right of the 21st Brigade. The brigade was more than ready to go. Since dawn they had been standing to in the old front line where the Turkish artillery had ranged on them; as a consequence, even before the order to advance was given, one of the battalions, the 51st Sikhs, had already lost 80 men. It was easier when they started to advance; the strain of waiting was over and the fire was not so accurate. Indeed the brigade reached its objectives with very little difficulty and at little cost. But once in position, like the 21st Brigade before them, they had to withstand a savage counterattack which took its inevitable toll in killed and wounded. There was a short spell of bitter fighting but the Sikhs and Leicesters managed to hold their ground, the Turks were driven back, and at dawn on February 23, the British were still holding the first and second positions which had constituted the old Turkish front line. And meantime, events on the far side of the river had been shaping the course of the battle for the rest of Sannaiyat.

Concurrently with the attack on Sannaiyat which was intended to divert Khalil's attention and commit his reserves if possible, it will be remembered that considerable efforts were being made to conceal from the Turks the fact that a crossing was imminent in the Shumran region. That Maude was going to attempt to cross the Tigris sooner or later was obvious, the only question, so far as the Turks were concerned, was where. A daring raid across the river at Magasis four miles downstream of Kut was made during the night before the Sannaiyat attack—as a part of the mystification program—and because it was so successful a feint it is well worth a mention. Forty men of the 27th Punjabis who were landed[2] on the left bank of the river rushed some Turkish trenches and then returned successfully with some prisoners and a variety of captured weapons. It was a daring stroke and the raiding party had very few casualties, but success was due only to it being a small scale raid. With the Tigris in full spate the swirling rush of the flood water had drowned the splashing of the oars of the three pontoons which were employed as ferries, and the Turks were unaware of the raid until they were faced with the Punjabis' bayonets. Once they were roused however, the Turks quickly went into action and as the raiders rowed back, star shells illuminated the darkness for the troops rushed up on the left bank to oppose a phantom bridgehead. Clearly the feint had had its effect, as next morning a B.E. 2Cs reported seeing more Turks than ever around Magasis; Kiazim had reinforced Sannaiyat and had deployed at least some of his reserves in order to defend the river before Magasis and the river bank in the proximity of Kut.

That night, as Marshall was completing his preparations for the real crossing, Maude ordered his airmen to ensure that no Turkish airplane flew over the area to see what was happening. Just before dawn the British aircraft took off and throughout the hours of daylight a Martinsyde orbited the Turkish airstrip at Shumran in order to prevent the Turks leaving the ground. Only two Martinsydes were available for the task and this meant that for most of the time only one could keep station over Shumran. The method employed was to drop a bomb, then dive and machine-gun any aircraft which attempted to start up, and one aircraft proved to be quite sufficient for the job. Until about five o'clock that night, the constant patrolling effectively curbed all Turkish or German flying activity; then a single aircraft managed to elude the vigil. But by

---

2. The river was 330 yards wide at the crossing point. The party was rowed over in twenty pontoons by men of the no. 1 Bridging Train and the round trip took about 20 minutes.

then it was too late, for as darkness started to shroud the battlefield little could be seen of the last minute activity on the ground. All the Turkish observer did see was some of the pontoons being towed in the direction of the licorice factory and this was a piece of intelligence that could only lend credence to the idea that the crossing was going to be downstream from Shumran.[3]

During the night the guns took up their positions in the pits which had been prepared around the Shumran Bend and the 37th Brigade, followed by the cumbersome bridging train, advanced cautiously toward the ferry points. The Tigris was about four hundred yards wide at the loop; the current of its swollen yellow stream was going down but it was still running at about six knots so that, without even considering the opposition, getting across to the other side was going to be no easy matter. And whatever the circumstances of crossing, enough men had to be got over in the first trip to seize a strip on the left bank while the pontoons were ferried back for the next party and so on, until a force, sufficient to hold off the Turks while the sappers built their bridge, had been assembled: to be effective this had to be done before the Turks could bring up their reserves. Then there were the problems of the bridge builders, one fear being that the two anchor-laying boats of the bridging train—two ships' dinghies equipped with Evinrude engines—would be unable to ride the current. Fortunately for those involved, the river steadied and the anchor-layers functioned correctly; for once, it seemed that the Mesopotamian elements were favoring the British.

At 5:15 a.m. the pontoons were lifted into the water and a quarter of an hour later all three ferries went into operation. In the half light of dawn, as the pontoons pushed off, the silhouette of the far bank was just visible although it was not possible to make out whether any men were there. So far the Turks had showed no sign of being aware of what was doing on and at no. 1 ferry the first party of Norfolks paddled across without much difficulty. A single rifle shot suddenly rang out as they approached the far bank and this was followed by a fusillade of shots with a machine gun joining in. But by now the Norfolks were across and had seized a strip of the bank before the Turks were fully alive to the threat. However, as soon as Kiazim's men did realize what was happening the surface of the river was churned by the hail of bullets from their rifles which was soon augmented by the fountain-like sprays of falling shells from the heavy artillery fire directed at the crossing places. Through the storm of bullets the pontoons weaved backward and forward between the banks,

3. It seems that the Turks absorbed this news; they were in no doubt that a crossing was imminent but they concluded that the raid at Magasis was a hoax and that the real crossing would take place somewhere near the licorice factory. At dawn next morning a column of Turkish infantry was seen moving in that direction, away from Shumran.

building up the strength of the bridgehead on the far side and bringing back wounded to regimental aid posts set up under the dike of the right bank. Within an hour a sizeable strip of land round the no. 1 ferry-head was in the hands of the Norfolks.

At the no. 2 ferry events did not go so well for the British and the 2nd/9th Gurkhas had a hot reception. Ten of the thirteen pontoons carrying the first assault wave got over to the far bank but of the ten, four were sunk on the return journey. First ashore was Major George Wheeler[4] who led a handful of Gurkhas in a mad rush up the bank. A rifle with its bayonet fixed, hurled from the top of the bank, halted him in his tracks and took the top off his scalp, but Wheeler was soon back on his feet and leading a foray which finally established the Gurkhas two hundred yards inland. Unfortunately, there was nobody to follow his little party, for although the six surviving pontoons at this ferry had tried to bring more Gurkhas across, every man in them was either killed or wounded before the pontoons even reached midstream.

At the terminal of no. 3 ferry the reception had been even hotter. The 1st/2nd Gurkhas, together with their rowers from the Hampshires, suffered a similar fate to that of the second wave at no. 2 ferry and afterward their story could be read in the mud. The Turks lining the bank at this point had used the dike as a parapet to steady their aim while they poured lead into the boats and wherever a pontoon had managed to reach the left bank lay the dead of Nepal and Hampshire. The bodies of the few Gurkhas who had managed to scramble out of the boats and on to the bank sprawled in the mud; the boats, one by one, either stranded or drifted downstream as the rowers became casualties. In the face of such opposition no. 3 ferry, like no. 2, had to be abandoned. There was no sense in going on; better to reinforce success and try to expand the Norfolks' bridgehead.

For a couple of hours the situation could best be described by that service cliché "fluid" but the Norfolks had got a definite footing on the far bank and Wheeler's Gurkhas were still clinging precariously to the little enclave they had carved out. By ten o'clock things were looking brighter. The whole of the Norfolk battalion was across the river; the 2nd/9th Gurkhas were following them and slowly, in the teeth of heavy machine gun fire, the grip on the toe of the peninsula was being extended. For a time the automatic fire of several machine guns had slowed things down, the most damaging being concealed in a nullah close by Wheeler's little party of Gurkhas. Realizing that the British guns were unable to knock out this particularly troublesome gun, Wheeler's

---

4. Major Wheeler was awarded the Victoria Cross for his gallantry in this action. He had arrived from India only the night before the attack and as he was invalided back to India after the action and never returned to Mesopotamia he earned his reward in a record short time of service.

Gurkhas now took a hand. With shouts of "Ayo Gurkhali," the little men got up, charged the nullah and the gun was captured. Once it was out of the way the Turks began to give ground. One attempt was made to counterattack down the middle of the peninsula but the Turks were quickly dispersed by the British artillery across the river as they started to collect for the assault. Meantime, a hundred and fifty yards upstream of no. 1 ferry, work on a pontoon bridge had already started. Six mules dragged up the first wagon of the bridging train while the battle was in full swing just across the river; cheeses, buoys, ropes and anchors were quickly flung on to the ground and a squad of sappers drove in the stakes of the land anchorage. The carts carrying the cumbersome pontoons were men called forward, unloaded—the working party was still under fire from the far bank—and gradually the boats were pushed into position. Fortunately for the Sappers, the Turkish gunners seemed to have no forward observation officers or else no telephones back to their guns; whatever the cause, they had failed to locate the site of the bridge and had registered on the nullah behind no. 1 ferry where the Norfolks had assembled for the assault crossing. Not until the afternoon did their howitzers start to sweep the bank and by that time it was too late, for by 4 p.m. when the bridge was completed the Turks were having to think of getting their guns away, or else losing them. Eight hours after the first stakes of the. land anchorage had been driven in, men and material were pouring across the thousand foot long bridge and forming up behind the Norfolks and Gurkhas who by this time were on the ridge astride the bend. Six hundred Turks had been captured and Kut, for so many months the lodestar of the Tigris Corps, was doomed.

Further downstream, the 7th Division had been expected to push on and occupy the third and fourth Turkish lines at Sannaiyat concurrently with the river crossing operation. In Maude's view, keeping the Turks occupied at Sannaiyat was the most efficacious way of ensuring that the crossing was a success. Provided the 7th Division maintained their pressure, not only would they be prevented from diverting troops to the crossing point, there was every chance that a large proportion of them would be cut off, but because no move was made until the early afternoon events did not work out as he had expected and during the morning considerable numbers of Turks were withdrawn.[5] They slipped away very quietly and every credit is due to them for the skillful way in which the withdrawal was carried out. At 7 p.m. a patrol sent out to ascertain whether they were still holding their fourth line got a hot reception, but at midnight another patrol found only dead and dying in the trenches. The Turks had

---

5. A column of at least four battalions moving away from Kut toward the Dahra Bend was spotted from the air during the afternoon.

gone, and so far as the men of the 7th Division were concerned that was all that mattered; the series of fruitless battles for this tiny stretch of barren land was over at last and they were glad.

The road to Kut and beyond was open and, at dawn on February 24, Maude issued his orders for the pursuit; there followed a series of blunders for an account of which it is necessary to go back to Shumran. Once across the river, the 14th Division had pressed on up the peninsula. That night the division was holding a line from bank to bank across the loop a thousand yards inland from the original bridgehead and soon after 6 a.m. next morning the infantry swept forward again. Their next objective was the one-storied huts of the Dahra Barracks and for three thousand yards the 36th and 37th Brigades advanced across the bare plain until they were checked by a Turkish rearguard dug in close by the barracks. In order to give the men pulling out of Sannaiyat time to get away along the road across the top of the Shumran loop Kiazim Karabekir had ordered a delaying action to be fought out here. The 26th Brigade, advancing on the right toward the northeast corner of the peninsula was stopped and the 37m Brigade, which was moving straight up the peninsula to cut the road, was counterattacked twice and also brought to a halt. But this was only a pause. As soon as Kiazim's rearguard had achieved its object and the tail of the retreating column from Kut had passed them, they too started to fall back along the Baghdad road. In the meantime, while this situation was developing, Crocker's Cavalry Division had been ordered "to cross bridge immediately and *take up vigorous pursuit along left bank in direction of Bughaila.*" From the Dahra Barracks, Bughaila was about twenty miles up the Baghdad road and so Maude's instructions were quite explicit: Crocker was to get after the retiring Turks as fast as he could and head them off. Failing to do this was the first blunder and the opportunity for the sort of cavalry action which could only have occurred about once in a hundred years was missed'.

The two cavalry brigades started to cross over to the Shumran peninsula at about 9 a.m.; Crocker's previous orders had told him to concentrate his force and wait at a rendezvous south of the bridge, so he can hardly be blamed for me late arrival at the bridge. But knowing that "vigorous action" was required once he had got over to the far side his subsequent actions are inexplicable. Instead of going off to the left, both brigades trotted off up the west bank of the peninsula and were soon mixed up in the 36th Brigade's infantry battle for the Dahra Barracks; only when the barracks had been captured two hours later were they able to get through. The 7th Cavalry Brigade, leading, continued on in a northerly direction for a couple of miles men wheeled off to the left; the 6th Brigade followed suit about a mile in the rear and, within a relatively short space of time, they were again embroiled in the rearguard infantry battle.

Columns of men and guns moving west across the top of the peninsula were a clear indication of the Turks' retreat and with all this movement going on across his front it hardly seems credible that Crocker should have made no attempt to make use of the one attribute his horses brought to the force—that of mobility. Admittedly it is always easy for any chronicler to pass judgment— yet from what is recorded it appears that Crocker made no determined attempt to push on around the Turkish flank either that day or the next—and after February 26, the opportunity had vanished. Just as soon as they had ridden clear of the infantry's line of fire the two brigades wheeled left, dismounted and stopped. It was an incredible performance that was bound to lead to a good deal of criticism of the Cavalry Division and indeed, even after close on half a century, it is still a sore issue with some people—not all of them cavalrymen. For this reason it is worthwhile digressing momentarily in order to try to make a fair appraisal. According to the war diaries of the two brigades, the cavalry *were* trying to outflank the Turks; in doing so they were heavily engaged—so much so that it was impossible to continue their outflanking movement. If these are the facts, this is a reasonable explanation. Those who accept it have pointed out that too much might have been expected of the cavalry in the pursuit, that the rifle and the machine gun—even in the hands of partially demoralized troops—were still powerful weapons. In 1902 a Colonel Henderson, wrote "It appears to be anticipated that the cavalry, if led with sufficient boldness, thundering forward in a close succession of steel-tipped lines, will have the supreme satisfaction of riding down a mob of panic-stricken fugitives whose bandoliers are empty, and who are so paralyzed by terror as to be incapable of using their rifles." Then he went on to explain that even beaten enemies are rarely reduced to such a prostrate condition that they completely lose faith in their weapons. Small bodies of infantry, he thought, armed with the magazine rifle of the day, could still hold up large bodies of mounted men. (After such an argument, one is tempted to wonder—apart from the social influence—why so many cavalry regiments had been retrained in the armies of Britain, India and all the great continental powers!)

In this instance, the fleeing Turks were by no means "a mob of panic-stricken fugitives," and this seems to confirm the application of Henderson's theory. Kiazim's rearguard, barring the road to Bughaila and Baghdad, was only about 2,500 men. Consequently the Turkish flank could not have extended far to the north; all Crocker had to do was to push on a couple more miles and he should have been in the clear. Furthermore the 6th Cavalry Brigade sustained only eight casualties—two killed and six wounded—throughout the whole day

(February 24)[6] and they were the first into action. Had they been handled boldly—as at Ramadi seven months later—the cavalry's action might have been decisive and large numbers of Turks cut off and rounded up. As it was, they got away. The cavalry themselves have laid the blame on their commanders: Maude, for keeping them so much on the move before the Shumran crossing that their horses were tired when they were really needed, and for his constant petulant demands to be kept in wireless touch with what they were doing and where they were (arising no doubt from his distrust of their performance); Crocker, for his lack of initiative. One vital quality was lacking in the cavalry at this time, and that was good leadership. That much hackneyed expression about leadership which is quoted so much to young officers today and which derives from the Chinese proverb "Under a good general there are no bad soldiers," was as true then as ever. No one could say that the cavalrymen in Mesopotamia lacked guts in 1917; when they got into action they invariably lived up to their traditions. Yet their outstanding failures up to the capture of Baghdad seem even more remarkable when compared with the extraordinary brilliance of their successes afterward. It was the same cavalry that was used, made up the same regiments, largely composed of the same men; the ground was not so different, the only thing that was changed was the leadership, so one can only assume that that is where the fault lay. Whatever the cause of it, this was the first blunder.

Before turning from the cavalry, their associates deserve a brief mention at tins stage. The "Lambs," as the Light Armored Motor Batteries were euphemistically called, were comparatively new to Mesopotamia and tins was the first opportunity they had had to prove their worth. During the rearguard action of February 24 and 25, 1917, the Turks probably suffered more from the action of the armored cars than from the whole of the cavalry division, and at a time when the cavalry should have been dismounted and dug in twenty miles behind the footsore Turkish infantry, the Lambs distinguished themselves and made an effective contribution to the battle.

So much for those who are usually associated with the dash and verve of battle. The most unfortunate effect of the cavalry's performance was the delay that was imposed when Caley's 13th Division eventually caught up with the Turkish rearguard at Sheikh Sa'ad, where the second blunder occurred. Finding the Turks dug in, the leading British brigade drove in their outposts but were checked when it came under heavy fire from the main Turkish position. Instead of pushing on around the enemy flank with his two remaining brigades

---

6. Casualties of the 7th Cavalry Brigade are not known. As they came into action later they were presumably less than those of the 6th Brigade.

and throwing the whole weight of his division on to Kiazim's rearguard, Caley now hesitated—because he was pinning his faith on the Cavalry Division's making an outflanking movement which would force the Turks to pull out. As may be adduced from the events so far, relying on the cavalry was not altogether a wise thing to do. Fortunately the Corps Commander was quick to appraise the situation and as soon as Marshall learned what had happened, Caley was ordered to attack with every available man. Unfortunately, unlike Joshua, Caley was unable to command the sun to stand still and by the time his troops were in a position to attack, it was dark. Nevertheless, the attack went in and could be counted a success in so far as it was the direct cause of the Turkish rearguard's abandoning their positions. But many of the Turks were able to slip away into the darkness and confusion when they might have been put in the bag. It was the last serious engagement between the two forces until the battle at the Diyala on March 7; several hundred Turkish prisoners were taken, losses on both sides were heavy but the Turks managed to get out the majority of their guns of the Sannaiyat force. Now came the final blunder, committed this time by the Royal Navy. Except for the fact that the sailors managed to turn it into a brilliant success its consequences might have been most serious; it was the action of the gunboats that finally converted the Turkish retreat into a rout.

For fifteen months the Navy had been waiting for their chance to resume what they considered to be their proper role. From the moment Townshend was locked up in Kut, the Tigris Fleet had been relegated to the role of a heavy battery in trench warfare; in this new phase they were to become cavalry and horse artillery combined, and they had been looking forward to the time when this opportunity should present itself. The day after the crossing at Shumran the three gunboats waiting at Sheikh Sa'ad were off, steaming up the river as fast as they could go. HMS *Mantis* stopped at Kut while the crew landed to hoist the Union Jack; after that all three boats were off again. All along their route the river banks hid the view and consequently from the decks of the ships it was only possible to get an occasional glimpse of the countryside, and then only a distant one. Believing that Marshall's columns were in hot pursuit the gunboats pushed on at full speed around the huge bends, getting only occasional glimpses of bodies of men moving in the direction of Baghdad, and these were mistaken for British troops. Suddenly just beyond Bughaila they ran slap into the Turkish rearguard and were received with heavy fire at point-blank range from almost every class of weapon from 5.9 inch howitzers down to rifles. At the Nahr-Al-Kalek Bend the river turns back in a complete hairpin bend and here the vessels came under fire from three sides as a Turkish battery and machine guns dug in at the apex of the peninsula raked the fleet as it passed. Casualties were heavy but, miraculously, none of the three vessels concerned—HMS *Tarantula, Mantis* and *Moth*—were sunk, although they were holed time and time again. "Retreat" is a word not found in the Royal Navy's dictionary; even if it had been, there could be no going back, and so with all guns blazing the three ships steamed on and in due course their gallantry was rewarded. Swinging around the next bend where they were clear of the deadly fire, they reached a point where the road swung in toward the river, and here their machine guns were able to play havoc with the Turkish transport slogging back to Baghdad. Shortly afterward the full benefit of running the gauntlet developed. What was left of the Turkish river fleet came into sight, running before them. Keeping up a brisk fire at the troops on the river bank with their machine guns, all three gunboats engaged the shipping with their heavier armament. The rearmost Turkish ship, one with a 4.7 inch British gun captured at Kut, was the first to sink; then the *Basra* was hit and ran herself ashore; then the *Pioneer* was set on fire and ran aground; finally the gunboats were able to concentrate on the *Firefly*, lost to Townshend at Umm-At-Tabul in the retreat from Ctesiphon. The *Firefly's* crew, chastened no doubt by what had happened to the other ships had soon had enough and as darkness fell they ran her nose ashore, landed, and escaped, leaving the *Firefly* intact and under full steam. This was the end of the action, during which the Turks' fighting fleet had been reduced to two Thorneycroft patrol boats carrying pom-poms—and they spent the summer in the shallows somewhere above Tikrit. In one day the Turks' river navy had been annihilated.

The Navy had done well. Apart from the ships, large numbers of prisoners had been taken, many of whom had come down to the river bank to surrender even while the ships were in hot pursuit. For many of them it was a choice between the mercy of the British or the vindictiveness of the Arabs. Seeing that the Turks were in a bad way the Buddhoos had turned on them in the same way as they had turned on Townshend's columns retreating from Ctesiphon, and some of Kiazim's soldiers presented themselves on the bank naked as they were born, to crave protection from their irregular allies. Together with those rounded up by the cavalry and the wounded who were collected, over 4,000 Turks were taken between the crossing of the Tigris on February 23, and the evening of the fight at Nahr-Al-Kalek on February 26. The bag, and its mode of collection in this last lap of the running fight, was almost a repetition of Townshend's advance from Qurna to Amara in June 1915. Most important was the fact that the crossing at Shumran and the capture of Sannaiyat meant an end to the long period of trench warfare with its detailed preparation and regular supply system; the future of the campaign was one of open warfare. But the change brought difficulties of supply and maintenance, and by the time

Marshall's troops reached Bughaila shortages were beginning to make themselves felt. Within three days of the crossing the chase had gone about as far as it could and when the cavalry rode into Aziziyeh on the 27th, and found that it was occupied, the first phase of the pursuit was over.

The Turks were in no real position to stay and fight; their retreat had become a rout and they were moving on a broad front in a disorganized rabble. But it was just not possible to follow them up. Maude himself was anxious enough to press the advantage but, unlike Nixon in his abortive attempt to reach Baghdad, he had a sound and sensible regard for logistics and was all too aware of the frailty of his supply line. Already the 7th Division had eaten its emergency rations; the animals had no food left at all, and it was only by the fortuitous arrival of a couple of motor launches and a camel convoy, carrying sufficient food for half rations to be issued, that the situation was saved. The difficulty was the time that it took to bring up supplies from Sheikh Sa'ad along the winding Tigris, since it took eight hours for the round trip from the base supply dump at Shumran. On February 28, the cavalry reconnoitered Aziziyeh again, and this time they found it unoccupied. But once more—this time because of the supply situation—they were obliged to fall back temporarily on Nahr-Al-Kalek. Finally, they returned next day; the gunboats moved up to join them, and that was as far as the pursuit could be carried for the time being. The infantry might have trudged on a bit further but there was little point in their doing so when they had no chance of catching up with the fleeing Turks. Until the extended line of communications could be reorganized a halt was inevitable.

Even so, much had been accomplished and because of its significance relative to future operations, the breakthrough at Kut might well be compared with that effected by Montgomery at Alamein. The Turks had been grimly hanging on to the positions barring an advance toward Baghdad, and me operation to eject them had succeeded beyond Maude's wildest hopes. Having captured over 7,000 of Khalil's men, it was evident that Khalil's force deployed across the road to Baghdad had virtually ceased to exist. In their flight they had thrown away, buried or abandoned guns, mortars, rifles, machine guns, and every other kind of military impedimenta in great profusion; four ships, barges, *mahelas,* launches, and an enormous quantity of bridging material had also fallen into British hands. Furthermore the strain to which the Turks had been subjected was evident in the appearance of the exhausted prisoners, and Maude was convinced that his own four divisions were completely capable of dealing not only with the wreck of the army in front of him, but also with the reinforcements which Khalil was reported to be rushing up to Baghdad. Maude's troops were in good heart, and as the news from the other fronts in

Mesopotamia was good, every prospect of the campaign pleased. At Nasiriyeh his men were expected to be able to start moving forward, and it appeared that the Persian situation had also been favorably affected by the recent success. If so, the Turks in front of Baratoff could be expected to withdraw and the Russians would also be able to drive on toward Baghdad. With a mind to the future Maude authorized the issue of a proclamation to the Arabs, pointing out what had already happened to the Turks, forecasting future British successes, telling them that the new conquerors came as friends who would be happy to trade with them—and warning them that stern reprisals would be exacted if there was any sign of aggression.

To those in Mesopotamia everything pointed to a resumption of the advance on Baghdad as soon as the supply line could be organized, and everybody from Maude down to his last private soldier was as optimistic as the Turks were pessimistic. There was one limiting factor, which was not directly attributable to conditions at the front but which precluded any immediate push; Whitehall, nervous of a repetition of the 1915 debacle had not yet given permission. Unless success could be assured, the War Cabinet was not prepared to give Maude carte blanche for a dash into the unknown. He had already exceeded his original directive, and the men in London did not want to face another loss of prestige. To Maude it might seem that Turkish resistance had crumbled, but they wanted the facts and time to consider them before he was given a free hand; the lesson of Nixon's optimism still smarted. However, on February 27, Maude had wired the Commander-in-Chief in India recommending that His Majesty's Government should be asked for instructions "for a further advance against a beaten enemy who could only reach Baghdad as a disorganized mob" and this wire had crossed with one from "Wully" Robertson to Delhi. In this, me Chief of the Imperial General Staff stressed that on no account should Maude allow himself to get into a situation which would necessitate his having to retire, and suggested that it might be safer to wait until the Russians were in a position to advance on Baghdad before any further move forward was made. Robertson had been led to understand that Baratoff expected to be able to move in four or five weeks time when the snows cleared, which would seem to be the opportune moment for a concerted drive on the capital. In the meantime, Maude might consider a cavalry raid on Baghdad—a suggestion which in the light of the cavalry's performance so far might be regarded as ludicrous.

Telegrams between London, Delhi and Mesopotamia now started to come and go thick and fast. Eventually, two days after Maude had wired to say that the Turks had evacuated Aziziyeh and that the road to Baghdad seemed to be open, he was at liberty to resume the advance. The final telegram from London explained that the War Cabinet had not understood that Maude's victory had been so complete and the future conduct of affairs was left to him; there was only one word of caution: he was not to overdo things and it was imperative that he should get in touch with the Russians.

One issue which at the time was possibly not clear to those who were advocating the advance is now worth considering. No matter how desirable it might be, from a prestige point of view, to capture Baghdad it must have been obvious that the pursuit could not stop there. To hold the capital meant blocking three approaches about sixty miles distant from it. This must inevitably mean that a considerable number of troops would be needed and a very great extension of the line of communications. Whether or not this was the most profitable way of employing Britain's resources is arguable, for it must be remembered that Mesopotamia was still regarded as a "secondary" theater of war. If it was supposed that the Turks would concentrate a force against Maude at least as big as his own, so drawing men off from other fronts the position was worth while. For the next eighteen months however, with a force of about fifty thousand men all told, the Turks in Mesopotamia were to hold down a British force with a ration strength nearly ten times as great—with all the consequent drain on British shipping resources; from the Turkish point of view this must have been very well worth while.

On March 4, Maude sent his appreciation of the situation to Robertson. In his opinion, he said, it was vital to move on Baghdad at once; the old Turkish Army had ceased to exist, a new one would take a long time to form, and he expected to get to the city with very little opposition. On the other hand, if no attempt were made to take Baghdad he considered that the effect on the Arabs would be adverse, and his existing line of communications would be in trouble. He added that he had little faith in any help being form coming from the Russians, but as his own force was equivalent to seven or eight Turkish divisions he had no fear that he would not be able to hold Baghdad once he got there. As soon as the supply situation was favorable—which he expected would be in a day or two—he intended to resume the advance. The reply from Robertson gave him his head; so far as Whitehall was concerned, Maude should act "as an Army Commander with a beaten and demoralized army in front of him."

Chapter 17

On to Baghdad

Khalil—now promoted to Pasha status—had been considerably shaken by the news that the British were across the Tigris. In a frenzy of despair, three days later, he was confiding to Kiazim Karabekir that there was little point in trying to defend Baghdad; it was indefensible anyway, lying as it did in a treeless plain with only the river as a defensive line. The one course open to him, he said, was to withdraw right back to Samarra, ninety miles beyond the capital. There, Kiazim's battered columns could regroup behind Ali Ihsan's 13th Corps. Twenty-four hours later however, Khalil had changed his mind and Kiazim was peremptorily ordered to stop the retreat, turn about, and fight it out with Maude at Aziziyeh. But it was too late; Don Quixote would have had a better chance tilting at windmills than Kiazim had of making a stand at this stage. The order was quietly ignored and the retreat continued to Lajj and Ctesiphon, where the lull caused by Maude's own stay at Aziziyeh afforded Kiazim's men a much needed respite until the Turkish Army Commander had made up his mind what to do next. As Khalil still had no plan, and the decision to defend the capital was taken only during the period when Maude was persuading Whitehall that the advance should go on, several valuable days were lost. And these were the only days when an effective defensive system could have been coordinated. With ten thousand[1] men, Khalil ought to have been able to hold off the British troops, but to do so would have meant making use of every natural and man-made obstacle which was at hand. It would have been possible, but time was the vital factor and for Khalil the sands were fast running out. From the south and southeast, the way to Baghdad was already barred by the Diyala River and the Mahsudiya Canal;[2] by breaking down the dikes of the Tigris north of the city and opening up the multitude of irrigation channels with which the countryside was intersected, the whole region between Baghdad and the Diyala could have been flooded and a huge area on the east and southeast side of the town turned into an impassable lake. At the same time, by sinking boats and otherwise damming the Diyala about twenty miles upstream, much of the country east of the Diyala could also have been flooded—so precluding any British out-flanking movement to the east or northeast. By scientific employment of the waters, all this was possible and the City of the Caliphs would have become. a citadel largely surrounded by a huge moat. Then Khalil would have needed to deploy his troops only on a very narrow front. But no such plan was adopted and so, as the dull flat countryside was broken only by the irrigation channels—which in themselves were not formidable obstacles—he was faced with the defence of an area which required a very large force to ensure its protection. Had Khalil made up his mind early enough there would have been just enough time to loose the waters over the countryside. As it was, he dithered for a week and when he finally decided to try and hold Baghdad it was too late.

This is not to say that no preparations whatsoever were made. While Khalil's ideas were frantically swinging between the extremes of offering battle as far forward of the city as possible—which, by this time meant Ctesiphon— and no battle at all this side of Samarra, some defensive works were being got ready. Even these suffered as a result of indecision and all too frequent changes of plan. Kiazim's men, tired though they were, set to digging new trenches around Ctesiphon; the newly arrived 14th Division started to prepare positions behind the Diyala and, on the right bank of the Tigris, some of the Baghdad populace were marched out to the sand hills at Umm-At-Tabul and put to work with pick and shovel on a short defensive line there. Before this last line could be completed however, Khalil had decided to hold a much longer line on the right bank, a line which ran from the confluence of the Tigris and the

---

1. According to Turkish estimates there were 9,200 infantry, 500 cavalry and 48 guns available for the defence. This included the Baghdad garrison troops.
2. Also referred to as the Khar Canal.

Diyala across to Tel Aswad. At this, the locals were marched forward from Umm-At-Tabul to be set to work on the new line, and Kiazim Karabekir was told that he would have the privilege of holding it. To Kiazim, this was as impossible a task as halting at Aziziyeh had been an impossible order for the 52nd Division—which was all he would have to man the trenches with—was down to less than 2,300 men. His vigorous protests eventually convinced Khalil that it was impossible and Khalil now turned back to the uncompleted Umm-At-Tabul position. The Tel Aswad position was abandoned, the men with the picks and shovels were solemnly marched back to their old digs and told to carry on where they had left off. But the dithering had gone on too long, for by now Maude's men were in contact with the 14th Division on the line of the Diyala.

So much for the Turkish scene; before going on to describe the sequence of events which terminated in the capture of Baghdad it is as well to consider the situation in regard to the Russians—with whom Maude was supposed to coordinate his operations. In theory, the whole of the Russian operations were being directed by the Grand Duke Michael, although so far his direction had not had much success. At this particular moment the Grand Duke's main army, the 7th Caucasus Corps under General Chernozubov, was snowed in two hundred miles northeast of Samarra. This was the army that the Turks had driven back from Mosul and pursued halfway to the Caspian Sea, and until the snows melted—which would not be for some time, it could hardly be expected to make any impression on the battle for Baghdad. The Grand Duke's other army comprised about twenty thousand men under Baratoff, and its activities have already been referred to in an earlier chapter. This was the force which faced Ali Ihsan's 13th Corps, and with which Khalil had hoped to sweep around through Persia to cut in behind Maude. Baratoff had steadily given ground in front of Ali Ihsan but, as soon as Ali started to pull back, Baratoff followed him up and "Wully" Robertson had relayed to Maude the information that the Grand Duke had ordered Baratoff to push on to Khanaqin with all speed; hence his concern about Anglo-Russian cooperation in the drive on Baghdad. It will thus be appreciated that Baghdad's prime importance stemmed from the fact that it was a common center from which the line of advance of three distinct Turkish expeditions radiated and pressure by both the British and Russians along all three lines seemed to be important. Because of the weather, Chernozubov in the north could do little, although he was tying down a large Turkish army, some of which might have been detached to reinforce Khalil. With the Russians in Persia it was a different matter, and any threat to Baghdad must necessarily affect the whole situation there. Ali Ihsan's recall was already having its influence on the Turkish strategical plan and this was the point that Whitehall had in mind in the plea for the coordination of Maude's plans with those of Baratoff. *If*—and it was a big if—the Russian and British blows were correctly timed, if a Russian column could cut the Mosul-Baghdad railway while another followed up Ali Ihsan's rearguard, the whole of the Turkish army retreating before Maude must inevitably be surrounded and captured. That was the most that could be hoped for; in practice it was anticipated that Maude, when he linked up with Baratoff, would be able to cut off the Turkish 2nd Division which was acting as Ali Ihsan's rearguard.

At this point, attention is drawn to the date. The Russian Revolution started on March 10, 1917 and already there were rumblings. For some weeks Whitehall had been aware of the scandals connected with the Russian Government and the Imperial Army, but there was no suspicion of the extent to which the troubles would spread, and certainly nobody had any conception of their momentous consequences. On the contrary; that Whitehall had every confidence in Russian cooperation is evident from the constant references in Robertson's telegrams to Maude, urging him to base his plans on cooperation. Any anxiety that was felt about the Russians stemmed from wholly different reasons. Those in Delhi and Simla were all in favor of cooperation but they did not want to see the Russians get to Baghdad before the British. Then, as now, Russian motives were suspect. Maude himself does not appear to have been overenthusiastic about the cooperation of which he was being constantly reminded. Probably his coolness originated from intelligence reports of the behavior of Baratoff's men in Persia; they were not doing much fighting but they were certainly doing plenty of eating—at the Persians' expense. In *the* long run Maude's lack of faith in his allies proved to be justified; Russian pressure diminished as the Bolshevik germ spread and it was not long before any hope of help from that quarter had evaporated in the eventual debacle. What is more, if he had lived only a few months longer he would have been concerned in pulling a few irons out of the fire on their behalf.

This, then, was the general background on the resumption of the British advance on Baghdad on March 8. The lull in the fighting had not stopped the activities of the Royal Flying Corps and, during the first week of the month, Baghdad Airport and troop trains on the Baghdad-Samarra stretch of line had been bombed; a couple of aircraft had even attempted to emulate T. E. Lawrence's train wrecking exploits. Two Sapper officers were landed within a few hundred yards of a railway culvert between Baghdad and Samarra. Leaping out of the airplanes they ran toward the culvert carrying explosive charges with which to blow it up, but as they ran mounted Arabs were seen galloping down on them from a village less than a mile distant. Halfway to their objective they saw that not only would they be cut off but also that the explosives they were carrying were quite inadequate for the demolition of the culvert. Back they doubled to the airplanes, whose propellers were still turning and as they climbed aboard the two pilots opened their throttles wide, taking off straight toward the approaching Arabs. As the undercarriages of the two machines skimmed over them, the Buddhoos scattered and both machines escaped. An all-out air effort had been planned for the day of the advance but a violent dust storm prevented any serious flying and two of the Martinsydes which did attempt reconnaissances crashed in the swirling fog of yellow dust.

Despite the conditions—and a hot day, as well as the blinding sandstorm which grounded the airmen, made life almost insupportable—the advance started as planned, and Marshall's infantry made an eighteen mile forced march from Zeur which brought them to within striking distance of the southwest corner of what the British troops called "the old Turkey cock's city of Haroun-al-Rothschild." In the dust fog the cavalry vanguard were the first to run into trouble and a sharp brisk action. Spotting what they took to be a Turkish convoy, the 13th Hussars drew their sabers, shook out into extended order and galloped down on the Turks in true cavalry style. Too late they realized that they were charging into an entrenched position, and as machine guns and rifles cut down men and horses, the commanding officer coolly edged his squadrons to the flank in the hope of finding a way around. But the Turkish line extended too far and eventually the decimated regiment was compelled to retire. They had sustained heavy losses but the Hussars extricated themselves with credit and their action was a very gallant affair. It showed that the cavalry certainly did not lack guts, whatever else may have been missing, and it did much for their prestige in the eyes of those whose confidence in the mounted arm had been shaken by their disappointing performance so far.

Early on the morning of March 9, Maude's infantry vanguard reached Bustan, seventeen miles beyond Zeur. The road they had followed was littered with the tell-tale debris of a broken army in flight. Guns and equipment had been dumped and, from the evidence of the skins and hooves which were all that remained, Kiazim's men had had little to eat except sheep—and even these had been devoured raw. Soon the great Arch of Ctesiphon came into sight and next morning found the British troops bivouacked on the scorching plain before it; on the river the naval gunboats were moored close by the Throne-room of the Chosroes. And now, as the troops moved up on the last leg of the long road to Baghdad, Buddhoos lined the route, bowing, gesticulating and waving white rags. These were the same people who had paraded for the Turks ten months before and had made another great show of jubilation when the ill-fated garrison of Kut had passed them by in different circumstances.

As expected, the first check to Maude's advance came at the Diyala River which, a hundred and twenty yards wide, in flood and unfordable, presented a formidable obstacle. Men of O'Dowda's 38th Brigade were spearheading the vanguard and when they tried to move up to the near bank it was to be greeted with a hail of lead. The fire of the divisional artillery and that of the gunboats on the river was called for but, even when shells crashed down on what could be seen of the Turkish positions on the far bank, it was still not possible to get down to the water's edge. O'Dowda decided to wait until darkness fell before trying to force a passage. There was a full moon that night and the visibility, together with the width of the river and a two knot current all made the prospects of a crossing somewhat doubtful and so his sappers advised him against it. But in spite of their technical appraisal O'Dowda was still set on making the attempt. If he expected the Turks to retire as soon as they realized an assault crossing was imminent his hopes were soon to be dashed, and as soon as the first pontoon was lowered into the water the whole of the launching party from the 6th King's Own was cut down. The moonlight on the water was more than sufficient for a man to take aim, the range was short, and the Turks had concentrated machine guns and rifles at first-class vantage points in houses on their side of the river. Three pontoons were launched but none got even halfway across; nothing could live in the hail of lead spewed out by the Turks across the river, and such covering fire as there was utterly failed to keep it down. Two of the pontoons[3] drifted helplessly down past the junction into the Tigris, with their freight of dead and wounded, and next morning they were still drifting past the camps at Ctesiphon, a grim warning to the waiting troops that the Turks still had plenty of fight in them.

O'Dowda had intended two simultaneous crossings of the Diyala on that first night, one by the King's Own near the junction of the tributary with the Tigris and the other by the East Lancashires further upstream. The East Lancashires crossing was delayed because of the struggle they had to carry their boats nearly a mile over rough broken country, and after the failure of the King's Own their attempt was prudently abandoned. The King's Own lost fifty killed in this almost forgotten little action. Since there had been no proper reconnaissance for it, next to no organization, no feints, no alternative crossing places and very little covering-fire, this can be considered a shining example of how a river crossing should not be carried out; only the need to press on quickly can provide any justification for it. It was the Turks who came out best in this sorry little affair and they had administered a sharp lesson. Fortunately

---

3. There was one unwounded man in the third pontoon, *Private Jack White,* a signaller. Swimming ashore with his cable he hauled the boat to safety and so saved the lives of several of the wounded occupants. For this act White was awarded the Victoria Cross; he was one of the few Jewish V.C.s of the war.

the lesson was not lost on either Marshall or Maude and next day the Cavalry Division was sent off up the Diyala to try and locate the Turkish flank where the next attempt to cross might have more success. Once again the cavalry failed in their mission because the flank was never located. After the battle it was learned that the Diyala was held in strength for only ten miles from the junction; for a further fifteen miles north its protection was the responsibility of a Turkish cavalry force, two hundred and fifty sabers strong. Yet, when the British cavalry trotted back to base, they reported finding the river occupied all the way along the fourteen mile stretch they had tentatively explored and the outcome of this information was a decision to continue with attempts to force a passage in the defended area.

In the meantime, while the cavalry were cantering about the bank to their north, the infantry of Christian's 36th Brigade had moved up the river to a position about six miles above the junction where it was hoped that a crossing might be effected that night. Patrols sent down to the bank soon found that the Turks were watching the prospective crossing place, and Christian was told not to commit himself unless he could take advantage of any success further down the river. (O'Dowda, whose brigade was still deployed near the confluence, was planning another assault for that night.) Concurrently with this activity the Sappers were busy building a bridge over the Tigris at Bawi, four miles above Ctesiphon, which would permit Maude to pass troops and heavy equipment—especially guns—over to the right bank. Thompson's 35m Brigade was already across, having been ferried over on the night of March 8, and this brigade was steadily working its way up the Tigris toward the Turkish positions north of Tel Aswad. Having already passed the Diyala junction on this opposite side, Thompson was now in a position to give a certain amount of support to any fresh attempt by O'Dowda to get across the Diyala. Theoretically, from his side of the river, machine guns could enfilade the Turkish position opposite O'Dowda although in practice it turned out that such fire must necessarily be considered more in the nature of a prophylactic rather than deliberate support.

From the information which he had received from his airmen, Maude knew that the Turks' defenses on the right bank were nowhere near as strong as those on the Diyala. Being firmly of the opinion that Khalil was only fighting a delaying action, and that Baghdad would be left to its fate as soon as the situation had reached a point where the British were threatening to cut his escape route, Maude concluded that his best plan would be to exploit the weakness of the defence system on the right bank of the Tigris. His idea was to transfer the Cavalry and 7th Division over to the right bank where Thompson's brigade already provided a firm base over the new bridge. In order to keep the Turks occupied on the left bank while this was going on, O'Dowda's and Christian's assault crossing operations on the Diyala were to continue. The real blow would then come in as a hook to the Turkish right, directed toward the railway station.

If Maude had hoped for an element of deception or surprise in his plan he had failed to make allowance for the extraordinary efficiency of the German airmen under Khalil's control. Several new aircraft with a complement of German pilots to fly them and mechanics to service them were based on the Baghdad airfield and these kept the Turkish commander well informed of all Maude's troop movements. Consequently when Khalil was told that the Cavalry Division, and possibly two other infantry divisions, appeared to be getting ready to cross over to the right bank of the Tigris, he promptly started to adjust the dispositions of his troops to cope with a threat to this flank. The key move was for Kaizim Karabekir's 51st Division to cross the river, leaving the defence of the Diyala to the 14th Division. As will be seen shortly, this move was upset by O'Dowda's attack that night.

Soon after midnight on March 9, the Loyal North Lancashires launched their pontoons just above where the King's Own had come to grief the night before. Under a heavy bombardment the ferries worked well for a short time; there were quite a few casualties but within an hour a company of the Loyals—about 100 men all told—had started to form a bridgehead on the far bank. Then the trouble started. The Turks, realizing the dangers attendant on the British getting a footing over the Diyala threw everything they had into the fight. As the pontoons were sunk, the ferrying ceased and the little company of Lancashiremen on the far side were left holding a small semi-circular bend in the river bank not more than fifty yards across and twenty-five yards deep. No less than five attacks were thrown in against their position but the Loyals hung on grimly and the Turkish regiment concerned—one of those of the 51st Division which was supposed to be moving across to the left bank of the Tigris—was virtually wiped out by small arms fire. Arrangements for covering fire were still inadequate, so the Loyals were more or less dependent on their own resources, and it was not long before it could be seen that their difficulty was going to be a lack of ammunition. Attempts to get some across from the other side of the Diyala proved fruitless. Everything was tried, men swimming across with a cable by which boxes of ammunition could be hauled across—even firing the cable across by rocket—but the swimmers were killed in the water and the rockets failed to carry the line over. By the following night, when eventually they were relieved, the forty men that remained of the original company in the bridgehead had been reduced to their last clip of ammunition. Further upstream the men of Christian's brigade had also tried to cross the

Diyala, and they too had failed. Unlike the Loyals they had been unable to get anyone established on the far bank and seeing that it was hopeless to go on, Christian called off the operation.

On the other side of the river, the Cavalry Division had started out toward where it was thought the Turkish flank lay some hours before the Diyala attacks went in. The multitude of irrigation channels which crisscrossed their route made the going slow but at daybreak on the morning of March 10, after a short advance on foot, they ran up against the right of the Tel Aswad trenches and were pinned to the ground. The 28th Brigade, plodding on behind, eventually came up and took over, enabling the cavalry to extricate themselves, pull back out of range of the Turks' rifles and regroup for another attempt to get around behind. Realizing what was going on, the Turks' reaction was to draw their line back toward the old Umm-At-Tabul position. Thwarted, baffled and thirsty the cavalry took themselves off back to the river to water their horses. The infantry was still in action but no further progress was made before dark, and this was a state of affairs with which Maude was anything but pleased. Apparently nobody had sent back much information and he was not clear what exactly was happening; all he did know was that the 7th and Cavalry divisions had incurred more than 600 casualties between them, and that Khalil seemed to have stabilized a front line. He had no way of knowing that the Turks were in a bad way. But they were. The maneuvers on the right bank of the Tigris—especially those of the cavalry—had alarmed Khalil, and despite the fact that the battles on the banks of the Diyala were still raging he had insisted that Kiazim should shift the whole of the 51st Division across to the right bank of the river which he felt was the weak link in his defensive chain. Consequently only one regiment was left to guard the Diyala and most of it was concentrated around the Loyals tiny bridgehead. As this particular regiment had lost over a thousand men and practically all its officers in the space of two days, the morale of the remainder was very low; most of its men had had their bellyful of fighting—for the time being, at any rate.

That night, when the river-crossers renewed their assault the Turks gave way. The depleted bridgehead of Loyals, almost at the proverbial stage of "last man and last round" was relieved and the bridgehead rapidly expanded. Further upstream the Wiltshires effected a second crossing against very little opposition and only the third attempt came to grief and, happily, the set back was not serious. Two armored motor barges of a pattern designed for the Gallipoli landing and generally known as "Beetles," had been brought up from Basra in the belief that they might serve a purpose sooner or later. They were offered to Lewin who saw in them the opportunity for the sort of piratical expedition more usually undertaken by Marines, and he accepted with alacrity.

His plan was for the Beetles, carrying five hundred men of the Cheshires from his own brigade, to motor up the Tigris past the Diyala junction. Half a mile above the confluence of the rivers the Beedes were to turn in to the left bank and the Cheshires would disembark. Once ashore they would rush any trenches to their front, work around behind the Turks facing O'Dowda and finally link up with the Loyals' bridgehead. Lewin, never a man to miss a fight if he could help it, was so keen on the idea that he proposed to go along with the expedition himself. In any other circumstances the result might have been laughable; the Beetles only got about five hundred yards before they became stuck in the mud and while Lewin fumed, one of the gunboats had a trying time towing them off. The Beetles had been anything but a success. Whether the Cheshires could have contributed much to the battle even if their aquatic adventure had not ended in disappointment is doubtful. By 9:30 a.m. on the morning of March 10, the whole of O'Dowda's brigade was across the Diyala, a bridge[4] had been completed by 11:00 a.m. and the infantry were assaulting the trenches at Tel Mohammed, the last defended position before Baghdad.

On the other side of the Tigris the Turks had fallen back toward the Mahsudiya Canal, with the 7th Division treading on their heels, and one of the Cavalry Brigades was moving around their left to close the ring around Baghdad. Except for some intermittent shelling and a certain amount of rifle fire there was very little fighting, and even this tapered off when a dust storm, which blew up about 9 a.m., cloaked the battlefield and reduced visibility to about fifty yards. The gunners could not see to shoot and Maude decided that it would be best to stand fast and resume the attack that night. Since many of his men had no water left in their water bottles and nobody had had anything to eat during the past twenty-four hours his men badly needed a break. Furthermore, as a result of the sand storm, all communications were, to use an apt phrase, "in the air" and not only he, but very few of the units knew exactly where they were, let alone where anyone else was.

For Khalil, Kiazim Karabekir, and their respective staffs, watching the progress of events from a vantage point at the Iron Bridge across the Mahsudiya Canal, the situation must have seemed even worse. As the thick yellow fog descended, they could see a British column moving at a snail's pace across their front toward the northeast. This was the British Cavalry Division, but it was moving so slowly that nobody present could make up their minds as to whether what they could see was a cavalry or an infantry division. If it were

---

4. The permanent structure which now spans the Diyala near the original crossing place was given the name "Lancashire" Bridge. A memorial close by reads: "To the Glorious Memory of the Heroic Dead who are buried near this spot and who gave their lives to carry out a brilliant feat of arms which resulted in the crossing of the Diyala River on March 10, 1917, in the face of a strongly entrenched enemy. *Pro Patria.*"

the latter, the situation was serious indeed, but even if it were the cavalry it was quite obvious that the railway which served as their main avenue of retreat would be cut if it were allowed to get much further north. One of Khalil's German staff officers suggested that the 51st Division should attack it without further ado and, until Kiazim was able to convince him that it would be a hopeless venture, Khalil was all for it. With the 51st Division tired, dispirited and well below strength, Kiazim expressed the opinion that Khalil was merely snatching at a straw—as indeed he was. Khalil, despite his earlier vacillations, and the subconscious realization that the battle for Baghdad was already lost, was concerned at the disgrace which would reflect directly on him if he gave up the city without a struggle. By fighting, he could save sizeable shreds of his reputation, even if it did mean incurring a few thousand casualties. But his staff were opposed to any heroics, and probably little concerned about Khalil's reputation. They all knew that the Turkish force was not strong enough to hold off the encircling movement to which Maude's troops had evidently been committed, and that if the decision to retreat was left much longer the safety of what remained of Khalil's army would be jeopardized. Apart from this, ammunition at the front was reportedly running low and its resupply was giving cause for alarm. All these facts were heatedly reiterated to Khalil and he was advised to break off the battle and withdraw forthwith.

Faced with these inexorable facts, Khalil retired to deliberate with his Chief of Staff and in less than ten minutes he announced his decision; he agreed to withdraw that night. That he had been reluctant to take the decision is understandable enough. Apart from his own loss of face, Baghdad which had been occupied by the Turks for centuries had many historical, religious and sentimental associations for them. Furthermore, without Baghdad they would find it very difficult to retain any hold on what was left of their Mesopotamian empire. But the decision was inevitable; Khalil had to order a retreat or face the alternative of the complete annihilation of his battered army.

At 8 p.m. that night orders were issued for a general withdrawal to a line about nineteen miles north of Baghdad, and from that moment on, until the last train left Baghdad station early on the morning of March 11, the city was a scene of organized pandemonium. For nearly three weeks—ever since the Shumran crossing which had sealed the fate of Baghdad, in fact—the Ottoman authorities had been requisitioning stocks of merchandise and sending them off by rail to Samarra. By now the bazaars were nearly empty and a great deal of the military stores had also been evacuated. But large quantities—including seven new airplanes still in their crates—still remained. These had to be burned or disposed of in some other way and for the next few hours, as the Turkish infantry pulled out of their positions and tramped back through the city, base troops were engaged on the frantic implementation of a scorched earth policy. As the Turkish guns fired salvoes to get rid of their remaining shells, a deep red glare from the fires of organized destruction lit the horizon—to Maude's men a sure sign of the Turks' impending departure. In the city itself, where an endless procession of weary Turkish troops was wending its way through the streets toward the Northern Gate, orders had been given that any man who fell out en route would be shot. But the comforts of a British prison camp and comparative idleness clearly appealed to many of them, for a large number did creep away to hide until Maude's men marched in, despite this threat of the final penalty if they were caught.

In 1917, the population of Baghdad was about a hundred and forty thousand people of mixed races, and religions, most of whom were crowded and packed into the small, airless jerry-built slums, which had seen little change since the days of the Caliphs. That night it is doubtful if any of them had much sleep and the Muezzin had little need to call the Faithful to prayer next morning since a large proportion of the Faithful had already filled the mosques to overflowing the night before. Not all of them, however, for as the Turks moved out the riff-raff of the town moved in, and by the time the British troops arrived these gentry had gutted many of the shops and removed almost everything that could be moved—even to the seats and benches in the public gardens.

Shortly before midnight, when patrols found that the Turkish trenches on their front were empty, the 35th Brigade set off up the right bank of the river. Only a few riflemen had been left behind to cover Khalil's retirement and by 6 a.m. on the morning of March 11, a patrol of the Black Watch was searching the railway station for trophies appropriate to the occasion.[5] The British had arrived at long last and if the railway station is considered to be Baghdad proper, then the Black Watch had the honor of being first into the capital. The men themselves were not particularly conscious of any solemnity in the occasion, they were too tired for that. Even so, they were elated by the inscription "BAGHDAD" in large letters on the wall of the terminus, for it marked the end of a long, long trail. For some days, the empty station was a place to see, almost a place of pilgrimage and "BAGHDAD" was not the only writing on its walls. In great red paint daubs the Turks had left numerous ironic messages and texts for their successors—some grossly humorous, some strangely pathetic. Those like "100 Tommies = 1 Askeri," and "It is a long way to Baghdad" seem singularly inappropriate for the occasion; more sensitive

---

5. Officers of the Black Watch will always regret that they failed to appropriate the station bell as a historic piece of loot; the Regiment made up for it with the station bell at Samarra.

imaginations would merely have arranged for the station nameboard to be obliterated.

On the left bank, while men of the 38th and 39th Brigades had been clearing the Turks from the palm groves round Tel Mohammed at the point of the bayonet, the 40th Brigade had been making a wide turning sweep to bring them right around the flank of this last of the Turkish redoubts. With the rearguard falling back all the time, they made rapid progress. Soon after dawn the road was clear and two squadrons of British Cavalry were trotting toward the city. Outside the Southern Gate they were met by a black robed deputation of Arab and Jewish notables, bringing a petition from the merchants of Baghdad and a plea from the American Consul for British troops to take over control of the city without delay. With the Turks gone Arabs and Kurds were now tearing the place to pieces and the well-to-do feared for their property and hidden stocks. Scarcely an hour passed before three battalions of the 35th Brigade (the Buffs, 37th Dogras, 102nd Grenadiers) were crossing the Tigris in commandeered *gufahs;* half an hour later the Union Jack had been hoisted in the Citadel and soon after that British and Indian soldiers were patrolling the bazaars, dispersing the crowds of looters and firing over the heads of any of the rabble who showed resistance. Apart from the removal or destruction of the military stores, by fair means or foul, the Turks had appropriated as much other material as they had been able to lay their hands on. This had all been got away; nevertheless the merchants had taken good care to secrete quite large quantities of consumer goods and valuables and it was on the basis of these stocks that the Bazaars were doing a roaring trade within three days of the city's being taken over. The merchants complained bitterly of their losses, of course, saying that the eight hours which elapsed between the departure of the Turks and the advent of the British cost them something like a quarter of a million pounds sterling at today's rate of exchange! Trading under Turkish rule, it had been difficult enough to make a profit and the Turks had a nasty habit of commandeering stocks or buying them with paper money. For this very reason the merchants had taken the precaution of hiding sizable quantities of their merchandise. When the news of the crossing at Shumran reached the city it was obvious that as far as business was concerned there were a few rainy days ahead and they wanted to be ready for them. But hiding things from the Turks was one thing, stopping the Arabs getting hold of what was hidden was another. When they were set on getting their hands on some loot the Arabs were prone to employ even nastier methods than the Turks.

Because of all this the men smiled, the women clapped and the children danced as Maude's men marched in. They saw nothing extraordinary in the scene; invading armies had marched into Baghdad a dozen times before; here was a guard for their persons and property. To the British troops, knowing nothing of the background, it was a bewildering reception. Persians, dressed like Joseph in long silken coats of many colors; red-fezzed Oriental Jews in misfit European clothing; handsome Armenian refugees who had spent the night huddled in the Christian churches, fearful of their fate if any of the fleeing Turks learned of their existence; lordly turbanned Muslims in black flowing robes—all turned out to cheer them as they tramped in through the Southern Gate. It was a gala display, a fiesta—something which had *not* taken place when Townshend's men had tottered painfully through the same streets. Dirty, unwashed, unshaven and unfed, the men of the 35th Brigade thought it was fantastic. The Turks had only just gone and yet here were the inhabitants of one of the major cities in their Empire greeting their enemies like long lost brothers. What they did not understand was that although the Turks had been the rulers in Baghdad, to the bulk of the Arab and Jewish population they were almost as alien as the British. However, if they failed to understand the politics of the situation, there was one thing they certainly did understand. Here were women—attractive women, even some blondes among them—unveiled, smiling and apparently friendly. To men who, for over a year, had seen nothing in the shape of a woman, other than black bundles filling their pitchers on the Tigris bank, Baghdad seemed to have distinct possibilities for the World War I equivalent of today's American "R. and R." Men's shoulders straightened, packs grew lighter, weariness was forgotten and the dust of Baghdad became a lenitive for sore feet. It had been a long hard march but here they were at last, about to sample some of the delights of "The Thousand and One Nights." Regrettably, most of them were to be disappointed and lusty anticipations were confined to dreaming.

That day, not surprisingly, things were seen through a rose-tinted mist. Subsequently, Baghdad's alleys and minarets, at close quarters, turned out to be just the same as those of any other Eastern city. In the first few days of the occupation not even calls to all Al Rashid's djinns could raise a glass of beer and as for the women, they proved to be just as inaccessible as anywhere else in the world. However, very few of the troops were to rediscover the facts of life at this time since only a very small proportion of the Tigris Army was allowed into the city, and many of the men who passed by without entering it in March 1917 never saw the place at all, or if they did, it was but a brief glance from an ambulance taking them back "down the line." Maude had given strict orders; there was still work to be done and there could be no rest yet. The Turks were not yet beaten; Khalil was regrouping his shattered columns and there were nearly a hundred miles to go before there could be any relaxation.

On March 11, only the King's Own and three battalions of the 35th

Brigade saw the inside of the city on the left bank. Of the rest; the three brigades[6] of the 13th Division, who had fought their way across the Diyala, were ordered to march around and not through the city; the 14th Division halted just north of the new Diyala bridge; the 3rd Division waited at Bawi. After a year in the trenches it was a sad disappointment for British and Indians alike. The peacock blue and old gold of the minarets was plainly visible—yet they were not allowed to approach them; for them, it seemed, there were to be no bright lights, no relaxation—all they could look forward to was more hard marching and more fighting. But that was the way of the war; in the manner of the British soldier there was plenty of grumbling but the order was obeyed.

Considering that he followed in a cycle of conquerors which included Nebuchadnezzar, Alexander, Cyrus, Julian, the Chosroes and Haroun-Al-Rashid, Maude's own arrival at Baghdad was remarkably unassuming. On the evening of March 11, his ship drew up and anchored opposite the British Residency which was to become his GHQ. Most other British property had been reduced to heaps of dust and rubble but the fact that the old Residency was serving as a Turkish hospital when he arrived and filled to capacity with wounded Turks, is probably the only reason the building had not been destroyed. The wounded Turks had been left without anybody to look after them—no doctors, no orderlies—and in twenty-four hours conditions had degenerated to a near-Crimea state. That the medical service of any nation could blandly desert its own wounded in this fashion was beyond British comprehension. Yet this was another illustration of the curious Jekyll and Hyde complexity of the Turkish character. The Turks would be quite prepared to abandon his wounded, inflict untold horrors on the unfortunate wretches who became his prisoners, and to accept corruption and extortion as an official's prerogative. Yet on other occasions he could show great kindness equally well, and behave in the fashion which is simply described in the Western world as that of a gentleman. In the case of the Armenians, he was prepared to organize a wholesale massacre and then adopt those children who had managed to survive—rather as one takes in a stray puppy or kitten. Once in his home the youngsters would be given all the privileges of his own family, treated kindly and well cared for. Allah approves of a child being brought up as a true Muslim; the Turk was aware of that, nevertheless this curious quirk in his make-up cannot all be explained away as religious fervor. Then, when it came to fighting, while the Turk went into battle in a spirit of "may the best man win"—he never stooped to take unfair advantage and always observed the

---

6. The 6th King's Own from O'Dowda's 38th Brigade was the only battalion in these three brigades to take part in the triumphal entry. The 40th Brigade, which had enveloped the Tel Mohammed position, was halted in the palm groves outside the city.

customary international courtesies and decencies in regard to dead and wounded. On the field of battle, which is a pretty bestial scene anyway, this is something that is easily understood and because the Turks accepted the conventionalities of what was once called civilized warfare, the British soldiers had a sneaking affection for him. And if this should seem strange it must be remembered that the news of the brutish neglect of the Kut prisoners had been largely suppressed. Even when accounts of Turkish inhumanities did start to appear in the newspapers they were regarded as officially inspired; the British soldier always prefers the evidence of his own eyes.

Maybe the explanation of this paradoxical character of the Turk was rooted in the past. Half Tartar, half European; perhaps his ego was flattered by an exhibition of the polished side of his nature to an Englishman and his inclination to revert to the barbarian only became apparent when dealing with Arabs, Kurds or others whom he regarded as inferior. In the Germans there was probably something of a kindred spirit and perhaps this had something to do with their unhappy and unholy alliance. Clearly all this is controversial. Any Turcophile would argue that it is never possible to generalize in issues of this sort and that the majority of Turks have since looked upon their crimes against humanity with as much dismay as any European. Furthermore, anything done by the Turks in World War I pales into insignificance beside the horrors of Belsen and Buchenwald in World War II. Like the Germans the Turks have long been an enigma.

Back to Baghdad: in the half apologetic way that the British seem to have excused so many of their actions in the Empire building days, one of the first things that was done as soon as a semblance of order had been achieved in the city was the issuance of a proclamation explaining the presence of British troops to the people of Baghdad.

Its flowery style and stilted phrases are redolent of another world and one wonders where the romantic was found who wrote it. It was an extraordinary document, yet the text was endorsed by the British Cabinet. On Maude's behalf it purported to express the wishes of "my King and the people over whom he rules," "my King and his peoples . . . and the Great Nations with whom he is in alliance," "the British people and their Allies," "Great Britain and the Great Powers allied to Great Britain," and finally "the British people and Nations in alliance with them." It promised nothing but hoped that the people of the Baghdad province would "prosper even as in the past" and it invited "through your Nobles . . . may unite ... in realizing the aspirations of your Race." There was nothing in it to contradict the general belief that when the moment was ripe Britain would declare Mesopotamia a British Protectorate as she had done with Cyprus in November 1914. On the other hand it did suggest that the Allies benevolently accepted the concept of a United Arabia, so that the proclamation cut straight across the agreement between them that a settlement of the Ottoman Empire should await the outcome of the war.

To the people of Baghdad the document meant absolutely nothing, and even less to the population of Mesopotamia as a whole. But elsewhere it came in for considerable criticism; this was "politics" in the American sense. None of the political representatives in Mesopotamia, including Sir Percy Cox, had been consulted as to its make-up and Lord Cromer remarked tartly that "it was not necessary for His Majesty's Government to emulate the Hebrew Prophets, but they would have been well advised before its issue, to enlist the help of Muslims in touch with Islamic opinion."

In the House of Commons it was received with mixed feelings; the Speaker referring to it as a document containing a great deal of oriental and flowery language not suited to our western climate. One Irish protagonist suggested that a similar proclamation might well be suitable for issue in Ireland, another that Maude—who was an Irishman—was probably thinking of Ireland when he addressed the people of Baghdad. As for the soldiers, they were baffled. Very few of them in Mesopotamia had any time at all for the Arab; their experience was confined to Buddhoos and, if there were any choice they preferred the Turk. The "greatness and renown" of the past with which the Arabs were credited left them completely indifferent. In its happy oriental vein, the proclamation might be diplomatic, designed to impress the Arabs with a beneficial change in fortune consequent on their arrival. But it is doubtful if any British soldier cast himself in the role of Crusader and those who thought about the manifesto at all felt it was all rather ridiculous, pure nonsense and totally unnecessary. The answer was simple enough, when the time came Mesopotamia would become another jewel in the King Emperor's Crown— that was the logical reason for the fighting which had taken them to Baghdad. Very few were concerned with deeper issues of the war; to them the problem was simply a matter of defeating the Turks. If in doing so the British Empire gained a large slice of territory, so much the better. But this was the viewpoint of those too close to the scene, too involved to rationalize the capture of Baghdad with the world situation. It is for this reason that a pause is desirable here, in order to review what the loss of the Ottoman Empire's center of three great provinces implied in terms of its effect on the Allied war effort.

The most immediate effect was to disrupt the operations of Ali Ihsan's force in Persia, and what *this* implied will be obvious. With his Baghdad base gone, Khalil's Persian expedition collapsed; supplies could no longer go forward and there could be no further advance on Baratoff's front. However, the ramifications of the fall of Baghdad went much further afield than Persia.

But first it must be realized that the capture of the capital city did not mean the whole of Mesopotamia[7] had been conquered. While two of the major vilayets, Basra and Baghdad, were in British hands, that of Mosul was still held by the Turks, although with Maude in Baghdad and the Russians poised above it in the north, Mosul was in a particularly precarious position. Materially the Turks had lost heavily for, in a strictly military sense, Maude's victory had meant the destruction of a sizeable Turkish army. In December 1916 Allied intelligence had estimated that there were forty-two Turkish divisions in the field. Of these, twenty-two opposed the Russians on the northern front and in Persia, six were in Arabia or Egypt, five in Anatolia and European Turkey, two in Rumania and one in Macedonia; the remaining six had not been identified and so were considered to be deployed as a general reserve. Thus it was reckoned that about twenty-six divisions—Approximately two hundred and forty thousand men—opposed the combined Russian and British forces converging on Mesopotamia. The strength of the five divisions which Khalil controlled was estimated at between forty-five and sixty-three thousand bayonets[8] and it was calculated that in the fighting from Kut to the Diyala between twenty-five and thirty thousand casualties had been sustained, i.e., about half the force. To these losses must also be added the effect on the morale not only of the Turks themselves but also on those of their allies whose interests depended on Turkey's success and her ability to pin down a large army on the Tigris front.

To Germany, it spelled the end of. a twenty-year-old dream of a new India and "a place in the sun." With the end of the Berlin-Baghdad railway in British hands the scheme was finished. If only for this reason March 11, 1917 should be a memorable date in the historian's calendar.

---

7. Baghdad is only on the edge of the real Mesopotamia. Rather than refer to "Lower" or "Upper" Mesopotamia, the name has been used as a generic term` covering the whole country. Literally "between the rivers"—Euphrates and Tigris—what is now Iraq, consists of about fifty-five thousand square miles of land.
8. Post war Turkish sources quoted strengths of about half these figures; the truth probably lay somewhere between the two.

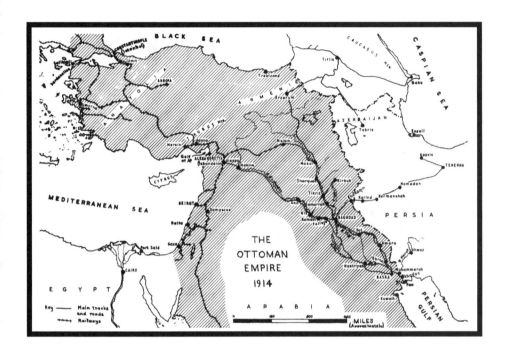

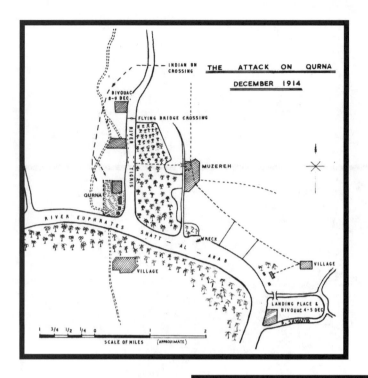

THE ATTACK ON QURNA

DECEMBER 1914

INDIAN BN CROSSING

BIVOUAC 8-9 DEC.

FLYING BRIDGE CROSSING

RIVER TIGRIS

MUZEREH

QURNA

RIVER EUPHRATES

SHATT — AL — ARAB

WRECK

VILLAGE

VILLAGE

LANDING PLACE & BIVOUAC 4-5 DEC

R. SUWANIB

3/4 1/2 1/4 0   1   2

SCALE OF MILES   (APPROXIMATE)

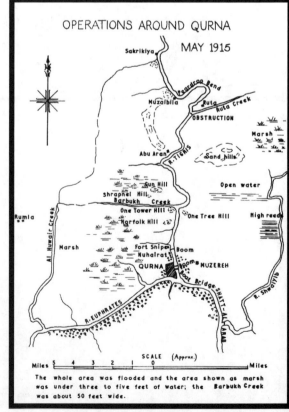

OPERATIONS AROUND QURNA

MAY 1915

Sakrikiya

Peardrop Bend

Muzaibila

Ruta
Ruta Creek

OBSTRUCTION

Marsh

Abu Aran

R. TIGRIS

Sand hills

Open water

Gun Hill

Shrapnel Hill
Barbukh Creek

One Tower Hill

High reeds

Rumia

Norfolk Hill

One Tree Hill

Al Huwair Creek

Marsh

Fort Snipe

Boom

Nuhairat

Boom

QURNA

Boom MUZEREH

Boat Bridge SHATT-AL-ARAB

R. Shwaiyib

R. EUPHRATES

Miles 5   4   3   2   1   0   Miles

SCALE   (Approx.)

The whole area was flooded and the area shown as marsh
was under three to five feet of water; the Barbukh Creek
was about 50 feet wide.

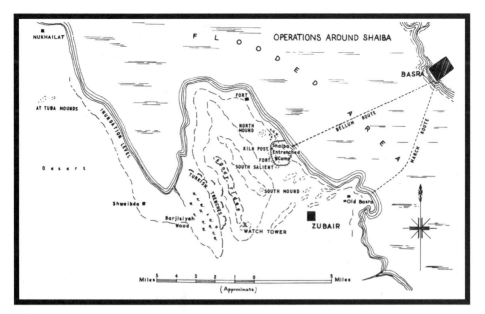

OPERATIONS AROUND SHAIBA

NUKHAILAT

F L O O D E D   A R E A

BASRA

AT TUBA MOUNDS

INUNDATION LEVEL

FORT

NORTH MOUND

BELLUM ROUTE

MARCH ROUTE

Desert

KILN POST
Shaiba
Entrenched
Camp
FORT

SOUTH SALIENT

Shweibda

TURKISH TRENCHES

SOUTH MOUND

Old Basra

Barjisiyah Wood

WATCH TOWER

ZUBAIR

Miles 5 4 3 2 1 0   5 Miles
(Approximate)

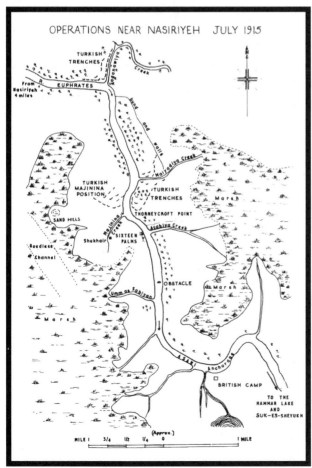

OPERATIONS NEAR NASIRIYEH   JULY 1915

TURKISH TRENCHES

Sadanaiya Creek

From Nasiriyeh 4 miles

EUPHRATES

Mind and walls

Majrudiya Creek

TURKISH MAJININA POSITION

TURKISH TRENCHES

Marsh

SAND HILLS

THORNEYCROFT POINT

Majinina Creek

Atabiya Creek

Reedless Channel

Shukhair

SIXTEEN PALMS

Umm es Tabison

OBSTACLE

Marsh

Marsh

A K A R   Anchorage

BRITISH CAMP

TO THE
HAMMAR LAKE
AND
SUK-ES-SHEYUKH

MILE 1   3/4   1/2   1/4   0   1 MILE
(Approx.)

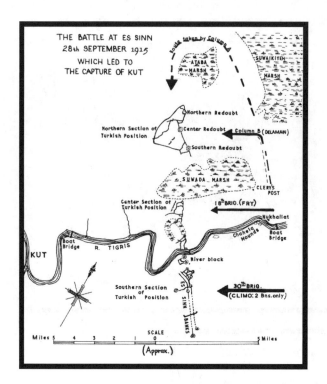

THE BATTLE AT ES SINN
28th SEPTEMBER 1915
WHICH LED TO
THE CAPTURE OF KUT

Route taken by Column A

ATABA MARSH

SUWAIKIYEH MARSH

Northern Redoubt

Northern Section of
Turkish Position

Center Redoubt

Column B (DELAMAIN)

Southern Redoubt

SUWADA MARSH

CLERY'S POST

Center Section of
Turkish Position

18th BRIG. (FRY)

Mukhailat

Chahela
Mounds

Boat
Bridge

Boat
Bridge

KUT

R. TIGRIS

River block

Southern Section
of
Turkish Position

ES SINN BANKS

30th BRIG.
(CLIMO: 2 Bns. only)

Miles 5   4   3   2   1   0   SCALE   5 Miles
(Approx.)

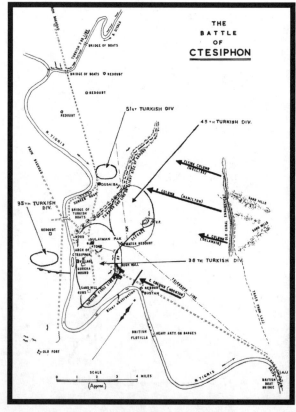

THE
BATTLE
OF
CTESIPHON

BRIDGE OF BOATS

BRIDGE OF BOATS   REDOUBT

REDOUBT

REDOUBT

51st TURKISH DIV

45th TURKISH DIV.

R. TIGRIS

FLYING COLUMN (MELLISS)

COLUMN (HAMILTON)

35th TURKISH
DIV.

MOUSAIBA

REDOUBT

BRIDGE OF
TURKISH BOATS

V.P.

WOOD   SULAIMAN PAK

ARCH OF
CTESIPHON

WATER REDOUBT

B. COLUMN (DELAMAIN)

SAND HILLS

SAND HILLS

38th TURKISH DIV.

VILLAGE
GURKHA MOUND

HIGH WALL

SAND HILL
GUNS

TURKISH FIRST LINE

TELEGRAPH LINE

TRACK FROM LAJJ

C. COLUMN (HOGHTON)

REDOUBT

BUSTAN

River obstruction

BRITISH
FLOTILLA

HEAVY ARTY. ON BARGES

OLD FORT

R. TIGRIS

BRITISH
BOAT
BRIDGE

SCALE
0   1   2   3   4   MILES
(Approx.)

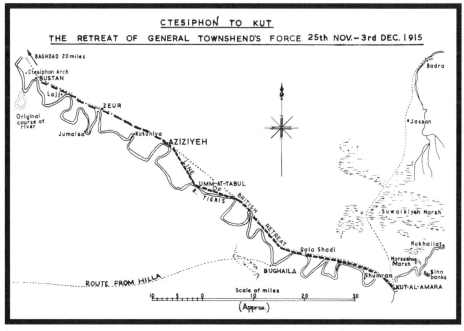

CTESIPHON TO KUT

THE RETREAT OF GENERAL TOWNSHEND'S FORCE 25th NOV.–3rd DEC. 1915

BAGHDAD 20 miles

Ctesiphon Arch
BUSTAN

Badra

Lajj

ZEUR

Original
course of
river

Jassan

Jumaisa

Kutuniya

AZIZIYEH

UMM-AT-TABUL

R. TIGRIS

LINE OF BRITISH RETREAT

Suwaikiyeh Marsh

Nukhailat

Horseshoe
Marsh

Qala Shadi

Sinn
banks

ROUTE FROM HILLA

BUGHAILA

Shumran

KUT-AL-AMARA

Scale of miles

10 5 0 10 20 30

(Approx.)

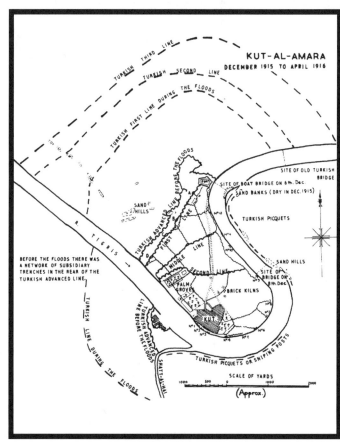

KUT-AL-AMARA

DECEMBER 1915 TO APRIL 1916

TURKISH THIRD LINE

TURKISH SECOND LINE

TURKISH FIRST LINE DURING THE FLOODS

SITE OF OLD TURKISH
BRIDGE

SITE OF BOAT BRIDGE ON 6th. Dec.

SAND BANKS (DRY IN DEC. 1915)

SAND
HILLS

TURKISH PICQUETS

R. TIGRIS

TURKISH ADVANCED LINE BEFORE THE FLOODS

FIRST LINE

MIDDLE LINE

SAND HILLS

SITE OF
BRIDGE ON
8th Dec

SECOND LINE

BEFORE THE FLOODS THERE WAS
A NETWORK OF SUBSIDIARY
TRENCHES IN THE REAR OF THE
TURKISH ADVANCED LINE.

PALM
GROVES

BRICK KILNS

KUT

TURKISH ADVANCED LINE BEFORE THE FLOODS

TURKISH LINE DURING THE FLOODS

SHATT-AL-HAI

TURKISH PICQUETS OR SNIPING POSTS

SCALE OF YARDS

1000 500 0 1000 2000

(Approx.)

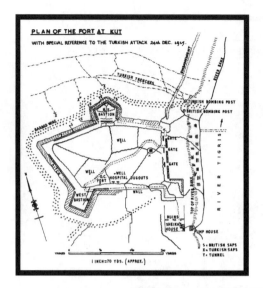

PLAN OF THE FORT AT KUT

WITH SPECIAL REFERENCE TO THE TURKISH ATTACK 24th DEC. 1915.

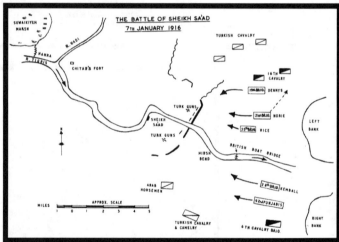

THE BATTLE OF SHEIKH SA'AD

7TH JANUARY 1916

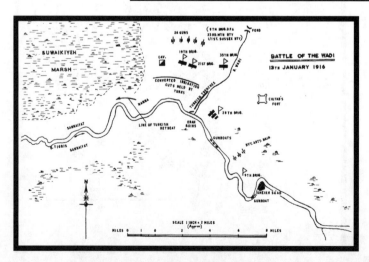

BATTLE OF THE WADI

13TH JANUARY 1916

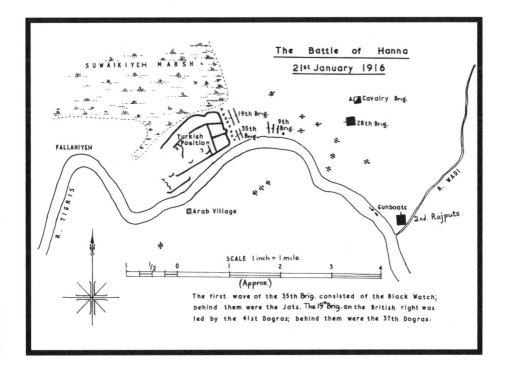

The first wave of the 35th Brig. consisted of the Black Watch; behind them were the Jats. The 19th Brig. on the British right was led by the 41st Dogras; behind them were the 37th Dogras.

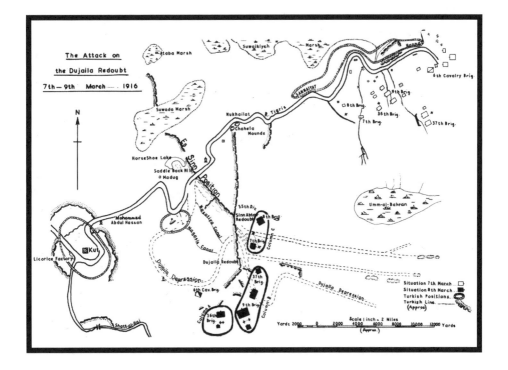

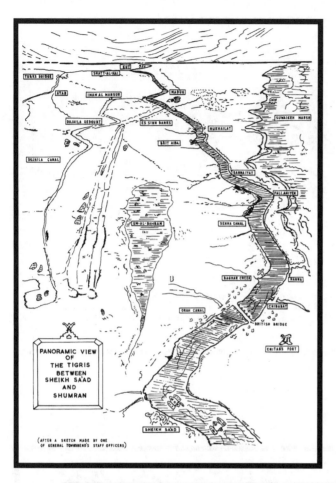

PANORAMIC VIEW OF THE TIGRIS BETWEEN SHEIKH SA'AD AND SHUMRAN

(AFTER A SKETCH MADE BY ONE OF GENERAL TOWNSHEND'S STAFF OFFICERS)

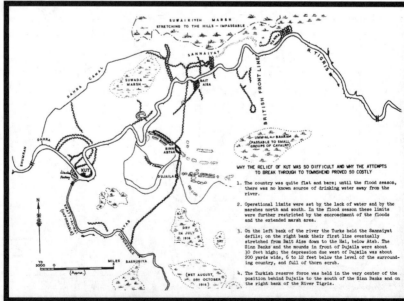

WHY THE RELIEF OF KUT WAS SO DIFFICULT AND WHY THE ATTEMPTS TO BREAK THROUGH TO TOWNSHEND PROVED SO COSTLY

1. The country was quite flat and bare; until the flood season, there was no known source of drinking water away from the river.

2. Operational limits were set by the lack of water and by the marshes north and south. In the flood season these limits were further restricted by the encroachment of the floods and the extended marsh areas.

3. On the left bank of the river the Turks held the Sannaiyat defile; on the right bank their first line eventually stretched from Bait Aisa down to the Hai, below Atab. The Sinn Banks and the mounds in front of Dujaila were about 30 feet high; the depression due west of Dujaila was about 200 yards wide, 6 to 12 feet below the level of the surrounding country, and full of thorn scrub.

4. The Turkish reserve force was held in the very center of the position behind Dujaila to the south of the Sinn Banks and on the right bank of the River Tigris.

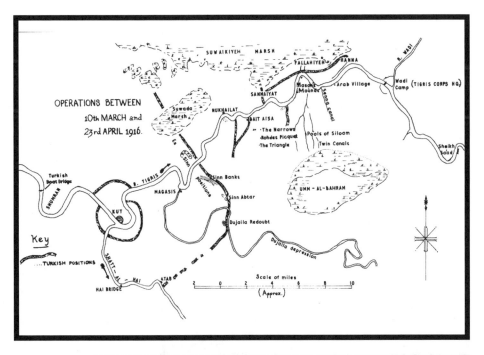

OPERATIONS BETWEEN
10th MARCH and
23rd APRIL 1916.

SUWAIKIYEH MARSH

FALLAHIYEH HANNA
R. WADI

Masons Mounds
SANNAIYAT
Arab Village
Wadi Camp (TIGRIS CORPS HQ)
Sanq Canal

Suwada Marsh
NUKHAILAT
BAIT AISA
The Narrows
Rohdes Picquet
The Triangle
Pools of Siloam
Twin Canals
Sheikh Saad

Turkish Boat Bridge
SHUMRAN
R. TIGRIS
MAGASIS
Sinn Banks
Sinn Abtar
UMM-AL-BAHRAM

KUT
Dujaila Redoubt

SHATT-AL-HAI
Dujaila depression

Key
....Turkish positions

ATAB
HAI BRIDGE

2 0 2 4 6 8 10
Scale of miles
(Approx.)

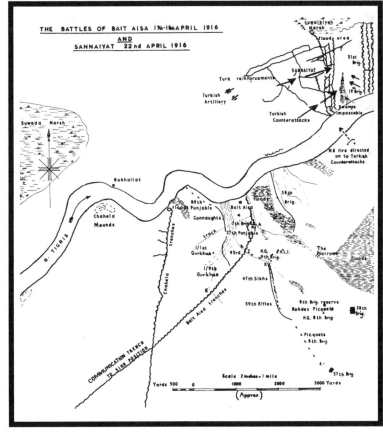

THE BATTLES OF BAIT AISA 17th-18th APRIL 1916
AND
SANNAIYAT 22nd APRIL 1916

Suwaikiyeh Marsh
Flood area
21st Brig.

Turk reinforcements
SANNAIYAT
19th Brig.

Turkish Artillery
Swamps impassable

Turkish Counterattacks
N6 fire directed on to Turkish Counterattacks

Suwada Marsh

Nukhailat

Chahela Mounds

R. TIGRIS

89th Punjabis
Connaughts
floods
Bait Aisa
39th Brig.
7th Brig. A
27th Punjabis

Trenches

Chahela
1/1st Gurkhas
93rd
1/9th Gurkhas

H.Q. 9th Brig.
9th K.L.I.
XV
The Narrows
floods

47th Sikhs
E
59th Rifles

8th Brig. reserve
Rohdes Picquets
H.Q. 8th Brig.
38th Brig.

Bait Aisa trenches

Picquets 8th Brig.

COMMUNICATION TRENCH TO SINN POSITION

37th Brig.

Yards 500 0 1000 2000 3000 Yards
Scale 2 inches = 1 mile
(Approx)

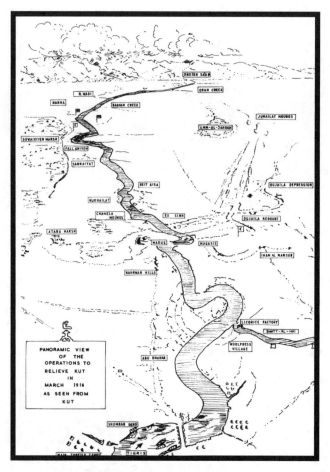

PANORAMIC VIEW
OF THE
OPERATIONS TO
RELIEVE KUT
IN
MARCH 1916
AS SEEN FROM
KUT

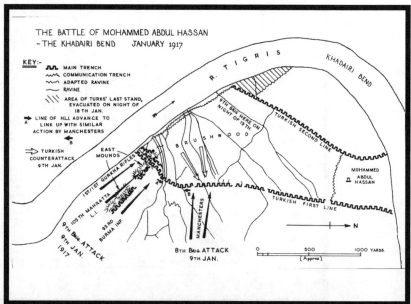

THE BATTLE OF MOHAMMED ABDUL HASSAN
- THE KHADAIRI BEND   JANUARY 1917

KEY:-
━━━ MAIN TRENCH
〰〰 COMMUNICATION TRENCH
⌒⌒ ADAPTED RAVINE
─── RAVINE
▨▨▨ AREA OF TURKS' LAST STAND,
      EVACUATED ON NIGHT OF
      18TH JAN.
➡ LINE OF H.I.I. ADVANCE TO
A   LINK UP WITH SIMILAR
B   ACTION BY MANCHESTERS
⇨ TURKISH
   COUNTERATTACK
   9TH JAN.

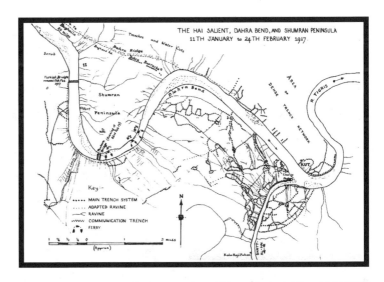

THE HAI SALIENT, DAHRA BEND, AND SHUMRAN PENINSULA
11TH JANUARY to 24TH FEBRUARY 1917.

Key:—
···· MAIN TRENCH SYSTEM
···· ADAPTED RAVINE
⌐ RAVINE
ᴠᴠᴠ COMMUNICATION TRENCH
⥮ FERRY

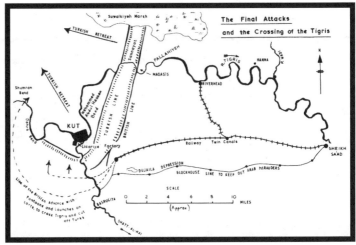

The Final Attacks
and the Crossing of the Tigris

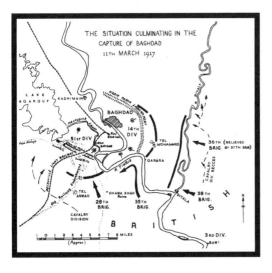

THE SITUATION CULMINATING IN THE
CAPTURE OF BAGHDAD
11TH MARCH 1917

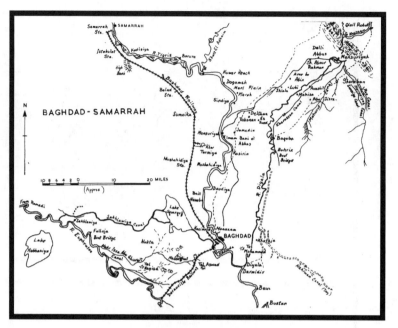

BAGHDAD – SAMARRAH

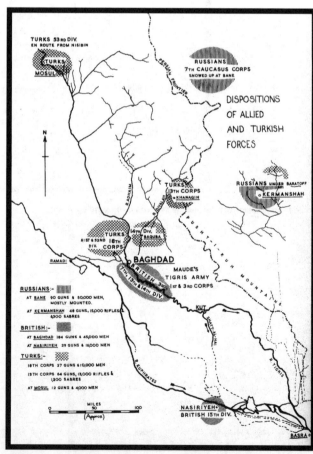

DISPOSITIONS OF ALLIED AND TURKISH FORCES

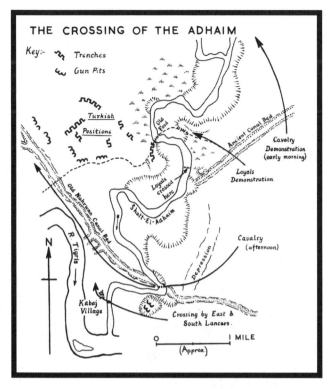

THE CROSSING OF THE ADHAIM

Key:- ∿ Trenches
      ⌇ Gun Pits

Turkish Positions

Old Ford

Cavalry Demonstration (early morning)

Ancient Canal Bed

Loyals Demonstration

Loyals crossed here

Old Nahrwan Canal Bed

Shaft-El-Adhaim

R. Tigris

N

Depression

Cavalry (afternoon)

Kabaj Village

Crossing by East & South Lancers.

0   1 MILE
(Approx.)

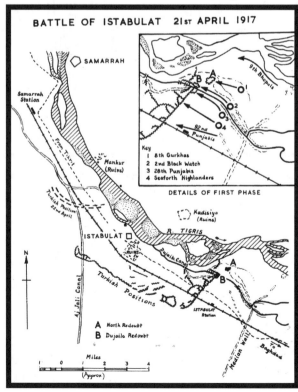

BATTLE OF ISTABULAT 21ST APRIL 1917

SAMARRAH

Samarrah Station

A

B

9th Bhopals

1

2

3

4

92nd Punjabis

Key
1 8th Gurkhas
2 2nd Black Watch
3 28th Punjabis
4 Seaforth Highlanders

DETAILS OF FIRST PHASE

From Tigris

Mankur (Ruins)

Turkish Position 22nd April

Kadisiya (Ruins)

R. TIGRIS

ISTABULAT

RUINS

Dujaila Canal

A

B

Al Jali Canal

Turkish Positions

ISTABULAT Station

Median Wall

To Baghdad

N

A North Redoubt
B Dujaila Redoubt

Miles
1   0   1   2   3   4
(Approx.)

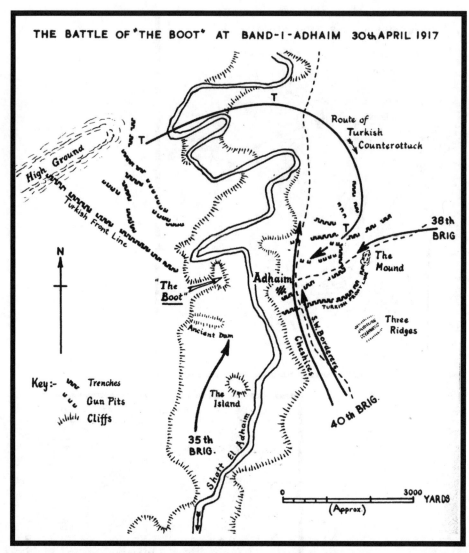

THE BATTLE OF "THE BOOT" AT BAND-I-ADHAIM 30th APRIL 1917

High Ground

Route of Turkish Counterattack

Turkish Front Line

T

T

T

38th BRIG

The Mound

N

"The Boot"

Adhaim

Three Ridges

Ancient Dam

TURKISH FRONT LINE

S.W. Borderers

Cheshires

Key :— Trenches
Gun Pits
Cliffs

The Island

40th BRIG.

35th BRIG.

Shatt El Adhaim

0   3000 YARDS
(Approx.)

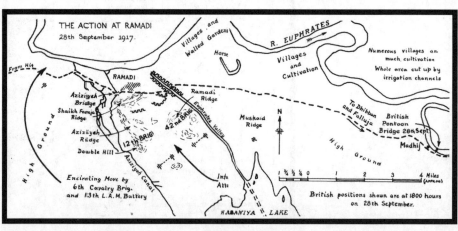

THE ACTION AT RAMADI
28th September 1917.

Villages and Walled Gardens

R. EUPHRATES

Numerous villages an. much cultivation

From Hit

RAMADI

Horse

Villages and Cultivation

Whole area cut up by irrigation channels

Aziziyeh Bridge

Ramadi Ridge

Shaikh Faraja Ridge

Euphrates Valley

To Dhibban and Falluja

British Pontoon Bridge 28th Sept

High Ground

Aziziyeh Ridge

42 nd BRIG.

Muskaid Ridge

N

Madhij

12 th BRIG.

Double Hill

Aziziyeh Canal

High Ground

Encircling Move by
6th Cavalry Brig.
and 13th L.A.M. Battery

Infa Atte

½ ¼ 0   1   2   3   4 Miles
(Approx.)

British positions shown are at 1800 hours
on 28th September.

HABANIYA LAKE

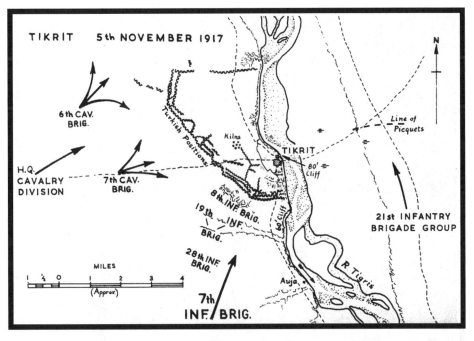

TIKRIT   5th NOVEMBER 1917

6th CAV. BRIG.

H.Q. CAVALRY DIVISION

7th CAV. BRIG.

Turkish Positions

Kilns

TIKRIT

80' Cliff

Line of Picquets

N

8th INF. BRIG.

19th INF. BRIG.

28th INF. BRIG.

7th INF. BRIG.

21st INFANTRY BRIGADE GROUP

Auja

R. Tigris

MILES
1 ¼ 0   1   2   3   4
(Approx.)

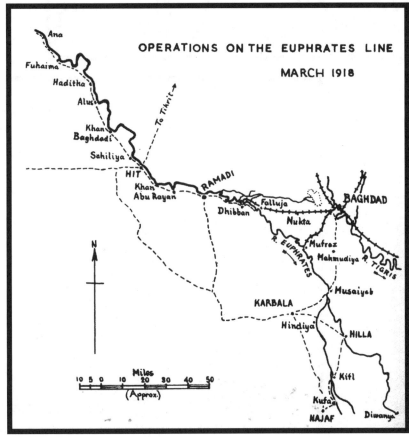

OPERATIONS ON THE EUPHRATES LINE

MARCH 1918

Ana

Fuhaima

Haditha

Alus

Khan Baghdadi

Sahiliya

To Tikrit

HIT

Khan Abu Rayan

RAMADI

Dhibban

Falluja

Nukta

BAGHDAD

R. EUPHRATES

Mufraz

Mahmudiya

R. TIGRIS

Musaiyeb

N

KARBALA

Hindiya

HILLA

Kifl

Kufa

NAJAF

Diwanya

Miles
10 5 0   10   20   30   40   50
(Approx.)

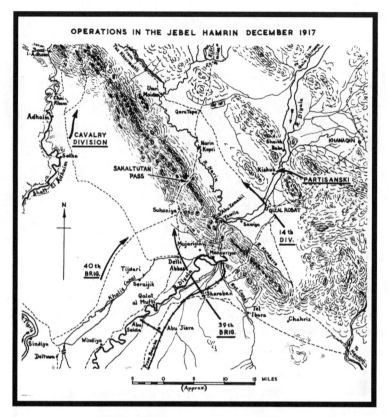

OPERATIONS IN THE JEBEL HAMRIN DECEMBER 1917

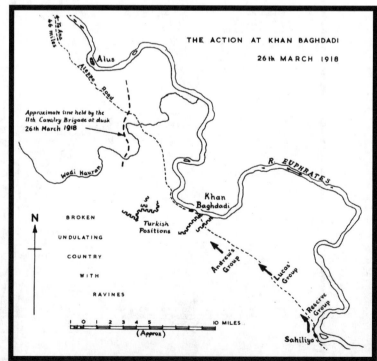

THE ACTION AT KHAN BAGHDADI
26th MARCH 1918

Chapter 18

Samarra

Before turning to the course of events in the field beyond Baghdad, a brief review of the strategic situation as it appeared at the end of March, 1917, should serve to put the Mesopotamia campaign in its correct perspective vis-à-vis the rest of the war. In England, where conscription had been in force for nine months and the limits of British manpower were painfully apparent, the most momentous news of the whole war had come during the previous month. The United States had joined the Allies at long last and, although it could hardly be hoped that her strength would develop for at least another year, an Allied victory now seemed certain. There might still be a long way to go, but Germany and her allies would be crushed eventually. In the meantime, the intensified submarine campaign which had been running for less than a month was already causing great anxiety—not only with regard to the supplies for the United Kingdom, but also because of its possible effect on the sea communications to Palestine and Mesopotamia. In France another great offensive was being prepared; in Italy and Serbia the fighting had bogged down in trench warfare; in Palestine, El Arish had been occupied by British troops and preparations were being made for the first battle of Gaza. Baratoff, slowly following up the retreat of Ali Ihsan near Kermanshah, had been told by the Grand Duke that he would be getting two divisions of Cossacks as reinforcements and to go as fast as he could. The rumblings coming out of Russia were getting more persistent but on the Caucasus front where the much vaunted Russian Army steamroller was expected to have its real effect, Trebizond, Erzerum and Erzingyan in Armenia, had all been occupied and Whitehall continued to be confident of future Russian cooperation. Winter conditions had brought Chernozubov operation to a standstill for the time being, but as soon as the weather improved he was expected to roll on toward Mosul. In less than a few months it was to become apparent that this was a hope which could never be realized. Those officers of the Caucasus Army who managed to escape being put down a hole in the ice were soon fleeing for their lives, many with their epaulettes nailed to their shoulders; no advance ever materialized and Russian pressure on the Turks diminished and finally melted away in the general debacle of the revolution. But that was not the picture in March 1917, and at that time there seemed to be very clear advantages to be obtained by Maude's cooperation with the Russians in a two-pronged drive on Mosul.

Certainly it was of little use Maude's figuratively sitting back in Baghdad; the Turks were containing large numbers of troops—British and Russian—who could be usefully employed in other theaters, just as soon as the Turks were defeated. In any case he would not be able to regard Baghdad as the end of the road. Baghdad had such political and strategic importance, the Turks could hardly be expected to acquiesce in its loss and, even if it involved standing on the defensive in the Caucasus and withdrawing troops from other theaters, it was almost certain that considerable effort would be devoted to its recapture. With Baghdad open to attack by columns advancing up any or all of the three river lines of the Tigris, Euphrates and Diyala, to hold the city it would be necessary to secure outposts up these lines of approach. That Baghdad was not the limit of the Mesopotamian theater was to prove only too true; events were to show that Maude's men still had some of the stiffest fighting of the campaign in front of them.

In what, but for its Biblical associations, might truly be called Godforsaken country, communications were, as always, the biggest problem facing an army undertaking military operations in Mesopotamia. Fear of the administrative consequences of a breakdown in the communications not only set the limits on the operations but also decided the general plan of the campaign. The occupation of Baghdad had already doubled the length of Maude's supply line from Basra and the strain was such that considerable improvements would have to be effected quickly if operations were to continue—especially if the two hundred and forty mile advance on Mosul was a serious proposition. The German railway stopped at Samarra; beyond it the Tigris was unnavigable. Stocks of railway material in India were not enough to allow the section between Baghdad and Basra to be completed, let alone to extend the line beyond Samarra, so that if Maude were given Mosul as his next objective there was bound to be a very considerable delay before he could reach it. There was an alternative; operations up the Euphrates might exert pressure on the Turks, but a railway was as vital there as it was along the Tigris and the distances involved would be greater, so that taking all this into consideration, it seemed to those responsible for directing the British war effort from Whitehall that the army in Palestine was in a much better position for turning the screw on the Turks than Maude in Mesopotamia. Consequently Maude was told quite firmly that his job was to consolidate the British position in Mesopotamia and tighten his grip on Baghdad; with this end in view, military operations should be confined to the Baghdad province.

Irrespective of any political considerations—and it must be apparent from the proclamation issued soon after the occupation of the city that there were plenty of these—Maude saw that Baghdad's administrative services had to be put on a sound footing. They had been neglected by the Turks for too long and much of what had to be done was not only militarily necessary but also politically expedient. Measures for effective sanitation and a properly organized water supply were put into effect; a pontoon bridge (subsequently named after Maude) was built across the Tigris to connect the eastern and western sectors of the city; political officers were brought in from India. All this gave Maude's flair for organization full scope and besides initiating many of the schemes he went fully into the details of each one himself. But apart from his preoccupation with civil administration he was still directing operations designed to consolidate the British hold on the Baghdad province. Tactically, there were still four clear objectives to be realized before his latest directive was fulfilled. First, Khalil's beaten army had to be chased up the Tigris, cleared out of the province and crushed before it could be reorganized; second, the railhead at Samarra had to be captured; third, Ali Ihsan's troops had to be intercepted before they could join up with Khalil. All three objectives would lead to the establishment of outposts on three lines along which the Turks could strike back at Baghdad while the fourth and most vital objective—that of gaining control of the areas from which the Tigris and Euphrates waters could be used to flood the countryside, and so bring operations to a standstill—was essential to the other three. Both rivers were rising and whoever held their banks at certain points north and northwest of the city could flood the Baghdad region as Khalil might have done to hold it. Near Falluja, the Euphrates flood level was about fourteen feet higher than the level of the rest of the countryside between there and Baghdad, and by opening a dam at the mouth of the Sakhlawiya Canal, five miles upstream of Bustan, the whole of Lake Aquarquf could be filled. If this happened all the countryside south of the lake could be flooded and the suburbs of Baghdad on the right bank of the Tigris submerged. As the left bank could also be opened at several places north of Baghdad, releasing other flood water, it was possible to turn the whole area into a vast lake, in the middle of which the old part of the city would be left standing as if on an island. Once this happened the British force would be water-logged while the Turks would still be able to move quite freely six miles inland. Thus, control of the points from which the flood water could be released was a military necessity; Baghdad would not be secure until the Turks were driven right back to a position where they could do no damage.

Following the withdrawal from Baghdad, Kiazim Karabekir had ordered his men to fall back all the way to Istabulat, to a position which would cover the railway terminus at Samarra. Not being a man to fritter away his men unnecessarily he could see that the only course now open to the Turks was to get back to the shelter of a tactically sound position which had some strategic worth and where he could reorganize his battered units. But Khalil thought otherwise; he was not prepared to yield any more ground than was absolutely necessary. So far as he was concerned Maude would have to fight every inch of the way and, as Kiazim and he could not see eye to eye, Kiazim had to go. In his place came Shefket Pasha—a good soldier but not in the same class as Kiazim—and the result of the change was a series of battles between Baghdad and Istabulat. Events were to justify Kiazim's assessment of the situation. These battles brought absolutely no benefit to the Turks, whereas Kiazim's plan would have enabled the Istabulat defenses to have been put into a state which would have made resistance there far more profitable for the Turks. With Shefket in command, the bulk of Kiazim's old corps retired along the Tigris while a detachment of the 14th Division was sent off to Baquba, forty miles from Baghdad up the Diyala.

Khalil's aim was to reunite his 6th Army, by linking up Shefket's Corps with that of Ali Ihsan. For this, it was essential that Baquba, where the Khanaqin road from Persia crosses the Diyala, should be held until Ali's troops could reach it and get across the river. At this stage, Ali's 2nd Turkish Division which was facing the Russians in the Pai Taq pass was retiring fast, but the advance guard of the 6th Division had already crossed the Persian border into Mesopotamia and a party had been sent ahead to cooperate with Shefket's men at Baquba. The route his force was taking ran past Qizil Robat, through the Jebel Hamrin mountain range and along the Diyala from Sharaban and as Ali was engaged in the highly dangerous process of a transfer from one front to the other while still in contact with the Russians he faced the danger of having to fight in two directions at the same time. Once across the Diyala his position should ease however, for he would be able to swing around and have a clear route via Kifri and Kirkuk back to Mosul and only one front. Ali Ihsan Bey—known to the British troops as "Old Sandbag"—was one of the ablest of the Turkish generals, a man of great initiative and foresight—and the fact that he was able to cope so competently with the situation which was now developing is greatly to his credit. As will be seen he was soon to be committed to fighting two simultaneous rearguard actions—the very circumstance he had hoped to avoid.

Maude's aim was the opposite of Khalil's. What he hoped to do was to prevent any junction between Ali Ihsan and Shefket; separately the two Turkish Corps could be destroyed in detail; operating together they would be far more difficult to deal with. On the face of it, the advantage seemed to lie with Maude as numerically his army was about twice as strong as that of Khalil—the combined strengths of the Turks being about twenty thousand while Maude had about forty-five thousand combatants whom he could deploy north of Baghdad. The first move made was designed to harry Shefket's troops when, on the night of March 13, two days after the capture of the city, the 7th Division, under command of Major General Sir Vere Fane set off north along the railway to attack a Turkish position reported as being "somewhere near Bait Nawab"—one of the places which was a potential flood menace. Losing direction during the night, the column floundered about for a time, but eventually the Turks were located dug in about four and a half miles south of Mushahidiya station where their trenches had been sited in the expectancy of the British attacking from the east. The railway lay about six miles inland at this spot and the Turks appear to have sited their defenses to cope with an approach from the direction of the river rather than from the desert. In fact, if their reasoning was based on the belief that Maude's men would cling to the water, they miscalculated. The 28th Brigade, closely followed by the 19th, moved in on them from the east to attack the front of the position, as the Turks had expected. But Norie's 21st Brigade, on which Fane was relying for the decisive blow, was sent across the railway to work around the Turks' right flank. As the two brigades who were attacking frontally deployed and started their advance, the Turks opened fire. Although there was better cover for this attack than the division had known for a long time, losses were still heavy and there was much hard fighting before the railway station was captured. As Fane had anticipated, it was the flanking move of the 21st Brigade which decided the action. The Black Watch lost half their strength in the initial advance,[1] but most of the Turks made off soon after the main position on one of the sand

---

1. In this action the Black Watch lost ten officers—five killed or died of wounds—and two hundred and twenty-seven men; the lst/8th Gurkhas lost every officer except one.

hills known as "Sugar Loaf Hill" had been successfully assaulted by the 9th
Bhopals and shortly before midnight the action was over. After a twenty-one
mile march, followed by a stiff fight the British were in no condition to follow
them up and so they were allowed to go. In thirty hours marching and fighting
the troops had had only the water in their water-bottles and so, after clearing
the battlefield, the 19th and 28th Brigades returned to their bivouacs outside
Baghdad while the 21st Brigade was left to watch the river dikes. Despite its
comparatively high cost, it had been a very successful little action. British
casualties totaled six hundred, as against the Turks eight hundred. But one of
the flood danger points had been secured and Fane had forced the Turks into
another retreat; the following morning an air reconnaissance reported seeing
stragglers from the action fully twenty miles north of Mushahidiya.

The next important subsidiary operation followed almost immediately and
this, like the attack on Mushahidiya, was undertaken to safeguard Baghdad
from the floods. Maude had wanted to seize Falluja, whose importance has
already been explained, as soon as he got to Baghdad. Supply difficulties had
precluded his making any move in this direction earlier, and it was not until
March 19, that the 7th Brigade reached Falluja. There was little fighting; most
of the opposition came from the Arabs, as the Turks fell back on Ramadi,
twenty-five miles upstream, when they saw the British troops approaching. The
objective had been reached at virtually no cost but, unlike the Mushahidiya
operation, the underlying object had not been attained. When the mouth of the
Sakhlawiya Canal was reached it was only to find that the Turks had cut the
dam before they fled and that there was no hope of repairing it. But for the
fact that the Tigris flood water was exceptionally low that year, and the dike on
the right bank protected the railway and suburbs of Baghdad by holding back
the water, the situation would have been even more serious than it was. To
preserve the Decauville railway and the road, so maintaining communications
with the Euphrates, a dike had to be built along the Nukta road. The same
effect might have been achieved more simply by cutting the dikes on the right
bank above Sakhlawiya and diverting the river waters into Lake Habbaniya. But
this would have flooded the land of the Dulain Arabs, and Maude had no wish
to stimulate their hostility—there was trouble enough with them as it was,
although they gradually came to terms when they found there was no support
forthcoming from the Turks.

Apart from directing these operations to stop Baghdad being flooded out,
and supervising the grand plan for reorganized city administration, Maude was
busying himself with steps toward more effective Anglo-Russian cooperation.
Linking up with Baratoff was the ultimate objective and if, in doing so, he
could prevent Ali Ihsan getting back across the Diyala, so much the better.

Like Khalil, Maude had appreciated the importance to Ali of Baquba, and on March 14, a small party of infantry from the 14th Division was packed into Ford vans and sent off post-haste to occupy the village. Khalil's men were ready for them; greeted with a rattle of small arms fire and finding the bridge down, the commander of the party settled down to await the advance guard of what had been dubbed the "Khanaqin Column."[2] The main body of this column, under command of D'Urban Keary, was assembling outside Baghdad while the 8th Brigade with some Sappers and a bridging train had already set out for Baquba. D'Urban Keary had been given a dual object: to establish contact with Baratoff and to crush Ali Ihsan between the British and Russians in the process. That Maude was confident Ali Ihsan could be smashed is evidenced by his signal to Whitehall on March 19, two days after the 8th Brigade had succeeded in capturing Baquba. Stating that he had concentrated eight thousand men at Baquba, that his supply situation now was "excellent" and that he was doing everything he could to cooperate with Baratoff, he asked for the boundaries of British and Russian spheres of influence to be laid down. Once Ali had been crushed between the British and Cossack nutcrackers, his troops and those of Baratoff would be facing each other and it was desirable to know the precise limits of each other's territory. A time was coming when he and Baratoff would be cooperating in joint operations against the Turk and he wanted everything right. Little did he know that a political upheaval was paralyzing the sinews of the Imperial Army and that Baratoff was short of ammunition, transport, supplies—everything, in fact, which an army needs to move and fight.

He believed that Baratoff was steadily driving a broken mob of Turks before him; that it was only the weather, the terrain—and perhaps an element of Russian sloth—that was delaying Ali Ihsan's coup de grace. What he did not know was that Ali Ihsan's troops were far from being dispirited, that their morale was high and their tails were up. Nor did he expect D'Urban Keary to be met by a Turkish force numerically superior to the "Khanaqin Column"—a force which would be capable of holding off the British until they had got all their men and equipment across the Diyala. Consequently the realization of these facts came as a shock. Ali Ihsan was retiring all right but in an orderly fashion, and as he was little troubled by Russian pressure his withdrawal turned out to be a form of offensive. With Shefket's 18th Corps and Ali Ihsan's 13th both converging on Baquba, it was Maude's flank that was threatened, not that

---

2. It comprised the 7th Cavalry Brigade (less the 13th Hussars); two batteries of the 4th Royal Field Artillery Brigade (twelve 18-pounder guns); the 215th R.F.A. Brigade (eight 18-pounder guns); one Howitzer Battery (four 4.5 inch howitzers) two companies of the 3rd Sappers and Miners, the 8th and 9th Infantry Brigades, 34th Pioneers and a wireless set. Four light armored motor cars joined the column toward the end of March.

of Ali Ihsan.

By March 20, D'Urban Keary had concentrated the column at Baquba and his cavalry had gone on to occupy Abu Jisra, fifteen miles further up the Khanaqin road. After the initial scuffle to capture the village, things had been remarkably quiet, and even the cavalry had not met any opposition. However, the first check came soon after the column had advanced to Sharaban, for here the Turks were holding a position which was to delay D'Urban Keary until Ali Ihsan had established a proper defence, where the ground would favor the Turks. Such a place was not far away, and where the Khanaqin road entered the first low range of hills, Ali Ihsan was prepared to offer battle. Here at the foot of the Jebel Hamrin range, his troops were holding a potentially strong position behind two canals whose existence was not even known to the British troops until they reached them. On the night of March 23, men of the 8th Brigade crossed the first of these canals, the Nahrunia, but when they came to the second—the thirty foot wide, high banked Balad Ruz—no further progress was possible. Apart from the physical difficulties of getting across the canal, the Turks were occupying three tiers of traversed fire trenches which had been dug in the ridge overlooking it, and had a line of outposts stretching right down to the water. Behind the ridge the rocks of the Jebel Hamrin rose eight hundred feet from the plain and from the activity among them it looked as if Ali was here in considerable strength: six thousand men was the estimate made at the time.[3]

Clearly, this was going to be a hard nut to crack but, as D'Urban Keary was committed to it, he decided that there was nothing to be gained by waiting. His plan was for two battalions of the 8th Brigade to attack frontally and so "hold" the Turks, while the 9th Brigade made a flank attack from the east. By crossing the Balad Ruz well to the south, the 9th Brigade should be able to strike at Ali Ihsan's left flank at dawn on March 25. But if the attack was to succeed, surprise was essential; the attackers would have to be on the hills by dawn or the plan would fail. And it was the terrain that decided the issue, for to get across the Ruz a bridge had to be built. This disclosed D'Urban Keary's intention, and on the morning of March 24, an air reconnaissance reported the Turks were moving guns along the ridge to cover the route which the 9th Brigade would have to follow. After all the time and labor put into building the bridge, D'Urban Keary did not consider that a change of crossing place was reasonable at this late stage. Nevertheless the operation was doomed before it started.

As the troops formed up for the attack, dawn revealed a thoroughly unwarlike setting—reminiscent almost of an English spring scene—with a blue

---

3. In fact it was occupied by 4,500 rifles, and 20 guns.

sky, a willow-fringed stream and banks bright with buttercups and clover. Beyond the rolling plain, the Jebel Hamrin appeared as a scalloped ridge of rock; in the far distance, forty miles or more away the snow capped mountains. All seemed very peaceful, until the Turks artillery started to register on the bridge. Then, as the 1st/1st Gurkhas started to advance on the left, the Dorsets in the center, and the 1st/1st Mahrattas on the right there was the vicious crack of bursting shrapnel, and on the rock-strewn plain the shrapnel and shell splinters soon proved to be much more lethal than ever they had been on the yielding clay of the Tigris valley. The battle that ensued was one that demanded North-West Frontier tactics and one with which the men of the original Expeditionary Force would undoubtedly have been familiar and would even have welcomed. But of those who went into action on this day it is doubtful if there was one who had seen any service on the frontier; these men had learned their trade in the trench warfare of the Mesopotamian plain and this sort of battle was new to them. Even worse than their ignorance of the correct tactics was the situation which developed as a result of the flanking attack hitting the ridge, not at the limit of the Turks trenches, but at a point which Ali Ishan had reinforced; in consequence the 9th Brigade was severely handled. Only with considerable difficulty and by using every available man in the 8th Brigade to cover the withdrawal was the brigade extricated, and then only at a cost of nearly 1,200 casualties—more than a third of the troops engaged. That this was a different sort of war to that which they had been fighting may be deduced from the fact that for the first time in nearly a year the casualty list included a large number of "missing," many of whom were wounded who had had to be left behind in the retreat. It was the Turks who came out best in this battle and Ali Ihsan had proved quite conclusively that his men were not a beaten and demoralized force.

For Maude, the next few days were a period of uncertainty. Not only was he unsure of Ali's movements and purpose, but he was completely in the dark as to what Baratoff was doing. In point of fact, the Russians were doing very little and Ali, having already got most of his troops across the Diyala, was already moving southwest with the intention of effecting a junction with Shefket's Tigris force, somewhere near Deltawa. The action before Sharaban having served its purpose, his rearguard pulled out after the battle and the 8th Brigade was able to continue up the road, through the Jebel Hamrin to Qizil Robat. The advance guard arrived on April 1—April Fool's Day, although nobody thought much about tomfoolery in these circumstances—and here contact with the Russians was finally established. Until they actually met neither side quite knew the whereabouts of the other; with no wireless sets except those at the respective Army Headquarters messages between the respective vanguards had to go via Baghdad and Kermanshah and this was necessarily a tedious business. Consequently, when the two forces did meet, contact was unexpected and quite dramatic. As the 13th Lancers, riding ahead of the 8th Brigade's marching infantry neared the village of Qizil Robat, cavalry were seen on the horizon to be galloping toward them and they turned out to be a sotnia of Cossacks which Baratoff had sent forward. After a long ride from Hamadan they had crossed the Persian frontier the day before and bivouacked ten miles northeast of Qizil. Wearing jack-boots and Persian lamb caps they were riding in true Cossack style with short stirrups—toes down, heels up. Their small horses, loaded down with equipment looked thin and spent, but the men themselves were a hard-bitten, cheery lot of individuals, who were soon fraternizing with the Indian troopers while their officers were drinking a bottle of English rum at the 8th Brigade headquarters.

The meeting signified the end of a phase. There were no Turks east of the Diyala and Persia was clear of them. But the British-Russian nutcrackers had failed to work, since they had closed on nothing; Ali Ihsan's troops had got away and had not even been badly mauled. For this the blame lies with the Russians; they had failed in their part of the offensive, and the British in Mesopotamia could gain little comfort from rumors that a revolution in Petrograd had liberated humanity. Maude's men were concerned with smashing the Turk, not with the greater philosophical problems. They could only conclude that if the Russians had applied their steamroller tactics to drives on Mosul and Khanaqin, Ali Ihsan and Khalil would have been crippled.

Ali Ihsan's force was far from being crippled. He was now aiming for the Marl Plain and the route he had chosen followed the Khalis Canal via Delli Abbas. To help him, Khalil had transferred Shefket's Corps across the Tigris to the Shatt El Adhaim, and while the battle of Jebel Hamrin was being fought out a force of about 5,000 infantry and 500 cavalry was moving down toward Sindiya to secure Ali's flank. Realizing what was afoot, and determined to prevent Shefket and Ali joining forces at any cost, Maude now set two simultaneous operations in motion. The 7th Cavalry Brigade, already with Keary's column at Baquba was joined by the rest of the Cavalry Division and Jones the divisional commander was ordered to stop Ali moving beyond Delli Abbas. At the same time Caley's 13th Division was sent up the Tigris to deal with Shefket's column near Sindiya. Finding the Turks dug in near Dogameh, Caley attacked and what was to become known as the "Battle of the Marl Plain" ensued. Over ground which has the surface of a concrete floor, smooth as congealed toffee, and figuratively speaking hotter than "the burning Marl" that received Lucifer and his fallen host, the 39th and 40th Brigades attacked frontally. Caley's intention had been that only the 39th Brigade would make a frontal attack; this would serve to hold the Turks while the other brigade swung around and enveloped the Turks left flank. However, finding that this flank extended far beyond expectations, the 40th Brigade was also committed to a frontal assault. The strongest battalion in the brigade was the 5th Wiltshires, so they were put in to lead the attack, and of the 500 men of Wiltshire who went into the assault, nearly 200 fell before they got to the first line of advanced Turkish rifle pits. Since it was not known for certain where the main Turkish front line actually was and they had incurred so many casualties, they were now ordered to stop where they were until the other brigade's attack had had a chance to develop. Fortunately, the 9th Royal Warwicks, 7th Glosters and 7th North Staffords had more success on the 39th Brigade's sector and after some hard fighting the position fell, the Turks withdrawing to the Adhaim. For the time being a junction of the 13th and 18th Corps had been prevented and Ali Ihsan, after running into the Cavalry's block at Delli Abbas, was assumed to be retiring along the Kifri Road toward Mosul.

Having been foiled in his attempt to unite the two Corps of the 6th Army west of the Jebel Hamrin, Khalil now hoped to attain the same object further back. Reinforcements of two divisions were on their way to him together with some German airplanes, although by this time he was getting short of ammunition, supplies were running out, and the morale of Shefket's Corps was very shaky. Maude, who had appreciated these facts from Intelligence reports, was keen to take advantage of them, and anxious that the Russians should act vigorously in support of his operations. In a message to Whitehall,[4] relayed to Alexieff, who had taken over from the Grand Duke Michael as Commander-in-Chief of the Russian Army, Maude pointed out that he could not hope to operate against both Shefket and Ali Ihsan in two different directions at the same time; he had not enough transport to be able to do so. The Russians, he suggested, should deal with Ali Ihsan, while he attended to Shefket's troops.

If Maude really had hoped for any help from the Russians on these lines, such help soon proved to be a myth. The seventy thousand strong Caucasian Corps remained where it was, and in the middle of April its commander, Chernozubov resigned—excusing himself on the grounds that his men did not like him. From Persia, Baratoff bluntly answered Maude's requests for cooperation with a statement to the effect that he could do nothing, unless supplies were forthcoming for sixteen thousand men. Whitehall, passing this message back to Maude, said that on their information these numbers could safely be halved; subsequently it turned out that Baratoff only had about three thousand

---

4. Presumably by cable or wireless from Whitehall to St. Petersburg; there by shaky telegraph right across Russia, through Turkestan into Persia, despite revolutionary activities. One wonders how long it took to get to its destination.

men all told, and these were of very inferior caliber. When pressed to do something, Baratoff asserted that he had done all that was expected of him; he had cleared Persia and he was going no further. His reply was indicative of the times; the Russian revolution had had its effect and it was becoming clear that there would be no further help forthcoming from this direction. Worse still, there was every possibility that something like 200,000 prisoners captured by the Russians might be set free and that some of these would eventually be redeployed on the Mesopotamia front. In the meantime, however, Maude had decided to follow the suggestion he had put to Whitehall, and D'Urban Keary's Khanaqin Column had been ordered back to Baghdad while he prepared to deal with Shefket's troops on the Tigris. Maude's intentions were essentially aggressive; he believed in harrying the Turks whenever the opportunity presented itself. If Whitehall was correct in assuming that Baratoff would be induced by his superiors to take the offensive, his troops would be best employed in driving up the Tigris. If Whitehall was wrong, then he would still be furthering the Allied cause.

The operations which followed now had this object, and Marshall, the 3rd Corps Commander, was given the task of forcing a passage across the Adhaim as an opening gambit. By April 5, a force had been concentrated on either bank of the Tigris. Caley's 13th Division on the left bank was supplemented by a weak composite cavalry brigade. (Made up of two squadrons of the 32nd Lancers, a squadron of the Herts Yeomanry and one of the 21st Cavalry [an old Indian Frontier Force Regiment]. This force was entrusted to a dashing and ambitious staff officer from the headquarters of the 14th Division, Colonel R. A. Cassels).[5] On the right bank, near Sumaika, Fane's 7th Division, with a squadron of cavalry, 44 guns, a bridging train and a flight of the Royal Flying Corps, was waiting to advance as soon as the 13th Division were across the Adhaim. Conditions were anything but ideal for an advance and were deteriorating rapidly. The weather was getting hot and the area was infested by a plague of locusts which had spread over the countryside, leaving a desolate track in their wake and causing the Arabs by the river bank hurriedly to cut their half-ripe corn in an endeavor to save as much as they could from the voracious horde. The Tigris was in flood and it was still difficult to navigate[6] so that getting supplies up to the forward area was more than usually difficult. Yet there was nothing to be gained by delay and Marshall made his plans for a

---

5. Later, General Sir Robert Cassels, K.C.B., Commander-in-Chief, India.

6. Pilots of the boats coming up the river kept to the channel by steering along the line where vast numbers of snow-flies—akin to the English may-flies—lay over the deep channel. At this time of the year these flies covered the stream but lay thickest over deep water, so that by following the line of the most numerous flies it was possible to avoid running aground.

crossing of the Adhaim on the night of April 11. However, a report from the Cavalry Division on the previous day, to the effect that the Turks were advancing in strength from Jebel Hamrin along the Khalis Canal, gave him reason to pause and think again. Ali Ihsan was threatening his flank and prejudicing the operations up the Tigris; Maude's premonition that Baratoff's force would not contain Ali Ihsan had been justified. The cavalry were retiring slowly in front of Ali Ihsan's column but it was obvious that until this threat had been dealt with, to attempt a crossing of the Adhaim would be foolish. Putting aside his plans for the following day, Marshall turned to deal with Ali, and two brigades, the 39th and 40th, were sent across the desert to help Jones.

Meanwhile the cavalry were falling back before Ali Ihsan's infantry and the Turkish 2nd Division had started an enveloping movement designed to turn their flank in order to get in behind them. However, as the Turks swung around to close the net, Marshall's two brigades who had made a twenty mile forced night march from Adhaim suddenly appeared on the scene. Neither side was aware of the presence of the other until they actually clashed and the result was the rare experience of a true encounter battle in the open. They met near Shiala, and there was a race for the nearest rise, the one dominant piece of ground in the plain. By doubling up the ridge, the Cheshires and the Royal Welsh Fusiliers managed to reach the crest while the Turks were still six hundred yards away on the far side. At the top they lay down and opened up a steady fire against the waves of Turkish infantry, whose numbers—because of a mirage—seemed greater than they were in reality. Meantime, the Commanding Officer of the 55th Brigade R.F.A., realizing the importance of the ridge, galloped up his batteries and brought his sixteen 18-pounder guns into action at fifteen hundred yards range. This tipped the scales and as the gunners blazed away, the Turks broke and the fight developed into a running battle. Ali's men withdrew in good order but after three days hard fighting they had melted away into the foothills of the Jebel Hamrin beyond Delli Abbas, where Marshall was not prepared to follow. And so, leaving the Cavalry Division with the two infantry brigades near Arar bu Abin to watch this flank, Marshall returned to the Adhaim.

Now that his flank was clear, he could carry on with his plan for crossing the Adhaim. The place for it had already been selected by O'Dowda, a few miles from where the river flowed into the Tigris. No one supposed that getting a foothold on the far side would be easy. The Turks were holding the right bank with about two thousand men and, although the river was only about three feet deep and about ten yards wide, its quicksand bottom meant that it was safe to cross only at the fords. The stream itself meandered about in a bed about two thousand yards wide, which was about fifty feet below the general level of the plain; in most places the walls of the bed were sheer cliffs.[7] Marshall's plan was based on making the Turks believe that he intended to cross on their left flank—not a particularly difficult problem because that is what they would have expected anyway—while the real attack was to be put in between the Turks and the Tigris. This should drive them away from the water. A few miles from the river junction there was an old ford and this was selected as the site for a "demonstration" by the Loyals1 while Cassels's cavalry went off to maneuver upstream in another feint. On the night of April 17, with the Turks' attention riveted on their left flank, the two Lancashire battalions—the East Lancashires and Prince of Wales's volunteers—made a night approach march which brought them to the river bank at the lower ford without their presence being suspected. Not a casualty had been sustained and the Turks were completely unsuspicious of the menace at this point. Each company had carried a pontoon to the river and just before dawn the Lancashiremen scaled the cliff on the far side, and rushed the Turkish picquets. Then, having gained a position in the broken ground on top of the cliffs, the final assault against the Turks first line trenches was made undercover of a heavy barrage. To flash their positions to the artillery the troops were carrying pieces of metal (cut out from jam tins and worn on the back), a trick that had been learned at Gallipoli, and the gunners were able to put down a curtain of steel within a few yards of their front.

The Turks did not offer much resistance and, after a dog-fight which lasted only a few minutes, most of them threw down their rifles and, surrendered. With the bridgehead firmly established, the King's Own were ferried over— not at the original crossing point but further up the river, near the extinct bed of the Nahrwan Canal—and the sappers were able to start work on a bridge. Owing to the quicksands near the far bank having to be solidified with brushwood, the bridge took much longer to build than had been anticipated. Consequently the cavalry pursuit was delayed and Cassels, who had returned from his maneuvering, and watered and fed his horses, was stamping around impatiently waiting to get on with the next phase of the operation—rounding up the flying Turks. However, just as soon as the bridge was completed, Marshall gave him the all clear: "Now you can go," he said, "pursue as far as the outskirts of Samarra and keep between the enemy and the river." Cassels was off as hard as he could go, galloping over the soft sandy country; to return at dusk with over 700 prisoners and a considerable number of mules. To his chagrin the Turks

---

7. The ancient bed of the Nahrwan Canal, the big distributing canal of Nebuchadnezzar's time which took off from the head of the delta when Nimrod's great barrage was in existence, ran through the Turkish position. Originally this canal crossed the bed of the Adhaim over a mile long aqueduct as broad as the Suez Canal.

had got their guns away, but in spite of this his effort had been an outstanding success. Indeed, the whole action had been completely successful. At a cost of 73 casualties, over 1,200 prisoners had been taken and, allowing for killed and wounded, it could be assumed that the original Turkish force of two thousand men on the Adhaim had practically ceased to exist.

On the right bank of the Tigris, Fane's column now moved forward and on April 16, the Median Wall—an ancient ruin about thirty feet high, which lay just over three miles southeast of Istabulat station on the Baghdad railway— was in British hands. Two days later Cobbe arrived to take over command of the operations on this side of the river and Cassels, with his cavalry, was sent to join him. The next objective was Istabulat where the Turks were holding a strongly entrenched position across the Dujaila canal, covering the Samarra terminus of the railway. The canal itself "was a narrow water-course, about twenty feet deep with very steep banks, and spanned by three small bridges behind the Turkish line. The main line of Turkish trenches ran along a ridge south of the railway for about a mile, and then parallel with it in a north-westerly direction, for several miles. From these trenches the Turks could command the flat open plain across which Cobbe's troops would have to advance if they were to assault it, the key to the position being two redoubts north of the canal, standing on hillocks forty feet above the level of the plain. From the Median Wall on April 19, Cobbe sent out fighting patrols north and south of the canal and, during the night, the ground which the patrols gained was consolidated by building four strong points about four hundred yards from the Turks advanced positions and two thousand yards from their main defenses. Next morning the troops who were to assault the position were concentrated in and around them. From there, in the early morning of April 21, the 19th Brigade was to attack across the open country south of the canal while the 21st Brigade attacked along the north. On the 21st Brigade's front, the Black Watch would advance on the Dujaila Redoubt—the nearest of the two Turkish strong points to the canal—while the 1st/8th Gurkhas made for the North Redoubt; the Black Watch and Gurkhas were attacking frontally, but on their right flank the 9th Bhopals were to strike at the flank. South of the canal, a company of the 28th Punjabis (of the 19th Brigade) would advance in line with the 21st Brigade but the Seaforths who were to attack on their left, would not assault until three hours later. The plan was not so complicated as it may seem and there were sound reasons for the operation being done this way, for in deciding to stagger the timings it was Cobbe's intention to give the Turks line of retreat a bias to his left. Not only would the 21st Brigade's attack distract their attention from the more open ground which the 19th Brigade had to cross, but eventually it should have the effect of driving them away from the water and on to Cassels's cavalry.

The first move was made in the early morning of April 21, when the 92nd Punjabis successfully assaulted Istabulat Station and dug themselves in half a mile from the Turks front line. Then, soon after 6 a.m., the Black Watch and Gurkhas moved in open order across the bare plain north of the canal toward their objectives. Both were reached almost at the same moment and some stubborn fighting with no quarter given or taken now ensued. But by 6:45 a.m. the Black Watch had occupied the Dujaila Redoubt. However within a quarter of an hour the Turks had put in a heavy counterattack and reoccupied it. Once again they were evicted by the Highlanders and at 7:15 a.m. the Redoubt was again in British hands. Still the Turks were not prepared to give up. Counter-attack after counterattack was launched along the banks of the canal and it took two hours of hand-to-hand fighting, bombing and bayoneting, before the Redoubt was finally held. And, owing to some of the British guns changing their positions at the time when the first Turkish counterattack was delivered, the Black Watch was left without any effective artillery support; as a result more men were lost than need have been the case. Meanwhile, on the flank the 9th Bhopals, who had overshot their objective and come under a devastating fire from the banks of the canal had lost two hundred of their men and all but one of their officers mowed down in less than ten minutes. South of the canal the Seaforths had the easiest time, and when their attack went in shortly after 10 a.m. they were completely successful.

At 4:30 a.m. on April 22, patrols reported that the Turks were evacuating the position and this was the signal for the cavalry and the armored cars to take up the pursuit. But the Turks were not beaten yet. During the night they had retired four and a half miles northwest to another position in front of the Samarra railway station, and this they were evidently prepared to hold. As it ran along a ridge which commanded the open plain it was obvious that another bout of hard fighting was necessary before it was captured. The 28th Brigade moved up and by mid-day this brigade, fresh to the battle, had reached the ruins of old Istabulat, from where they could see the railway station and in the far distance across the undulating plain, the golden dome of the Mosque of Samarra. It was an intensely hot and sultry day and while the troops rested prior to their next trial, the ridge which was to be their objective was shelled. Cobbe's plan was to pry the Turks off the river by attacking their left, while Cassels's cavalry and the armored cars worked around their right flank.

With the 51st Sikhs following close behind, the Leicesters led in the attack during the late afternoon, and as their first waves came under heavy fire, the Sikhs swung over to the left to extend the line of advance. Heavy casualties slowed the pace of the attack and it was past midnight before the two battalions were actually in the position from which the final assault on the ridge was to be launched. Here there was a pause for a breather and a reorganization of the thinning ranks. Then soon after 1:30 a.m. a tremendous barrage crashed down on the Turkish positions and, when the guns lifted, the Leicesters and Sikhs swept forward up the slope. By the light of a full moon Shefket's men could see the gleaming bayonets of the British troops and when the assault was less than fifty yards from their trenches they were scrambling out and bolting back toward Samarra. The Leicesters, their blood up and encouraged by the sight of the Turks racing down the hill, scarcely checked at their objective and followed. A mile beyond the ridge a battery of Turkish guns were still firing and the gunners were so astonished by the sudden appearance of British troops that they offered no resistance. The battery commander, stepping out to meet the breathless company commander of the leading Leicester company, shook him by the hand and surrendered his seven guns and fifty men without further ado while on the right and left of this battery, other guns were limbering up and galloping away. So far as the Leicesters could see the Turks had had enough and they were pulling out; the obvious thing to do now was to dig in and this is what they started to do.

It was not long before the Leicesters were to pay for their precipitate, if apparently successful, performance. Shefket, hearing of the loss of his seven guns, reacted violently and the whole of his reserves were thrown in against the flank of the 28th Brigade. Two thousand men took part in the counterattack, and as they had no hope of holding them, the handful of Leicesters was compelled to fall back toward the ridge. With no means of getting the captured guns away, these had to be abandoned and in a few hours time the survivors of the original attack were grinding their teeth with chagrin at sounds which indicated that their trophies were being pulled back toward Samarra. For some time the British troops were in a ticklish situation. The impetus of the counterattack had carried the Turks back onto the ridge and it was only the 56th Punjabi Rifles and the 136th Company of the Machine Gun Corps that saved the British from losing everything that had been won in twelve hours hard fighting.[8] But while possession of the ridge was being disputed, Cassels was probing the Turkish flank, and his armored cars had even managed to get up as far as Samarra Station. Not that his maneuvering was unopposed; running into a Turkish position, the 32nd Lancers promptly charged toward the trenches and as the cavalry tore down on them me Turks occupying the trenches threw down their rifles as a gesture of surrender. Seemingly a gallant action on the part of the cavalry, it was a typical example of the risks attached to a mounted

8. In this action Lieutenant Graham of the Machine-Gunners earned his Victoria Cross.

assault against entrenched troops, for no cavalry charge in the open against riflemen had worked since 1870. The impetus of the charge had carried the troopers well beyond the forward trenches and the Turks in the reserve line were quick to react. In a clamor of machine gun fire men and horses started to fall and, seeing the Lancers in difficulties, the Turks in the forward trench picked up their rifles and opened up on them from the rear. Caught between the two lines of trenches, the Lancers extricated themselves with great difficulty and with heavy loss of life. Yet their attack was not a complete failure. Coming as it did at the very moment when the counterattack against the 28th Brigade on the ridge was having some success, it caused Shefket to look over his shoulder. If only the Lancers had been supported by the armored cars undoubtedly their wild charge would have been a complete success. They would have broken through and Shefket's flank would have gone—a fact which he was quick to appreciate. Fighting continued into the night but he had already decided that it was time for his troops to pull out.

Probably what frightened him more than anything else was one factor which has not so far been mentioned. From across the Tigris, the guns with Thompson's 35th Brigade had been supporting Cobbe's troops and had done some bloody execution. They were recalled to the Adhaim battle that night, but Shefket was worried by their presence on the left bank; if he dallied he might well find that Marshall would be in Samarra before he could get his men away through the town. Consequently on the morning of April 23, Shefket's force was retiring along the Tikrit road, leaving Samarra free to be occupied by the British. Two days fighting had cost Maude over 2,000 casualties; the Turks had left 500 dead on the field and 259 of their men had been captured, together with considerable quantities of material.

While all tins was happening on the right bank, more Turks on the left were threatening Marshall's flank on the other side of the river. The indefatigable Ali Ihsan, by dint of hard marching behind the screen of the Jebel Hamrin mountains, had transferred the bulk of his force to the Adhaim gap and was now marching down the Adhaim in a last desperate hope of saving Samarra. He arrived too late to prevent Marshall crossing the Adhaim but, by the night of April 23, his troops were digging in at Dahubu, less than twenty-five miles away from where the crossing had taken place. Ali had hoped that his presence on the Adhaim would be undetected until he was ready to attack Marshall, and to conceal his intentions a force of about two thousand men had been dropped off at Delli Abbas, to keep the Cavalry Division occupied while the main force moved against Marshall. It was a well conceived ruse but, unfortunately for Ali, one which did not work; from the ever-present Buddhoo British intelligence was getting accurate information as to his whereabouts and movements and Maude, appraised of the threat, ordered Marshall to attack and destroy the column "forthwith." The order put Marshall into a quandary. At that moment all he had available was O'Dowda's 38th Brigade—now only about 1,200 strong—and about 350 cavalry; most of his artillery was with Thomson supporting of Cobbe's attack on Istabulat. Yet it was clear that he had to do something quickly as an air reconnaissance had reported Turkish troops digging in on the right bank of the Adhaim only about twelve miles away. His decision to attack with every man he could muster consequently meant withdrawing Thomson from Cobbe's battle.

From the map, it appeared that there was a broad deep nullah running down to the Adhaim about a mile from where the Turks had been seen and, as this seemed to be as good a concentration area as any other, Marshall ordered Thompson to make a compass march on it, timing his arrival for daybreak next morning. At the same time Caley was instructed to send up Lewin's 40th Brigade and as much of the 14th Division's artillery as Caley could spare from Deltawa; they were to join Marshall next day some five miles upstream of the advanced Turkish position which was the point he estimated he would have reached. At 9 p.m. on April 23, Marshall set off with O'Dowda's Brigade, walking at the head of the column with the brigade commander. Nothing untoward occurred until just before dawn when lights, which were taken to be the fires of an Arab encampment, were seen ahead. In the first glimmer of dawn however, when Turkish soldiers could be seen silhouetted against the sky and machine guns opened up, this illusion was soon dispelled; the brigade had walked straight into the Turkish positions. Surprise was mutual and the battle broke with sudden abruptness. Fortunately, as the Loyals advanced due east toward the Turks, the dust raised by Thompson's marching infantry could be seen coming up on the left flank. Marshall now had two weak infantry brigades at his disposal.

The Turks had also seen the dust and when a concerted attack was put in against them they hurriedly withdrew across the Adhaim. None of Marshall's infantry was capable of taking up the pursuit and so the cavalry was sent on to harry them while he rested and reorganized his reunited force. But next day Marshall was on the move again and the Turks were found to be holding a position on both banks of the river near what was locally called Band-i-Adhaim—the "Gate of the Adhaim"—not far from the foothills of the Jebel Hamrin. Here, thirty-six miles from its mouth, the Adhaim degenerated into a small stream which meandered in a bed two or three thousand yards wide, bordered by cliff-like banks, thirty feet or more high; in the middle of the river was a large island, and about a mile beyond this island the cliffs of the right bank of the Adhaim jut out into its bed in the shape of a boot. On the irregular mound of this "boot" lay the center of the Turkish position. To the left of it, a line of trenches ran back toward a hill for about four thousand yards; on the right, the Turks had dug other trenches which ran across the river bed and over the banks circling Band-i-Adhaim village and effectively screened their left flank. The whole position covered about seven or eight miles of front and from it the Turks had a wide field of fire over an almost level plain. As on other occasions Ali Ihsan had selected ground for the defence which would give his troops every advantage.

The battle of Band-i-Adhaim, or "The Boot" as it was called, which was fought on April 30, turned out to be the bloodiest action in Mesopotamia—if the losses in proportion to the force engaged are counted. Having closed up to the position, Marshall moved the 38th Brigade out to the northeast at dusk on April 29; at daybreak the main attack was launched covered by all his artillery. At 5 a.m., as dawn broke, two battalions of the 40th Brigade, the Cheshires and the South Wales Borderers, started their advance. After five months of continuous fighting the strength of the Cheshires had dwindled to 330—this in spite of the reinforcements they had received and the South Wales Borderers went into action only 340 strong; by the end of the day the Cheshires had been reduced to 204 and the South Wales Borderers to 137. The objectives of the two battalions lay on either side of the empty, mud-hut village which stood on the high banks of the stream, and the Cheshires on the left drove the Turks out of their line at the point of the bayonet; on the right, where the trenches had suffered heavy punishment from the British barrage the Turks surrendered en masse to the Borderers. And it was at this point that things started to go wrong. Elated at their initial success, both battalions now swept on for nearly two miles, overrunning the Turkish second line at which they were supposed to halt and consolidate. With their blood up, the Turks seemingly on the run, and two batteries of guns in front of them, this was too good an opportunity to miss. By 6:30 a.m. the guns had been captured, and three hundred prisoners taken. Then the weather took a hand in the battle and a sudden dust storm completely obscured the landscape to shut out the whole scene. The "fog of war" had descended with a vengeance and Ali Ihsan, always an opportunist, quickly turned the situation to his advantage. Realizing that the Cheshires and South Wales Borderers would be disorganized and that they could expect no support from their artillery in the blinding dust, he brought the whole of his reserves across the river; wheeled, moved across the front of the 38th Brigade, invisible in the fog, and struck at the remnants of the two battalions with a force which outnumbered the British by six to one. The result could never have been in doubt; seven of his eight guns were recaptured, the majority of the prisoners recovered, and 150 British soldiers taken. What was left of the combined force of Cheshires and Borderers was driven back through the village until the pursuing Turks were held up by the fire of the remainder of the 40th Brigade, now moving up in support. The storm abated about 4 p.m. but by that time Ali Ihsan had made good his retreat into the mazes of the Jebel Hamrin; once more he had got away.

This was the last engagement until the British offensive was renewed in the autumn. For the time being Ali's force had been immobilized and Marshall's men, who had lost heavily in this final engagement, were not much better off. Having almost fought themselves to a standstill, the hot season—that period which runs from May until September in Mesopotamia and which to the British, signified the "close season" for the Turks—brought to both sides a welcome lull in the operations.

The Mesopotamian summer in 1917 turned out to be more severe than those of the two previous years; it was according to the people of Baghdad, "the hottest season in the memory of man." As the weeks passed the temperature steadily rose; by July official thermometers in Baghdad were showing 123° and, as tents and dug-outs were often as much as ten degrees higher man this, it will be appreciated that conditions were anything but pleasant. Even in May the temperature in Samarra was reaching 110° and the troops were still clad in their winter uniforms of thick serge. For British, Indians, and Turks alike, the enemy now was the sun, the dust and the flies. Every day was a period of burning torment, by 8 a.m. the sun's glare was unbearable and by mid-day it was a fireball in the heavens. Only the cool nights brought relief and the troops "aestivated" just as the old Romans had hibernated. Battle casualties in Maude's force had been about eighteen thousand, out of a total fighting strength of about forty-five thousand—a very high percentage, although considerably less than that suffered in the four months trying to break through to Townshend at Kut. To these were now added the casualties of the climate, over thirty-seven thousand men admitted to the hospital between the middle of March and mid-April.

But the balance sheet was not all written in red. Baghdad was securely British; much of Khalil's 6th Army had been destroyed; Kut, Baghdad and Samarra had all been captured and the road to Persia was open. The objectives of driving back Khalil's force, disorganized after the battle for Baghdad, preventing Ali Ihsan joining forces with it, and seeing Samarra had been attained and—what was vital to the security of Baghdad—the areas from which the countryside of the province could be flooded had been secured. The troops, sweltering in their tents and trenches, were hoping that the war would have been won on other fields before a new campaigning season opened in September.

Chapter 19

Winter 1917: A New Offensive and the Death of General Maude

Although there was very little fighting during the summer months of 1917 it became increasingly clear, as the months slipped past, that not only was peace still a long way off, but also that the future might well contain some difficult moments for the Mesopotamian Army. What was happening in Russia was extremely disturbing, and Intelligence sources in Turkey reported a new Turco-German force assembling at Aleppo. Enver Pasha was obsessed with the idea of recapturing Baghdad, and in his resolve the Germans saw a chance to resuscitate their own aims of an Eastern Empire. British prestige would suffer a severe set back if Baghdad were recaptured, an invasion of Persia could follow and, now that the Russians were faltering, all old plans for German domination of the East could be dusted off, ready for use. Here was a fine new opportunity to break the impasse on the Western Front and the men in Berlin were sufficiently enthusiastic to set aside five million pounds worth of gold for its backing.

An impressive name does not of itself make an impressive army and the "Yilderim Group"—Thunderbolt Group—as the new force was called, was not particularly impressive, even on paper. But the Germans felt that an army on which grand hopes were based deserved a grand title, and there is a

Wagnerian ring of threatening portent about the name thunderbolt. Two Turkish infantry divisions, stiffened by a contingent of the German Asiatic Corps, comprising three infantry battalions supported by machine gun companies, mortars and artillery batteries, made up the Group. Compared with the numbers of Turks, the German contingent of fighting men was small but— according to Ludendorff—they were picked men who would serve to provide the Yilderim's backbone. Command was given to a German general, von Falkenhayn, and other Germans filled all the key staff and command appointments—a situation that was bound to lead to friction sooner or later.

Early in June, von Falkenhayn reported to Enver Pasha—and presumably to the German High Command at the same time—that an operation to recapture Baghdad was now practicable, and his staff was told that the Yilderim would march down the Euphrates when everything was ready. The Group would concentrate at Hit prior to an attack against the British left flank which would sever Maude's line of communications to Baghdad. But no offensive was possible for at least six months, since success would depend on von Falkenhayn's own line of communications. The railway to Baghdad had not yet been completed and until trains from Aleppo could run through to Mosul the supplies needed for the operations could not be assured. The trouble was that the tunnels through the Taurus and Amanus mountains had not been completed and to complete them by December would be a Herculean task. Nevertheless, von Falkenhayn reckoned that it could be done, and the German railway engineers set about trying to meet his target date with the usual Teutonic thoroughness and zeal. They failed because the work necessitated wholehearted Turkish cooperation, and temperament alone made the Germans and Turks incompatible bedfellows. Furthermore British successes in Palestine had changed the whole strategic picture in the Middle East. In November the Turks holding the Beersheba-Gaza line were fleeing for the hills around Jerusalem and von Falkenhayn, who had had second thoughts about Baghdad, was trying to persuade Enver that the Yilderim could be used to far better effect in Palestine. It was not that von Falkenhayn was against the principle of attacking Baghdad and an offensive drive into Persia; the underlying reasons for such an offensive were still valid. But he considered that German interests could now be better served, and more expeditiously, in another part of the Ottoman Empire. Prospects for a German take-over of Arabia and Syria seemed brighter than those of any expedition down the Euphrates. As he told Mustafa Kemal, when asked to explain his intriguing activities designed to enlist Arabs to the German cause, he was "a German before anything else." Enver was still obsessed with Baghdad and wanted to stick to the original plan, but von Falkenhayn had already written it off. In the welter of arguments which raged between the

German, who openly declared that he was a patriot first and an ally second, and the Turk, who had done so much to put his country into Germany's clutches in the first place, the threat to Baghdad evaporated. The Yilderim never operated in Mesopotamia and all the preparations made for it to do so only served to develop the growing friction between the two allies.

Meantime, however, the Germans were trying to finish the railway and to build up supply dumps along the proposed line of advance down the Euphrates. At the same time considerable improvements were being made in the British communication system. By the end of July the meter-gauge railway from Kut to Baghdad had been completed, as had narrow gauge lines between Baghdad and Baquba, and Sumaika to Sindiya. A meter gauge line from Qurna to Kut was under construction; other lines from Baghdad to Falluja and Musaiyeb, and an extension of the old Turkish line beyond Samarra were also being planned. Roads had been built, floods controlled and river transport had increased to such an extent that daily deliveries to Baghdad often exceeded two thousand tons of supplies. A measure of the development of the administrative machine may be deduced from the fact that in July 1916—only a year previously—it had been a struggle to land three hundred tons daily at Sheikh Sa'ad, and Sheikh Sa'ad was less than half the distance of Baghdad from Basra. At Basra, where more wharves and facilities for ships at Nahr Umar, twelve miles beyond the town, had also been built, the whole region had been so transformed that any of the original I.E.F. "D" languishing in prison camps in Anatolia would have been utterly astounded by the developments.

Maude himself was not unduly worried by reports of the Yilderim Army and he was dubious about any advance down the Euphrates. If von Falkenhayn were to attack in Mesopotamia it was Maude's view that the Yilderim would concentrate at Mosul and then advance through the fertile country to the east, via Kirkuk, to Baquba, along a route where local supplies would be obtainable. To Maude, by far the most worrying problem was that which the Russians had created. After the meeting with the Cossacks, it will be recalled that the "Khanaqin Column" had fallen back on Baquba, and that Baratoff had been left to look after the Persian end of the Dujaila. Early in June however, Baratoff withdrew to Kermanshah, leaving a military vacuum on the Persian frontier—a situation of which Ali Ihsan was quick to take advantage. It was not that he had given up, Baratoff declared, merely that he was not able to feed his troops in the forward area. Perhaps he believed his equivocation, but as he never contributed anything further to the campaign, Baratoff had given up. Flowery promises of future Russian operations came to Maude's headquarters during the course of the summer by various members of his staff, but nothing ever came of them. The Russians remained in Persia, living off a country which could ill provide for their needs, but they did nothing useful. They were rapidly becoming more of a liability than an asset, as was forecast in a message from their British military liaison officer:

> British gold may help the Russians in Persia but it will not make them fight. The old Russian Army is dead, quite dead. Our efforts, therefore, to resuscitate it, stand useless.

The message only confirmed Maude's suspicions that he could not count on any concerted action with the Russians. His difficulty was that Baratoff's supineness had left the field open for the Turks, and from their Jebel Hamrin eyrie, Ali Ihsan's men were moving down into the Russian created vacuum, to cut the Khanaqin road and edge down the Diyala toward Sharaban. Maude was not prepared to tolerate the loss of Sharaban. Egerton's 14th Division advanced from Baquba, and as a counter-measure after an interval of six weeks, occupied Sharaban. Air reconnaissances had reported that Turks were digging in southwest of the town and Egerton had expected to have to fight for it. However, when the British troops were seen to be converging on them Ali Ihsan's men melted away back to the relative safety of their hill positions in the Jebel Hamrin. So far as the British were concerned the capture of Sharaban was bloodless success—a hard march but no battle.

The only operation during the hot weather of 1917 in which both marching and fighting were necessary, was the attack on Ramadi in July; and, as it was the first serious attempt that had been made to use motorized infantry[1] in this theater, it is particularly interesting. After Falluja the Turks had withdrawn up the Tigris to Ramadi, where about a thousand men with 6 guns were occupying positions covering the Madhij Defile, eighteen miles west of Falluja. Maude decided to attack, primarily because work on the Sakhlawiya dam was a prerequisite of the flood protection scheme, and to safeguard the working parties meant occupying Dhibban twenty miles south of Ramadi, which in turn, suggested a need to evict the Turks from Ramadi. Getting troops up to a position from which an attack could be launched was the main problem. A force could be collected at Dhibban by easy stages, but from there the infantry would face a twenty mile march. In the intense heat marching was an agonizing hardship, even at night, and for this reason it was decided to rely on a measure of mechanization. By using vehicles to ferry the troops up to the position from which they could attack, it was hoped that they would arrive reasonably fresh

---

1. The need for a permanently organized force of motorized infantry to exploit the gains of armored cars had come about as the result of the first attempt to seize Baquba. Armored cars which had preceded the lorry-borne infantry were unable to drive off the combined detachments of Shefket and Ali Ihsan and in the interval between their action and the arrival of the infantry, the bridge across the Diyala had been destroyed.

and unaffected by the heat. Two squadrons of cavalry, 14 horse-drawn guns, two sections of Light Armored Motor Batteries (LAMBS), half a company of Sappers and Miners and the 7th Infantry Brigade, were assembled as a striking column, and three airplanes detailed to cooperate with it. The 127 Ford vans and lorries available were capable of lifting 600 men at a time, and it was planned to move the column at night, to take tents for shelter against the sun during the day, and for ice to be carried for the immediate treatment of heat stroke. Time was to show that all these precautions would be needed, since thermometers in Baghdad on the day selected for the attack read 160° in the sun and 122° inside a tent. In two days the force was concentrated at Dhibban and the staff in Baghdad was confidently predicting that as soon as the Turks got wind of the attack, Ramadi would be evacuated. The cavalry and armored cars moved out early in the evening of July 8, and, except for a small detachment remaining to hold Dhibban, were followed by the rest of the force. The Madhij Defile was reached and occupied without incident by midnight and the cavalry was approaching the outskirts of Ramadi about sunrise; opposition came only when the rearguard started to move through the gardens along the river bank just outside the town. There, a combination of bad going, Turkish artillery fire and the canal, brought the advance to a rude halt. Reinforcements were rushed up but a dust storm, which interrupted communications and prevented the gunners seeing their targets, together with a heavy toll of casualties, resulted in an abortive attack. Battle casualties were severe enough but, as the day wore on, the heat caused almost as many losses and it was soon appreciated that the Turks had never had any serious intention of evacuating their positions. Consequently, under the cover of darkness that night the British withdrew to the river bank, completely exhausted and incapable of further efforts. Total casualties amounted to 566, of which 321 had been caused by the heat—some men dying of heat stroke, some of thirst, and others going mad.[2] On July 14, the withdrawal was continued to Dhibban and although the Turks did nothing to impede the retirement, about fifteen hundred Buddhoos repeatedly attacked the British rearguard. The expedition had achieved nothing and the moral to be drawn from it was that only the very gravest military urgency justified any offensive in the height of the Mesopotamian summer.

The Royal Flying Corps tried to keep flying during the summer months but, like the ground troops, its activities were restricted by the heat. In Basra, a few days of the heat and humidity soon played havoc with the unclimatized airmen of 63 Squadron which arrived during August, and the wooden frames of

---

2. No doubt many who succumbed died of heat exhaustion. At that time there was no understanding of the need to replace the salt lost to the body through perspiration; the reason why wild animals went daily to salt licks had not yet been appreciated.

new airplanes—RE 8s[3] and Spad Fighters—shrank. Many of them were rebuilt, but accidents resulting from their disintegrating in flight continued for some months. Invariably such accidents were fatal for these were the days before parachutes (the only people who had them were the observers in observation balloons). In spite of difficulties, however, the RFC prepared for the future and as crews recovered and aircraft were pronounced safe to fly, 63 Squadron flew up to the Samarra front, to engage in routine reconnaissance and air-photography from which maps could be prepared for the next advance.

South of Falluja the country was penetrated without opposition as far as Hilla and Musaiyeb, and political officers were sent into the great desert shrines of the Shilah at Karbala, Najaf and Kadhimain. The district was almost clear of Turks but it was not until the cold weather that communications were established between Hilla and Nasiriyeh. Here and there small Turkish garrisons still held out though usually not for long; either they abandoned their posts and took to flight when supplies ran low, or surrendered to the locals. One such post at Diwanya, south of Baghdad, did not give up until the end of the summer but this was unusual. Some of the garrison surrendered to the locals during July but one officer and thirty men, Tartars from the Caucasus, held on stubbornly.

To police the roads, villages and towns now under British control Arab levies were raised and gradually the country was cleared of the marauding bands of Buddhoos, whose hey-day was now past. Work on an irrigation scheme connected with the Hindiya barrage was also started. Not only would this help to provide more food for the invading army, it would also be a valuable post-war asset. Those responsible for the political aspects of the campaign had an eye to the future, and if Britain was going to administer the country after the war the scheme promised tremendous economic benefit. The earlier experiences of the campaign had shown the importance of local supply and this knowledge was accentuated by the difficulties consequent on the German submarine campaign taking its toll of British shipping. This barrage, designed by Sir William Willcox and constructed by the British firm of Sir John Jackson as the basis of a great cultivation scheme, had been finished before the war but under the Turks the vast area to be brought under cultivation had never been irrigated. At Hindiya, the Euphrates divides into two branches—the Shatt-al-Hilla on the east, and the Shatt-al-Hindiya to the west—the two channels joining up a few miles above Samawa. Until the nineteenth century the Shatt-al-Hilla constituted the main channel, but sometime during this

---

3. Called by the RFC "Harry Tates" in accordance with rhyming slang, and after a popular music hall comedian of the day.

period the bulk of the river was diverted into the Hindiya off-shoot which, in point of fact, had been the main channel more than a thousand years previously. It was to re-divert some of the waste Hindiya water back to the Hilla channel, which had been silting up over the years since the barrage had been built. The actual barrage had been completed before the war, but the Hilla irrigation channels had never been developed. As soon as these were dug out, three hundred thousand acres of hitherto unproductive desert came under cultivation, and the summer of 1918 saw the greatest harvest in this part of the world since the days of Nebuchadnezzar. The Shatt-al-Hilla development was only part of a much greater ploughshare scheme, however, and in May, as soon as the Tigris operations were completed, irrigation schemes throughout the length of that part of the Euphrates which was under British control were put in hand, labor being provided by the locals and direction by the British. During the hot weather the work was delayed by the gap in the communications between Nasiriyeh and Hilla but once this was bridged the administration of the whole country from Basra to Baghdad became increasingly effective. Because it brought profit to them, the Arab cultivators welcomed the land development schemes brought by the administrators; because they resulted in enough grain being grown to feed Maude's army, their military benefits also were far reaching. By utilizing local supplies, the tonnage of foodstuffs on the lines of communication was reduced and this freed rolling-stock and river transport for other supplies as well as effecting a much needed economy in overseas shipping.

But not all the local produce was going to the British. Some of it, grown in the lower Euphrates region, was getting through to the Turks by routes which converged on Ramadi and until this place was occupied by Maude's troops it was apparent that there could be no effective British blockade of foodstuffs from the south. Once Ramadi was in British hands however, the desert road to Karbala would be cut and the Turks' source of supplies denied to them. But apart from the fundamentally administrative reasoning, Maude now had a sound tactical basis for seizing Ramadi—the threat of the Yilderim Group. Furthermore, with two new divisions[4] added to his Order of Battle he was in a stronger position than at the beginning of the summer. The decision to capture Ramadi was taken in the middle of September and the task was given to Brooking, commanding the 15th Division, recently formed by amalgamating the units which had been garrisoning the Nasiriyeh district since 1916. Always,

---

4. The 15th Division, under command of Major General Sir H. T. Brooking, had already been formed from units in Mesopotamia, and Major General W. Gillman's 17th Division, was in the process of forming. The advance elements of a third division, the 18th, had also arrived in Mesopotamia but it was not ready until the end of the year.

it seemed, there were excellent reasons for reaching out further and further into Mesopotamia. In this case two other factors served to reinforce the primary argument for an attack on Ramadi. First, the town was a convenient center from which to control the desert tribes—and this, it appears, was always a good subsidiary reason for any advance. Secondly, at Ramadi, the Habbaniya "escape" takes off; this escape enabled the flood waters of the Euphrates to be diverted into the storage reservoir provided by the Habbaniya depression and so it had considerable importance in the irrigation schemes. But these were subsidiary reasons; Maude's prime aim was to smash the Turk whenever he could do so.

Brigadier General A. W. Andrew's 50th Brigade,[5] which had been holding Falluja, was joined there by the rest of Brooking's division which marched up from Baghdad. By September 20, Brooking had established outposts forward of Madhij eighteen miles west of the town and he had learned from Arab agents and air reconnaissance reports that the Turks were dug in along the Muskaid Ridge, a low line of sand dunes between the Euphrates and Lake Habbaniya. This was their forward line of defenses; the main position was about a mile further on, just south of Ramadi itself. His plan followed what seems to have been the popular Mesopotamian pattern, a frontal attack from the south, while the 6th Cavalry Brigade made a wide outflanking detour to the west, to cut the Aleppo road two or three miles beyond the town. Tactically it was soundly based. With no bridge across the Euphrates at Ramadi, the Turks were fighting with their backs to the river. If they could be hemmed in, the garrison had only two alternative escape routes, swimming the river, or smashing a way through the cavalry block. Though it may seem odd, the idea of being cut off had never occurred to them. Lack of water away from the river, and the consequent difficulties entailed in getting it to a force operating on their southern or right flank, together with their experience of the attack in July had led them to believe that a fresh attack would repeat the previous tactics. If so, the British would seize the Muskaid Ridge and then work methodically along the river banks; it was for an attack of this nature that their defenses had been organized and their trenches covered an arc, east from the river to the south. If the situation became really difficult they counted on being able to fall back along the Aleppo road toward Hit. It was miscalculating Brooking's ability to supply his troops with water by means of his Ford vans that led to their undoing. Nor, apparently, did they see through the deception created by ostentatious preparations at Madhij since all these—a pontoon bridge, dumps of supplies, and troop movements—lent color to their own pre-

---

5. Then comprising the 6th Jats, 14th Sikhs, 24th Punjabis, and 97th Infantry.

conceived ideas of the direction of a British attack.

Brooking's assaulting force moved out of Madhij during the night of September 22. With Dunsford's 12th Brigade on the right and Lucas's 42nd Brigade on the left, the infantry made straight for the Muskaid Ridge, their first objective, and this was reached and occupied with very little opposition. So far everything had gone the way the Turks had expected. But then, instead of trying to force their way along the river bank both brigades swung to the left and by 3 p.m. they had reached the Euphrates Valley Canal. Meanwhile, keeping clear of the infantry engagement, Holland-Pryor's cavalry had swept around south of the Muskaid Ridge, across the Euphrates Valley and Aziziyeh Canals and by 4 p.m. they were astride the Aleppo road. Then, five miles west of Ramadi, they dismounted and started digging in for all they were worm. It was the last moment when the Turks might have found a way out, for once Holland-Pryor's men were entrenched, they were cornered. Their only chance then would have been to counterattack and breakthrough the cavalry cordon, before Brooking tightened the ring and they were pounded out of the trenches by the British guns. But the opportunity slipped by and with the road blocked, Brooking's infantry now started to close in toward the town. On the right, the 42nd Brigade attacked Ramadi Ridge while the 12th Brigade, which had been pulled back, swung west behind the 42nd, and worked around to Aziziyeh Ridge. Neither ridge offered much cover, and the advance of the 5th and 6th Gurkhas and the Dorsets up the long pebbled gradient of Ramadi Ridge had to be made in the teem of heavy machine gun and rifle fire from the top, and through a hail of bursting shrapnel from Turkish artillery sited on their left front. Despite casualties the Ridge was taken, and by nightfall the British were holding the Turks on the south and southeast between the two canals, while the cavalry was firmly entrenched astride the only road out of the town.

By now the Turks were alive to their peril and an attempt to break out of the trap came soon after 3 a.m. A column of Turkish infantry tried to force its way through Holland-Pryor's positions between the road and the river bank but was stopped by machine guns, adeptly handled by men of the 14th Hussars, the few Turks who did manage to get through were rounded up next day by cavalry, patrols and armored cars reconnoitering up the road toward Hit. This action continued until dawn (September 29) and in daylight it was obvious that Brooking's plan had succeeded; the Turks were well and truly trapped. During the morning the 12th Brigade resumed its attack on the Aziziyeh Ridge and despite heavy fire and repeated counterattacks the 39th Garhwalis, 90th Punjabis and the Queen's carried the last outlying defenses, and then pushed on to clear the Shaikh Faraja Ridge. The only means the Turks had of getting out of the slowly tightening net now lay across a bridge over the Aziziyeh Canal, a thousand yards from this last ridge. To break out, they would have to get their guns and wheeled transport across the bridge, and once this bridge was in British hands, the fish was in the net. So-, the Aziziyeh bridge was assigned to the Garhwalis as their next objective and the little hill men from the Nepal border charged across open ground from the Shaikh Faraja Ridge toward it. As they ran, three Turkish guns, firing over open sights at almost point-blank range poured shrapnel into their ranks and for every Indian who got through, two fell. But they captured the bridge—and the guns—and when the guns had ceased firing the three assaulting companies were barely a hundred strong. Though they were unaware of it at the time, behind the mud walls of the town in front of them were two thousand Turks.

The Garhwalis élan did more than carry their objective. Ahmed Bey, the Turkish Commander, had served on the Euphrates front since the battle of Shaiba, and he had concluded that they were but the advanced sections of a much greater force; such a spectacular charge could only be made with the absolute confidence that comes from knowing the odds are heavily weighted in favor of the attack—or so he thought. The battle was over, the garrison finished. White flags appeared on the walls, and before long the Turks were trooping out of the town to make their way to captivity. Practically the whole of the garrison was captured; 3,545 prisoners, of whom 145 were officers, 13 guns, much ammunition and considerable quantities of equipment were taken. Only a detachment of cavalry and a few infantrymen, who succeeded in swimming the Euphrates, escaped. West of the town a deep nullah was strewn with litter—saddles, weapons and all the other impedimenta of war; there also was a great herd of sorry-looking horses and mules, left behind at the last moment when the attempt to break-through the 6th Cavalry Brigade's cordon had failed. During the day a German aircraft flew over and was on the point of landing at Ramadi when the pilot suddenly realized that there had been a change in occupation and flew off. The news of the defeat had not yet reached the Turkish higher command; when it did it came as an unpleasant and unexpected shock. Fearing reprisals if the Turks ever managed to reoccupy the Baghdad province, the Arabs north of Falluja had been openly hostile toward the British after their ineffectual operation against Ramadi in July. But after this success they decided that the British had come to stay and that it would pay them to cooperate with the new masters. Everything, in fact, suggested that it was the right time to exploit success in this part of the country, and Brooking decided to strike at the next Turkish stronghold up the Euphrates without delay. What he proposed was a raid on the biblical city of Hit, a town which occupied the same relative position on the Euphrates as Tikrit on the Tigris seventy miles to the east, and which is famous for its bitumen wells. Here also

the Euphrates leaves its rocky bed and emerges into the alluvial plain of Mesopotamia. A desert road, which linked the Turkish forces on the Euphrates with
those on the Tigris, connected Tikrit with Hit, so that this town represented
another start-point for further operations; once again were the British being
lured on by the advantages of somewhere further up the road. A few days
elapsed before the raiding party could be assembled but, by October i, a
motorized column of 365 men of the Dorsetshire Yeomanry and 24 officers
and men of the Royal Engineers had been collected. The striking force was to
be carried in Ford vans; four armored cars, which would protect the column en
route, and several heavy motor ambulances were to accompany it. In the late
evening the convoy moved off and no sooner was it on its way than there was
trouble. No one had anticipated that the going would be so slow, nor that the
road would have to be repaired; because the convoy was moving without
lights, the guides repeatedly lost direction and the heavy, clumsy motor ambulances slowed the pace of the lighter and more maneuverable personnel-
carrying vans. To have had any real chance of success, surprise was essential
but when dawn broke on October 2, and the raiders were still five miles short
of Hit with all chance of surprise gone, the commander of the force decided to
turn back. Lack of experience and foresight had resulted in both this raid on
Hit and the first attack on Ramadi being failures; the plain fact was that nobody
knew how to handle motorized columns. For Ramadi, the vehicles were merely
used to ferry the troops to the forward area, but the raid on Hit was a
deliberately planned action by a mechanized force and no one had given any
thought to the state of the road or stopped to consider the different
mechanical properties of heavy and light vehicles. Any hastily organized force
is apt to fail because of the unforeseen eventuality, and this is particularly so
with mechanical equipment. Improvised columns of mechanized transport
have no better chance of success in a difficult mission than a force of infantry
suddenly mounted on horses or camels might have; for the raid on Hit, a
smaller force of armored cars and vans would probably have provided a more
powerful and flexible instrument which would have stood a better chance of
success. Wisdom comes easily after the event, and at least it is true to say that
the British were learning by their failures, and the staff was already evolving an
improved organization for the use of motorized transport in Mesopotamia.

The next move was made on the Diyala front, where Marshall had been
concentrating the greater part of his Corps with the intention of clearing the
Turks out of the Jebel Hamrin. With Sharaban already occupied, Maude's plan
was for Marshall to seize the pass through the Jebel Hamrin on the left bank of
the Diyala and to occupy Mendali—a town on the Persian frontier lying southeast of Sharaban and roughly thirty miles due east of Balad Ruz, famous for the

excellence of its dates. Mendali was under the influence of a local potentate with the comic opera title of "Wali of Pusht-i-Kuh" and, although the Wali had not actually committed himself, he was known to have strong leanings toward Turkey and Germany, largely through the influence of a German doctor; for this reason Maude considered that it was desirable to impress on the Wali that the British had come to Mesopotamia and proposed to stay. For the operation, Marshall had the 13th and 14m Divisions, and the 7m Cavalry Brigade, now under command of Brigadier General Norton. On the night of October 18, the cavalry was sent off on a forced march from Balad Ruz, to cut off and capture the small Turkish garrison in Mendali while Egerton, leaving the Thompson's 35th Brigade at Sharaban, marched the 36th and 37th Brigades due east, toward the eastern end of the mountain range. All went according to plan; Mendali was occupied and at dusk the following evening Norton's cavalry trotted up the road from Mendali, around the north side of the Jebel Hamrin, toward Qizil Robat. There, it was presumed, they would be across the Turks' line of retreat when Egerton attacked their positions in the hills. Meanwhile Egerton was still marching east toward the end of the mountain range, and Thompson, also moving by night, had advanced from Sharaban to the Ruz Canal. Having arrived at the canal in front of Ali Ihsan's positions, Thompson bridged it at three different points and men halted to await orders. What was to be attempted was a concerted converging drive on the Turks, and the 35th Brigade had to wait until the rest of the troops taking part in the operation were in position. Apart from the cavalry and the two columns of Egerton's division, Caley's 13th Division also had a part to play and his columns, advancing along the right bank of the Diyala, were closing in on Mansuriyah to provide a back-stop when Egerton's men closed the trap. At daybreak on October 20, it was sprung; Egerton's infantry moved westward along the ridge, and Thompson advanced frontally to meet them. But the pincers closed on thin air; the quarry had fled—not toward Qizil Robat and the waiting cavalry either, but across the Diyala. The river was very low at this time of the year and most of the Turks got across the gorge, safely away through the fastnesses of the northwestern section of the mountain range and out along the Qara Tepe Road. Next day parties of them were seen by the scouting aircraft of the Royal Flying Corps, scurrying north.

Metaphorically a hammer had been used to swat a fly and the fly had gotten away; consequently Marshall's bag was small. Nevertheless, in dislodging Ali Ihsan from a very strong position, much had been achieved at a negligible cost, since only three casualties had been incurred. The Sakaltutan Pass, through which the Delli Abbas-Qara Tepe Road ran was still held by the Turks, but the Jebel Hamrin on the left bank of the Diyala was now completely clear. And, since Mansuriyah had been occupied, the British could control the height of water in the four main canals carrying the waters of the Diyala south of this point. To evict the Turks from the Sakaltutan Pass might now appear as a desirable objective, but an attack in the muddle of hills in which they were entrenched would undoubtedly have incurred a large number of casualties and so, for the time being, they were allowed to stay.

On this front the troops now enjoyed a few weeks welcome break. The Turks were mostly out of harms way and, after the drab and featureless table-land around Baghdad, the rocky gorge of the Diyala and the sandstone rocks of the Jebel Hamrin were a pleasant break. There was plenty of game—partridge, snipe and duck—for those who had the means and ability to shoot. Fishing was easier; there was plenty of fish in me river and in the absence of rods, grenades would always ensure a good haul. The countryside was delightful and for a few brief weeks it was almost an idyllic existence, described by a Scots-man as "a bit of the auld country," by a South African as "like somewhere on the Basuto frontier," and by a New Zealander simply as "home." There was even wild pig for the cavalry to stick and doubtless the thoughts of those who had known the joys of pre-war soldiering in India, drifted back to the pleasant days among the Simla hills, when the officers shot and fished, played polo and cricket, and danced at the club, while the men—the "soldier-Sahibs—walked about in their scarlet coats. But that was another world, far removed from the Jebel Hamrin. The old days had gone, never to return, and most of the men who had known them were either dead and buried along the Tigris, or languishing in Anatolia as "guests" of the Sultan.

Life was not so pleasant on the Tigris front, nor so peaceful. In the middle of October Khalil's men moved forward from Tikrit and dug in eight miles north of Samarra. Cobbe, whose troops were guarding this front, was uncertain whether this move presaged a new Turkish offensive and when airplanes were sent to reconnoiter, the reports which came back seemed to indicate that the Turks had been heavily reinforced. Islands in the Tigris were reported to be "packed with the enemy" although it transpired afterward that what the un-trained observers had taken to be masses of Turks were flocks of sheep. Cobbe was not to know this, however, and to meet the threat he asked Maude to send up the Cavalry Division and began to concentrate his own Corps; while he was doing so, the Turks retired as suddenly as they had come. This was another opportunity which seemed too good to miss and Maude ordered Cobbe to cut off the Turks before they got back to Tikrit.

Cobbe set off, following up along both banks of the river, and it soon became clear that the Turks had no intention of being caught as they had been at Ramadi. After a brisk action against the 21st Brigade at Daur, twenty miles beyond Samarra, they successfully eluded the encircling British cavalry, retired to their positions in front of Tikrit where, in an elaborate trench system, seven miles in circumference whose ends rested on the river, they doubtless felt relatively secure. On the morning of November 5, Cobbe launched his attack; the first assault being delivered on the center of the Turkish position by the 8th Brigade shortly before noon. On the right the 59th Rifles, and on the left the 47th Sikhs, with the 124th Baluchis in support, advanced over a thousand yards with great dash to capture the Turks' first line of trenches. Then the Manchesters went in and for three hours they were heavily engaged in some sticky fighting while the complicated warren of trenches was cleared. Twice during this period the Turks counterattacked and were driven off. Then the Seaforths and the 125th Napier's Rifles were thrown into the battle on the left of the Manchesters, and when the Turks saw the familiar tartan of the Highlanders advancing toward them they either threw up their hands or scrambled over the parados of their trenches and bolted. They were not prepared to wait for the bayonets of "Abu Reish"—the Father of the Feather—the name by which the Black Watch and Seaforths were known to them and the Arabs.

But the battle was not over; as the Seaforths and 125th Napier's Rifles swept on to carry the Turks' second line of trenches, they came under fire from their left—opposite where dismounted patrols of the 13th Hussars had been containing the Turks' flank throughout the day. Seeing this as one of the rare moments for a mounted action the order was given for two squadrons of the Hussars and a squadron of the 13th Lancers to mount, draw swords and prepare to charge. Jumping the trenches to gallop in at the point, and scattering the Turks who were fleeing from the Seaforths and 125th Napier's Rifles, the cavalrymen charged to where wire prevented them going any further, a thousand yards beyond the front line. Wheeling about they then covered their withdrawal by dismounted action. Like the charge at Lajj and that of the 32nd Cavalry at Istabulat, it was a magnificent affair, a splendid example of military spirit. But, in the words of the French general "It was not war," and the wisdom of Norton, the Brigade Commander who gave the order which doubtless every cavalryman dreamed of hearing in those days, can be disputed. If the charge had attained any tangible result, its advisability would be less questionable. But the Turks, demoralized by the infantry attacks in the center, were already falling back toward Tikrit where a pall of smoke was a clear indication that the destruction of their stores preceded a full scale retreat. A few snipers and outposts remained to be mopped up but early next morning Cobbe's troops were in possession of the picturesque old walled town. White flags were flying from the roofs of the buildings as they entered and a few Arabs were pilfering what little the Turks had left behind; aground in the river below the town was the old *Julnar*, the ill-fated steamer which had made the gallant but hopeless attempt to get through to the starving garrison of Kut during the Relief Force operations. There was little else, certainly no food, for it seemed that Khalil's men had been living from hand to mouth. The Turks themselves almost got clean away and only 320 prisoners were taken. In a skillful rearguard action they had made good their retreat to the Fadiah Gorge, where the Tigris cuts through the hills, and the chance of any real coup on the Tigris front was now lost.

Now, in the middle of what had seemed to be a run of British victories came a dire stroke of misfortune, for on November 18, General Maude died of cholera.

Until only four days before this tragic event he had been in perfect health and the troops in and around Baghdad were accustomed to seeing him on the morning gallops which were part of Maude's almost ritualistic keep-fit exercise program. Consequently the news that the Army Commander was seriously ill came as an intense shock. Not a man in Mesopotamia could be unaffected by the news, for he was the man who had brought the army out of chaos, salvaged the campaign for the British and led them to victory. Because so many thousands of men had already died for the Allied cause in Mesopotamia and many more were destined to make the supreme sacrifice before the war ended, perhaps any stress on Maude's death may seem out of place. No man is indispensable—least of all generals in wartime. But Maude had special qualities and his demise must be judged in the light of his accomplishments, not as a unit in the wholesale slaughter of those years. It was under his leadership and by his initiative that the battered Tigris Corps had recovered its morale and his personality influenced the whole field of operations from the Persian Gulf to the foremost outposts up the Tigris and Euphrates. When he fell sick his habits of personally controlling details of operations which are normally relegated to subordinates and of seldom confiding his plans to others now resulted in an effect analogous to the sudden shut-down in the power-house controlling a vast electrical scheme.

How he contracted the disease is something of a mystery. The idea that he might have been poisoned was pooh-poohed; nevertheless certain suspicious circumstances were present. Anonymous threats against his life had been made; in itself this was nothing unusual since threats had been made against other British notables in Baghdad, including the Military Governor, Brigadier General C. J. Hawker. About ten days before Maude's death, however, one of Hawker's staff officers deputized for his chief at some function where he partook of refreshments, served by the same contractor who provided them at the concert which Maude attended with Mrs. Eleanor Egan, a visiting

American reporter, and he died of cholera. The entertainment which Maude attended was a theatrical performance of Hamlet, played in Arabic, under the auspices of the "Alliance Israelite of Baghdad" and as it was attended by Persians, Arabs, Kurds, Syrians and Chaldeans as well as Jews there can be no sane suggestion that it was a Jewish plot. Coffee was served during the preliminary courtesies and, according to Mrs. Egan, Maude diluted his with "a large quantity of cold raw milk" while she drank hers black. Nothing untoward occurred at the party which, for Maude, concluded happily enough with the singing of a chorus in Arabic extolling the virtues of "Sir Stanley Mod." Next morning, however, he complained that he was "feeling a bit cheap" and that afternoon was told by Colonel Willcox, his doctor, to go to bed. Apparently Maude was not prepared to give up quite so easily, but eventually he was persuaded to put down his pen and retire to bed; on the evening of the third day he died.

Immediately after his death, the bazaars of Baghdad seethed with rumors that the Army Commander had been poisoned, and it was largely because of this that Marshall, on whose shoulders the command now fell, ordered an investigation. Detectives of the Civil Police spent three months trying to uncover evidence which would implicate the contractor who had provided the coffee at the concert, but at the end of that time they still had nothing which even suggested foul play. Nevertheless Marshall decided to have the contractor and his assistant deported as undesirables—a decision of which he wrote with disarming candor "I was probably, indeed almost certainly, unjust. Still, though there was no epidemic of cholera in the city, it is always endemic, and the contractor should have been particularly careful about a thing like milk on such an occasion." Willcox, the doctor, refused to accept the suggestion of anything unusual or abnormal about the circumstances of Maude's death. "There is no reason to suspect," he wrote, "that the infection of the milk was other than an accidental infection from the water of the area, which was known to be under great suspicion at the time, cholera being present in that part of the city." Marshall, it seems disregarded Willcox's testimony and acted according to his conscience and in the circumstances he can hardly be blamed. Maude was an old friend and, if there was a suspicion of murder, the British justice must be seen to be done. Unfortunately the political effect of the deportation of the contractor and his assistant was that of a slur on the Jewish section of the Baghdad population, and as the attitude and behavior of these people toward the British had been above reproach this was sorry treatment.

One other aspect of Maude's untimely death perhaps calls for comment, since the "Official History of the War" merely states that the Army Commander died of cholera "after two days illness" and makes no mention of the circumstances. None of the doctors protested against the Army Commander or anybody else attending functions in the notoriously infected parts of Baghdad. Hawker's deputy had died of cholera and the disease was known to be endemic; yet none of the medical officers suggested that Maude should restrict his activities. In a prophetic story published in 1909, under the title "The Green Curve" it was said of the general who was the chief character "it was no part of the scheme that he should share the hardships of his troops, or any hardships. . . . Even against his natural tendencies he was to be preserved from every possible danger which might lead to his loss, and from every physical discomfort or exposure which might injure his health and so affect his judgment." Many other generals had followed or been advised to follow this precept but not Maude. Preventive and prophylactic measures which he had been instrumental in introducing into Mesopotamia saved the lives of others, but he died. Like Alexander the Great and the Emperor Julian before him, he was a victim of Mesopotamia. Since a convenient scapegoat had been found to cover the cause of his death no further inquiry was considered necessary and the case was closed.

To the army in Mesopotamia Maude had become what Kitchener had been to the British armies in Europe and it felt his loss keenly. In eighteen months, under his leadership, the morale of a defeated army had been raised to the pitch of confidence which had brought the spectacular successes of 1917 and it was by his powers of organization that comforts which had never been dreamed of in the days before he took over command had been brought to it. He was an austere man but chivalrous also. "The soul of chivalry" said Lord Curzon in a tribute to his memory at Westminster, "he was not less strict in the discipline that he applied to himself than in that which he applied to others. A non-smoker, almost a total abstainer, he set an example of conscientious self-control which profoundly affected the conduct of those who served under him." He had done well for his country and, though the inhabitants probably did not realize it at the time, much for Iraq—the country that was to rise and spring into independence from the ashes of the old Mesopotamia.

> Batteries have told the listening town this day[6]
> That through her ancient gate of his last resting place
> Maude has gone north.

---

6. Maude was buried in the Military Cemetery outside the North Gate of Baghdad. These lines are attributed to one of his staff, Colonel Dixon.

Chapter 20

Finale

From his deathbed, Maude's last coherent instruction to his staff was that they should "carry on." His successor was all too willing to continue in the ways of his revered chief, but Marshall soon found that his ability to do so was strictly limited. Not only was he now faced with a rapidly changing tactical situation impressed on Mesopotamia by the momentous tide of events outside the theater, but if Maude had been pursuing any set policy and not an extemporary series of improvisations, such a policy had been kept strictly to himself. Nor, apparently, was the Home Government prepared to allow Marshall the freedom of action his predecessor had enjoyed, and from hereon the extent to which he was able to "carry on" was firmly dictated by Whitehall. And powerful factions in Whitehall were suspicious of the new Army Commander. When the possibility of Maude's replacing Sir Archibald Murray in Egypt had cropped up some months earlier, Maude had strongly recommended Marshall's being appointed to take his place in Mesopotamia. "A grand little fighting soldier," Maude had said of him. At the time, "Wully" Robertson had grudgingly accepted the recommendation. Nevertheless he was uneasy about a "soldier's soldier"—and as Marshall had never been employed on the staff, he could be considered nothing else—for a post which demanded political understanding as well as military skill. Even before the notes of the *Last Post* had resounded across Maude's grave, Robertson seemed to be having second thoughts about confirming Marshall in the appointment. Then, when he had concluded that Marshall was probably the most suitable man for the job, the C.I.G.S. was determined to see that *his* men controlled the key positions on Marshall's staff. Since Marshall had no staff experience himself, it was essential that he should be served by people who had; there was going to be no repetition of the earlier administrative failings if Robertson could avoid it.

Major General Hopwood, Maude's old Chief of Staff, was the first on the list of those to be replaced. As Hopwood was but a name in the Army List to Robertson, Marshall was peremptorily ordered to replace him with someone whom Robertson knew personally and could trust. It was hardly an encouraging start for Marshall and his resentment is understandable. To Robertson's cable he replied tartly that he had "every confidence in Hopwood," whom he was "not prepared to sacrifice to his own ineptitude." But his plan cut no ice with the C.I.G.S. Hopwood was ordered back to Britain, Gillman, who had only just taken over command of the 17th Division, taking his place. Robertson was determined that Marshall should abide by the rules—his rules, the Whitehall rules—and in his next cable he laid down the framework of the policy to which Marshall should work. Basically, this directive was a recapitulation of Maude's earlier instructions: the oil supplies were to be safeguarded, British influence maintained in the Baghdad province; Arab cooperation to be encouraged; Baratoff's cooperation to be enlisted; there were to be no rash offensives. There was one important extra clause however; Marshall was to consider how he could reduce the size of his army in Mesopotamia.

The limitations of British manpower were worrying the politicians as well as the service authorities in England, and Robertson was being compelled to cut the unfruitful secondary theaters of war to the bone. And Mesopotamia, where a huge army was being tied down by comparatively small forces was an obvious area in which to seek economies. Operating along short, radial lines of communication, the geographical and strategical advantages all lay with the Turks, while the British scattered over a wide area, with the 15th Division up the Euphrates; the 1st Corps well up the Tigris with a front at Tikrit; and the 3rd Corps on the Diyala, between Delli Abbas and the Jebel Hamrin—were at the end of long vulnerable supply lines. Administratively, the situation was a strain; militarily it was unrewarding, for the fighting seemed virtually to have come to an end. Even in England it was quite obvious that getting a blow in at the Turks was becoming more and more difficult as time passed, for whenever the British advanced, the Turks merely receded, like the mirage—leaving another stretch of sand and dust to be garrisoned and pacified. Far better, thought Robertson to concentrate the war effort where the prospects were more promising.

It was a sound appreciation, for the plain fact is that whatever was done in Mesopotamia at this juncture mattered little. This was a period when disturbing events elsewhere were shaping the course of the war, and the Mesopotamia Expeditionary Force had attained its purpose long ago; the Land of the Two Rivers was now just an expensive drain on the war effort. Right from the day of the original I.E.F. "D" it had been expensive, but never more than now. Particularly now, for in October a counterrevolution in Russia had overthrown the Provisional Government and instituted what was later to be known as Bolshevism; by December, Russia was breaking away from the war, and before the year was out the Bolsheviks had opened peace negotiations at Brest-Litovsk and the Russian Army had largely disintegrated.

In Europe, France was war-weary; Italy, after the debacle of Caporetto was looking to Britain and France for help; Britain's Army on the Western Front, exhausted by the Third Battle of Ypres, was a hundred thousand men short of Haig's estimated requirements, and brigades were being reduced from four to three battalions. With Russia's defection, prospects for Germany seemed brighter than at any time since 1914 and it was conceivable that she could switch between thirty and forty divisions from the Eastern Front for a renewed onslaught in Flanders. Viewed from Whitehall, the need to concentrate every possible resource in Europe and allow theaters like Mesopotamia to simmer seemed very logical.

Few of those serving in Mesopotamia can have been aware of the background, but one event on the Persian border toward the end of November was directly related to the crumbling Russian efforts. In an aura of secrecy, a party of about twelve hundred Russians, calling themselves the Partiskanski, arrived at Mendali, having ridden down from Persia through *the* Wali of Pusht-i-Kuh's territory. The detachment was commanded by a hardbitten old soldier, Colonel Bicharakov, and because of his partial disablement he was compelled—like Sulaiman Askari of Shaiba fame—to exercise his authority from a litter. His unit was primarily a Cossack[1] force; the men, all picked volunteers from the various regiments of Baratoff's army in Persia, had sworn allegiance to their officers, to uphold the traditions of the old Imperial Army and never to desert their allies. Like their commander they were tough, hard men and, so far they had not been affected by the Bolshevik bug, although they had adopted the revolutionaries' method of deciding punishment by "Soldiers Council" trials.

---

[1] The Cossacks had been the armed police of the Tsar and, in general, they remained loyal to the Monarchy during the early stages of the Revolution.

On arrival at Mendali, Bicharakov announced that he was placing himself and his men unreservedly under Marshall's orders. His supplies obviously had to come from British sources and so Marshall ordered him to march the detachment across to Sharaban where transport was easier. However, before leaving Mendali there was a minor fracas and an account of this may serve to illustrate the Russians' peculiar ideas on discipline. Smallpox was raging in Mendali when the Partiskanski arrived, and the town had been placed out of bounds to troops; since the Russians were now under British orders this restriction was taken to apply to them equally as much as British troops, and Bicharakov accepted this fact. Consequently, when British military police caught a couple of Russians in the "out of bounds" zone they were handed over to Bicharakov for summary punishment, and trial by "Soldiers Council" resulted in the two malefactors being condemned to death by shooting. Fortunately Marshall came to hear of the sentence before it was carried out, complained that the penalty was, to say the least of it, excessive, and when the council met again the sentence was reduced to three days' confinement to camp!

By this time, as the Turks had retreated well over thirty miles and out of immediate striking distance on both the Tigris and the Euphrates front, the Diyala area seemed to offer most promise for an immediate offensive. Since he knew the region so well Marshall probably favored it anyway, and no doubt he saw an opportunity to test the reliability of Bicharakov's detachment under fire. Securing the Sakaltutan Pass was a desirable objective in itself, and if the Turks who were holding it could be surrounded and destroyed at the same time, so much the better. This is what Marshall decided to try to do and the task was given to the new commander of his old Corps, Egerton. Egerton's plan was to direct three converging columns onto the pass, while the cavalry demonstrated up the Adhaim River, in order to deter the Turks from bringing reinforcements down from Kirkuk. The 14th Division was to cross the Diyala upstream of Qizil Robat on the night of December 2, while the Partiskanski crossed five miles still further north of Kirkuk; at dawn on December 3, both would advance toward the village of Narin Kopri, to get behind the Turks' positions in the hills covering the pass. Meanwhile, the 13m Division would seize Suhaniya—the approach to the pass on the west side of the Jebel Hamrin—in preparation for a full scale offensive next day, up and through the pass itself. The Turks' line of communications lay along the Kifri Road and, even if the Cavalry Division were not able to penetrate the mountains twenty miles north of the Sakaltu-tan pass and occupy Umr Maidan as it was hoped, the operations of the 13th Division should still stand a very good chance of herding the Turks who were deployed in the pass into the arms of the 14th Division and the Russians.

Unfortunately the plan did not work out as Egerton had expected. Bichara-kov, directing the Russian contribution to the operation from his litter collapsed from a bout of dysentery and, at a crucial stage of the battle, the Partiskanski retired across the river. Nor was the Cavalry Division able to complete the circle. Immediately prior to the battle, Marshall received information that Ali Ihsan had got wind of the Cavalry Division's move up the Adhaim, and had ordered his troops to let the cavalry get well into the mountains toward Umr Maidan, and then attack them on ground where mounted men would be helpless. As a result, Jones was ordered to confine himself to "demonstrating" on the near side of the mountain range. It was not a complete failure however, for the rest of the plan went smoothly enough and when the two divisional columns met at dusk on December 5, 250 Turkish prisoners had fallen into British hands at a comparatively small cost in British casualties. But the offensive had fallen far short of Marshall's hopes, and so could not be counted as anything more than a partial success. But it did have a demoralizing effect on the Turks. Even before the action, deserters had been coming in, and during the advance up the Sakaltutan Pass most of the Turks who were taken had surrendered after a very little show of resistance—clear evidence that Turkish morale was flagging. Deserters and prisoners alike all had the appearance of tired, hungry, ragged and ill-equipped troops and so, at long last, it looked as if the Turkish Army was cracking. Reports from German prisoners taken on the Euphrates who said that "chaos abounded" on their lines of communication, tended to confirm the impression given by the Jebel Hamrin prisoners. According to the Germans all the old Turkish traits of dishonesty, peculation and incompetence were reasserting themselves; grain and ammunition were being stolen; friction between the Turks and their German allies was increasing rapidly.

It was all very true; the Turks were apathetic and their German allies exasperated, for Mesopotamia was not the only front showing signs of Turkish demoralization. In Palestine, where Allenby was now operating in the Judaean Hills, the Turks were on the run. Jerusalem fell on December 9, and this not only gave the deathblow to the Yilderim scheme for recapturing Baghdad, but also suggested that, strategically, Palestine was the most suitable theater in which to crush Turkey. To Robertson and Haig, busily scraping men from anywhere, to replace the losses sustained by the exhausted armies on the Western Front, the news that Turkey was reeling must have come as a welcome gleam in an otherwise somber outlook. There could now be no doubt whatsoever that Mesopotamia could safely be relegated to the second rank of the "sideshow," and Marshall was ordered to release troops for Palestine forthwith. Consequently, the 7th Division at Tikrit was immediately replaced by Leslie's

17th Division, moved to Basra, and shipped off to Egypt; it was followed in March by the 3rd (Lahore) Division, whose place on the Tigris front was taken by the 18th Division.

As might be expected these moves resulted in a reshuffle of the rest of the troops in the theater, and Marshall toured his Command during December, seeking manpower economies and the release of fighting troops from duties on the lines of communication. From Ahwaz to Tikrit and Ramadi to the Jebel Hamrin was a vast area and it is hardly surprising that some strange anomalies should have come to light during the Army Commander's inspection. It was not only some of the developments which had taken place ostensibly for military purposes, which came in for his criticism—though many of these were to come in for severe censure from India Command within a very few months. Some of the troops themselves were a very mixed bag. In Baghdad one extra-ordinary unit, the 49th Bengalis, immediately became his pet *bête noire*. This battalion, composed (as he records) of "a lot of stunted, immature Bengali boys," had been raised and sent to Mesopotamia as a sop to Bengali politicians. To add weight to their agitation for self-government these politicians wanted to be able to say that the population of Bengal had done its bit for the Empire, and the 49th Bengalis was the outcome. Since most of its members were totally unfit for any form of service, the unit was useless, even for duties on the line of communications, and Marshall wanted to send it back to India. But the political situation in India precluded such a simple solution, and he was ordered to convene a board of combatant and medical officers which would report to the Commander-in-Chief in India, on the battalion's fitness.

The board, with Holland-Pryor as president, was duly assembled, and its report appears to have vindicated all that Marshall had said about the battalion. Of close to a thousand men, not more than sixty were capable of marching five miles when fully equipped. Delhi accepted these findings and Marshall was told that he could send the battalion back to India, but at a rate of not more than thirty men a month—an instruction which was virtually equivalent to saying that it would stay in Mesopotamia.[2]

Criticisms of the quasi-military developments in the Mesopotamian hinter-land came largely as the result of a visit by General Sir Edward Altham, India

---

2. While the signals deciding the fate of the 49th Bengalis were passing to and from Delhi, two Indian officers of the battalion were murdered by their own men. When the telegrams announcing their deaths reached their next of kin in India the news spread like wildfire through Calcutta and processions, carrying banners "Bengali patriots the for their King and Country," marched through the streets! After the Armistice the Indian Government decreed that the 49th Bengalis should be one of the battalions to be retained in Mesopotamia. Marshall protested that such a decision could only have been made on political grounds, and consequently India should bear the cost of the battalion's upkeep, not the British taxpayers. In a terse reply he was told to mind his own business.

Command's Quartermaster General, and Sir Thomas Holland, the Civil Head of the Munitions Board. Holland, who considered that India had been "bled white" by the demands of Mesopotamia made no secret of his views to Marshall. According to him, the "MacMunn" bridge at Amara was hardly necessary and much railway material and rolling stock had been wastefully employed. The fact that the Indian Railways had been recompensed by the Home Government's exchequer seems to have been ignored, and when the two visitors returned to India their report was one of reckless expenditure. This led to a Commission of Inquiry being sent to Mesopotamia for a full investigation, but its report justified all the criticized projects as being essential to the conduct of military operations, and exonerated both Marshall and Maude from allegations of extravagance.

The investigations on Mesopotamian administration are, however, in advance of the narrative and it is necessary now to return to the operational area. The next fighting took place on the Euphrates front. After Ramadi the Turks holding Hit had been reinforced, and by March they were holding a strong position at "Broad Wadi" two miles north of the town, with the bulk of their force fifteen miles further upstream. Marshall was now intent not only on capturing Hit, but also on trapping its Garrison as he showed in his dispatch of April 15, 1918: "There would be no difficulty in capturing the town and driving the Turks out of their positions; but the capture of the Turkish force would be a matter of extreme difficulty in consequence of their previous experience at Ramadi." This was to prove an accurate forecast. On March 9, after patrols of Brooking's 15th Division had discovered that the town had been evacuated, Hit was occupied. Built of grey limestone on the edge of a limestone and clay plateau where the Euphrates winds through a valley between low hills, from a distance Hit looked like many a town in Italy. Its minaret stood out like a campanile, the palms below its walls looked like cypresses, and the arched aqueducts in the river were reminiscent of Roman architecture. But at close range all such illusions were dispelled, and Hit was seen to be just another unsavory, biblical city like Tikrit. The tightly packed honeycomb of miserable dwellings, steep narrow alleys, open sewers and the basic smell were the same as in so many other places in Mesopotamia—with only one major difference: the smell of age-old ordure was overlaid by the foul reek of the sulphuretted hydrogen emanating from the bitumen wells—the wells which the Arabs called "the mouths of hell." In normal times its orchards, where peaches, apricots and figs grew among the mulberries for which the town is famous, provide a slight attraction. But in March 1917 the orchards had been wrecked, to provide wood with which the Turks could revet their trenches.

When the Turks evacuated Hit they had fallen back on Khan Baghdadi and their commander, Subri Bey, was deprived of his command for making no attempt to stem Brooking's advance. With Subri's example before him, his successor Nazmi Bey was not expected to quit with quite the same readiness as his predecessor and if, as Brooking predicted, he showed greater temerity, then this was a situation which could be exploited. If an offensive could be staged quickly enough, Brooking reckoned that it ought to be possible to surround and destroy the whole Khan Baghdadi garrison. Very little was known about the country beyond Hit, but British mobility had been increased since Ramadi, and Brooking was relying on this for a quick and cheap success. To this end, traveling by night and hiding by day, Cassels's Cavalry Brigade, armored cars and Ford vans moved up to the forward area and, to prevent any suspicions being roused, the RFC was ordered to keep away from the area. For the operation, Brooking planned to split his force into four columns. Andrews' 50th Brigade was to advance along the Aleppo road; the 42nd Brigade, under Lucas, was to follow Andrews; Cassels's cavalry with the greater portion of the Light Armored Motor Batteries, under Hogg, was to circle around the Turks' right flank, and a special mobile column consisting of four companies of infantry,[3] engineers and two machine-gun sections, all carried in three hundred Ford vans was to operate directly under Brooking's orders, This last group was to be supported by the 8th Light Armored Motor Battery and a battery of field artillery which was provided with double-horsed teams for greater mobility.

The operation was scheduled to start on March 26, and on the day before everything was due to swing into action, an incident occurred which is worth recording, if only because of its outcome. Major Tennant, the commander of the RFC in Mesopotamia suddenly elected to fly over Khan Baghdadi in a new DH4, taking Major Hobart the Brigade Major of Edwards' 8th Brigade of the 3rd Division with him. Ostensibly Tennant was visiting some of his squadron waiting at Hit to take part in Brooking's operations next day, but Hobart apparently had never seen the Euphrates and so the Khan Baghdadi part of the trip appears to have been more in the nature of a joy-ride than anything else. That it was possible for such an event to occur was undoubtedly due to Tennant's determination to establish the independence of the air arm. Differences of opinion had arisen earlier as a result of Maude's staff, who had little or no knowledge of aircraft maintenance, expecting aircrews to do more than their decrepit airplanes could achieve. In consequence, senior staff officers ordering junior RFC ranks to do as they were told resulted in tempers flaring on both sides, and Tennant had appealed to the Army Commander Maude, who realized the limitations of a single squadron trying to fulfill the

---

3. Half the 1st/5th Queen's and half the 2nd/39th Garhwalis.

demands of an army fighting three campaigns simultaneously, smoothed out the tension. Tennant's authority was established and probably on this occasion he overstepped it.

Low cloud caused him to fly low over the Khan Baghdadi positions and his aircraft was brought down by machine-gun fire. Neither Tennant nor Hobart was hurt but both were captured, and after an interview with Nazmi Bey they were sent off down the Aleppo road, under the escort of a dozen renegade Russians. Meantime Brooking's attack had started. After a long and circuitous march, Cassels's group arrived at the Aleppo road five or six miles north of Khan Baghdadi, and by 5 p.m. on March 26, they were dug in ready to stop any flight from the town. The signal for the other columns to advance was then given and the general lines of the Ramadi action were repeated. After a brisk fight the Turkish positions in front of the town were breached, and the Turks themselves retired rapidly along the Aleppo road, closely followed by Brooking's infantry. Finding they were unable to break through Cassels's block the Turkish resistance suddenly collapsed and Nazmi Bey surrendered the whole of his force of over 5,000 men; the defeat had been even more complete than that of Subri Bey at Ramadi. Nazmi's men had made some attempt to destroy their equipment but Brooking's advance was so quick that the Turks had very little time to effect much damage. As a result, 12 guns, 47 machine guns, ambulances, field kitchens, water-carts, convoys of bullock wagons and vast quantities of ammunition and stores were all captured and the Turkish troops, who were exhausted and completely demoralized, surrendered freely.

Nor was this the end of the operation so far as Brooking was concerned. Orders were issued for the Cavalry Brigade and armored cars, with as many troops as could be carried in the hundred Ford vans then available, to push on up the Aleppo road to Ana,44 where Cassels was to destroy the Turkish storage dumps and wireless station. At this point, Cassels seems to have had one of his rare moments of caution. To get the order to Hogg, impatiently waiting to drive on up the road, the Cavalry Brigade commander had to motor forward, and his orders to Hogg were for the armored cars to go half-way to Ana and then await the arrival of the horsed cavalry before going further. Why such a pause was considered necessary is difficult to understand. However, Ana was reached next morning and the 8th Light Armored Motor Batteries continued along the Aleppo road with orders to capture as many high-ranking Turkish and German officers as could be found; seize 18,000 gold liras which the retreating Turks were said to have with them; and, if possible, rescue Tennant and Hobart. Since a number of prisoners, including Herr Preusser, the head of the German mission on the Euphrates, was picked up in the pursuit, the first part of the mission was completely successful. So, too, was the rescue of the two airmen. Nearly thirty-two miles west of Ana, as the cars were winding their way along the narrow round between hills and the river they suddenly came on the Cossack prisoners' escort. The cars opened fire; Tennant and Hobart who had run down the river bank for cover from their guards when they heard the noise of Rolls-Royce engines, were hastily hauled into one of them and that was the end of their captivity. The cars then continued for some miles further up the road but no gold was found and the raid—for it was nothing more—came to an end when the cars returned to Ana. From there, Tennant and Hobart returned to Baghdad under arrest; Marshall, with considerable justification, being of the opinion that their disastrous flight had never been necessary. However a Court of Inquiry exonerated both and they were released, Tennant to return to India and Hobart to go to Palestine where he rejoined his brigade.

Since the raid on Ana was the third operation in which motorized infantry was employed in Mesopotamia, and it led to some reorganization that was important later, it is appropriate to conclude the narrative of the successful Khan Baghdadi operation with a brief digression on this topic. The two previous operations, the first attack on Ramadi and the raid on Hit, were unsuccessful and this last was only partially so. But as a result of the experience which had been gained in all three, Marshall decided to create a permanent cadre of motorized units which could operate with the armored car brigade. Known as "Lewis gun detachments" and made up of a company strong force (a hundred and fifty men), equipped with thirty Lewis light machine guns in addition to the men's rifles, they were transported in fifty Ford vans.5 As such detachments expected to fight dismounted as ordinary infantry, their role was quite different from that in which the light-car patrols operating in Egypt and Palestine were eventually used. With the armored cars, each "Lewis gun detachment" was expected to constitute a quick hard-hitting, quick-striking mobile column. Since the Hit raid had provided ample evidence that engineers would be needed if they were to be successful, it seems strange that the need for a sapper or pioneer element in their make-up appears to have been overlooked. Possibly a shortage of engineers in Mesopotamia militated against their inclusion.

And now it is necessary to make some mention of an aspect of the concluding stages of the campaign which became the subject of considerable criticism in the closing stages of the war.

Toward the end of 1917, rumors began to circulate in Mesopotamia of a mysterious side-show, a "Hush-Hush Push," somewhere beyond the borders of the theater. Volunteers from the Army in France, as well as picked men from the British regiments in Mesopotamia began to assemble at a special camp near Baghdad and, although their preparations were shrouded in security,

it was soon common talk that their destination was Persia.[4] Nor did this conclusion emanate from loose talk; the fact that people in the "Special Force"
camp were buying clothing suited to Arctic cold, studying. Persian, and
changing rupees for Persian kran was a clear enough indication. Finally the
rumor was laid in the first week of January, when the Russian-speaking Major
General Dunsterville—the original of Kipling's Stalky—arrived to take
command of the force and it became known that his mission lay beyond
Northern Persia. And, from this moment began one of the strangest missions
ever undertaken during the First World War. "Dunsterforce," as it came to be
known, was to get through to the Caucasus and help the Armenians, Georgians
and Azerbaijanis, evict their Turkish masters, and form a buffer state between
revolt-torn Russia and Turkey. Then, when the political issues had been settled,
those of the new states who were capable of bearing arms were to be drilled
and disciplined into an army capable of resisting a Turco-German force which
was said to be forming somewhere "up there" near the Caspian. In so far as
the expedition was out of the ordinary run of the war, it combined the attrac-
tions of a well-paid military adventure and a crusade. Not only was a new republic to be founded from peoples saved from the Turk on one side and
Bolshevism on the other, but a new threat to the British Empire was to be
countered almost at its source.

According to the British Foreign Office, the combined Turkish and
German force that was forming had India, Persia and Afghanistan as its objectives; as Baratoff's army was rapidly disintegrating it had deduced that the
road through Persia to India was wide open. Such information was more than
sufficient to frighten the men in Delhi. Denuded of troops, India saw a recrudescence of that old bogey—an invasion across the North-West Frontier. Yet
it was only a bogey, for Russia's defection had not really opened the road to a
Turco-German offensive on a European scale. Moving large bodies of troops
through Persia was a military impossibility in 1917; even in the 1960's such an
offensive would be difficult enough. A realistic assessment should have concluded that any danger to India lay in political penetration, in the subversive
work of the diplomat-agent and spy, not in a military threat. So long as Britain
and her Allies held on in France, diversions in the Caucasus and Persia were
nothing more than minor embarrassments; the absence of good roads, insufficient transport and a dearth of supplies were insuperable obstacles to the con-

4. All were of a very high caliber; Australians, New Zealanders, Canadians, British; all NCOs with "Military
medals." As inducements for hazardous service, subalterns were given the temporary rank of Captain, a £30
kit allowance and £1 day subsistence allowance; the men were given the rank of sergeant and an allowance of
12/6 a day. By present standards these allowances may seem paltry but their 1966 equivalents would probably be six or seven times as much.

centration of any force in Persia greater than brigade strength. Compared with the life and death struggle in progress on the Western Front, India's problems may be judged insignificant; nevertheless, the "Eastern Committee" of the British War Cabinet had decided that any Pan-Islamic offensive directed toward India must be stopped. Furthermore the Georgians had asked for help and, it was for these reasons that Dunsterforce was to set up a new republic and save India.

At this point it must be made clear that although Marshall had been ordered to give Dunsterforce every possible assistance, Dunsterville's mission was entirely independent of the Mesopotamia Expeditionary Force. Marshall was against it from the start; to him it was obvious that the expedition was going to need assistance totally disproportionate to its value. Not only would three hundred and thirty miles of execrable road separate Baghdad from Dunsterville's forward base at Hamadan, but another hundred and fifty miles of unguarded, unpaved highway, containing a 7,500 foot mountain pass that separated Hamadan from Kazvin; then from Kazvin to Enzeli, on the southern shore of the Caspian, the road deteriorated into a track fit only for horses. He did not underestimate the difficulties. Even when the road surface had been improved and some of the worst gradients eased, it still took a daily convoy of seven hundred and fifty lorries to feed a force at Hamadan of less than a thousand men, and far from there being any question of living off local supplies—as had been suggested in London—the people of Karind, Kermanshah and Hamadan had to be fed from British sources. In eighteen months Cossacks and Turks had reduced the country to a state of famine; trees had been felled, crops burnt, granaries destroyed and thousands were starving; not even any seed grain for the next harvest was available. On top of this came a drought; either the British had to supply food or the Persians would starve.

These were the conditions that provided the backcloth. What remained of Baratoff's army had withdrawn to the Caspian by this time and Bicharakov's Partiskanski detachment, the only disciplined force that remained to Baratoff, had been released by Marshall to cover the withdrawal—not that the Partiskanski could exercise much control in these circumstances. Despite these difficulties—some of which he had anticipated and some which were to be a rude surprise—in January Dunsterville set off from Hamadan with a small advance party and eventually, after much perseverance arrived at Enzeli. There he found the town occupied by the remnants of the Russian Army of the Caucasus: three thousand Bolsheviks angry, hostile and suspicious, who demanded to know where he was going and why. "To Tiflis," he replied, explaining that by leaving the war Russia had left the British flank exposed to invasion by the Turks, and that the British Government had ordered him to go to the Caucasus to report on the situation. As neither this explanation nor further argument proved acceptable to the Bolshevik "Council," and Dunsterville's party was hopelessly outnumbered, the situation looked ugly. Only Dunsterville's silver tongue and his knowledge of both the Russians and their language, persuaded the Bolsheviks to let him and his party go, and they were only allowed to do so on condition that the mission retraced its footsteps and made no attempt to cross the Caspian.

This spelled the end of the mission, for there could now no longer be any hope of making Armenia a buttress against the Turks. Dunsterville returned to Hamadan, where he employed his gifts of eloquence trying to persuade the Persians that they really did want the British to stay in their country, and Dunsterforce with Bicharakov and his much reduced Partiskanski detachment, deployed across the Enzeli-Kermanshah road, and served as a thin outpost line barring the way between the Caspian and Baghdad. Meanwhile, the Georgians, finding that the English were not coming, invited the Germans—who promptly sent a smart division to occupy Tiflis which, during its stay, squeezed the wretched town dry. Then another element intervened. Under the terms of the Brest-Litovsk Treaty, Russia's new Red Government ceded the whole Caucasus region to the Turks, a measure which, because of its Armenian population, might be, considered to be one of Bolshevik brutality. The result was that the Turks began to occupy the Caucasus, pushed on to Tiflis and were reported to be making for the oil-rich area of Baku. To counter this, the Eastern Committee in Whitehall, working presumably from small-scale maps, calmly ordered Marshall to send a force up to the Caspian and occupy Kirkuk. As the Caspian expedition meant a seven hundred mile mountain road, extension of the already enormous line of communications up the Tigris and Diyala rivers, and to Kirkuk another two hundred miles, Marshall was anything but enthusiastic. However, his cable, sarcastically drawing a parallel with the only other attempt to operate on a large scale at the end of seven hundred miles of road— that of Napoleon's Moscow campaign—and suggesting that the latter could "hardly be called an unqualified success," drew a stern rebuke from Whitehall and, he was compelled to initiate a Persian expedition.

Bicharakov, accompanied by the armored cars of Dunsterforce and a detachment of the Hampshire Regiment provided the vanguard and started off for Enzeli from Kazvin.[5] At this point a certain Kuchik Khan, ambitious Chief of the Jangalis tribe that lived in the forest-clad hills between Resht and Enzeli decided to take a hand and hold up the column. But his Jangalis were quickly

---

5. Marshall had sent the Hampshire Regiment up in lorries with a detachment of Gurkhas to bolster the strength of Dunsterforce while the road to Kazvin was being hastily developed.

brushed aside and Enzeli was occupied without difficulty. (Some weeks later Kuchik Khan attacked the garrison at Resht but was beaten off with heavy losses. After being bombed by what they called the RFC's "flying devils," the Jangalis surrendered, and were disarmed and dispersed. Thereafter they gave no trouble.) The next move came in July, after Bicharakov, taking his Partiskanski with him, had left Enzeli to take over command of the "White" Army in the Caucasus. Like their Tsarist predecessors the local government in Baku, who were attempting at this time to stem the Bolshevik tide, were averse to anyone other man Russians controlling the oil fields. Yet they had no troops on whom they could rely apart from those of Bicharakov; unless he were called in it meant either British or Turkish intervention. No sooner had Bicharakov left Enzeli man a coup d'état took place and the Mensheviks in Baku were succeeded by an Armenian-Russian bourgeois regime, only too willing for British troops to help solve their problem. A request for British aid, backed by an urgent plea from Bicharakov, was sent to Dunsterville now firmly established in Enzeli with the greater part of Andrus's 39th Brigade, and on August 4, Dunsterville landed at Baku. Getting there was the difficulty. The Bolshevik troops who had opposed him on his earlier visit had melted away to their homes by this time, but the shipping on the Caspian was under Bolshevik control, and although the Baku Government sent transports to lift the force, the ships were run not by their captors but by crew committees. Consequently negotiations for using the ships for a particular purpose or time were invariably protracted. However, despite the trans-port difficulties and the scarcity of local supplies, a British force consisting of detachments of the Worcesters, Warwicks and North Staffords was concentrated at Baku and considering that the column was at the end of a thousand miles of difficult communications between Basra and the Caspian, getting even this small force there was a remarkable achievement. Unfortunately events were to prove that it was not sufficient for the task to which it had been committed. Dunsterville's declared object in occupying Baku was to prevent the Turks establishing a base on the Caspian, to protect the Armenians and—probably the most important reason of all—to lay hold of Baku's oil supply. Already oil was fast becoming the dominant factor in the thoughts of those concerned with the future of the Middle East and allied interests extended to the oil field at Baku.[6] But apart from this, it cost twenty pounds a gallon to bring petrol to Dunsterforce from

6. In September 1917 an American mission, styling itself "The Persian Famine Relief Commission" arrived in Baghdad and went on to Persia. It did good work fighting the famine but as it returned to the U.S.A. with valuable concessions for the Standard Oil Company, it appears that oil, as well as famine relief, had been among its objectives. Marshall himself recalls that in London in 1919, "while one could freely discuss the possibilities of cotton-growing in Mesopotamia with Government officials, the bare mention of the word 'oil' created a chilly atmosphere."

Abadan so that the Baku wells would bring welcome relief to the tenuous supply line through Mesopotamia. However, the Turks had got to Baku before Dunsterville and although the locals,[7] armed with a variety of weapons, had turned out in force and driven the Turks out of the actual town, by the time Dunsterville's troops got there the Armenians and Russians had had enough fighting. Already some of the garrison was negotiating for a surrender. As the parties of Dunsterville's men arrived, a scrappy defence line was taken up around the town and by August 25, about a thousand British troops had been deployed in support of the Baku garrison. But by now the Turks had been reinforced and next morning when they attacked the Armenians fled. The attack was held by men of the North Staffords and Worcesters but to do so they had had to fall back on the town with no reserves and no prospect of reinforcements; the British position was hopeless. The Armenians themselves were no longer prepared to help; the English had come to save them they said, let them get on with it. Within a few days Dunsterville was forced to accept that he had no chance of holding the port. Fourteen thousand Turks were already arrayed against him and with their shorter line of communications there was every reason to suppose that they would be able to assemble an even greater force before long. On September 1, the decision was taken to evacuate the British force, but although the Russian staff was prepared to allow Dunsterforce to go, the Bolshevik Navy was not so agreeable and when the withdrawal did take place on September 14, the three ships carrying the force had to move stealthily out of the harbor under the guns of the Bolshevik warships of the Caspian fleet. As the Turks had attacked that night and were storming into the town most of the force got away safely; only the last transport was fired on but the captain, with a British revolver at his head, continued on course and all three ships got safely back to Enzeli. Getting away had been a close shave and much of the equipment, including all Dunsterville's motor transport and the horses accompanying the column, had to be abandoned.[8] And nothing had been achieved.

At Enzeli, crowded with Armenian refugees who had to be fed and housed by the British Government, Dunsterville got his orders to return to England. The situation looked black and now, for the first time, news of the existence of Dunsterforce, and the intervention at Baku appeared in the British Press. Not unnaturally it provoked considerable criticism. The wisdom of British presence

---

7. About 10,000 volunteers (7,000 Armenians, 3,000 Russians), with no military training.

8. To complete the Partiskanski story: after helping to subdue Kuchik Khan, Bicharakov went on to occupy Petrovsk on the Caspian, 200 miles north of Baku, which he held against the Turks until the end of October. He then successfully evacuated his force to Enzeli and returned with the British force in Baku in November. Apart from the award of a British decoration (G.B.) he received large sums of money for his services to the British Government.

in Persia was questioned, the Baku expedition was condemned as a quixotic adventure, and Marshall who in all fairness had been against any extension of the campaign outside the borders of Mesopotamia from the outset also came in for a share of the blame. He had failed to give adequate support to Dunsterville, his critics said. As for Dunsterville himself; he was blamed for going to Baku with a there handful of troops when it was quite obvious to any armchair critic that a division would be necessary. Dunsterforce's lavish expenditure in Baku and Persia also brought its commander into disrepute. A considerable sum of money had been spent, much of it going as bribes; misdirection and misappropriation of funds could all be proved although the real trouble was that Dunsterville's officers were men of grit, unsuited to the role of staff officers which circumstances in Persia had forced on them. Those who spoke up for the principle of this tragic expedition talked gloomily of the German menace to India, directed from Baku. Yet, as has been stressed already, their assessment of its value was as faulty as that of those who wholeheartedly condemned the Dunsterforce activities. Dunsterforce was defeated by what Napoleon called "the secret of war"—communications. When it came to consideration of an armed invasion of India, the Turks would have been just as impotent as a sizeable British force trying to operate from Mesopotamia. in the Caucasus region.

Not that the Germans or Turks themselves ever seriously considered a Turco-German-Bolshevik force, self-supplied and equipped with all the artillery and ammunition it would have needed for such an expedition, descending by way of the Caspian to attack India. German ideas of penetrating India centered on political infiltration; it was by stirring up trouble in Afghanistan, among the Pathan tribes of the North-West Frontier, and engineering a mutiny among the people of India that Germany hoped to disrupt the British Raj; a military campaign was not a practical proposition. Some of the Persians had accepted German gold but they had been able to do little to further German aims; and the Emir of Afghanistan, "the chosen of God," had consistently turned a deaf ear to political missionaries preaching a Jihad and held down the fanatical elements of his State with extraordinary firmness.

While this account of the adventures of Dunsterforce and the situation in Persia may seem to have been a digression from the Mesopotamia campaign proper, the story would be incomplete without them. But, because they are part of the background, no attempt had been made to make more than a cursory appraisal of their effects other than on the main theme, to which we must now return for the final act. By the summer of 1918, the Mesopotamia Expeditionary Force had undergone considerable changes. Apart from the two divisions which had been sent to Palestine, an Indian battalion had been taken from each of the remaining brigades in the theater for service in Salonika, and a company had also been taken from each of the Indian battalions to form the nuclei of new units then being raised in India. Replacements had been drafted from India, but Marshall's army was now a much diluted force. Considerable reorganization had also taken place. The Cavalry Division had been broken up into its constituent brigades and the ineffective 13-pounder guns of the Royal Horse Artillery relegated to base defenses, being replaced by the longer ranged and more effective 18-pounders. No one could yet predict the end of the war and all this reorganization was necessary if the Army in Mesopotamia was to be ready for the next campaigning season after the hot weather. On the civil side, agricultural development schemes were forging ahead, as were countless other plans designed to make Mesopotamia self-supporting and self-contained. Crude oil was replacing the firewood which formerly had to be imported from India; new industries were started to manufacture many other items, including soap, which had previously to be procured from outside the country; and even the troops in the rear areas were growing crops. Militarily there was little that could be done, particularly as the general war situation appeared so complicated. The Ottoman Empire might seem exhausted, as indeed it was, but the spectacular successes of the Germans in France and Flanders were adrenalin to the Sick Man of Europe and Enver's regime. At dawn on July 18, with the start of the great Allied advance in France which was to drive the Germans back to their own frontier, the whole tide of the war finally turned. On September 19, Allenby struck in Palestine, and a few days after the fall of Baku a realistic and prophetic summary of events was sent to the British Minister in Teheran:

> The complete destruction of the whole Turkish Army in Palestine leaves Syria open to invasion. Every anti-Turkish element in the country will support the advancing British. The communications of the Turkish force in Mesopotamia are thus seriously threatened, and in all probability it will be forced to abandon Mesopotamia altogether. Arabia is completely lost to them and the fall of Medina is now imminent. Turkey, in addition to being faced with the loss of three-quarters of her Asiatic territory, is gravely threatened in Europe by the Allied advance in the Balkans, which since September 15 has continued uninterruptedly. To meet all these dangers on so many fronts the Turks have only one army left, which is now in the Caucasus and Persia. General Allenby's victory has already compelled them to transfer to Constantinople a division which was destined for Tabriz; and the situation in the Balkans and Palestine will completely paralyze Turkish operations in the Middle East, and in all probability will lead very soon to the evacuation of Persia. Thus the whole situation has been transformed in the last few days, and the Turks must now think only of protecting their own territory, and not of further aggression.

Allenby, at Aleppo, had unlocked the door for Marshall; the Turks were beaten to a standstill in Palestine and now it was up to Marshall to administer the coup de grace in Mesopotamia. But Marshall was short of transport; maintaining the supply line to Persia needed almost every available vehicle in Mesopotamia, and the extension of the Baghdad railway as far as Tikrit had been vehemently opposed by Delhi. To advance on Mosul, which is what he was now ordered to do, therefore necessitated the slow build up of supply depots forward of Tikrit and doing this gave warning to the Turks of an impending attack in that direction. On other grounds, it did not seem as if the operation would be easy. The Turks had been occupying the position covering the Fathah Gorge for over a year and its defenses, both natural and artificial, were formidable; moreover, because of the dilution of the Mesopotamia Army, most of the troops who were available for the attack had no previous experience of war. And as final preparations were being made, a serious outbreak of Spanish influenza which was sweeping through Europe at that time provided an additional handicap.

Cobbe was given charge of the main operation for which, in addition to his own 17th and 18th Divisions, he was allotted Norton's and Cassels's Cavalry Brigades and the Light Armored Motor Batteries, while two squadrons of aircraft were detailed to support him. As a flank guard to protect the main operation, a mixed force under Lewin was detailed to move up the right flank with Kirkuk as its objective. Between October 18 and 29, Cobbe's force moved steadily forward and by the morning of October 29, the Turks had been driven back to a position just north of Sharqat. An attack on this position was launched early in the afternoon and the Turks responded with a vigorous counterattack. This was held, and that night loud explosions were heard coming from the Turkish position. Arrangements had been made to renew the attack next morning, but at daybreak white flags could be seen fluttering all along the Turkish lines and shortly afterward Ismail Hakki, the commander of the Tigris force, surrendered in person. (This officer had commanded the troops on the right bank of the Tigris opposite Kut in the early part of 1917 and had been one of the last to make good his escape across the river when the remnants of his force were captured in the Dahra Bend.) As nearly twelve thousand prisoners and 50 guns were taken, this represented a crushing defeat for the Turks. Yet it was not enough and orders were issued for a column, under General Fanshawe (the commander of the 18th Division), comprising the 7th and 11th Cavalry Brigades and the 54th Infantry Brigade, and some artillery, to push on and capture Mosul.

At noon on November 1, a general armistice was concluded with Turkey and next morning when Fanshawe's advance guard was within twelve miles of

Mosul it was met by a flag of truce, sent by the indefatigable Ali Ihsan. The bearer of the flag had brought a letter from Ali, telling Fanshawe of the terms of the armistice and asking him to fall back to the point he had reached at noon the previous day—when the armistice had been concluded. Marshall was having none of this; he was not going to be thwarted at this late hour, and Fanshawe was told to push on to Mosul. Ali Ihsan had little option but to give way and, to save face, he announced that he would welcome the British in Mosul.

With Ali posing as Commander in Chief of the Mosul region, and British troops bivouacked outside the town, a comic situation prevailed during the next few days. A Turkish band played "God Save the King" outside Fanshawe's` headquarters, while Turkish flags flew from the public buildings and this was a situation which Marshall was not prepared to tolerate. Inviting Ali to a conference, he announced that no matter how Ali Ihsan interpreted the terms of the armistice, he, Marshall, was determined to take over the whole Mosul region and if Ali resisted he would be held responsible for any blood that might be shed. After much specious argument, Ali, seething with rage, accepted the terms which Marshall laid down but later next day, wrote to say that he had sent in his resignation to the new Turkish Minister of War. Marshall's retort was to provide him with an escort to leave Mosul. After Ali's departure things went smoothly; the war in Mesopotamia was over.

So ends the chronicle of the campaign which General Gorringe had so bitterly described as being "No Man's Child." Four years, almost to a day, elapsed from the time the guns of HMS *Odin* silenced the Turkish battery at Fao until General Townshend, acting as a Turkish emissary, carried Marshal Izzet Pasha's request for a general armistice to Admiral Calthorpe at Mudros. Not counting materials and hopes, the cost of victory was nearly one hundred thousand casualties,[9] of whom close to one third were killed or died of wounds. And between the armistice and the beginning of 1922, the cost of Iraq to the British taxpayer was said to be £100,000,000. Whether the inheritors of the Turk reaped the harvest of all this sacrifice is another story; Mr. Bonar Law gave his opinion in the House of Commons: "I wish we had never gone there!"

---

9. Actual casualties were: Officers 4,335 (killed or died of wounds or disease 1,340); other ranks, 3,244 (killed or died 29,769).

Epilogue

We cannot undo the past, but we are bound to pass it in review, in order to
draw such lessons as may be applicable to the future.

Winston Churchill

By the spring of 1916, the ugly rumors circulating in Britain about the
sufferings of the wounded, and the inadequate administrative arrangements in Mesopotamia, had aroused considerable feelings of anxiety, indignation and alarm. During the anxious weeks when Kut lay under siege, criticism
of the way the campaign was being run swelled to a volume that the authorities
in Whitehall found impossible to ignore. Largely to propitiate the press, a
Commission of public inquiry, was appointed to "examine the origin, inception
and conduct of the operations"[1] in Mesopotamia and, where the evidence
warranted it, "apportion" blame and responsibility. The Commission's report
was published in August 1917 and the storm of indignation which it created
can only be compared with that which followed the loss of the Minorca in
1756 and resulted in the execution of Admiral Byng on the quarterdeck of the
Monarque. If only for this reason, therefore, a short digression on the facts
behind the outcry is necessary.

There can be little doubt that a public inquiry into the causes of what had
gone awry was warranted; whether autumn 1916 was the time for such an

---

1. Official History, Vol. IV.

inquiry is another matter, however. Shaken by the turn of events following the abortive attempt to reach Baghdad, and the storm of criticism aroused by the reports reaching India—mostly by men who had seen something of conditions at Ctesiphon—the Indian Government, in March 1916 had already initiated their own inquiry[2] into what lay behind the scandal of the medical arrangements. By August the evidence collected by the "Vincent-Bingley" Commission had had its effect, and most of the shortcomings were in the process of being put right. Lord George Hamilton, the Chairman of the Whitehall Commission, was one of those who had doubts about the timing of the British inquiry, and in a letter to the *Times*, a month before the Commission's report was published, he blandly announced that he had only agreed to take the job on in order to avert a political crisis. As may be appreciated from such behavior, Hamilton was clearly motivated primarily by political considerations and, as the composition of the rest of the Commission had a strong political bias also, it is not surprising that political rather than military factors appear to have dominated its deliberations. Eight men were appointed to it. Of the seven members besides Hamilton, one, Lord Donoughmore, was the chairman of various committees in the House of Lords, four were members of Parliament, and one was an Admiral; there was only one soldier, General Neville Lyttleton. Lyttleton had served in India but only as a young officer; "none of the others had any practical experience in that country, of military or civil administration."[3]

The aim of the Commission—according to its members own interpretation of the Government's terms of reference—was to investigate the efficiency of the administrative arrangements in Mesopotamia, and to report on the conduct of those responsible for the higher direction of the campaign. Wisely enough, they decided that it was no part of their duties to act as a supra-military court of inquiry, or to function as a court-martial; their findings were to be purely factual, disciplinary action was outside their aegis.

Because the evidence of the Vincent-Bingley Commission was already available to them, and a large number of sick or wounded officers who had served in Mesopotamia had returned to the U.K. in addition to the fact that those of the senior officials who were not then in England could be brought home without much difficulty, the Commission decided that there was no need for any of its members to visit either Mesopotamia or India. Without question this was a most unfortunate decision; some time and a little money was saved by conducting the inquiry in London, but only at the cost of sacrificing any

---

2. The "Vincent-Bingley" Commission—after the Honorable Sir William Vincent, K.t, I.C.S., Major General A. H. Bingley, C.B., C.I.E., two of its three members.
3. Official History, Vol. IV.

proper appreciation of the difficulties involved—the very factors which were of primary importance. As it was, the Commission had very little idea of the reality of the circumstances behind the words they collected, when a visit to the scene of the operations should have enabled them to draw more complete and accurate conclusions.

For the sake of legality, witnesses appearing before the Commission gave evidence on oath, but the customary rules of evidence were not observed and those whose conduct was questioned during the hearing were given little or no opportunity to clear themselves. Naturally enough, the exigencies of the war made it impossible to examine everybody whose evidence might have contributed to balanced conclusions—Townshend, for instance, was obviously a key witness, and he was a prisoner. But some, who undoubtedly should have given evidence, were not called upon to do so. For example, neither the Quartermaster-General in India, whose department was directly responsible for all the transport arrangements, nor any of his staff gave evidence. Such a blatant omission lends force to the criticism that the members of the Commission, sitting on soft seats in London, never grasped the significance of some of the issues they were supposed to be investigating.

However, between August 1916 and the following April, the evidence and opinions of a hundred witnesses was recorded and, when the Commission's report was published it hit the headlines. No doubt a public outcry had been expected; in all the circumstances, one was inevitable. What the wounded had had to endure was quite sufficient in itself to raise a storm, and the press clamored for disciplinary action against those whose conduct had been criticized—despite the fact that many of the Commission's conclusions were not legally proved. The gist of them was censure of the Secretary of State for India, the India Office, the Viceroy and several of the former commanders, including Generals Sir Beauchamp-Duff, and Sir John Nixon, who were all blamed for the tragedies leading to the fall of Kut; little recognition was paid to the way individuals had been handicapped by the lack of pre-war preparation and the strain on India's resources in August 1914. At a stormy debate in the House of Commons, Mr. Chamberlain, whom the Commission held partially responsible for the abortive advance to Ctesiphon, announced his resignation as Secretary of State for India. "It is not possible that I, who am named in the Report . . . and whose responsibility is sole and undivided in other matters where the Commission administers rebuke or censure, should continue as head of that office in which my conduct has been censured . . ." he declared. In actual fact Chamberlain's responsibility may be regarded as being little more than technical, but his resignation was regarded as an honorable gesture, in keeping with the precedents and traditions of the Mother of Parliaments, and it was accepted. Lord Hardinge, who was far more blameworthy than Chamberlain, had also been indicted by the Commission but his resignation was refused on the grounds that it would be detrimental to the public interest.

Because enough of the truth emerged, it might be argued that none of these factors are really important. Yet, when the findings of the Mesopotamia Commission are compared with those of the Dardanelles Commission, which investigated a disaster comparable with that which befell I.E.F. "D," it becomes apparent that the outcry about Mesopotamia was motivated by political considerations. The attempt to seize the keys of the Dardanelles was lauded as a brilliant strategic conception and when the Army Commander, General Sir Ian Hamilton, was relieved of his command the point was made that "seeing how much he had done with wholly insufficient means, the blame of the failure could scarcely lie heavily upon him."[4] Yet Nixon had also had to make do with "wholly insufficient means" but he was blamed. The planning of the Gallipoli operation is often described as "bold"; and a less suitable adjective would be difficult to find, since administrative arrangements were as inadequate as the individuals responsible for them were incompetent. Admittedly, the planning for the Mesopotamia campaign was as bad as at Gallipoli but, in spite of it, I.E.F. "D" accomplished wonders—as evinced by the amazing run of successes preceding Ctesiphon. An element of bad luck influenced both campaigns, as it always will, but while Hamilton proved to be totally ineffective in the field, Nixon showed that he was prepared to take risks in order to achieve success. Boldness, in other circumstances, is usually regarded as the fundamental requirement of a commander; he cannot hope to be "lucky" if he is not daring. Only when success does not follow the bold approach is criticism voiced, and this is what happened in Mesopotamia. Yet most of the senior commanders in this theater: Barrett, Nixon, Delamain, Townshend, Mellis, Gorringe and Aylmer—despite their age—and later Maude, Marshall, Cobbe and Brooking were far superior in imagination, energy and sheer guts to the comparable commanders at Gallipoli. They had the customary failings of the time, due largely to the system in which they had been brought up. Nevertheless they compare very favorably with their booted and spurred counterparts on the Western Front, who, from their French chateaux were more concerned with Whitehall intrigues than the battles.

But, even if it is argued that the generals were of the same calibera, there was one major difference between the Dardanelles and Mesopotamian expeditions which undoubtedly influenced the judgment of the two Commissions; the former was controlled by the Home Government, the latter by the Govern-

---

4. *Naval Operations,* Vol. III—Sir Julian S. Corbett, p. 171.

ment of India. Behind the charming, ineffective Hamilton and the romance of Troy lay the whole political might of Whitehall; behind Barrett and Nixon, a collection of individuals totally unfitted to control any sort of campaign, civil or military. "Apportioning blame and responsibility" comes easy when it lies outside one's own aegis and in the case of Mesopotamia the blame could so easily be laid at India's door. When Whitehall took over direction of the campaign it was quite certain that there could be no further inquiries as to its conduct, if only because it is difficult to conceive the authorities ordering a Commission to investigate the Government's own shortcomings. If it were not so, Commissions inquiring into the operations of the Somme, at Passchendale, and of operations in March 1918, or on the causes of the fall of Singapore and the ill-fated Suez venture in 1956, could have resulted in disconcerting dis closures, whose reverberations around the corridors of power in Whitehall might well have rocked the seats of politicians and service chiefs alike.

After the war, the Official British Historian was sufficiently moved to comment on the workings of the Mesopotamia Commission: *"That the Commission did not always appreciate the true significance of what it learnt, lends force to the criticism often made that, generally speaking the members of the Commission were lacking in the technical and up-to-date knowledge of military operations and military war organization required in an inquiry of this nature. It is undoubtedly true that in a military sense, its report was incomplete and in a few cases inaccurate."* That his *official* voice should be permitted to criticize in this fashion suggests that the post-war government was inclined to have second thoughts as to the value of the Commission's report. But the damage had been done; the scalp hunters with facile pens called for the punishment of those cited as being responsible by the Commission and the military reputations of most of the earlier commanders were destroyed.[5]

That there were scandalous failings on the part of the authorities responsible for the campaign, and of certain individuals in particular, is unquestionably true. But whether the Mesopotamia Commission apportioned blame correctly is another matter. It is not proposed to labor the point; apart from this general summary, criticisms and comments have been offered throughout this narrative, and the reader will have already appreciated that the two most important factors were administrative shortcomings and the effect of the terrain. Shortage of transport, supply difficulties and poor medical facilities have all been discussed at length, and it is not proposed to dwell on them; for the most part such failings stemmed from pre-war Governmental parsimony or inadequate preparations. The terrain comes into a different category however,

---

5. Not that of Townshend. When he returned to England after the war he was still regarded as "the Hero of Kut" by everyone, except powerful factions behind the scenes in the War Office. Nixon died, of a broken heart it was said, in 1921.

and because it is peculiar to the "land of Sweet F.A. with a river up it," some comment on its effect is necessary. First, it must be remembered that these were the days before the tank had made its appearance on the battlefield, and when it came to infantry attacks the ground favored the defence. Moving across the open, attackers were subject to the devastating effect of long range small arms fire, and heavy casualties brought attacks to a standstill at ranges of over a thousand yards, time and time again. Irrigation channels close to the river, lack of landmarks, mirage, and the fact that the ground was easy to dig, all helped the defender. The vast distances; the flat, bare, featureless plain; lack of cover, and the floods all added enormously to the difficulties of the attackers. Poor maps, lack of information, and the complete absence of drinking water away from the river during the hot weather, all handicapped movement; and in the cold season the whole plain turned into a morass of sticky mud. As an obstacle, as a vital supply line and, above all, as the source of water to which the troops on both sides were tied, the Tigris was all-important, and its paramount influence on the operations will have been obvious. However—except in the unique conditions afforded by the Suwaikiyeh Marsh in front of Kut—the Tigris did normally provide one exploitable feature; because the defenders were tied to it, there was always an "open" flank. Townshend had grasped this simple fact very early, and that is why his bold operation at Es Sinn, leading to the capture of Kut in September 1915, was so successful. Later in the campaign, "turning" the outer flank became almost a battle drill and the actions at Ramadi, Khan Baghadi, and Tikrit were all fought on this basis.

It might have been expected that the cavalry would have done more to exploit the open flank, and nothing could have been more disappointing in the early part of the campaign than its absolute failure. That it did so badly is largely due to the fact that India had sent some of the best of her regular cavalry to France, and only an ill-organized, scratch brigade to Mesopotamia. Apart from their poor equipment and old horses, the units themselves were second-rate, and caste questions and feeding methods all detracted from their efficiency. And there is little doubt that the wretched animals suffered appallingly. Their corn and fodder all had to be brought up from Basra and occupied much space in the scanty river transport. As the line of communications lengthened these supplies were more and more apt to run short at critical times and by the time of Es Sinn, every rib of me horses could be counted. It was not their war but they were worn out by the flies, the short rations and overwork. Still, it must be remembered that Mesopotamia was, in many respects, cavalry country "par excellence"; the going was good and favored the mobility which was supposed to be the one outstanding advantage that the mounted arm brought to the field. By moving swiftly, making use of the mirage, and sweeping around the flank the advantage seemed to lie with mounted men; if opposition were met, a wider sweep should have enabled them to retain their striking power and still hold the advantage. But not until late in the campaign was this fact grasped; right up to the occupation of Baghdad the cavalry always seems to have moved at its slowest pace, hanging on to the infantry, and at a crucial stage of any battle, taking the first opportunity of either returning to water its horses or getting rid of them and coming to a standstill.

One of the prime difficulties facing both cavalry and infantry was that of determining precise locations, and in maintaining the direction of an advance; compasses were indispensable but very few were available. Attacking an unseen enemy through a hail of bullets, whose source was invisible; acutely conscious of being conspicuous against the skyline, and baffled by not knowing exactly where they were—all these factors induced a depressing sense of importance in the British and Indian troops. And this feeling was exacerbated by the difficulty of distinguishing friend from foe, and inability to judge distances across the flat shimmering plain. As always the brunt of the fighting was borne by the infantry, and in the early days the troops tried to advance in the way they had been trained. The method used was one which had been developed and proved successful during the Boer War—one section providing covering fire, while another party ran forward. But such tactics were of little use in Mesopotamia, where a concealed machine-gun could sweep vast areas of open ground and control any covered approaches. Add to this the retrogressive attitude and insane rigidity of those in command—elderly brigadiers to whom the Boer War was the pattern and who, for the most part, were possessed by a "dress by the right" complex—and it is easy to understand[6] why British and Indian casualties were so heavy. Despite losses, frontal attacks were regarded as the most normal method of securing an objective; a solid column would be directed on to it and despite the blasting of the successive front ranks, the column kept on until either the objective was taken or flesh and blood could stand no more. Troops coming from France, to whom long advances across open ground with little or no artillery umbrella were novel, were often regarded as trench-minded, and lacking in offensive spirit by the old guard in Mesopotamia, trained and accustomed to war on the North-West Frontier of India.

On the Western Front, it had been quickly appreciated that frontal attacks could only hope to be successful if they were supported by enormous artillery bombardments. But artillery support of this nature was never possible in

---

[6] This was not peculiar to Mesopotamia, of course; nor to the British Army. Similar hide-bound rigidity was seen with the Germans when the steamroller advance of 1870 was employed against the firepower of 1914.

Mesopotamia. It is unnecessary to emphasize the effect of difficult observation, the mirage, and lack of accurate maps; some of these problems might have been overcome by use of aerial observation—if the airplanes had been available. Air photographs could and did help, but generally it was extremely difficult to shoot at the right place at the right time, unless airplanes located the targets and then ranged the guns. Getting shells onto the correct location is a self-evident necessity but often it just did not work out that way. At Dujaila, for example, the Mound offered a good, clear target and it was heavily shelled; but the trenches just below it escaped any damage. And in the first battle of Sannaiyat, the guns fired not on the infantry's objective but only on the second and third line trenches. Apart from a shortage of high explosive ammunition there were no smoke shells at all. In the dry hot weather, shrapnel was found to be reasonably effective in raising a screen of dust which served as smoke cover, but in the wet weather, and in many of Marshall's early actions, only smoke shells could have provided a screen. Yet there were none—not merely because of transport and climatic deterioration difficulties, but because smoke was new and its possibilities had not yet been realized in Mesopotamia. But all these causes were merely contributory. The plain fact is that the British artillery never attained its "Queen of the Battlefield" status in Mesopotamia; not only was it hopelessly insufficient to give even the necessary covering fire to the infantry, but it could rarely do any counter-battery work, which usually had to be left to the warships on the river. For the first and probably the last time in the campaign the Turkish artillery was mastered at Qurna, but this only happened because the Turks had so few guns in such a restricted area. At Ctesiphon, and again in the Spring of 1916 when the ships were unable to get within range of the British objectives, the Turks were able to shell the attacking columns without let up or hindrance. Even as late as April 1917 at Istabulat, when many more guns and plenty of ammunition were available, the British artillery was still inferior to that of the Turks. It would be possible to detail the effect of many of the shortages, but as most things were in short supply there seems little point. The lack of guns has been chosen, not because any stigma is attached to the gunners themselves—under the greatest difficulties they performed magnificently—but because they were so few, the infantry casualties were correspondingly great. Something must now be said about the much maligned Buddhoos, who also exerted a considerable influence on the campaign. Leaving out any consideration of religious affinities it could be expected that the Turks should have more influence over them than the British; when I.E.F. "D" landed at Fao, the Turks were, after all, the men in possession. Probably the Arabs were not hostile to the British as such, it was just that they objected to anyone who came to their country or tried to control them. And as true sons of Ishmael they were out for loot, not glory. Since both sides ruined their fields, dug trenches in their crops, cut down their dates, destroyed the irrigation cuts and, more often than not, treated them like dirt, the war was a great nuisance. All they could hope for was profit by loot; it really mattered little which side provided it. Many of them were mounted, and although their ponies were small they could ride rings around the heavily accoutred British and Indian cavalry. Preferring not to risk a fight unless the odds were heavily weighted in their favor, they would tag along behind British columns in crowds, keeping just out of range but surging forward occasionally to fire their rifles into close formations, and always alert for the chance to ambush small parties. Expert thieves, they could get through almost any obstacle at night without being discovered, and were even known to crawl under the barbed wire perimeter fences of British camps and tie the legs of horses together, prior to dragging them back under the wire—all undetected. Even the best known achievements of the Pathans on the North-West Frontier of India could rarely compare with the exploits of the Buddhoos in this direction. With plunder their sole object, they had no compunction about despoiling the dead, and would dig up corpses for the sake of their clothing and boots, which meant that burial places had to be concealed. Unquestionably they were a great nuisance, particularly in the first two years of the campaign. If it had been possible to take vigorous action against them in the early days, no doubt their nuisance value could have been severely curtailed; but the political situation, the hopeless lack of transport and the ineffectiveness of the British cavalry precluded this. Consequently, throughout the campaign troops had to be confined in perimeter camps, large numbers of guards had to be found and extra care taken to protect the flanks of any advance.

Since the material difficulties under which the campaign was undertaken could hardly have been worse, it must be regarded as an epic of guts and improvisation. There was a shortage of almost everything needed for its prosecution and so, up to Ctesiphon, the amazing successes which *were* achieved were little short of miraculous; after that followed a period of failure. It is not proposed to go over the arguments as to whether or not the siege of Kut should ever have taken place. Townshend's judgment was that an advance beyond Kut was foolhardy, but an officer may not repeat a rejected protest and after Ctesiphon he had to make the best of a bad job. Until then, his role had been that of the commander of a striking force, with Baghdad as his objective; after Ctesiphon he was supposed to play for time and cover Basra until problematical reinforcements could arrive from France and India. The alternatives facing him were to turn Kut into a defended camp, and be prepared to withstand a siege; or to retire down the Tigris and stand at Ali Gharbi—the most suitable forward area for the fresh troops to concentrate for another British offensive. Since Nixon ordered him to stand siege in Kut the decision may be considered to have been taken out of Townshend's hand and it may be argued that this was the only choice open to a far-sighted general with a depleted force in ill-health. Yet one cannot escape the impression that in the early stages, Townshend himself considered the idea of a siege preferable to a further retirement; always at the back of his mind there was the memory of his success at Chitral.

Against the background of the difficulties and shortages which have been discussed, far from its being surprising that Townshend's garrison was never relieved, the more astonishing do the achievements of the troops of the Tigris Corps appear. And this can be put down to two things. First, in four black months, both Aylmer and Gorringe made superhuman efforts to overcome insuperable obstacles with inadequate means and secondly, the extraordinarily high morale and the first rate quality of the troops concerned—particularly those who came from Egypt, but above all the superb Indian Corps from France. The latter divisions had seen much hard fighting in the mud of Flanders and, despite heavy casualties, a camaraderie had developed between British and Indians which was probably not excelled even by that engendered by the 4th Indian Division in Eritrea and North Africa twenty-five years later. Their performance in the bitter battles of Hanna, the Wadi and Dujaila speak for themselves; never before had the Indian Army had to fight under such heartbreaking conditions and accept such monstrous casualties. As was so well said in an official telegram "They did all that flesh and blood could do."

After the fall of Kut, when Whitehall took over direction of the campaign and Maude assumed command, the technique of destruction began to build up. Until that time, as General Gorringe said, Mesopotamia "was believed to be a sideshow and no man's child." In the Nile campaign, Gordon's death in Khartoum gave the British Government a definite objective. Transport, materials, and troops were collected in that order and a methodical preparation finally resulted in Omdurman. Similarly it was Townshend's surrender that produced a definite object for this campaign. Until Kut fell, its direction had been under the control of India where a regressive atmosphere was unfavorable to reform or change, and whose government was totally unfitted to control a large expedition overseas. Lack of cooperation between India and Britain, and between civil and military executives in both countries was the underlying cause of the failures. Disunity of purpose is common to many campaigns—not only British. And one can usually trace three distinct periods in the actions of the governments concerned. First, the period of reluctantly learning the meaning of cooperation; a second period when they were being forced to make such cooperation possible; and finally a third period when the hard earned and expensive lesson was put into effect with dramatic effect. In his book *Before the War,* Lord Haldane wrote: "It is our gift to be able to apply ourselves in emergencies with immense energy. Our success in promptly pulling ourselves together has often suggested to outside observers that we had long ago looked ahead, but we were merely inefficient." (In 1940 Winston Churchill was to echo these very sentiments.)

The campaign in Mesopotamia was an excellent example of British ability to "muddle through" for the "ill-found expedition," after its preliminary defeats, was finally crowned in victory. But after Kut, what did it really accomplish when the oil supply at Ahwaz had been made safe? What of lasting value did it achieve? According to modern historians, the Ottoman Empire was broken by the Arab revolt, and histories of Iraq written today make little or no mention of the I.E.F. "D," the Mesopotamian Expeditionary Force, Maude or Marshall; Townshend and Kut are largely forgotten; many people are not even quite sure where Mesopotamia is—or was. Yet Iraq exists now largely because of what the British Indian Army did. Half a million men, fighting under the British flag, brought freedom to a nation and the benefit of Iraqi oil to the rest of the world; to shatter the German dream of an Oriental Empire and "a place in the sun" over thirty thousand of them died in the Mesopotamian wastes.

After Kut was further sacrifice really necessary? Indeed was any campaign ever necessary in Mesopotamia at all? To both of these questions a negative answer might have been provided by what is usually known as "the Alexandretta Project." Had this scheme been put into effect there might never have been any campaign in Mesopotamia, and certainly the Gallipoli disaster would have been averted. Doubtless there are some who will say that any alternative could have proved even more costly than both the Gallipoli and Mesopotamia "side-shows" combined. But no one can possibly say what the outcome might have been and as it was viable and seemingly, at fifty years distance, an attractive alternative, a brief outline of what was envisaged makes a fitting conclusion to this story.

The idea was the ingenious brain-child of that far-sighted soldier, Lord Kitchener, who suggested that a force landed in the Gulf of Alexandretta in the Mediterranean could cut the Baghdad railway, which skirts the Gulf, and sever Turkey's main line of communications to the east. Once this was achieved, the Ottoman Empire would have been cut in two and as the railway tunnels through the mountain ranges east and west of the Gulf were still unfinished in 1915, it would have been extremely difficult for the Turks to mount an effective counter-stroke. Any force, advancing either from the west or east to attack the invaders entrenched across the railway, would have had to operate from railheads beyond the mountains and across eighty miles of difficult roads and mountain tracks. Under such circumstances, since Turkey was known to have very little mechanical transport, her army's supply problem would have been very difficult, while the fact that the local population was mostly Armenian should also have helped the invaders.

It was a plan ideally suited to a nation whose power and prestige rested on the Royal Navy and, if the Alexandretta scheme had been carried through with the whole might of India, Australia and New Zealand behind it, it is reasonable to suppose that Turkey would have collapsed before the end of 1915. Admittedly all this is conjecture but if it had succeeded, there would have been no Mesopotamian campaign, no Armenian massacres, no toiling through Sinai sands, no Gaza battles and no fighting in Palestine. In all probability Bulgaria would never have joined the Central Powers; Serbia would have been saved, and the Russian debacle might never have occurred. Lastly Britain would have been spared the humiliation of Kut and the Dardanelles defeat and the vast sacrifice of human life that the Gallipoli-Mesopotamia ventures entailed. Nor is such conjecturing entirely without foundation from "the other side of the hill"; as the following extracts from Field Marshal von Hindenburg's reminiscences of the war make clear:

> Perhaps not the whole course of the war he wrote but certainly the fate of our Ottoman Ally, could have been settled out of hand, if England had secured a decision in that region, or even seriously attempted it. Possession of the country south of the Taurus would have been lost to Turkey at a blow, if the English had succeeded in landing in the Gulf of Alexandretta.

> In so doing they would have severed the main artery of Trans-Taurian Turkey, through which flesh and blood and other revitalizing forces flowed to the Syrian, Mesopotamian and a part of the Caucasian armies.

> The protection of the Gulf of Alexandretta was entrusted to a Turkish army which contained scarcely a single unit fit to fight; every man who could be of use in the fighting line was gradually transferred to Syria or Mesopotamia. Moreover, coast protection by artillery at this point was more a figment of the Oriental imagination than a military reality.

> Enver Pasha exactly described the situation to me in the words: "My only hope is that the enemy has not discovered our weakness at this critical spot." It seemed impossible that the English High Command should not know the true state of the coast defenses in this theatre.

> If ever there was a prospect of a brilliant strategic feat it was here. Such a campaign would have made an enormous impression on the whole world, and unquestionably would have had a far-reaching effect on our Turkish Ally.

> Why did England never make use of her opportunity here?

The answer to von Hindenburg's question is tragically simple. In February 1915 (which, it will be recalled, was before Nixon had taken over in Basra) General Bird wood's army in Egypt was preparing for this very operation; orders for the action after landing had actually been issued. But on February 16, the decision was taken in Whitehall to divert all the available troops in Egypt for the support of the naval attack against the Dardanelles and "K. of K's" plan was abandoned. Later, when the decision to evacuate Gallipoli was taken he tried to resuscitate it. But by then the military and naval staffs of both France and Britain, as well as the statesmen, had had their fill of amphibious warfare and after the Aegean experience no scheme of this nature, however enticing, would tempt them a second time. And not only were the Allies now deeply embroiled in Mesopotamia; they were also committed to the Salonika venture. The opportunity was gone and it is for posterity to say whether this was a mistake. Fifty years after the events, Britain still has an enviable share in the oil of the Middle East, but it is hard to say whether the "ill-found" campaign in Mesopotamia contributed much toward this state of affairs.

Yet it is fitting to conclude with a reminder that history has a strange way of repeating itself. At the beginning of the Second World War, Britain faced the same problems in this part of the world, as she had faced in 1914; Middle East oil was vital, Iraq—as Mesopotamia had been renamed—was still a *Drang nach Osten*. Fortunately, the lessons of the neglected campaign of two and a half decades before, had been absorbed by the succeeding generation of administrators—some of whom had fought in Mesopotamia and grimly recalled their own experiences of a bastard country, and a bastard war. Iraq was secured and held *before* the Germans and their allies could once again cause it to be the theater of a difficult and costly campaign at a time when Britain's resources were, once again, at their lowest ebb.

Appendix

Notes on the Organization and Equipment Used

1. *General*

The campaign in Mesopotamia must be considered in the context of the whole war destined to be called the First World War. Certain limitations, such as the fact that Mesopotamia was regarded as a secondary theater directed from Delhi and that certain personalities were involved have a special significance. But, when one takes a sober look at armament, equipment methods, and even prevailing attitudes of mind in regard to such issues as attrition, it will be appreciated that certain factors were equally as applicable to the Western Front (or Gallipoli) as to Mesopotamia.

To begin with, no one really had any idea of what a "big" war was going to be like, and very few people prophesied the effect of the machine gun or that the war would be one of entrenchments. The importance of artillery had been made clear by the Russo-Japanese War, but even so the need for heavy artillery with which to pound successive lines of trenches in depth behind the front line had been overlooked. The standard British 18-pounder field gun closely resembled the weapons of all the other great powers. With an effective range of about 5,300 yards, it had a maximum rate of *sustained* fire of eight rounds a minute. A British infantry division in 1914 had fifty-six 18-pounders and eighteen 4.5-inch howitzers, but I.E.F. "D" was less well equipped than this. Indirect fire by artillery was in an experimental stage compared with what we know today. The use of flags, helios, and signal lamps was attended with obvious disadvantages, and in Mesopotamia the mirage often precluded their use at all. Telephones functioned well so long as the wires remained uncut, but the disadvantage was the distances involved.

Demands for increased infantry firepower led to the arming of battalions with light machine guns, but none reached Mesopotamia until the autumn of 1916; in the fierce battles to relieve Kut in April of that year the Vickers gun had to be used in an LMG role. As the Vickers tripod weighed 48 lbs. and the gun itself another 38 lbs., it did not make for mobility.

In 1914 the airplane was only beginning to make its military debut in Europe. No one had resolved whether it was better to use the French method of *rafales* (squalls) of shells to overwhelm resistance by rapid fire and sheer weight of metal or to rely on the method preferred by the British of slow, carefully ranged concentrations of fire on the most important target.

Experience soon showed that concealment and cover for the guns were vital; direct fire was found to be impracticable except in special circumstances, and guns were controlled by Forward Observation Officers (F.O.O.) by means of a telephone. To cope with entrenched defense and machine guns, attacks had to be made under barrages—moving walls of steel splinters that crept forward ahead of the infantry assault. Communication systems were weak. The wireless was capricious; radios in the field had only a short range, while portable sets were still only in a developmental stage. Development was quick but, as might be expected, it was 1917 before any of the new techniques really made themselves felt in Mesopotamia. Except for a few in Palestine, tanks were never used anywhere except on the Western Front, but armored cars did have an opportunity to prove their worth in Mesopotamia in the closing stages of the war.

2. *Organization of the British Army*

For the benefit of the serious student of military history, the organization of the British and Indian troops has been given in some detail. This conspectus is a theoretical one and its interpretation is accompanied by the difficulty, well known to all soldiers, of distinguishing between "ration," "combatant," and "rifle" (or "bayonet") strengths. This organization is also the one the British War Office aimed for after its take-over from the Indian Government.

According to *The Field Service Pocket-Book of 1914,* an Indian Division- of three infantry brigades and divisional troops was composed of 3,548 British "bayonets" and 8,606 Indian: a total of 12,154 fighting men, including officers and armed men, in the administrative services. There were also 3,212 "camp followers"—sweepers (sanitary men), *dhobis,* cooks, and servants—who did not carry arms. To support them, there were 1,750 animals—pack mules, ponies, and camels. A Cavalry Division consisted of a headquarters, four cavalry brigades, two horse artillery brigades, a field engineers squadron, a signal squadron, and four cavalry field ambulances (total: 439 officers and 8,830 men under a Major General).

A Cavalry Brigade had a headquarters, three cavalry regiments, and a signals troop (about 1,700 all ranks, under a Brigadier General). When not allotted to a Cavalry Division, the Brigade also had a horse artillery battery, an ammunition column, a troop of field engineers, signals, and a cavalry field ambulance (total strength 2,300).

3. *Transport*

The Tigris served as the only real line of communication for the British and Turks alike. The British, with access to the sea, were in a position to increase and replenish their river transport; the Turks were left with what was upstream when Basra was captured. When Kut was besieged, Khalil Pasha had five large river steamers at his disposal, but these could only carry goods as far as his base at Shumran, five miles north of Kut; therefore, supplies for the troops facing the Tigris Corps had to be conveyed from Shumran by means of camels and donkeys.

From Mosul Turkish troops and equipment were carried downstream to Baghdad on *kelleks*—enormous skin rafts, still used on the Tigris reaches. They were broken up at Baghdad and the skins taken back to Mosul by land to be made up again into rafts for repeated use.

So far as the British were concerned, the carrying capacity of the Tigris fleet at the time of Townshend's fateful advance to Ctesiphon never equaled that of a working, single-line railway with adequate rolling stock. Yet the river could have offered advantages over a railway running through potentially hostile Arab territory; up to Qurna the Shatt-al-Arab was navigable for ocean-going steamers of up to 14-feet draft and, above it vessels drawing feet of water could usually get as far as Amara, if not beyond. Most of the paddle steamers were of 400 to 500 tons and drew between 3½ and 5 feet of water. They worked with a lighter attached to both sides—a system that not only increased the carrying capacity but also protected the steamer at the numerous bends in the tortuous Tigris.

Since considerable reliance had to be placed on native craft, a description of the types used is pertinent:

Mahela (Mahaila). This was a crude, primitive, piratical-looking craft akin to the *dhow,* with high forward sloping masts, huge rudder, and lateen sail; it was painted like a Chinese junk but had Arab designs and characters. These boats varied considerably in size; their capacity ran from 15 to nearly 100 tons, but the most common ones carried about 30 to 35 tons. Towed against a current, a *mahela* could make about 10 miles a day; under sail with a following wind she could do about 5 or 6 knots.

Bellum. This is the Arab name for the long, canoe-shaped boat that still abounds around Basra. In appearance the *bellum* resembles a gondola; it is poled or paddled according to the depth of the water and was capable of carrying 15 to 25 men. A fleet of bellums was converted into assault craft (referred to in official dispatches as "war bellums") by armoring them with iron plates.

Mashoof. This was a cheap and very flimsy version of the *bellum.* The *Danack* was a cross between the *bellum* and *mashoof* but propelled by paddles rather than by poles.

Gufah (Goofah). The cauldron-shaped *gufah* of Baghdad, indigenous to the Tigris, is a round coracle of dried reeds coated with bitumen; it varies in size between 4 and 12 feet in diameter. (The usual diameter was 7 feet and this size could carry 15 to 20 men.) Below Amara *gufahs* were seen infrequently, but they were used in increasing numbers between Kut and Baghdad. Probably the oldest vessel in the world, Herodotus said they were "round as bucklers" taking merchandise and a donkey each from Nineveh to Babylon. At Babylon the merchandise would be unpacked, and the *gufah* would be stripped and carried back to Nineveh by the donkey passenger.

Two other craft are also wormy of mention: the *Safina*—a large flat-bottomed wooden barge, shaped like a pontoon, and a *Gissara*—a type of boat used in Turkish and Arab bridges. *Gissaras* invariably formed the pontoons of Turkish boat-bridges.

Land transport started off by being that which might be expected to support a North-West Frontier campaign. First- and second-line transport was provided by pack mules; "A.T." carts were drawn by mules, ponies, or camels, and a bullock train pulled the heavy guns. In the roles for which they were intended, the mules and ponies, as well as their drivers, lacked nothing; there were just not enough of them. The camels were not so successful; apart from the problems of feeding them in the Basra region, they are not as hardy as mules: they are sensitive to damp, cannot stand snow, and must be tactfully treated if they are to work well.

In spite of Mesopotamia's resources in cars, none was made available to her by India until after the War Office had assumed control of the theater. General Maude, when he relieved Sir Percy Lake, immediately demanded mechanical transport from the United Kingdom, and during 1917 motor ambulances, cars, lorries, and armored cars started to arrive. In fact, there was a very good reason why mechanical transport was substituted for animals: fuel and oil were available locally, while fodder had to be imported from India. Half-ton Ford vans were selected as the most suitable general-purpose vehicles, and by the end of the war nearly 7,000 vehicles were in Mesopotamia, as compared with 100 heavy lorries in use when Baghdad fell.

4. *The Royal Naval Air Service and the Royal Flying Corps in Mesopotamia*

Early in 1915, to provide a means for air reconnaissance, a flight of four naval seaplanes was sent out from Egypt to set up a seaplane base at Basra. Three of the aircraft were Short seaplanes (150 h.p. Sunbeam engines) and the other a Sopwith (100 h.p. Gnome engine). It was soon found that land-based aircraft were of more use than seaplanes, and so two of the Shorts were converted to "hydro-airplanes" by stripping their floats and substituting wheels. For the operation on the Tigris in April 1916, Gorringe had eight aircraft of the Military Wing and three seaplanes. Thirty Squadron came into being in March; before that all aircraft were under the command of Major Massey (of the 29th Punjab Regiment). The aircraft that accompanied Townshend's force up to Lajj comprised five different types: the three Short seaplanes, B.E. 2G (90 h.p. engine capable of about 85 miles per hour), Maurice Farman Longhorn (70 h.p. engine), Maurice Farman Shorthorn (70 h.p. engine), and Martinsyde—Martin Handyside—(80 h.p. Gnome engine). Eight machines in all were available at the time of Ctesiphon, as well as the two converted seaplanes. Of these, one B.E. 2C crashed on landing at Lajj, one Maurice Farman Shorthorn was sent to cut the telegraph lines beyond Baghdad (see page 103) and was lost, and a Longhorn was shot down near Ctesiphon before the battle started. After the battle the five remaining machines flew back to Kut, where the two seaplanes were dismantled and sent downstream on a barge. None of the aircraft that remained in Kut during the siege ever worked, and the pilots and crew were given non-flying duties.

In March and April the food dropped into Kut was flown in by B.E. 2C's—50-lb. bags being slung on each side of the fuselage and 25-lb. bags on the undercarriage. There were 140 food-dropping flights, and a total of about 16,800 lbs. was dropped from heights of 5,000 to 8,000 feet between April 15 and April 27; German aircraft and Turkish gunfire prevented the supplies being dropped from lower altitudes. Besides food and mail, a 70-lb. millstone and £10,000 in gold and silver were successfully dropped. Needless to say, all these items were "free" dropped; no parachutes were available.

5. *The Turkish Army*

In 1914 the Turkish Empire contained a heterogeneous mixture of races and creeds, including Arabs, Armenians, Kurds, and Syrians. However, the backbone of the Turkish Army was the sturdy Anatolian Turk. Courageous, with a certain inherent aptitude for war and an extraordinary power of endurance—particularly under stress and conditions of hardship and privation—he made a first-class fighting soldier. He was limited only by his poor education and consequent inability to handle complex weapons and equipment.

Just before the war an attempt was made to reorganize the Turkish Army on German lines under a German military mission headed by General Liman von Sanders, but there had been little time to effect any marked change. In August 1914, 36 weak divisions were able to take the field, and as the war progressed other divisions were formed, but not more than 43 divisions were ever mobilized at the same time.[1]

A division normally consisted of three regiments (brigades)—each of three battalions and a machine-gun detachment, supported by 24 to 36 field guns and the usual ancillary services, but the divisions varied considerably in strength. There were grave deficiencies in heavy artillery, technical units, transport, medical and supply services, and there was no effective air service. As the war progressed the Germans endeavored to remedy these deficiencies; they also took over all the principal staff appointments and ran the Turkish railways. These German actions, coupled with the disparities in rations, clothing, and amenities that existed between the Germans and Turks, and a typical Teutonic attitude toward their Turkish allies aroused considerable friction.

Leaving all these considerations to one side, the Turkish soldier showed qualities that made him a formidable adversary, particularly on the defensive. Defensive positions were invariably skillfully planned and well constructed; once the Turks were in them, they would hold on stubbornly until the end. (Townshend commented on more than one occasion of the Turks' "beloved" trenches.)

---

1. Over 2½ million Turks were said to have been called up, but losses and desertions were so heavy that the total army strength was probably never more than 650,000. Only the Anatolian Turks kept their morale and fought well to the end; disaffection and desertion were rife among the other races.

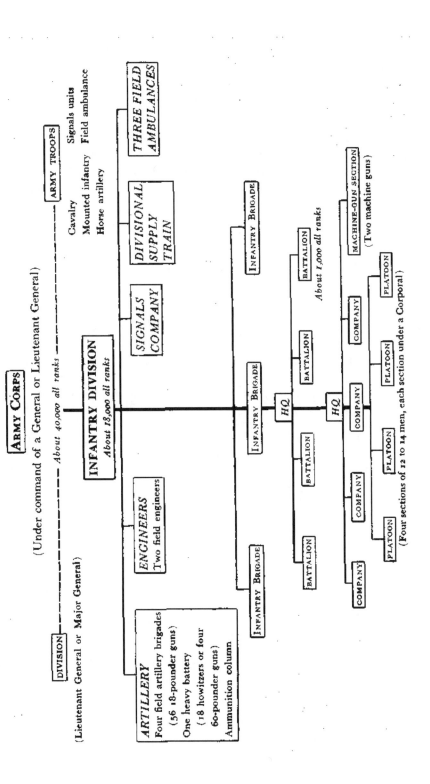

ARMY CORPS

(Under command of a General or Lieutenant General)

About 40,000 all ranks

DIVISION — — — — — — — — **ARMY TROOPS**

(Lieutenant General or Major General)

Cavalry   Signals units
Mounted infantry   Field ambulance
Horse artillery

INFANTRY DIVISION
About 18,000 all ranks

ARTILLERY
Four field artillery brigades
(56 18-pounder guns)
One heavy battery
(18 howitzers or four
60-pounder guns)
Ammunition column

ENGINEERS
Two field engineers

SIGNALS COMPANY

DIVISIONAL SUPPLY TRAIN

THREE FIELD AMBULANCES

INFANTRY BRIGADE   INFANTRY BRIGADE   INFANTRY BRIGADE   INFANTRY BRIGADE

HQ   HQ

BATTALION   BATTALION   BATTALION   BATTALION

About 1,000 all ranks

COMPANY   COMPANY   COMPANY   COMPANY   MACHINE-GUN SECTION

(Two machine guns)

PLATOON   PLATOON   PLATOON   PLATOON

(Four sections of 12 to 14 men, each section under a Corporal)

Bibliography

This is *not* a comprehensive bibliography; for the most part it is but a list of books and articles referred to while compiling the account. One book not listed that contains much relevant background material is that consistent best seller, the Bible. Many of the books listed are not easy to procure; for the reader who wishes to pursue the subject of Mesopotamia, the best sources in the United Kingdom are the libraries of the British Museum, the Imperial War Museum, and—for members—the Royal United Service Institution.

Books have been listed with date of publication; regimental histories have been denoted only by their main title. Apologies are offered in advance for any inconsistencies in ranks and initials.

1. *General*

Barber, Major C. H., I.M.S., *Besieged in Kut and After* (Edinburgh: Wm. Blackwood & Sons, 1917).

Bell, Lady, D.B.E., *The Letters of Gertrude Bell,* 2 vols. (New York: Boni and Liveright, 1927).

Birch-Reynardson, Capt. H., *Mesopotamia 1914–1915* (London: Andrew Melrose, 1918).

Bird, Major-Gen. W. D., *A Chapter of Misfortunes* (The Battles of Ctesiphon and Duj'ailah), (London: Forster Groom & Co., 1923).

Bishop, H. C. W., *A Kut Prisoner* (New York and London: John Lane & Co., 1920).

Bray, Major N. N. E., *Shifting Sand* (London: Unicorn Press, 1934).

Buchanan, Sir G., *The Tragedy of Mesopotamia* (Edinburgh: Wm. Blackwood & Sons, 1938).

Bullard, Sir R., *The Camels Must Go* (London: Faber & Faber, 1961).

Callwell, Major-Gen. C. E., *Field Marshal Sir Henry Wilson.,* 2 vols. (New York: C. Scribner's Sons, 1927).

——, *The Life of Sir Stanley Maude* (London: Constable & Co., 1920).

Candler, Edmund, *The Long Road to Baghdad,* 2 vols. (London: Cassell & Co., 1919).

Cato, C., *The Navy in Mesopotamia 1914–1917* (London: Constable & Co., 1918).

Churchill, Rt. Hon. Winston S., *The World Crisis 1916–1918* (Vols. 3 and 4), (New York: C. Scribner's Sons, 1927).

Cook, Sir E., *The Press in War Time* (London: Macmillan & Co., 1920).

Corbett, Sir Julian, *Naval Operations* (*History of the Great War, Based on Official Documents,* Vols. 2 and 6), (London: Longmans, Green & Co., 1922 and 1923). (Published for the Historical Section of the Committee of Imperial Defence.)

Dunsterville, Major-Gen. L. C., *The Adventures of Dunsterforce* (London: Edward Arnold, 1920).

Eady, Major H. G., *Historical Illustrations to Field Service Regulations* (London: Sifton Praed, 1930).

Egan, Eleanor Franklin, *The War in the Cradle of the World* (New York: Harper & Brothers, 1918).

Ellison, Lieut.-Gen. Sir Gerald, *The Perils of Amateur Strategy* (London: Longmans, Green & Co., 1926).

Erdman, Hugo, *In Heiligen Kersien* (Berlin: Mittler, 1918).

Evans, Lieut.-Col. R., *Brief Outline of the Mesopotamia Campaign* (London: Sifton Praed, 1926).

Ewing, Rev. W., *From Gallipoli to Baghdad* (London: Hodder and Stoughton, 1917).

Fortescue, Sir John, *Following the Drum* (Edinburgh: Wm. Blackwood & Sons, 1932).

Fraser, Lovat, *India Under Lord Curzon and After* (New York: H. Holt & Co., 1911).

Gawry, Gerald De, *Three Kings of Baghdad* (London: Hutchinson & Co., 1961).

Hall, Lieut.-Col. L. J., *The Inland Water Transport* (London: Constable & Co., 1921).

Hankey, Lord, *The Supreme Command 1914-1918* (Vol. 2) (London: Allen & Unwin, 1961).

Hindenburg, Marshal Paul Von, *Out of My Life.* (Translated by F. A. Holt. London: Cassell & Co., 1920).

Ismay, Lord, *Memoirs* (New York: Viking Press, 1960).

Jones, E. H., *The Road to En-Dor* (New York and London: John Lane & Co., 1919).

Kearsey, Lieut.-Col. A., *A Study of the Strategy and Tactics of the Mesopotamia Campaign* (Aldershot: Gale & Polden, 1934).

Kiesling, Oberstleutnant Hans von, *Mit Feldmarschall von der Goltz Pascha in Mesopotamien und Persien* (Berlin: Mittler, 1926).

Kutz, C. R., *War on Wheels* (Harrisburg, Pa.: The Military Service Publishing Co., 1940).

Leland, Bt. Lieut.-Col., F. W., *With the M. T. in Mesopotamia* (London: Forster Groom & Co., 1920).

Long, P. W., *Other Ranks of Kut* (London: Williams & Norgate, 1938).

Macmillan, N., *Tales of Two Air Wars* (London: G. Bell & Sons, 1962).

MacMunn, Lieut.-Gen. Sir. G. F., *Afghanistan: From Darius To Amanullah* (London: G. Bell & Sons, 1929).

——, *Behind the Scenes in Many Wars* (London: John Murray, 1930).

——, *From the Outbreak of War with Germany to June 1917. (History of the Great War, Based on Official Documents, Egypt and Palestine,* Vol. 1.), (London: John Murray, 1928).

Marshall, Lieut.-Gen. Sir W., *Memories of Four Fronts* (London: Ernest Benn, 1929).

Morgenthau, Henry, *Secrets of the Bosphorus* (London: Hutchinson & Co., 1918).

Moukbil, Commandant M. Bey, *La Campagne de L'Irak, 1914–1918. La Siege de Kut-el-Amara.* (Paris: Berger-Levrault, 1933).

Mousley, E. O., *Secrets of a Kuttite* (London: John Lane & Co., 1922).

Murphy, Lieut.-Col. G. G. R., *Soldiers of the Prophet* (London: J. Hogg, 1921).

Neave, Dorina, *Remembering Kut* (London: Arthur Barker, 1937).

O'Dwyer, Sir M., *India As I Knew It* (London: Constable & Co., 1925).

Philby, H. St. J., *The Heart of Arabia* (London: Constable & Co., 1922).

Phillips, Sir Percival, *Mesopotamia—The Daily Mail Inquiry at Baghdad* (London: Daily Mail Publications, 1922).

Repington, Lieut.-Col. C., *The First World War 1914-1918.* 2 vols. (Boston: Houghton Mifflin Co., 1920).

Robertson, Field Marshal Sir W., *From Private to Field Marshal.*(London: Constable & Co., 1921).

——, *Soldiers and Statesmen* (London: Cassell & Co., 1926).

Ronaldshay, Earl of, *The Life of Lord Curzon.* 3 vols. (New York: Boni & Liveright, 1928).

Roosevelt, Kermit, *War in the Garden of Eden* (New York: C. Scribner's Sons, 1919).

Sandes, Major E. W. C., *In Kut and Captivity with the 6th Indian Division* (London: John Murray, 1919).

Sherson, Erroll, *Townshend of Chitral and Kut* (London: Wm. Heinemann, 1928).

Smith, Sir C. B., Bt., *Territorials in Mhow and Mesopotamia* (Privately printed in 1920 and only a very few copies were produced. One of these is held by the Imperial War Museum and another by the Ministry of Defence [Army] Library in London).

Swinton, Capt. E. D., *The Green Curve and Other Stories* (London: Wm. Blackwood & Sons, 1909).

Sykes, Major-Gen. Sir Fred, *From Many Angles* (London: G. G. Harrap & Co., 1942).

Tennant, Lieut.-Col. J. E., *In the Clouds Above Baghdad* (London: C. Palmer, 1920).

Thomas, Sir Miles, *Out on a Wing* (London: Michael Joseph, 1964).

Thompson, Rev. E. J., *Beyond Baghdad with the Leicesters.*(London: Epworth Press, 1921).

Townshend, Major-Gen. Sir Charles V., *My Campaign in Mesopotamia* (New York: J. A. McCann & Co., 1920).

Toynbee, A. J., *The Islamic World* (London: Ernest Benn, 1926).

Wilson, Sir Arnold T., *Loyalties: Mesopotamia 1914–1917* (London: Oxford University Press, 1930).

Wilson, H. W., (ed.). *The Great War* (Vols. 5, 6, and 7: 1915-1918), (London: Amalgamated Press, 1916).

Woodruff, P., *The Guardians (The Men Who Ruled India,* Vol. 2.) (New York: St Martin's Press, 1954).

Yale, W., *The Near East* (Ann Arbor, Mich.: University of Michigan Press, 1958).

Yeats-Brown, Capt. Francis, *The Lives of a Bengal Lancer* (New York: Viking Press, 1930).

2. *Regimental Histories* (Most regimental histories have been published privately for limited circulation by regimental associations.)

a. *British Service*

History of the Dorsetshire Regiment 1914-1919. Part 1: *The Regular Battalions.* Compiled by the Regimental Historical Committee and published by Henry Ling, Dorchester, 1933.

History of the Hampshire Territorial Forces Association and War Records of Units, 1914-1919. Compiled and published by the Hampshire Advertiser, Southampton, 1921.

Atkinson, Capt., C. L. *The Devonshire Regiment, 1914-1918* (Exeter: Eland Bros., 1926).

——, *History of the South Wales Borderers, 1914-1918* (London: Medici Society, 1931).

——, *The Regimental History of the Royal Hampshire Regiment* (Vol. 2) (Glasgow: Macklehose & Co., 1952).

——, *The Queen's Own Royal West Kent Regiment, 1914-1919* (London: Simpkin, Marshall, Hamilton, Kent & Co., 1924).

Campbell, Capt. G. L., *The Manchesters. (The History of the Regular, Militia, Special Reserve, Territorial and New Army Battalions Since Their Formation with Records of Officers Now Serving and the Honours and Casualties of the War of 1914-1916.),* (London: Picture Advertising Co., 1916).

Gowper, Col. J. M., *The King's Own* (Vol. 3: 1914-1950) (Aldershot: Gale & Polden, 1957).

Crookenden, A., *The History of the Cheshire Regiment in the Great War.* (Chester: W. H. Evans & Co., 1938).

Durand, Sir H. Mortimer, *The Thirteenth Hussars in the Great War.* (Edinburgh: Wm.

Blackwood & Sons, 1921).

Jourdain, H. and E. Fraser, *The Connaught Rangers* (London: Royal United Service Institution, 1924).

Kenwick, Col. N. C. E., *The Story of the Wiltshire Regiment* (Aldershot: Gale & Polden, 1963).

Kingsford, C. L., *The Story of the Royal Warwickshire Regiment* ("Country Life Series of Military Histories."), (London: Country Life, 1921).

Millett, Major J. A. T. (ed.). *Historical Record of the 14th (King's) Hussars 1900–1922* (Vol. 2). (Compiled by Brig. J. Gilbert Browne and Lieut.-Col. E. J. Bridges.), (London: Royal United Service Institution, 1932).

Missen, Capt. L. R., *History of the 7th (Service) Bn. Prince of Wales's North Staffordshire Regiment 1914–1919* (Cambridge: W. Heffer & Sons, 1920).

Neville, Capt. J. E. H., *Mesopotamia and North Russia. (History of the 43rd and 52nd Light Infantry in the Great War, 1914–1919,* Vol. 1.), (Aldershot: Gale & Polden, 1938).

Nicholson, Major-Gen. Sir Lothian and Major H. T. McMullen, *History of the East Lancashire Regiment in the Great War 1914–1918* (Liverpool: Littlebury Bros., 1936).

Nunn, Vice Admiral W., *Tigris Gunboats* (London: Andrew Melrose, 1932).

Oatts, Lieut.-Col. L. B., *Proud Heritage: The Story of the Highland Light Infantry* (Vol. 3), (Glasgow: House of Grant, 1963).

Pearse, Col. H. W. and Brig.-Gen. H. S. Sloman, *History of the East Surrey Regiment* (Vols. 2 and 3: 1914-1919), (London: Medici Society, 1934).

Petre, F. Lorraine, *History of the Norfolk Regiment* (Vol. 2: 1914-1918), (Norwich: Jarrold & Sons, 1924).

Stacke, Capt. H. Fitz., M., *The Worcestershire Regiment in the Great War* (Kidderminster: G. T. Cheshire & Sons, 1929).

Stevens, F. E., *The Battle Story of the Hampshire Regiment 1702-1919* (Southampton: Hampshire Advertising Co., 1919).

Sym, Col. John M., *The Seaforth Highlanders* (Aldershot: Gale & Polden, 1962).

Tallents, Major H., *The Sherwood Rangers Yeomanry in the Great War, 1914-1918* (London: Philip Allan & Co., 1926).

Ward, Major C. H. Dudley, *Regimental Records of the Royal Welsh Fusiliers* (Vol. 4) (London: Forster, Groom & Co., 1929).

Wauchope, Major-Gen. A. G., *A History of the Black Watch (Royal Highlanders) in the Great War 1914–1918* (London: Medici Society, 1925).

Whalley-Kelley, Capt. H., *"Ich Dien." The Prince of Wales's Volunteers (South Lancashire) 1914–1934* (Aldershot: Gale & Polden, 1935).

Wylly, Col. H. C., *History of the 1st and 2nd Battalions: The Leicestershire Regiment in the Great War.* (Aldershot: Gale & Polden, 1928).

——, *History of the Manchester Regiment* (Vol. 2: 1833-1922), (London: Forster, Groom & Co., 1925).

——, *History of the Queen's Royal Regiment* (Vol. 7: 1905-1923), (Aldershot: Gale & Polden, 1925).

——, *The Loyal North Lancashire Regiment* (London: Royal United Service Institution, 1933).

Wyrall, Everhard, *The Die-Hards in the Great War—History of the Duke of Cambridge's Own (Middlesex) Regiment* (London: Harrison & Sons, 1930).

——, *History of the Somerset Light Infantry 1914–1919* (London: Methuen & Co., 1927).

b. *Indian Army*

A Brief History of the 3rd Battalion 1st Punjab Regiment (formerly 16th Punjabis), (Aldershot: Gale & Polden, 1927).

Historical Record 110th Mahratta L.I., now 3rd/5th Mahratta L.I (Calcutta: Government of India Press, 1927).

History of the 5th Royal Gurkha Rifles (Frontier Force) 1858–1928 (Aldershot: Gale & Polden, 1930).

Anderson, M. H., *With the 33rd "Q.V.O." Light Cavalry in Mesopotamia* (Harangabad: Published by the Regiment, 1913).

Atkinson, Capt. C. T., *A History of the 1st (P.W.O.) The Dogra Regiment 1887–1947.* (Southampton: Camelot Press, 1950).

Condon, Brig. W. E. H., *The Frontier Force Rifles* (Aldershot: Gale & Polden, 1953).

Evatt, Brig.-Gen. J., *Historical Records of the 39th Royal Gurhwal Rifles* (Vol. 1: 1887–1922 Mesopotamia), (Aldershot: Gale & Polden, 1922).

McClintoch, Lieut.-Col. R. L., *Historical Records of the 2nd "Q.V.O." Sappers and Miners* (Vol. 2: 1910-1919), (Bangalore: 2nd "Q.V.O." S and M Press, 1921).

Maunsell, Col. E. B., *Prince of Wales's Own: The Scinde Horse 1908–1922* (Delhi: Published by the Regimental Committee, 1926).

May, Capt. C. W., *History of the 2nd Sikhs, 12th Frontier Force Regiment 1846–1933* (Jubbulpore: E. C. Davis Mission Press, 1934).

Quereshi, Major Mohammed Ibrahim, *History of the 1st Punjab Regiment* (Aldershot: Gale & Polden, 1958).

Rawlinson, H. G., *Napier's Rifles: History of the 5th Battalion 6th Rajp-tana Rifles* (London: Oxford University Press, 1929).

Ryan, Major D. G. J., Major G. C. Strachan, and Capt. J. K. Jones, *Historical Record of the 6th Gurkha Rifles* (Aldershot: Gale & Polden, 1925).

Shakespear, L. W., *History of the 2nd K.E.O. Gurkhas* (Aldershot: Gale & Polden, 1925).

Stoney, P. S., *A History of the 26th Punjabis* (Aldershot: Gale & Polden, 1924).

Tugwell, Lieut.-Col., W. B. P., *History of the Bombay Pioneers* (London: Sidney Press, 1938).

3. *Official Publications*

a. Published in Great Britain by H. M. Stationery Office, London.
   History of the Great War: Principal Events. 1922.
   Official History of the Great War: The Campaign in Mesopotamia 1914-1918 (ed. by Brig.-Gen. F. J. Moberly). Vols. I–II: 1923-1927.
   Report of the Mesopotamia Commission (Cd 8610). 1917. (The Commission was appointed by Act of Parliament by the Government of Great Britain, and its report includes that of the "Vincent Bingley" Commission appointed by the Government of India.)

b. Published in Great Britain by H. M. Stationery Office, London, for limited War Office Distribution.
   Handbook of the Turkish Army. 1915.
   Naval and Military Dispatches. (All published and printed as supplements to the *London Gazette.*)

i. *Relating to operations in all theaters of the war.*

Part I	September–November 1914. Issued	1915
Part II	November 1914–June 1915.	"	1915
Part III	July–October 1915.	"	1915
Part IV	December 11, 1915 (Gallipoli).	"	1915
Part V	January–April 1916.	"	1916
Part VI	May–December 1916.	"	1917
Part VII	December 1916–July 1917.	"	1917
Part VIII	July 1917–June 1918.	"	1918
Part IX	July–December 1918.	"	1919
Part X	January 1919–January 1920.	"	1920

ii. *Relating only to operations in Mesopotamia and Persia.*[*]

November 1919–January 17, 1920 (Sir G. F. McMunn)
January 18, 1920–June 30, 1920 (Sir J. A. Haldane)
July 1, 1920–October 19, 1920 (Sir J. A. Haldane)
October 20, 1920–August 20, 1921 (Sir J. A. Haldane)

c. Printed or published in India.

The Army in India and Its Evolution. Delhi: Government of India Press, 1924. Critical Study of the Campaign in Mesopotamia up to April 1917. Compiled by Officers of the Staff College, Quetta. October-November 1923. Printed by the Government of India Press, Calcutta, for G.H.Q. India and issued as an "Official Use Only" document.

"Yilderim" by Lieut.-Col. H. H. Amir Bey (Published originally by the Turkish General Staff; translated by Capt. G. O. de R. Channer, M.C.) (Printed by the Government of India Press for G.H.Q. India, 1923).

4. *Articles in Periodicals and Journals*

a. *The Army Quarterly* published quarterly in London by Wm. Clowes & Sons. "Mesopotamia: A Political Retrospect." Vol. ii, April 1921.

Dewing, Major R. H., "Lessons from Experience with Irregulations." Vol. ix, October 1924.

———, "Some Aspects of Maude's Campaign in Mesopotamia." Vols. xiii and xiv, January and April 1927.

Rimington, Major-Gen. J. C., "Kut-al-Amara." Vol. vi, April 1923.

b. *Journal of the Royal United Service Institution,* published quarterly by the Institution in London.

Bird, Major-Gen. W. D., "Things Are Not Always What They Seem." November 1922.

c. *Journal of the Royal Central Asian Society,* published quarterly by the Society in London (12 Orange Street, Haymarket, London, W.C.2).

Brooke-Popham, air Comm. H. R. M., "Some Notes on Aeroplanes with Special Reference to the Air Route from Cairo to Baghdad." 1922.

Gheradame, M., "The Baghdad Railway." 1911.

Wilson, Sir Arnold T., "Mesopotamia 1914-1921." 1922.

---

[*] These dispatches were published with the *London Gazette* (32379) of July 1, 1921.

d. *Journal of the Royal Engineers,* published quarterly by the Regimental Association at Chatham.
Molesworth, Capt. F. G. "Mesopotamia." December 1916.
Witts, Major F. V. B. "Light Floating Bridges in Mesopotamia." December 1923.

e. *Journal of the Cavalry Association,* published quarterly by the Association in London.
Fanshaw, Sir H. D. "Cavalry in Mesopotamia in 1918." Vol. x, 1920.

f. *Blackwood's Magazine,* Edinburgh.
Hobart, P. C. S. "Three Days with the Turks in Mesopotamia." July 1918.
Wauchope, Brig.-Gen. A. G. "The Battle That Won Samarra." April 1918.

g. *The Oxfordshire and Buckinghamshire Light Infantry Chronicle.* (Published for the Regiment by various publishers at London, Aldershot, and Southampton between 1915 and 1920.)

5. *Anonymous Authorship*
On the Road to Kut (by "Black Tab"). London: Hutchinson & Co., 1917.
"The Times" History and Encyclopaedia of the War. 21 vols., and index. London: The Times Publishing Co., 1920.

6. *Unpublished Material*
"47th Sikh's War Record." (Typescript held by the Imperial War Museum.)
Blackwell, E. and E. C. Axe. "War Record of 'B' Battery 271st Brigade, R.F.A." 1926. (Copy held by the Imperial War Museum.)

Index